ZELDA FITZGERALD

By the same author

ZELDA FITZGERALD

Her Voice in Paradise

SALLY CLINE

JOHN MURRAY
Albemarle Street, London

A catalogue record for this book is available from the British Library

ISBN 0-7195-5466 7

Typeset in 11/12.5pt Palatino by
Servis Filmsetting Ltd, Manchester

Printed and bound in Great Britain by
Butler & Tanner Ltd, Frome and London

This book is dedicated

to **Marmoset Adler**
Vic Smith, Esme Ashley-Smith, A. Het Shackman
'Everybody was so young' (Sara Murphy)

to **Ba Sheppard**
'They were banking in gods those years' (Zelda Sayre Fitzgerald)

to **Marion Callen**
'Once Again to Em' (after F. Scott Fitzgerald)

to **Rosemary Smith**
'[S]he knew everything' (Zelda Sayre Fitzgerald)

In memory of **Larry Adler** 10 February 1914 – 7 August 2001
'Life seemed so promissory always when he was around'
(Zelda Sayre Fitzgerald)

CONTENTS

ILLUSTRATIONS

(between pages 236 and 237)

Readers who wish to see Zelda Fitzgerald's paintings can:

- read *Zelda: An Illustrated Life*, ed. Eleanor Lanahan, Harry N. Abrams Inc., New York, 1996;
- contact the Visual Materials Division, Department of Rare Books and Special Collections, Princeton University Library, where there are copies of the slides of Zelda's paintings;
- contact Sally Cline (c/o John Murray (Publishers) Ltd) who also has copies of the slides.

The author and publisher would like to thank the following for their kind permission to reproduce illustrations: 1, 2, 4, 5, 6, 7, 8, 12, 13, 14, 20, 28, 29, 33, 34, 35: photographs from the F. Scott Fitzgerald archives at Princeton University Library used by permission of Harold Ober Associates as agents for the Fitzgerald Trustees, reproduced courtesy of Princeton University Library; 3: by permission of Sally Cline, Cambridge, UK; 9: courtesy of Edward Pattillo, Montgomery, Alabama; 10: Estate of the late Grace Gunter Lane, courtesy of Fairlie Lane Haynes, Montgomery, Alabama; 11, 19, 32: by kind permission of Pat Sprague Reneau, California; 15, 16: Lloyd C. Hackl, Center City, Minnesota; 17, 18: courtesy of Enoch Pratt Free Library, Baltimore. Reproduced by permission; 22: © 1997 Meryle Secrest, Washington DC; 23: Papers of Djuna Barnes, Special Collections, University of Maryland Libraries; 25: copyright 2002 Estate of the late Honoria Murphy Donnelly, courtesy of John C. Donnelly, Florida; 26: courtesy of the John F. Kennedy Library, Boston; 27: from the Scribner Archives. Courtesy Scribner/Simon & Schuster (reproduced courtesy of Princeton University Library); 30: used by permission of Harold Ober Associates as agents for the Fitzgerald Trustees, courtesy of Cecilia Ross (also courtesy of Princeton University Library); 31: used by permission of Harold Ober Associates as agents for the Fitzgerald Trustees, courtesy of Samuel J. Lanahan Jnr (also courtesy of Princeton University Library); 36: (photograph by Koula Svokos Hartnett, Columbus, Ohio, 1990) copyright Koula Svokos Hartnett in *Zelda Fitzgerald and the Failure of the American Dream for Women*, 1991, Peter Lang Publishing, Inc., New York; 37: used by permission of Harold Ober Associates as agents for the Fitzgerald Trustees, courtesy of Eleanor Lanahan; 38: courtesy of Mary Parker, North Carolina; 39: North Carolina Collection, Pack Memorial Public Library, Asheville, North Carolina.

ACKNOWLEDGEMENTS

This is in no way an authorized biography but without the unstinting support of Zelda Fitzgerald's granddaughter Bobbie (Eleanor) Lanahan, and through her the Fitzgerald family and Estate, it could not have been adequately researched. My most significant acknowledgement is therefore to Bobbie, herself a painter, for showing me Zelda's paintings, analysing her artwork, sharing her knowledge, spending several weeks talking to me and giving me photographs and slides of Zelda's paintings. For five years she has facilitated my access to the wide network of Fitzgerald friends and relations across the USA. Bobbie did not necessarily agree with my findings but with rare generosity she guided me, removed obstacles from my path and was a constant source of encouragement.

An initial interest in my work came from Henry Dunow of the Fitzgerald Estate, which was followed by unprecedented help from Zelda's other granddaughter Cecilia Lanahan Ross who exchanged ideas and gave me the gift of Scottie's memoir. I am further indebted to their father the late Samuel Lanahan, to their brother Samuel Lanahan Jnr and to Scott Fitzgerald's nieces Courtney Sprague Vaughan and Pat Sprague Reneau, for photographs, paintings, memoirs and family information. I am most appreciative to Chris Byrne of the Harold Ober Literary Agency for his initial help over permissions and to Craig Tenney, also of Harold Ober, in the later stages.

I have been fortunate in being given six awards for this biographical research. I owe special debts of gratitude to the British Academy for their Independent Scholar's Research Award; to the Society of Authors for their Writer's Award; and to the Eastern Arts Board for three bursaries, all of which enabled me to travel and work in Europe and America with time to peruse archives, to live in cities inhabited by the Fitzgeralds and to view Zelda's paintings in private collections and museums throughout the USA.

I thank Princeton University for their Fellowship and two years' access to the Rare Books Department in the Firestone Library where the major Fitzgerald archives and photographs are held. The Rare Books Curator of Manuscripts, Don Skemer, shared with me his invaluable knowledge and came to my aid warmly and cleverly many times. Great gratitude is given to John Delaney (Chairman, Fellowship Committee), Ben Primer (Fellowship Committee) and to William Joyce (former Associate University Librarian) most especially for his generosity over permissions for the use of slides and photos. I thank also Jennifer Bowden, Chris Dupin, Charles Eyre Greene (Keeper of the Reading Room), Monica Ruscil, Jane Snedeker, Susan Waterman. For AnnaLee Paul's hours of patient photoduplication and her lasting friendship I am very appreciative. Above all I thank Peggy Sherry, the Reference Librarian and Archivist, who gave me several months of professional help and who, together with Stuart Rich, made my long stay in Princeton feel like home. During my Princeton sojourn I was fortunate in meeting the scholar Raymond Cormier, who enlivened my days with fascinating ideas on Zelda and who untiringly maintained a further three-year stimulating correspondence.

I thank John Hurley and Jane Raper for helping me find accommodation in Princeton, Judy Thompson and Al and Betty Cohen for providing it, Ann and Mitsuru Yasuhara and Liz Socolow for their local knowledge and hospitality.

I wish to thank those Fitzgerald scholars and biographers who have gone before me from whom I received illuminating insights. They include the premier Fitzgerald scholar Matthew J. Bruccoli and his assistant Judith Baughman who were constantly courteous and informative, Jackson R. Bryer, Scott Donaldson (a memorable lunchtime talk on Hemingway and Fitzgerald), Koula Svokos Hartnett (five years' discussions and communications), Nancy Milford (who put aside her own writing for a lengthy interview), Ted Mitchell for a riveting exchange of ideas over *Caesar's Things* and Zelda's death, Ruth Prigozy (who gave me food, drink, contacts, articles, information, advice and guidance), Frances Kroll Ring (two long interviews and two years' correspondence), Jacqueline Tavernier-Courbin (several *Save Me The Waltz* discourses), and James West. The late James Mellow's biography of Zelda and Scott was a constant source of inspiration.

From the many people involved in the Fitzgeralds' lives who showered me with kindness, conversation and counsel I would mention particularly Waverly Barbe, Tony Buttitta (who gave me two long interviews and a marvellous tea when he was gravely ill), Lucy Dos Passos Coggin, Carol Lobman Hart, the late Grace Gunter

Lane, Ring Lardner Jnr, the late Ida Haardt McCulloch, Sally Wood Millsap, Mary Parker, the late Dr Irving Pine, Landon Ray, Budd Schulberg, Joanne Turnbull and Janie Wall. Exceptional help in the shape of family photographs, afternoon teas, tapes, slides, videos, letters, documents, memories and conversational enchantments came from Fanny Myers Brennan and the late Honoria Murphy Donnelly.

Institutions, librarians, curators, archivists, journalists, academics who have contributed information, interviews, materials include: Alabama Department of Archives and History; Anglia Polytechnic University Library, Cambridge; Arbury Court Library, Cambridge; Asheville Chamber of Commerce; Asheville Charter Hospital; *Asheville Citizen Times*; Asheville Fire Department; *Atlanta Constitution and Journal*; Atlanta Fulton Public Library; Birmingham Public Library, Alabama; Cambridge University Library; Lana Burgess (Assistant Curator, Montgomery Museum of Fine Arts); Mitchell Dakelman (Hoorman Library, Wagner College, New York); Harvard University; Vincent Fitzpatrick and Averil Kadis (Enoch Pratt Free Library, Baltimore) for wonderful photographs and information on the Menckens; Kim Korby Fraser (*Ladies Home Journal*, New York); Chandler W. Gordon (Captain's Bookshelf, Asheville); Antonia Hodgson (for help with Dolly Wilde information); Chris Jakes and his team at the Cambridgeshire Collection, Cambridge Central Library, who provided weeks of help with archival microfilms; the John F. Kennedy Library; *Journal of the American Medical Association*; Frances Kessler (*Esquire*); Dr Levington, Medical Superintendent, Charter Hospital (formerly Highland Hospital); Nancy Magnuson (Librarian, Julia Rogers Library, Goucher College); Malaprop's Bookstore, Asheville; Maryland Historical Society, Baltimore; Nancy McCall (Archivist, Johns Hopkins Medical Institutions); the endlessly helpful out-of-print team at Micawber Bookstore, Princeton; Minnesota Historical Society; the *Montgomery Advertiser*; New York Public Library; Don Noble (University of Alabama, Tuscaloosa); the *Princeton Packet*; Princeton University Bookstore team; Rebecca Roberts (Sara Mayfield Collection, University of Alabama); Shannon Scarborough (*Birmingham News*, Alabama); Kathy Shoemaker (Special Collections, Woodruff Library, Emory University, Atlanta); Dr James Stephenson (Assistant Dean, University of West Virginia); *Town Topics*, Princeton; Troy State University, Montgomery; University of Georgia Library; J. Willis (*New York Times*); Ann S. Wright (Special Collections Librarian, Asheville Buncombe Library).

For manuscript reading, advice, networking, medical help, and encouragement of many kinds I thank: Tim Barnwell (for exceptional photos of the fire), Davina Belling, Larry Belling, Carl Brandt, Stephen Bristow, Heidi Bullock (Zelda's art), the Cambridge Women Readers Group, Tracy Carns (for her enthusiasm over a Zelda lunch), Gwynneth Conder, Kirk Curnutt (discourse on fundamentalism and madness), Heather Dearnaley, Michelle Dodsworth, Kay Dunbar, Olga Foottit, Mary Gordon, Wayne Greenhaw, Katherine Grimshaw, Allan Gurganus (for the typed version of his talk on 'Sacrificial Couples'), Ann Henley, Jan Hensley (for recovering news reports and making me tapes), Jane Jaffey, Joel Jaffey, Carol Jones, Jean Kesler, Stella King, Heidi Kuntz, Cheryl Lean, Alan Margolies, Nancy Marlen, Josie McConnell, Eileen McGuckian, Bonnie McMullen, Graham Metson, Jane Miller, Linda Patterson Miller, James Moody, Kathy Mullen, Erin Murphy, Andrea Porter, Aliye Seif, Ruth Shaw, Gail Sinclair, Keith Soothill, Deborah Thom, Eleanor Vale (who in my absence sustained my house during a massive burglary with great courage), Nancy VanArsdale (many interesting talks in Asheville), Linda Wagner-Martin, Ralph Ward, Alison West, Alisa Hornung Weyman. I owe special thanks to Kathy Bowles and Chris Carling for their unending enthusiasm, encouragement and wise counsel.

The infectious optimism of several writers and artists has sustained me: I thank the Cambridge Women Writers Group (Joy Magezis, Chris Carling, Geraldine Ryan, Marion Callen), Julia Darling, Millicent Dillon (for six years' long distance writerly support), Helen Dunmore (for the gift of her 'Zelda' poem), Kathryn Hughes, Christina Johnson, Neil McKenna, Cliff McNish, Marion Meade (for spirited discussions about Dorothy Parker), Wendy Mulford, Michelle Spring, and especially Marion Elizabeth Rodgers for her intriguing biographical insights into H. L. Mencken and Sara Haardt and her constant optimism. I am also grateful to Andrew Lownie and the stimulation of the Biographers' Club. For advice on Zelda's art I thank Frankie (Frances) Borzello, Julia Ball, Carolyn Shafer and Jane S. Livingston.

In Montgomery I thank Julian and Leslie McPhillips, who direct the Scott and Zelda Fitzgerald Museum, for accommodation, entertainment, enormous Southern hospitality and constant chauffeuring, and at the Museum Elena Aleinikov for her valuable assistance and several meals. I owe a major debt of gratitude to Eddie Pattillo, my encyclopaedic wise and funny guide, who more than anyone helped me to comprehend the nature of the Deep South. In

Tuscaloosa Camella Mayfield (literary executor of the Sara Mayfield Collection) spent many months minutely tracking documents and offering personal and professional insights into the relationship between Zelda, Sara Mayfield and Tallullah Bankhead.

In St Paul and Center City Minnesota I am grateful to Lloyd Hackl and Barbara Paetznick for city tours, historical research, a folder of unpublished Kalman letters, accommodation and incredible warmth and hospitality. Lloyd trod in Scott's trails with me and helped me understand Scott's community. In Burlington, Vermont, I am grateful to Susan O'Brien for accommodation, information and the freedom to write and roam through her lovely house. In New York I thank Anne Gurnett and Jonathan Bander for accommodation, unstinting guidance, laughter and several exciting art tours. For five years' writing space in Sennen Cove, Cornwall, where much of this book was written, I thank Jean Adams and Susan Willis.

I feel remarkably fortunate that John Murray, my London publishers, genuinely love books and are concerned for their authors' well-being. Thank you to John Murray, Grant McIntyre, Stephanie Allen and my patient resourceful copy editor Anne Boston. Caroline Westmore has stood between me and trouble many times with delightful good humour and superb skill. My editor Caroline Knox is always courteous, sometimes critical (usually correct!) and knows just how to get the best from her author.

Barbara Levy, my good friend and perceptive literary agent, has rigorously read and analysed every chapter. I thank her and her lively helpful assistant Lindsay Schusman for critical comments, tact and always being on my side. For typing, photocopying and editorial assistance I thank Caroline Middleton and Stephanie Croxton Blake in Britain and Karen S. Doerstling in Princeton, and for hours of hard work on the bibliography I thank Jo Wroe.

I have relied on the excellence of my talented research assistant Rosemary Smith more than on anyone else. Scholarly, clever and kind, she has an encyclopaedic memory for detail and with perseverance and meticulous craft she has transcribed hundreds of tapes, typed all the research notes, devised charts, organized research systems, sorted photographs, done sterling work on the bibliography, cut, edited and helped structure every draft and the final version and kept me afloat.

I am indebted to the Royal Literary Fund, London, for its awards of two Writers' Fellowships (2000–2001 and 2001–2002) which have enabled me to write up the research with a strong measure of security.

I am continuously grateful to Hilary Spurling, originator of the Fellowship Scheme, and to the imaginative thoughtful Steve Cook, its director. My Fellowship has been tenable at Anglia Polytechnic University Cambridge, where my time in the English Department has been joyous. At Anglia I thank my three student researchers: Jason Austen Guest (for editorial aid), Sally Peters (illuminations about Zelda's art), most of all Miranda Landgraf (for clarity, constant attentiveness and sensitive skilled cutting). I thank Shirley Prendergast for research insights, Clare Bruges for her warmth and fortitude, the Dean, Rick Rylance; and my colleagues Rick Allen, David Booy, Peter Cattermole, Nora Crook, Mark Currie, Simon Featherstone, John Gilroy, Ted Holt, Mary Joannou, Kim Landers, Kate Rhodes, Anna Snaith, Carol Thomas, Gina Whisker, Vicki Williamson, Sue Wilson, for their encouragement. In particular Tory Young (for her vivacity), Ed Esche (for his daily supportive, often political conversations), Nigel Wheale (for his poetic wisdom and friendship) and most of all my writer friend and Head of Department, Rebecca Stott. Rebecca has read and edited many chapters, has spent long hours after work discussing the book's minutiae. She has made a significant sparkling professional contribution to this book for which my gratitude is beyond formal words.

On the domestic front one person is owed a benediction: my friend Angie North who runs my house and cares for my cat and deals with all emergencies during my research trips abroad. There could not be any research without her formidable kindness.

As always I could not have written this biography without the inspiration, love and support of my family and extended family.

First I thank Em Marion Callen, who knows every line of Zelda's art, who trod in Zelda's footsteps with me throughout the Deep South and in Scott's footsteps in Princeton and New York. When I faltered she didn't. Her very presence cheered me on.

I thank next Jonathan Harris, Joan Harris, Miles Ashley-Smith, Beth Callen, Aaron Callen, Molly Smith Callen and Elsie Sheppard. Laura Williams kept me going when she was perilously ill herself with a bravery Zelda would have admired. Jane Shackman was always ready to listen to drafts; and at hard moments Manda Callen calmed me down and Vic Smith cheered me up. Aunt Het (Harriet) Shackman rang me four times a week for five years to console or congratulate. Larry Adler, who knew most participants in the Fitzgeralds' drama, encouraged the project for years and was still encouraging when he died just before I wrote the last chapter. My stepchildren, Peter Adler, Wendy Adler Sonnenberg, Carole Adler

Van Wieck, were wonderfully supportive during those last weeks. Ba Sheppard, after twenty-four years of faithfully challenging and enthusing me, this time read every page of the final draft and suggested pertinent provocative cuts and edits. She enhanced the text and empowered the writer. My daughter Marmoset Adler, who has had the hardest year of her young life, never once stopped showering me with cuttings, photocopies and clever ideas. I thank her most of all.

The author and publisher would like to thank the following for permission to reproduce quotations. Quotations from the Fitzgerald holdings in the Manuscripts Division, Department of Rare Books and Special Collections, Princeton University Library, are published with permission of the Princeton University Library. Excerpts from *Save Me The Waltz* by Zelda Fitzgerald: reprinted with permission of Scribner, an imprint of Simon & Schuster Adult Publishing Group, from *Zelda Fitzgerald: The Collected Writings*, edited by Matthew J. Bruccoli. Copyright 1932 by Charles Scribner's Sons. Copyright renewed © 1960 by Frances Scott Fitzgerald Lanahan. Excerpts from short stories, articles and letters by Zelda Fitzgerald reprinted with permission of Scribner, an imprint of Simon & Schuster Adult Publishing Group, from *Zelda Fitzgerald: The Collected Writings*, edited by Matthew J. Bruccoli. Copyright © 1991 by The Trustees under Agreement Dated July 3, 1975. Created by Frances Scott Fitzgerald Smith. Excerpts reprinted with permission of Scribner, an imprint of Simon & Schuster Adult Publishing Group, from F. Scott Fitzgerald: *A Life in Letters*, edited by Matthew J. Bruccoli. Copyright © 1994 by The Trustees under Agreement Dated July 3, 1975. Created by Frances Scott Fitzgerald Smith. Excerpts reprinted with permission of Scribner, an imprint of Simon & Schuster Adult Publishing Group, from *Dear Scott/Dear Max: The Fitzgerald-Perkins Correspondence*, edited by John Kuehl and Jackson Bryer. Copyright © 1971 Charles Scribner's Sons. Reprinted by permission of Scribner, an imprint of Simon & Schuster Adult Publishing Group: excerpts from *Tender Is The Night* by F. Scott Fitzgerald. Copyright 1933, 1934 by Charles Scribner's Sons. Copyright renewed © 1961, 1962 by Frances Scott Fitzgerald Lanahan; from 'The Adjuster', in *All The Sad Young Men* by F. Scott Fitzgerald. Copyright 1926 by Lanahan; from *The Letters of F. Scott Fitzgerald*, edited by Andrew Turnbull. Copyright © 1963 by Frances Scott Fitzgerald Lanahan. Copyright renewed © 1991; from *The Great Gatsby* (Authorized Text Edition) by F. Scott Fitzgerald. Copyright 1925 by Charles Scribner's Sons. Copyright renewed 1953 by Lanahan. Copyright © 1991, 1992 by Eleanor Lanahan, Matthew J. Bruccoli, and Samuel J. Lanahan as Trustees under Agreement Dated July 3, 1975. Created by Frances Scott Fitzgerald Smith; from Introduction by Frances Scott Fitzgerald Lanahan to *Letters To His Daughter*, edited by Andrew Turnbull. Introduction Copyright © 1965 by Frances Scott Fitzgerald Lanahan. Copyright renewed © 1993 by Eleanor Lanahan, S. J. Lanahan, and Cecilia Ross; from *The Beautiful and Damned* by F. Scott Fitzgerald (New York: Scribner, 1922). Excerpts from F. Scott Fitzgerald, *The Crack-Up*, copyright © 1945 by New Directions Publishing Corp. Reprinted by permission of New Directions Publishing Corp. By permission of Harold Ober Associates Incorporated: Extracts from *Dear Scott/Dearest Zelda. The Love Letters of F. Scott and Zelda Fitzgerald*, edited by Jackson R. Bryer and Cathy W. Barks, St Martin's Press, New York, to be published in

England by Bloomsbury. Heretofore unpublished letters copyright © Eleanor Lanahan, Thomas P. Roche and Christopher T. Byrne, Trustees under Agreement dated July 3, 1975, by Frances Scott Fitzgerald Smith; extracts from Eleanor Lanahan, *Scottie The Daughter Of . . . The Life of Frances Scott Fitzgerald Lanahan Smith*. Copyright © 1995 by Eleanor Lanahan. Rights in text by F. Scott and Zelda Fitzgerald in the United Kingdom and Commonwealth (excluding Canada) is reprinted by permission of David Higham Associates Limited. 'The Hours' from *The Collected Poems of John Peale Bishop*, edited by Allen Tate. Copyright © 1948 by Charles Scribner's Sons; copyright renewed © 1976. Used with the permission of Scribner, an imprint of Simon & Schuster Adult Publishing Group. Extracts from *The Best Times: An Informal Memoir* by John Dos Passos, published by the New American Library, New York, 1966, reprinted by permission of Brandt and Hochman Literary Agents, Inc. 'Zelda' by Helen Dunmore, from *Short Days, Long Nights*, Bloodaxe Books, 1991, reprinted by permission. Extracts from an unpublished essay by Sara Haardt based on her 1928 interview with Zelda Fitzgerald (Haardt Collection, Julia Rogers Library, Goucher College, Baltimore) published by permission of the Enoch Pratt Free Library of Baltimore, in accordance with the terms of the will of H. L. Mencken. Excerpts reprinted with permission of Scribner, an imprint of Simon & Schuster Adult Publishing Group, from *A Moveable Feast* by Ernest Hemingway. Copyright © 1964 by Mary Hemingway. Copyright renewed © 1992 by John H. Hemingway, Patrick Hemingway and Gregory Hemingway; extracts from *A Moveable Feast* by Ernest Hemingway, published by Jonathan Cape, reprinted by permission of The Random House Group Ltd. Excerpts reprinted with permission of Scribner, an imprint of Simon & Schuster Adult Publishing Group, from *Ernest Hemingway: Selected Letters, 1917–1961*, edited by Carlos Baker. Copyright © 1981 The Ernest Hemingway Foundation, Inc.; reprinted with permission of Scribner, an imprint of Simon & Schuster Adult Publishing Group, and the Hemingway Foreign Rights Trust from *Ernest Hemingway: Selected Letters, 1917–1961* edited by Carlos Baker. © The Hemingway Foreign Rights Trust. Excerpt reprinted with permission of Scribner, an imprint of Simon & Schuster Adult Publishing Group, from *The Only Thing That Counts: The Ernest Hemingway-Maxwell Perkins Correspondence*, edited by Matthew J. Bruccoli. Ernest Hemingway's letters to Maxwell Perkins: Copyright © 1996 by The Ernest Hemingway Foundation; reprinted with permission of Scribner, an imprint of Simon & Schuster Adult Publishing Group, and the Hemingway Foreign Rights Trust from *The Only Thing That Counts: The Ernest Hemingway-Maxwell Perkins Correspondence*, edited by Matthew J. Bruccoli. Ernest Hemingway's letters to Maxwell Perkins: © The Hemingway Foreign Rights Trust. Extracts from Sara Mayfield, *Exiles from Paradise: Zelda and Scott Fitzgerald* and *The Constant Circle: H. L. Mencken and His Friends*, and from unpublished documentation held in the Sara Mayfield Collection, University of Alabama, Tuscaloosa, reprinted by courtesy of Camella Mayfield, Literary Executor. Reprinted by permission of Farrar, Straus and Giroux, LLC: excerpts from *Letters on Literature and Politics 1912–1972* by Edmund Wilson, edited by Elena Wilson. Copyright © 1977 by Elena Wilson; excerpt from 'Weekend at Ellerslie' from *The Shores of Light* by Edmund Wilson. Copyright © 1952 by Edmund Wilson. Copyright renewed © 1980 by Helen Miranda Wilson; excerpts from 'After the War', 'France, England, Italy' and 'New York' from *The Twenties* by Edmund Wilson. Copyright © 1975 by Elena Wilson.

Every effort has been made to contact copyright-holders, but if any have been inadvertently overlooked the author would be glad to hear from them.

'ZELDA'
by Helen Dunmore

At Great Neck one Easter
were Scott
Ring Lardner
and Zelda, who sat
neck high in catalogues like reading cards

her hair in curl for
wild stories, applauded.
A drink, two drinks and a kiss.

Scott and Ring both love her –
gold-headed, sky-high Miss
Alabama. (The lioness
with still eyes and no affectations
doesn't come into this.)

Some visitors said she ought
to do more housework, get herself taught
to cook.
Above all, find some silent occupation
rather than mess up Scott's vocation.

In France her barriers were simplified.
Her husband developed a work ethic:
film actresses; puritan elegance;

tipped eyes spilling material
like fresh Americas. You see
said Scott   they know about work, like me.

You can't beat a writer for justifying adultery.

Zelda
always wanted to be a dancer

she said, writhing
among the gentians that smelled of medicine.

A dancer in a sweat lather is not beautiful.
A dancer's mind can get fixed.

Give me a wooden floor, a practice dress,
a sheet of mirrors and hours of labour

and lie me with my spine to the floor
supple   secure.

She handed these back too
with her gold head and her senses.

She asks for visits. She makes herself hollow
with tears, dropped in the same cup.
Here at the edge of her sensations
there is no chance.

Evening falls on her Montgomery verandah.
No cars come by. Her only visitor
his voice, slender along the telephone wire.

INTRODUCTION

Mythical voices: mapping the myth

A Jazz Age Icon or a Renaissance Woman?

Paradoxically, Zelda Fitzgerald embraced both definitions yet was imprisoned by neither. Zelda, who arrived with the twentieth century, had an impressive array of untamed talents. She was a powerful painter; an original writer; and a ballerina who began late but achieved substantial success.

However, it is Zelda's character which has assumed symbolic status, her life the stuff of myth, her romance with Scott Fitzgerald which has enabled her spectacular rise and emblematic fall. As her creativity and brains were backed by beauty, rebelliousness and a flair for publicity, it is hardly surprising that in terms of her talents the legend makers sold her short.

Zelda must bear some responsibility. Her childhood escapades caused such intense gossip in Montgomery that myths about her wildness started early. Later she made it easy for mythmakers to prioritize her role as flamboyant flapper rather than hardworking artist. With her help, at least in the early years, mythmakers invented and reinvented Zelda Fitzgerald as American Dream Girl, Romantic Cultural Icon, Golden Girl of the Roaring Twenties and most often as a Southern Belle, relabelled the First American Flapper by her husband Scott Fitzgerald, the quintessential novelist of the Jazz Age, which he named.[1] When as a bride Zelda jumped in the Washington Square fountain, danced on tables in public restaurants, performed cartwheels in a New York City hotel lobby, it was not surprising that the media gambolled with her exploits.

Zelda and Scott flourished as capricious, merciless self-historians writing and rewriting their exploits. They used their stormy partnership as a basis for fiction which subsequently became a form of private communication that allowed fiction to stand as a method of discourse about their marriage. That discourse was then rewoven into their legend.

Recently myth has likened Zelda to those other twentieth-century icons, Marilyn Monroe and Princess Diana. With each she shares a defiance of convention, intense vulnerability, doomed beauty, unceasing struggle for a serious identity, short tragic life and quite impossible nature.

During a dazzling period of American culture, Zelda, as artistic creator and as object of Scott Fitzgerald's literary creations, spoke for a generation of bright young women. Yet she was out of step with it. Her painting and writing, too, are out of step. Their oddness jolts the reader or viewer. The legend misses that out.

Her literature and art with their hallucinatory connections between ideas are unsettling: transgressive, like their creator. When I saw her vivid, unpredictable paintings they stirred my imagination, but gave rise to a strange anxiety.

I looked at a nursing mother with a red blanket, an agonized portrait which flies in the face of acceptable motherhood. The mother has half her head severed while the baby sucks at what looks like the mother's entrails. Powerful but hardly comforting, it set me off on an untrodden trail to discover Zelda's overlooked relationship to her daughter Scottie.

Zelda's paintings and her writings, like Zelda herself, are enigmatic but it is not their labyrinthine quality alone which skews the legend.

The way Zelda's gifts panned out provides a second motive. Our society awards higher status to artists engaged fulltime on a single creative pursuit than to artists engaged on multiple forms of art. Being gifted in three directions – painting, writing, ballet – smacks of dilettantism.[2]

That Zelda's legend is unbalanced is also rooted in how our society rates literature and painting. Generally we credit art produced consistently and continuously, which provides us with a complete body of work by which to make judgements.

Zelda's does neither.

Zelda's writing is not continuous. She was most productive during two periods: 1929 to 1934, when intermittently hospitalized, and 1940 to 1948, after Scott's death, until her own. Between those periods Zelda was often ill or prevented from writing. As her biographer I had to ensure these two problems were separated.

Zelda's art is not a complete body of work, nor is much of it dated. It lacks the habitual artistic 'progression' or linear development by which one can sometimes date paintings. I have therefore, like several art critics, identified paintings by subject or theme.[3] I have also managed to match up several paintings with life events or with ideas occupying Zelda's imagination at a particular time.

Although her visual art is the most successfully refined of her three gifts, and although she produced paintings continuously from 1925 until the day before her death in 1948, many have been lost, burnt or otherwise destroyed. Fire and destruction remain two significant linked themes in Zelda's life.

Though Zelda's artistic legacy is substantial – more than 100 paintings – it still represents only part of her total production. This may be why Zelda's two early biographers gave it only token consideration. I have given her invisibilized art considerable attention. I was fortunate in being able to see more than two-thirds of Zelda's paintings in public and private collections, and was given slides of the rest by Eleanor Lanahan, Zelda's artist granddaughter, and by various owners of Zelda's work.

Today her painting and fiction are both attracting a new wave of critical attention. Her second novel, *Caesar's Things*, unfinished at her death in 1948, is about to be published; and there will be several major exhibitions of her paintings in the USA, Paris and London.

When we turn to Zelda's ballet career, the facts are incontrovertible but the legend deals with them selectively. Although Zelda began her apprenticeship in the Diaghilev tradition very late at twenty-seven, within a mere three years she was invited to perform a solo role with the Italian San Carlo Opera Ballet Company: an invitation which brought her the chance she had been awaiting but which for complex reasons she reluctantly declined.

Because Zelda's first doctor, and Scott, perceived her dance career as the cause of her first breakdown, and because Scott and her doctors banned her from dancing, this was the biographical view adopted subsequently. Zelda's ballet therefore has been consistently viewed as obsession rather than as artistic commitment. One of my aims has been to scrutinize these two polarized perspectives.

However, during Zelda's life her ballet, like her writing and painting, was subsumed under the greater interest of her marriage. As Zelda's biographer I have tried to balance the account.

Starting one's own creative life as 'the wife of' a famous writer often presents problems of comparison at best, invisibility at worst, for the less powerful writer and partner. But Zelda's case was more complicated. Unlike Antonia White and Jane Bowles, who also wrote out of their mental suffering, she never had writer's block.

Instead she fought the block on her writing imposed by a fellow writer. Her work is often seen as one of promise and the enemies of promise as those within. One enemy however was without. Scott, confusingly, tried to help her even as he stood in her way.

Being Fitzgerald's wife offered Zelda artistic opportunities she might not so easily have acquired alone, but being Fitzgerald's wife made it harder for his public to rate her talents in their own right.

I have scrutinized her marriage, which surprisingly soon was dominated by Scott's increasing alcoholism and her own mental suffering, each of which nourished the other. This led them to a litany of loss. Zelda, no longer able to inhabit the identities which Scott had offered her as glamorous wife and flapper incarnate, grew first resentful, then uncertain of who she was. Her fractured ego meant her identity was constantly in flux. Though Scott admired her for her physical fearlessness, she began to betray great emotional anxiety. She feared her own sexual ambiguity and they both feared the possibility of his. She revealed the struggles within her marriage and the struggle to maintain her uncertain identity through her writing and her ballet, which Scott struggled to repress.

Zelda felt it would be healthier to leave the marriage. But devotion and dependence led her time and again to stay. Scott felt the same ambivalence. For years they battled through a labyrinth of love and loyalty, tearing resentment and extreme bitterness. Finding a way out seemed as impossible as finding a way to stay in. Despite Scott's affairs and escalating alcoholism and despite Zelda's illness, neither entirely gave up on the marriage. They kept hold of its reality, and when that faded they kept hold of the fictions they had woven about it.

In analysing the relationship they connived at, I had to analyse the very nature of marriage and the balance of power between the sexes central to any marriage, integral to this one. The Fitzgeralds' challenges illuminated the times in which they lived. Though Zelda's struggles were those of many women in the early twentieth century, trying to find an artistic identity in the face of pressure to remain in feminine domestic roles, Scott too was impeded by his era's restrictions on his role as husband and male expert. In order to show alternatives open to the Fitzgeralds, I have given space to a comparison between their marriage and that of Zelda's Montgomery friend, Sara Haardt, and Scott's mentor, the critic H. L. Mencken.

The Menckens' civilized, more equal marriage attracted less media attention because legends thrive on dissipation. Thus as alcohol soaked Scott and Zelda's menage a new, not unfavourable myth granted Scott a weary dispensation for his drinking while ignoring possible effects on Zelda. Her sense of self floundered as life in rented houses and hotels degenerated into binges, bizarre behaviour, dissipation, drunkenness and no ground beneath their feet.[4] Later, Zelda's screaming red and yellow paintings would caricature in terrifying ways that lack of ground.[5]

Both Zelda and Scott began to use the word 'ominous' about their marriage. By September 1928 Scott had headed his Ledger entry with the word underlined three times in black. When Zelda later fictionalized those unsettling years in *Caesar's Things*, in about 1938, the word 'ominous' occurs on almost every page.

I examined the way the legend recorded these tragic notes. I observed how the labels progressed from 'eccentric' to 'mentally disordered' to 'schizophrenic', finally to 'the crazy wife of Scott Fitzgerald'.

Sadly, during Zelda's lifetime, other arcane, gifted but fragmented women (including Janet Frame, Vivien Eliot, Sylvia Plath, Antonia White), who displayed similar esoteric nonconformist behaviour, were deemed more suitable for sojourns inside mental institutions than for life outside.[6] It comes as no surprise to discover that Zelda the artist was also the holder of entry and exit passes to seven of the world's most expensive mental asylums for the last eighteen years of her short life.

Those breakdowns, crudely labelled 'madness', form a great part of the Fitzgerald mythology; while the evidence of Zelda's art forms only a small part of her legend.

What is extraordinary is that the years of Zelda's greatest discipline as a writer, dancer and visual artist coincided exactly with those years when she was first hospitalized, then diagnosed as schizophrenic.

I explored in depth the way one hospital[7] became, in 1932, the setting for one of the most contentious battles in literary history between an artistic husband and wife. From her hospital bed, Zelda completed her first novel *Save Me The Waltz* in a mere four weeks, drawing on some of the same autobiographical material which Scott was trying to plot into his novel-in-progress *Tender Is The Night*, which took him nine years to complete. Scott, incoherent with fury that anyone other than he should use their joint life experiences as literary fodder, first insisted the publishers cut large sections of *Save Me The Waltz* in 1932, then a year later during a three-way discussion with Zelda and her psychiatrist forbade Zelda to write any fiction which drew on shared autobiographical incidents.

This ban, which followed swiftly on Scott's stringent prohibition on her ballet, meant Zelda's rights to her own material and forms of self-expression were severely curtailed.

Following this Scott used Zelda's speech, letters, diaries, personal feelings and episodes of mental illness in his own fiction, and sometimes with Zelda's assent, sometimes without, encouraged her articles and stories to be published under joint names or his name alone.

Subsequently these undisputed facts became an issue over which supporters line up under two dramatic banners as diametrically opposed as the Plath and Hughes literary camps. Flags are waved, protests are shouted. There seems to be no middle ground.

From one perspective Zelda has been hailed by the Women's Movement as a feminist heroine, oppressed by a relentlessly ambitious husband who plagiarized her writing and exploited her personal experiences for his literary gains.

The opposing perspective sees Zelda as a sick selfish tyrant, writing lively but derivative fiction, holding her loyal husband hostage financially, impeding and dragging down his magnificent literary progress through her trivial desire for autonomy.

Exponents of both sides have raised her up or cut her down in biographies, memoirs, academic dissertations, critical studies, articles and reviews. They have turned her into a cult figure in other writers' novels, dramas, movies and stage plays.

I have tried to steer a steady course between these two polarized positions.

I have scrutinized the reasons why Scott felt he had the artistic right to silence Zelda's voice. Scott and subsequent biographers have suggested that, because Scott was the 'professional' and Zelda the 'amateur', the interests of professionalism can be used to legitimate Scott's actions. Zelda herself internalized the idea that those who are not professional cannot be equally talented.

Today we recognize that professionalism may have to do less with talent and more with financial rewards and status. Since the term 'professional' in Zelda's time rested, as it does today, on the way artists could or could not define themselves by their work, I have examined how Zelda fought for that self-definition.

I was also curious about why one writer's silencing of another writer's voice should have been labelled by critics as 'artistic rivalry'. Artistic rivalry implies a competition between equals, as opposed to 'silencing' which implies one artist has more power than the other, so it seemed worth exploring not only the definitions but also the effects of this 'rivalry' on the Fitzgeralds' domestic partnership.

Living with a famous artist can make for a tough relationship. In the Fitzgeralds' case Scott's fame rested on his writing while Zelda's ambition rested on *her* writing; thus they fought on the same ground. Zelda inevitably experienced feelings of admiration and frustration, rivalry and invisibility. Living with a man of publicly acknowledged talent who was necessarily self-focused engendered in Zelda a real desire to protect and support that man's talent, but also provided little breathing space in which to nurture her own.

Although this aspect of their story parallels late twentieth-century gender roles, I have attempted consistently to see Scott and Zelda within their own period.

Previous writers have focused a spectacular white spotlight on this particular literary controversy.[8] I aimed to view it within the context of the whole of Zelda's art and life. I have concerned myself as much with the rest of her painting and writing as with the literary row which brought her prominently to public attention. There was no lack of material. I have been fortunate in having access to everything she wrote, published and unpublished, a literary legacy which includes two novels, a dozen short stories, a galaxy of sketches, essays and magazine articles, spiritual and artistic notebooks, a stage play, and autobiographical and fictional fragments in the Princeton University Library, where there are also scrapbooks, albums and a monumental archive of letters.

I trawled through hundreds of unpublished painful illustrated letters, many from Zelda to Scottie which show an absentee mother's story not previously told in full. I was fortunate in being given Scottie's own unpublished memoir about Zelda by Scottie's daughter Cecilia Ross.

Zelda's hospital letters, haunting for their traumatic honesty, are particularly startling less for Zelda's awareness of what she sees as an unjust incarceration than for her pragmatic acceptance of hospital censorship. If she was ever to be released she was forced to write in an acceptable way. Untwining these two positions has been a hard task.

This Letters Archive allowed me to engage with Zelda's relationship to her mother, Minnie (a more ambivalent one than the legend logged), and with her women friends, few of whom are mentioned in earlier biographies, especially Sara Murphy, Sara Mayfield and Xandra Kalman. By good fortune I was generously offered a whole file of largely unpublished letters between Zelda and the Kalmans.[9]

I was also given an unpublished manuscript of Sara Haardt's which contained conversations and an interview with Zelda.

Though an important diary of Zelda's and eight further stories have been lost, evidence of their themes and content has been helpful.

Fitzgerald biographies have given the impression that after the tragedy of Scott's early death in 1940 absolutely nothing else happened to Zelda until her own tragic death in 1948. Plenty happened to her. I suggest she came into her own artistically during those eight years.

I have faced several problems. One problem was that a few of my older interviewees found it hard to distinguish between their memories and their readings of what has become an abundance of Fitzgerald material. A second problem was the delicate issues which have surrounded biographies of Zelda Fitzgerald. For more than thirty years no full length life of Zelda Fitzgerald and no literary biography at all had appeared. After Nancy Milford's controversial biography (1970) and Sara Mayfield's memoir (1971), both of which disturbed the Fitzgerald family, there was a long literary silence. Scottie, Zelda's daughter, was extremely distressed by what she saw as an unnecessary focus on Zelda's mental condition and her sexuality in the earliest biography. Milford was 'urged' to remove many of those references before her biography was published.[10] Despite Scottie's dislike of Mayfield's book, she generously gave that book also her permission. After Scottie's death her children, though equally generous over permissions, nevertheless felt they should honour her views so retained certain biographical impediments by restricting a considerable amount of medical material in the Princeton archives. I was fortunately able to see all of that material.

During those thirty-one years the Estate gave permission to one academic study (Hartnett 1991), one study of the Fitzgeralds' marriage (Kendall Taylor 2001) and several papers on Zelda's writings. In 1996 Zelda's granddaughter Eleanor Lanahan edited an illustrated book which focused on Zelda's art. What was still missing was a full length literary biography which saw Zelda as an artist as well as in her other roles.

I therefore approached the Trust initially with a request centred on Zelda's overlooked art. After long discussions, Eleanor Lanahan and other family members recognized that in order to grapple with the social and psychological as well as artistic forces that shaped Zelda's work, I would need maximum information and help. My path was cleared, my task unimpeded. I was given full access to all papers available, to family members and to people still alive who had known Zelda, including some of her Southern Belle girlfriends.

Zelda's medical condition plays a key part in this biography. I was fortunate in being given access to most medical records now available and was allowed to read those hitherto under seal.[11] I also spoke twice to Zelda's last psychiatrist,[12] who held a different view of her diagnoses from that recorded in the legend.

I looked at how the label 'schizophrenia' was applied to women. Evidence suggests that Zelda's failure to conform to a traditional feminine role has, to some extent, been buried within a diagnosis of mental disorder. Zelda was a courageous woman who struggled to maintain her sanity in the face of the horrific treatments she was forced to undergo. It became obvious that she suffered as much from the treatment as from the illness itself. My particular challenge was to try to separate illness from treatment.

Zelda's hospital label in the Thirties was schizophrenia; by the Fifties her last psychiatrist suggested (too late) that it might have been manic depression. Though the treatments for these mental diagnoses in periods separated by two decades were somewhat (though curiously, not entirely) different, that difference had less to do with diagnoses than with methods of control considered appropriate during each era. If letters and journals from other women patients in the Fifties/Sixties/Seventies are compared with Zelda's of the Thirties/Forties, we see that emotions engendered in all absentee mothers and artists inside closed institutions were remarkably similar. Fear, frustration, resentment and despair attached themselves to incarceration, imprisonment, enclosure. Bewilderment, guilt and powerlessness clung to the role of absentee motherhood. The evidence from Zelda's writings and comments from people close to her show such feelings led to incompetence over practical matters and swings from extreme harshness to wild indulgence towards her daughter Scottie.

Reading Zelda's notebook, which concentrated on making patterns from chaos, seeing her need for 'aspiration' (this word occurs on almost every page of one of Zelda's notebooks) as if by writing it she could realize it, I understood her feelings of being out of control which any prisoner or asylum resident would recognize.

Another challenge was to balance Scott's lifelong loyalty to a wife diagnosed as suffering clinical 'madness' with his constant refusal to take her out of hospital because he feared the disruption it would cause to his work.

The biographer's role is first to enter imaginatively into her subject's world, then to recognize that writer and subject are separate people, and that her task is to provide one version of possibly significant events and possibly significant motives which have impelled the subject's life and influenced their art.

In threading the narrative of her life through her painting and writing, aided by the memories of those who knew her, I have tried to give Zelda a life of her own, separate from Scott Fitzgerald's, but to acknowledge where the intertwining and complicity have been purposefully tangled by the two participants.

In Paris and New York she was spoken of as aloof, yet in her home town I heard repeatedly how warm, accessible and loyal she was, how her character was 'shot through to the bone with a strong vein of kindness'. Certainly during this research I have been most impressed by Zelda's moral bravery. Throughout her troubled, sometimes tormented, life she exhibited qualities of endurance and courage with what her particular enemy and Scott's friend, Ernest Hemingway, would have called grace under pressure if he could have brought himself to praise her at all.

Zelda shared with all four of Hemingway's wives, though not with his heroines, the qualities of resilience and relinquishment. But her graciousness and stoicism, unlike theirs, were those of a Southern lady. Though Zelda was sometimes more irritatingly confrontational than was appropriate in the South, where difficult issues are delicately approached by stealth, she was never once accused of vulgarity.

Everyone I met in the Deep South (where I learnt more about Zelda than anywhere else) told me that 'ultimately Zelda was a Southern lady'. Yet in the Deep South, in her childhood, Zelda behaved as no ladies dared. It was one of the contradictions in her character she would never lose.

To understand Zelda and her work it is imperative to look closely at her roots. So it is in that place, the Deep South, at that time, the early 1900s, doing what ladies did not dare to do, that we first meet Zelda.

PART I

Southern Voice
1900–April 1920

CHAPTER I

Zelda Fitzgerald's life was made for story. It had page-turning qualities even before Zelda and Scott amended it for the legend.

The tale begins with the indisputably Thespian timing of her birth, which coincided with the start to the new century. Later she saw the dramatic possibilities of a life that paralleled an era.

Even her name had already been fictionalized. When Zelda was born on Tuesday 24 July 1900 at 5.40 a.m. in the Sayres' house on South Street, Montgomery, her forty-year-old mother Minerva, herself named for a myth, was known locally as an avid reader. Perusing romantic novels, Minnie had twice run across the unusual name Zelda.[1] In Jane Howard's 1866 *Zelda: A Tale of the Massachusetts Colony* the heroine was a beautiful gypsy. In *Zelda's Fortune*, written in 1874 by Robert Edward Francillon, the second Zelda, again a gypsy, 'could have been placed in no imaginable situation without drawing upon herself a hundred stares'.[2] Francillon's line could have been written expressly for Zelda Sayre.

Zelda's rhapsodic looks matched her artistic temperament. Her hair, long and loose, 'was that blonde color that's no color at all but a reflector of light'.[3] And it was the lighthearted Machens, her sunny mother's relations, that Zelda took after, while her brother and sisters were dark like her father's temperament and Montgomery's history.

Zelda always said that her home town's controversial history strengthened her. Although (or perversely because) prolonged civil war tore the South apart and massacred an entire generation of Southern men, Montgomery citizens were proud that a nation had been born there. Today, more than half a century after Zelda's death, they still are. Montgomery was the Cradle of the Confederacy and its first flag had been raised from the staff of the state Capitol.[4] In Zelda's girlhood ghosts of the late Confederacy drifted through sleepy oak-lined streets.

The Civil War, the defining historical event of the Deep South, still vibrated in people's minds. It created a distinctive Southern culture often at odds with itself and the country. During this blood-letting of 1861–5 the Confederate states in the South which wished to secede from the Union fought to maintain certain rights, not least the right to determine state law on the institution of slavery, the mainstay especially in the South of an agricultural plantation economy. Thus the South ran counter to the moral beliefs of its time in perpetuating slavery just when the rest of the Western world was decisively giving it up. Traditionally there had been a gulf between black fieldhands and black house servants: black women for instance, in the houses of Zelda and her friends, cooked and wet-nursed and raised the children.

In Zelda's birth year, only thirty-five years after slavery was abolished in America, some historians believe the secret heart of the South still carried an uneasy but powerful sense of the rightness of their nineteenth-century position on slavery. In adolescence Zelda *saw* period advertisements which proved lynching, mutilation and the mark of the branding iron had been incontestable methods by which black fieldhands and house servants were kept in check. But what Zelda *heard* was that these shocking brutalities disturbed the élan of white Montgomery families less than the tragedies that had befallen their own brave youths. For in this volatile environment, the resentments of the blacks were stifled beneath the white romanticization of antebellum plantation life built on slavery.

In her childhood Zelda never questioned the fact that the respectable white families with whom she mixed had been instrumental in upholding laws that penalized Negroes. In her own family her father, Judge Sayre, had even *created* such laws. Zelda's daughter Scottie later wrote: 'I am sorry to say that while he was a just man, known for his unshakable integrity, he was probably one of the sturdiest pillars of the unjust society . . . he was author of the "Sayre Election law", which effectively prevented Negroes from voting until the Civil Rights Act of 1964. So he was one of the heroes of the established order . . . but then if you weren't, in those days and in this place, you would have been an outlaw from society.'[5]

What Zelda learnt from the Judge and her mother, Minnie Sayre, was that Southerners were fanatical about their Southern beauties, the chivalry of their Southern gentlemen, Union General Sherman's devastating raids which were instrumental in the Confederacy's defeat.[6] Because she came from an old-established white Southern family, she understood the symbolism of the South's luxuriant blossoms which atrophied into perfumed decay. She grew up acutely aware that casualty and spoilage could always occur at a moment of great promise to any of the young men who courted her.[7] Zelda's heritage was the proximity of youth and beauty to death and annihilation.

Talking about the dead was therefore common amongst Zelda's circle. She knew her ancestors were spirited, quixotic and rash. Pioneers and speculators, politicians and lawyers, they raced to the brink and didn't pull back. Zelda felt she took after them. The Sayres and the Morgans on her father's side were illustrious and property-owning while the Cresaps and the Machens on her mother's side were powerful and romantic.

After Zelda's death, when Scottie investigated the Maryland Cresap line that stretched from Zelda's maternal grandmother Victoria Cresap Mims back to the seventeenth century, she said it became clear why Zelda emerged from a conservative Southern background as one of the Twenties' most flamboyant figures: 'my mother was descended from some of the most audacious, impetuous, picturesque and irrepressible figures in all of Maryland's colorful history'.[8]

The most audacious was Colonel Thomas Cresap, born 1694 in Skipton, Yorkshire. This quintessential frontiersman had emigrated to the York County side of the Susquehanna River in Maryland, where he ran a ferry across to the present-day town of Washington Boro. Cresap was known as 'The Maryland Monster' to the Pennsylvanians among whom he settled.[9] Rumoured to be Lord Baltimore's secret agent, he had been granted 500 acres and appointed surveyor, magistrate and captain of the militia in competition with the Pennsylvanian officials. So obnoxious was he to them that finally they sent him to jail. As he was led in chains to the courthouse hundreds gathered to see the infamous Maryland Monster.

Once released, he impertinently borrowed from his lawyers to move his family to Oldtown, an abandoned Indian village near today's Cumberland.[10] He founded the massive Ohio Company and became guide, explorer, politician and protagonist in the wilderness drama. Depending on which version you credit, the Monstrous Frontiersman died at the age of 96, 100 or 102.

It was Thomas's 'perfect mate' Hannah Johnson, married to him in 1727, who particularly fired Zelda's imagination. Born in Prince George's County, Hannah, a 'darkly handsome Amazon', defended her disputed territory on the old Indian lands of Conejola. When arrested by Lancaster County's sheriff in 1736 she 'carried a rifle, two pistols, a tomahawk, a scalping knife, and a small dagger in her boot'.[11]

Of Hannah's three sons, one was killed by Indians and another died serving in George Washington's army in 1775. Her oldest son, Daniel Cresap, fought in the French and Indian War and was buried in Maryland in 1798 at the foot of Dan's Mountain, named after his own glorious exploits. His son Daniel Jnr, born 1753, who commanded a regiment to put down the 1794 Whiskey Rebellion,[12] died from hardships on the campaign without the benefit of whiskey.

The last of Zelda's bold Maryland ancestors, Daniel Jnr's eldest son Edward Otho, his courageous wife Sarah Briscoe[13] and two small daughters travelled down the Ohio river on a flat boat to Kentucky. Within six years Sarah was widowed with five tiny children. A tame version of Edward's death suggests he caught pneumonia but Zelda always preferred the version that he was killed by Chickasaw Indians. One anecdote on which all versions agree is that because of the tangled position in which his body was found he had to be squeezed into his coffin. Then when it was opened at the wake, out sprang the body of Edward Otho.[14]

Sarah's daughter Caroline Cresap, Zelda's great-grandmother, who married John Mims of Kentucky, inherited the Cresap bravado. Caroline's daughter Victoria married Confederate Senator Willis B. Machen, twenty-eight years her senior and already twice widowed, with whom she had two daughters: Zelda's mother Minnie and the younger delicate Aunt Marjorie. Minnie would tell Zelda how during the Civil War her intrepid grandmother Caroline, on a visit to the Machens' Kentucky home Mineral Mount, on the Cumberland River, insisted on flying the Confederate flag from the roof. A passing Yankee gunboat instantly splintered the house with shells.[15]

In Zelda's home in Pleasant Avenue, Minnie, five years old at the time of the incident, still kept Senator Machen's carved mahogany *secretaire* whose corner had been blown off by the gunfire. She riveted young Zelda with tales of their Machen ancestors' earlier exploits. There was John Machen, who boldly emigrated to Virginia from Scotland in the early seventeenth century.[16] There was his son Thomas Machen, still restless, who left Virginia for South Carolina then finally settled to marriage with a Sayre cousin, Mary Chilton.[17] There was Thomas's son Henry Machen I, a man still on the move. A lieutenant during the Revolution, he went to Kentucky with an English immigrant, Grace Greenwood. By 1802 Zelda's great-grandfather, tobacco planter Henry Machen III, and his wife Nancy Tarrant had formed a Scottish colony on Kentucky's Cumberland River. Minnie showed Zelda a sepia photo of herself on which an admirer had scrawled 'The Wild Lily of Cumberland'.

Henry Machen III's son Willis, raised in Kentucky when the state was a frontier, was energetic, enterprising and multi-talented like his granddaughter Zelda. Initially an iron-refiner, when his business failed, to everyone's astonishment he became a successful lawyer in Kentucky's South West, served in the legislature and helped frame Kentucky's constitution.

Willis's major rebellion came during the Civil War when Kentucky's allegiance to the Union was challenged by a provisional state government set up by secessionists, amongst whom Willis was pre-eminent. He was elected to the Confederate Congress[18] and appointed President of the Council of Ten, the Governor of Kentucky's advisory board.

However, in 1865 as a secessionist he was forced to flee with a price on his head to Canada, where Victoria and their daughters joined him, until he was pardoned by President Grant in 1869 and returned to Kentucky to rebuild his plantation.

In 1872 Willis served for four months on the US Senate, during which time young Minnie visited Washington with him. His name was presented by the Kentucky Democratic Delegation for the Vice Presidential nomination that year, though he did not win it. By 1880 he was a powerful member of the Kentucky railroad commission. Minnie, like Zelda a rebel, did not always agree with her father but remained proud of him.[19] It was that pride which Zelda absorbed and which she saw in her home, a veritable seat of justice presided over by *her* father, Judge Anthony Dickinson Sayre. Zelda learnt from her father that blood and breeding were more significant status symbols than house ownership. The Judge's home became a 'shining sword [which] sleeps at night in the sheath of his tired nobility'. In Zelda's first novel, her father becomes a retributory organ, the force of law and order, the pillar of established discipline. He was a 'living fortress' who offered his children such a sense of security that it absolved them 'from the early social efforts necessary in life to construct strongholds for themselves'.[20] This made her despise 'weaklings' without the 'courage and the power to feel they're right when the whole world says they're wrong'.[21]

Yet when she *was* in the wrong her father's reputation protected her from open criticism. In his thirties he was asked to serve as a member of the Alabama House of Representatives. Four years later he was elected President of the State Senate for a term. By 1897 he had become a City Court Judge in Montgomery.

In 1909 he was appointed to the Alabama Supreme Court as

Associate Judge. 'Though judges were elected, he refused ever to campaign, which fortunately became unnecessary for he early on ceased having any opponents. The thing he is most famous for in legal circles is never having had an opinion overturned.'[22] From 1910 he was re-elected each year, and by 1928 he was awarded the degree of Doctor of Laws. Throughout Zelda's childhood, 'he was considered a great judge, so much so that when it rained, the conductor of the streetcar . . . which he caught every morning, would stop the streetcar and walk for two blocks with an umbrella to fetch him'.[23]

Zelda's father, Judge Anthony Sayre, had grown up in his father Daniel's book-lined house on Court Street, Montgomery, where Daniel had inspired his children with a love of learning. Daniel Sayre had founded and edited a Tuskegee newspaper, then moved to Montgomery to edit the *Montgomery Post*. Anthony, his youngest son, was sent to a small private school, then in 1878 to Roanoke College in Salem, Virginia, from where he graduated with honours in Greek and mathematics.[24] He spent a year teaching at Vanderbilt University, then returned to Montgomery to read law and be admitted to the Bar. He earned little during his first few years as a practising attorney. However in 1883, at twenty-five, when he was appointed clerk of the city court he knew he was in a position to marry.

As the nephew of the distinguished United States Senator John Tyler Morgan (his mother Musidora's younger brother), he spent some leisure time with the Morgans. On New Year's Eve his uncle John's family gave a ball. A young Kentucky woman, Minnie Buckner Machen, who was staying with her Montgomery cousin Miss Chilton, was invited. The Chiltons were also cousins to the Sayres, which gave shy young Anthony a reason to approach her. He noticed her mass of curling hair, her firm bones that held her jewel-like face, her determined chin, which Zelda inherited.

Minnie was less interested in flirting with him than in hurrying back to Kentucky, for her father, Senator Willis B. Machen, had promised she might go to Philadelphia for elocution and music lessons. Minnie's chin was determined on a stage career. She was talented: she wrote poetry, acted, sketched and sang soprano. She gave music lessons to friends and her first story had been published.

Life on a big stage held greater interest than life as a small-town lawyer's wife. Minnie left Anthony for Philadelphia, where she read for Georgia Drew, head of the Barrymore-Drew theatrical family and, offered a role, was determined to accept. But when

Willis Machen discovered her unseemly actions, he hurtled after his daughter, dragged her off the stage, put her on a train back to Kentucky. Once home she discovered the reason for his rage. The Southern Democrats were talking of nominating him as their Presidential candidate. He certainly could not afford to have a daughter who was an actress. It would be more seemly for her to marry a lawyer with prospects. Mineral Mount, Machen's red-brick mansion on his three-thousand-acre tobacco plantation, would be a fine place for a wedding.

And so it was, on 17 June 1884.

Minnie told Zelda that she never entirely got over her disappointment at not going on the stage: a disappointment heightened after a Kentucky publisher asked her to consider writing a novel, when the most she could manage was occasional poems or stories for the *Montgomery Advertiser*. For by then she was running a household of ten, which included her five children: daughters Marjorie, Rosalind and Clothilde, fourteen, eleven and nine when Zelda, always known as Baby, was born in 1900, her one surviving son, Anthony Dickinson Sayre Jnr, born 1894, whom she treasured, and several relatives.

The death at eighteen months of her elder son, her second child Daniel, threw a permanent shadow over her life. After the birth in 1886 of Marjorie, frail, fretful, always subject to illness, Minnie had been heartened by the birth in 1887 of strong robust Daniel. But the boy child who raced through their home one day was stricken by spinal meningitis the next. 'When he died I wanted to die too,' Minnie said. 'I shut myself up in my room. I wouldn't see anyone or eat. I lay on the bed and turned my face to the wall. It might have gone on like that for no telling how long. But then . . . our family doctor . . . made me look at him. "Minnie", he said. "I know how you feel. But you've got a poor lonely girl downstairs who needs you. What's past is past. You've got to live for the living."'[25]

It was a phrase Minnie was to use often in a life so shaken by tragedies that a friend suggested an epitaph: 'Tragedy was an old familiar acquaintance of Mama Sayre's, one to whom she could say calmly, I know you and I am not afraid.'[26]

Still grieving when Rosalind (Tootsie), born in 1889, and Clothilde (Tilde), born in 1891, confirmed her disappointment that her family had 'hatched into girls',[27] Minnie's energy returned with Tony's birth. On him she lavished love to be surpassed only by her extravagant affection for baby Zelda. Six when Zelda was born, similarly highly strung, Tony became her competitor. When Zelda uses

Tony to depict 'Monsieur', the older brother of her autobiographical heroine Janno in her second novel *Caesar's Things*, he is allowed more licence than Janno and is 'angry at his rights being contested'.[28] Although Zelda later grew particularly close to both her brother and her father, as a child she contested all Tony's rights and battled against her father's.

A family friend said that the Judge, a 'severe and rather humorless disciplinarian', would send his children from the table without supper 'if they were late in arriving or unmannerly in conduct'.[29] Though Marjorie, Rosalind and Clothilde, even Tony, respected him for fear of reprisals, Zelda felt it was her right to disobey his rules and never accepted his icy detachment. She constantly goaded him as if she thought a bleeding wound would bring him closer to her. Her mother confessed that the Judge might have borne a closer relation to his girls had he not lost his boy in infancy;[30] Zelda, shaken, pretended she couldn't care less. She escaped out of her bedroom window despite being forbidden to go out at night. When her father called her a little hussy for kissing a date goodnight she said caustically: 'isn't that the way hussies do?'[31] The Judge was outraged that Zelda believed she was one of those girls who 'think they can do anything and get away with it', like her later fictional heroine Alabama Beggs, who said: 'I will be troublesome, too, if I can't do as I please.'[32] Pleasing herself was Zelda's most significant childhood trait.

To her friends she referred to solemn Papa as 'Old Dick', a ribald shortening of his middle name Dickinson, and continued to taunt him. One story suggests that Scott Fitzgerald, at his first dinner at 6 Pleasant Avenue, watched in amazement as Zelda provoked her father to such uncharacteristic rage that he chased her round the table with a carving knife.[33]

Minnie never provoked him. It was thought in the family that she poured out so much love on her children because she found her husband wanting in the affection *she* needed: 'he was known to be a very dry, silent type, without a shred of gregariousness'.[34] There must have been many times when, having seen herself as an actress, Minnie was irked by the reality of her role as a housewife. There must have been many times when Judge Sayre emerged from 'his cerebral laboratory', where he 'better provide[d] for those who were his'[35], and noticed a flicker of regret in his attentive wife's eyes.

How happy, then, were Zelda's parents?

'When I was a child, their relationship was not apparent to me,' Zelda later recalled. 'Now I see them as two unhappy people; my mother was dominated and oppressed by my father and often hurt by him; he forced her to work for a large family in which he found neither satisfaction nor a spiritual link.'[36] So little satisfaction did he find that Zelda bitterly portrays him as saying: "'I will build me some ramparts surrounded by wild beasts and barbed wire on the top of a crag and escape this hoodlum."'[37]

Neither of Zelda's parents, however, complained about each other. Her father complained so insistently about lack of money that in her first novel, *Save Me The Waltz*, Zelda makes it the predominant feature of her heroine's father. Her own father's anxiety about insufficient funds meant that for most of his life he did not own his own ramparts but rented other people's.

The Judge's parents, who originally lived in the Capitol area, had resettled in the top hat district known as 'The Hill', though not in its stateliest homes. In 1885, a year after his marriage, the Judge sold his father's Court Street house and bought a small cottage west of Sayre Street near their family Church of the Holy Comforter, where Minnie played the organ and sang in the choir. After their son Daniel's death, the house, already too small for six children, was now haunted by grief. When several relatives moved in with them the Judge decided to sell. Though his Supreme Court salary was a respectable $6,500 a year, his financial commitments and his many dependent relatives made him uneasy about another purchase. In 1907 he rented first a house in Montgomery Avenue, then two further houses nearby. In 1909 the family moved to 6 Pleasant Avenue, which he continued to rent until his death in 1931.

It was in this airy white house filled with flowers that Zelda grew up. In *Save Me The Waltz*, she describes it as having 'an affinity with light, curtain frills penetrated by sunshine . . . Winter and spring, the house is like some lovely shining place painted on a mirror.'[38] The many green-shuttered windows of this grey frame house looked out on the deep porch that ran along the width of the house. Zelda's mother, an ardent gardener, trailed clematis vines and Virginia creeper across the porch, where Zelda entertained her friends, to screen it from the sun. From the porch with its creaking swing, the family's focal point, a flight of steps led down to the front garden, and a second flight from the garden to the sidewalk.

Inside the house, the large rooms were distinguished by polished pine floors and oriental rugs. Zelda used the red velvet *portières* which separated the back hall from the front as stage curtains for her theatrical performances.

Zelda's parents always employed a cook, laundress, gardener

and when necessary a children's nurse. This meant Zelda grew up with virtually no domestic skills. Zelda's nurse was a large, handsome black woman called Aunt Julia, who wore a cap and apron and lived in a tiny cottage in the rear yard.

All the servants were black, so Zelda and her white girlfriends were tended by 'unfailingly loving, efficient black women' to whom they were close.[39] In later years this produced conflict, because in Montgomery they moved in a society where the parallel isolation of Southern black and white women was intensified by the cult of the white woman as 'soul of the South [who] must remain untainted by association with inferior classes and races'.[40]

Montgomery, that stronghold of segregation whose early settlers came from Virginia and South Carolina as well as from Europe, was built upon seven hills, high on the tawny red bluffs above the wide brown swirling Alabama River. Zelda always recalled the deep elm trees overhanging the brown foam at the water's edges and the shadows which slept under the Spanish moss. Brown mud oozed between the cobblestones of the main streets which curled down to the riverside lined with decaying wharves. Blue and white octagonal blocks paved the sidewalks. Zelda would later fictionalize the town as so hot, with breezes so seldom, that young girls would shelter behind thick flowering vines or struggle for centre place under ubiquitous electric fans.[41]

Those girls were modelled on girls from two kinds of white Montgomery families: Old Money (like the long-established Perry Street and Cloverdale families) and New Money (often from business, recent residents trying in vain to buy themselves into the inner circuit).

All Zelda's friends were Old Money, mostly with good addresses. The well-bred Haardt sisters, Ida, later Zelda's classmate, and the older Sara, who despite two years' seniority would share with Zelda a number of beaux, lived in fashionable Perry Street. Sara's Bavarian grandparents had come to Alabama in the 1840s cotton-boom days.[42] Her mother, descended from two distinguished Virginian families, 'fanatical about the South',[43] was proud of their address. Occasionally Zelda persuaded studious Sara to cartwheel down the elegant avenue. Later, when Zelda was a young mother and Sara a writer, Zelda reminded her: '[I remember] sailing wildly down the middle of Perry Street hill, screeching at the top of my lungs and catching hold of the backs of automobiles as they dashed up the hill again.'[44]

Katharine Elsberry Steiner, Zelda's close friend and cousin by

marriage, was supremely 'Old Montgomery', for her great-grandfather had been private secretary to Jefferson Davis and Assistant
Secretary to the Confederate Congress. But while Katharine lived in
Cloverdale's Gilmer Avenue and Felder Avenue, Zelda's family,
equally renowned but insufficiently wealthy, did not.[45]

Lack of wealth did not hinder Zelda from occupying a dominant
role within her group of friends. Her sisters Marjorie, Rosalind and
Clothilde were too old to be in the running. Zelda's friends all ran
behind. 'She was our leader, and when she said "Jump!" we all
jumped,' said Katharine. She and Zelda considered themselves soul-
mates because 'we were in and out of each other's houses. We were
very much alike. We dressed alike, and even looked alike.'[46] In a photograph of the two girls taken in their early teens, they have identical
flyaway curly bobs and floating lawn skirts, but what distinguished
Zelda was her hoydenism. Most Montgomery girls were interested in
attracting the attention of boys. Zelda was interested in being one of
them. 'I have always been inclined towards masculinity. It's such a
cheery atmosphere boys radiate – And we do such unique things.'[47]

She saw her mother as a free spirit whose fire had been quenched,
but her father stood for independence. 'Zelda looked at her sisters
and her mother and saw ladies in their traditional role. Then she
looked at her father who had the freedom of the Southern male. She
decided to be her father.'[48]

'From earliest childhood she was the neighbourhood tomboy,'
said Scottie, Zelda's daughter, 'the agent provocateur who dared
other little girls to race down the middle of the street on roller
skates, or jump from the rocks into the swimming hole as only boys
were supposed to do.'[49]

Zelda fictionalized her own 'original and devil-may-care attitude'[50] in Save Me The Waltz, where her autobiographical heroine
Alabama admits: 'I never let them down on the dramatic possibilities of a scene – I give them a damn good show.'[51]

Montgomery gossip thrived on the show. Zelda thrived on the
gossip. Years later, she told a doctor that as a child she did not have
'a single feeling of inferiority, or shyness, or doubt, and no moral
principles'.[52] This allowed her to run counter to the repressive
Southern ideology about women at the turn of the century.
Elaborate male courtesy masked rigid restrictions. Women,
expected to see domesticity as paramount, had to exhibit ladylike
behaviour. So Zelda's mother tried to instil the 'No Ladies' rules
into her brood. According to Sara Mayfield, five years younger than
Zelda and her devoted follower, there were six cardinal maxims.

No lady ever sat with her limbs crossed. Young ladies said 'limbs' instead of the crude four-letter word 'legs'. Ladies' backs did not touch the backs of chairs. Ladies never went out without clean linen handkerchiefs. No lady left the house until the last button on her gloves was fastened. No lady ever let her bare feet touch the bare floor.

Zelda, unlike the other girls, flouted all six. She used cruder words than 'legs'. She swung on the chairs, didn't bother with buttons because she didn't bother with gloves, climbed trees with bare feet and with bare hands fought Tony's male friends. To entertain the boys she double-somersaulted, cartwheeled and competed with daredevil Tallulah 'Dutch' Bankhead in backbends. Tallulah, the only girl to rival Zelda's flamboyance, bent so far backwards she could pick up a handkerchief with her teeth, rousing the boys to cheers. While Zelda, determined to be a dancer, started ballet in 1909,[53] and took top billing in young people's recitals at the Grand Theatre, Tallulah was preparing herself for an acting career.

Crowds of youngsters gathered to watch Dutch and Zelda hold court in the appropriately named Court Square where both Zelda's and Sara Mayfield's fathers, who served on the Alabama Supreme Court for twenty years, had offices. Presiding over the Department of Archives and History in the square was Tallulah's uncle Dr Thomas Owen, Sara Mayfield's cousin. Tallulah and her sister Gene (Eugenia), left motherless early, had run wild at their grandparents' in Fayetteville until their aunt Marie Bankhead took them back home to Montgomery.[54]

Zelda's set also hung around the State Capitol, spellbound by the Greek Revival building with its imposing dome and gleaming white porticoes supported by Corinthian and Doric columns.[55] Sara Haardt, who would major in English and history at Goucher College, stood awed, with her poetry book, beside the brass star that marked the spot where Jefferson Davis had taken the oath of office as President of the Confederate States. Zelda, never awed, flashed past the star, raced to the top of the stone steps that led to the dome, then, as defiant as Davis himself, sat astride the guns before sliding down the banisters of the famous rotunda circular staircase.[56]

Zelda's defiance conflicted at all times with Southern society's protective attitude towards all its women and in particular with her father's protective attitude towards her: 'it's very difficult to be two simple people at once, one who wants to have a law to itself and the other who wants to keep all the nice old things and be loved and safe and protected'.[57]

More often she saw herself as confident: a child in motion. 'I walked on the open roofs . . . I liked to dive and climb in the tops of trees.'[58] Zelda used her backyard swing like a circus trapeze artist. When the Ringling Brothers Circus came to Montgomery she raced down to Judge Sayre's office to hang out of his window and watch the gaudy painted parades pass by. Years later she would paint circus artists from those memories. The acrobats she drew turned the somersaults she had turned. 'I was a very active child and never tired, always running with no hat or coat even in the Negroid district and far from my house,'[59] an act of daring at a time when there was considerable if unofficial geographical segregation in Montgomery. The blacks (only one-tenth of the population) still suffered the indifference to their injuries of the largely white North and the hatred of the largely white South.[60] This had produced an almost mythic terror of black sexuality amongst white Southern adults. Though that fear affected most of Zelda's young girlfriends, she herself responded boldly. In *Caesar's Things* she writes about her child-heroine Janno's 'fear of the black-hand',[61] yet one of the *least* aggressive scenes in the novel, which is saturated with images of mutilation and death, is Janno's accidental meeting with a negro man. He is patently more scared than Janno of the consequences to *him* if he behaves badly. The child registers that she *should* feel terror, yet this interaction of a black man and a small white girl seems relatively safe to both Janno and the readers.

Though she read a great deal, not surprisingly she preferred books with action. 'The fairy tales were my favourite,' she said, because their creatures twisted, contorted and rushed through the pages. The three little pigs, Hansel and Gretel and Alice in Wonderland, which she copied as a child, she later formally painted. In Judge Sayre's extensive library she dipped into his encyclopaedias, Shakespeare, Thackeray, Dickens, Scott, Wilde, Galsworthy, Kipling, Plutarch, Aristotle, Aeschylus and Gibbons. She read Victorian children's books, gobbled up fiction slightly too old for her: 'popular tales for boys, novels that my sisters had left on the table . . . all I found about the civil war'.[62]

However, books alone could not replace a sound education, and in her late twenties Zelda regretted her inattention to early school life. Judge Sayre, a member of the Montgomery Board of Education, felt his children should be educated in public schools, so Zelda did not go with Tallulah Bankhead and Sara Mayfield to Miss Gussie Woodruff's Dame's School. Instead her mother sent her at six to the Chilton Grammar School behind Zelda's home.[63] Zelda did not like school, came home, told her parents it was worse than prison, and refused to return. Although Minnie Sayre, a student of theosophy, valued education – she had herself graduated from Montgomery Female College on 26 June 1878 and 'spent a winter being "finished" in Philadelphia'[64] – she indulgently allowed her daughter to stay off school until she was seven, after which Zelda returned until her graduation.

Scott Fitzgerald believed that Minnie's indulgence[65] had spoilt Zelda's character and encouraged what he saw as her selfish reck-lessness. Zelda's friends and relations sturdily refuted this perspective. Their view was that while Zelda received Minnie's constant praise, she was also taught to be kind and considerate. Sara Mayfield, who became her biographer and knew her for forty years, delineated her as compassionate, thoughtful and tender. Zelda never patronized anyone younger or weaker and protectively showed youngsters how to skate or dive. She was generous with time and money and never condescended. As one Montgomery child said: 'She didn't look down on me as little but made me feel as big as she.'[66]

From her father Zelda inherited secrecy and reflectiveness, for she was not always the madcap of legend. Zelda carried about her an air of urgency and mystery that made her elusive,[67] dreamy and sensual.[68] She would go on solitary walks, veer into strange silences or bubble out a stream of free association that whizzed through her brain, which later characterized her remarkable epistolary technique.

Even with friends she spent some evenings in reverie. In the powder-blue dusk that replaced the scorching sultry afternoons, Zelda, the Haardt sisters, Katharine Elsberry and her schoolfriend Eleanor Browder would catch lightning bugs. The others talked as they put them in bottles to make lamps, while Zelda's silence seemed louder than their conversations.

When she felt most unsettled or most alone, Zelda wandered down to Oakwood's Confederate Cemetery, where many of her ancestors lay. In that place of memories and secrets she would smell the lush decay from the bruised petals of poppies and roses which drifted over the grey headstones and grey gullies. Southerners still see those short-lived tissue-paper poppies and parchment magnolias as nostalgic reminders of lost childhood, fallen dead and family silences. It was Zelda's inheritance from a land of unlayable ghosts.

Sara Haardt's mother used to tell the girls: 'The South wants to forget.'[69] But the South never forgot. 'The past is never dead. It's not even past.'[70]

Consequently the cemetery, in Zelda's youth, was a place people treated like a park, bringing flowers, chatting to the dead. Today Old Montgomerians take researchers around the cemetery and point proudly to the six gleaming white Confederate graves that relate to Zelda, their local heroine. That the bodily remains of the Sayres lurk inside is not disputed; but the accuracy of the inscriptions is as puzzling as the portions of their lives that are omitted.

The first tombstone, adorned with fresh flowers, is Minnie's: the gravestone merely informs visitors she was born in Eddyville 23 November 1860, died 13 January 1958 and was the Judge's wife.

Next to Minnie's grave is a tomb for two: Zelda's eldest nervy sister Marjorie Sayre Brinson, born according to the tombstone in 1885 (but according to the Family Bible in 1886), who died two years after their mother in 1960, and her husband, Minor Williamson Brinson, who died in 1954. Locals say breezily: 'It was Marjorie who went crazy you know not Zelda, but then you could say it ran throughout their family.' Scottie recalled her Aunts Clothilde and Rosalind as constantly nervous and ailing, though not as depressed as Aunt Marjorie, who spent time in a sanatorium in 1945 with a nervous breakdown. When Marjorie's daughter, little Marjorie, stayed with the Sayres during her mother's breakdowns the child was told her mother was away on 'visits'.[71] Not until 1933, when Zelda's brother Tony had *his* breakdown during Zelda's own nervous illness, did their mother open up. She wrote to Zelda: 'Morgan blood is a pest since it means unstable nerves,' revealed how she had nursed Marjorie for two years 'and was with Tilde at her worst last summer'.[72] Scottie herself, determined to deny the family's melancholy stain, remained relentlessly resilient.

Tony has the next grave, with a neat plaque recording his birth, 9 March 1894, and his death, 27 August 1933. One would not expect it to mention his dissolute behaviour or the fact that he left Auburn University without a degree. But curiously, it removes any trace of his marriage. Tony married Edith, known by locals as 'a girl from the wrong side of the tracks', who 'disappeared' after Tony's final illness and was never spoken of again. The gravestone fails to record that Tony killed himself after many months of recurring nightmares of killing his mother.

The imposing grave next to Tony's is that of Judge Anthony Dickinson Sayre, born 29 April 1858 in Tuskegee Alabama, died 17 November 1931. Visitors notice that seventy years after his demise this grave, too, is swept and the stone polished. Zelda's friend Katharine reported that Minnie 'had to keep an eye on the Judge because he was given to terrible dark depressions'.[73] But no graveyard guides talk about this. They tell you proudly that the responsible Judge took several family members into his home, but they never mention that his subsequent anxiety led to a severe nervous break-down. For fifteen years Minnie never mentioned it either, until she forced herself to tell Zelda she had nursed the Judge 'through nine months of prostration in 1918'.[74]

Next to the Judge's memorial is another twin tomb containing two of his brothers: Daniel Morgan, the second Sayre child and eldest boy,[75] born 1839, whose death is shown by research to be 1862 but is given on the tombstone as 1888;[76] and John Reid Stonewall Sayre, sixth child and third son, who died 17 February 1940.[77] He was well known to Zelda, for the Judge had given him a home at 6 Pleasant Avenue.

The sixth Sayre tomb contains the Judge's parents: Daniel, born Franklin, Ohio, 1808, and Musidora Morgan, whom he married on 26 November 1835 in Benton County, Alabama. Daniel the journal-ist, who died in 1888, was also a democrat and landowner.

The Sayres, early settlers on Long Island, had moved via New Jersey and Ohio to Alabama. By the time of the Civil War they had become completely Southern in outlook and politics. Daniel's elder brother William had built the White House of the Confederacy for Jefferson Davis, and had become a founder of the first Presbyterian church in Montgomery.

Musidora's death, recorded as 4 March 1907, is firmly established by research, but her birth, given on the tombstone as 1818, was in fact 1817. None of the townsfolk, however, care much about the birth date, as 'Musidora wasn't from here. Born in Huntsville you know.' Zelda's grandmother, a respected schoolteacher,[78] was eccentric, forthright and didn't care whom she upset. Locals still talk about the day the widowed Musidora, also given a home by the Judge, intentionally muddled up two friends of the Sayres, both called Mrs Bell. As the wealthier Mrs Bell walked past the Pleasant Avenue porch Musidora exclaimed: 'Are you the nice Mrs Bell or are you the wealthy, ordinary and very common Mrs Bell?'

Graveyard guides inform visitors that such behaviour was due to Musidora's many griefs. She bore nine children but saw four die very young and two in early adulthood. The girls were particularly vulnerable.[79] Of the three surviving children, one was Zelda's Uncle Calvin, a silversmith, whose silver was kept in Scottie's closets until she died. In June 1871 Uncle Calvin married Zelda's friend Katharine Elsberry's great-aunt Kate. Zelda and Katharine were nine when he died in Los Angeles.[80]

The second surviving child was John Reid Stonewall; the third, Zelda's father, was treasured as the youngest. The miracle of his survival in part accounted for his overweening sense of responsibility.

On a graveyard tour one hears of the prestigious reputations of Musidora's brothers Irby and Philander, but most especially of the eminence of another brother, US Senator John Tyler Morgan.[81] What one never hears is that in his blood, too, ran the nervous disposition that haunted both sides of Zelda's family. After getting his Panama Canal scheme through the Senate he suddenly killed himself.[82]

In Oakwood Cemetery one gravestone is patently missing. That is the grave belonging to Marjorie Machen, Zelda's aunt. After suffering a series of tragedies she too was invited by Zelda's dutiful father to live with them. Had Aunt Marjorie died elsewhere, the absence of a grave would occasion no surprise. But Marjorie killed herself in the outhouse next to the kitchen of 6 Pleasant Avenue, the Sayres' 'pleasant house on a pleasant street, filled with pleasant people'.[83] Katharine Elsberry said: 'That suicide was hushed up even more than most of them were.'[84]

If you ask the graveyard guides where Aunt Marjorie's grave is, or exactly what happened to Aunt Marjorie, they shake their heads and look surprised, as if vanishing graves or repressed insanities are nothing to do with them.

In Zelda's favourite Oakwood Cemetery, there are as many omissions as there are memorials.

Zelda's previous biographers have written very little about the strains that affected Zelda's family because mental illness is one of the least discussed, if most common, occurrences in Old Montgomery. Zelda's mother had never mentioned that *her* mother, Victoria, had suffered mental illness in the harsh Canadian conditions. Minnie never told Zelda that two years after Grandfather Willis's death Victoria, griefstricken, committed suicide. It was one of several suicides not spoken of in Zelda's family.

Montgomery people point out that 'the Civil War did something terrible to Southern men'. Suicides were more common amongst Montgomery men than was ever publicly acknowledged. Sara Mayfield's brother, and the father of Zelda's cousin Katharine, both committed suicide. Both deaths were hushed up. This was the dark side to the vivid life of the South in which Zelda grew up.

'In the South most of our good families are tainted with insanity. We handle it by thinking of the insane as "special". But we don't talk about anything considered "unpleasantness" and insanity would be unpleasantness. So Montgomery families create incredible facades. Entire blocks and neighbourhoods support each other in the lie of stability. Southerners don't like those who are willing to wrestle with their demons in public. You can be sure if you don't deal with the South it will deal with you.'[85]

But in the Northern life Zelda was to lead she would have to face those inherited troubling instabilities.

She would need great courage. How fortunate that from her ancestors Zelda also inherited resilience and a sense of the romantic.

CHAPTER 2

As an adolescent Zelda embodied the 'romantic readiness', the heightened sensitivity to the promises of life which Scott Fitzgerald would one day write about.[1] Her romantic qualities embraced a love of nature, a love of the past and – even in these early years – a primitive imagination. Her Southern schooldays always seemed to her to be fragile.

When she and Sara Haardt were living in the North many years later, Zelda reminded her friend: 'It always seemed to be Spring . . . the whole town filled with the smell of kiss-me-at-the-gate . . . at night we were skating again, . . . or dancing violently. For us, life had become spectacular, bombastic, almost unbearably exciting . . . then . . . we had the inescapable feeling that all this beauty and fun – everything – might be over in a minute.'[2]

As Zelda blossomed into a young woman, many people remarked that there was something theatrical about her eyes. They changed colour: sometimes blue, sometimes green; most often Confederate grey. Young men stared at Zelda and she stared right back. Her appearance with its peaches-and-cream complexion was also archetypically romantic.

At Zelda's co-educational school, Sidney Lanier High,[3] to which she moved after graduating in 1914 from the Sayre Street School, when her classmates listed the qualities of a composite Ideal Senior Girl, Zelda rated top marks for a kissable mouth. In *This Side of Paradise* Scott uses both Zelda's peaches-and-cream complexion and her 'eternal kissable mouth, small, slightly sensual, and utterly disturbing' for his heroine Rosalind Connage.[4]

Zelda, with a figure that 'fitted together with delightful precision, like the seeds of a pomegranate',[5] looked tall, an illusion of height due to her erect posture and her dancer's grace.[6] She had finely-tuned strong bones, a hawk-like nose which gave her face great strength and a low voice with an attractive Southern drawl.

Adults remarked on her convoluted vocabulary. Her idiosyncratic speech pattern, bursting with high-flown metaphors and disconnected associations, had become habitual and had never troubled her family. Scott, who met her four years and many metaphors later, found her unusual connections curious but copied them into his notebook for use in his fiction. Later, however, her language jolted her Northern doctors. Her sensuous Southern allegories became an integral part of the way psychiatrists diagnosed her symptoms as schizophrenia.

Zelda's speech was in fact rooted in traditional Southern dialect which is characterized by that same concrete sensual detail, vivid dramatic imagery and sly humour. It arose from the mixture of both black and white folk speech which Zelda heard as she grew up tended by black mammies and overseen by white educators.

Zelda spent her high school years lightheartedly dashing off the classic curriculum of history, geography, English literature, French, Latin, physics, chemistry, maths and physiology. She had a consistently high B average and did even better in English and maths. Considering her low class attendance her aptitude was dazzling, but her long-term interest was nil. 'We played hookey almost every day from school . . . Sometimes we'd stop at old Mr McCormack's grocery store . . . and buy a lot of loose crackers and dill pickles and chocolate nigger babies . . . When we were tired . . . we would go in a picture-show and sit in the dark of the theatre while the janitor swept around us and picked up the peanut shells . . . [or] we went swimming in some inconceivably muddy hole.'[7] What *did* interest her was art and ballet. She shone at painting lessons *in* school and *out* of school she enrolled in Professor Weisner's dancing class.[8]

On her few days in school she inventively talked her way out of trouble. In her senior year she was chosen to represent England in a public wartime pageant. Sara Haardt remembers rehearsing Zelda in the dressing room. 'She had recited her speech, letter-perfect: "Interrupted in these benevolent pursuits for over three years I have been engaged in bloody warfare" . . . [Then] with a shining helmet and sword, she marched on the stage and faced the tense, waiting crowd . . . her tongue was suddenly paralyzed. "Interrupted –" she began. "Interrupted –" she began again. "Interrupted –". It was hopeless. Zelda went on repeating it like an irritating gramophone record until with supreme confidence she made an exit line that brought the cheering house to its feet: "Gentlemen, I've been permanently interrupted!" '[9]

Her schoolfriend Livye Hart recalls Zelda's complete disregard for propriety. During the last part of their school years there was an unbreakable taboo on any mention of childbirth, especially out of wedlock. Zelda broke it on Armistice Day 1918. A mixed crowd milled around scattered with confetti. Zelda said in a stage whisper to Livye so that the boys could hear: 'I'm so full of confetti I could give birth to paper dolls.' The men heard too and wanted to laugh but their wives were tutting. Days later, Zelda, fresh from a date, went further: 'I liked him so much that he will probably be the father of my next child.'[10] Zelda pasted into her scrapbook a school magazine item that said: 'What would happen if Zelda Sayre ever said anything serious?'[11]

Some evenings, when bored, Zelda would borrow one of the boys' cars and drive past Madame Helen St Clair's, the local whorehouse, flicking the spotlights on boys she recognized as they entered or left the establishment.

She was voted prettiest girl in class – but not the best dressed. The Belles who looked drab at school also looked dull in the evenings. The majority, who looked trim at school, looked elegant at nights. Their clothes were consistent. Zelda's were not. As with everything else there was something slightly askew. Out of line. A beat away from the norm.

Her school clothes were deliberately careless, pleated skirt bunched up round her waist to shorten it so that her slip showed, tie hung the wrong way. But at night her melodramatic finery outclassed everyone else's. Her mother was an excellent seamstress, so Zelda stood on the stage lending an air of importance to two yards of green tulle. The first thing you noticed was 'that manner she had, as though she was masquerading as herself'.[12]

Zelda knew it was mandatory for Southern Belles to define themselves by their looks. Zelda's daughter Scottie told *her* children: 'In the South the sense of femaleness is implanted at a very young age . . . Southern girls [have] long hair in tumbled curls . . . high heels and fetching make-up.'[13]

Zelda's set felt keenly their fashions were inferior to New York. 'We were all little Alabama girls, kinda greenhorns, but Zelda was more up for the show,' commented Grace Gunter, two years younger than Zelda, who went to the same schools, became a Belle with her and would remain a friend when Zelda returned to Montgomery in 1940. 'You felt as if you had to compete. I had flannelling pyjamas with feet in them but Zelda . . . soon changed to negligées with big lace. During the day we all wore middy blouses . . . but at nights we might wear lawn with lil pink roses. Alabama girls were meant to look very feminine. We all wore high heels . . . had long hair and didn't smoke. Later some of us did bob our hair but our parents would be very fierce.'[14]

It was 1919 before Zelda cut hers, at which point she wrote to Scott: 'I'm going to bob my hair, and that may evoke a furor.'[15]

Minnie Sayre told her daughters a lady was meant to create a quality of life, not question it. Zelda's three attractive sisters never questioned it. What they *did* flout was the Old Montgomery expectation that they should not work before marriage. Both Marjorie and Rosalind chose interesting careers cut short by engagements. Marjorie was a good pen-and-ink artist and a schoolteacher before she married Minor W. Brinson in 1909 and resigned.[16] On graduating from Sidney Lanier High School Rosalind worked as a teller at the First National City Bank, the first Montgomery girl of a 'good family' to hold a non-teaching job. Later Rosalind, always pragmatic, told Scott that she firmly believed in bourgeois values, but at the time she enjoyed the frivolous job of Society Editor for the *Montgomery Journal* before she married Newman Smith in 1917. Two months later, dark and serious Clothilde, reputed to be almost as attractive as Zelda, married John Palmer who, like Rosalind's husband, served as an officer in the American Expeditionary Force in Europe.

As Tony, the sibling she was closest to, was working in Mobile as a Mississippi River Civil Engineer, by the time Zelda finished high school in 1918 she was the only child left at home.

Zelda's bedroom was the smallest of five. It was pink, white and magical. The white bed covered with a Marseilles counterpane looked on to starched white muslin curtains that let in the sunlight. Pink flowers climbed over white walls, matching the pink chintz-covered dressing table. Her grandmother Musidora's desk and a slat-backed rocking chair stood near the bed.

Years later she recreated her bedroom colours in her first novel and suffused the pages with the smell of pear trees, for opposite their house was an orchard where overripe fruit tumbled down and split open.

In summer she had a perfect view of her mother's pink geraniums, yellow peonies and purple verbenas. In spring she gazed on a lake of blue hyacinths edged by sunshine jonquils and Mexican primroses. Her bedroom also overlooked the grounds of the landlady's estate in which grew camellias, boxwood and kiss-me-at-the-gate. Her particular love was for giant cape jasmines and voluptuous magnolias which would become memorable signatures in her paintings.[17]

But Zelda's romantic relationship to flowers was edged with something strange. She watched her mother tame ferocious tiger lilies and arrogant iris until they grew quietly alongside the crepe myrtle, then years later drew those lilies with petals like tentacles and a phallic arrogance. Later she said that beneath their surface beauty she saw an underlying fragmentation and despair. It was a grown-up viewpoint and a provocatively Southern vision.

If Zelda's intuitive responsiveness to natural beauty was partly influenced by the profusion of Alabama flowers, it was also marked by some of North Carolina's lushest landscapes where the Sayres took their summer vacations. Zelda accompanied the Judge and Minnie to a hilltop inn in Saluda, North Carolina.[18] They picked blackberries and walked, dwarfed by towering mountains. Later, Zelda's paintings braced those same mountains with highly coloured visible tension.

Though as an adult Zelda lived in the North, her creative insights were for ever Southern: there were no cold colours, her most striking landscapes were scorching.

Legend suggests that Zelda had few women friends but in fact she was extremely popular. Her friends were of course all white: Old Montgomery Belles were never permitted friendships with young black women. Even white Southern women were somewhat isolated from each other by the dictum of competing for male attention. Nevertheless Zelda moved with a strong female team as vivacious and beautiful as herself: Livye Hart, a dark gypsy, Eleanor Browder, a Modigliani portrait,[19] Grace, 'eldest of the six beautiful Gunter girls' and daughter of Montgomery's Mayor which gave her a slight edge. All had the characteristic Old Money appreciation of their own worth but Zelda's belief that her way of doing anything was the best was even stronger than her peers'.

There is a photo of Grace, Zelda and their set leaning against a motor on their way to a picnic, all in regulation white middy blouses with neat black ties, all laughing except Zelda who stands taller than the rest, her tie knotted more carelessly, unsmiling. 'We always moved around in groups,' Grace said holding the photo nostalgically. 'That day the chaperone made a pass at my boyfriend so I've got my head down I was so furious . . . Zelda was our natural leader. It didn't happen to her.'[20]

Zelda later reminded Sara Haardt: 'We were never conscious of chaperones or disapproval of any sort. If we were criticized one place we simply went to another. We had . . . no sense of guilt . . . nothing seemed unnatural. It was only when the older generations made us conscious of what we were doing that we grew confused and wild.'[21]

On Friday nights Zelda's set went out with their dates to teenage dances over May's Confectionery shop because Zelda adored May's pineapple drops and sugared perfume balls. Sometimes Zelda suggested dances at the pavilions in nearby Oak Park or Pickett Springs.[22] Sara Haardt recalls the last Christmas dance she and Zelda attended at the ballroom of Montgomery's Exchange Hotel where Mrs Jefferson Davis received visitors. 'I saw her [Zelda] . . . wearing a flame dress and gold-laced slippers, her eyes starry and mocking, flirting an immense feather fan. Her bronze-gold hair was curled in a thousand ringlets, and as she whirled about, they twinkled enchantingly like little bells. Around her flashed hundreds of jellybeans . . . [with] pearl-studded fronts and hundreds of other flappers . . . but they seemed somehow vain and inarticulate beside her. Beauty, they had, and grace, and a certain reckless abandon – yet none of them could match the gleam of gay derision that flickered beneath the black edge of her eyelashes – and none of them could dance as she did, like a flame or a wind.'[23]

Virginia Foster Durr, later a Civil Rights activist, also described Zelda's popularity: 'Zelda always did things to shock people . . . she was just gorgeous. She had a glow around her. When she came into a ballroom, all the other girls would want to go home because they knew the boys were going to be concentrating on Zelda. The boys would line up the whole length of the ballroom to dance with her for one minute. She was pre-eminent and we recognized it . . . Zelda was like a vision of beauty dancing by. She was funny, amusing, the most popular girl; envied by all the others, worshipped and adored, besieged by all the boys. She did try to shock. At a dance she pinned mistletoe on the back of her skirt, as if to challenge the young men to kiss her bottom.'[24]

Zelda had more freedom than her friends. She could go straight from school to the ice-cream parlour without checking in. Rosalind said that, apart from the 'No Ladies' rules, 'we were not brought up on "Don'ts" but were allowed to think for ourselves.'[25] They owed this to their mother, who though she lived in Montgomery for seventy-five years always felt an outsider, with an outsider's eccentric privileges. Minnie saw her neighbours as provincial and dull. They saw her as 'artistic' or odd. Montgomery residents still tell the tale of how Minnie permitted her four daughters to bathe nude on her back porch, a place that could be overlooked by keen-eyed local boys. When the respectable ladies suggested to Minnie that she found them a more modest location she is reputed to have said tartly: 'Why should they? God gave them beautiful bodies!'

In view of this maternal example it comes as no surprise that Zelda herself should later have chosen to wear a tight flesh-coloured Annette Kellermann one-piece bathing suit and to encourage the rumours that she swam nude.

According to Katharine Elsberry and Grace Gunter Lane those rumours were quite untrue.[26] Ida Haardt told a friend: 'Zelda was spirited. But nevertheless we thought of her as a lady. She was not thought of as wild or immoral. Zelda was well liked and well respected. The tales of her being "fast" came from people's jealousy.'[27] Alabama Judge John P. Kohn said: '[Zelda was] attractive, vivacious, daring . . . No one to my knowledge ever questioned her good reputation as to morals.'[28] How then were reputations made or lost?

Grace Gunter explained:

> We were coy and we expected the boys to be courteous . . . unless a girl already had a bad reputation. Zelda did not have a bad reputation . . . She just had a reputation as a tomboy who did daring things. Like once Zelda got up on a table in the Country Club and did a dance. Everyone was shocked. Another time she commandeered a street car and drove it off like a crazy person. Daring and more boyish she was but she never drank, none of us did, none of us smoked, nor did Zelda. She wasn't wild sexually, she did not have that kind of reputation. She was very independent. She got bored and restless quicker than the ordinary girls. Zelda was different from everyone else.[29]

All her set agreed that Zelda was 'different'.

Sara Mayfield believed that as 'flirtation was an old Southern custom but "going the limit" was not, the evidence was against Zelda being 'a speed'. But even loyal Sara had to admit that when Zelda's beaux slipped away from her one night because they wanted to swim naked, she followed them and tied their clothes in knots. True or false, Zelda at fifteen did nothing to discourage tales of her outrageous behaviour.

At fifteen Zelda would have liked the newspaper publicity she achieved at twenty, but she rarely made the Montgomery newspapers before 1918, owing to the rule that 'A lady's name should never appear in print but three times: when she is born, when she marries, and when she dies.'[30]

To Zelda's chagrin it was Tallulah Bankhead, her childhood rival in daredevilry, who managed to break that embargo. In the interests of decorum and public safety, as one girl put it,[31] Tallulah had been removed from Montgomery and sent with her sister Eugenia to

New York's Academy of the Sacred Heart where she pressed to go into the theatre.[32] At sixteen she finally got a small part in the play *The Squab Farm*. Montgomery was so appalled that the newspapers ran the horrified headline: 'Society Girl Goes on Stage'. When Tallulah's aunt Marie Bankhead read it she was so shocked that she immediately wired Tallulah: 'Remember you're a Bankhead!' The telegraph office got it wrong and Tallulah received the message: 'Remember you're a blockhead!'[33]

Once she finished schooling, Tallulah lived alone at New York's Algonquin hotel where later Dorothy Parker, Robert Benchley and other wits would set up their circle. The Sayres would have insisted Zelda had a chaperone before setting foot in such a place. But Tallulah employed a French maid who, she assured her Montgomery friend, was just as effective for she was 'still a technical virgin'.[34]

Montgomery women adhered to the same rules as New Yorkers. Under the 'New Freedom' Zelda's set could have a good time as long as they preserved their technical virginity. Confederacy codes meant no gossip. The sin lay in the saying. That was where Zelda differed from the rest. None of them were 'speeds' but Zelda couldn't resist the temptation to appear one, to tell the tale. So while Sara Haardt confined her dancing to the more dignified waltz, foxtrot or tango, Tallulah in New York and Zelda in Montgomery raised their hemlines to the knee and danced the sensuous shimmy and the Toddle cheek to cheek. To be thoroughly rebellious they tackled the Charleston, which originated as an African American South Carolina dance. In New York Tallulah was one sophisticate amongst many; in Montgomery Zelda was one on her own.

It was a relief to Zelda's teachers when in 1918 she graduated from Sidney Lanier. Under Zelda's graduation photo run the lines:

Why should all life be work, when we all can borrow.
Let's think only of today, and not worry about tomorrow.[35]

Sara Haardt had graduated two years previously but though trained like Zelda to become a Belle, she had merely gone through the motions.[36] Sara's intransigence was intellectual. She knew that ladies were not expected to hold radical opinions or speak out and that if they did they could be punished. But when the Northern Suffragettes arrived in Montgomery and spoke from soapboxes Sara and some other Belles, though not Zelda, joined them. Within minutes they were hauled off by the police.

Sarcastically Sara said later: 'If you have a mind, and you don't want to use it – or you can't use it – the place to live is the South.'[37] But Zelda wasn't quite sure what to do with her mind. As an intelligent young woman she felt stifled by the way Southern Belles were pressed towards uniformity. She knew from her mother's experience that artistic women had to conceal any commitment to free their creative voice. But as Grace pointed out: 'Zelda wasn't serious or studious like Sara Haardt . . . there was all the difference in the world between Sara and Zelda, they were not the same kind of girl. Zelda was clever too but they had different goals.'[38]

When Sara, never strong, overcame bouts of illness to enter Goucher College, Baltimore, in fall 1916, she began a life that would enable her to become a writer.[39] Sara had taken the path which sharply divided the Brains from the Belles; it was a path that Zelda, brainier than most, later wished she had taken.

When Zelda graduated she wanted to escape, but the idea of college never entered her head. Though bolder than Sara in most respects, she would conventionally accept the route through marriage. To achieve that, eligible beaux must become her priority. She was never short of male admirers whom she constantly encouraged to take the risks she took, on motorcycles, in cars, or diving into seas from high cliffs, and she was contemptuous if they failed.

Zelda was not a 'tabloid sort of person. From the first, the men who liked her were very distinguished.'[40] Two of the most distinguished were John Sellers and Peyton Mathis, whom she had known since childhood and who courted both her and Sara Haardt for several years. On the surface they appeared to be Southern gentlemen, labelled the Gold Dust Twins because of their wealth, renown and inseparability. Peyton was the proprietor of the Montgomery Marble Works and creator of several distinguished monuments in the cemetery. Older than Zelda's other beaux and known as 'The Pride of the Confederacy', Peyton behaved as if he had a romantic past. Sellers was tall, chestnut blond and from a society background.[41] Along with Leon Ruth, Lloyd Hooper and Dan Cody[42], all Zelda's ex-beaux, these two men were endowed with physical magnetism and money. However, the smooth-talking Sellers and Mathis played a highly destructive role in one of the most savage scenes in Zelda's adolescence.

It was a sexually abusive scene which Scott later euphemistically termed a 'seduction'. In the 1930s, during bitter recriminations about their marriage breakdown, Scott reminded Zelda that though at the time of their marriage 'the assumption [was] that you were a great prize package – by your own admission many years after (and for which I never reproached you) you had been seduced and provincially outcast. I sensed this the night we slept together first, for you're a poor bluffer.'[43] In 1938 Scott went further in a letter to Zelda's sister Marjorie and offered chapter and verse: 'Your mother took such rotten care of Zelda that John Sellers was able to seduce her at fifteen.'[44] Scott's biographer Jeffrey Meyers confirms that Zelda lost her virginity at fifteen.

Further evidence of Sellers' violence comes from Sara Mayfield's later relationship with him. Despite Sellers' courting of both Zelda and Sara Haardt, it was young Sara Mayfield whom he married in 1924 when she was nineteen; but within three years his drinking, cruelty and sexual violence forced Sara to divorce him. This would have taken great courage as divorce in the South in the Twenties was heavily stigmatized. But when Sellers violated a particular Act which forbade men to cross state lines for immoral purposes such as prostitution or sex with young girls, Sara had little choice.[45]

Zelda never at any time refuted Scott's accusation. As a girl who did *not* have a bad reputation her shock at being treated like one who did would have secured her silence. She did however leave one account which implied Scott's accusation was almost certainly correct and probably took place in the girls' schoolyard. In Zelda's version, in her second novel, Mathis as well as Sellers was implicated.

Montgomery and her schooldays, often represented as a golden time in a peaceful place, are depicted in the autobiographical *Caesar's Things* as dark and threatening. The town initially wears 'an air of bounty'. Janno, Zelda's confident heroine, darts through the sunny hours, a rebel like herself. Then suddenly 'a penderant cumulative doom hangs latent in the air'; a 'great fear of the black-hand covered the town'; people talk of an impending 'cataclysmic event'. There is blood on the sidewalks. As the sickly-sweet summer vines fade Janno/Zelda's terror increases. She has forgotten 'all about this year of her life until she was grown, and married, and tragedy had revivified its traces – as she then saw, carved from the beginning'.[46]

Forbidden activity for girls and violence from boys crowd the chapters. On Janno's porch, the creaking swing is jammed with boys, as proprietorial and powerful as those Zelda grew up with. When the gang rush off, four, including handsome Dan and Anton, who hang around like the Magnetic Twins, with the obvious attributes of Sellers and Mathis, stay with Janno. They 'subscribed to heavy petting' and did not believe that sex 'should be the expression of an inward emotion'.

Anton, with chestnut hair, is 'a rich boy and knew the criteria. He killed himself later but you never could have told it at the time. He was debonair, insouciant, and he went to church with prestige.' The boys turn on her: come with us. One of the mothers has told the girls not to 'go like that' with boys. Janno wishes fervently it had been her mother. That might have given her the strength she needed to refuse.

Lacking 'rules and prescriptions for right', she tries: 'It's not right. I don't want to go.' Dan won't argue with a mere girl; Anton feels 'girls went where boys told them and were glad of the attention'. And he wants Janno. 'The boys looked wisely at each other; turned ominously . . . "Then if you don't want to go with us, nobody will have anything further to do with you."' Zelda suggests Janno is intimidated not only by the boys' menacing lines but also by their superior clothes and manners. 'It was clearly a threat, an ominoys [sic] world. It was not clear in her mind just what ominous rendez-vous with other orientations they proposed; but it was quite clear that this was a step from which irrevocable consequence would result.'

Like a Greek chorus the boys intone: 'If you didn't go with us where will you be?' They assume the air of an 'authorized commit-tee': 'You won't have any friends – nobody else will come to see you.' Janno 'looked over the threat of doom – and followed the judg-ment of men'.[47]

Zelda, who from childhood was familiar with Greek tragedy, allows something horrible to happen offstage as Janno is led away by the Magnetic Twins.[48] Some sinister sexual violence occurs.

They went up to the haunted schoolyard so deep in shadows and creak-ing with felicities of murder to the splintery old swing and she was so miserable and trusting that her heart broke and for many years after she didn't want to live: but it was better to keep going.

Janno proudly pretends not to care. She will try to be attractive, to ensure she is 'well received'. She will strive for popularity, make the best of the broken circumstances. But in her mind something says: 'But what you do is to suffocate the soul because you do care and it would be better to cry.' Zelda believes that self-respect and survival ensure a traumatized woman forgets. She 'relegates that sort of thing to the ash can until years later'.[49]

Though this very strong evidence for Zelda's early tragedy is fic-tional, it would seem to be autobiographically accurate; but it will also have been influenced by later clinical traumas. Most significant incidents in Zelda's fiction do have autobiographical triggers. Black moments patently clouded the well-documented Alabama sunshine. The Gold Dust Twins are substantial models for Dan and Anton, her imaginative creations.

Another piece of factual evidence relates to this very important incident. Zelda was known for her extreme coquetry, which can be explained in two relevant ways. To some extent Zelda was influenced by the Southern code that demanded flirtatiousness in women, and by the effects of World War I on modern American women which deterred them from exclusive commitment.[50] But her purposefully capricious sexual style could also be rooted in the violent girlhood incident Scott refers to. Recent research shows that most girls who have been sexually abused grow up sexualizing their friendships, sometimes physically, usually emotionally and often verbally through heavy sexual banter. As Janno in Zelda's novel explains, the original trigger for this behaviour is often suppressed for many years.

It is also relevant that the young beaux' code of courtesy and honour in a town where the Bible was read and memorized was set against their knowledge that possum hunting, military escapades, adulation of male violence and lynchings were as routine as courting and weddings.

These of course were to be abruptly changed by the war, as indeed was Zelda. She recalled how before the war 'there was scarcely a ripple in our lives; life itself seemed serene and almost smugly secure.'[51] Montgomery, which she later fictionalized as Jeffersonville in 'Southern Girl', was a sleepy town: 'Nothing ever seems to happen . . .; the days pass, lazily gossiping in the warm sun. A lynching, an election, a wedding, catastrophes, and business booms all take on the same value, rounded, complete, dusted by the lush softness of the air in a climate too hot for any but sporadic effort.'[52]

Then on 6 April 1917 the USA declared war on Germany.

'Suddenly, almost the next day – everything was changed. Life had suddenly become exciting, dangerous; a crazy vitality possessed us . . . the War came . . . we couldn't afford to wait, for fear it would be gone forever: so we pitched in furiously, dancing every night and riding up and down the moonlit roads and even swimming in the gravel pools under the white Alabama moon . . . Oh, we did wild, silly things – often incredible things – but oftenest with a sense of tragedy.'[53]

Montgomery was besieged by soldiers from nearby Camp
Sheridan and aviators from Camp Taylor. 'The war brought men to
town like swarms of benevolent locusts eating away the blight of
unmarried women that had overrun the South since its economic
decline.'[54]

Belles' habits changed. They hurried through their self-conscious
rituals of five o'clock swims when the sun went down followed by
languid six o'clock sodas in order to join 'the taller, broader, older
youth in uniform'. According to *Caesar's Things*, 'the town smelt of
khaki', there was a 'general air of the felicity of romance about. The
girls were prettier than the shop windows . . . One had to be in love
. . . the city staggered with the impact of love.'[55]

Zelda's circle entered new kinds of courtships. Katharine
Elsberry recalled: 'We had a date with a different boy each night of
the week.' By 1918 Katharine had eloped with a Canadian stationed
at Camp Sheridan, partly because Northern soldiers were a novelty
but also, as she told Zelda, because of 'sexual curiosity'. Afraid to
break the news to her family, she called Zelda and asked her to tell
them.[56]

'There weren't enough girls to go round,' wrote Zelda. 'Girls too
tall or too prim . . . were dragged from their spinsterly pursuits to
dance with the soldiers . . . You can imagine how the popular ones
fared!'[57]

The most popular was Zelda. Admirers from Auburn University
had already founded a fraternity based on her initials: Zeta Sigma.
Zelda now added the military to fraternity boys and football heroes.
Uniformed beaux swarmed her sagging veranda, which looked like
a recruiting station. In her glove box she collected the soldiers' gold
and silver insignia which they threw down before her as tributes.

'It was strange what things the war did to us . . . Of course I
suppose, it goes back further than that, but it was as if everything in
the air, in life, sort of led up to it.'[58] For Zelda war intensified the
feeling of life's fragility. A youth spent in Montgomery is time spent
in a past that is always present, where the only currency is the imminent possibility of death. Zelda had both always known it yet never
known it until now. Once the war began, soldiers left and did not
return. Aviators were flung from the skies and did not rise.
Suddenly her particular Southern past had converged with the
national wartime present.

But she was only seventeen. She did not yet want to think about
it. In time she would acknowledge those feelings in her fiction and
painting, but for now she is off to the wartime dances.

'I danced every night,' she recalled, '. . . but the ones I enjoyed most were the privates' dances down in the dirty old City Hall auditorium. Only a few girls went . . . it was supposed to be rough . . . there were no officers present – there weren't even any intermissions because there weren't enough girls to go round.'

At those dances she still could not dismiss that sense of tragedy. 'We even danced by sad, wailing tunes, for it was just about then that the blues came in,' she said.[59] But there was a new element at the dances: something not tragic at all.

As the leading Belle at the Country Club, Zelda had the pick of the Montgomery bluebloods. But her romantic sensibility had attached itself to wider horizons, more sophisticated dreams of urban glamour, worldly success, swimming in a larger pond than Montgomery. When the Yankee army came to Camp Sheridan her attention was caught by new kinds of officers. There were midwestern Babbitts, Southern sharecroppers and rich Yankees. One night there was a young fellow from St Paul, Minnesota. He was a blond first lieutenant in the 67th Infantry whom she would later draw as a paper doll with pink shirt, red tie and brown angel's wings.

Zelda was performing a solo, 'The Dance of the Hours'. He stood at the edge of the dance floor and watched her.

She didn't ask his name. But he told her anyway. He was Scott Fitzgerald.

CHAPTER 3

Zelda later fictionalized that first meeting with Scott Fitzgerald in July 1918 by writing: 'There seemed to be some heavenly support beneath his shoulder blades that lifted his feet from the ground in ecstatic suspension, as if he secretly enjoyed the ability to fly but was walking as a compromise to convention.'[1]

It was an incorrigibly romantic line.

Scott matched it. His first impression of Zelda was that of 'a saint, a Viking Madonna'[2] whose beauty so stunned him that he changed his portrait of Rosalind Connage in *This Side of Paradise* (1920) to base her partly on Zelda. Then he wrote: 'all criticism of Rosalind ends in her beauty'.[3]

That too was a romantic line.

When Dorothy Parker encountered Zelda and Scott she thought they looked like a couple who had just stepped out of the sun.[4] But Zelda and Scott each had another side: a less sunny side, and one that synchronized. Not long after they met, Zelda wrote to Scott: 'You know everything about me, and that's mostly what I think about. I seem always curiously interested in myself, and it's so much fun to stand off and look at me.'[5]

Much less romantic: definitely egotistical; yet Scott found it provocative.

What was more, he could surpass it. One of the finest – if intermittent – marks of both his fiction and his character is his clear and honest self-appraisal. In a flash of insight many years after their first meeting, he wrote: 'I didn't know till 15 that there was anyone in the world except me, and it cost me *plenty*.'[6]

In time their egotism and self-centredness would damage their relationship, but in their first few months Zelda and Scott inflamed each other by flaunting those very qualities.

Their personal evaluations had a dangerous symmetry, as did their fierce judgements on other people. After dating Scott for some time Zelda wrote: 'People seldom interest me except in their relation to things, and I like men to be just incidents in books so I can imagine their characters.'[7]

Less openly in his Notebook Scott wrote: 'When I like women I want to own them, to dominate them, to have them admire me.'[8]

He had already voiced this view before he met Zelda. Like all infantry lieutenants in that period, Scott expected to die in battle. In the Officers Club he had begun writing a novel for posterity: 'The Romantic Egotist'. Among the 120,000 words[9] ran the lines: 'I was convinced that I had personality, charm, magnetism, poise, and the ability to dominate others. Also I was sure that I exercised a subtle fascination over women.'[10]

As Edmund Wilson said later, Zelda and Scott's fantasies were precisely in tune. Curiously, their appearance as well as their ambitions had a strange congruence. If Scott Fitzgerald looked like an angel he also looked absurdly like Zelda. People would soon mistake them for brother and sister. There are several photos of Zelda and Scott during the year they first met. They both have that gold-leaf hair that sets off their similar black one-piece swimsuits. She lounges lazily on a bank of flowers or is poised near a pool. She holds her breath before she dives in. The only difference is that whereas Scott's appearance at least in photos remains consistent, Zelda's changes from photo to photo, even in those taken the same year. She had as many faces as she had voices. Both Zelda and Scott had a gift for self-dramatization which often disguised their self-awareness. Both spent extravagantly, drank heavily, spelt badly, were spoiled children of older parents. Both had disliked their first schools and been allowed to withdraw from them by indulgent mothers.

Both liked to exchange sexual roles. Scott had dressed up as a showgirl for Princeton's Triangle Club. When Scott was temporarily out of reach, Zelda put on men's clothing and went to the movies with a group of boys. Scott, who was always surrounded by women, admitted: 'I am half feminine – that is my mind is.'[11] Zelda by her own assertion had always been inclined towards masculinity.[12] When Scott suggested that she met his mother, she wrote nervously: 'I am afraid I am losing all pretense of femininity, and I imagine she will demand it.'[13]

From early on they enacted dramas in order to attract attention. On getting it, Scott became excited by people's response while Zelda was indifferent.

Most versions of Zelda's legendary first meeting with Scott suggest it was at Montgomery's Country Club. J. Winter

Thorington, a cousin of her family, believes that they met earlier at a teaparty at his Great-Aunt Bessie's. In that version neither Zelda nor Scott took much notice of the other.[14] A few days later they met again at the Country Club, when Zelda's utter disdain for Scott first engaged his attention. He stared at her bewitched as she ignored the line of stags crowding around her.[15] Without asking anyone to introduce him, he cut in on her, astounded at her popularity. Not once could he dance across the room with her before another man cut in. In the intermission, frustrated at his low ranking, he asked her for a late date but she replied: 'I never make late dates with fast workers.'

She was prepared to give him her phone number, which he rang so often that he remembered it as long as he lived. He also remembered that her date book was filled for weeks ahead.

Despite her apparent coolness however he *had* made a visual impression on her. Scott looked like a jonquil. His golden hair, parted in the centre, was slicked down with tonic. He swaggered as he walked, rated himself a good dancer, and hid a slightly tense mouth with an engaging smile.[16]

His classical features, straight nose, high wide brow, heavy dark lashes, were striking, and his eyes, like Zelda's, changed colour. Though Zelda saw them as green, when Montgomery's Lawton Campbell met Scott at Princeton in 1916, he saw them as lavender. He thought Scott 'the handsomest boy I'd ever seen'.[17] Hardly surprising that at Princeton Scott 'collected a painful number of votes as the prettiest member of his class'.[18] Scott himself boasted that though he did not have John Sellers' and Peyton Mathis's envied qualities of great animal magnetism or money, he did have the two lesser requirements, 'good looks and intelligence', so he always got 'the top girl'.[19]

Zelda immediately noticed Scott's smart attire. Brooks Brothers in New York had tailored his officer's tunic. His sunshine yellow boots and spurs gave him a kick start over his fellow officers who wore ordinary issue puttees. When Zelda fictionalized him as David Knight in Save Me The Waltz (1932) she said he smelled like new goods. This apt simile matched Scott's own preoccupations. In his writings haberdashery is symbolic. Jay Gatsby and Scott Fitzgerald both see connections between their wardrobes and their wealth.

After checking out his clothes Zelda agreed to date him. She did not agree to stop dating other men.

Scott began to call regularly at the Sayres'. He sat with Zelda on the grey frame porch screened with clematis and vines from the sun.

He swayed with her on the creaking swing to the scent of honey-suckle, while Miss Minnie sat in her peeling rocker and the Judge ostensibly read his evening paper while observing him.

But Scott was not the only man to share the swing. He was but one of many officers who called regularly, all of whom Zelda knew 'with varying degrees of sentimentality'.[20] Dashing young aviators from Taylor Field routinely performed aerial stunts over the Sayre house to amuse Zelda. One moustached suitor, Second Lieutenant Lincoln Weaver, who had been kissed by Zelda, amused her for weeks until he proposed. At that point she instantly rejected him. Utterly astonished, he asked why had she kissed him? As testing the unknown was Zelda's passport to excitement she replied flippantly that she had never kissed a man with a moustache before.[21]

The aviators' flattering performances suddenly took a nasty turn. Two planes crashed while paying tribute to Zelda, one piloted by Weaver, the rejected moustached suitor who made the headlines as 'badly injured'.

For Zelda the tragedy of that aviator becomes a symbol of lost love which in her fiction she reuses several times. For Scott too, the rejected lover who falls like Icarus from heaven and dies becomes an enduring fictional symbol. Zelda and Scott pasted the death of Weaver neatly into their scrapbooks and their respective legends. But Weaver himself did not die. He survived and collected his army separation pay the following year. For Zelda and Scott, even in these early years, imagination was always more powerful than fact.

In Zelda's *Save Me The Waltz*, one of the captains courting Alabama tells her that he intends to get transferred to avoid being one of her beaux who falls out of planes and clutters up roadsides. When she asks who fell out, he tells her it was 'your friend with the Dachshund face and the mustache'. She is unmoved: 'we must hold on to ourselves and not care . . . There isn't any use worrying about the dog-one.' Alabama's careless response is characteristic of Zelda's own attitude towards suitors.[22]

Scott's rivals for Zelda were not pilots alone. There were golf-ing beaux, Southern halfbacks, rich university students and the wealthy and well-born boys she had grown up with. Scott however was a Yankee, his family were in trade, he was only an infantry lieu-tenant. As Sara Mayfield said: 'He was no great catch by Zelda's standards.'[23]

The self-styled 'great Southern catches' Peyton Mathis and John Sellers, who had been dating Sara Haardt during her vacations, began to rush Zelda when Sara returned to Goucher College and

Scott arrived on the scene. Sellers, who felt he still had a hold on Zelda, began to goad Scott. As he and Mathis disliked Scott more than the other Northern invaders who dated 'their' girls, when they noticed his drinking habits they mockingly dubbed him Scotch Fitzgerald. Worse still, they openly exhibited their financial superiority. On his army pay of $141 a month Scott could hardly afford to give Zelda a $10 bottle of bonded whiskey or a $6 dinner at the Pickwick Café, and he could never treat her to taxis. The Gold Dust Twins naturally had cars in which they drove Zelda to the cemetery to admire the art works, but when Zelda took Scott there to show him the Confederate graves she had to walk.

The Twins' Southern courting approach made them disdainful of Scott's Yankee wooing tactics. Southerners, in theory, put Belles on pedestals. Scott, in practice, certainly did not. One evening he carved his and Zelda's initials on the pillars of the Country Club, but in a bad error of judgement made his initials large and Zelda's small. That it rankled with her for years showed in her first novel, written in 1932, when David Knight carves words on the club doorpost. '"David", the legend read, "David, David, Knight, Knight, Knight, and Miss Alabama Nobody." '24

The way Zelda treated her men appalled yet fascinated Scott. He felt she treated men badly. She abused them, broke appointments with them and looked bored – yet they returned to her time after time.

In an early letter to Scott, Zelda said women should 'awake to the fact that their excuse and explanation is the necessity for a disturbing element among men – [if they did] they'd be much happier, and the men much more miserable – which is exactly what they need for the improvement of things in general'.25

Scott, who soon saw 'borrowing' Zelda's words as a neat way to improve his fictional characterizations, lifted her lines for his description of his heroine Rosalind in *This Side of Paradise*: 'She once told a roomful of her mother's friends that the only excuse for women was the necessity for a disturbing element among men.'26

Scott found Zelda's behaviour disturbing and erotic. At a dance soon after they met, knowing Scott was observing her, she took her escort into a lighted phone booth and kissed him. Though provoked, he desired her more. Fully aware of this, she took advantage of it. Or perhaps she could not help it. Whatever her motives, the consequence was the same: her behaviour stimulated them both to fictionalize it. Zelda not only understood Scott's tendency to live a fictional life, she created one for herself.

Perceptively she wrote later in *Caesar's Things*: '[He] was proud of the way the boys danced with her and she was so much admired . . . [It] gave [her] a desirability which became, indeed, indispensable to [him].'[27]

Scott had already written something similar in *The Great Gatsby* with Gatsby's response to Daisy: 'It excited him, too, that many men had already loved Daisy – it increased her value in his eyes.'[28]

Twice in his Notebooks Scott explored a deeper reason for the way his erotic drive for Zelda was stimulated by another man's interest. First he wrote the phrase 'Proxy in passion', later he enlarged on it: 'Feeling of proxy in passion strange encouragement'.[29]

That Zelda did not mind his voyeuristic ardour says something about her own alienation from her sexuality. She too had a private sexual vision: she liked watching him watching her with other men.

Despite her large number of beaux and her seemingly heartless behaviour towards them, Scott began to captivate her. They began to hold intimate conversations which gave her an uncanny feeling of exposure and closeness. No man had ever talked to Zelda quite like that before. In comparison with the sportsmen she was used to, Scott was intellectual, artistic and gentle, and Zelda had a 'quality which you couldn't help feeling would betray her sooner or later . . . the quality that made her like intellectual men'.[30]

Though he never fared well with men, Scott knew how to make women respond to him. His most remarkable characteristic – a genuine talent for intimacy born from an unguarded spontaneity – became irresistible to Zelda, as it did to many women, though it could cause confusion or hostility in some men. Zelda discovered that Scott preferred to emulate men rather than empathize with them.

'When I like men', he wrote, 'I want to be like them – I want to lose the outer qualities that give me my individuality and be like them.'[31]

In this dual approach to the two sexes, in his ambitions and insecurities, Scott was undoubtedly influenced by his relationship with his parents.

He talked to Zelda about them. Told her he identified with the Fitzgeralds who were genteel but impoverished. He did not say much about the McQuillans, on his mother's side, because he despised them for being wealthy but not well bred. Unlike Zelda, who was socially secure, this ambivalence made Scott feel highly insecure: 'I developed a two-cylinder inferiority complex,'[32] he told his friend John O'Hara later.

His parents had high ambitions for him, upon which he built. They began just after his birth on 24 September 1896 at 481 Laurel Avenue, St Paul, Minnesota, when they christened him Francis Scott Key Fitzgerald after his relative, the Maryland lawyer Francis Scott Key, who wrote 'The Star-Spangled Banner'. Scott loved the name and was quick to inform Zelda and all her friends. A month after Zelda met him, she took him to the Capitol to show him the star on the steps where Davis had taken the oath of office and to meet Sara Mayfield and Sara Haardt. Scott's introductory line to them was that he was Francis Scott Key's great-grandson – a somewhat inflated connection as they were merely second cousins three times removed.[33] This ploy fits the revealing anecdote that Scott's first credited word was 'up' at a mere ten months old.

Zelda's parents did not approve of the fact that Scott was a Roman Catholic Irish Midwesterner, even if as the son of Edward Fitzgerald he could trace his heroic Scott and Key ancestors back to seventeenth-century Maryland. While Zelda was proud of her mother, Scott was always slightly ashamed of his – for Mary (Mollie) McQuillan was the granddaughter of an Irish immigrant carpenter. That Edward Fitzgerald and Mollie married on 12 February 1890 in Washington DC when Mollie, nearly thirty, was already considered a spinster, must be credited to her assertiveness. Dramatic like her son, she got Edward to propose by threatening to throw herself into the Mississippi if he didn't.[34] Scott inherited from his mother a propensity for absurd antics that annoyed his friends but at the start amused Zelda.

Mollie's father, Philip F. McQuillan, was a shrewd example of the American Dream to which Scott himself would respond so avidly in his novels. Philip, born in Ireland's County Fermanagh, moved first to Illinois then to St Paul, Minnesota, also moving up the ladder from impecunious bookkeeper to wealthy renowned wholesale grocer.[35] On his death at forty-three from Bright's Disease complicated by tuberculosis – the spectre of the latter would haunt Scott throughout his life – he left an estate of nearly $300,000 which allowed Scott's mother (the eldest of five) a sound education and several European trips.

Scott, attracted by the indisputably beautiful Zelda, confessed that Mollie according to Edward Fitzgerald 'just missed being beautiful',[36] but according to him missed it by a mile. Mollie was vivacious, bright and eccentric: she frequently wore different coloured shoes, believing it was better to break in one new shoe at a time. She read, in Scott's opinion, a heap of bad books, and was constantly to be seen holding her umbrella aloft as she hurried to the public library to exchange one bad book for another.

Zelda and Scott were both spoiled as children, for similar reasons. Having lost two daughters, aged one and three, in an epidemic in 1896 while pregnant with Scott, Mollie, grief-stricken and hysterical, coddled him from birth. After the death of another infant girl in 1900, Mollie did not have a daughter until Annabel was born in July 1901. Scott's possible guilt about surviving may have led him to hypochondria in his adulthood. Publicly he turned his sisters' deaths into something mystical and mythic: 'I don't know how it worked exactly. I think I started then to be a writer.'[37] He may have meant he had been born out of suffering and singled out for special talents. His mother, hostile to his literary ambitions, nevertheless recorded every significant event in his childhood. This habit may have encouraged Scott to historicize himself, for from an early age he listed his partners on dancing school programmes, collected and collated his valentines, and at thirteen wrote a private 'Thoughtbook', the start of his lifelong list-making compulsion, delineating amours and recording highs and lows on the popularity scale. It was also the first example of the way he recorded every experience. From his schooldays nothing was real to him until he had written about it. Unlike Zelda, Scott was always concerned with his image, so he analysed what he thought of other people and cared deeply what they thought of him.

Scott's brains, vitality and often out-of-place directness of speech came from his mother whose frankness caused much local embarrassment. She once alarmed a woman whose husband was dying by saying: 'I'm trying to decide how you'll look in mourning.'[38]

Scott disparaged and resented her and turned for moral guidance to his father, whom initially he admired. Edward Fitzgerald loved literature, read poetry aloud to his son and encouraged him to write. A handsome man with Southern manners, he had a gentle ineffectual unambitious nature. The Fitzgeralds were Southern in sympathy. Edward Fitzgerald's first cousin Mary Surratt was hanged for conspiracy in Lincoln's assassination. As a boy Edward guided Confederate spies during the Civil War. Scott grew up listening to his father's tales of the lost South, and 'acquired an extended and showy, if very superficial, knowledge of the Civil War' which helped to enhance his reputation in Zelda's eyes.[39]

When Scott was born, Edward, who had attended Georgetown University without graduating, owned a doomed wicker furniture business,[40] was drinking too much, which horribly embarrassed

Scott, and was already cushioned by his wife's wealth. By Scott's second birthday his business had failed, after which he became a salesman with Procter and Gamble in Buffalo, New York. After several more moves which left Scott feeling anxious and dislocated, Edward finally lost his job in July 1908.[41] Scott was at home when the phone call came for his mother. The boy knew from the tone of her voice a disaster had occurred. Perhaps unaware of his mother's money, he prayed: 'Dear God ... please don't let us go to the poorhouse.' Eleven-year-old Scott knew the worst when his father came home. Edward had been fired. He had left home that morning a confident young man. He had returned that evening a broken old man. He felt a failure the rest of his life.

That incident coloured all Scott's relations with those wealthier than himself and, in the case of Zelda's family, those whose values were less materialistic than his. (The context of Scott's anecdotes is always as important as the content. Therefore it is significant that Scott first recounted that touching incident to a journalist who saw him as an alcoholic and forgotten writer.[42] This touching narrative was also pragmatic and self-serving.)

His father's failure fuelled Scott's determination to succeed, yet his creative mind responded more readily to tales of failure. He would always spin stories from lost causes. From his father Scott also inherited his romantic love of the past, his good looks, his impeccable tailored style and his honour, which even in the worst stages of his marriage to Zelda would never allow him to desert her.

As a boy Scott had lived with a 'great dream' with which now as an adult he tried to captivate Zelda. It was the dream of success as a writer which started in 1908 when his defeated family returned to St Paul, where they lived in the most fashionable Summit Avenue area of the city, but in a series of rented houses or apartments on the edges. This situation bears a remarkable similarity to Zelda's, for her family too lived on the margins of a silk-hat section. There were so many coincidences in their lives it is as if their conspiratorial natures had a historical precedent.

Scott's parents finally settled at the end of the finest street. Scott revelled in the symbolism, which was almost too neat. One biographer felt this made Scott feel an outsider whose sense of difference sharpened his skills as a social observer, but Lloyd Hackl, a St Paul historical researcher, points out, and St Paul residents confirm, that actually his mother's wealth gave him an *entrée* to the best in that society.[43] It was perhaps his self-consciousness and conceit that initiated and made him cling to his idea of isolation and difference. On

entering St Paul Academy in September 1908 he began to realize his
literary ambitions but did not achieve equal success in his social life.

In October 1909 his first published story, 'The Mystery of the
Raymond Mortgage', appeared in *St Paul Academy Now and Then*;
another, concerning the heroic behaviour of a Confederate soldier,
was the only juvenilia to interest Zelda.[44]

In August 1911 he wrote, directed and starred in his first play for
St Paul's Elizabethan Dramatic Club, *The Girl from Lazy J*. These
early writings, like his conversations, had a joyous childlike quality
that he never lost because he never buried the past. His imagination
reached out and responded to every experience, a quality Zelda
from the first found alluring.

As a young girl Zelda always won popularity contests, whereas
Scott as a young boy was desperately unpopular. Not one invited
child turned up to his sixth birthday party, forcing the small soulful
Scott indoors where he solemnly consumed the whole birthday
cake, including several candles. As an adolescent he fared worse.
Though he struggled for recognition, playing football, basketball
and enrolling in Professor Baker's dance class, he was labelled a
show-off. He would memorize titles in bookstores then discuss
books he had not read; he would observe his classmates' faults then
publicly criticize them, or he would see through them then write
about it. He also expected others to be as interested in him as he was.
This lifelong narcissism flawed his novels, adversely affected his
later friendships and damaged Zelda.

But during his early years in St Paul he made several lasting
women friends, including Marie Hersey, who would help Zelda
buy her first New York wardrobe.

Scott's grades at St Paul were so poor that he was sent to the
Catholic Newman School in Hackensack, New Jersey, in September
1911 to make a fresh and better start. The gamble failed. At Newman
his grades sank lower, he was thought fresh, and on home visits
began to be known as 'a man who drank'.[45]

He had a capacity for hero worship, usually for athletic and
socially self-assured men. It brought him the friendship of quarter-
back Charles (Sap) Donahoe, with whom he later roomed in
Princeton – but when he ventured out on to the Newman football
field himself he was labelled 'yellow'. After his failure he wrote a
poem called 'Football', whose success made him feel writing was an
adequate substitute for real action.

Scott's most important influences were two like-minded men:
Father Cyril Sigourney Webster Fay,[46] a trustee of Newman, and

Fay's friend, the Catholic convert and Anglo-Irish novelist Shane Leslie. Scott saw Shane, who had sat at Tolstoy's feet and swum with Rupert Brooke, as a romantic hero.

Fay, whose friends moved in high places, took Scott under his wing and served for some years as mentor and substitute parent. The thirty-seven-year-old priest and the sixteen-year-old student shared an egotistical absorption in self-analysis. Scott, impressed with Fay's social class and Catholic elitism, temporarily considered the priesthood. But entering the world of wealth through Fay's connections, about which he would always feel ambivalent, began to attract him more.

In his last year at Newman he met a well-heeled younger boy, Stephan Vincent Parrott (nicknamed Peevie), with whom he would vie for the priest's affections and to whom he would later show Zelda's private diary, which he considered brilliantly written. Father Fay encouraged Peevie and Scott to see themselves as spiritual brothers, though Fay's letters to Scott indicate less a fatherly feeling than a homosexual one. If Scott registered this at the time, his affection for Fay would have made him repress that recognition, because his attitude at all times towards male homosexual behaviour was a loud insistent melodramatic repulsion.

Scott's self-esteem in his last months at Newman had been somewhat salvaged by producing more plays in St Paul, by trips to the New York theatre, and by inventing ideas for musical comedies. He had discovered a musical score for a show called *His Honor the Sultan* produced by Princeton's Triangle Club. In that instant he determined to go to Princeton, the Southerner's Northern University. Despite flunking all the entrance exams he argued his way to acceptance in September 1913.

Enthralled by the university's Gothic architecture, he schemed to become one of the 'gods of the class'[47], but his fastest route was closed by a knee injury at football practice. He decided instead to achieve prominence via the Triangle Club, whose key members were Bunny Wilson, the shy scholar with the whiplash mind who would become Scott's literary mentor and 'intellectual conscience',[48] and poet John Peale Bishop, four years older than Scott. Bishop felt Scott was determined to be a boy genius even if he had to trim his age to look precocious. When their talk turned towards books Bishop, admitting he had not read many, commented that Scott had read even fewer, but 'those he said he had read . . . were many, many more'.[49]

Scott's other Princeton friends, all wealthy, were more interested in intellectual and literary excellence than in social aspirations. They included Alexander McKaig, Townsend Martin and Montgomery's Lawton Campbell, who became frequent visitors of the Fitzgeralds in their early married days, and John Biggs Jnr, who became a lifelong friend of both Fitzgeralds and who occupied a special place later in Zelda's life.

Wilson, a virgin, was like Scott painfully shy about sex. Bishop and McKaig were womanizers. One anecdote locates Fitzgerald, Wilson, McKaig and Bishop strolling down Nassau Street when two girls known to McKaig as 'hookers' passed them. Instantly he and Bishop rushed after them leaving Scott and Bunny flummoxed. Scott remarked prudishly: 'That's one thing Fitzgerald's never done!'[50]

Scott's fiction during this period is marked by the same caution about sex. His heroes have a puritanical restraint. Girls are lightly kissed by men who see a mere kiss as a commitment to an engagement. Once he uses Zelda as his role model, Scott's heroines emulate her spirited self-centredness: men are women's prey. Even in his apprentice work Scott's female characters illustrate these role reversals. In 'The Debutante' (1917) Helen, his selfish protagonist, said that she enjoyed controlling situations though it became tedious being in charge. Helen was stimulated by chasing men but when they responded she enjoyed it less.

In 'Babes in the Woods', written in 1917, Scott's college freshman courts Isabella, a 16-year-old 'speed', grants her the right to destroy him, waits for her high-handed 'mask to drop off, but at the same time did not question her right to wear it'.[51] Scott's quintessential theme of the gifted man ruined by a selfish woman had begun. The Fitzgerald heroine was the writer's inspiration so long as she was unattainable.

When Scott finally met Zelda in 1918 he came face to face with the woman of his early fiction.

Scott's real-life bid for social favours mirrored his fictional seesaw. Each social success at Princeton was followed by an academic catastrophe. He was made a member of Cottage, Princeton's prestigious eating club,[52] joined the *Tiger*'s editorial board in 1915, his stories appeared in the *Nassau Lit* and he became Triangle's secretary for 1915–16, writing the lyrics for *Fie! Fie! Fi-Fi!*, a much vaunted Triangle show. However when he tried to build on this by writing lyrics and offering to play a beautiful showgirl in Bunny Wilson's production *The Evil Eye*, which he hoped would lead him to the prize of Triangle President, he failed yet again. His scholastic record was so appalling he was made ineligible for the Triangle show tour, which would have included his solo performance in drag, and for the Presidency.

His Ledger registered the words 'Drunk', 'Passed Out at Dinner', 'Drunk', with tedious regularity. His habit of using alcohol to console himself for failure was one with which Zelda would grow increasingly bored and angry during their romance. She saw it as it was: a sign of terminal weakness.

It was not drunkenness however but a sickness diagnosed as malaria (which he preferred to think of as tuberculosis) which forced Scott to withdraw from Princeton on 3 January 1916. The University tagged his exit with the label 'withdrawn for scholastic deficiencies' but Scott successfully nagged the authorities for a letter saying he had left voluntarily on grounds of ill-health. Twenty years later, writing up his miseries for a *Crack-Up* essay, he said: 'I had lost every single thing I wanted . . . and that night was the first time I hunted down the spectre of womanhood', his classy name for the prostitute he had earlier ignored.[53]

But there was yet more to lose.

Over Christmas 1914 in St Paul, Scott had attended a party given by Marie Hersey for her friend Ginevra King, a strikingly beautiful sixteen-year-old socialite from Lake Forest, Illinois. Ginevra, as dark and brown-eyed as Zelda was fair, but neither as daring nor as dashing, like Marie was at Westover Girls' School in Connecticut from where she dated a string of Ivy League conquests. For Scott she had a magical glory, was rich and radiant, became his winter dream, his summer evanescence. She accepted Scott's usual invitation for a next-day date, after which, utterly in love, he wrote daily, sent telegrams, whizzed her to the Ritz in New York, invited her to Princeton. During a two-year courtship there was ever-growing ardour on his side and ever-growing indifference on hers. Slowly, painfully, he recognized that Ginevra, 'infinitely rare and to be marvelled at',[54] never asked him to Westover and was courted by men in a far superior social set. At her Lake Forest home in August 1916 he was made aware that poor boys should not think of marrying a girl 'whose voice is full of money'.[55]

One of Scott's oddest ideas – yet one that appealed to Zelda – had been to try and impress Ginevra by his performance as a glamorous showgirl in the tour of *The Evil Eye*. When he became ineligible to perform, he had to make do with his posed publicity stills, which were carried by newspapers around the country including the *New York Times*. There he was in blond wig, elegant off-the-shoulder gown, lace picture hat, diaphanous stole, carrying flowers, looking every inch as feminine as Ginevra herself. He received fan letters from men who wanted to date him and an agent offered to book him a vaudeville tour as a female impersonator.

Zelda, who revelled in outrageousness, would probably have posed with him attired in a gentleman's suit. But not Ginevra.

With his new love waning, Scott significantly mailed his thirteen-year-old sister Annabel, at convent school, a long letter that was in essence a charm course on how to get and keep men. He advised her on conversation, couture and cosmetics, how to sit, move and above all how to listen: 'Boys like to talk about themselves.'[56]

He told Annabel that Ginevra was a specialist in how to gaze at a beau effectively: mouth drooping, head hanging slightly, wide-open eyes fixed on the man in question. What he didn't tell Annabel was that the pathetic appealing look he advocated was the one he had used on his publicity photos!

Scott made even better use of his advice to his sister. He dressed up in women's clothes, sneaked a powder compact in the top of his blue stocking, accompanied a male friend to a fraternity hop at Minnesota University, danced his way through the evening with several eligible bachelors and was not unmasked until he had to go to the men's room.

Scott returned to Princeton in September 1916 to repeat his junior year. Though he invited Ginevra to the Yale game that November she had lost interest in him. In January she broke with him, broke his heart, then announced her engagement to the wealthy Ensign William Hamilton Mitchell, and finally entered Scott's world of fiction as the rich unobtainable heroine. By another fortuitous coincidence Mitchell, a good-looking young aviator, was able to harden up Scott's most consistent symbol: the aviator risking death.[57]

Scott kept all Ginevra's letters and typed and bound them into a book. Ginevra thought his letters were clever, bulky but unimportant. She destroyed them in 1917.

However, the loss of Ginevra and his multitude of failures did wonders for his fiction. It grew up, had a new resonance, hinted at power.

America entered the war, Scott's friends joined up, he took his exams for the army and received his commission on 26 October 1917. There seemed nothing left in his life except to read more good books and think about writing one. Thus it was in his first Officers' Training Camp at Fort Leavenworth, Kansas, he started 'The Romantic Egotist', which he sent to Shane Leslie who had offered to show it to his publishers Charles Scribner's Sons. Leslie corrected the grammar and spelling and sent a covering letter suggesting that Scott was a prose Rupert Brooke. 'Though Scott Fitzgerald is still alive it has a literary value. Of course when he is killed, it will also have a commercial value.'[58]

Instead of getting killed Scott met Zelda Sayre in July 1918 while Scribner's were still considering his manuscript. On 19 August Scribner's rejected it, overruling the enthusiasm of Max Perkins who would soon become Scott's editor and most loyal friend. Scott rapidly revised it but in October Perkins sent another rejection. Scott captioned the telegram 'The end of a dream' and stuck it in his scrapbook. Meanwhile he had posted Zelda one of the chapters telling her 'the heroine does resemble you in more ways than four'.[59]

It was a sharper wooing line than even those Scott had recommended to Annabel. The fact that he cautioned Zelda to secrecy about the chapter appealed to her sense of mystery. She elevated him to her top beau. The myth reports that Zelda and Scott fell in love at first sight. Not at all. On 4 September Ginevra King got married.[60] Three days later Scott entered these serious words in his Ledger: 'Fell in love on the 7th.' Scott had been unable to offer Ginevra anything she did not have or could not acquire. But Zelda wanted to escape from the claustrophobia of Montgomery gripped by its past. With Scott she saw a chance of a life in New York – though for that she needed the conditions to be right.

CHAPTER 4

Zelda threw herself into their courtship, playing the Deep South baby doll. Letters using the Southern Belles' courtly code winged their way to Scott:

'Nothing means anything except your darling self' . . . 'Don't you think I was made for you? I feel like you had me ordered – I want you to wear me, like a watch-charm or a button hole boquet' . . . 'Sweetheart I want to always be a help.'[1]

Those lines offer some evidence that her mother's training in femininity had at least reached Zelda's pen if not her intentions, but in case they were insufficient to impress Scott with the strength of her desire, Zelda outdid herself with this line:

'I'm all I'll ever be without you – and there's so much more room for growth – with you – all my mental faculties are paralysed with loving you – and wanting you for mine.'[2]

Her mental faculties of course were far from paralysed. She ended that letter briskly with a description of a helpless movie heroine who had stimulated her scorn for the way 'most women regard themselves as helpless'.[3]

Although in love with Scott, she preserved a wry detachment. 'Being in love', she wrote later, '. . . is simply a presentation of our pasts to another individual, mostly packages so unwieldy that we can no longer manage the loosened strings alone. Looking for love is like asking for a new point of departure, . . . another chance in life.'[4]

The couple held hands in pine groves and discussed poetry and seduction. But in wartime, loving Scott was not Zelda's only interest. She was preparing a war benefit ballet and according to Sara Haardt they danced all night, then spent every day working for the Red Cross. When Sara and Zelda talked about it later Zelda said: 'Some of the older girls . . . thought that because we talked so much we of the younger generation would never get any work done, but we sold more tags[5] and folded more bandages than all the rest . . . It was as if we were possessed with an insatiable vitality.'[6]

In October 1918 Scott received orders to go North, after which he hoped he would be sent to France. Zelda resisted his attempts to pressure her into commitment before he left. She was cautious of throwing in her lot with an insecure unpublished writer. A Southern Belle's expectation was rarely love on a budget; but more significantly, Zelda despised weakness. She needed Scott to feel *realistically* self-confident before *she* could feel secure about leaving her safe Southern world. Later, Scott rewrote and simplified Zelda's viewpoint until it became an avaricious girl's refusal to marry until the beau attained New York success. But at the time he knew Zelda's stand was consistent with her refusal to compromise on her desires. 'Here is my heart' were his last words before leaving.[7] Zelda would remember them until her death.

'Zelda was cagey about throwing in her lot with me before I was a money-maker . . .' Scott wrote later. 'She was young and in a period where any exploiter or middle-man seemed a better risk than a worker in the arts.'[8]

Rosalind later wrote to Sara Mayfield: 'I do not believe that Zelda's hesitancy about marrying Scott was prompted by any mercenary motive . . . it was rather her uncertainty about the wisdom of leaving her known world for a strange new one that restrained her.'[9]

Rosalind's analysis seems accurate. Despite her dashing ways Zelda had a tense uncertain side of which Scott appeared unaware, even though he had criticized her nervous habit of biting the skin on her lips. She needed the rock-solid protection of her family and community in order to rebel.

Zelda had a remarkable understanding of the way in which Scott inextricably linked his attitude to money with his attitude to her.

'There's nothing in all the world I want but you – and your precious love,' she wrote. 'All the material things are nothing. I'd just hate to live a sordid, colorless existence – because you'd soon love me – less and less.' She reassured him that money did not matter, whilst acknowledging that if she was not adorned like a material girl he would think less of her.[10]

Years later Scott would admit that he had 'never been able to stop wondering where my friends' money came from, nor to stop thinking that at some time a sort of droit de seigneur might have been exercised to give one of them my girl'.[11]

In Camp Mills, Long Island, as Scott anxiously waited to be posted, the Armistice was signed. Disappointed at not getting overseas he went on a drinking marathon, missing his unit's sober departure for Montgomery. However when the troop train pulled into Washington, there, sitting on a baggage truck with two girls and a bottle, was Scott. He told Zelda he had commandeered a locomotive on the plea that he was a courier with papers for the White House.[12] Zelda listened with amusement as another Fitzgerald fabrication passed into legend.

Her family neither encouraged the match nor took it seriously. Though there was Southern anti-Catholic feeling, the Episcopalian Sayres had become less opposed to Scott's Yankee Catholicism than to his lack of money and future prospects. Scott had not graduated, had no real career and drank too much. The Judge, seriously ill for nine months with 'nervous prostration', was not at his most tolerant, so when Zelda said Scott was sweet her father curtly replied: 'He's never sober.'[13]

Scott's harshest critics were Minnie and Rosalind, who both felt strongly that their Southern Baby needed more protection than Scott offered. Later Rosalind would hold Scott and the Southern uprooting largely responsible for Zelda's breakdowns.

For years Scott, ill at ease with the socially skilled Sayres, bitterly resented their judgemental opposition, particularly Minnie's. He retaliated by accusing Minnie of poor parenting: 'For a long time I hated *her* mother for giving her nothing in the line of good habit – nothing but "getting by" and conceit.'[14]

That Zelda, surrounded by beaux, *did* seem able to get by made him despair. She swam with boys in icy spring waters, she and Eleanor Browder formed a syndicate to buddy 'more college boys than Solomon had wives'[15] and she irritated Scott by retelling her mother's tales of penniless young authors turned out on dark stormy nights. Zelda's lack of faith in him provoked quarrels.

In December 1918 Scott wrote to a confidante that he was determined not to marry Zelda. But determined though he was he had to acknowledge that Zelda was extraordinary.[16]

That is the only evidence that Scott ever seriously tried to give up Zelda. But within two weeks, his resolve weakened. He wrote the bold word 'Love' in his Ledger before once more falling into it, this time decisively. 'The most important year of my life. Every emotion and my life work decided.'[17]

They spent romantic hours in restaurants, at vaudeville at the Grand Theatre, anywhere they could be alone and hold hands. Several biographers suggest they went further than holding hands.[18]

Scott wrote in retrospect that Christmas 1918 at the Sayres was a time of Zelda's 'sexual recklessness'[19], though this is questionable. One piece of evidence is a note pinned to Scott's 1934 'Count of Darkness' Philippe stories: 'After yielding [she] holds Philippe at bay like Zelda + me in summer 1917'. However Scott and Zelda had not yet met at that point so Scott's memory appears to be faulty.[20]

Stronger evidence points to the date being spring or summer 1919 when Zelda's letters have a heightened sensual intimacy.[21] They may have made love in April 1919 on one of Scott's three trips to Montgomery from New York where, trying to make sufficient money to marry Zelda, he lived in one room and worked as a copy-writer for the Barron Collier advertising agency.[22] At this time in a letter to Scott Zelda wrote these subtly passionate lines: 'Sweetheart, I love you most of all the earth – and I want to be married soon – soon – Lover – Don't say I'm not enthusiastic – You ought to know.'[23]

Whatever date is assigned to their lovemaking, it was a brief sexual experiment after which Zelda again held back.

On 9 January 1919 Scott had a premonitory seizure of trembling; neither Scott nor Zelda knew why. The following day, Scott learnt that his mentor Monsignor Fay had died. After Fay's death Scott had no further supernatural experiences though he continued to scatter them through his fiction. His Catholicism also died with Fay. Scott indicates that Zelda replaced the influence of Fay and the Church. 'Zelda's the only God I have left now,' he wrote on 26 February.[24]

During the spring Scott wrote nineteen stories and received 122 rejections with which he papered his walls, hoping that when he became famous biographers would relish and retell that story. Indeed they do.

Zelda was given the star part of Folly in the April Folly Ball held by *Les Mystérieuses*, a society of prominent Montgomery girls and matrons. Minnie and Rosalind had written the play which preceded the complex ballet. Zelda sent Scott a photo of herself amongst the roses in Minnie's backyard, poised on tiptoe in her black and gold costume trimmed with tiny bells. In an auditorium decorated with baskets of sunshine roses entwined with gold and black ribbons that matched her Folly outfit, Zelda expertly performed intricate sequences. Her ethereal beauty haunted the audience long after she stopped dancing.

Her practice had not been without pain. In March she had written to Scott: 'Your feet – that you liked so much – are ruined. I've been toe-dancing again and nearly broke my right foot . . . The doctor is trying . . . but they'll always look ugly.'[25] Curiously, Scott too had a strange view of his naked feet, which since his youth had been a source of erotic shame.

Zelda and her schoolfriend Livye Hart also performed in the Seague Musical. Irritatingly, she told Scott one actor was so impressed he 'tried to take me and Livye on the road with him'.[26] When dancing, she assured Scott, she felt 'self-reliant'.[27]

Though Livye and Eleanor shared Zelda's dance life, other friends were taking new directions. Katharine Elsberry, who had initially moved North with her wartime bridegroom, bore a son, and returned to Alabama where Zelda frequently visited her and the baby. With no support beyond her family's generosity, Katharine became a dental receptionist and the first divorcee of Zelda's set to do work other than schoolteaching.[28]

At Goucher College Sara Haardt was encouraged by her English instructor Harry T. Baker to write short stories that would soon be noticed by the literary critic H. L. Mencken.[29] Since October 1914 Mencken and drama critic George Jean Nathan had been co-editing *The Smart Set*.[30] Both Sara and Scott submitted some early stories. Mencken initially rejected Sara's stories until he met her in 1923, when he published 'Joe Moore and Callie Balsingame', the tale of a Montgomery girl and boy who grew up in the neighbourhood where she and Zelda met their beaux. When Scott revised and submitted his 1917 *Nassau Lit* story 'Babes in the Woods' Mencken published it in 1919. At $30 this became Scott's first and only commercial sale that year. Immediately he bought himself a pair of white flannels and knowing her love of finery, a luxury for Zelda. One story suggests it was 'moon-shiny' pajamas in which Zelda felt 'like a Vogue cover' and wished Scott's pajamas 'were touching'.[31] Another suggests it was a magenta fan with 'those wonderful, wonderful feathers [that] are the most beautiful things on earth'.[32]

Throughout their separation in spring 1919 they wrote constantly. Zelda seldom dated her letters scrawled in her large 'sun-burned, open-air looking script'.[33] Her punctuation was restricted to a series of dashes and a scattering of exclamation marks.

Zelda pasted Scott's telegrams into her scrapbook as they held a certain glamour. But (like Ginevra) she did not keep any of Scott's letters. Zelda wasn't sentimental.

Scott, who constantly catalogued, classified and preserved, did keep Zelda's letters. Every one of them. He wasn't sentimental either. He knew they would come in useful.

Take the letter Zelda wrote to him after one of her visits to
Oakwood Cemetery.

> I've spent today in the grave-yard . . . trying to unlock a rusty iron vault
> built in the side of the hill. It's all washed and covered with weepy,
> watery blue flowers that might have grown from dead eyes sticky to
> touch with a sickening odor.

Zelda had been moved by thoughts of long-dead passions.

> Why should graves make people feel in vain? . . . somehow I can't find
> anything hopeless in having lived – All the broken columnes and
> clasped hands and doves and angels mean romances and in an hundred
> years I think I shall like having young people speculate on whether my
> eyes were brown or blue . . . I hope my grave has an air of many, many
> years about it – Isn't it funny how, out of a row of Confederate soldiers,
> two or three will make you think of dead lovers and dead loves – when
> they're exactly like the others, even to the yellowish moss?[34]

Zelda's letters at nineteen were remarkable for their sensitivity to
place and her visualization of her emotions. Unlike Scott, she wrote
spontaneously without regard for audience or effect. Her letters are
significant because for two important years before they married we
see Zelda, a frivolous, loving, acutely sharp woman, through her
own words and eyes rather than through Scott's.

To Scott the letters were a gift in more ways than one. He inserted
Zelda's graveyard description into the penultimate page of *This Side
of Paradise*, which he had been rewriting in summer 1919. His editorial acumen assured him there was little need to alter Zelda's words.

> On an impulse he [Amory Blaine] considered trying to open the door of
> a rusty iron vault built into the side of a hill, a vault washed clean and
> covered with late-blooming, weepy water-blue flowers that might have
> grown from dead eyes, sticky to the touch with a sickening odour . . . He
> wondered that graves ever made people consider life in vain. Somehow
> he could find nothing hopeless in having lived. All the broken columns
> and clasped hands and doves and angels meant romances. He fancied
> that in a hundred years he would like having young people speculate as
> to whether his eyes were brown or blue, and he hoped quite passion-
> ately that his grave would have about it an air of many, many years ago.
> It seemed strange that out of a row of Union soldiers two or three made
> him think of dead loves and dead lovers, when they were exactly like
> the rest even to the yellowish moss.[35]

Zelda never revealed her reaction to this plagiarism. Young, in love with love, riding high on excitement, still professionally uncertain, she was probably more flattered by the attention paid to her words than offended at their appropriation.

Zelda trusted Scott enough to show him her personal diary.[36] He found it so extraordinary that he borrowed it for several months. In an act of betrayal he loaned it to Peevie Parrott, after telling him intimate details of his affair with Zelda. Parrott reported: 'As you say, it is a very human document, but somehow I cannot altogether understand it . . . It is hard for me to picture it [love] anywhere but in a book.' Parrott, like Scott, *did* picture Zelda's *diary* in a book, and thought it worth publishing.

Parrott, Zelda, Scott and all subsequent biographers agree on that first stage of the diary's travels. There are however several versions about the next stage.

Sara Mayfield said that in late 1918 Scott, 'with the diary in hand', accompanied by Wilson and Bishop, besieged Mencken's co-editor, the critic and writer George Jean Nathan, in his Royalton apartment, where Scott, who 'proposed to turn Zelda's journal into a novelette called "The Diary of a Popular Girl"', asked Nathan to read it'. Nathan immediately wanted to publish it and meet Zelda. According to Mayfield, Scott seemed keen, until Zelda broke off her engagement to him in June 1919, when, 'in an embarrassing position in regard to publishing her diary . . . [he] quietly diverted it to his own purposes in *This Side of Paradise*.'[37]

Curiously, when Mayfield later wrote Zelda's biography she revised the story. Scott, she says, had agreed to rewrite Zelda's diary for Nathan as 'The Journal of a Young Girl' but withdrew from his verbal contract, realizing he could put the diary to better use.[38]

One Fitzgerald biographer suggests that Scott had always intended to use Zelda's letters and diary in his first novel *This Side of Paradise*, to ensure his hero Amory Blaine's affair with Rosalind Connage resembled his own affair with Zelda.[39] When Scott later sent his editor, Maxwell Perkins, a segment of his manuscript containing parts of Zelda's diary, he confessed that much of the dialogue was Zelda's.[40]

Nathan himself recorded the episode quite differently for *Esquire* thirty-eight years later. His version does *not* implicate Scott as the instigator of the deal. On a visit to the married Fitzgeralds in Westport in 1920[41] he wandered down to the cellar and 'discovered' Zelda's diaries. He talks about them in the plural. '*They* interested me so greatly that in my capacity as a magazine editor I later made her an offer for *them* [author's emphasis]. When I informed her husband, he said that he could not permit me to publish them since he had gained a lot of inspiration from them and wanted to use parts of them in his own novels and short stories, as for example "The Jelly Bean".'[42]

Evidence suggests there were several diaries, all of which Zelda seemed prepared to give to Scott. Certainly she offered no resistance to Scott's high-handed refusal of Nathan's offer. Zelda may not have realized at the time that through her silent acquiescence *her* literary property became and remained Scott's.

What *is* known is that later Scott used diary extracts in *The Beautiful and Damned* as well as in 'The Jelly Bean'.

What is *not* validated is the view proposed by some that Scott, fearful of losing Zelda to a prosperous rival, was determined to win her by writing a successful novel in which he would express his love by including her diaries and portraying her character.[43] We have Scott's fictional appropriations but we do *not* have Zelda's diary or diaries. Perhaps in the course of the Fitzgeralds' changing addresses they were accidentally mislaid or removed from public perusal, if not deliberately, at least conveniently.[44]

Zelda, aware of the extent to which Scott drew on her writings and ideas, was led to try out some fiction herself. 'Yesterday I almost wrote a book or a story,' she wrote Scott, '. . . but after two pages on my heroine I discovered that I hadn't even started her, and, since I couldn't just write forever about a charmingly impossible creature, I began to despair. "Vamping Romeo" was the name, and I guess a man would have had to appear somewhere before the end. But there wasn't any plot, so I thought I'd ask you to decide what they're going to do.' She wished she had sufficient ambition to carry on but was 'much too lazy to care whether it's done or not'. At this stage she did not want to be 'famous and feted', but preferred to be 'very young always and very irresponsible and to feel that my life is my own – to live and be happy', and (she added with unconscious irony) 'die in my own way to please myself'.[45]

She told Scott she hoped 'I'll never get ambitious enough to try anything. It's so much nicer to be sure I could do it better than other people – and I might not . . . that, of cource, would break my heart.'[46] Already she had an insight into how much ambition could cost her.

During spring 1919 Scott posted Zelda an engagement ring which had belonged to his mother. 'Scott Darling, it really is beautiful. Every time I see it on my finger I am rather startled – . . . but I love to see this shining there so nice and white like our love – and it sorter says "Soon" to me all the time – Just sings it all day long.'[47]

Zelda told him she hardly ever took off the 'darling ring' except to swim, but the truth was she hardly ever put it on. 'She soon relegated it to her trophy box,' said Sara Mayfield, 'because . . . to exhibit it flagrantly would have impeded her conquests.'[48]

Zelda's letters swung Scott this way and that on a seesaw of emotion. She assured him of her love, then confessed to an escapade when she dressed in men's clothes to have fun in the movies with a gang of boys, followed by a crazy drive 'with ten boys to liven things up'.[49]

Protestations of everlasting passion compete with 'amusing' encounters with other beaux. Typically she tells Scott an 'old flame from the Stone Ages is calling' but remembers to add: 'He'll probably leave in disgust because I just must talk about you.' By April 1919 Scott's Ledger registers 'hysteria'. Zelda stayed cool: 'Scott, you're really awfully silly – In the first place, I haven't kissed anybody goodbye, and in the second place, nobody's left in the first place – . . . If I did have an honest – or dishonest – desire to kiss just one or two people, I might – but I couldn't ever want to – my mouth is yours.'

Ruthlessly she continued: 'But s'pose I did – Don't you know it'd just be absolutely nothing – Why can't you understand that nothing means anything except your darling self and your love – I wish we'd hurry and I'd be yours so you'd know.'[50]

Scott wished he could keep Zelda locked up like a princess in a tower and told her so incessantly.[51] Finally in exasperation she responded: 'I'm so damn tired of being told that you "used to wonder why they kept princesses in towers" – you've written that verbatim in your last six letters! . . . I know you love me, Darling, and I love you more than anything in the world, but if it's going to be so much longer, we just can't keep up this frantic writing.'[52]

But when, to placate her, he paused, Zelda chastised him: 'The only thing that carried me through a [trip to Auburn] . . . was the knowledge that I'd have a note from you when I got home – but I didn't . . . I hate being disappointed day after day.'[53]

Her view of Scott was piercingly accurate: 'I know you've worried – and enjoyed doing it thoroughly . . . [but] it's all right I rather hate to tell you that – I know it's depriving you of an idea that horrifies and fascinates – you're so morbidly exaggerative – Your mind dwells on things that don't make people happy.'[54]

What Zelda did not realize was that while besieging her with attention and becoming infuriated at her flirtations, Scott was dating another three women.

The first was the curly-haired Montgomery Belle May Steiner. May, popular with officers, fitted the pattern of Fitzgerald's lovers. Scott's Ledger for 1918 testifies to May's consistent appearances if not to the correct spelling of her name: July: 'May Stiener. Zelda . . . May and I on the porch. Her visiting bows'. August: 'Zelda and May'. In September there is no entry for May, presumably because he 'fell in love [with Zelda] on the 7th'. But in October the Ledger again registers: 'May Steiner. Reunion on 26th . . . left for North on 26th.'

Months later, May and Scott were still in contact. Zelda, unaware of Scott's entanglement, told him in her chatty April 1919 letter that after a severe bout of Spanish 'flu 'all her [May's] beautiful hair came out' so she was going to New York to have it treated and would phone Scott.[55] This was the hair admired by Scott, who was secretly aware of May's impending visit.

May, who entered Zelda's close-knit set when later she became Katherine Elsberry's sister-in-law, also entered Scott's fiction. Naturally he heightened their drama, so that in *The Beautiful and Damned* (1922) May, as Dorothy Raycroft, has an affair with Anthony Patch (the Scott hero), who jilts her when she becomes seriously ill.

Zelda, unaware also of Scott's romance with a second woman called Helen Dent,[56] was more significantly kept in the dark about his brief but passionate affair in New York with Rosalinde Fuller, an English actress. Scott's Ledger entry for October 1919 states: 'Went to see Zelda. New York. Rosalind.' Biographers have generally assumed this referred to Zelda's sister, but it is more likely to have been Fuller.

Rosalinde, at twenty-seven four years Scott's senior, was small, dark, with something of Ginevra's pert attraction. Edmund Wilson later told Rosalinde that Scott had considered his sexual encounter with her to be 'his first serious love affair'. At their first meeting at a Plaza Hotel party, Scott introduced himself, then suggested they leave at once. Unlike Zelda who refused late dates with fast workers, Rosalinde, an emancipated believer in free love, agreed immediately. Fitzgerald called a hansom cab, jumped his date inside, pulled a rug around their legs, and according to Rosalinde's racy account 'the clip-crop of the horse's hoofs made a background to our discovery of each other's bodies'.[57]

In the cab Scott's 'eager hands' felt 'in warm secret places under

the old rug'. Once out of the hansom he met Rosalinde frequently
for brief but intensely sexual assignations. Though in 1935 Scott told
Tony Buttitta that he had had no sexual experience before Zelda,
Rosalinde's diary refutes this: 'We made love everywhere, in theatre
boxes, country fields, under the sun, moon and stars . . . no end to
our delight and discovery of one another.' Rosalinde temporarily
succeeded in abolishing Fitzgerald's sexual inhibitions.[58]

Though Scott ceased to correspond with Rosalinde after their
affair, its repercussions continued. The erotic hansom cab ride
enters his fiction. His story 'Myra Meets His Family' (1920) includes
the heroine's romantic carriage ride up Fifth Avenue. In another
1920 story, 'The Lees of Happiness', his heroine Roxanne Milbank,
known as the 'Venus of the Hansom Cab', was at least partly based
on Rosalinde. In *The Great Gatsby* (1925) the narrator, Nick
Carraway, chooses a hansom cab ride through Central Park in
which to kiss Jordan Baker. In 1934 in *Tender Is The Night*, Dick Diver
(partly based on Scott) is in a Paris cab when he kisses Rosemary
Hoyt, the young woman who comes between Dick and Nicole Diver
(partly based on Zelda).

Whether Scott wished to retaliate for Zelda's flirtatiousness or
whether he wanted a final fling before marriage, he felt a 'sense of
shame at having let himself go so far in yielding to his physical proclivities'.[59] Curiously, Scott records no sense of shame about deceiving Zelda while berating her for what were, according to relevant
Montgomery beaux, far less sexually explicit flirtations.

It is interesting to speculate on Zelda's response had she known.
She might well not have minded. For when Scott, attempting to
make her jealous, dwelt on an attractive girl in New York, she
parried with: 'if she's good-looking, and you want to, one bit – I
know you could and love me just the same'.[60]

But what Zelda might have minded was his self-righteous deceit.

In June 1919 the climax to their roller-coaster romance came with
Zelda's involvement with Perry Adair, an Atlanta golfer. Invited by
him to the Georgia Tech dance, she returned home wearing a fraternity pin as a sign of their commitment. Realizing she had gone too
far, she returned his fraternity pin with a warm note. Unfortunately,
possibly by mistake, possibly not, she sent Adair a letter to Scott and
posted Scott the note to the golfer. Fitzgerald was incensed and told
her to cease writing to him.[61]

In June 1919, still angry with Zelda, with his lack of success and
with himself, Scott swung into the Sayres' parlour where he tried to
intimidate Zelda into an instant marriage, first with threats, then

with tears. She could not bear to see him demean himself. Marriage and New York was how Zelda planned to change her life, but she would not stand for any change founded on failure. Sad but resolute, she returned his ring and told him to leave.

He commemorated his personal tragedy first with a three-week binge, during which time he quit his advertising job and returned to St Paul,[62] later with a fine story, 'The Sensible Thing', 'about Zelda + me',[63] in which the anti-hero George O'Kelly seized Jonquil Cary in his arms 'and tried literally to kiss her into marrying him at once'. When that failed he broke into a long monologue of self-pity and ceased only when he saw he had made himself 'despicable in her sight'.[64]

Though Scott would never forget Zelda's rejection, he used it to his best advantage as he metamorphosed from amateur to professional. During July and August 'I dug in and wrote my first book.'[65] In rewriting he discovered his style, his voice and his subject.

Scribners finally accepted *This Side of Paradise* on 16 September 1919. Scott wrote immediately to Perkins asking for a fast publication: 'I have so many things dependent on its success – including of course a girl.'[66]

In November Wilson, Scott's literary mentor, suggested that Fitzgerald cease the cheap effects of commercial stories and substitute the serious work necessary for high art.[67] Temporarily ignoring this issue, Scott recalled his words to Wilson when they left Princeton: 'I want to be one of the greatest writers who ever lived, don't you?' Now on his way, he needed to see Zelda again.

In October he wrote asking if he could come to Montgomery, telling her of his success. She responded she was 'mighty glad' he was coming. 'I've been wanting to see you . . . but I *couldn't* ask you.' With her old wicked touch she told him she was recovering from a 'wholesome amour' with Auburn's 'startling quarter back' and asked him for a 'quart of gin'. He might find her mentally 'dreadfully deteriorated' but 'you never seemed to know when I was stupid and when I wasn't, anyway . . . 'S funny, Scott, I don't feel a bit shaky and "do-don't"ish like I used to when you came – I really want to see you – that's all – Zelda.'[68]

Zelda had taken pride in men not being able to fathom her intelligence. She had already written to Scott: 'Men think I'm purely decorative, and they're just fools for not knowing better . . . I love being rather unfathomable . . . Men love me cause I'm pretty – and they're always afraid of mental wickedness – and men love me cause I'm clever and they're always afraid of my prettiness – One or two have even loved me cause I'm lovable, and then, of cource, I was acting.'[69]

She believed Scott was the one person who knew and loved all of her. He wasn't quite so sure.

In November 1919 he became a client of Harold Ober at the Reynolds Agency, who remained his friend and agent for years. Ober's coup was to persuade the prestigious *Saturday Evening Post* to buy Scott's story 'Head and Shoulders' for $400 before Scott left for Montgomery in late November.[70] Thus he went with some triumph and some trepidation, but the reality of encountering Zelda could not live up to five months' fantasies. Scott wanted to repeat the past, but realized that 'There are all kinds of love in the world, but never the same love twice.'[71]

Although informally they renewed their engagement, Scott left Montgomery feeling they had lost what they had. Though Zelda wrote saying she would release him from any marriage obligation, she was the more optimistic. Earlier she had told a friend that she was not romantically in love with Scott but that she felt it was her mission to help him realize his potential as a writer.[72] Unlike Scott, she now felt a more realistic romantic resurgence. She felt they were building their love castle on firmer foundations. That first abandonment couldn't last. She thought it foolish to mourn for a memory when they had each other. '"When love has turned to kindliness" doesn't horrify me like it used to – It has such a peaceful sound – like something to come back to and rest – and sometimes I'm glad we're not exactly like we used to be.'[73]

Between November 1919 and February 1920 Scott's stories about bright upper-class adolescents were accepted fast. *The Smart Set* published 'The Debutante' in November, 'Porcelain and Pink' in January, 'Benediction' and 'Dalyrimple Goes Wrong' in February. He cabled Zelda with each success.

In December she read *This Side of Paradise*. Her response was: 'Why cant I write? I'd like to tell you how fine I think the book is and how miserably and completely and – a little unexpectedly – I am thine.'[74]

By January Scott had made sufficient money to leave cold New York for warm New Orleans, from where he visited Zelda.[75] When he said she had inspired his novel she responded: 'It's so nice to know you really *can* do things – *anything* – and I love to feel that maybe I can help just a little.'[76]

Scott wrote formally to the Judge for her hand[77] and they resumed their sexual relationship. During February Zelda suspected she was pregnant. Earlier, on seeing Katharine's baby, Zelda had told Scott: 'It's darling . . . I felt like I'd sorter like to have it',[78] but faced with a possible baby herself she was initially unsure whether she *would* 'sorter like to have it'.

Yet when Scott, who was very sure he did not want the responsibility of fatherhood, sent her pills for an abortion Zelda refused to take them. 'I wanted to, for your sake, because I know what a mess I'm making and how inconvenient it's all going to be – but I simply *can't* and *won't* take those awful pills – so I've thrown them away. I'd rather take carbolic acid . . . I'd rather have a *whole family* than sacrifice my self-respect . . . I'd feel like a damn whore if I took even one.'[79]

Before Zelda discovered that she was after all not pregnant, Scott had already repeated Zelda's key phrase 'self-respect' in a note to a friend's sister. If a young woman smokes and drinks in public, tells hair-raising stories to shock people and admits that she has kissed thousands of male admirers and certainly does not intend to stop, that girl is hardly a lady. But Scott confessed he had fallen for Zelda's bravery, honesty and 'flaming self-respect.'[80]

Between March and May Ober sold 'Myra Meets His Family', 'The Camel's Back', 'Bernice Bobs Her Hair', 'The Ice Palace' and 'The Offshore Pirate' to the *Saturday Evening Post*, which raised his fee to $500.

Scribner's Magazine paid Scott $150 for 'The Cut-Glass Bowl' and 'The Four Fists', more serious pieces. Then in February, having sold movie rights of 'Head and Shoulders' for a staggering $2,500, he sent Zelda a diamond and platinum wristwatch. She wrote back exuberantly: 'O, Scott, it's so be-au-ti-ful – and the back's just as pretty as the front . . . I've turned it over four hundred times to see "from Scott to Zelda".'[81]

Myth says the success of *This Side of Paradise* reassured Zelda so that she decided to marry him. Zelda said it was because Scott had renewed confidence in himself. When his novel was accepted she knew nothing about it. When she agreed to marriage it had still not been published and she had no way of knowing its outcome.

Six days before Scribner's published on 26 March 1920, Scott sent H. L. Mencken a review copy inscribed on the flyleaf with the words: 'This is a bad book full of good things, a book about flappers written for philosophers, an exquisite burlesque of Compton Mackenzie with a pastiche of Wells at the end.'[82]

Five days before it was published, the *Montgomery Advertiser* celebrated the twin achievements of two Montgomery Belles. It announced Zelda's engagement, and on the front page of the society section of the same 21 March issue it ran the headline: 'Sara Haardt elected to Phi Beta Kappa.' On Sara's graduation in June, the Goucher yearbook hailed her as 'a soulful highbrow'.[83] The two women writers-to-be had decisively taken different paths.

Scott sent Zelda her first corsage of white orchids. She sent him her most loving letter:

> Darling Heart, our fairy tale is almost ended, and we're going to marry and live happily ever afterward just like the princess in her tower who worried you so much . . .
>
> I DO want to marry you – even if you do think I "dread" it – I wish you hadn't said that – I'm not afraid of anything. To be afraid a person has either to be a coward or very great and big. I am neither. Besides, I know you can take much better care of me than I can, and I'll always be very, very happy with you – except sometimes when we engage in our weekly debates – and even then I rather enjoy myself. I like being very calm and masterful, while you become emotional and sulky.

Then, perhaps feeling she had tipped her hand a bit, she hastily finished with another courtly codeline: 'I'm absolutely nothing without you – Just the doll that I should have been born – You're a necessity and a luxury . . . you're going to be a husband to your wife.'[84]

Zelda's wedding was to take place in New York, where Scott insisted on being married in the Catholic church. He favoured St Patrick's Cathedral because he had a cousin, Father William B. Martin, on the staff there who would marry them. Zelda's family had always attended Montgomery's Church of the Holy Comforter, where Minnie played the organ, Rosalind had sung in the choir, Marjorie had been married, and Zelda herself who went regularly to Sunday School had been baptized, a little late, in 1910. Zelda told Sara Mayfield she did not feel sentimental about the Holy Comforter and thought it more exciting to be married in Manhattan. The Sayres, who avoided the turmoil and expense of a Southern wedding, apparently raised no objections.

Zelda left Montgomery wearing a Confederate-grey suit, almost – according to Sara Mayfield – the colour of her eyes. 'Some of the people with her thought they had never seen her look so beautiful before,' said Sara.[85] A crowd of her friends laden with flowers for her saw her off at the station. Astonishingly, not one of Zelda's many friends had been invited to the wedding. Apart from the bride and groom there were to be only Zelda's three sisters – Marjorie Sayre Brinson, Clothilde (and her husband John Palmer), Rosalind (and her husband Newman Smith) and Scott's Princeton friend

Ludlow Fowler. He was to be best man while Rosalind stood as matron of honour.

Zelda's parents had decided not to attend. They were not overtly opposed to a Catholic wedding, as long as it was in the North. Family members thought that as devout Episcopalians they would have felt uncomfortable about a Catholic ceremony in Montgomery. The Sayres' main concern was that Zelda should be accompanied by her sister Marjorie and would stay with her sister Clothilde. Indeed, the announcement in the *Montgomery Advertiser* stated that Zelda and Marjorie would be guests of Clothilde and John Palmer.[86] Events did not turn out as the Sayres had planned.

Zelda and Marjorie were met by Rosalind and Newman Smith at Pennsylvania Station, but instead of going to Clothilde's home in nearby Tarrytown, they found Scott had arranged for them to stay at the Biltmore Hotel.[87]

Zelda and Scott were married on 3 April 1920 in the Rectory of St Patrick's Cathedral. Scott, nervy and impatient, insisted that the wedding start even before the time at which Clothilde and John Palmer were due to arrive.

Zelda wore a blue-grey spring suit adorned by the single corsage of white orchids Scott had sent her. She had a matching hat trimmed with leather ribbons and buckles. She was the only ornament at her own wedding – for there was no music, no flowers, no photographer, and no lunch for the out-of-town visitors. After the ceremony the priest said: 'You be a good episcopalian, Zelda, and, Scott, you be a good catholic, and you'll get along fine.' Scott said later to Ludlow Fowler that it was the last advice he got from a priest.[88]

Immediately after the wedding, Zelda and Scott hurried away to suite 2109 at the Biltmore Hotel, a favourite amongst Princetonians. It was noticeable that Scott had not thought to ask any Princetonians apart from Fowler to his wedding.

Zelda, who had been treated as a princess most of her life, must have been shocked by the tiny, hurried wedding about which she had barely been consulted and in which her family had not been taken into account. She was painfully aware that Rosalind, Marjorie and especially Clothilde were disconcerted, distressed and angry. 'Scott had done all the planning without consulting me,' said Rosalind. 'Marjorie and the Palmers, and Newman and I lunched together, then Marjorie went home with Tilde.'[89]

Years later Scott described his emotions as a bridegroom: 'The man with the jingle of money in his pocket who married the girl a year later would always cherish an abiding distrust, an animosity, toward the leisure class – not the conviction of a revolutionist, but the smouldering hatred of a peasant.'[90]

Zelda never openly described *her* emotions. But she would have known, then, that her family's feelings were not important to her new husband.

PART II

Northern Voice
April 1920–April 1924

CHAPTER 5

Romance in Montgomery had seen Zelda as a celebrity dominating a struggling writer. Marriage in New York changed that. Scott was no longer struggling and she was no longer a celebrity. He had friends while she had none. Nor her family.

Scott's career had taken a meteoric curve upward. *This Side of Paradise* had hit bestseller lists around the States. Serious papers serialized abridged versions. By the end of 1921 twelve printings totalled 49,075 copies. Although earnings of $6,200 for 1920 did not make him wealthy his book, reviewed everywhere, became a conversational subject. Considered ground-breaking, it captured youth's essence as did its author. New York autograph-hunters loved F. Scott Fitzgerald and F. Scott Fitzgerald loved them. His wit and style caught the mood of the moment. As Zelda later wrote: 'New York is a good place to be on the upgrade' – especially for those who possess 'a rapacious, engulfing ego'[1] which Scott had, and used, to become youth's incandescent spokesman.

And Zelda?

She became his consort. A witty consort. An articulate consort. But for the first time in their relationship a decorative accessory, an epiphenomenal adjunct known as 'the wife of Scott Fitzgerald'.

Their marriage began what was to become in certain respects a dramatic role reversal. Suddenly in control of his professional life, Scott exerted a new control over his personal one. The wedding with its lack of consideration for Zelda's family was the first sign Zelda received. Neither Rosalind nor Clothilde ever forgave Scott or – for a long time – Zelda.

Zelda's wardrobe was the second sign of the Fitzgeralds' revised relationship. The flouncy organdie frocks in Zelda's trousseau suddenly seemed out of place to Scott. From adoring her Southern Belle appearance he was now embarrassed by it. He telephoned his St Paul friend, Marie Hersey, who after her years as Ginevra King's classmate at Westover had moved from Vassar graduate to New

York sophisticate. 'You've got to help me! . . . Zelda wants to buy nothing but frills and furbelows and you can't go around New York in that kind of thing.'[2] Take her shopping, he said to Marie. Get her the right kind of outfit. Marie did. They bought Zelda an original Jean Patou suit. Zelda, humiliated and incensed, bit back a retort until fourteen years later, when she reported to *Esquire* readers that she had never worn it, had stored it in trunks, and was 'oh, so relieved, to find it devastated at last'.[3]

After shopping, she and Marie had tea in the Plaza Grill, where gusts of expensive perfume streamed from the coiffeur on the way to the elevator, and the hotel flowers, according to Zelda and Scott's writer friend John Dos Passos, resembled goldbacked ten dollar bills.[4] As Marie steered Zelda towards the Grill, the smell of creamy sweet butter prefaced teatimes far from those in Montgomery. Assorted teas melted indiscernibly into Bronx cocktails and coloured liqueurs. Stylish New York women taking tea would soon become Zelda's models. In beaded dresses with hats like manhole covers they tapped tippy toes while sipping from tiny teacups before trotting off to the dance floors of the Lorraine or the St Regis. Girls with marcel waves dangled powder boxes, bracelets and lank young men from their wrists as they made their way from the warm orange lights of the Biltmore Hotel's façade to the elegant silver teapots of the Plaza or the Ritz.[5]

Although during 1920 Zelda went regularly with Scott and his friends to the Plaza, it was that first unfamiliar, humiliating teatime with Marie that left its mark on her prose. Ten years later, in her story 'A Millionaire's Girl', she recreates an indelible impression of fashionable New York where at dusky teatimes those girls inhabited the Plaza.[6]

Although Zelda soon discarded her small-town innocence and acquired a big-city gloss, becoming one of 'the halo of golden bobs' in those fashionable hotels,[7] that occasion with Marie was the first in a series of shivery performances as Scott Fitzgerald's wife.

Their life in New York in spring 1920 was a round of theatres and nightspots, for many celebrity names Zelda had merely conjured with were now eager to meet them. They lunched with George Jean Nathan in the Japanese Gardens of the Ritz where the Fitzgeralds, both stage-struck since adolescence, were particularly impressed by Nathan's companion, Ziegfeld *Follies* star Kay Laurel. At the Montmartre nightclub they watched another *Follies* star, Lilyan Tashman, weave her way around the dance floor. The famous vamp Theda Bara was at the Shubert Theatre in the comedy *The Blue Flame*.

All three Barrymores were starring on Broadway and the reigning theatrical queen was Marilyn Miller, whom Rosalind Sayre had seen the previous year and who Rosalind said could pass as Zelda's twin.

The Fitzgeralds behaved appallingly during performances. They laughed at their own jokes, and at one comedy, *Enter Madame*, Zelda fell off her seat in hysterics of giggles and the management asked them to leave.

Zelda's splashy displays were partly an overdose of high spirits, partly a feeling of being out of control in a new world.

Scottie told a friend later that her mother's Southern upbringing made enormous difficulties for her in New York: 'In the South, life was cosy and so full of love that it formed a cocoon. To step out into the world of New York . . . constantly exposed to parties where mother was supposed to be the witty and glamorous companion to a famous, difficult and demanding man, was something she was ill-equipped to cope with.'[8]

Outwardly Zelda did not acknowledge those difficulties. She exchanged her velvet lounging pants for slick city suits; her natural wit sustained conversations. Temporarily she hid any resentment about her role as 'companion'.

Their marriage coincided with the beginning of the Boom, the era of the Roaring Twenties that Fitzgerald, though knowing little about jazz, inventively named the Jazz Age, in order to connote a mood of music, dance and reckless stimulation.

Zelda found herself inhabiting not one New York world but two. There was Bohemian New York: the Washington Square area of Greenwich Village, with its winding streets, crumbling brown-stones turned into communal housing, its Bowery theatre, its cheap Italian and Hungarian cafés. In 1920 Bohemia's marginal pleasures were becoming marketable. It was strident, dusty, full of racket and reporters, speakeasies, illicit alcohol, hushed whispers and promise. Zelda and Scott visited in yellow taxis or walked through it like photographers with flashing camera-eyes rather than as residents who bought their groceries in brown bags from the corner shop. Zelda wrote repeatedly she was not a kitchen sort of person.[9] As she never exhibited any desire to tackle even the most rudimentary domestic chores she was delighted that their first few weeks were spent in the luxurious Biltmore Hotel, set in the second New York world, north of 42nd Street.

In this exclusive segment of the city bordered by Times Square, Central Park and the fashionable hotel and shopping districts, to which Fitzgerald restricted himself in his first novel and early stories, skyscraper windows sparkled in the sun. Zelda's eye for colour saw a glowing city, a fantasy palace where the 'tops of the buildings shine like crowns of gold-leaf kings in conference'.[10] She saw Park Avenue flowing smoothly up Manhattan as a masculine avenue, subdued, subtle, solid, a fitting background for the promenades of men.[11] She glimpsed Charlie Chaplin in a yellow polo coat, girls with piquant profiles who were mistaken for Gloria Swanson, shop assistants who looked like her idol Marilyn Miller, and bandleader Paul Whiteman who looked like his press photographs and played 'Two Little Girls in Blue' at the Palais Royal.

In both New York societies Zelda heard the sounds of the Twenties: monologues littered with adjectives, spoken by people who saw themselves as thoroughly amusing; conversations as sharp as her own with one wisecrack following another.

As a young woman from Alabama she had accurately imagined New York as a city of breathless postwar celebrity: 'Moving-picture actresses were famous . . . Everybody was there. People met people they knew in hotel lobbies smelling of orchids and plush and detective stories . . . everybody was famous. All the other people who weren't well known had been killed in the war; there wasn't much interest in private lives.'[12]

Zelda fastened early on two symbols of the city that later she repeatedly used in her writing and painting. The first was the notion of a city in perpetual motion where life was lived at high speed. Bred on the dawdle and deliberations of the Deep South, she satirized the smart people spotting smarter people disinclined to be spotted; the relentlessly elegant people ruthlessly ignoring ignorable people who were dying to be spotted. ' "We're having some people", everybody said to everybody else, "and we want you to join us", and they said, "We'll telephone." All over New York people telephoned. They telephoned from one hotel to another to people on other parties that they couldn't get there.'[13]

The city's visual delights provided Zelda with twilights, the second significant symbol which fed her art. She imprinted their bluish haze, the way they shone on 57th Street where she and Scott held hands and swooped like hawks in and out of the traffic. She would recall spectacular violet-grey dusks which hovered mistily above the hood of a taxi on which she rode the breeze while Scott perched on its roof as they became the living, breathing, toe-tapping embodiment of the Roaring Twenties.

Zelda later used those New York gloamings in her fiction as a context to their escapades. Zelda's dusks both hid and revealed the way the beautiful pair did appalling things with an air of breeding. Of course she had seen some pretty good twilights in Montgomery. She immortalized Montgomery's incandescent globes, black inside with moths, with a 'time and quality that appertains to nowhere else'.[14] But those were old-hat twilights, too suffocatingly hot to enjoy. So magnetized was Zelda by her honeymoon twilights over Brooklyn Bridge, Fifth Avenue, Times Square and Central Park that she first fictionalized them, later painted them.[15]

One 1920 honeymoon sky stayed with her for years. In her short story 'A Millionaire's Girl', written in 1929, she recalled: 'Twilights were wonderful just after the war. They hung above New York like indigo wash, forming themselves from asphalt dust and sooty shadows under the cornices and limp gusts of air exhaled from closing windows, to hang above the streets with all the mystery of white fog rising off a swamp.'[16]

In 1932 she rewrote this for her first novel[17] for, like Scott, Zelda was never averse to recycling a witty phrase – though usually she repeated her own, while Scott often repeated hers. Maybe in those twirling twilight Twenties they both saw her words as hanging in a communal closet. Maybe it was only later that Zelda wanted separate wardrobes.

Scott, spellbound by New York as a child, drew *his* symbolic New York landscape from three glimpses of New York prior to his arrival there in 1920.[18] Scott's first reported glimpse was when as a ten-year-old he saw a ferry boat at dawn moving slowly from the Jersey shore towards Manhattan. His second occurred when as a fifteen-year-old Newman schoolboy he saw two New York theatrical shows starring Gertrude Bryan and Ina Claire, who 'blurred into one lovely entity, the girl. She was my second symbol of New York. The ferry boat stood for triumph, the girl for romance.'[19] Scott found his third symbol as an adult when he saw his Princeton intellectual mentor, Bunny Wilson, striding confidently along a New York street, drawing strength from the city pavements and from a force Scott called 'that new thing – the Metropolitan spirit',[20] a dynamic movement like a 'tall man's quick-step'.[21]

Scott links these three symbols through the idea of a romantic quickened pace, which parallels Zelda's notion of romantic dusks hovering over a city constantly in motion. The Fitzgeralds shared the insider's excitement mixed with the outsider's awe. Zelda also shared, at one level, Scott's frontier viewpoint of New York. She acted as a glamorous model for his Western tourist image of New Yorkers which he presented so skilfully in *This Side of Paradise*.[22]

In Scott's words: 'It was an age of miracles, it was an age of art, it was an age of excess, and it was an age of satire.'[23] At this level, Zelda was as amazed as Scott that overnight he was hailed not merely as the chronicler of an age he saw as the greatest, gaudiest spree in history, but also as the city's laureate. Through his work and their joint escapades, they now embodied the spirit of a particular New York which bore little resemblance to Theodore Dreiser's poor person's New York or to Edith Wharton's aristocratic New York. Changed by the building boom, it was a postwar luxurious metropolitan place, peopled by a new generation who arrived with ambition and riches from all over the States. Minnesota's apprentice writer had become the 'arch type' of what New York wanted.[24] 'I, who knew less of New York than any reporter of six months standing and less of its society than any hall-room boy in the Ritz stag line, was pushed into the position not only of spokesman for the time but of the typical product of that same moment.'[25]

Although enjoying her role as a famous Fitzgerald, at a deeper level Zelda saw through it. Intelligently she pointed out that New York, speakeasy city of metallic urgency, was more full of reflections than of itself, that the only concrete things in town were the abstractions.[26]

There was nothing concrete about their domestic life during their first months. Zelda told Sara Mayfield it was fortunate her parents had decided not to accompany her to New York as they would have been shocked at Scott's 'monumental spree' in the Biltmore Hotel, where he called up bellboys to bathe him and left taps running till they flooded the hotel.[27] Before the management moved them on, several of Scott's college chums came to visit them.

In 1919 Edmund Wilson had gone to New York to work for *Vanity Fair*, and as managing editor there he hired his Princeton friend John Bishop. By the time of the Fitzgeralds' marriage Bishop was often staying at the opulent apartment of another Princetonian, Townsend Martin, a suavely dressed globe-trotting screenwriter. Unlike his uncle, the wealthy philanthropist Frederick Townsend Martin, young Martin, a womanizer, had no intention of becoming a reformer.

Wilson and Bishop were the first to meet Fitzgerald's bride in room 2109. Zelda offered the bachelors Orange Blossom cocktails spiked with bootleg gin, then spread herself elegantly on a sofa. Wilson saw her initially as 'very pretty and languid', but soon decided she had a forceful interesting personality accompanied by wit, beauty, recklessness, unpredictability and Southern exoticism.[28] Bishop saw her as a 'barbarian princess'.[29] Only later (when married himself to a wealthy efficient woman who encouraged his career) did he blame Zelda for encouraging Scott to drink and waste his talent.

Since their wedding both Fitzgeralds had begun drinking heavily. In their first few months together they often fell asleep when drunk, so they might arrive at a party and immediately take a nap. Zelda, who had annoyed her parents by rebellious drinking in Montgomery, now drank more because there were no parental checks. Scott drank because he was an incipient alcoholic. Scott admitted that when he first became rich he discovered that after a few drinks he was able to hold forth and please his audience. So he began to drink more heavily to attract a bigger audience.

Though this is not Scott speaking but one of his characters in 'A New Leaf' (1931), it aptly sums up his attitude in the early Twenties, when his desperate need to please people ran alongside his increasingly unpredictable drinking behaviour.

Zelda had mixed memories of her honeymoon, some glamorous, some rueful. Too much alcohol soaked the moonlight and roses. 'People in the [hotel] corridors complained; there was a tart smell of gin over everything; for years the smell of her trousseau haunted [her] . . . corsages died in the ice-water tray and cigarettes disintegrated in the spittoon.'[30]

Among regular Princetonian visitors to the Fitzgeralds' hotel suite was John Biggs Jnr, Scott's former room-mate, ex-editor of the Princeton *Tiger* and Triangle Club collaborator, now an aspiring writer who would publish two novels with Scribner's in the 1920s before settling firmly into his law career. He was often accompanied by Lawton Campbell, a writer and business executive, and Alex McKaig, who worked in advertising.

A former editor of the *Daily Princetonian*, Alex had a pudgy baby face with curly hair parted in the centre, and still lived with his mother. He had a waspish nature which came from envying his more gifted friends. He kept a constant diary of the Fitzgeralds' movements which provides valuable glimpses of their first few weeks. His first entry, nine days after their marriage, is unflattering to Zelda and offers poor prospects for their marriage. 'Called on Scott Fitz and his bride,' he recorded, 'latter temperamental small-town Southern belle. Chews gum – shows knees. I do not think marriage can succeed. Both drinking heavily. Think they will be divorced in 3 years. Scott write something big – then die in a garret at thirty-two.'[31] McKaig's and Wilson's views of Zelda as a hick Southerner out of place in a big city say as much for their Northern stereotyped attitudes about the Deep South as they do about Zelda.

Lawton Campbell, a tall blond Southerner who had been in Princeton's Triangle Club with Scott, felt great affection for Zelda. His aunt Margaret Booth ran the school of that name in Montgomery, and linked by their Alabama connections he and Zelda remained friends for years. She felt close enough to him later to give him one of her paintings, which he treasured and refused to sell after her death. In 1920 he was a wealthy executive with General Foods and author of two successful plays, *Solid South* and *Immoral Isabella*. He told Sara Mayfield that 'Of all the people who ever came out of Alabama . . . Zelda Sayre Fitzgerald and Tallulah Bankhead [were] the most fascinating.'[32]

Several of their circle noticed Zelda's curious speech patterns filled, according to Bunny Wilson, with 'felicitous phrases and unexpected fancies'.[33] Wilson observed: 'She talked with so spontaneous a color and wit – almost exactly in the way she wrote – that I very soon ceased to be troubled by the fact that the conversation was in the nature of a "free association" of ideas and one could never follow up anything. I have rarely known a woman who expressed herself so delightfully and so freshly; she had no ready-made phrases on the one hand and made no straining for effect on the other.'[34] Although 'it was difficult to talk to her consecutively about anything,' said Wilson, 'you were not led . . . to suspect any mental unsoundness'.[35]

Years later, Campbell also recollected Zelda's singular speech. 'She would stretch out on the long sofa in my living room . . . and recount some fabulous experience of the night before . . . If her remarks were occasionally non sequitur one didn't notice it at the time. She passed very quickly from one topic to another and you didn't question her. It wouldn't occur to you to stop and ask what she meant.'[36]

It is important to recognize that Campbell's delineation of Zelda's speech patterns as 'non sequitur' or disordered, and Wilson's determination to include (even if then to deny) hints of mental unsoundness, occurred not merely forty years after conversations with Zelda but after her many years of being publicly labelled as a schizophrenic whose medical diagnosis had used her *ordinary* speech patterns to indicate the disintegration of her thinking processes. It would have been hard for Campbell or Wilson so many years later to recall Zelda's speech without that mental illness framework.

Lacking female friends, Zelda relied particularly on Ludlow Fowler, Scott's best man, for company. Ludlow, wealthy and generous, spent time with Zelda and Scott at the theatre and the *Follies*. On the weekend of 24 April 1920 several friends, including Ludlow, who had been active in the Triangle Club with Scott, accompanied the Fitzgeralds to the Cottage Club, one of Princeton's most prestigious eating clubs, to which Scott had belonged. On arrival Zelda somersaulted down sacrosanct Prospect Avenue then, on reaching the Cottage Club, insisted on having her breakfast omelette flamed in brandy with applejack which she provided.[37] In order to shock the academic community Scott introduced her as his mistress, got drunk, started a fight and wound up with two black eyes. 'We were there three days, Zelda and five men in Harvey Firestone's car, and not one of us drew a sober breath,' he confided later to Marie Hersey, adding it was 'the damnedest party ever held in Princeton'.[38] That Scott still had good women friends as confidantes whereas she suddenly had none was another blow to Zelda.

When the Biltmore evicted the Fitzgeralds they moved to the Commodore Hotel, two blocks down 42nd Street, and celebrated their arrival by whizzing round the revolving doors for half an hour. In mid-May they were forced to leave there too because of rowdy behaviour.

They filled their first weeks with antics, and the newspapers filled their pages with the Fitzgeralds. Scott undressed at George White's *Scandals*, Zelda dived fully dressed into the Union Square fountain.[39] The media watched as the Fitzgeralds lived life on the wing. What could be better for headlines than a couple who did not go in for self-preservation? Journalists turned their bizarre behaviour into myth, which in turn encouraged the Fitzgeralds to invent further unseemly exploits. They were caught in a vicious circle which left them confused and alienated. Zelda wrote that in New York they needed 'to absolve themselves in the waters of each other's unrest'.[41] Scott wrote retrospectively that within a few months of arriving in New York he and Zelda no longer knew who they were or what they were expected to do.

As *enfants terribles* they *did* provoke people, but they were never vulgar and often funny, so they got away with it. One writer friend said: 'I couldn't get mad at him and particularly not at Zelda; there was a golden innocence about them and they were both so hopelessly goodlooking.'[41] Scott's appeal lay in his charm and intuitiveness. This allowed people initially to look kindly on his clowning before he botched up their approval with even worse behaviour. His desire to

impress people led him into some conspicuous acts. Take the afternoon in the Scribner Building when Scott, knowing Edith Wharton
was in Charles Scribner's office, rushed in and fell at Wharton's feet
in a parody of homage. Legend has it that despite Wharton's stiff for-
mality she took it well.

Their whirlwind antics of those first few months meant Scott
accomplished very little new writing. But he reaped benefits from
stories written earlier which together with sketches, plays and features appeared every month in the *Saturday Evening Post*,
Metropolitan, *Vanity Fair*, the *Nassau Lit*, *Scribner's Magazine*. *The
Smart Set* in July published his brilliant naturalistic story 'May Day',
whose core was the 1919 May Day Riots and the suicide of sensitive
Gordon Sterrett, an artistic failure.

He did very little work on his second novel either, but despite this
by June 1920 *Metropolitan* had advanced Scott $7,000 for serial rights
for the as yet unwritten book *The Flight of the Rocket*, which became
The Beautiful and Damned. Scott, under the literary influences of
Joseph Conrad, Mark Twain and especially Theodore Dreiser's
deterministic realism, intended his new novel to emphasize, as
'May Day' had done, the idea that human behaviour is determined
by forces beyond the characters' control.

During 1920 his price for short fiction rose from $400 to $900 and
eleven stories earned him $4,650. He was paid $7,425 from the
movies for three stories ('Head and Shoulders', 'Myra Meets His
Family' and 'The Offshore Pirate') and he was offered an option on
future stories. That year, his first full year as a professional writer,
he earned $18,850.[42] He and Zelda were incapable of covering their
expenses with his earnings; thus he began his lifelong habit of borrowing from Harold Ober and Scribner's.

Both Fitzgeralds enjoyed thinking up new ways to burn money.
Scott used five-dollar bills to light his cigarettes and folded five-
hundred ones to show the figures when he wore them in his vest
pockets. Though Zelda's father had brought her up to see money as
unimportant, suddenly exhilarated by the sheer amount they
appeared to have, she consumed it eagerly on Manhattan-style
expensive clothes.[43] Neither of them knew how to manage finances.

Though Scott remained obsessed with and critical of the rich he
was never averse to consorting with them, so he enjoyed their visits
to Ludlow Fowler's family's rich New York mansion. Zelda was
particularly intrigued by the elevator, having never seen one inside
an ordinary house before.[44]

For Scott this was a time of storing up images, characters and situations which he would use after August when he started writing again. Zelda's role was primarily as Scott's muse, subsequently as his editorial eye. Scott's literary friends were aware that he leant on her for invention and literary direction. McKaig, who assessed Zelda's mind as undisciplined yet intuitive, asserted that she supplied Scott with all his copy for female characters. He also felt Scott was too absorbed in Zelda's personality, indisputably the stronger of the two.[45] This image, popular with Scott's friends, was not entirely accurate. Zelda kept hidden those areas of dependence on Scott – her need for friendship and emotional support.

Scott based his protagonists almost entirely on Zelda and himself. As McKaig recorded in his diary, Scott 'made another true remark about himself . . . cannot depict how any one thinks except himself & possibly Zelda. Find that after he has written about a character for a while it becomes just himself again.'[46]

Campbell, like McKaig, believed Zelda was the dominant influence on Scott's writing. 'I have always thought that Zelda did more for Scott than Scott did for Zelda. I have seen him many times write down the things she said on scraps of paper or the backs of envelopes.'[47]

Being a muse is not much of a job for a bright young woman and Zelda, isolated from her kin, grew bored. An outdoor person, never happier than when swimming, she was now living an entirely city life. One of Scott's worries was the extent to which his male friends found her physically exciting. John Peale Bishop flirted openly with her in front of Scott who, voyeuristically, at first found it sexually stimulating.[48] Zelda told John: 'I like you better than anybody in the world; I never feel safe with you! – I only like men who kiss as a means to an end. I never know how to treat the other kind.'[49]

Scott's short stories had achieved a certain notoriety for their lushly described passionate kisses, so Zelda's remark might have been a specific marital goad; more likely, she was exhibiting her Southern role of a woman who erotically disturbed men. Certainly she also flirted with McKaig, who had entirely changed his negative impression of Zelda and now declared her the most brilliant, beautiful young woman he had ever known.

Wilson, formerly as sexually reticent as Scott himself, did not flirt with Zelda. He already coveted the poet Elinor Hoyt Wylie, while also in an impossible three-cornered romance with a second poet, Edna St Vincent Millay, and Bishop, his fellow editor at *Vanity Fair*.[50] However, he did fall under Zelda's mesmeric influence and was intrigued when she told him that hotel bedrooms erotically excited her.[51] At this point Wilson gauged Fitzgerald to be 'neurotically jealous' of Zelda.[52]

Zelda flirted more seriously with screenwriter Townsend Martin, whose good looks and globe-trotting tales she admired. At first on the grounds that Townsend and John Bishop, who shared an apartment, had missed out on wedding kisses, Zelda playfully kissed both men whilst Scott remarked tolerantly: 'Oh, yes, they really have kisses coming to them, because they weren't at the wedding, and everybody at a wedding always gets a kiss.'[53] Then, going further, Zelda captured Townsend in the bathroom where she asked him to give her a bath, and walked into John's bedroom suggesting she crawl into bed with him – though only to sleep, she reassured everyone. Wilson reported that Scott's tolerance faded and he became worried and huffy.[54]

Scott's jealousy about Townsend Martin increased that summer when Zelda became, as she later admitted in a letter to Scott, 'romanticly attached'.[55] Scott's Ledger for June 1920 thankfully records 'Townsend goes abroad' but it also discreetly mentions the 'Jean Bankhead fuss'. Possibly in retaliation, Scott had gone further than Zelda and had a brief affair with Gene (Eugenia) Bankhead, who was engaged to the alcoholic Morton Hoyt, a drinking buddy of Scott's and a *Vanity Fair* writer. This affair was close to home, as Gene of course was the elder sister of Zelda's friend Tallulah, and Morton the brother of Wilson's 'poetic romance', Elinor Hoyt Wylie.[56]

Zelda later expressed her complex feelings in *Caesar's Things*: 'Janno had always been jealous. Situations which had to be faced with dishonesty and endured for the sake of a code to which she did not subscribe made her sick. She couldn't say to Jacob, "I don't want you to go, you're obligated to me. Anyway, she's not as nice as I am." She sat being . . . courageous . . . saying to herself . . . such was all in the game.'[57]

The game intensified when Zelda's suspicions were accurately aroused about Scott's affair with another Montgomery Belle, actress Miriam Hopkins. That this 'game' appeared part of a life of freedom confused her. In both her novels Zelda's heroines, Alabama and Janno, equate lack of restrictions with lack of security. On her wedding night Alabama lies awake, thinking that 'no power on earth could make her do anything, she thought frightened, any more except herself'.[58] Janno says, 'fright makes one realize [one's] dependence on the formulas'.[59] Initially a lifestyle where she was no longer tied down by tradition or taboos was what Zelda thought she wanted. But a life without limits brings its own fears.

Zelda flirted heavily with Scott's friends partly from habit, but also partly because attracting men seemed the only familiar talent left to her. As well as lacking girlfriends with whom to share confidences, she had no mother to spoil her, no father to rebel against. Zelda's role as a Flapper for Scott's writing was exhausting, but she had not yet found an alternative. Without a solid base she settled for male admiration. She had regarded flirting as harmless so long as Scott remained loyal. But when *his* explorations led to sexual relationships her world rocked. Having no other support she had to suppress any anger and lean on Scott.

Already in their first few months of marriage the Fitzgeralds were encountering problems which would intensify. But they still had one constant bond: precious talks and dreams. This intimacy allowed them to guard against intruders and remained the one safeguard they never entirely lost. Scott recalled that the lengthy conversations he and Zelda had at bedtime which sometimes lasted until dawn were crucial to their relationship. During the daytime he felt they never achieved that same intimacy.[60]

After their heavy city socializing Scott felt a rural retreat would enable him to finish his second novel, promised to Perkins for September. In May 1920 Zelda's Montgomery friend Leon Ruth, one of Scott's early rivals, now studying at Columbia, helped them buy a second-hand Marmon sports coupé. They hoped a car would enable them to search for a house near water because, as Scott wrote to a friend, 'If Zelda can't swim, she's miserable.'[61]

Zelda played havoc with the car but managed to find a suitable house near Long Island Sound in Westport, Connecticut, fifty miles from New York, in 1920 still country not suburbia. When Westport was constructed in 1835 as a new town along the Sangatuk river with pieces from neighbouring towns Fairfield, Norwalk and Weston, river and seafront took on a new significance as wharves, warehouses, mills, factories and, later, luxurious country estates, inns and restaurants sprang up. By the time the Fitzgeralds moved there, summer visitors and New York commuters swarmed the beaches. Their house, built in 1758, was originally the home of Wakeman Couch, an early farmer who grew onions on the surrounding acres. 'Burritt Wakeman's place' was a two-storey grey shingled farm cottage on Compo Road which took its name from the old Compo Tide Mill building.[62] The year before Zelda arrived, a wooden bathing pavilion opened at Compo beach, and wooden bath-houses lining the boardwalk could be rented by the hour, but Zelda ignored those facilities as their house had its own garden and stretch of beach. From a photograph taken in May 1920 we can see the house, its imposing veranda supported by elegant pillars, was set in a spacious garden surrounded by trees. It was a house of many windows, all with an attractive rural aspect. Another photo dated July 1920 shows Zelda in a black one-piece swimsuit stepping off their landing stage into the water.

They rented Wakeman Cottage from May through to September 1920. Domestic life there was no more orderly than it had been in Manhattan hotels. Dirty laundry piled up in closets. Neither Zelda nor Scott cooked. A servant was desperately needed. Zelda wrote to Ludlow Fowler that as soon as they acquired a servant and 'some sheets from Mama' he would be very welcome. 'We have a house with a room for you and a ruined automobile because I drove it over a fire-plug and completely de-intestined it.' This incident may have been partly caused by Zelda's poor eyesight. The Montgomery family doctor had suggested that the retina of her right eye was missing.

Believing that she was pregnant, she added anxiously: 'Only by the time you do come I'll probably have grown so fat like this [drawing of fat stick woman] that you wont be able to recognize me . . . I'll have to wear a [measure of music with words 'Red, red rose' beneath] to disclose my identity – or condition . . . But it's a deep secret and you *must* keep very quiet and not laugh too hard and be *very* sympathetic.'[63] In the event she was not pregnant.

They hired a houseboy, Tana, from the Japanese Reliable Employment Agency, but having a houseboy did not materially improve their domestic situation. In late June or early July Wilson visited Westport, told that 'Zelda had decided to change her style and behave like a conventional lady, paying and receiving calls and making polite acknowledgments'.[64] Wilson wrote that Zelda's reform was shortlived as revels restarted in their rustic retreat. The Fitzgeralds and their friends were 'revelling nude in the orgies of Westport'.[65] Zelda's later recollection bears this out: 'The beach and dozens of men'.[66]

At one party given by theatrical producer John Williams, their Westport neighbour, Nathan, who accompanied them, flirtatiously played several choruses of 'Cuddle Up A Little Closer' for Zelda on the piano.

During another party in this quiet place they upset the authorities when they reported a false fire alarm. Legend has it that when the firemen asked where the fire was, Zelda pointed dramatically to her breast and said 'Here!'

These alcoholic weekends often ended in rows. On 13 June 1920 McKaig noted: 'Visit Fitz at Westport . . . terrible party. Fitz and Zelda fighting like mad. Say themselves marriage can't succeed'.

In Westport Scott began on a new plot for *The Flight of the Rocket* (eventually *The Beautiful and Damned*), in which Westport served as the model for Marietta, New York. The Fitzgeralds' grey shingled house becomes the model for Gloria and Anthony Patch's rented grey honeymoon cottage, which was established at a time when any woman who kept a cat was thought to be a witch.

Zelda told Sara Mayfield she found Westport depressing and began to persuade Scott to attend parties in Gotham to break the monotony.[67] Zelda as a restless woman did not fit easily into either of the two conflicting images prevalent during 1920 of her and Scott. One was the public image sponsored by the media of the golden couple glowing with success, happy in each other's company. The other was the private image held by McKaig and other friends that their rows were so frequent and so embittered that their marriage seemed to be breaking up.

Scott and Zelda half-believed and lived out both images. Meanwhile Zelda, homesick for Montgomery, told Scott she hankered for Alabama peaches and biscuits for breakfast. Underneath, she wondered if her parents missed her as much as she missed them.

She hoped a return South would not only allow her to show off her new marital style and clothes, but also give her some stability and improve the elements that had unexpectedly started to go wrong. Scott suggested a trip to Montgomery in the car they had rechristened The Rolling Junk. They set off on 15 July 1920. Typically, they had not informed the Sayres of their plans.

CHAPTER 6

Zelda was a reckless driver with few automotive skills and defective vision. Scott was equally incompetent. During the July 1920 trip their broken axles, flat tyres, speeding fines and high garage bills[1] gave Scott sufficient material for 'The Cruise of The Rolling Junk', a witty travel series. Zelda told Ludlow Fowler their inability to read maps meant Connecticut to Montgomery (1,000 miles as the crow flies) 'took us a week . . . The joys of motoring are more or less fictitious.'[2]

In Virginia their matching white knickerbocker suits were considered so shocking that a good hotel initially refused them entry. By Greensboro, North Carolina, Zelda felt obliged to pull on a skirt over her knickerbockers.[3]

As they finally neared Montgomery, the floral Southern scents and the sight of young belles in organdie dresses filled Zelda with nostalgia. Scott understood: 'Suddenly Zelda was crying, crying because things were the same and yet were not the same. It was for her faithlessness that she wept and for the faithlessness of time.'[4]

Predictably, they were locked out of the Sayres' house as Zelda's parents were away. Swiftly they drove to Livye Hart's, where Peyton Mathis gawped at Zelda's knickerbockers. 'What's happened to you?' he asked. 'You went away in long skirts and you've come back in short pants.'[5]

Though displaced in the North, Zelda found, like Thomas Wolfe who also left the South for New York City, that on returning there is a deep sense in which you *can't* go home again.

In the Sayres' temporary absence they stayed initially at the Country Club before moving on to Katharine Elsberry's in prestigious Felder Avenue. Zelda wandered through Katharine's garden amongst familiar camellias, magnolias and roses before characteristically monopolizing Katharine's bathroom. Before breakfast Katharine heard Zelda call out: 'Scott, what did you do with the toothbrush?' Later Katharine told Zelda's granddaughter: 'Didn't

have but one. I thought that was the sweetest, most romantic thing
I had ever heard of.'[6]

Sharing a toothbrush was strangely untypical of Zelda, who was
obsessive about cleanliness. 'Zelda . . . looked like she'd always just
had a bath,' said one Montgomery friend.[7] Bathrooms for Zelda
were often a context to romance. Before she saw Katharine, she had
already held court publicly from her own bath and preferred to
have Scott nearby when she was bathing.[8]

Zelda believed that women who bathed constantly were morally
pure, a symbolism borrowed by Scott for the novel he was writing
about marriage.[9] His heroine Gloria Gilbert cries: 'I loathe women
. . . They never seem clean to me – never – never.'[10] When Gloria's
fiancé Anthony Patch asks why she is prepared to marry him,
Gloria, modelled on Zelda, replies: 'Well, because you're so clean.
You're sort of blowy clean, like I am. There's two sorts . . . one's . . .
clean like polished pans. You and I are clean like streams and winds.
I can tell whenever I see a person whether he is clean, and if so,
which kind of clean he is.'[11] In 1920 Zelda felt most men were more
likely than women to be 'blowy clean', which might be why she felt
able to share Scott's toothbrush.

On the Sayres' return Zelda re-settled into her baby role, noticing
Scott's coolness towards her parents. Scott felt Zelda's home town
no longer appreciated him, while her parents still saw him as unreliable. Feeling ill at ease in Montgomery, after only two weeks they
sold the broken-down Marmon and departed by train. Zelda, sad to
leave her parents, persuaded them to visit Westport later.

Scott returned North determined to work seriously on his novel,
for which he had already signed a contract with *Metropolitan
Magazine* for serialization. He told Harold Ober he would deliver
the manuscript by October.

In mid-August Zelda wrote to Ludlow Fowler: 'Scott's hot in the
midst of a new novel and Westport is unendurably dull but you and
I might be able to amuse ourselves – and both of us want to see you
dreadfully.'[12]

Though Zelda told Ludlow how glad she was to see her parents
when they visited that month, they were less happy. Collected from
New York by Zelda and Scott, they discovered two drunken friends
of Scott's asleep in the hammock who arose and danced drunkenly
at the dinner table. Zelda was forced to borrow $20 from her mother
to send them to a roadhouse. To her dismay they returned at 3 a.m.
whereupon Scott began drinking gin and tomato juice with them.
When Zelda appeared the kitchen was in a shambles; she tried to

remove the gin bottle from Scott, he fended her off and her face caught in the swinging door. Her nose bled and her eyes swelled up. At breakfast when her parents saw her the Judge was stony with disapproval.

Matters worsened when the Sayres, having expected Zelda and Clothilde – who lived nearby in Tarrytown – to visit each other regularly, discovered Zelda had not seen her sister since Clothilde had borrowed Zelda's new pigskin suitcase to carry away her baby's wet diapers.[13] Zelda, who even as a child had never wanted to share her toys with her siblings, was disproportionately annoyed. But there were also underlying reasons for the sisters' estrangement: Clothilde was still seething over Scott's treatment of the Sayres at the wedding, while the Fitzgeralds were angry that she had subsequently reprimanded them for overspending.

When the Sayres left in late August, a week earlier than planned, to visit their 'good' daughter, Zelda realized 'she hadn't been absolutely sure of how to go about anything since her marriage had precluded the Judge's resented direction'.[14] But despite the Judge's disapproval, Zelda told Sara Mayfield she was 'desolate' at their departure.[15]

Scott renewed serious work on his novel in the Wakeman cottage while Zelda instigated a whirlwind social life in New York. First they saw Bunny Wilson and John Peale Bishop, who both still coveted the poet Edna St Vincent Millay. Edna was a brilliant, beautiful woman around whom clever men flocked but who, unlike Zelda, had learnt to escape from romantic messes by using her intellect. Whilst being courted by Wilson and Bishop, she carefully ensured they printed her poems in *Vanity Fair*. The two men were not above giving public displays of three-cornered heavy petting with Millay, who complained that her two 'choir boys of Hell' managed to maintain their joint affair with her without splitting up their own friendship. Sober observers noted that when petting on a couch Wilson, despite his Puritan rearing, 'was assigned the lower regions of the poet, while Bishop was entrusted with the top half'.[16]

Edna and Zelda shared the quality of elusiveness, forceful personalities and serious natures beneath their wild frivolity. But when they met in 1920 Edna, already focused on her writing, drew male professional admiration, a possible obstacle to friendship with Zelda.

Though Bishop was attracted to the volcanic Millay, as a Southern aristocrat it was Zelda rather than Edna whom he understood. Bishop's Southern background ensured he was never entirely at home in New York, but merely masked his insecurities by witty discourse, as did Zelda.[17]

In St Paul in 1919 Scott had read his work aloud to Donald Ogden Stewart, who, newly arrived in Manhattan, engaged Zelda with his wit. Scott introduced him to Wilson at *Vanity Fair*, where Stewart was subsequently offered work.[18] Scott's introduction of one friend to another who might prove useful professionally was characteristically generous.[19]

That season in New York Zelda and Scott met most of the established literati: popular novelist Edna Ferber (who later numbered Fitzgerald amongst her 'Ten Dullest Authors' in a *Vanity Fair* article);[20] critic Burton Rascoe, who had given *This Side of Paradise* an excellent review in the *Chicago Daily Tribune*; James Branch Cabell, author of *Jurgens* and in 1920 among the most famous of living American novelists, with whom Scott entered into a correspondence. They also met 44-year-old Sherwood Anderson, who like Scott had moved from advertising to acclaimed fiction which exposed the damaging passions that underlay outwardly ordinary Americans.[21]

A friend of Anderson's, Theodore Dreiser, eminent author of *Sister Carrie*, was giving a quiet publication party for a recent novel.[22] Though Dreiser was another of Scott's heroes, Anderson couldn't procure him an invitation so the Fitzgeralds gatecrashed the party at St Luke's Place. Scott, tipsy, waving a bottle of champagne, sang out: 'Mr Dreiser, my name is Fitzgerald. I have always got a great kick out of your works.' Dreiser curtly put the bottle and his disorderly guest on ice.[23]

Scott and Zelda kept up this constant round of party-going even though Scott told a journalist: 'Parties are a form of suicide. I love them but the old Catholic in me secretly disapproves'.[24] They met members of the Round Table, known as the Vicious Circle, the infamous weekday lunch club for irreverent humorists including Robert Benchley, Robert Sherwood, George S. Kaufman, Dorothy Parker and Alexander Woollcott, dramatic critic of *The World*. The Fitzgeralds frequented their gatherings at the Algonquin Hotel on West 44th Street.[25] Sherwood and Kaufman were writing a string of successful musical comedies, and Tallulah Bankhead was one actress associated with the group.

When Parker got fired from *Vanity Fair* for a contentious dramatic review her colleagues Benchley and Sherwood had resigned in protest. The vacancy was filled by Edmund Wilson, the solitary son of a moody melancholic lawyer father and deaf mother, who had turned to books for comfort from his oppressive background. Wilson saw the group as shallow and incestuous because they had all read the same children's books and 'all came from the suburbs and "provinces"'[26], which of course enabled them successfully to promote each other's literary reputations. Their caustic queen, Dorothy Parker, exemplified their tone of debunking bitchy wit which mocked their own or other people's provincial upbringings.

Parker's first glimpse of the Fitzgeralds was the now legendary one of Zelda riding on the hood of a taxi while Scott hung on to the roof. Parker, seven years older than Zelda, was a talented satirist whose barbed aphorisms delighted New York journalists. A short-story writer, playwright and essayist, her lasting work has been her light verse which cleverly mocked at failure, loneliness and despair, themes currently engaging Fitzgerald's imagination. Parker said that after glimpsing the zany honeymoon pair she was introduced to them by Robert Sherwood. But Wilson claimed that *he* was the first to arrange a meeting because Parker, who had already met Scott briefly in 1919,[27] 'was beglamoured by the idea of Scott Fitzgerald'.[28] Wilson said he arranged dinner at the Algonquin where they all 'sat at one of those Algonquin tables, too narrow to have anyone across from you, so that one sat on a bench with one's back to the wall', and Parker quipped: 'This looks like a road company of the Last Supper.'[29]

Wilson found Dorothy 'fairly pretty' but with a vulgarity which came from using too much perfume,[30] less to his taste than Zelda, whom no one ever considered vulgar. Scott however was flattered by Parker, three years his senior. He did not mind her lethal drama reviews in *Vanity Fair* or her habit of warmly greeting presumed friends then later making acid comments about them. He did, however, record a joke about someone asking whether Parker had injured anyone that day. The answer was: 'No, but don't remind her. Maybe she hasn't done her bad deed for the day.'[31]

Though Parker was later kind to Zelda, in general she had no use for dependent women. 'Her view of Zelda,' said Parker's biographer Marion Meade, 'formed in 1920 . . . was negative – and I don't believe she ever changed her mind . . . She was also put off by Zelda's foreign [Southern] accent which to a rabid Manhattan chauvinist meant the person must be a hillbilly.'[32]

Parker also disliked Zelda's looks: 'I never thought she was beautiful . . . candy box face and a little bow mouth . . . something petulant about her. If she didn't like something she sulked.'[33]

Parker's poisonous wit caught only part of Zelda's personality. Momentarily Zelda *would* sulk, as she did when she noticed the fulsome attention Parker paid to Scott, but then with a strange shift of direction she would lose interest in what had gripped her and a remote evasiveness would subsume the petulance.

After the summer Scott wished to write seriously for the theatre, so the Fitzgeralds began to see more of playwrights Lillian Hellman and Charles MacArthur (a former journalist), film and stage actresses Lillian Gish (a year older than Zelda) and Helen Hayes (Zelda's age), and screenwriter Anita Loos (born 1893), who in 1925 would write *Gentlemen Prefer Blondes*. Gish, more positive than Parker about Zelda, said: 'They were both so beautiful, so blond, so clean and clear – And drinking strait whiskey out of tall tumblers . . . Zelda could do outlandish things – say anything. It was never offensive when Zelda did it, as you felt she couldn't help it, and was not doing it for effect.'[34]

Zelda's particular friend was rough-haired Carl Van Vechten, then in his forties, a hulking, highly successful novelist, critic and photographer. The writer Djuna Barnes told Edmund Wilson she thought Carl was a 'prissy' literary name-dropper,[35] but Zelda found Carl a 'divine' party host. Despite his devoted marriage to Russian actress Fania Marinoff, Carl had several well-established homosexual relationships, which possibly accounted for Zelda's lasting non-flirtatious friendship with him. 'Our relations were very impersonal,' she said years later, 'but Carl was a fine friend.'[36]

Early in their friendship, Van Vechten noticed Scott's inability to hold alcohol. 'He could take two or three drinks at most and be completely drunk . . . he was nasty when he was drunk, but sober he was a charming man.' What he noticed about Zelda was her uniqueness. 'She was an original . . . she tore up the pavements with sly remarks . . . She didn't actually write them down, Scott did, but she said them.'[37]

Van Vechten summed up how friends saw the Fitzgeralds in his novel *Parties*, where David and Rilda Westlake, modelled on the Fitzgeralds, 'love each other desperately, passionately. They [cling] to each other like barnacles cling to rocks, but they want to hurt each other all the time.'[38] Rilda influences most of David's behaviour: he acts only to aggravate or to please her. One complaint of Rilda's to David shows genuine insight into the Fitzgeralds' bond: 'Our damned faithfulness . . . our clean "fidelity", doesn't get us very far. We follow each other around in circles, loving and hating and wounding. We're both so sadistic.'[39] Van Vechten has even replicated Zelda's use of 'clean' to imply sexual purity.

Certainly Scott and Zelda were intensely jealous of each other.

Zelda felt excluded by the literary attention he received; Scott felt excluded by the male admiration she received. Before their marriage Scott had confided to Wilson that 'I wouldn't care if she [Zelda] died, but I couldn't stand to have anybody else marry her.'[40]

The rising tensions between the Fitzgeralds often exploded into heated disputes which either began in Westport, continued on the New Haven train and were sustained at friends' Manhattan apartments, or began in New York and were maintained on the train journey home.

Alex McKaig, who that August had returned to reporting the Fitzgeralds' activities in his diary, recorded one row he witnessed on 15 September 1920: 'In the evening Zelda – drunk – having decided to leave Fitzgerald & having nearly been killed walking down RR track, blew in. Fitz came shortly after.'[41] Sara Mayfield takes up the story. 'Fitzgerald had boarded the train without money or a ticket. The conductor threatened to throw him off but finally let him stay when Scott promised to pay him upon his arrival in Westport. After Scott tore into Zelda for walking the tracks, she refused to give him the money for his ticket, and they joined in a verbal battle that was to continue intermittently for two decades.'[42] McKaig's judgement was: 'Fitz should let Zelda go and not run after her . . . he is afraid of what she may do in a moment of caprice.'[43]

After this incident Zelda wrote Scott a letter which Mayfield considered a typical 'passionate reconciliation':

> I look down the tracks and see you coming – and out of every haze & mist your darling rumpled trousers are hurrying to me – Without you, dearest dearest I couldn't see or hear or feel or think – or live – I love you so and I'm never in all our lives going to let us be apart another night. It's like begging for mercy of a storm or killing Beauty or growing old, without you. I want to kiss you so – and in the back where your dear hair starts and your chest – I love you – and I cant tell you how much – To think that I'll die without your knowing – Goofo, you've got to try [to] feel how much I do – how inanimate I am when you're gone – I can't even hate these damnable people – Nobodys got any right to live but us – and they're dirtying up our world and I can't hate them because I want you so – Come Quick – Come Quick to me – I could never do without you if you hated me and were covered with sores like a leper – if you ran away with another woman and starved me and beat me – I still would want you I know – Lover, Lover, Darling – Your Wife.[44]

Though the letter idealizes the incident it also reveals Zelda's dependency, an emotion that would have surprised their friends.

If readers of Fitzgerald's novels who have never read Zelda's letters find this particular note familiar, it is because Scott reproduced it almost word for word in *The Beautiful and Damned*. Zelda herself had no idea that Scott had used both the episode and her exact words until she saw the published version of *The Beautiful and Damned* in 1922.[45] She bit back her shock and, unable at the time to voice her resentment over this appropriation, later did express her increasing discontent with her status as Scott's assistant-wife. In *Caesar's Things* she immortalizes Scott as the painter Jacob: 'Jacob went on doing whatever it was that Jacob did . . . He was more important than Janno; she always felt as if she should be helpful about his tinkerings; they were intricate enough to need an assistant. She didn't really do anything but wait on his will. While Jacob painted she went to the hair-dresser and bought things . . . She stated and tabulated and compared the shoes of 42nd Street with the shoes of Upper Broadway.'[46] In 1920 Zelda felt shoe-shopping was insufficient for a young woman with brains, but still she hid her frustration while flirting wildly to arouse Scott's jealousy.

She succeeded with George Jean Nathan, one witty constant visitor. Nathan, thirty-eight, short, dark and melancholic, was Scott's model for the brilliantly original Maury Noble in *The Beautiful and Damned* whom Scott compares to 'a large slender and imposing cat'. Nathan, according to biographer James Mellow, was also a self-acknowledged chauvinist who preferred under-educated women. He tested a woman's capabilities by asking her directions to Grand Central Station. 'If her answer was 50 percent correct she was intelligent enough for normal use.'[47]

Zelda, confident of her own intelligence, flattered by Nathan's obvious interest, ignored this displeasing characteristic. Nathan soon addressed letters just to Zelda, beginning notes 'Fair Zelda' or 'Dear Blonde', signing them 'Yours, for the Empire, A Prisoner of Zelda'.[48]

Acknowledging the seriousness of Zelda's addiction to chewing gum, Nathan wrote: 'I am very sorry to hear that your husband is neglectful of his duties to you in the way of chewing gum. That is the way husbands get after five months of marriage.'[49]

At one of Nathan's excellent parties Zelda came to grief – typically when taking a bath. 'At present, I'm hardly able to sit down owing to an injury sustained in the course of one of Nathan's parties in N.Y.', she reported to Ludlow Fowler. 'I *cut* my *tail* on a broken bottle and can't possibly sit on the three stitches that are in it now – The bottle was bath salts – I was boiled – The place was a tub somewhere.'[50]

Scrutinizing Nathan's bathroom, Zelda found other women's golden hair in Nathan's combs, then discovered to her chagrin that he spent time with at least two other 'dear blondes'. One was Hollywood screenwriter Anita Loos, the other Ruth Findlay, star of *The Prince and the Pauper*, a Mark Twain doppel-gänger tale of rags and royalty in sixteenth-century England.[51]

Unabashed, Nathan continued their correspondence: 'Dear Misguided Woman: Like so many uncommonly beautiful creatures, you reveal a streak of obtuseness. The calling of a husband's attention to a love letter addressed to his wife is but part of a highly sagacious technique . . . It completely disarms suspicion . . . Why didn't you call me up on Friday? Is it possible that your love is growing cold? Through the ages, George.'[52] By October Scott's jealousy of Nathan temporarily cooled his friendship with him.[53]

Despite annoying Scott, Nathan enabled them to meet Scott's 'current idol',[54] the critic H. L. Mencken, who, disliking New York and its literati, only visited the *Smart Set* offices for a few days once a month from his home in Baltimore. He would book in at the Algonquin, then nip over to Nathan's suite at the Royalton or share a hearty German lunch and beer at Luchow's nearby. At the end of July Nathan laid in three cases of gin then invited Scott and Zelda to a New York party at his Royalton apartment to meet Mencken. The critic was enchanted by Zelda, whom he called 'the fair Madonna',[55] but encountering the Fitzgeralds at their most extreme presented him with a challenge. All Mencken's friends, according to his biographer Marion Elizabeth Rodgers, led 'sane, systematic lives, their own personal code of conduct, like Mencken's, being based on the avoidance of extremes'.[56] Mencken recalls that in 1920, when he and Nathan gave cocktail parties, Zelda and Scott would drive over then, despite being drunk, to Mencken's horror would insist on driving home.[57]

Baltimore born, two years older than Nathan, with a squat face and hair plastered back and parted down the middle, Mencken could hardly be termed handsome. Yet in 1920 he had become one of America's most eligible bachelors, well-known for such cynical remarks as 'any man who marries after 30 is a damn fool'.[58] This light side, labelled The Bad Boy of Baltimore, contrasted with his serious side, tagged The Sage of Baltimore, which reflected his position as America's most respected critic, journalist and editor. As the writer Sherwood Anderson said, receiving a letter from Henry Mencken felt 'like being knighted by a king'.[59] Mencken at the time was the only person in the USA for whom Fitzgerald had complete admiration.

Though Mencken's comments were feared by authors, remembering his own first rejections the Sage treated writers with courtesy. Zelda's friend Sara Haardt who, after graduating from Goucher College, was now back in Montgomery teaching history at the Margaret Booth school, had already submitted several stories to the *Smart Set* and had received several of Mencken's gentle rejections. As Sara's fiction focused on Southern culture she was not well disposed towards the Sage, who had recently labelled Alabama 'The Sahara of the Bozart', his teasing term for Beaux Arts.

Scott, being Northern, was better disposed than Sara to Mencken. He had already, in his own phrase, 'bootlicked' the great man, who would soon become one of his intellectual mentors, by sending him a flatteringly inscribed copy of *This Side of Paradise* and by adopting some of Mencken's positive views on Dreiser and Conrad.

Flappers and Philosophers, Scott's first volume of stories, which included 'Benediction' and 'Dalyrimple' already published by Mencken, came out on 10 September 1920, dedicated to Zelda.[60] He nervously awaited Mencken's review.[61] Although it was a commercial success,[62] Mencken now publicly called attention to the split in Fitzgerald's work between serious fiction and entertainment.[63] The Sage felt Scott had great talent but a suspect lifestyle, possibly influenced by Zelda's extravagant tastes. Privately, he noticed Zelda's enjoyment of money and Scott's preoccupation with it: 'His wife talks too much about money. His danger lies in trying to get it too rapidly.'[64]

Scott wished to be a serious artist but he was drawn to money. He had been thrilled when in May 1920 *Metropolitan Magazine* had taken an option on his stories at $900 each while the *Saturday Evening Post* paid only $500.[65] High-paying popular magazines, however, wanted bland optimistic tales, while Scott's real interest was in astringent satire or pessimistic fiction. Zelda, who could not see the profound difference between popular and literary fiction, was proud of him for making money from magazine stories. Whether this severe misjudgement was rooted in her lack of literary training or in her father's disapproval of writers who could not pay their way, so that she assumed high fees were a sound criterion, is not clear.

Despite earning almost $20,000 that year, Scott owed $600 in outstanding bills and a further $650 to the Reynolds Agency.[66] In desperation he wrote to Maxwell Perkins, who also blamed Zelda for Scott's financial crisis, for a loan. 'She wanted everything,' he complained.[67] Certainly, when Scott had been reduced to drawing steadily against future royalties for *This Side of Paradise*,[68] Zelda's request for a fur coat had not helped. Scott's generosity meant they rapidly ran out of funds. His scheme of borrowing ahead from his publisher and agent had already established an insecure life pattern.

Though Zelda spent money easily, she had none of her own, and no bank account. Sara Mayfield felt Scott needed the power he gained from Zelda's dependency but Zelda resented it. There is curious conflicting evidence. One anecdote suggests Zelda felt comfortable with the situation: she took Rosalind to lunch at the Plaza, pulled out a roll of banknotes the size of a baseball and said: 'Scott gave it to me as I went out the door, so what else could I do with it but bring it along.'[69] But sometimes 'money vanished mysteriously'.[70] In July 1920 Scott notes: 'Zelda hides $500', followed in November by: 'Zelda hides $100 from Dorothy Parker.'[71] This suggests that Zelda was resentful both about her lack of independent finance and perhaps about Parker.

Their dire finances left Zelda in a quandary about Scott's Christmas present. With habitual ingenuity she wrote to James Branch Cabell, enclosing her photo, saying that when trying to steal Nathan's first edition of *Jurgens* as a Christmas present for her husband 'under pretence of intoxication', she had been foisted off with a fencing foil which she would gladly exchange for a copy of the book.[72] Cabell, highly amused, sent her an autographed copy.

As Scott attempted to complete *The Beautiful and Damned* his irritation with Zelda, who wanted to party, increased. The beady-eyed McKaig reported she was 'increasingly restless – says frankly she simply wants to be amused and is only good for useless pleasure-giving pursuits; great problem – what is she to do? Fitz has his writing of course – God knows where the two of them are going to end up . . . If she's there Fitz can't work – she bothers him – if she's not there he can't work – worried what she might do.'[73]

Scott's writer friends who encouraged Zelda nevertheless believed that women should be helpmates not distractions. McKaig reported Zelda's next visit to New York:

> September 16: Zelda came in & woke me sleeping on couch at 7.15 for no reason. She has no sense of decencies of living . . . Fitz picture and an article to go in Vanity Fair. Autobiographical note about him in Metropolitan this month – got $900 for it . . . His vogue is tremendous.
>
> September 27: John [Bishop] spent weekend at Fitz – new novel sounds awful – no seriousness of approach. Zelda interrupts him all the time – diverts in both senses . . .

McKaig also kept up a running report on the affairs of Wilson, Bishop and Edna St Vincent Millay:

> September 17: Bunny Wilson and Edna Millet in intolerable situation. He wants her to marry him. She tempted because of great poverty and the financial security he offers . . . However . . . she is making eyes at another man. It nearly kills her but she can't help it.
> September 20: Bunnie has repeated to Edna . . . things John [Bishop] said about her . . . John is very distressed.

But when John poured out his woes to Alex, McKaig remarked that Bishop was damn stupid, interested only in himself, poetry and women. Bishop, like Scott, was presumably insufficiently interested in McKaig's attempts to leave advertising.

During the summer of 1920 Scott, overlooking these undercurrents, had written three stories: 'The Jelly Bean' (sold to *Metropolitan*), 'The Lees of Happiness' (*Chicago Sunday Tribune*) and an unsold story, 'IOU', focused on marital relationships.

Scott drew on Zelda's Southern world, 'a grotesquely pictorial country', for the backdrop.[74] 'The Jelly Bean', he told Ober, was 'the first story to really recreate the modern southern belle',[75] Nancy Lamar, inspired of course by Zelda. Reckless Nancy meets and kisses Southern pool-hall loafer Jim Powell at a country club dance. In love, Jim decides to reform. But the following day, learning that Nancy got drunk and married her date from Savannah, he returns to loafing.

In 'The Lees of Happiness' writer Jeffrey Curtain, happily married for one year to former chorus girl Roxanne Milbank, suffers a stroke, lives like a vegetable for eleven years and is tended devotedly till death by Roxanne.[76]

A later story, 'The Adjuster', carries forward this miserable marital theme. Luella and Charles Hemple are drifting towards divorce when Charles suddenly has a nervous breakdown and Luella is forced to assume domestic responsibility. In *The Beautiful and Damned* too, Gloria's husband Anthony is seized by 'a sort of madness' and ends up a ruined man being pushed along in a wheelchair.[77]

Though Scott professed himself content with their 'revelry and marriage' in his 1920 Ledger,[78] his fictional treatment of marriage at this time is curiously ominous.[79]

By October 1920 the Fitzgeralds felt fall in Westport would be dreary, so they moved into an apartment at 38 West 59th Street between Fifth and Sixth Avenues, conveniently near the Plaza Hotel from which they could order meals. Campbell and McKaig, as frequent visitors, were again made painfully aware of Zelda's lack of housekeeping skills.

Campbell spent his one-hour lunch break there:

> When I entered the room was bedlam. Breakfast dishes were all about, the bed unmade, books and papers scattered . . . trays filled with cigarette butts, liquor glasses from the night before . . . Scott was dressing and Zelda was luxuriating in the bath-tub. With the door partly open, she carried on a steady flow of conversation. 'Scott,' she called out, 'tell Lawton 'bout . . . tell Lawton what I said . . . tell Lawton what I did . . .'[80]

Lawton's lunch hour was over before Zelda was dressed. Her egotistic interruptions from the bathroom have a demented note as she fights for recognition.

That fall the Fitzgeralds smoked on their beds or those of their friends, ordered sandwiches from nearby delicatessens and entertained in their luxury slum. In October McKaig's waspish diary records: 'Went to Fitzgeralds. Usual problem there. What shall Zelda do? I think she might do a little housework – apartment looks like a pig sty.'[81]

As a man addicted to constant changes of shirts Scott grew irritable with his Southern Belle's inability even to organize the laundry.[82] His testiness may have increased because so many friends witnessed the increasing disorder.

Later, Zelda regretted how little she knew about marital responsibilities or Scott's Northern expectations of Minnesota wives. 'People really ought to be taught about marriage in the schools: what they expect as its rewards and which of the responsibilities they are willing to carry. Then they would be able to choose which pattern in which to pursue their destinies.'[83]

Fitzgerald alternated wild parties with bursts of energetic work. In November he wrote Perkins he had 'done 15,000 words in last three days which is very fast writing even for me who write very fast'.[84] Scott's hard work meant that Part I of *The Beautiful and Damned* was finished by January 1921, a month later he gave Part II to Wilson to criticize. He completed it just before they sailed for Europe at the beginning of May.

McKaig, hitherto cynical towards Zelda, suddenly fell in love with her.[85] On 27 November he told his diary: 'I spent the evening shaving Zelda's neck to make her bobbed hair look better . . . She is lovely – wonderful hair – eyes and mouth.' But he would not betray Scott. On 4 December he recorded: 'Lunch at Gotham. T. [probably Townsend Martin] Zelda, Scott and I. Then took Zelda to cocktail party . . . and then tea in Biltmore. In taxi Zelda asked me to kiss her but I couldn't. I couldn't forget Scott – he's so damn pitiful.'[86]

During that winter of dissipation there were two more bathroom incidents. When McKaig arrived home after that taxi ride with Zelda on 4 December he found a telephone message from Scott: the most awful thing had happened, would he go to their apartment immediately, it would be a test of friendship.

'I rushed up expecting to find a death or serious accident,' McKaig reported. 'When I got there . . . he said hello casually and went on talking . . . I asked him in Christs [sic] name what the matter was – it seemed they had a quarrel. Zelda went into the bathroom, turned on the water to hide noise of footsteps & walked out the door. Instead of trying to find her himself he . . . telephoned all his friends. Finally Zelda called & I went for her.'[87]

McKaig's account is curious. It seems odd that the Fitzgeralds' row should have occurred immediately after McKaig rejected Zelda's advance, if indeed he had done so. It seems odd that Scott should have phoned McKaig instead of looking for Zelda himself. It seems odd that it was McKaig rather than Scott who finally went to fetch her. It is possible that McKaig's diary offers an incomplete record for reasons of discretion. Or had Scott become suspicious of McKaig and phoned him at his home in case Zelda was there?

Certainly, during another quarrel that tense winter Scott broke down the bathroom door. In Zelda's version he 'hurt' her eye; in Scott's Ledger he notes the bathroom door incident and 'the black eye', but he puts a January rather than December date which, if accurate, may imply two fierce bathroom rows.[88] Scott became so sensitive to the way Zelda always fled to a bathroom when distressed that later he picked the bathroom for a suicide attempt by Nicole Diver (partially based on Zelda) in *Tender Is The Night*.

On 11 December McKaig joined Scott in arguing with Zelda about the 'notoriety they are getting through being so publicly and spectacularly drunk. Zelda wants to live the life of an "extravagant". No thought of what world will think or of future . . . I told them they were headed for catastrophe if they kept up at present rate.'[89]

A few days later Bishop and McKaig decided cynically the Fitzgeralds' drunken performances were possibly all contrived to 'hand down [the] Fitzgerald legend'.[90]

That honeymoon year amply fed their increasing notoriety. Zelda

later described the life they led as a 'rickety world of aftermath . . .
a rackety world of brow-beating the heart'. In her second novel she
fictionalizes Scott's friends as men who all knew what kind of cold
cream she used, who confessed their preferences in women to her
and who 'slumbered over the grill-stairs and left their hats all over
town and spent hours putting more acceptable interpretations on
things . . . sensitive the while [to] a precariousness of the whole
arrangement'. Precarious was an accurate word for that first year of
marriage. In *Caesar's Things* Zelda later reflected on what it had
meant to be a star's wife: 'He owned her, bundled her up and set her
in taxis beside him . . . showed her off to an inclusive set of college
friends and made a big success of being impresario.'[91] The star's
wife was expected to be compliant, courageous and ingratiating.
Being seen as her husband's glamorous possession after years of
stardom as a Southern Belle was painful yet not unusual for a
married woman.

Zelda had little time, however, to dwell on any discontent with
her present role before she was thrust into a very different one. In
February 1921 she discovered she was pregnant, and immediately
went back to Montgomery where Scott joined her in March. For
Zelda the transition from a lifetime of being her family's 'baby' to
thinking of herself as a baby's mother was thorny. Still wishing to
be considered a belle rather than a mother-to-be, she was delighted
when asked to dance at the annual *Les Mystérieuses* Masked Ball,
which that year was a Hawaiian pageant. Lawton Campbell, visiting his family in Montgomery, attended the ball:

> one masker was doing her dance more daring than the others . . . Finally
> the dance . . . turned her back on the audience, lifted her grass skirt over
> her head for a quick view of her pantied posterior and gave it an extra
> wiggle for good measure . . . Everybody was whispering 'That's Zelda!'.
> It was Zelda and no mistake! She wanted it known . . . and she was
> happy with the recognition.[92]

Back in New York in April, Zelda's bewilderment about motherhood increased. She felt incompetent and recognized that Scott and
their bachelor friends were hardly more knowledgeable. Most of the
ex-Princeton set knew where to find the blank verse in Cabell or how
to get seats for the Yale game but knew nothing about having a baby.[93]

When Zelda was two months pregnant the Fitzgeralds decided to
pack their incompetence and ignorance into a suitcase and take
their first trip to Europe, returning before the birth.

They sailed for Europe on the Cunard liner *Aquitania* on 3 May 1921. From May to July 1921 they scanned life and culture in England, France and Italy. In London, after checking into the Cecil Hotel, Zelda's greatest thrill came when Shane Leslie, Scott's early mentor and Winston Churchill's first cousin, took them on a night walk through Dockland along the waterfronts of Stepney, Limehouse, Wapping and on to the haunts once taken by Jack the Ripper. Zelda, dressed in men's clothes, added the remarkable twilights along the Thames to her collection which she would paint later. It was an area with no taxis, no police, more appealing to Zelda's sense of adventure than the staid lunch hosted by Lady Randolph Churchill, the famous Jenny Jerome, Winston's mother. Though Zelda talked at length to Winston, what she recalled were dessert strawberries 'as big as tomatoes'.[94] The Fitzgeralds met Jack, the younger Churchill son, who took them to a cricket match which bored them; they left early. Tallulah Bankhead, then the toast of London, introduced them to the Marchioness of Milford Haven who Scott said indignantly was as near to royalty as they came.[95]

Zelda, an avid reader since childhood, was excited that Maxwell Perkins had arranged for them to meet John Galsworthy, who invited them to dinner in Hampstead[96] with the Irish playwright Lennox Robinson and St John Ervine, the novelist and dramatist. Scott said sycophantically: 'Mr Galsworthy, you are one of the three living writers that I admire most in the world,' but told Wilson later Galsworthy hadn't approved. 'He knew he wasn't that good.'[97]

They moved on to Paris, arriving on 17 May. Disappointed at not seeing Anatole France, another of Scott's heroes, after waiting for an hour outside his house, they tried the *Folies*, Versailles and Malmaison, then decided sightseeing bored them.

Wilson, also on a European tour, reaching Paris on 20 June after the Fitzgeralds had drifted to Venice, felt the Fitzgeralds lived as tourists in France, as they had in New York. Zelda certainly did not feel at home in France until she had learnt French for her second trip. Scott's view of France summed up their attitude to Europe: 'France is a bore and a disappointment,' he wrote to Shane Leslie, 'chiefly, I imagine, because we know no one here.'[98]

Wilson, who had broken up with Edna Millay, decided to visit her in Paris that July and discovered that she had been his one romantic passion. 'She was tired of breaking hearts and spreading havoc ... she can no longer intoxicate me with her beauty or throw bombs into my soul ... but ... some glamour of high passion had gone out of life when my love for her died.'[99]

The Fitzgeralds glossed Venice from 26 May, Florence by 3 June and Rome by the 22nd, where 'Zelda and I had an appalling squabble'.[100] Zelda laconically took photos in each place with such labels as 'Me and Goofo in a Gondola' and 'Goofo at Fiesole', but their facial expressions show little enthusiasm for their surroundings. Italy brought some fierce words from Scott: 'God damn the continent of Europe. It is of merely antiquarian interest.'[101]

Their last European stop was a return to London on 30 June, where they drifted from a gloomy room at Claridge's to the Cavendish. Scott wanted to see if *This Side of Paradise*, published by Collins on 26 May in Britain, had been well received. He was disappointed to find most English critics dismissed it as trivial.

From London they went to Windsor, then on 4 July to Cambridge, where they sought out Rupert Brooke's Grantchester haunts and took snapshots of each other. Scott took one of Zelda in sedate hat and long plaid skirt outside Trinity College. Zelda shot Scott in three-piece suit strolling down a leafy Grantchester path and labelled it with a Brooke quote: 'The men observe the rules of thought' . Under her own Grantchester photograph she scribbled: 'And is there honey yet for tea?'[102]

Mencken describes how Scott had confided to him and Nathan that their

> coming child deserved to be born in some historic . . . romantic place. Paris seemed a likely choice, but when they got there they found it dull and shabby . . . Algiers and Tunis turned out to be even worse . . . Spain and Italy also disappointing, they began a frantic chase over Europe, looking for an ideal place for the nativity. In the end Zelda approached her time without any such ideal place being found, and in a sudden panic they sailed for home.[103]

Mencken depicted the Fitzgeralds' feelings of *ennui* correctly as they scampered through Europe establishing one temporary base after another, Zelda's restlessness increasing. As they migrated from America to Europe, and within the States from Northeast to South, then from Midwest to West, in search of Utopia, their marriage resembled nothing so much as a twenty-year odyssey. Zelda and Scott's rootless wandering existence was a significant contribution – both a symptom and a cause – to Zelda's later instability.[104]

For Scott this relentless travelling felt familiar, for his childhood pattern had never included security. His constant moves with parents searching for improved residences led him to expect in adulthood psychological and practical improvement with every move. But for Zelda their transitory life, albeit exciting, made her feel displaced. She came from an area where place is important, but so is standing still. As Eudora Welty and William Faulkner emphasized, Southerners move around less than Northerners, often remaining rooted to land, family and community. Faulkner said he would never live long enough to exhaust the stories that sprang from his 'little postage stamp of native soil'. Zelda and Scott, who rarely stayed long enough in one place to till its soil, achieved their stories by obsessively mining their own lives and each other's for material and created their fiction almost entirely from personal experience.

They travelled back to the USA in July on the *Celtic*, going first to Montgomery, where they felt a new confidence as proud parents-to-be. Scott, proud of Zelda's new form, showed it off to Katharine Elsberry, who later told Zelda's granddaughter the story. Zelda posed in a new handmade French slip from Paris. 'Scott said: "Katharine, look at that." . . . [I] looked and there was the bulge: Scottie was on the way.'[105]

Scottie herself recalled: 'I was supposed to be born in Montgomery, Alabama, but there was a terrible heat wave in September of 1921 . . . and my father – I'm sure it was my father because he seems to have made all the decisions at all times – decided to wait for the event in St Paul, Minnesota, instead.'[106]

Zelda told Sara Mayfield's mother: 'Scott's changed. He used to love to go to the cemetery to see the Confederate graves and say he loved the South, but now he wants to get as far away from it as he can.'[107]

Scott demurred, but after less than a month in Montgomery he and Zelda moved to Minnesota. Like New York it was, as Zelda had feared, a world away, psychologically as well as geographically, from Alabama.

CHAPTER 7

Zelda, seven months pregnant and steadily gaining weight, arrived with Scott at St Paul, Minnesota, in August 1921. 'There were the Indian forests and the moon on the sleeping porch and I was heavy and afraid of the storms.'[1] She felt acutely miserable in the cold North that seemed perpetually wet. Everywhere she looked she saw water, for Minnesota lives up to its Sioux name 'land of sky-tinted water'. Now-extinct glaciers had gouged out more than 15,000 lakes, so that with the major rivers running along the eastern and western borders 95 per cent of its population live within ten minutes of a body of water. Abundant waterways and dense forests made it an ideal breeding ground for beavers and muskrats, ensuring that fur-trading, fishing and lumbering flourished from the sixteenth century.

When Zelda arrived with Scott, St Paul had grown from a frontier outpost to great prominence.[2] From 1870 the railroads that augmented river craft had used St Paul as a railhead, so Zelda saw a significant example of the continuing transformation of America from a rural to an urban culture, from a society based on breeding and inherited wealth to one built up by salaried executives with images fostered through the new advertising industry, in which several of the Fitzgeralds' circle worked. Though St Paul is a beautiful city, Zelda saw it permeated by Ibsenesque melancholy and perpetual chill. Its lack of ancestral roots felt alien. St Paul *was* only a three-generation town – though proud of the fact, like the town in Scott's 'The Ice Palace' where 'everybody has a father, and about half of us have grandfathers. Back of that we don't go ... Our grandfathers ... founded the place, and ... had to take some pretty queer jobs while they were doing the founding.'[3] When Scott's Irish emigrant grandfather, Philip Francis McQuillan, settled in St Paul in 1857, the Minnesota Territory was only in its eighth year. As it expanded, with a speculative boom that attracted 500 immigrants a day, McQuillan prospered by trading his first 'queer job' of bookkeeping for, in Zelda's view, the more peculiar one of wholesale grocery.

Scott, the grocer's grandson, always retained a homey feeling about St Paul. Later he wrote to his former sweetheart Marie Hersey that 'in spite of a fifteen year absence, it is still home to me'.[4] Zelda, the grocer's granddaughter-in-law, never saw St Paul as home, not least because Scott had a shared history with Marie Hersey from which she was excluded. Marie and Scott, dancing partners at Professor Baker's dancing class, had acted together in the Elizabethan Dramatic Club and in 1915 Marie had accompanied Scott to a Triangle Club dance.

There were other things, too, that made Zelda feel left out.

In Montgomery, the Sayres' social standing had assured Zelda's place. In New York, Scott's overnight fame had given them access to a highly regarded artistic milieu. But in St Paul, though there *was* a high society, it was created by business executives rather than landowning aristocrats familiar to Zelda. Most of those Northerners found Zelda's Southernness alien. The first Northern woman Zelda met from that society, and the only one she liked, was Scott's schoolfriend Xandra Kalman, now twenty-three, who though a Catholic had in 1917 married the divorced wealthy banker Oscar Kalman, twenty-five years her senior. As soon as the Fitzgeralds arrived at the end of August 1921, the Kalmans found them a rented house[5] in Dellwood, a rich resort on White Bear Lake ten miles north-east of St Paul where they spent the summer.

'All the people came who liked to play golf or sail on the lake,' wrote Zelda, 'or who had children to shelter from the heat. All the young people came whose parents had given them for wedding presents white bungalows hid in the green – and all the old people who liked the flapping sound of the water.' When Zelda described those 'summer people' she admitted her contradictory feelings of safety and ensnarement. The visitors lived in 'long, flat cottages . . . so covered by screened verandas that they made you think of small pieces of cheese under large meat safes.'[6]

Like Scott's sister Annabel, Xandra had attended the Visitation Convent School, in her case from 1906 until 1912, and like Scott himself had joined Professor Baker's dancing class[7] and the Elizabethan dramatic group. The Kalmans frequently invited the Fitzgeralds to their large summer home in Dellwood. Scott, having known the couple for years, did not need to impress them and Xandra's warmth meant that Zelda unfurled and became less aloof. Zelda called Xandra Sandy; they swam regularly together and played golf. 'I was one of the few women that Zelda got close to,' Xandra said. 'We were together practically every day.'[8]

Xandra and Zelda, alike in their frank direct manner, also had similar backgrounds. Xandra came from one of St Paul's most notable families. Her New Yorker great-grandfather Aaron Goodrich, who had become one of Tennessee's most prominent lawyers and legislators, was appointed by President Zachary Taylor as Minnesota's first Supreme Court Chief Justice in 1849. Like her great-grandfather Xandra was clever, energetic, artistic and highly organized. She inherited her wide-ranging knowledge from her grandfather, Canadian Daniel A. Robertson, who in 1850 served as a delegate to the Ohio constitutional convention, was a colonel in the Minnesota State militia, and as a lawyer and scholar served in Minnesota's legislature before becoming mayor of St Paul in 1860 and three years later its sheriff.[9] From her father, William C. Robertson, who was in real estate and finance, she learnt sound business sense. She and Oscar instantly took charge of the Fitzgeralds.

But when Zelda left the Kalmans and the lake and drove into St Paul, everywhere she looked she saw Scott's footprints.

Walking with Scott along prestigious Summit Avenue, whose towering elms, leaded glass windows, stone façades and pillars make it one of America's best surviving examples of Victorian Boulevard architecture, she knew that Scott, Marie and their circle had played outside 475, Marie's family house, or near 623, where Scott's widowed grandmother Louisa McQuillan had lived.[10]

In a small triangular park bordering Summit, Scott had played touch football with several boys now active in St Paul's literary life. Thomas Boyd, a columnist with *St Paul Daily News*, immediately interviewed the returned celebrity and persuaded him to write book reviews. Other newspapers played up the arrival of his bride. A charming photo headlined 'Bride On First Visit to St Paul' shows Zelda's hawk-like profile looking pensive.

As Boyd was a partner in the Kilmarnock Book Store at 84 East 4th Street, Scott spent free afternoons with him and his writer wife Peggy Woodward, catching up on literary gossip. Scott, in his role as talent scout, generously encouraged Scribner's to publish both Boyd and Woodward. Scott was less generous (or consistent) about the phenomenal success of *Main Street* (1920) by the other local hero, Sinclair Lewis, who lived on Summit and who with visiting novelist Joseph Hergesheimer made up this tight-knit literary circle. Scott's respectable bestseller *This Side of Paradise* achieved 49,000 copies in its first year, compared with *Main Street*'s phenomenal 300,000 copies. Though Scott wrote to Lewis that it was the best

American novel so far, to critic Burton Rascoe he wrote, 'Main Street is rotten.'[11] However, now they were all St Paul literary boys together, rivalry was temporarily forgotten.

Zelda, not one of the boys, was seldom included in their afternoon club. Instead she read widely and hardly drank. Possibly influenced by meeting Galsworthy, she devoured his novels. Max Perkins sent her *To Let*. '[I]t makes our Galsworthy so complete', Zelda answered immediately, 'that we're both quite impressed with the long line of purple books – I don't do much but read so I'm awfully glad you sent it to me – We are quite popular out here and are enjoying our importance and temperance . . . but I'm homesick for Fifth Ave.'[12]

Meeting Scott's parents, Edward and Mollie Fitzgerald, and his sister Annabel for the first time did little to reduce her homesickness. All three Fitzgeralds unendingly exhibited 'Minnesota niceness'.[13] Zelda, though appreciative, felt she had nothing in common with them. She told Sara Mayfield they had neither Southern charm nor New York sophistication, that Mollie Fitzgerald was badly dressed and painfully eccentric while Scott's father with his cane, flowing cravats and Vandyke beard struck her as an ineffectual cardboard figure from a bygone age.

Annabel, born in 1901 in Syracuse, New York, was like her parents a staunch member of St Paul's Catholic community, in whose Visitation Convent School Annabel had been enrolled from 1909 to 1913. Zelda saw her as a conventional convent girl who even returned as an adult to the convent for retreats. Annabel tried to be helpful to her sassy new sister-in-law but never saw her as a friend.

It came as a relief to the family as well as to Zelda when she and Scott settled into the young married circle who attended the White Bear Yacht Club, the University Club, the Town and County Club, and the Minnesota Club which held dances, discussion groups and golf tournaments. Zelda, secure in her friendship with the Kalmans, once again disturbed the peace. She smoked on the back platforms of trolleys, commented out loud at the movies, outraged young men who danced with her by whispering flirtatiously: 'My hips are going wild; you don't mind do you?'[14] At that time pregnant women were expected to remain discreet if not to hide away. Though 1921 was the first year that American women enjoyed full voting rights, Zelda's bold behaviour shocked Scott's community.

To her horror Scott began to notice and comment on her increasing weight. In his September Ledger he described her as 'helpless' because of her extra pounds. In December his Ledger again tartly recorded 'Zelda's weight' alongside a mention of 'cottillion' dances and bobsleigh rides which she was now more self-conscious about attending. Without her slim figure Zelda felt like 'Alabama nobody'.[15]

Completely unprepared for the birth, she depended heavily on Xandra, who bought diapers, bassinet, cot, bathtub, booked doctor, nurse, hospital room, even a nanny, and made Zelda laugh at the bizarre baby business. Zelda wanted Xandra, her first woman friend since leaving Montgomery, to be her baby's godmother, but Fitzgerald family intervention foiled this plan and Annabel was chosen. But neither this nor any subsequent setback disrupted Zelda's lifelong friendship with the Kalmans, documented by the massive file of letters between them.[16]

The Fitzgeralds had rented the Dellwood house for a year, but in October 1921 they were asked to leave because their landlord claimed they had damaged the plumbing. They moved downtown to the Commodore, an apartment hotel near the Kalmans' lavish residence on Summit, to await the birth.

On 26 October 1921, in the Miller Hospital, Frances Scott Key Fitzgerald was delivered. It was a hard long labour. Xandra said 'Scott kept popping in and out of the delivery room jotting things down in the little notebook he always carried. When I asked him what he'd hurriedly scrawled during Zelda's labor, he replied: "'Help!' and 'Jesus Christ!'" When I asked why he wrote it down he said, "I might use it some time!"'[17]

Scott, told to wait outside the delivery room, threatened to kill himself if Zelda died. When he discovered suicide was unnecessary he collected his pencil, notebook and wits and, as Zelda emerged faint from the anaesthetic, coldly recorded her first comments: 'Oh God, goofo, I'm drunk.[18] Mark Twain. Isn't she smart – she has the hiccups. I hope it's beautiful and a fool – a beautiful little fool.' Zelda ruefully acknowledged that her own life might have been simpler if she had been less sharp.

Two years later Scott coolly recycled her remark in *The Great Gatsby*, when Daisy says about the birth of *her* daughter: '"I'm glad it's a girl. And I hope she'll be a fool – that's the best thing a girl can be in this world, a beautiful little fool."'[19]

Zelda never forgot Scott's detachment.

The security Zelda gained from her father's protection meant she had never acquired necessary protective mechanisms. This had contributed to her belief that those close to her held her best interests. This episode with Scott was the first of several dents in that belief.

Zelda's granddaughter Eleanor Lanahan said: 'The little girl was called Scottie and was no fool. Zelda named her Bonnie in *Save Me The Waltz*. Scott called her Honoria in "Babylon Revisited". She arrived in her parents' lives not only as a baby whose life they scripted, but as an artist's model with a fictitious persona and a fictitious world they invented as they went along.'[20]

Zelda, initially disappointed about the sex of the baby, within days wrote to Ludlow: 'She is awfully cute, and I am very devoted to her.'[21]

Scott telegrammed everyone: 'LILLIAN GISH IS IN MOURNING CONSTANCE TALMADGE IS A BACK NUMBER AND A SECOND MARY PICKFORD HAS ARRIVED.'[22]

Minnie Sayre behaved just like the mother in Zelda's *Save Me The Waltz*: '"My blue-eyed baby has grown up. We are so proud."'[23] Zelda, now a mother in Minnesota, missed the slow creak of her garden swing. She missed the rusty croaking of the frogs in the cypress swamps. She felt strongly that 'home' was still Montgomery.

Zelda did not lose weight or self-consciousness. 'Scottie was born and we went to all the Christmas parties and a man asked Sandy "who is your fat friend?"'[24]

She closeted herself with the baby, pasting into her scrapbook every 'devoted mother and baby' photograph taken by the St Paul newspapers. Meanwhile Scott produced short stories and a winter show for St Paul's Junior League. When he invited friends home, Zelda would say: 'You won't come, will you? The baby wakes up and yells and the place is too small. We don't want you.' If Scott overheard he would say: 'Zelda's got this silly notion that we can't have anyone in the place . . . you'll come up, won't you, and help me cure her of this idea.'[25] But if they actually arrived, Zelda waved them away.

The only visitor Zelda consistently welcomed was Xandra, who came regularly for lunch or to play golf. Zelda pasted into her scrapbook a newscutting of them both outside the club house, under the headline 'Society Women Compete in Golf Tournament'.[26] Though Xandra had helped Zelda find a nanny, neither she nor Zelda was prepared for the tyrannical Anna Shirley, who acted like the baby's warder. It was a dispiriting start to a series of bad relationships between Zelda and Scottie's nannies.

In November 1921, again coming to their rescue, Xandra enabled them to lease the Victorian frame house at 626 Goodrich Avenue[27] which belonged to Xandra's parents, on vacation abroad. Zelda's homesickness increased as she rattled about with only the baby and Nanny for company, because that winter Scott rented a room downtown to work with a stenographer on revisions to *The Beautiful and Damned*.

Scott insisted on having the baby baptized a Catholic in the Visitation Convent chapel[28] and, never a precise chronologist, dates the baptism as November in his Ledger. But St Paul historical researcher Lloyd Hackl gives the date as 8 December 1921, borne out by the baptismal certificate which gives the baby's sponsors' names as Annabelle [*sic*] Fitzgerald, Scott's sister, and Joseph Barron, who officiated.[29] The baby's name is listed as Frances Scott Fitzgerald but on the birth certificate it appeared as Scotty.[30]

Baptisms generally bring to mind pictures of attentive parents and friends gathered together solemnly. *This* baptism of Zelda's only child was as curious as was her only wedding. According to Hackl, Zelda did not attend because Scott's parents, who considered her eccentric, feared how she might act. Though others were nervous about how much the equally unpredictable father might drink, he did attend.[31] More alarming was the fact that Anna Shirley refused to let the godparents hold the baby.[32] She allowed only Annabel as godmother to place her hand on baby Scottie.

Zelda did not publicly reveal her feelings of exclusion, but watched as her husband's pride in their child became more possessive. It was as if, by being born in St Paul, the baby had become more Scott's than Zelda's, with ultimate authority left to Anna Shirley. Xandra recalls how one evening she and Oscar stopped by and found that the baby, whom Zelda was breastfeeding, had hiccups. The angry nanny loudly blamed it on Zelda's excessive gin consumption the previous night. Zelda, herself breastfed for years by Minnie Sayre, was uncomfortably aware of subtle pressure from both Scott and the nanny to adopt the more distant mothering style of his Northern culture.

The harsh winter of 1921, when biting cold infiltrated every pore, further dragged down Zelda's spirits. There is a photo of her smiling bravely on a bone-chilling sleigh-ride over 'grey and glassy'[33] snow, but she wrote Fowler: 'This damn place is 18 below zero and I go round thanking God that, anatomically + proverbially speaking, I am safe from the awful fate of the monkey . . . Ludlow, I certainly miss you + Townsend + Alec – in fact I am very lonesome.'[34] When in January 1922 novelist Joseph Hergesheimer[35] told Zelda he had lived off hominy grits in the wild Appalachians, she responded tartly: 'But at least you didn't have to live in St Paul on the edge of the Arctic Circle.' She also told Hergesheimer that she felt lonely because Scott was immersed in writing his play *The Vegetable*.[36]

Zelda's reaction to her first Northern winter was curiously anticipated by Scott in his 1920 story 'The Ice Palace', where Southern Belle Sally Carrol Happer wants to leave the South to 'live where things happen on a big scale'. On a January trip to visit her Yankee fiancé, Sally Carrol Happer nearly freezes to death in an ice palace at the Winter Carnival. She gratefully returns to the familiar South, to the spangled dust over which the heat waves rise.[37]

Zelda, however, cannot return.

After the *Metropolitan* serialization of *The Beautiful and Damned*, heavy revisions were necessary for the book publication.[38] Zelda suggested cutting the serial's didactic conclusion. Scott cabled Perkins on 23 December 1921: 'LILDA [Zelda] THINKS BOOK SHOULD END WITH ANTHONY'S LAST SPEECH ON SHIP SHE THINKS NEW ENDING IS A PIECE OF MORALITY.' Perkins decided Zelda was artistically 'dead right'.[39]

Scott had told his publisher, Charles Scribner II, that his hero was a man with the tastes and weaknesses of an artist but with no creative inspiration who, with his beautiful young wife, is wrecked on the shoals of dissipation.[40]

The protagonists, Gloria Gilbert and Anthony Patch, move from their spoiled life as beautiful people to damnation caused by drinking and idle expenditure of unearned wealth. As Anthony's alcoholism escalates his marriage to Gloria declines, a theme that aptly reflected the problems Scott and Zelda faced daily.

Zelda, more interested in abstract thought and descriptions than in emotions, found that concepts of beauty, damnation, and moral degeneracy came easily.[41] Scott, who needed them in the writing of *The Beautiful and Damned*, 'had almost no capacity for abstract ideas or arguments and could enter into other people's attitudes only when he had known them [emotionally] in his own experience'.[42] Scott therefore found this talent of Zelda's very useful, and indeed told Alex McKaig 'Her ideas largely in this new novel.'[43]

The novel's autobiographical theme was pointed up by W. E. Hill's recognizable Fitzgerald portraits on the jacket which depicted a fashionable young couple seated side by side but with heads and bodies turned away from each other. They appear bored, lifeless, sulky. Scott wrote a virulent letter to Perkins: 'The girl is excellent . . . somewhat like Zelda but the man . . . is a sort of debauched edition of me.'[44]

After listening to Scott's complaints Zelda painted an alternative book jacket: a witty depiction of a nude with bobbed hair, exactly like herself, splashing in a champagne glass. This was Zelda's first professional drawing. In bright red, yellow and blue crayon over pencil, it vividly expresses the Roaring Twenties tempo. Crackling flames in the same hectic colours spurt and sizzle round the title. Unlike Hill's world-weary illustration, Zelda's 'The Birth of the Flapper' offers a dizzy symbol of the prosperous, youthful, insouciant mood.[45] Scott loved its vivacity, typical of Zelda's early sketches, which showed an illustrative skill she never lost. Unfortunately Zelda's earliest surviving artwork was never used.

The Beautiful and Damned was published on 4 March 1922, dedicated to three early mentors: Shane Leslie, Maxwell Perkins and George Jean Nathan, to whom Scott had become reconciled despite Nathan's insistence that baby Scottie looked like Mencken! Scott had written to Charles Scribner: 'it's really a most sensational book + I hope won't disappoint the critics who liked my first one'.[46] H. L. Mencken, the critic Scott most admired, wrote: 'There are a hundred signs in it of serious purpose and unquestionable skill . . . Fitzgerald ceases to be a *Wunderkind*, and begins to come into his maturity.'[47]

The Fitzgeralds' friends enjoyed the book not least because several saw themselves inside it. Nathan was Maury Noble; screenwriter Ted Paramore, whom Zelda labelled fun to be with,[48] did not even get a name change when fictionalized.

Some believed the novel was an accurate portrait of the Fitzgeralds' marriage. Edmund Wilson felt 'It's all about him and Zelda.'[49] Others felt it was a cleverly vamped up version.

In several significant ways it *did* mirror their life.

Gloria discovers Anthony is 'an utter coward toward any one of a million phantasms created by his imagination'. Anthony discovers Gloria is 'a girl of tremendous nervous tension and of the most high-handed selfishness . . . almost completely without physical fear.'[50] Gloria, suckled until she was three, nervously chewing gumdrops, is reminiscent of Zelda chewing gum or her lip. Film magnate Joseph Bloeckman's courtship of Gloria is based on Nathan's wooing of Zelda; Gloria's movie test on an offer made to Zelda to star in a film version of *Damned*; and Gloria has a fling with aviator Tudor Baird, who suffers the habitual aviator fate in Scott's novels: 'Afterwards she was glad she had kissed him, for next day when his plane fell 1500 feet . . . gasoline engine smashed through his heart.'[51]

There are some distortions. While Scott's ambitions were closely defined, Anthony wastes his days over ill-defined goals. Whereas Zelda's thoughtfulness was constantly remarked on in Montgomery[52], Gloria is utterly thoughtless. But one scene showing Anthony as a dilettante and Gloria as an obstruction has a wicked authenticity: '"Work!" she scoffed. "Oh, you sad bird! You bluffer! Work – that means a great arranging of the desk and the lights, a great sharpening of pencils, and 'Gloria, don't sing!' . . . and 'Let me read you my opening sentence' . . . Two weeks later the whole performance over again."' It is razor-sharp in its depiction of Scott's expectation that 'Gloria would play golf "or something" while Anthony wrote.'[53]

Over time, Scott vacillated about how close a marital portrait the book was. In 1920 he had written: 'I married her [the flesh and blood Rosalind-Zelda] eventually and am now writing a . . . more "honest" book about her.'[54]

Years later he wrote to Zelda: 'I wish The Beautiful and Damned had been a maturely written book because it was all true. We ruined ourselves – I have never honestly thought that we ruined each other.'[55]

Later still, Fitzgerald told Scottie that Gloria had a more frivolous and certainly more vulgar nature than Zelda. Though Scott admitted he had drawn on events in their married life he denied any real resemblance between Gloria and Zelda except in facial beauty and style of speech. He told Scottie the focus was quite different. For instance, he said reassuringly, he and Zelda enjoyed their life together much more than Gloria and Anthony had.

The 'truth' lurks in the interstices. The Gilbert-Patches were not the Fitzgeralds, rather they were Scott's internal fears of what they could become.

Several critics saw the relationship between Gloria and Zelda as merely superficial. John Peale Bishop felt Scott had created 'a Fitzgerald flapper of the now most famous type – hair honey-colored and bobbed, mouth rose-colored and profane . . . he has as yet failed to show that hard intelligence, that intricate emotional equipment upon which her charm depends, so that Gloria . . . remains a little inexplicable, a pretty, vulgar shadow of her prototype.'[56]

Zelda pasted Bishop's review in her scrapbook.

Lawton Campbell told Sara Mayfield: 'The Beautiful and Damned was pure Zelda.'[57]

Scott had sent a manuscript copy to Wilson, who said it represented an advance over his earlier writings but, curiously, ignored the crucial influence he knew Zelda had on Scott's work. He suggested that the three significant influences on Scott's writing and character were firstly that he was Irish (romantic but cynical about romance); secondly that he came from the Midwest, so overvalued the East's sophistication; thirdly that he drank heavily.[58] Scott asked him to delete the reference to alcohol and to add in Zelda: 'The most enormous influence on me . . . since I met her has been the complete, fine and full-hearted selfishness and chill-mindedness of Zelda.'[59] It was a cold remark that captured an unnerving, even bleak, facet of Zelda's nature, the antithesis to the effervescent artist who had drawn the champagne nymph.

In the last quarter of *The Beautiful and Damned* Scott used passages from novels and projects aborted in 1919. One project, 'The Diary of a Literary Failure', included the fifty-page 'Diary of a Popular Girl' based on Zelda's journal, which Scott, without consulting Zelda, had not permitted Nathan to publish. Scott's biographers who state that key passages in his novel were *inspired by* Zelda's letters[60] overlook the fact that it was not a matter of 'inspiration' but a direct borrowing of Zelda's lines, which were then revised with the minor transposition of a few words. Scott admitted his practice to Perkins: 'I'm just enclosing you the typing of Zelda's diary . . . You'll recognize much of the dialogue. Please don't show it to anyone else.'[61]

Without acknowledging Zelda as his primary source Scott had sanitized one letter from spring 1919. Zelda had written that she and Scott were 'soul-mates' who had been mated since the time when people were 'bi-sexual', an idea Zelda had absorbed from her mother's theosophical doctrines. Scott redesigned it: ' "We're twins! . . . mother says that two souls are sometimes created together and – and in love before they are born." '[62]

In Scott's novel the 'Diary' section rushes through in precisely Zelda's style. Take these lines:

> April 11th . . . I'm gradually losing faith in any man being susceptible to fatal injuries . . .
> April 21st . . . Anthony . . . called and sounded sweet on the phone – so I broke a date for him . . . I feel I'd break anything for him, including the ten commandments and my neck . . .
> April 24th . . . What grubworms women are to crawl on their bellies through colorless marriages! Marriage was created not to be a background but to need one.[63]

Quickwitted Zelda, though somewhat slow to catch on to the implications of this practice of unacknowledged 'borrowing', had begun to do so by the time she was asked by Burton Rascoe, the *New York Tribune*'s book critic, to review her husband's book.

In her first published signed article, 'Friend Husband's Latest', she remarked acidly: 'on one page I recognized a portion of an old diary of mine which mysteriously disappeared shortly after my marriage, and also scraps of letters, which, though considerably edited, sound to me vaguely familiar.'

In her review Zelda pointed out pleasantly: 'Mr Fitzgerald . . . seems to believe that plagiarism begins at home.' Though Zelda's review was partly a joke she made a serious criticism: 'The other things I didn't like . . . I mean the unimportant things – were the literary references and the attempt to convey a profound air of erudition. It reminds me in its more soggy moments of the essays I used to get up in school at the last minute by looking up strange names in the *Encyclopaedia Britannica*.'[64] Matthew J. Bruccoli says Zelda's 'criticism is just, for the novel is intellectually pretentious'.[65]

Scott, amused and proud of Zelda's review, ignored any serious undercurrent. Edmund Wilson wrote to Scott: 'Convey all my recommendations to Zelda, whose review of The Damned I thought fine and whose thing in The Metropolitan I liked less.'[66] Wilson was referring to *Metropolitan Magazine* which together with *McCall's* had been sufficiently impressed by Zelda's review to invite her to contribute articles on the Flapper. She wrote four features: 'Eulogy on the Flapper', 'Does A Moment of Revolt Come Sometime To Every Married Man?', 'The Super-Flapper' and 'Where Do Flappers Go?' All four were paid for, three were published.

It was the slow small start to her professional writing life, though it was hard for both Fitzgeralds to see it like that yet. However, Scott did devote a page of his 1922 Ledger to 'Zelda's earnings', which totalled $815. She was paid $15 by *New York Tribune* for her review; $50 by *Metropolitan Magazine* for 'Eulogy on the Flapper' (June 1922), $250 by *McCall's* for 'Does A Moment of Revolt Come Sometime To Every Married Man?' (March 1924) and $500 for 'The Super-Flapper', which remains unlocated, presumably unpublished. The articles appeared under Zelda's by-line, but alongside ran the explanation that she was Scott Fitzgerald's wife.

McCall's commissioned her to write a 2,500-word article on the Flapper at ten cents a word. In October 1922 they sent her $300 for a feature, 'Where Do Flappers Go?', but did not publish it. There are two curious points: firstly, this $300 is not listed in Scott's careful notes; secondly, *McCall's* in October 1925 *did* publish 'What Became of the Flappers?', possibly the same article, with Scott's piece 'Our

Young Rich Boys', under the joint title 'What Became of Our Flappers and Our Sheiks?' by F. Scott Fitzgerald and Zelda Sayre Fitzgerald.[67]

It is worth examining 'What Became of the Flappers?' to see how similar Zelda's writing style was to her speech: witty, rhythmic, highly descriptive. Each sentence is balanced, with substantial repetition and a jaunty edge. 'The flapper springs full-grown, like Minerva, from the head of her once-déclassé father, Jazz, upon whom she lavishes affection and reverence, and deepest filial regard ... The best flapper is reticent emotionally and courageous morally. You always know what she thinks, but she does all her feeling alone.'[68]

In 'Eulogy' Zelda held that the Flapper was deceased. Her outer accoutrements had been bequeathed to girls' schools, shop girls, and small-town belles. Nothing could replace 'the dear departed ... who will live by her accomplishments and not by her Flapping'. Never again would a girl say ' "I do not want to be respectable because respectable girls are not attractive." ' Never again would a girl arrive at the knowledge that ' "boys *do* dance most with the girls they kiss most" ' or that ' "men *will* marry the girls they could kiss before they had asked papa" '.

Zelda lamented the death of the Flapper who bobbed her hair, put on 'a great deal of audacity and rouge', 'flirted because it was fun to flirt', 'refused to be bored chiefly because she wasn't boring'.[69]

Above the 'Eulogy' article is a marvellous sketch of Zelda by Gordon Bryant, who caught both her intense gaze and the flicker of regret in her eyes. The regret was about to intensify.

CHAPTER 8

Zelda's desperation to go East was satisfied when a *Beautiful and Damned* publication party was held in New York in March 1922. They left Scottie behind with her nurse for two weeks.[1] They stayed at the Plaza, Zelda's favourite: 'an etched hotel, dainty and subdued'.[2] Like the Plaza, the Fitzgeralds were subdued when Wilson met them. He felt Zelda was 'more matronly and rather fat (about which she is very sensitive)' but was more mellow and he liked her the better for it. He spotted that relations with Scott were strained.[3] After New York Scott wrote to Wilson: 'I couldn't seem to get sober enough to be able to tolerate being sober . . . the whole trip was largely a failure.'[4]

Scott's regrets were echoed by Zelda. The strain and failure (and her weight) may have been due to her discovery in late January or early February that she was pregnant again. One possible cause could have been that modern contraception was not freely discussed until the early 1920s and was not yet widely available. Zelda did not want a second child so soon. After all, Scottie was only three months old.

Despite the horror Zelda had shown *before* marriage about taking termination pills, she decided to have an abortion. In a later letter to Scott which analysed the events that led to her first asylum incarceration, Zelda specifies 'pills and Dr Lackin' in New York during a house-hunting stay while still officially resident in St Paul.[5] While Scott's March 1922 Ledger merely records: 'Zelda and her abortionist', Sara Mayfield states firmly that 'this was the first of three similar incidents, each of which drove another wedge into their marriage'.[6] Zelda's sister Rosalind confirmed that there was more than one abortion and later asked Scott whether the abortions had contributed to Zelda's mental breakdowns, a relevant question. Although Scott agreed to this abortion, it seems that years later he still resented it; just as Zelda deeply regretted it. There is a grim undated entry in Scott's Notebooks where he states harshly: 'His son went down the toilet of the XXXX hotel after Dr X – Pills.'[7] As far as Zelda's health was concerned, the termination was to have tragic effects on her ability to conceive and would result in many years of gynaecological problems.

The facts were hard for both Zelda and Scott to deal with but Scott, as so often, wove his fiction around the facts.

In *The Beautiful and Damned*, written during 1921, he focuses on Gloria's pregnancy and the conflicts surrounding it. Though the dating of Zelda's 1922 pregnancy meant it could not have provided the novel's raw source, either Scott was illustrating the uncanny talent for prophecy which he had already shown in 'The Ice Palace', or his fictional scene did not reflect Zelda's 1922 pregnancy but was based on her suspected pregnancy in Westport, which she mentioned to Ludlow at exactly the time Scott was writing his first draft.[8]

In Scott's *published* novel, Gloria suspects she is pregnant and discusses the possibility of abortion with Anthony. He says: '"I'm neutral. If you have it I'll probably be glad. If you don't – well that's all right too."' The decision is left to Gloria who is seen as a selfish woman: '"Afterward I might have wide hips – and no radiance in my hair."'[9]

This published fictional interpretation of Gloria/Zelda's reaction to another pregnancy is considerably more extreme than Zelda's real-life response. In an earlier manuscript version, in which significant differences occur, Scott more accurately portrays Zelda's responses. In that version Gloria is genuinely distressed. Anthony suggests she gets help: '"Why can't you talk to some woman and find out what's best to be done? Most of them fix it some way."'[10]

This *earlier*, stronger manuscript version shows Anthony sharing the decision and stresses Gloria's human qualities. In the published novel the problem is shelved rather than resolved when Gloria learns she is not pregnant.

It is also tenable that Scott might have based this episode in *The Beautiful and Damned* on Zelda's fierce pre-marital denunciation of an abortion. Either way, Scott's lingering Catholic beliefs and Zelda's change of attitude feed into the changes in treatment from manuscript to publication.

Zelda and Scott returned from New York to Goodrich Avenue, St Paul, where Zelda, according to Xandra, was 'not at all interested in going out with the girls, and when Scott wanted to remain at home, Zelda stayed with him.'[11] Xandra later suggested to Lloyd Hackl that what kept Zelda at home in St Paul was the company of two literary men. They were Sinclair Lewis, at 516 Summit Avenue, whose *Babbitt* (1922) was repeating the success of *Main Street*, and humorist Donald Ogden Stewart opposite him at 513. Zelda told Xandra that both were more mentally stimulating than most Minnesota society women.[12] Zelda said Stewart, still a clerk with the American Telephone Company in Minneapolis, who wrote comedy at nights on his return to Mrs Porterfield's Boarding House, offered her intellectual stimulus. Xandra recalled that Zelda 'wasn't a belle-butterfly, that she was an extremely intelligent person' whose intelligence largely serviced Scott's work. Scott, 'then writing religiously', would go over everything he had written with Zelda, incorporating her suggestions.[13]

Zelda and Scott had been the first of their set to marry; but Bishop now announced his intention of marrying Margaret Hutchins, a wealthy Chicago socialite, before going abroad. Margaret was already the target of sour appraisals by the Fitzgeralds' circle. Wilson wrote to Scott: 'She [Margaret] will supply him with infinite money and leisure but, I fear, chloroform his intellect: I think her a prime dumb-bell with . . . an all too strong will which may lead John around by the balls.'[14] Scott replied: '[H]aving the money, she'll hold a high hand over him. Still I don't think he's happy and it may release him to do more creative work.'[15] Zelda recognized that Scott felt distressed because after John's marriage, his friendship with Scott waned.

Wilson himself, his passion for Edna Millay spent, had become attracted to Mary Blair, a successful actress in the Provincetown Players productions of Eugene O'Neill's plays. Despite his mother's disapproval of actress-wives, Wilson too was contemplating matrimony.

By the time Bishop married Margaret on 17 June 1922 the Fitzgeralds and Scottie, nanny in tow, had moved from Goodrich Avenue to the White Bear Yacht Club for Zelda to swim and sunbathe.

Xandra Kalman played golf daily with Zelda. 'She was . . . rather a good golfer . . . far better than Scott.'[16] Years later Zelda reminded Oscar: 'I so often think of the happy times . . . the caddy house . . . the long somnolent summer hours at the lake.'[17]

Xandra respected Zelda because she seemed different from other women. 'Certainly she enjoyed being different': she was not a Southern 'clinging vine', yet despite those differences 'she was a natural person'.[18] Later Xandra told her friend Hackl that Zelda's 'naturalness' included extreme frankness. 'There weren't many people whom she liked. I won't say she was rude, but she made it quite clear. If she didn't like someone or if she disapproved of them, then she set out to be as impossible as she could be.'[19] Xandra suggested that another part of Zelda's naturalness was that she had no affectations, no exaggerated Southern drawl.[20] But most friends highlighted Zelda's pronounced Southern speech: when mentioning Mayfield, Murphy or Haardt she drawled the name Sara so that it sounded like her own maiden name 'Sayre-ah'.[21] Xandra, perceptive however about Zelda's remoteness, said she 'never felt quite at "home" with Zelda'; she never reached the centre of Zelda's identity.[22]

By August the Fitzgeralds had been evicted from the Yacht Club for boisterous behaviour.[23] They never seemed to mind evictions, merely moving their rolling party on to the next location. Now they wheeled their pram laden with clothes a few blocks to another rented residence in Dellwood where partying continued while Scottie slept.

Financial strains beset them. Sales of *The Beautiful and Damned* were less good than Scribners' prediction.[25] They reached about 50,000 copies, similar to *This Side of Paradise*, but Scott was now indebted $5,600 to Scribner's. Despite publication in September 1922 of Scott's second story collection *Tales of the Jazz Age*,[26] which sold 12,828 in its first year, the Fitzgeralds were unable to break even. A film offer seemed imperative. Scott's ambiguous relation to Hollywood meant that sometimes he abjectly courted movie moguls, other times he patronizingly felt he alone could bring culture to commerce. Thus he jubilantly sold the film rights of *The Beautiful and Damned* to Warner Brothers for $2,500, but both he and Zelda disliked the movie when it appeared in 1922.[27] Scott thought it cheap, vulgar, ill-constructed and shoddy. Zelda was ashamed of it.

The fall's icy weather drove the Fitzgeralds back to St Paul's Commodore Hotel. Scott had finished writing his play *The Vegetable* but since then had received a batch of rejections. His depression over this, and Zelda's fears of ice floes and Arctic snow, made them decide to return to New York's Plaza in September. They left Scottie with her nanny in St Paul and began house-hunting in Westchester and Long Island.

Wilson saw them in New York and reported Zelda had lost her fat, both were behaving rationally and Scott had hit on a scheme for preventing Zelda 'from absorbing all his time, emotion and seminal juice . . . a compact . . . by which each is bound not to go out alone with another member of the opposite sex.'[28]

Scott was still preoccupied with the progress of *The Vegetable*. Sara Mayfield met Zelda for tea in the Palm Court,[29] found her tanned, fit, 'theoretically on the water wagon' and thrilled that her plunge into the fountain had been commemorated by artist Reginald Marsh for his Greenwich Village Follies curtain. It also portrayed a truck-load of literary celebrities including Scott, John Dos Passos, Gilbert Seldes, John Peale Bishop, Edmund Wilson and Don Ogden Stewart, zooming down Seventh Avenue. When Scott joined Sara and Zelda at the Palm Court he was determined to discuss *The Vegetable*. Despite its rejections he said 'It's going to be a big money-maker.'[30]

In New York the Fitzgeralds met everyone and everyone wanted to meet them. Later *Hearst's International* ran a full-page photo-graph, circulated countrywide, of the couple posed dramatically, pouting charm. A long strand of pearls falls from Zelda's neck. Her dress has ice-white fur trims. Her hair is waved and sleek. She called her image her Elizabeth Arden Face.

Scott had become reconciled with Townsend Martin, probably because Zelda no longer flirted with him, and at his 'long long party' they met Gilbert Seldes, editor of *The Dial*. Seldes, hung over, had lain on Townsend's bed to recover. 'Suddenly . . . this double apparition approached me. The two most beautiful people in the world were floating toward me . . . I thought to myself, "If there is anything I can do to keep them as beautiful as they are I will do it".'[31]

For Zelda, the glamorous contrast between Minnesota's harsh-ness and New York's soft focus made Manhattan seem like a palace. She wrote: 'the city huddled in a gold-crowned conference. The top of New York twinkled like a golden canopy behind a throne.'[32] John Dos Passos, whom she first met that October, agreed. Shy, stammer-ing Dos Passos, ex-Harvard, born in Chicago the same year as Scott,[33] wrote: 'lunching at the Plaza with Scott and Zelda . . . marks the beginning of an epoch . . . it was a crisp autumn day. New York is at its best in October . . . The clouds are very white . . . Windows of tall buildings sparkle in the sun. Everything has the million dollar look.'[34]

Despite his shyness, radical views and dislike of stardom, Dos Passos was going through a million-dollar phase himself, having just leapt to fame with *Three Soldiers* (1921), based on his ambulance corps service in France and Italy, for which Scott envied him. Bishop had written to Wilson that *Three Soldiers* was a marvellous book and made 'FSF look like a hack writer for Zelda's squirrel coat'.[35]

Fortunately Scott had not sighted that phrase before he wrote a favourable review in the *St Paul Daily News*,[36] but he did feel rivalrous towards him. Yet with typical generosity the Fitzgeralds invited writer Sherwood Anderson to meet Dos Passos at lunch.

To impress their guests the Fitzgeralds served Bronx cocktails then champagne, followed by lobster croquettes. 'Scott always had the worst ideas about food . . . They were celebrities in the Sunday supplement sense of the word,' recalled Dos Passos, '. . . the idea of being that kind of celebrity set my teeth on edge.'[37]

Dos Passos found the shaggy-haired unkempt Anderson with his gaudy Liberty silk necktie 'an appealing sort of man'[38], with greying curls and strangely soft wrinkles in his face. Zelda, said Dos Passos, was 'very beautiful [with] a sort of grace . . . very original and amusing. But there was also this little strange streak.'[39]

The Fitzgeralds' interrogations also struck him as strange. 'Scott and Zelda both started plying me with questions. Their gambit was to put you in the wrong. You were backward in your ideas. You were inhibited about sex . . . my attitude was that they were nobody's goddamn business.'[40]

After lunch Dos Passos and the Fitzgeralds, who had rented a scarlet touring car and chauffeur, househunted on Long Island. In Great Neck Dos Passos suggested they call on the humorist and short-story writer, thirty-seven-year-old Ring Lardner, and his wife Ellis.[41]

Lardner's reputation was rooted in his use of American vernacular, admired by Scott and Dos Passos. He also had a reputation as an alcoholic. When they arrived the American lingo was not in evidence but the whiskey was. Dos Passos recalls: 'A tall sallow mournful man with a high arched nose stood beside the fireplace – dark hollow eyes, hollow cheeks, helplessly drunk. When his wife tried to get him to speak he stared at us without seeing us . . . Scott kept saying that Ring was his private drunkard; everybody had to have his private drunkard.'[42] When they left, Zelda initially disliked Ring and told Sandy he was a typical newspaperman who happened to play the sax while Ellis was 'common' but more likeable.[43] On becoming the Lardners' neighbours their opinions rapidly improved. Scott particularly admired Lardner for bruises gained representing the Yale football team against Harvard.

En route back to New York they stopped for Zelda and Dos Passos to visit a carnival while Scott, drunk and morose, waited in the car. The carnival pair rode a Ferris wheel, but according to Dos Passos: 'Zelda and I kept saying things to each other but our minds never met.'[44] As this infamous Ferris Wheel Incident has become legendary for its first glimpse of Zelda's 'madness', it is worth comparing two versions both authored by Dos Passos.

In 1963 he produced what appeared to be a straightforward, rather general account.

> We were up in the Ferris wheel when she said something to me. I don't remember anymore what it was, but I thought to myself, suddenly, this woman is mad. Whatever she had said was so completely off track; it was like peering into a dark abyss – something forbidding between us . . . from that first time I sensed there was something peculiar about her.

Dos Passos, who fails to give a specific instance of their conversation, without any evidence suggests to readers Zelda is mad. He continues:

> She would veer off . . . Zelda did have a manner of becoming personal that wasn't really very amusing . . . she'd go off into regions that weren't funny anymore. There were also things about which one didn't tease her . . . Sometimes she would go on, but there was always a non-sequitur in it. It stunned one for a moment. She seemed in such complete self-possession.[45]

The crucial point in this first account is that nowhere is there a hint of anything sexual between them.

Three years later in 1966 Dos Passos published a memoir which when focusing on the Ferris wheel ride firstly intensifies his belief in Zelda's madness, but secondly introduces an ambiguous sexual undercurrent.

> It wasn't that she wanted me to make love to her: she was perceptive enough to know I wouldn't make a pass at Scott's girl. She may have thought it bourgeois but that was the way it was at that time. We'd only known each other ten hours, but for all our misunderstandings the three of us were really friends . . . The gulf that opened between Zelda and me, sitting up on that rickety Ferris wheel, was something I couldn't explain . . . years later . . . it occurred to me that, even the first day we knew each other, I had come up against that basic fissure in her mental processes that was to have such tragic consequences. Though she was so very lovely I had come upon something that frightened and repelled me, even physically. Zelda kept insisting on repeating the ride and I sat dumb beside her, feeling more and more miserable. She was never a girl you could take lightly. Through it all I felt . . . a puzzled but affectionate respect.[46]

This version begs more questions than it answers. In a mere first meeting of ten hours, what were the misunderstandings? If it was bourgeois to make a pass at Scott's girl 'at that time', was it less so later? Dos Passos states that Zelda had not wanted him to make love to her. He does not state whether he had wanted to. If he had, and if Zelda had ignored an outright advance or a subtle sexual hint, a 'gulf' might have opened between them.

The significant fact is that by the mid-Sixties writers like Dos Passos, who provided early evidence of Zelda's bizarre behaviour, were already feeding their memories into a validated clinical framework.

Soon after the Ferris wheel incident, Zelda told Sandy that for $300 a month they had found 'a nifty little Babbit-home'[47] at 6 Gateway Drive, Great Neck, on the north shore of Long Island, fifteen miles from New York City, where they stayed from mid-October 1922 to April 1924. The Island's lush farmland and sandy beaches, stretching 125 miles to the east of Manhattan, were an obvious target for a quick break. As you headed out from Brooklyn and Queens, sand dunes and countryside replaced dour urban boroughs. The north shore, less developed than the south, had a rural rugged feel as it cascaded in a series of bluffs, coves and wooded headlands. Magnificent cliffs were topped with estates built by wealthy New Yorkers. Labelled the Gold Coast, it became the hunting ground of the rich.

Zelda went West and fetched Scottie, relieved to be leaving Nanny Anna Shirley in St Paul. Zelda later recalled to Scott: 'I brought Scottie to New York. She was round and funny in a pink coat and bonnet and you met us at the station.'[48] At the time Zelda wrote to Sandy: 'Scott met me with a nurse which I promptly fired and since then I have had the Baby myself'.[49] The replacement nurse ($90 a month) failed to get on with the live-in servant couple ($160 a month) but the part-time laundress ($36 a month) pleased Zelda. The Fitzgeralds still couldn't get their maths right. Nor were their finances helped by constant commuting to sample Manhattan night life. Scott wrote a witty article for the *Saturday Evening Post*, 'How to Live on $36,000 a Year', to show that they couldn't and that $12,000 remained unaccounted for.

In Great Neck Scott revised *The Vegetable*, published in April 1923. In summer 1923 Sam M. Harris agreed to produce and direct it. Scott told Wilson: 'Zelda and I have concocted a wonderful idea for Act II of the play.'[50] Zelda's 'wonderful idea' did not pay off, for when the play, scheduled for Broadway, opened in Atlantic City at the

Apollo Theatre it failed dismally.[51] Zelda, Scott and the Lardners, who had arrived to watch, were forced to see how badly the second act fantasy in particular worked on stage. Zelda wrote to Sandy that 'the show flopped as flat as one of Aunt Jemima's famous pancakes'.[52] Scott admitted: 'People left their seats and walked out.'[53] Though he attempted improvements it never reached Broadway and Scott never wrote another play.

Both Fitzgeralds soon became close friends with the Lardners. Mid-Westerners Ring and Scott shared a dedication to writing and alcohol. Scott successfully promoted Ring's literary reputation but failed to put brakes on Lardner's drinking or his own. Zelda and Scott wrote to the Kalmans that Scott and Ring had got drunken and debauched a few nights earlier and stayed up for twenty-four hours. Zelda told Sandy that she was living in a town full of drunken people, many of whom were actresses.[54] Ring's drunken influence on Scott so distressed Zelda that she warmed to him only slowly, though according to Ring Lardner Jnr his father very soon became extremely fond of Zelda.[55] Whereas Ring became more staid after drink, Scott became more abusive which gave Zelda a new role: apologizing to guests after parties in Great Neck, which Zelda described to Sandy as 'Times Square during the theatre hour'.[56]

Though not especially interesting, Great Neck became Scott's West Egg, the mysterious Gatsby's home. In Zelda's time palatial houses spawned show-business and press celebrities who included Herbert Bayard Swope, executive editor of *New York World*, Eddie Cantor, actors Leslie Howard and Basil Rathbone, theatrical producers Arthur Hopkins and Sam Harris, and millionaire songwriter Gene Buck and his wife Helen. 'We drank Bass Pale Ale,' Zelda recalled, 'and went always to the Bucks or the Lardners or the Swopes when they weren't at our house.'[57] Zelda did not take to Helen Buck, who had the legs and mind of a 'Dulcy-type chorus-girl'.[58] This view was doubtless tainted by Scott's interest in Helen, for according to biographer Scott Donaldson Helen was a 'significant encounter'.[59] Zelda later recalled: 'In Great Neck there was always disorder and quarrels . . . about Helen Buck, about everything.'[60]

The biggest party they gave was for Rebecca West, whom Zelda never liked.[61] Scott, anticipating West's arrival with delight, told Thomas Boyd Zelda was scared.[62] Though Scott had told West someone would drive her from New York to Great Neck, due to a misunderstanding no one collected her. Not knowing the Fitzgeralds' address, West waited all evening in her hotel room to be fetched. Scott, insulted by his guest's failure to appear, made loud fun of her. Scott and West were finally reconciled on the French Riviera in 1925, but by then Zelda, who had met West, thought she looked 'like an advertisement for cauliflower ears and [was] entirely surrounded by fairies – male.'[63]

Ring Lardner, with Ellis's approval, began an elaborate satirical courtship of Zelda, fascinated by her free speech and unconstrained behaviour. Perhaps in retaliation for the Helen Buck incidents Zelda encouraged Ring's flatteringly witty poems. In *What of It?* he wrote: 'Mr Fitzgerald is a novelist and Mrs Fitzgerald is a novelty'; in his fairy tale burlesque, Scott became Prince Charming and Zelda merited the line: 'Her name was Zelda but they called her Cinderella on account of how the ashes and clinkers clung to her when she got up noons.'[64] One Christmas Ring sent her a poem whose first verse ran:

> Of all the girls for whom I care,
> And there are quite a number,
> None can compare with Zelda Sayre,
> Now wedded to a plumber.[65]

Despite new friends Zelda missed Sandy, wrote to her regularly with appreciation for the way Sandy and Oscar had helped and amused her in St Paul, and in one note added seriously that 'there's something more that isn't so easily expressed'.[66]

When the *Baltimore Sun* interviewed her the following fall in Great Neck, Zelda had started writing three short stories. 'I like to write,' Zelda said. 'I thought my husband should write a perfectly good ending to one of my tales, and he wouldn't! He called them "lop-sided", too!' Zelda called Scott to join the interview. Immediately the journalist moved on to discuss *Scott's* stories and insisted Zelda did too. Did she admire 'The Offshore Pirate'? Did she love Scott's books and heroines? 'I like the ones that are like me!' said Zelda. 'That's why I love Rosalind.' Yet again Zelda, with her own connivance, had been relegated to the role of Famous Author's Wife.

Scott told the journalist Zelda 'is the most charming person in the world . . . she's perfect.' Zelda said: 'You don't think that. You think I'm a lazy woman.' Scott replied: 'I think you're perfect. You're always ready to listen to my manuscript, at any hour of the day and night . . . You do, I believe, clean the ice-box once a week.'

Then Scott took over the interview. He asked Zelda if she was ambitious: 'Not especially, but I've plenty of hope . . . I'm not a "joiner".' She wanted to 'be myself and enjoy living'. When Scott asked what Zelda would do if she had to earn her own living, she said prophetically: 'I've studied ballet. I'd try and get a place in the Follies . . . If I wasn't successful, I'd try to write.'[67]

Scott had summed up 1922 as 'a comfortable but dangerous and deteriorating year . . . No ground under our feet.'[68] By February 1923, when deterioration merited a Ledger entry of 'still drunk', a violent note entered his drunken rages. Once when Anita Loos dined at Great Neck Scott locked Zelda and Anita in the dining room and threw a wine cooler, a lighted candelabra, a water carafe and a leg of lamb at them screaming 'Now I'm going to kill you two!' Anita, shaking and incredulous, and Zelda, highly distressed but still loyal to Scott, were forced to flee to Ring Lardner's.[69]

In March 1923 Bunny Wilson married Mary Blair, and the Kalmans visited the Fitzgeralds. Zelda was so excited that the evening passed in a haze of alcohol, ending when Zelda rode out of the Kalmans' hotel room in a laundry cart. Zelda and Scott's third anniversary began 'on the wagon' but they finished April 'tearing drunk'.[70]

In May they made two significant new friends: Esther Murphy and Tommy Hitchcock. Tommy, Zelda's age, from a wealthy upper-class family, attended the Fay School and St Paul's before Harvard. A military aviator awarded the *Croix de Guerre*, he became a celebrated polo player, idolized by Scott for the qualities he himself desired. Hitchcock became one of Scott's models for Tommy Barban in *Tender Is The Night*.[71]

Zelda found Esther Murphy more radical because she had broken away from her family's conventional Fifth Avenue leather-goods firm Mark Cross, worth two million dollars. They met through Edmund Wilson, who thought highly of Esther's literary talents, and Alex McKaig, who for a time wanted to marry her. Esther's circle included her brother Gerald, sister-in-law Sara and the Parisian lesbian feminist set dominated by writer Natalie Barney and painter Romaine Brooks, who would all play a significant part in the Fitzgeralds' lives.

In July to Zelda's delight Scottie began talking, and as Scottie developed Zelda found motherhood easier. Visitors swarmed the house: John Biggs, Scott's lawyer friend, and Max Perkins visited in May and July, Scott's Aunt Annabel and Don Ogden Stewart arrived in August.

Suddenly Scott forswore his role as Demon Lover. Zelda wrote sadly to Xandra: 'Scott has started a new novel and retired into strict seclusion and celibacy. He's horribly intent on it.'[72]

Left on her own, Zelda appreciated Montgomery visitors, who included Livye Hart's mother and Eleanor Browder in June, and Rosalind in July and August. Several visits were disasters. Eleanor was appalled by Gateway Drive notices that announced 'Visitors are requested not to break down doors in search of liquor, even when authorized to do so by the host and hostess.' When Mrs Hart invited Zelda and Scott to tea at New York's Astor Hotel, they arrived separately, too drunk to locate each other in the hotel lobby. Horrified, Mrs Hart forbade Livye, still at home in Montgomery, to visit Zelda.

Rosalind's visits were worse. The first involved a 'happening' comparable to that which had greeted the Sayres in Westport; the second a raucous overnight party which Scott refused to leave. When Zelda and Rosalind, thoroughly exasperated, left without him, Zelda whispered: 'I never did want to marry Scott.'[73] Though Zelda did not explain or repeat the remark it was one her sister never forgot.

Montgomery visitors told Zelda that Sara Haardt had left her teaching post to return to Goucher as their youngest English instructor.[74] In July 1922 her 'Strictly Southern' sketches of Alabama folk were bought by Emily Clark's *The Reviewer*, whose advisers were James Branch Cabell, Joseph Hergesheimer and Mencken. The following spring Sara met Mencken for the first time when he presented the prize for the Goucher Freshman short story contest, won by Sara Mayfield.

Mencken, about to give his lecture 'The Trade of Letters' to the '250 virgins' in the hall, suddenly spotted amongst the 'no less than 27 appetizing cuties'[75] the exquisite japonica-pale Sara Haardt. Instantly he changed his talk to 'How to Catch a Husband'. Then he asked Sara Haardt to chaperone young Sara Mayfield (usually called Little Sara) for dinner with him.

Over dinner the Sage said diplomatically: 'Miss Haardt, didn't you send me a story for *The Smart Set* once?' Sara's diplomacy matched his: 'Yes, and you read it very promptly.' Mencken began their seven-year courtship: 'As I recall, I found it most impressive. Unfortunately it didn't fit our needs just then. Send me some more stories and mark them for my personal attention.' Their conversation turned to Zelda: 'What a girl!' Mencken said. 'Cleverer than Scott, if the truth were known.'

The following day Sara Haardt showed Little Sara Mencken's *In*

Defense of Women, which she found brazenly anti-women. Despite this, Sara Haardt was soon lunching with Mencken.[76]

Unlike the Fitzgeralds, Haardt and Mencken were each cynical about love and marriage. Mencken defined love as 'the delusion that one woman differs from another' while Sara said: 'I would advise any woman to wait. There is so much in life — so much for a woman to see and do . . . marriage is a career, but it isn't life, it isn't everything.'[77]

Nevertheless stumpy dishevelled middle-aged Mencken and young reticent Sara were soon a familiar sight in Baltimore's bars. That October Mencken bought Sara's first story for *The Smart Set*.[78]

One month later Zelda finished *her* first serious story. She wrote the bulk of 'Our Own Movie Queen'; Scott added the climax and revised it. Its satirical underlying message is that Hollywood stardom does not require brains or talent. Zelda's heroine Gracie Axelrod was the daughter of a disreputable Swede, 'the sole owner of a tumbledown shanty where fried chicken of dubious antecedents might be washed down by cold beer.' Gracie's talent was she 'fried the chicken with such brown art that complaints were unknown'. Zelda's talent was to show with wit, metaphors and intellectual bite that a nonentity in that society could rise to become the city's movie queen.[79]

Though written in November 1923 the story was not published in the *Chicago Sunday Tribune* until 1925, when it won two stars in O'Brien's short story collection. Zelda however received no credit at all. Her story was published under Scott's name and Scott received $1,000, minus 10 per cent, which he shared with Zelda.

At the time Zelda made no comment but after publication she scored out Scott's solo by-line and wrote in heavy black print 'ZELDA'.[80]

Both Sara Haardt's and Zelda's stories were clever: the difference was not in their fiction but in their identity as writers. Sara's serious work had been bought by a leading critic. Zelda's work was still being produced under Scott's by-line.

Zelda, Sara Haardt, Sara Mayfield and Tallulah Bankhead were products of a youthful upper-middle class that had 'fermented since 1900 [and] exploded with passionate fervour during the 1920s'.[81] Though Mayfield saw them as rebels born in a smug time and an ultraconservative place in which revolt was long overdue,[82] Zelda's three contemporaries were already practising the disciplines of their trade which would shape their rebellion while Zelda was not.

Scott's Ledger noted his writing assistance to Zelda but he did not

keep a similar record of Zelda's assistance to him. This was doubt-
less due to their respective positions as professional and amateur.
Professionals record and often charge for the help they give.
Amateurs don't.[83]

He used Zelda as a model, trusted her editorial skills, leant on her
literary judgements and confessed he should stop 'referring everything to Zelda – a terrible habit; nothing ought to be referred to
anybody until it's finished'.[84]

They were again $5,000 in debt, so Scott hibernated all winter in
a chill room over the garage until he had produced eleven stories
which netted him $17,000, enough to pay his debts and return to the
novel.

By Christmas 1923 Sara Mayfield, in Montgomery, told Zelda that
Sara Haardt had succumbed to the first of her serious illnesses; for
months she would write little. The Fitzgeralds spent Christmas Day
with Esther Murphy, Gilbert Seldes, Dos Passos and Mary and
Edmund Wilson. Bunny wrote to Bishop: 'I like Zelda better and
better every year and they are among the only people now that I am
always glad to see.'[85] He spoke for most of the Fitzgeralds' friends
when he said: 'the lively imaginations and entertainment value of
Scott and Zelda preserved them through a certain amount of trouble
making.'[86]

But Scott, tired of his friends, wrote: 'The most miserable year
since I was 19, full of terrible failures and acute miseries.'[87] By April
1924, exhausted with drink and debt, they rented their house and
sailed for France, where they felt they could live more cheaply and
have better adventures.[88]

PART III

Foreign Voices
May 1924–December 1926

CHAPTER 9

'Paris was where the twentieth century was,' Gertrude Stein assured the world.[1] In May 1924 the Fitzgeralds arrived to take their place there with seventeen pieces of luggage and $7,000. The luggage would last longer. Zelda reported to Maxwell Perkins that their boat journey was 'a weird trip haunted by such tunes as "Horsey, keep your tail up . . ." played by an aboriginal English orchestra'.[2]

In Paris Lawton Campbell spotted Zelda racing down the Champs-Elysées like a streak of sunshine while Scott strolled sedately holding a silver-topped cane. 'They were so smartly dressed and striking . . . They were beautiful.' Zelda, who matched the pure spring sky in a bright blue frock she had designed, ran towards him: 'This, Lawton, is my Jeanne d'Arc dress.'[3]

Renewing old friendships was important to the Fitzgeralds. They lunched in the Bois with John and Margaret Bishop, last seen two years earlier. Scott wrote to Wilson that 'John seemed to us a beaten man – with his tiny frail mustache – but perhaps only morally.' As Scott was self-confessedly 'drunk and voluble' his judgements may not have been entirely reliable.[4]

Scott planned to finish *The Great Gatsby* while Zelda aimed to lead a more orderly life. But within days disorder set in. At the Hôtel des Deux Mondes they mistakenly bathed Scottie in the bidet, noticed too late in a restaurant that Scottie had drunk gin fizz instead of lemonade, and finally decided wisdom lay in nannies. They chose Lillian Maddock, English, upright, able to render the Fitzgeralds' chaos into military precision. They also hired a cook and a maid and began their onslaught on the $7,000.[5]

Though Zelda proudly wrote to Max that in Paris they were a 'complete success – found a good nurse and resisted the varied temptations that beset our path,'[6] the new nanny's dominant nature, like Anna Shirley's, distressed her. If Zelda intervened Maddock, whom Zelda called the 'old buzzard', complained to

Scott. Probably that year, Zelda drafted her bitter story 'Nanny, A British Nurse', set in Paris and the Riviera. Two themes from Zelda's painful experience stand out: first, the malevolence of servants who insinuate themselves into, then take over households; second, the notion that compromise lies at the heart of a 'good' American marriage. Zelda also drafted a play version, on which is a note explaining that all is well until Nanny 'manoeuvres' people into 'disturbed matrimony'. With her perfect nose for scandal, Nanny knows that in a troubled household she will have control. She tells another nurse how important it is not to allow their masters any responsibility. Sally, the victimized mother, says sardonically about her baby: 'Bless its little heart. Is its cruel, cruel, parent going to take away its Nanny? No darling, it shall never have to live with only its family to bring it up.'

Zelda's description of her fictional nurse 'doing whatever it is that nurses do which gives them such an official air'[7] wittily evokes her line about her fictional Scott in *Caesar's Things*: 'Jacob went on doing whatever it was that Jacob did'[8] – a reminder that nannies, like husbands, have a more important role to play than mere wives and mothers.

That Zelda was still smarting several years later over the behaviour of Nanny Maddock and the nurses who preceded her is clear from her account in *Save Me The Waltz*, where David patronizingly suggests Nanny should help Alabama with her household accounts.

In Paris during their nine-day stay Zelda met Esther Murphy's brother Gerald and his wife Sara, with whom she and Scott formed a lifelong friendship.[9] The Murphys at that time were living in a gracious old house in St-Cloud. When Esther introduced these two outwardly dissimilar couples, she could not have foreseen the extraordinary attraction they would hold for each other.

The Murphys found the Fitzgeralds' all-American freshness irresistible while the Fitzgeralds were intrigued by this stylish unconventional pair who balanced artistic adventures with mature family life. The Murphys' son Baoth was a sturdy blond five-year-old, little Patrick was three, and demure Honoria at six swiftly settled into her role as Scottie's older best friend. It was both a friendship of equals and a tie between children and parents. Gerald, twelve years older than Zelda, and Sara, seventeen years older, shone with good parenthood while Zelda and Scott, despite having a two-and-a-half-year-old, still sparkled with adolescent rebelliousness. Zelda, who later fictionalized Gerald as Corning in *Caesar's Things*, precisely captured Gerald's fatherly attitude: 'When he was being charming Corning floated around in a hushed blooming of impersonal parental solicitude.'[10]

Sara Murphy was one of three cultured, well-travelled Wiborg sisters, unconventional daughters of a rich Cincinnati ink manufacturer. Sara, Hoytie and Olga sang three-part harmony at recitals, were considered a sensation in Europe, were presented by Lady Diana Cooper at the Court of St James in 1914. 'That year the Wiborg girls were the rage of London,' wrote Lady Diana.[11] The following year Sara, who owned twenty-seven substantial acres in East Hampton, Long Island, and had a fortune of $200,000, married Yale graduate Gerald Murphy, wealthy son of the owner of the Mark Cross leather-goods company.[12] Gerald, who had already known Sara for eleven years, said she remained so original that 'I have no idea what she will do, say or propose.'[13]

Sara, like Gerald restricted by staid family pressures, disapproved of American materialism, so when he refused to enter his father's firm they decided to move to Paris. With independent means and three infants, they arrived in 1921 to study painting with Natalia Goncharova and Russian futurist Mikhail Larionov and to make an art of living.

They arrived in Paris at the point when the twentieth-century artistic revolution, emerging before the First World War, was exploding into new forms. Cubist force had given way to Dada's crazy inspirations and erotic Surrealism. Intellectuals had fallen for *le jazz hot*, popular movies and the circus. Diverse arts were excitingly linked to one another. The Murphys, who had taken as a motto the Spanish adage 'Living Well Is The Best Revenge', became a nexus for the Parisian cultural community. Scott said that to be included in their world was a remarkable experience, for the Murphys, who focused on their children as well as on the widest possible culture, stood apart from the bohemianism of Montparnasse Americans whose expatriate life had a determinedly self-conscious intellectual fever. They found anything 'Jamesian' stuffy, preferring to seek out experimental artists like Miró and Juan Gris. Their European intimates included the most prominent Modernist figures: artist Fernand Léger, the burly butcher's son from Normandy; poet Jean Cocteau; Georges Braque, Cubist, and Igor Stravinsky, creator of *Le Sacre du Printemps* for Diaghilev's Ballets Russes, whom the Murphys had met through their scenic designs for Diaghilev's company. Picasso was a good friend, with a particular affection for Sara whom he painted nude with her famous rope of pearls, which Scott later hung around his heroine Nicole Diver's neck. Scott hung the personality of Nicole on the twin characters of Sara and Zelda.

Sara described Paris as a great fair, where everybody was so young and 'you loved your friends and wanted to see them every day'.[14] Among the friends they *did* see regularly were three writers already in the Fitzgeralds' circle, Dorothy Parker, Alexander Woollcott and Robert Benchley, as well as poet Archibald MacLeish and soprano Ada MacLeish, his wife, who had arrived in Paris in 1923.[15] Through the Murphys the Fitzgeralds met Broadway playwright Philip Barry, who had just made a splash with his comedy *You and I*, his elegant wife Ellen, whose father had given them a villa on the Riviera, the young journalist-writer Ernest Hemingway and his wife Hadley, and songwriter Cole Porter, formerly at Yale with Gerald, with whom he now had an intense emotional bond. Gertrude Stein reputedly called this circle the 'lost generation'[16] but once Scott got to know them he more accurately saw them as a generation *found* and *embraced* by the remarkable Murphys, whose money and encouragement enabled artists to transform twentieth-century culture.

Gerald, generous to every person he called his friend, was matched by Sara, whose serene beauty, described by MacLeish as 'like a bowl of Renoir flowers',[17] was rooted in deep concern for people.

The Fitzgeralds' friends Donald Ogden Stewart, the humorist, and Gilbert Seldes, critic and editor of *The Dial* who had come to Paris to write a book,[18] had both met the Murphys in 1923. Stewart, a Yale graduate like Barry, Porter and Murphy, unlike them felt an outsider, so was dazzled by the Murphys' glow. 'Once upon a time there was a prince and princess,' he wrote, '. . . they were both rich; he was handsome; she was beautiful; they had three golden children. They loved each other . . . they had the gift of making life enchantingly pleasurable for . . . their friends.'[19] Understandably Stewart was keen that the Fitzgeralds and Dos Passos should meet them.[20]

Dos Passos was initially as wary of them as he had been of Zelda and Scott. Typically, they were giving a party for Diaghilev's entire cast. Though Sara 'was obviously a darling' Dos Passos's first view of Gerald, 'Irish as they come', was that of a dandified dresser, cold, brisk and preoccupied.[21] 'There was a sort of film over him I couldn't penetrate.' Dos Passos, who had been hanging around the Left Bank with a rough press crowd led by Hemingway[22] after serving in France as a wartime ambulance driver, now peered ner-vously at the Murphys' lifestyle through his thick spectacles, then slunk off, prickly as a porcupine. But he was won over by Sara's knack for arranging food, furniture and people's lives for the better.[23]

His second impression of Gerald, on a long walk with him and the painter Fernand Léger, was positive. Gerald, who would be Zelda's first artistic influence, had studied with Léger and had already embarked on huge Cubist paintings of machinery. Dos Passos said Gerald's comments changed the hackneyed pastel-tinted Tuileries and the Seine's *bateaux mouches* into a freshly invented world of winches, anchor flukes and startling red towboat funnels.[24]

When Zelda met Gerald, she immediately shared Dos Passos's view that Gerald's mind had an 'uncommitted freshness'.[25] Though she believed 'people were always their best selves with the Murphys'[26] she gently mocked Gerald's emotional need for his friends to behave well and love each other, seeing it as a storybook imperative: 'Corning [Gerald] said "I want all these people to love one another because I love all of them" . . . and the guests obediently loved him.'[27] Zelda was particularly fascinated by the life of origi-nality and beauty the Murphys had created while Scott, sometimes baffled by it, found his admiration for Gerald tinged with envy. Gerald saw their relationship with the Fitzgeralds as mystical and symbiotic. 'We four communicate by our presence rather than by any means,' he said later. 'Currents race between us regardless: Scott will uncover for me values in Sara, just as Sara has known them in Zelda through her affection for Scott.'[28]

The Murphys had a special fondness for Zelda. They were first struck by her eyes. Gerald said of Zelda's illegitimate beauty: 'It was all in her eyes. They were strange eyes, brooding but not sad, severe, almost masculine in their directness.'[29] Sara added: 'Zelda could be spooky. She seemed sometimes to be lying in ambush waiting for you with those Indian eyes of hers.'[30] They respected Zelda's 'own personal style . . . her individuality, her flair . . . her taste was never what one would speak of as à la mode – it was better, it was her own . . . I don't think we could have taken Scott alone.'[31] Scott's drinking behaviour together with his schoolboy antics put them off and mini-mized their belief in him as a serious writer, an accolade they reserved for Hemingway.

Sara, Zelda's most affectionate supporter, recognized her as a similar 'cat who walked alone' and understood Zelda's central contradiction: that she was both intensely private and publicly out-rageous. But even to Sara, highly sensitive to nuance, Zelda remained a mystery. In a letter to Scott, Sara suggested that Zelda probably had 'terribly dangerous secret thoughts'.[32]

Zelda understood Gerald's quicksilver disposition, sometimes unabashedly friendly, other times withdrawing into a black Celtic mood, for it mirrored her own.

Whereas Zelda's friendship with Xandra Kalman had been based on shared sports and her reliance on Xandra for practical help, her friendship with Sara was rooted in a mutual interest in painting, ballet and literature. Sara was one of the first people to take seriously Zelda's creative potential.

Through the Murphys Zelda became conversant with the experimental Parisian art scene. In 1944 she wrote to Scottie recalling her exposure to the theories of the art world's most provocative figures, who included Miró, Gris, Matisse, Léon Bakst and Picasso:

> We knew Picasso (a dear friend of Gerald Murphy) . . . Léger – whom we met at the Murphys in Austria – and other modern geniuses whom we met at Gertrude Stein's left-bank salon. They were interesting and sympathetic and indeed I have never known a painter whose intuitive responsivity was not acute and immediate & I liked them very much. We also knew Brancusi & have visited his studio in the rue Monsieur with great wonderment and awe.[33]

This constant exposure constituted Zelda's earliest if most informal training. Without Gerald's artistic influence, it is less likely that she would have taken her first formal painting lessons a few months later.[34]

That spring the Riviera was on everybody's mind. Cole Porter drew Gerald's attention to the lushness of the Riviera off-season, so the Murphys planned to return that summer to Antibes, a few kilometres away from Ellen and Philip Barry's new house along the Corniche in Cannes. They knew the beaches would please Zelda while its remote tranquillity would attract Scott, so the two families decided to meet there. Gerald planned to clear away the seaweed on the small beach, Plage de la Garoupe, that 'bright tan prayer rug' which would become one of the most famous beaches in American literature.[35] During the summer the Murphys bought a plot on which stood a tumbledown villa with a spectacular garden. They used 350,000 francs, a quarter of Sara's annual income, and hired two Ohio architects to remodel the house into what would become the Villa America, immortalized in Fitzgerald literature.[36]

At the end of May the Fitzgeralds left for the Riviera, pausing at

Grimms Park Hotel, Hyères. From there Zelda wrote to Perkins that Scott was showing 'the most romantic proclivities' and they hoped to find a villa next week. Hyères had 'a forced atmosphere of pictur-esqueness and beauty for English sketchers'. Zelda's own artistic preference was for the vivid, even vulgar: 'I always suspect any place that isn't blatant – Venice, to me, is perfect.'[37]

They moved on to the Ruhl in Nice, where Zelda wrote that during dinner on the terrace stars fell in their plates; then the Hôtel de Paris, Monte Carlo, 'like a palace in a detective story';[38] then lin-gered at the Continental in St Raphaël to be near the Murphys at the Hôtel du Cap at Cap d'Antibes, awaiting renovations on Villa America. Finally the Fitzgeralds stopped whirling and settled in Villa Marie in Valescure, 2.5 kilometres above St Raphaël.

High above the sun-drenched beach the villa stood like a Moorish fortress with terraced gardens of palm, lemon and olive trees, pro-tected from the sun by groves of eucalyptus and parasol pines. Zelda recalled: 'Keeps crumbled on the grey hillsides and sowed the dust of their battlements beneath the olives and cactus. Ancient moats slept bound in tangled honeysuckle; fragile poppies bled the causeways.'[39]

Unlike New York where most of their friends were single, on the Riviera most were married. Among their frequent companions were Philip and Ellen Barry, Dick and Alice Lee Myers, and later that summer, Gilbert and Amanda Seldes. The Myers' daughter Fanny became the third in Scottie and Honoria's triumvirate. Alice, ex-nurse and Chicago graduate, had married Dick in 1921. Humorous, bear-like Dick had studied piano with Nadia Boulanger and com-posed songs while working for American Express in Paris. Zelda had an easy intimacy with the Myers who felt parental towards Scottie. One time Scott flirtatiously gave Alice an enlarged edition of Marie Stopes' *Contraception* wittily inscribed: 'I felt you should have this. So that Dick should never have an awful surprise – he is too nice a fellow. Yours in Sin, but, I hope, *sincere* sin. F. Scott Fitzgerald.'[40]

The Fitzgeralds, lacking French, lived like tourists who neither took part in the community nor visited churches or museums; but during the summer Zelda bought a French dictionary and a copy of Raymond Radiguet's *Le Bal du Comte d'Orgel* to learn the language by painstakingly reading the novel. During the long hours when Scott was rewriting *Gatsby*, Zelda read Henry James, and Van Vechten's latest book, *The Tattooed Countess*. When her eyes bothered her again she reverted to swimming, becoming as deeply tanned as in her Southern girlhood. She also became restless. The servants managed the villa (while padding the grocery bills), so she had no domestic chores.

Scottie remembers Nanny Maddock, who instilled in her discipline and manners. She was made to observe bedtimes and eat up everything on her plate.[41] Zelda's relationship with Maddock, as with Anna Shirley, made her feel increasingly incompetent at motherhood. When Scott locked himself away to write Zelda felt in need of company.

Stationed nearby at Fréjus air base were a group of young Frenchmen with whom the Fitzgeralds drank and danced in the beach casino. Several make it into Scott's Ledger and Zelda's novels. Aviators Paulette, Montague, 'fat and greasy Bellandeau' get passing mentions. René Silvy (Zelda's 'artistic son of a Provençal *avocat*', Scott's Silve[42]) and Bobbé (Zelda's fictionalized Bobbie, Scott's Bobby Croirier[43]) are described with luscious camp undertones by Zelda as 'very nice boys' who 'protruded insistently from their white beach clothes and talked in undertones of Arthur Rimbaud . . . [René's] eyes were . . . consumed by the cold fire of a Tintoretto boy.'[44]

One man makes it into the Fitzgeralds' lives. Edouard Jozan, 'the flying officer who looked like a Greek god',[45] becomes the catalyst for a major crisis in the Fitzgeralds' marriage.

Zelda, flattered when, like the aviators of Taylor Field, he swoops low over their villa as a tribute to her, casually lazes on the beach with him. There are occasional cocktails and dinners. Jozan found Scott and Zelda 'brimming over with life. Rich and free, they brought into our little provincial circle brilliance, imagination and familiarity with a Parisian and international world to which we had no access.'[46] At first Scott admired Jozan, who as an athletic assured aviator had all the qualities he most envied.

Zelda glamorizes Jozan in *Save Me The Waltz* as Jacques Chevre-Feuille (honeysuckle), but curiously in *Caesar's Things*, though he features as Jacques, occasionally she misnames him as Jacob, her Scott figure. Is there some indissoluble link between the two men? Certainly Alabama in *Save Me The Waltz* sees Jacques as a coin (the lieutenant with 'the head of the gold of a Christmas coin') and David as its reverse side. She tells David that Jacques looks 'like you – except he is full of sun, whereas you are a moon person'. Jacques 'moved his sparse body with the tempestuous spontaneity of a leader'.[47]

According to Sara Mayfield Jozan *was* a born leader coming from a tradition of bravery, honour and nobility.[48] Born at Nîmes, a year and two days older than Zelda, the son of a French army officer, a graduate from Brest's naval college, when he met Zelda he was about to embark on a distinguished career.

Jozan saw Scott as a proud domineering man, sometimes tender, sometimes cruel, who appeared more concerned with commercial than artistic success, despite talent and imagination.[49] Scott's focus on social status and the power and burden of money clashed with Jozan's ideal of human bravery and knowledge unsullied by commercial profit.[50]

About Zelda he had few reservations. He found her vivacious, witty, lovely, someone who said and did unexpected things. But he insisted he never saw signs of craziness. Those who had 'wild ideas' about her were themselves 'raving mad'.[51] He saw her 'shining beauty', a woman who 'overflowed with activity, radiant with desire to take from life every chance her charm, youth and intelligence provided so abundantly'. Jozan thought Zelda liked simple pleasures, 'the relaxed life on beaches . . . trips by car, informal dinners'.[52] The pair began to enjoy those pleasures away from the crowd.

Immersed in writing, Scott did not at first observe his wife and Jozan[53] drifting closer. Others did. The Murphys, in Valescure from Antibes for the day, noticed the romance, but did not think it serious. Sara felt from her talks with Zelda that she resented having 'to chase around after Scott'. Jozan became 'someone for her to talk to . . . everyone knew about it but Scott'. Gerald said: 'I don't know how far it really went, I suspect it wasn't much, but it did upset Scott a good deal. I wonder whether it wasn't partly his fault?'[54]

Then suddenly Jozan and Zelda were no longer seen together. Their friends were not told why. When Zelda returned to the beach she swam alone.[55] According to Fitzgerald's Ledger there was 'The Big Crisis – 13th of July', less than six weeks since they had met the French group. Those are the only *facts* we have. But so much speculation and fiction are woven into the legend that it is difficult to tell how serious their relationship became.

That Zelda was increasingly attracted to him is clear in both her novels. In *Save Me The Waltz*, when Jacques and Alabama dance he 'smelled of sand and sun; she felt him naked beneath the starched linen. She didn't think of David. She hoped he hadn't seen; she didn't care.' Jacques invites her to his apartment. Alabama hesitates. David sulkily watches them swim together 'wet and smooth as two cats'.[56] He insists that Alabama stops seeing Jacques. Alabama asks a friend to tell Jacques she cannot meet him. She doesn't see him again. An aviator's wife gives her a picture from Jacques and a letter in French. Unable to read it, 'she tore it in a hundred little pieces . . . Though it broke her heart, she tore the picture . . . What was the use of keeping it? Jacques Chevre-Feuille had gone to China. There wasn't a way to hold on to the summer . . . Whatever it was that she wanted from Jacques, Jacques took it with him . . . You took what you wanted from life, if you could get it, and you did without the rest.'[57]

In *Caesar's Things*, sixteen years later, she goes further fictionally. Janno kisses Jacques, then one evening 'they kissed again – a long time before his friends . . . Janno loved him so that she never questioned his good faith.' Another night after dancing with him 'she kissed Jacques on the neck . . . the kiss lasted a long time . . . she did not mean to do this'. The young officer 'treated her preciously and she knew that no matter what it was it would be tragedy and death: ruin is a relative matter'. Janno recognizes 'she should never have kissed him. First she should never have kissed Jacques; then she shouldn't have kissed her husband; then after the kissing had become spiritual vivisection and half-masochistic there should not have been any more.'[58]

Whatever happened between his wife and Jozan, after recording the 'Big Crisis' in July Scott makes light of it. He runs to 'a sad trip to Monte Carlo' but otherwise there are merely routine notes that Zelda was 'swimming every day. Getting brown'; that they went to Antibes, there was 'good work on novel', followed by 'Zelda and I close together'. The only unpleasant things listed are 'rows with Miss Maddox [sic]'.[59]

In August 1924 when their friend Gilbert Seldes and his bride Amanda arrived on their honeymoon they noticed no marital discord, observing only that Scott was sad over the death of his hero Conrad. Then they noticed Zelda had a frightening new habit. When Scott drove them all to the beach, at exactly the point where the road narrowed and curved dangerously on a hairpin bend, Zelda turned to Scott and asked for a cigarette. Scott took one hand off the steering wheel, rummaged in his pocket, found one, straightened out the Renault and just kept it from plunging over the roadside. Zelda, filled with repressed anger, may have been cruelly testing Scott's courage.

The Murphys witnessed other dangerous exploits. The Fitzgeralds would leave parties and go to Eden Roc at the tip of Cap d'Antibes, where Zelda would strip off her evening frock and dive from 35-foot rocks. Sara told Zelda it was dangerous. Zelda fixed her friend with what Gerald called her 'unflinching gaze like an Indian's'[60] and said, 'But Say-ra, didn't you know? We don't believe in conservation.'[61] On those evenings Sara persuaded Zelda and Scott not to drive back to Valescure, but to stay over at the Hôtel du Cap.

Whatever had taken place between Jozan and the Fitzgeralds now diminished. Scott wrote 'trouble clearing away' in September, and in October with gratitude, 'Last sight of Josanne'. Yet the maze of fantasy around this episode has resulted in several wild versions.

According to one, years later Scott told a relative that Zelda had asked him for a divorce in July, saying she loved Jozan. Scott furiously insisted on a face-to-face showdown with Jozan. When Jozan refused, Scott locked Zelda in the villa. Jozan, faced with this version of events, insisted that no such confrontation took place, nor did he know of any such punishment.[62]

There is no mention of Zelda's imprisonment in her *Save Me The Waltz*, but we cannot draw a firm inference from its apparent omission since Scott insisted on heavy revisions and deletions of autobiographical material which might have cast him in a bad light. However, in 1930 Zelda told her doctor she *was* locked in her room. It is of course possible that by the 1930s Zelda had come to believe Scott's invention.

Certainly, in *Caesar's Things*, she validates Scott's version: Janno 'told her husband that she loved the French officer and her husband locked her up in the villa'. Jacob tells her not to leave the premises and Janno replies wearily, 'a locked door is not difficult of comprehension'.[63]

When Scott later described the incident to his mistress Sheilah Graham, he said he had challenged Jozan to a duel. Each had fired a shot but remained uninjured. Graham felt that the story sounded like material from a book, which indeed it was. Scott rewrote the episode for an illicit love affair and duel in *Tender Is The Night*.[64]

Jozan himself went even further than denying the divorce confrontation: he emphatically denied having an affair with Zelda. He told Sara Mayfield firmly that Zelda had merely flirted with him to make Scott jealous, and that Zelda's account of their romance in *Save Me The Waltz* was an almost exact report of what happened in St Raphaël – a mere summer flirtation, romantic, decorous and slightly comic.[65]

He also told Nancy Milford that he was at no time involved in any scenes between the Fitzgeralds. He was unaware that Zelda was being forced to make choices, if indeed she was. He left the Riviera without knowing what had passed between Zelda and Scott. He never saw either of them again. 'They both had a need of drama, they made it up and perhaps they were the victims of their own unsettled and a little unhealthy imagination.'[66]

This seems the most accurate analysis. The forgotten tale of the fallen Montgomery aviator who had died for love of Zelda was revived once more with a Riviera setting. It provided both Fitzgeralds with fictional material, heightening their anecdotal performances.

Hemingway recalls Scott telling several versions. The first version Hemingway recalled was a genuinely moving story of Zelda falling in love with a French aviator. The later versions, according to Hemingway, were less sad and seemed to be created as useful fictional material. Hemingway's first wife Hadley, a more unbiased source with reference to Zelda, recalls their duo-performance: 'It was one of their acts. I remember Zelda's beautiful face becoming very, very solemn, and she would say how he had loved her and how hopeless it had been and then how he had committed suicide. Scott would stand next to her looking very pale and distressed and sharing every minute of it.'[67]

Sara Mayfield described this alleged suicide as 'an absurd invention'. The tragic hero stood before her in the flesh, explaining that far from dying, he had held a long distinguished career in the French Navy; served in Indochina in his youth; commanded a flotilla at Dunkirk after the outbreak of World War Two; subsequently had been captured and interned by the Germans. On release he had returned to service, in 1952 becoming Vice Admiral of the French fleet in command of France's Far East naval forces. Far from collapsing into suicidal depression due to his failed romance he had been awarded the Croix de Guerre, the Grand Croix du Mérite de l'Ordre de Malte, the Grand Croix de la Légion d'Honneur, and had retired in 1960 as full Admiral to live splendidly in Paris, where he read the Fitzgeralds' fabrications about his lost youth.[68]

The reason why Scott fictionalized and heightened the romance to include these fabrications was that he was then able to share it, thus once more take over an important piece of Zelda's life. That she allowed him to do so illustrates her intense emotional dependency on him. As she says later: 'Then Janno grew indomitably loyal and devoted to Jacob . . . Jacob somehow was the center of the whole business.'[69]

Though Scott recovered from the blow to his ego and Zelda from the blow to her heart by using the incident as material, neither of them ever recovered completely. The Murphys recalled, albeit forty years later, an alleged suicide attempt of Zelda's. Gerald said that around three or four o'clock one morning Scott banged at their door having driven miles. He was trembling, green and carrying a candle. He said Zelda had taken an overdose. They returned with him and Sara walked Zelda backwards and forwards to keep her awake.[70]

If this suicide attempt *did* happen that year it would have taken place at the point Scott wrote 'Zelda and I close together', and therefore would challenge the idea of reconciliation and reinterpret how deeply Zelda was affected. But whether it *did* take place in 1924 is open to question. Mayfield debunked as 'equally incredible' the idea that Scott had driven the 52 kilometres from St Raphaël before dawn to get help from the Murphys.[71] Amanda Vaill, the Murphys' biographer, tries to make sense of it by suggesting that the incident might have occurred on a night when the Fitzgeralds were actually staying at the hotel.[72] However, set against all such speculations is the fact that Scott himself does *not* mention Zelda taking an overdose that year in his Ledger. This biographer believes the Murphys may have misremembered the date, for it is the *following* August (1925) that Scott's Ledger entry says 'Zelda drugged'. Honoria Murphy in an interview with this author said it was not impossible that her father Gerald had got the year wrong because so many Fitzgerald anecdotes had been overlaid with newer versions and memories.[73]

It is quite possible that Scott was less affected by the Jozan incident than has been supposed. In his article 'How to Live on Practically Nothing a Year' written for the *Saturday Evening Post* during the crisis,[74] he writes amusingly about his family relaxing on the Riviera and concludes with a description of the visit of René and Bobbé to the villa. Scott dwells affectionately on their romantic white uniforms growing dimmer 'as the more the liquid dark comes down, until they . . . will seem to take an essential and indivisible part in the beauty of this proud gay land'. Although Scott doesn't mention Jozan, it is certainly *not* the description of an emotionally wrecked betrayed husband. Or if it is, then Scott's supremely professional style could be read as unnervingly cool.[75]

Few of Scott's biographers however seem willing to accept that the 'big affair' was nothing more than a summer flirtation. One, adamantly opposed to any such idea, assumes Zelda guilty of 'infidelity' with its 'agonizing aftermath'. He states that 'Jozan, using his French charm . . . invited Zelda to his apartment and seduced her.' He goes further and fantasizes that Jozan 'found Zelda a delightful lover'.[76] Bold and dramatic words but founded on sand. There is *no* concrete evidence that Zelda slept with Jozan. What we do know is that for the morbidly jealous Scott, who still had mixed-up Irish Catholic monogamous feelings for Zelda, the fact that she was entertaining a *desire* to commit adultery would be almost as much a sin as actually committing adultery. This is borne out in Zelda's *Caesar's Things* where Janno quotes from the Bible: '"He who looketh on a woman to lust after hath committed adultery with her in his heart already" – in his heart already – in his heart already –.' Janno says: 'Adultery was adultery and it would have been impossible for her to love two men at once, to give herself to simultaneous intimacies.'[77]

More significant is the fact that for the first time in their marriage Zelda seriously took away her attention from Scott. That he more often than not was focused on his writing and sometimes on other women was not the point. He expected her to focus on him and his work. To remove her attention could be more important than to remove her body. It was enough of a blow to an egotistic writer to make him write: 'That September 1924, I knew something had happened that could never be repaired.'[78]

In a later letter Zelda wrote to Scott: 'Then there was Josen and you were justifiably angry.'[79] She too misspelled her supposed lover's name. The fact that neither Scott nor Zelda ever managed to spell the name of the alleged adulterer was probably due to their poor literacy skills, but it would be a neat touch if it was also a psychological indication of their marital faithfulness.

The crisis behind them, they placidly renewed work on Scott's novel, telling Max: 'Zelda + I are contemplating a careful revision after a week's complete rest.'[80] On 25 October Scott told Ober that he was posting *The Great Gatsby* for serialization. Two days later he sent a copy to Max, writing: 'I think that at last I've done something really my own.' He wanted to call the novel *Trimalchio in West Egg* or *Gold-hatted Gatsby* or *The High-bouncing Lover* but Zelda plumped for *The Great Gatsby* and Scott took her advice.

Zelda, who had been reading Henry James's *Roderick Hudson*, decided they should winter in Rome followed by a trip to Capri. During 1924 she recognized that acting as Scott's editorial assistant was insufficient to satisfy her. Her Southern upbringing had led her initially towards the lure of an alternative lover; however, when this failed, the models of hardworking artists with whom they now associated finally struck a chord. By 1925 she would be published again, though not in her own name, and she would take her first painting lessons and her first ballet lessons.[81]

CHAPTER 10

Italy, during winter 1924 and spring 1925, proved damaging for Zelda's health but surprisingly beneficial for her awakening creative spirit. In November their first hotel, Rome's Quirinal, was rated fetid by Zelda: 'The sitting rooms are hermetically sealed and palms conceal the way to open the windows. Middle-aged English doze in the stale air.' Rome itself was a city of 'jonquils and beggars'.[1]

Her letter to Max Perkins acidly suggested that Roman ruins were better in France.[2] Her next note thanked him for sending Galsworthy's *The White Monkey*, then described Rome's comic-opera streets 'jammed with men in sky-blue cloaks with faces like dentists and under-nourished priests and students. I do think, since the Church largely rests on a theatrical basis, that they should cast their parts better.'[3] Her antipathy to Rome intensified as she fell ill. Abortions frequently impair the ability to conceive and this appears to have happened to Zelda. In late 1924 she had an operation to help her conceive. It infected her stomach and ovaries and damaged her reproductive organs. As she later sadly recalled: 'Dr Gros said there was no use trying to save my ovaries. I was always sick and having picqures [injections].'[4] After this operation Zelda was plagued with painful attacks of colitis throughout 1925. More important, there seemed little hope of more children.

There were other tensions. She and Scott had not resolved their difficulties following the Jozan conflict. Scott acknowledged in his November Ledger there was still 'ill feeling with Zelda', exacerbated by his nervous state following months of work on *Gatsby*. Zelda knew her advice would be expected at the proof stage. Though stimulated by being part of Scott's literary progress, she needed an independent *public* achievement separate from Scott – to recover the dynamic she had lost since leaving Alabama. This desire had acted as an undercurrent to the *private* Jozan romance. Now she felt more confident.

Zelda's 'confidence' was a complex issue. In Montgomery she did exactly what she wanted and was applauded for brains, beauty, physical prowess. She wrote her own lines and audiences loved them. In New York, Minnesota, Paris and on the Riviera, Scott wrote the script, she acted it. She played the arrogant flapper of his fiction, the famous author's proud wife. She still radiated assurance but Scott exuded authority.

If she was to achieve parity it must come from an area that deeply interested her. Honoria Murphy and Sara Mayfield always said Zelda had a lifelong passion for painting,[5] and Zelda's time in France with the Murphys, watching international artists design scenery for Diaghilev's Ballets Russes, mixing with Picasso, Braque and Léger, had increased her appreciation of some of the finest art forms then available. She knew Gerald had leapt from dilettante artist to professional painter. She knew Sara, who like herself had leisure and a nanny, had taken painting lessons from the Russian émigrée Natalia Goncharova, and Goncharova's strong shapes and flamboyant colours appealed to Zelda. Honoria Murphy believed her parents had a strong influence on Zelda's decision to formalize her interest in art.

The Fitzgeralds moved to the less fashionable Hôtel des Princes near Piazza di Spagna where, according to Zelda's article on hotel life, they lived on Bel Paese cheese and Corvo wine and suffered damp sheets.[6] For these privileges they paid $525 a month for full board for three, including wine and service. The $7,000 the Fitzgeralds had brought to France had gone before they moved to Rome, so Scott telegraphed Perkins for a $750 advance, making his debt to Scribner's $5,000.

Financial imperatives meant Scott speedily wrote more short stories while Zelda trawled the city. 'It was exciting being lost between centuries in the Roman dusk and taking your sense of direction from the Coliseum.'[7]

Before the *Gatsby* proofs arrived, Perkins wrote on 20 November praising the novel but suggesting Gatsby's character was 'somewhat vague'.[8] Scott acknowledged on 1 December that 'Zelda also thought I was a little out of key'.[9] On 20 December Scott admitted to Max that Gatsby was vague because he himself hadn't known what Gatsby looked like or was engaged in. Zelda, he said, had been instrumental in putting this right. 'After having had Zelda draw pictures until her fingers ache I know Gatsby better than I know my own child.'[10]

The subsequent rewriting exhausted Scott, so to calm him Zelda read aloud from Will James's novel *Cowboys North and South*.

'Zelda's been reading me the cowboy book aloud to spare my mind + I love it – tho I think he learned the American language from Ring rather than from his own ear.'[11] Ring Lardner's racy idioms were one of the characteristics which had endeared him to Zelda.

Despite Scott's reluctance to re-embark on 'short stories for money (I now get $2000.00 a story but I hate worse than hell to do them)'[12] he wrote the bulk of three new ones. 'Love in the Night', published in the *Saturday Evening Post* in March 1925, employed an exotic Riviera setting, a forerunner for the backdrop to *Tender Is The Night*. 'Not in the Guidebook' and 'The Adjuster', also stories of marital discord, reflected the aftermath of the Jozan incident.[13]

In 'Not in the Guidebook' the young, spoilt, moneyed wife, modelled on Zelda, has her inheritance stolen by her husband who deserts her in France. Charles Hemple, the hero of 'The Adjuster,' has a nervous breakdown attempting to please Louella, *his* spoilt discontented wife. Confronted with her invalided husband, Louella is given instructions by a mysterious Dr Moon which read like a lecture from Scott to Zelda. 'We make an agreement with children that they can sit in the audience without helping to make the play,' he said, 'but if they still sit in the audience after they're grown, somebody's got to work double time for them so that they can enjoy the light and glitter of the world.'[14] As Zelda read all Scott's fiction she would have absorbed the message.

While Zelda was still suffering severe abdominal pains, Scott caught influenza and his drinking escalated. One evening, exploring the nightlife with Zelda, he became embroiled in a drunken row with some cab drivers who demanded an extortionate 100 lire to take them home. Scott struck out and knocked down a plain-clothes police officer who intervened. His version, colourfully rewritten for *Tender Is The Night*, was that two *carabinieri* beat him up as they hustled him off to jail. Zelda, aided by $100 and the US Consulate, freed him the next day. She was accompanied by journalist Howard Coxe, a Princeton graduate who had become attentive towards her. Scott, slow to recover from illness and from his humiliation, resented Coxe's attentions towards Zelda.

Zelda had met Coxe when an American movie crew, filming *Ben Hur* in Rome, had invited the Fitzgeralds and several journalists to join the movie's social life. Scott's professional interest in Hollywood scriptwriting was aroused, as was his interest in the film's young star, Carmel Myers, daughter of a San Francisco rabbi. Scott openly flirted with Carmel, whose film career had started in 1916 as the protégée of D. W. Griffith and who subsequently starred as a vamp with Rudolph Valentino, Douglas Fairbanks and John Barrymore. Scott saw her immediately as 'the most exquisite thing I have met yet . . . as nice as she is beautiful', as he wrote about her later. Perhaps in retaliation, Zelda allowed Coxe his inconsequential but gallant gestures. At the movie company's Christmas Ball Zelda, feeling ill again, asked Coxe to take her home, but made her indifference clear. This rejection might account for Coxe's extraordinary gaffe in front of Scott in a bar. Scott, about to return to their hotel with a Christmas present for Scottie, heard Coxe boast to the assembled drinkers: 'I could sleep with Zelda any time I wanted to.' Still recovering from the Jozan incident, Scott was enraged. When Coxe told Wilson about it later, Wilson wrote reflectively: 'Afterward [Coxe] couldn't imagine what on earth had made him [say that], felt terribly about it . . . Actually – my own comment – Zelda was not so loose nor Howard so dangerous as this implied. He was envious of Scott . . . the drinks had brought this to the surface.'[15]

Scott's December 1924 Ledger reported before the movie party 'depression', after the movie party a 'row in café', an 'Xmas row' and a 'reconciliation' followed by a period on the water wagon in order to be sober for revising the *Gatsby* proofs.

This Christmas, always a significant celebration for them, they had a glittering tree in their hotel room hung with silver bells.[16] But they expected too much from Christmas, tried too hard, drank too much, destroyed their festivities.

In January 1925 Scott as well as Zelda was sick but despite his influenza he managed the final revisions to *Gatsby* which would be published in April. He had already converted a discarded portion of *Gatsby*'s opening into 'Absolution', a story which dealt sensitively with the sensuous experiences of an imaginative boy, Rudolph Miller, who lies in the confessional to Father Schwartz, an ageing priest, who then faces his own sexual temptations.[17]

'Absolution' had been published the previous June by Mencken and Nathan in their newly founded *American Mercury*. Sara Haardt, who had accompanied Mencken to the launch party after her recovery from pleurisy and bronchitis,[18] was suddenly taken seriously ill with tuberculosis. While Zelda battled with ovarian attacks, Sara was forced to give up her doctorate and spend most of 1924 isolated in Baltimore's Maple Heights Sanitarium. Her illness served to increase Mencken's devotion and when Peyton Mathis, one of the Gold Dust Twins, returned enthusiastically to wooing Sara, Mencken competitively stepped up his courtship. Romantic feelings had not stopped Mencken earlier from rejecting Sara's story,

'Miss Rebecca', for *The Smart Set* on the 'dubious ground' that it dealt with old maids. Editors, he said, were tired of old maids and their moonings. However one prestigious female editor, Emily Clark, immediately accepted it for *The Reviewer*.[19] Mencken and other male critics at that time had a specific analytical approach to good fiction which favoured writers like Scott and penalized writers like Sara and Zelda. To meet standards of Northern male literary gurus, fiction had to be simultaneously a psalm and a criticism of life. Zelda and Sara with their shared Southern background wrote fiction that more often probed Southern passions and resentments through description and surface tracings; that revealed convoluted emotional relationships through appearances rather than through analysis.

During summer 1925 both Zelda and Sara had work published. In June, Zelda's 'Our Own Movie Queen' (written in November 1923) appeared in the *Chicago Sunday Tribune*. In September, Mencken *did* publish Sara's 'Alabama' and *did* accept her story 'Mendelian Dominant' for the *American Mercury*, both written whilst she was very ill in Montgomery. Yet again Sara's work appeared under her own name. Yet again Zelda's appeared under her husband's name.

During 1924, nineteen-year-old Sara Mayfield married the other Gold Dust Twin, John Sellers. Zelda's attitude towards Sellers, curiously in view of his abusive behaviour, had a fierce push-and-pull intensity. She never entirely lost interest in Sellers. When she met young Sara in Paris a few years later her first question was: 'What's going on at home? Tell me about John Sellers.' Sara explained that in 1924 she hadn't known that Sellers, like Scott, drank heavily. 'I married him – in the time of my innocence . . . and divorced him when I came of age.'[20] In 1924 Sara's innocence shielded her from the problem of Sellers' drinking while Zelda, no longer innocent, daily faced Scott's alcoholism.

Scott's drinking and Zelda's fragile health caused winter in the Holy City to turn sour. In January 1925 they took excursions to Tivoli, Frascati and Naples, then in February, with Zelda still sick,[21] they decided to flee to sunny Capri. They took a suite in the Tiberio Palace high on a hill overlooking the sea. The sun shone, their hopes were high, but frequent rows spoilt much of their two months' stay. Scott wrote to Bishop:

Zelda and I sometimes indulge in terrible four-day rows that always start with a drinking party but we're still enormously in love and about the only truly happily married couple I know . . . The cheerfulest things in my life are first Zelda and second the hope that my book has something extraordinary about it. I want to be extravagantly admired again.[22]

After five weeks in bed with her abdominal infection, Zelda recovered and began daily climbs up to the 'scalloped . . . high white hotel' through 'devious dark alleys that house[d] the island's Rembrandt butcher shops and bakeries'.[23] Her solitary walks were broken by Scott's Aunt Annabel, who arrived in Capri to spend time with them.[24]

Scott finally met his former literary idol Compton Mackenzie, whose influence on his work according to Wilson 'can't be over-estimated' and whose influence on Zelda's style, also according to Wilson, was considerable.[25] Scott told Bishop that the author of the much-admired *Sinister Street* was merely polite, handsome and pleasantly monotonous. Scott felt Mackenzie had been wrecked by the war in the way Wells had been. Yet Mackenzie appeared not to be aware his work had degenerated.

Mackenzie introduced the Fitzgeralds to Norman Douglas, E. F. Benson, Somerset Maugham and his friend John Ellingham Brooks, all prominent among Capri's thriving colony of literary homosexuals.[26] Scott, not having known of the circle's existence, felt his habitual curiosity and escalating repulsion towards the men.[27] 'This place is full of fairies,' he complained to Max Perkins.[28] Scott's tedious tallying of 'fairies' and his increasing voyeuristic interest in their sexual habits is at odds with the fact that he was often outrageously camp in his own letters to Bunny Wilson.[29] The previous year Scott had written to Bunny: 'I long to go with a young man . . . for a paid amorous weekend to the coast . . . Deep calling to deep.'[30] Nor was this a new habit, for when Wilson was serving in France during World War One, Scott had sent him some glossy photos of himself labelled: 'Give one to some poor motherless Poilu fairy who has no dream.'[31] Scott's contradictory feelings about homosexuality would soon intrude on his relationship with Zelda.

It was on Capri that Zelda first met forty-four-year-old Romaine Brooks, the wealthy, talented painter, who had just finished her affair with pianist Renata Borgatti. Romaine and American novelist Natalie Barney, her lifelong friend and often lover, were at the centre of the prominent artistic intellectual élite who became Zelda's friends. The group, who wrote and painted on Capri, also met regularly in Paris at Barney's rue Jacob salon.

Amidst Capri's breathtaking scenery, while Scott drank, Zelda drew. Infused by the creative stimuli of other artists, in February 1925 she took her first formal painting lessons. In March Scott notes in his Ledger 'Zelda's lessons'. In April he records 'Zelda painting, me drinking.' After five weeks she had learnt colour theory.[32] It is likely that before she left Paris Gerald Murphy, who acted as Zelda's informal painting mentor, suggested she begin instruction, although it is not known how many lessons she took or with whom. The art critic Carolyn Shafer thought it possible that Zelda had more than one tutor and that Romaine Brooks might have suggested a second instructor. Shafer also thought Dos Passos and Ogden Stewart, both painters themselves, might have helped Zelda to make a formal start on her painting.[33] Evidence relating to the obsessive feverish quality with which she worked at any art makes it almost certain that she painted daily.[34]

None of Zelda's Capri paintings are known to survive but several oils on canvas provide substantial hints of the work inspired by Capri and the Riviera. Shafer suggests Capri's tropical vegetation, dramatic vistas and colourful characters could have produced images similar to Zelda's undated vivid blue and orange *Mediterranean Midi*.[35] This painting depicts a typical Murphy picnic on a stretch of tan sand beneath a startling blue sky marked by wispy white clouds. In the top right corner a vivid orange beach canopy juts out. In the bottom left corner a still life of fresh fruit and wine goblets sits on a white blanket under a massive tree which stretches up the left side of the canvas. The giant trunk has the muscularity which from early on Zelda used for her figures' knotted legs and arms. For her still life, canopy and tree Zelda adopts the Parisian Cubist technique of fracturing then reassembling forms and surfaces from different angles so that even her modest Mediterranean beach scene jolts and surprises the viewer.[36]

An undue emphasis has been placed on the influence on Zelda's art of the Parisian Modernists she knew personally, mainly because she *did* know them personally.[37] In fact, the more she painted the fewer links there are between their work and hers, but initially she would have picked up two distinct styles from Picasso, who in Paris in the Twenties was still creating multiple perspectives that challenged the idea of coherent space. One style affected the way Zelda ordered pictorial space; the other style helped her to shape figures which occupied that space. Zelda also adapted the lustrous energy and colours which Picasso and his artist colleague Mikhail Larionov used for the sets and costumes Picasso designed for Diaghilev's Ballets Russes, in which his first wife Olga was a '*deuxième ballerina*'.[38]

On Capri Zelda probably began her first formal flower paintings which became one of two recurrent themes, the other being dance figures. Sara Murphy recalled Zelda's passion for flowers after the sojourn in Capri. 'She used to wander for hours through our garden by herself – touching or picking a flower here and there – once she wore a huge pink peony as a hat.'[39] Scottie, recalling Zelda's attraction to nasturtiums which Zelda constantly painted in Italy and on the Riviera, told a friend later: 'I can still see the nasturtiums on the [lunch] table.'[40]

Though Zelda painted several floral compositions under Italy's hot sun, her consistent and striking influence is the Deep South. They show the twin hallmarks of many Southern artists' primal sensuous pictures: fiery Southern light and exotic flowers that are passionately groomed and coddled in Southern neighbourhood gardens.[41]

The other notable element in Zelda's depiction of Italian, French and Deep Southern blossoms is that she painted them as a woman familiar with her subject. Minnie, a lifelong gardener, had taught Zelda the horticultural skills that grounded the hectic symbolism of her flower paintings.

Although Zelda continued formal art lessons in Philadelphia when she returned to the US, there is no evidence of instruction in the proper techniques for preparing canvases. Eddie Pattillo points out that as so many of her oil paintings have required extensive conservation it seems unlikely she was trained in glazes and varnishes.[42] Shafer's view is: 'Certainly she liked thick paint but I think her painting was guided more by her emotions than by any concern for conservation.'[43] – Further confirmation of Zelda's line to Sara Murphy that she and Scott took terrible risks because they didn't believe in conservation.[44]

While Zelda painted, Scott neurotically drank his way through the short time left before *Gatsby*'s publication on 10 April. Despite Perkins's earlier praise, Scott fermented with nerves. He felt the novel might fail on two grounds. Firstly critics might dislike it because it dealt with the rich and contained no peasants borrowed from Tess. Secondly women readers might dislike it because it contained no important woman characters. Although Daisy Fay Buchanan is never as important as the male heroes she does bear interesting resemblances to Zelda, on whom, together with Ginevra King, she is based.[45] Daisy's two betrayals of Gatsby were based on Zelda's broken engagement to Scott and her romance with Jozan. The confrontation scene at the Plaza between Gatsby, Daisy and Tom has strong echoes of Zelda, Scott and Jozan. Gatsby tries to force Daisy to deny the past, to tell her husband she never loved him, but Daisy, perhaps like Zelda after the Jozan episode, says 'the sensible thing': '"Oh, you want too much! . . . I love you now – isn't that enough? I can't help what's past." She began to sob helplessly. "I did love him once – but I loved you too." '[46] Gatsby is incredulous, desperate to repeat their first moments when Daisy loved only him.[47]

Several of Zelda's Montgomery friends who had upset Scott through perceived disloyalty or infidelity provided names for characters in *Gatsby*. Jordan Baker, Daisy's golf champion friend, was possibly based on one of Zelda's girlfriends, Jordan Prince, who had provoked Scott's jealousy by inviting Zelda to accompany her on a midterm date.[48] Dan Cody, Gatsby's drunken patron, is linked to an early 'infidelity' of Zelda's. Mayfield suggests Scott irritably lifted the name from Dan Cody, son of a wealthy banker, one of Zelda's Montgomery beaux. Scott dedicated the novel, with its ironic connections and undertones, 'Once Again to Zelda'.

While Zelda and Scott were touring Europe in April 1925, in Washington Scott's sister Annabel married Lieutenant Clifton A. Sprague of the US Navy. Scott missed seeing his sister, whose bad points as a girl he had enumerated as 'Pale complexion', 'Teeth only fair' and 'Only fair figure',[49] blossom into a slim rosy-faced woman wearing a powder-blue chiffon gown with a matching picture hat, carrying an arm-bouquet of Killarney roses. Scott admired Clifton who later, as Admiral Sprague, became a hero of the Battle of Leyte Gulf in World War Two, but felt no rapport with his brother-in-law and saw less of Annabel after their marriage.

In late April 1925 the Fitzgeralds left Capri. They sailed on the SS *Garfield* from Naples to Marseilles, where Scott received a cable from Perkins which announced that reviews for *Gatsby* were superb but sales were uncertain. The Fitzgeralds had put their Renault on board ship. The top had been damaged and Zelda, who preferred open-top cars, insisted it was removed. Zelda was not well enough to make a long car journey so when it broke down in Lyons they abandoned it and caught the train to Paris. By 1 May they had leased for eight months a gloomy furnished apartment on the fifth floor at 14 rue de Tilsitt on the Right Bank where Fitzgerald, equally gloomily, awaited reviews. They spent as much time as possible out of the apartment visiting Cole Porter, the Murphys and the Bishops, through whom they met the poet Allen Tate and his Southern novelist wife Caroline Gordon. Zelda marvelled at how those two married writers had established an equal supportive relationship.[50]

Despite Max's encouraging words, reviews were mixed. One critic said there was no 'chemical trace of magic, life, irony, romance or mysticism in . . . "The Great Gatsby"'.[51] An unsigned report in the *New York World* was headlined: 'F. SCOTT FITZGERALD'S LATEST A DUD'.[52] The *Herald Tribune* argued that though Scott had managed the exact tone and shade of contemporary life he had not yet 'gone below that glittering surface, except by a kind of happy accident'.[53] Even Zelda's fan Ring Lardner, who had read the book in page proofs, pointed out a series of inaccuracies and his praise was muted.[54]

Scott's ego was slightly appeased when the two critics whose words he most valued were approving. Wilson wrote to him: 'It is undoubtedly in some ways the best thing you have done – the best planned, the best sustained, the best written.'[55] Mencken wrote – 'I think it is incomparably the best piece of work you have done. Evidences of careful workmanship are on every page . . .' though 'it reduces itself, in the end, to a sort of anecdote'.[56]

Finally came unequivocal excellent reviews. In *The Dial* Gilbert Seldes concluded Fitzgerald had 'more than matured, he has mastered his talents and gone soaring in a beautiful flight, leaving behind him everything dubious and tricky in his earlier work, and leaving even farther behind all the men of his own generation and most of his elders'.[57]

When T. S. Eliot wrote: 'it seems to me to be the first step that American fiction has taken since Henry James',[58] Scott felt able to regard himself as 'the biggest man in my profession . . . everybody admired me and I was proud I'd done such a good thing'.[59]

Scott's satisfaction was justified, for *Gatsby* was and has remained an incandescently fine work.[60] At the time, however, it was not the financial success he had hoped for. He had predicted first-year sales of 80,000 copies but it sold fewer than 20,000. At one level prepared for this, he had written to Perkins that he had already prepared a book of fine stories for the fall. His next idea was to write some quick 'smart' stories to accumulate money for his next novel. If he failed at that then he would leave for Hollywood to learn to write movies. He loathed financial insecurity but he had no idea how to reduce their high living standards. He still felt that if you didn't work your hardest at your art there was little point in being an artist.

Fortunately for Scott and Zelda the dramatic rights to *Gatsby* were sold,[61] which meant they were temporarily released from financial anxiety and he could return to 'The Rich Boy', based on Ludlow Fowler; this would be published in *Redbook* in January/February

1926. With *Gatsby* behind him Scott continued to plan his next novel.[62]

In May 1925 the Fitzgeralds met fifty-one-year-old Gertrude Stein, the experimental writer, and her companion Alice B. Toklas, who were at the heart of a celebrated Parisian literary salon at 27 rue de Fleurus. It attracted such writers as Ford Madox Ford, Edith Sitwell and Sherwood Anderson, and the writer-publisher Robert McAlmon, who had made a marriage of convenience to the British heiress, writer Winifred Ellerman (known as Bryher). Another habituée was Janet Flanner, Paris correspondent for the *New Yorker*, who also frequented the opposing literary salon in rue Jacob led by 'The Amazon', Natalie Barney.

When the Fitzgeralds arrived, Stein and Toklas were about to leave Paris for their annual vacation. Stein always demanded the undivided attention of gentlemen guests while females were handed over to Alice. One suspects strong-minded Zelda found this situation irritating. However, as Stein had become a pioneering collector of the modernist art of her vanguard painter-friends, Zelda was able to retreat from Toklas's chit-chat to examine the paintings of Picasso, Matisse and Juan Gris adorning the walls.

Zelda, now regularly accompanying the Murphys to ballet, poetry recitals and avant-garde art shows, was fascinated by the Cubist still lifes and Picasso's massive glowing Rose Period nudes.[63] Though Zelda later wrote to Scott that Picasso's art was more about ideas than painting, at the time she decided that of all Stein's works the Picassos were 'the only ones worth having'.[64]

Scott presented Stein with an inscribed copy of *Gatsby* and on 22 May she replied warmly that she liked the 'melody' of his dedication 'Once Again To Zelda'. It showed he had a background of 'beauty and tenderness'. He wrote 'naturally in sentences', she said. 'You are creating the contemporary world much as Thackeray did his in *Pendennis* and *Vanity Fair* and this isn't a bad compliment.'[65] It wasn't.

Scott wrote back unctuously: 'My wife and I think you a very handsome, very gallant and very kind lady.'[66] If Zelda did think any such thing she kept it to herself. Out loud she told Sara Mayfield that Stein's conversation was 'sententious gibberish'.[67]

Three-year-old Scottie did not take to Stein either. The child, highly disciplined by her British nannies, recalled: '[When] Gertrude Stein came to call I made my appearance, curtsied as I'd been taught to do, and left the minute I was excused. I found her terrifying.'[68]

Zelda's friend Carl Van Vechten had become Stein's American agent for her complex experimental plays and poems which were hard to understand and harder to place. But it was not Carl who introduced the Fitzgeralds to Stein and Toklas. It was Ernest Hemingway, the man who would become Zelda's enemy.

Hemingway and his first wife Hadley had paid their first call on Stein in March 1922 when Gertrude discussed writing with Ernest, 'a delightful fellow',[69] and Alice had taken Hadley aside to chat about domestic matters. Such a close bond was forged between the couples that Alice and Gertrude became godparents to Bumby, the Hemingways' son. Since that first meeting, to confirm his literary standing, Hemingway had already brought to Stein's studio Ada and Archibald MacLeish, Dos Passos and Ogden Stewart. When Zelda first visited Stein, Hemingway was Stein's favourite writer.

Hemingway had previewed the Fitzgeralds' visit by writing to Stein and Toklas a very favourable report. He told them Zelda was 'worth seeing' and he planned to bring the Fitzgeralds to meet Gertrude and Alice the following Friday.[70] At that point Hemingway glowed with praise for Zelda – usually about her physical attributes, indicating that he thought of her in terms of a possible conquest. When she dealt a severe blow to his ego he rancorously rewrote his initial view of her.

Scott, who like Zelda had already met Hemingway in the Dingo bar in Montparnasse, had been immediately captivated. Hemingway, three years younger, considerably taller and more athletic, had a reputation as a war hero and acted the tough guy. Scott's impression of Hemingway was entirely favourable. He had already read his two slim volumes, *Three Stories and Ten Poems* (1923) and the incisive vignette collection *in our time* (1924), and was as impressed by Hemingway's dedication to writing, apparent openness and lack of affectation as he was by his undoubted talent.[71] Hemingway was highly conscious of Scott's well-established commercial celebrity but felt superior and virtuous about seeking artistic accomplishment irrespective of financial rewards. Scott, aware of the younger writer's patronizing attitude, was still ready to make a hero out of Hemingway.

Thirty-two years after their first meeting Hemingway wrote an unreliable report which describes Scott as effeminate, with a long-lipped mouth that 'on a girl would have been the mouth of a beauty ... the mouth worried you until you knew him and then it worried you more'. He portrays him as a nuisance, a fool and a pathetic drunk.[72] It seems Scott had overpraised Hemingway's work, embarrassed him with personal questions ('Did you sleep with your wife before you were married?'), then passed out.[73]

In May 1925 Scott invited Hemingway to go to Lyons with him to pick up the Renault he and Zelda had abandoned. This trip has given rise to competing versions. At the time Hemingway wrote to Max Perkins a very positive account: 'We had a great trip together . . . I've read his Great Gatsby and think it is an absolutely first rate book.'[74] In *A Moveable Feast*, not written until Scott had been dead nearly twenty years and Hemingway was on the edge of dementia that would end in suicide, Hemingway created a malicious semi-factual account of Scott's annoying behaviour during the drive. He reveals Fitzgerald as self-pitying, hypochondriac, unreliable, spendthrift, artistically flawed, sexually inexperienced, emasculated by Zelda and consistently drunk. He himself remains mature, manly and sober. Scott's behaviour could well have made that trip tedious, but this later scathing report of Hemingway's bears no resemblance to his earlier one. Similarly, at the time Hemingway told Ezra Pound that both he and Fitzgerald enjoyed an enormous consumption of wine.[75] But in his vitriolic *A Moveable Feast* he records only Scott's drunkenness.

If there *were* bitter undercurrents at the time, Scott ignored them. Instead he wrote to Gertrude Stein: 'Hemminway and I went to Lyons . . . to get my car and had a slick drive . . . He's a peach of a fellow and absolutely first rate.'[76]

Scott had already told Perkins six months before he met Hemingway that this peachy fellow had 'a brilliant future . . . He's the real thing.'[77] Zelda, after meeting Hemingway, told Gerald, who asked what she had against Hemingway: 'He's bogus.'[78] 'At the time,' Gerald said later, 'the word just didn't seem to fit; there wasn't anyone more real and more himself than Ernest. Bogus, Ernest? Of course, who knows how right she may prove to be?'[79]

For Zelda there appeared to be proof in every action Ernest took, every word he spoke. From the moment she met Hemingway, she disliked him with an unwavering unrelenting force equalled only by his own for her. The stage was set for the battle between Zelda and Hemingway for Scott's allegiance. None of the weapons they used were pleasant.

CHAPTER 11

At the first sight of Zelda, Hemingway behaved no differently from
many of Scott's male friends. He found Mrs Fitzgerald, the woman
'worth seeing', intensely physically attractive.

During the first lunch Ernest and Hadley Hemingway shared
with the Fitzgeralds, Hemingway displayed his attraction to Zelda.[1]
It was a gloomy lunch party which took place soon after Scott and
Hemingway's first meeting, supposedly at the Fitzgeralds' ornate,
badly furnished apartment, according to Sara Mayfield a 'depressing flat over a brasserie . . . a fifth-floor walk-up, with strange
purple-and-gold wallpaper'.[2] In fact, documentation shows the
famous lunch took place not at the Fitzgeralds' curious apartment
but at the Hemingways' humble flat.[3] Perhaps it was its humble
location that made the inventive Ernest change it to the Fitzgeralds'
superior one!

Zelda remembers an ornamental turtle on the lunch table brimming with white violets. Ernest remembers Zelda. But exactly what
he remembers depends on which of his versions you read.

In his earliest manuscript version of that lunch he gives this
picture of Zelda: 'very beautiful and . . . tanned a lovely gold color
and her hair was a beautiful dark gold and she was very friendly.
Her hawk's eyes were clear and calm.' Her skin is smooth and
tawny, her legs light and long as 'nigger legs', she is not drunk nor
is she jealous of Scott's work. Though Hemingway sees her as spoilt
and as saying curious things he admits to an erotic dream about her
the following night. 'The next time I saw her I told her that and she
was pleased. That was the first and last time we ever had anything
in common.'[4]

Maybe. Or maybe not. There is counter-evidence which shows that
at the start of the two couples' friendship, when Hemingway writes
to Scott he regularly sends affectionate greetings to Zelda: 'And how
is Zelda ?', 'Best love to Zelda' and similarly pleasant if perfunctory
remarks.[5] When Zelda was sick, Hemingway demonstrated concern.

He wrote to Scott that he understood how hard pain was and what a shame it was for Zelda to be ill.

Hemingway during this short early period was confident that Zelda as well as Scott would be fascinated by him. But Zelda, who often responded flirtatiously to male interest, did not respond to Hemingway.

Far from it. Cynical about Hemingway's display of aggressive manliness, she thought Scott's romantic admiration for his hard-boiled manner demeaning. Attracted to deferential, civilized, more polished men, Zelda felt menaced by Hemingway's brutish behaviour. Seeing his influence as a threat to her marriage, she shrewdly queried Ernest's sexual prowess. First she remarked to Gerald: 'Nobody is as male as all that!' Then she taunted Hemingway to his face: 'No one is as masculine as you pretend to be.'[6] She told Sara Mayfield and wrote to Perkins that Ernest was 'a sort of materialist mystic',[7] rather than a gentleman in their Southern sense. Indeed Hemingway was not a gentleman in any sense. Mayfield remembers Ernest derided polite conversation between men as 'damn women's talk'. His method of commending one male friend to another was to announce: 'You'll like him – he's tough.' Zelda told Sara this was suspicious camouflage, that beneath Hemingway's integrity as a writer there was base metal in the man that never rang true. She felt that under Ernest's well-publicized 'healthy' interest in sports, tippling and war, there was 'a morbid preoccupation with offbeat sex and the sadism and necrophilia that go with it' which she found 'repugnant'.[8]

One afternoon at the Deux Magots café Sara listened to the Fitzgeralds arguing about Hemingway. Scott reprimanded Zelda for insulting Hemingway. Zelda retorted: ' "I didn't insult him. I just said he was a phony." '

Sara, as amazed by the word 'phony' as Gerald had been at the word 'bogus', repeated incredulously to Zelda: ' "A phony? What makes you say that?"

' "She's jealous," Scott said.'[9]

If Zelda was jealous, Hemingway was certainly vindictive.

In his later published version of *A Moveable Feast*, Hemingway carefully contrives to rewrite that first lunch scene in the purple-and-gold wallpapered apartment to put both Zelda and Scottie in a very bad light. Three-year-old Scottie is portrayed with a strong Cockney accent acquired from an English nanny. Zelda is hung over with a drawn face, tired eyes, suffering a poor permanent wave which has ruined her 'beautiful dark blond hair'. Hemingway focuses on how Zelda encourages Scott to drink, calls him 'kill-joy' and 'spoilsport' when he demurs and smiles smugly as he drinks so much he will be unable to write later.[10]

Neither account – the version portraying Zelda as dissipated and manipulative, nor the version in which she is erotic and dream-worthy – is entirely to be trusted. But the rewriting to Zelda's detriment in that late account in *A Moveable Feast* after her death was the last in a long series of attacks which continued throughout her life.

Hemingway fired off the first of his charges in 1925.

Zelda was too independent. She was jealous of Scott's work. She didn't put Scott and his writing first. She encouraged Scott's drinking to further destroy his talents. Her greed was behind Scott's decision to devote more time to best-selling stories, less to literature. As for their luxuriant lifestyle (for which Hemingway held her responsible), it was shamefully brash compared with his and Hadley's. Hemingway paused. Breathed. Took aim again. This time he spotted signs of a lesbian orientation, well if not *that*, or not *that* quite *yet*, Zelda certainly mixed with women who mixed with women. Worst of all, Hemingway noticed definite signs of instability.

Legend suggests that on first meeting Zelda, Hemingway drew Scott aside and said brutally: 'She's crazy,' shocking Scott deeply.[11] Hadley, when questioned, had no memory of Ernest saying this though it is possible that Ernest spoke out of her hearing. Hemingway still insisted in conversations with Scott as late as 1934 that he had known in 1925 that Zelda was unstable. 'I thought Zelda was crazy the first time I met her and you complicated it even more by being in love with her and, of course, you're a rummy.'[12]

During 1925, Hemingway ensured Zelda heard his tales of her supposed craziness. Zelda said angrily to Scott in front of Sara Mayfield: 'He [Hemingway] thinks I'm crazy and says so. Why shouldn't I say anything I choose to about him?' To which Scott replied that if she said scandalous things about his big new friend she *was* crazy.[13]

The following year on the Riviera, when Zelda said ironically: 'Ernest, don't you think Al Jolson is greater than Jesus?', Hemingway saw this as confirmation of Zelda's insanity.[14] Neither Hemingway nor his biographers recognized Zelda's remark as typically idiosyncratic. In this case she repeated it: Gerald Murphy also recalls her saying, 'Don't you think that Al Jolson is just like Christ?' Gerald did not push Zelda further as other people were present, but he said such startling remarks 'gave her conversation a freshness and a certain edge that was part of her charm'. Honoria Murphy said that Gerald considered neither Hemingway nor Scott ever fathomed Zelda's complexity: 'her mind operated in a different way from other friends, she quite simply made different connections.'[15]

Sara Murphy thought that though Zelda's 'wit was sometimes barbed, it derived from the surprise of incongruity and from searching, humorous observation'.[16]

Many of the Fitzgeralds' friends did not believe Hemingway's canards. They told Arthur Mizener, Scott's first biographer, that Zelda saw more sanely than Scott how seriously their lives were getting out of hand. During 1925–6 Zelda had more stability than Scott and a greater strength of character to resist dissipation. Mizener suggested: 'A good deal of injustice has certainly been done to the Zelda of the twenties because she later went insane and it is difficult not to let the knowledge that she did so affect one's view of what she was like before 1930.'[17]

Some of the reasons for Hemingway's focus on these particular 'flaws' in Zelda can be seen in his childhood, early manhood and in his choice of marriage partner and style of marriage.

Hemingway was born in Oak Park, a Chicago suburb, on 21 July 1899, the second of six children. Like Scott he had a dominant mother and a father given to depression, who was passive with his wife but strict with his children, all of whom were regularly spanked. Dr Clarence Hemingway was an outdoor person who taught his children to hunt and fish. Strong-willed Grace Hall, Ernest's mother, was an indoor person, musical, artistic, determined to remain independent. A good soprano, she worked with a famous voice coach, auditioned for the Met and when married continued to give singing lessons, earning ten times more than her husband earned as a doctor. Grace treated her two first-born, daughter Marcelline and son Ernest, in an unusual manner that had a lasting effect on Ernest – and on his relationship to Zelda. Grace dressed them like female twins, in gingham dresses or fluffy lace tucked frocks with picture hats. She had their hair cut similarly in a Dutch dolly style with bangs across the forehead hanging prettily below the ears. Ernest wore dresses until he entered kindergarten, twice as long as any contemporary boy might have been attired in female garb. Moreover no boys in that period had girls' haircuts as well as girls' clothes.[18]

Both Ernest and Marcelline felt scarred by their father's mental illness and their mother's intimate companionship with Ruth Arnold, Grace's former favourite pupil, who was only three years older than Marcelline and had long lodged with the family. As she and Clarence became estranged, Grace decided to use an inheritance to build a cottage a mile away from the family summer residence. Ruth visited there constantly after Dr Hemingway forbade her to enter his family home. Dr Hemingway began to act 'insane on the subject' of Ruth, just as Ernest would begin to act insane on the subject of Zelda.[19] Ernest consistently depicted his mother as a villain in fiction and letters, but it seems Grace's greatest crimes were her artistic independence and her unapologetic unwillingness to become an ordinary housewife.[20] In this she was very like Zelda.

During the 1920s Ernest's hatred of his mother had intensified. He felt she had emasculated his father and later felt she drove him to his suicide in 1928, after which young Ruth moved in to live with Grace.[21] Incensed, Ernest would then forbid his sons to visit his mother on the grounds that she was 'androgynous'.

So by the time Zelda encountered Hemingway his hostility to domineering women, his anxieties about mental instability and his aggression towards lesbianism were strongly formed. All he needed was a target.

Towards male homosexuals he was less aggressive than intensely curious, as Scott was. Gerald Murphy noticed Hemingway would frequently say: 'I don't mind a fairy like so and so, do you? . . . He was extremely sensitive to the question of who was one and who wasn't.'[22] The teasing homoerotic letters Ernest and Scott wrote each other showed their shared attitude of antipathy yet attraction towards 'fairies' which escalated into crude banter when they drank.

But of course neither of them wished the outside world to view them as 'fairies', and Scott in particular was protective of Ernest's manly reputation. Zelda however had no such reservations. When Scott accused her of being jealous of Hemingway she shrieked: "'Of what? A rugged adventurer, big-game hunter, sportsman, and professional he man, a pansy with hair on his chest?"'

Scott's face went scarlet and his eyes bulged as he shouted

"'Zelda! Don't ever say that again . . . it's slanderous.'"

Zelda, calmer than Scott, pointed out that if calling Hemingway a pansy was slander, then Scott should sue the homosexual American writer Robert McAlmon, who was currently spreading the rumour that Scott and Ernest were homosexuals. Zelda told Sara that Scott and Ernest both fell out with McAlmon because of these – in their terms – unsavoury accusations.[23] Scott, deeply distressed, began to question his masculinity, which in turn had negative implications for his marriage.

Perhaps in retaliation for these rumours, Hemingway charged Zelda with seeking out lesbian company in Paris salons as a method of impeding Scott's work. He believed Scott was frightened that spring that Zelda would get so drunk that she would lose control. Hemingway admitted that Zelda did not encourage those who pursued her but the pursuers amused her and also made Scott so jealous he insisted on accompanying Zelda everywhere. That meant he could not work.

As Hemingway recalled and wrote about the incident many years later, several of Scott's biographers think he misremembered the date and that Zelda entered Natalie Barney's lesbian artistic set in 1929, a date which *is* substantially documented. However, if we consider the women Zelda mixed with in 1925–6 it is plausible that Hemingway was correct. Through the Hemingways and Murphys, Zelda met Pauline Pfeiffer, a *Vogue* journalist from Arkansas, rumoured to be on a husband-hunting expedition in Paris, who had become attracted to Ernest, and her small exotic sister Jinnie, who, by taking more interest in women suitors than in men, may have introduced other artistic lesbians into Zelda's circle.[24] However, during 1925 and 1926 Zelda would almost certainly have been drawn to these women because they were *artists*. Although her marriage was suffering sexually, both through her own lingering illnesses and through Scott's by now addictive alcoholism, she was not in search of specific sexual adventures with women. She was, however, angry with Hemingway who, she felt, ruthlessly encouraged Scott's drinking.

Hemingway seemed able to drink all day, half the night and still work well the next morning, whereas after three cocktails Scott was 'off on a spree that left him shot for a week'.[25] Ironically, in 1925, when Scott's writing began to suffer more severely from his alcoholism, Hemingway blamed Zelda, and later hand-wrote a sketch to show her again in a bad light.[26] In the sketch Fitzgerald frequently turns up drunk at the Hemingways'. Ernest's son Bumby asks his father whether M. Fitzgerald is ill. Ernest replies that Scott's sickness derives from too much alcohol and therefore too little work. Young Bumby wonders whether Scott still respects his own art. Caustically Ernest points out that it is Zelda who does not respect Scott's art and may well be jealous of it. Bumby the true son of Ernest suggests Scott should chastize Zelda

This was exactly what Ernest thought Scott should do. He thought Zelda should play out a traditional role like his wife Hadley. Despite a private income, Hadley did the cooking and cleaning whilst Ernest fixed bottles for baby Bumby and dramatized their reduced circumstances. Zelda of course always employed nannies and wherever she and Scott lived they lived extravagantly, while Hadley and Ernest lived frugally in a sparsely furnished apartment over a sawmill off the Latin Quarter at 113 rue Notre-Dame-des-Champs. Zelda's clothes came from Patou or Chanel, Hadley's from Au Bon Marché. Hemingway minded that more than did either Zelda or Hadley.

The Fitzgeralds took cocktails at the Ritz or the George V while the Hemingways drank at zinc bars in the Latin Quarter. The Fitzgeralds regularly dined on pressed duck at the Tour d'Argent or sampled *pâté aux truffes* at Maxim's, while Ernest and Hadley had been known to borrow money from their friend Sylvia Beach, who owned the famous Shakespeare and Company bookstore, to eat at the local brasserie. As the Hemingways possessed no evening clothes, if the Fitzgeralds met them after dinner outings had to be tempered to the Hemingways' tastes. These were primarily dancing at *bals musettes*, attending boxing matches or touring decadent and homosexual bars in the rue de Lappe.[27] Hemingway's fondness for these lends a certain irony to his accusation that year that Zelda was consorting with lesbians. Zelda in fact preferred to accompany the Murphys to a Diaghilev première, or one of Etienne de Beaumont's '*Soirées de Paris*', than to haunt bars with the Hemingways. Zelda confided in Sara Mayfield that she hated the friends Scott had picked up at the Dingo Bar. 'All they talk about is sex – sex plain, striped, mixed, and fancy. Nice life, sitting in a café all day and a *bal musette* all night. You have to drink yourself blotto to keep from being bored to death.'[28]

The couples' friendship was largely based on Scott and Ernest's shared interest in writing. Hadley and Zelda were merely writers' wives who did not particularly get on. Hadley found the Fitzgeralds 'inconvenient friends', as they called on the Hemingways at four in the morning: 'We had a baby and didn't appreciate it very much. When Scott wrote I don't know.'[29]

Temperament and marital goals were more serious differences between the two women. Hadley felt Zelda was fundamentally frivolous, though 'a charming, lovely creature . . . [who] lived on what Ernest called the "festival conception of life"'.[30] Hadley admired Zelda's beauty and style but recognized they had little in common. Zelda was bold and free spirited, Hadley shy and still insecure.

Born Hadley Richardson in 1891 in St Louis, the youngest of four, she was delicately reared and overprotected because of a childhood injury.[31] When she was twelve her beloved father committed suicide, as Ernest's father would do later. It was a cheerless household for a timorous adolescent. Musically talented like her domineering mother, she retreated into her music until she entered Bryn Mawr, but was forced to leave college because of illness. Her life became still grimmer when her oldest sister died giving birth to a stillborn child; then her mother contracted Bright's Disease, so Hadley nursed her until she died in 1921. At twenty-nine Hadley saw herself as a spinster. On a visit to Chicago an excitable twenty-one-year-old, 'hulky, bulky, something masculine',[32] noticed her diffidently playing the piano at a party. This hulky creature was Ernest Hemingway, unproven writer. Her shyness dissolved. Within three weeks Hemingway talked of marriage. Hadley adored the fact Ernest was devoted to his art. Ernest adored her red hair, sense of fun and her appreciation of him, his adventures, his writing. Before they married she wrote Ernest letters similar to those Zelda had written to Scott: 'I love your ambitions. Don't think I am ambitious except to be a balanced, happy, intelligent lady, making the man happy.' But Hadley, who understood Ernest's fears (which paralleled Scott's), assured him that though she had had a girlhood friendship with a lesbian he 'needn't fear on that side'.[33] Hadley's nurturing instinct suited Ernest. Hadley's trust fund suited him more.[34] Hadley decided she would use her fund to back Ernest's career. They married on 3 September 1921, after which Ernest saw himself as a teacher with Hadley as his brightest pupil, who would never be allowed to dominate him as his mother had dominated her father. Zelda, aware of Hemingway's determination, worried that he would further influence Scott in that direction.

Observantly she said to Hadley: 'I notice that in the Hemingway family you do what Ernest wants.' Hadley was honest enough to admit that although 'Ernest didn't like that much . . . it was a perceptive remark. He had a passionate, overwhelming desire to do some of the things that have since been written about, and so I went along with him – with the trips, the adventures. He had such a powerful personality; he could be so enthusiastic that I became caught up in the notions too.'[35]

Hadley did not tell Zelda that what she observed in the Fitzgerald marriage was two kinds of jealousy: Scott's jealousy of Zelda and Zelda's jealousy of Scott's work.[36] The fact that Hadley's ambitions were to service Ernest's skewed her view of Zelda so that she loyally echoed Hemingway's view that Zelda 'was more jealous of his

[Scott's] work than anything'.[37] Zelda's letters and fiction show clearly that at this time she was not jealous of Scott's achievements, but was growing resentful that her part in Scott's success was neither credited nor paid for; her attempts at independent writing were subsumed under Scott's name, while her painting was seen as frivolous.

When Hadley noticed that Zelda was not swept along by Ernest's charisma, she suggested: 'He was too assured a male for her. Maybe she . . . resented it . . . He was then the kind of man to whom men, women, children and dogs were attracted.'[38] Hadley was right about men liking him. Unlike Scott, who found male friendships difficult because he made heroes of his male friends, Hemingway inspired male companionship. But not all women liked him. One woman friend said he was 'in every way a man's man. I think he disliked women heartily; and in most cases they disliked him – excluding sex, of course.'[39]

Zelda was now painting steadily. What is more, she had a direct entry to Natalie Barney's rue Jacob art enclave, for she had already met Barney's lover, the painter Romaine Brooks. Now, through Esther Murphy and Esther's sister-in-law Noel, Barney's friend, Zelda met other female artists and writers. Gerald Murphy, irritated by the group's openly homosexual antics, distanced himself from his sister, particularly when Esther was fictionalized as Bounding Bess by novelist Djuna Barnes in her lesbian satire *Ladies Almanack*. Noel, married to Gerald's brother Frederick, found Gerald's attitude inexcusable, partly because she accurately suspected that Gerald was being dishonest about his own submerged homosexual feelings.[40]

Zelda found the group's artistic camaraderie stimulating and their willingness to take her art seriously a change from Scott's attitude, which vacillated between suggesting she did something for herself and giving her little credit when she did.

During 1925 she started on a self-portrait which she worked on for a year. She was using watercolour and gouache on paper, a medium which suited her life of travel. It would have been hard to transport and store vast stretchers, bulky canvases and oil paints whereas small gouaches on paper were easily portable.[41]

Zelda dated few of her paintings so it is difficult to be precise about which watercolour she worked on during 1925. The most likely is *Girl With Orange Dress* because it shows influences of Larionov and other Cubists and has some links with Murphy's paintings.

Zelda was thoroughly exposed to the work of Mikhail Larionov in 1925, when she viewed his sets, scenes and curtains for the Diaghilev ballet, all in the same intense powerful colours she used in *her* early paintings.[42] Like Larionov, Zelda uses a Cubist perspective to fracture pictorial space without allowing the scene to disintegrate. In *Girl With Orange Dress* her two main subjects, a girl in billowing skirts and a zany dog, are seen from different viewpoints on different planes. Then to achieve wild vibrations she explodes a bright orange colour on to the picture.[43] The girl's body sways off-centre, her billowing skirt makes the picture move, while the dog leaps about in the right foreground. Zelda's cockeyed angles and compositional movements force our gaze to move too, with an effect akin to an earthquake. Zelda's craft, still in its early stages, allowed her partially to restore the painting's balance by splashing reddish-orange on the fireplace and vase of flowers, to move the viewer's eye to the right of the composition.

The first impressions that Zelda's friends derived from her paintings were like their first impressions of the artist: no one quite knew what was going on in Zelda's head. Characteristically, Zelda produced ambiguities. It is not clear if the girl dressed in orange is dancing or just swaying like a plant. It is not clear if she is merry or sad.

Zelda had also seen many of Gerald Murphy's paintings. Though he was never a direct influence on her there are at this point some similarities in their work. Gerald used shifting perspectives to represent real objects together with abstract forms to achieve a haunting emotional intensity that unsettles viewers, much as Zelda's paintings do. In 1924 he had painted a remarkable picture, *Razor*, which influenced the Murphys' set.[44] He crossed a fountain pen and a safety razor like heraldic quarterings against a gigantic matchbox, balanced the matchbox on three other boxes and gave them oddly angled perspectives. When Zelda and other friends looked at it, they saw the matchbox top presented flat as if viewed from above; the part that held the matches receded from their gaze, while the razor was drawn in profile and in section from three viewpoints. What Gerald's and Zelda's dissimilar paintings had in common was the odd angles and strange brooding quality which gave them their sense of power. But while Gerald's work has precision, brevity and control, Zelda's is untamed.

Already painting and writing, Zelda now returned after a seven-year gap to her old love, ballet. According to Mayfield, in spring 1925 in Paris both Fitzgeralds met Lubov Egorova, the Princess Troubetskoy, who would become the single most significant artistic influence on Zelda.[45] Egorova, formerly a leading ballerina with the Russian Imperial Ballet, had emigrated to Paris and at Diaghilev's suggestion opened a studio in 1923, where she excelled as a ballet coach. One version of how Zelda and Egorova first met is that Scott, who thought Zelda needed something to do, suggested that Murphy arrange an introduction; more probably Zelda, who knew Egorova was teaching young Honoria Murphy, asked Gerald to arrange dancing lessons for her. Because of the Fitzgeralds' constant travelling Zelda did not begin her serious dance work until 1927. However, as Mayfield later remarked, the seeds of the Fitzgeralds' discord over Egorova were sown before Zelda and Scott left Paris to visit the Murphys in Antibes in August 1925.

Sara Murphy recalled that during that year 'She [Zelda] worked so *hard* at her painting and writing and dancing,' but added, 'We . . . only *wish* she had been happier.'[46]

Despite her fruitful activities Zelda was increasingly unhappy about the role of Hemingway in her marriage, while Scott certainly felt torn between his wife and his new friend. But he continued to advance Ernest's literary progress with great generosity. As self-appointed talent scout for Perkins, Fitzgerald successfully masterminded Ernest's move to Scribner's. He even lent money to Hemingway, who exaggerated his poverty.[47] Zelda objected to Scott's constant loans to Ernest. 'He's a pain in the neck – talking about me and borrowing money from you while he does it,' she said angrily to Scott. 'He's phony as a rubber check and you know it.'[48]

Hemingway accepted but never forgave Scott's benevolence.[49] His manipulative skill shows when after finishing *Gatsby* he wrote that he was suddenly aware that no matter how badly Scott behaved, he would regard such behaviour merely as sickness. Moreover Ernest would try, as a good friend, to help him. Those lines effectively established Hemingway as Scott's benefactor when it was largely the other way round.[50]

That spring and summer of 1925 Scott, with Hemingway's encouragement, and an assertive style not unlike Hemingway's own, completed a significant work, 'The Rich Boy'.[51] Scott wrote to their wealthy friend Ludlow Fowler that it was 'in large measure the story of your life, toned down here and there and simplified'.[52] In one of his most famous literary passages Scott divulges a deep-held belief:

Let me tell you about the very rich. They are different from you and me. They possess and enjoy early, and it does something to them, makes

them soft where we are hard, and cynical where we are trustful . . . they
think, deep in their hearts, that they are better than we are because we
had to discover the compensations and refuges of life for ourselves.[53]

Though Zelda was intermittently ill with gynaecological problems during the summer, for Scott it was a time of '1000 parties and
no work'.[54] He sipped cocktails with the Murphys and got drunk
with Hemingway, 'an equeal and my kind of idealist'.[55] His drinking increased so that even their friends' children became aware of
it. Fanny Myers recalls how one lunchtime Scott rang their doorbell,
staggered in drunk then fell on her bed. Alice Myers explained to
little Fanny that Scott was 'having a little lie down'. Fanny forgave
him because on his recovery he said she was exceptionally pretty,
her first ever compliment.[56]

Scott's debauched lifestyle was leaving physical effects. Sara
Mayfield reported: 'His hair was still yellow as a jonquil, but he had
lost the fresh-scrubbed look of an Arrow collar advertisement. His
hands were stained with nicotine, and he was constantly drumming
a tattoo with them or wiping the perspiration from them with a
damp handkerchief . . . his skin had a greenish tinge . . . he had
developed what he called "a pot".'[57]

Zelda still retained her lithe figure and classic beauty but her blue
eyes, according to Sara, were often sad. In unguarded moments she
nervously twisted her hands together or chewed the corner of her
mouth. The Murphys noticed a strange smile occasionally played
about Zelda's lips.

Scott's behaviour, even with the Murphys, became unreliable,
sometimes tasteless. One evening the Murphys took the Fitzgeralds
and Barrys to a new dance restaurant near the Champs-Elysées.
Scott, uninterested in food, music or dancing, remained sullen.
Ellen Barry recalls that when the Murphys rose to leave Scott sank
to his knees on the dance floor, clutched Gerald's hand and sobbed:
'Don't go! Take me with you – don't leave me here!' Gerald, furious,
pulled away. 'This is not Princeton, and I'm not your roommate,' he
said curtly.[58]

Despite Gerald's chastisement, Scott continued to ask him for literary advice and pester him with intimate questions.[59] Scott was
desperate to live inside Gerald's skin, but though he hero-
worshipped Gerald he never understood him. Zelda, watching,
empathizing, rarely asking questions, understood Gerald much
better. Though Sara chided Scott for his appalling behaviour she
also acknowledged: 'He *always* realized when he had gone too

far – & was sorry and mortified – not always, I am sorry to say, till much later . . . but he *did* feel badly about it.'[60]

Scott had what the biographer Scott Donaldson calls a 'severe crush' on Sara as well as Gerald. Gerald believed Scott was 'sentimentally disturbed' by Sara.[61] But what lay underneath Scott's idolization of the Murphys was their Eastern establishment privilege, their self-assurance.

A tricky area for Zelda was Sara Murphy's adoration for Ernest, which contrasted with her intermittent irritation with Scott. Sara would not hear a disparaging word about Hemingway, even from Zelda. Both Murphys reinforced Gertrude Stein's boundless admiration for Hemingway's work.[62] After reading an unfinished manuscript of *The Sun Also Rises*, Gerald wrote to Hadley: 'We read it the other day and were blown out of the water alive.' To Ernest himself, Gerald said: 'Those God-damn stories of yours kept me rooted and goggle-eyed all the way to Germany the other day . . . My God, but you've kept your promise with yourself.'[63] The Murphys' greater respect for Friend Ernest over Friend Scott stemmed from the fact that Hemingway rarely allowed anything to interfere with his promise whilst Scott did so constantly.

In contrast to his own disreputable antics, Scott kept an orderly eye on Scottie's, exercised strict overall control and cut Zelda out: a system he maintained throughout Scottie's youth. Scottie's least pleasant memory about life in France was Scott's insistence on catechism class every Sunday. 'Daddy made me go even though he no longer believed in the Catholic faith, but his family did and he feared that they might be offended if I wasn't brought up in the Church.'[64]

Zelda was offered only the role of creative games inventor or designer of unusual dolls. Her exclusion may have been another underlying cause for their escalating rows. Sara Murphy said it was obvious when quarrels reached a climax, for Zelda's trunk could be seen in the courtyard. A day later she would heave the trunk back upstairs. Sara emphasized Zelda's loyalty. She never spoke to the Murphys or other friends about their marital battles. 'It did upset her to hear Scott scolded or criticized – she flew to his defense & backed him up in everything – If Scott . . . pretended to make love publicly – or even once drove a taxicab away, leaving the driver behind, she would *only* chuckle indulgently.'[65]

Then matters deteriorated. Zelda told Mayfield that after a few drinks Scott would become truculent. In one drunken rage he struck her and Zelda told Sara she 'was physically afraid of him in his manic states'. Scott defended himself later by demanding of a group of male friends: 'Is there any man present who can honestly say he has never hit his wife in anger?'[66]

Zelda's repressed anger appeared to result in a further distancing from people. Sara Murphy said: 'I don't believe she liked very many people although her manners to everyone were perfect.'[67]

As their lives became more unruly, Zelda clung obsessively to personal cleanliness and order. That year Sara Murphy felt Zelda was even fresher and 'more exquisite': 'She was so beautiful always – glossy dark-gold hair and her delicate "Indian" face, and a fresh little cotton dress every day – cleanliness and order were a sort of fetish with her.'[68] Nathan recalls her as 'resolutely fastidious' but says it was because 'Scott would have it no other way'.[69]

In August 1925 the Fitzgeralds went to Antibes, where the Murphys had moved into their fourteen-room Villa America high above the beach of La Garoupe. Scott, fascinated by the villa's Moorish style, admired Gerald's success in scraping away the seaweed so that visitors could swim. Dinner parties were held on the flagstone terrace shaded by a linden tree. Waxed black tile floors contrasted with sheer white walls and gleaming chrome furniture. Black satin covered the chair seats. Tangerines, lemons and olives crowded the orchard near Sara's herb garden. The fragrance of eucalyptus and mimosa wafted through cedar trees and palms. The Murphys used a small Provençal farmhouse for guests, Gerald had a painting studio and seven-year-old Honoria entertained her brothers, Scottie and Fanny Myers in her playhouse.

Scott needed solitude to work on his new novel, then called *Our Type*, later *The Boy Who Killed His Mother*, based, he told Perkins, on the Leopold–Loeb murder. But he also confessed to Perkins: 'it is about Zelda & me & the hysteria of last May and June in Paris. (Confidential).'[70]

There was however to be no solitude on the Riviera, as Scott's name-dropping letter to Bishop illustrates:

There was no one at Antibes this summer except me, Zelda, the Valentino, the Murphy's, Mistinguet, Rex Ingram, Dos Passos, Alice Terry, the Mclieshes, Charlie Bracket, Maude Kahn, Esther Murphy, Marguerite Namara, E. Phillips Openhiem, Mannes the violinist, Floyd Dell, Max and Chrystal Eastman, ex-Premier Orlando, Ettienne de Beaumont . . .[71]

Scott's list (from which only the Hemingways, away in Spain, were missing) depicts the cultural invasion that was about to turn Antibes into an international playground.

In Antibes Zelda, though frequently ill, provided entertainments for Scottie. When the child said she'd like to get married, Zelda staged a wedding. Little Scottie wore a white dress and veil and carried a bridal bouquet. Scott gave her away and bought her ring. 'Not a real diamond,' Scottie complained, 'it was from the five-and-dime store'. Zelda produced a wedding cake, then sent her on a honeymoon ride along the Mediterranean coast in a car decorated with streamers and fresh flowers.[72]

Though Scottie's childhood was torn with rows, a drunken father and later a sick absent mother, memories like these meant she determinedly recalled it as 'romantic'.[73] Legend says Scottie was 'untouched by marital conflicts' but Scottie's daughter, Eleanor Lanahan, says this was merely Scottie's defence which she maintained throughout her life.[74] Playing these children's games, Zelda and Scott too lived for a time in a magical world.

Then one evening in August a disturbing incident occurred. The Fitzgeralds dined with the Murphys at an inn in St Paul de Vence in the mountains above Nice. The dining terrace was built 200 feet above the valley with a sheer drop from the outside walls of the terrace. Gerald sat in front of a flight of ten stone steps. Isadora Duncan, at forty-six somewhat heavy, with dyed red hair, was dining at a nearby table. When Gerald alerted Scott to her presence, he rushed over and knelt at Duncan's feet while she ran her fingers through his hair and called him her centurion. The Murphys later told Mayfield that when Duncan indicated to Scott he might visit her that night Zelda showed no resentment, but watched them silently for several minutes. Then suddenly she leapt from her chair, sprang across the table, across Gerald and flung herself down the stone steps. 'I was sure she was dead,' Gerald said. 'We were all stunned and motionless.' In fact Zelda reappeared within moments, standing still at the top of the steps. Sara ran to her and wiped the blood from her knees and dress. Gerald recalls thinking that, strangely, this violent incident had not appeared ugly: yet another example of Zelda's style which meant no matter what she did, she did it without vulgarity.[75] Mayfield's analysis was that 'if Zelda's eyes wandered, Scott's pride prompted him to attack her and the man to whom she was attracted; but if Zelda's *amour propre* was wounded by Scott's attentions to other women, she wanted only to destroy herself.'[76]

Scott's Ledger entry for August 1925 is laconic. He simply notes the name 'Eleanor Duncan', then scrawls out 'Eleanor' and replaces it with 'Isadora'. When Scott noted the Jozan incident he constantly misspelled the man's name. This time he casually gets the name entirely wrong and just as casually corrects it. In both cases Scott's use of language serves to minimize or gloss over a dangerous event.

Self-destructive actions on Zelda's part began to pepper meetings between the Fitzgeralds and Murphys. Gerald believed neither of the Fitzgeralds wanted 'ordinary pleasures, they hardly noticed good food or wines, but they did want something to happen'.[77]

On the Riviera Zelda and Scott became even closer to the Murphys and the MacLeishes. When the Fitzgeralds left for Paris in September, Gerald, forgiving Scott all lapses, wrote: 'There *really* was a great sound of tearing heard in the land as your train pulled out that day. Sara and I rode back together saying things about you both to each other which only partly expressed what we felt separately . . . Most people are dull, without distinction and without value, even humanely . . . you two belong so irrevocably to that rare race of people who are valuable.'[78]

This wildly generous letter stands as a witness to the good feelings both Zelda and Scott aroused in others, despite the tensions between them as a couple. Zelda's verdict on Antibes came in a letter to her friend Madeleine Boyd: 'We went to Antibes to recuperate but all we recooped was drinking hours. Now, once again, the straight and narrow path goes winding and wobbling before us and Scott is working.'[79] But that winter was not all work. The Murphys came to Paris at the end of September and saw the Fitzgeralds daily. In November the Fitzgeralds visited London and saw Tallulah Bankhead as the heroine in Michael Arlen's hit play *The Green Hat*.[80] Zelda wrote to Scottie: 'We went to London to see a fog and saw Tallulah Bankhead, which was, perhaps about the same effect.'[81] To Madeleine Zelda was as wittily acid about the playwright: 'just got back from bloody England where the Michael Arlens grow – hardy annuals it says in the seed catalogues'. Zelda told Madeleine that though in Paris she was 'not so amiable as I was before living in this seat of sin and literary learning', she was 'passing the winter agreeably among plagiarists who are always delightful . . . Civilization is not what it once was even for authors wives.'[82]

She did not tell Madeleine that severe stomach illnesses and repressed tensions had brought on a bout of uncontrollable nerves. Scott wrote to Hemingway that Zelda was suffering from 'a nervous hysteria which is only relieved by a doctor bearing morphine'.[83]

The Fitzgeralds needed a festive Christmas, and Scott had good news to celebrate. The *Saturday Evening Post* had raised his fees, New York theatrical producer Owen Davis had taken an option on *Gatsby* for production next February, Scott had a new short story collection, *All The Sad Young Men*, also coming out in February,[84] and his 1925 earnings totalled $18,333, only $2,000 less than 1924. So Zelda and Nanny decorated the tree with silver garlands, birds with spun-glass tails and cardboard houses shiny with snow, the ornaments they always travelled with. Then, smiling at their prosperity, Zelda, Scott and Scottie posed in a chorus line in front of their tree for one of those immortal photographs they sent their friends. They were still doing high kicks, but they were already falling.

CHAPTER 12

1926 was a year of change and experiment for several of Zelda's friends, but a year of sickness and danger for Zelda.

In Paris she discovered that three of her close friends also disapproved of Hemingway. Sara Mayfield, studying at the Sorbonne, frequently saw him strolling through the Luxembourg Gardens, Bumby at his hip and Hadley 'following him as silently as an Indian squaw', and told Zelda how much she disliked Ernest's attitude to Hadley.[1] Sara Haardt and H. L. Mencken were also furious with him, though for different reasons. Ernest had called Mencken 'that shit' and established him and Sara as permanent enemies.[2] Both Zelda and Sara Mayfield assumed this was because the Sage had not initially recognized Hemingway's talents. Though Mencken thought Hemingway 'knew how to shock women's clubs with dirty words' and produced great dialogue, he saw his stories as melodramatic and obvious. At the time Mencken felt that he was 'challenging, bellicose and not infrequently absurd'. Even later, Mencken wrote: 'My view of his work was never exalted.'[3]

Sara Haardt had recovered sufficiently from ill-health to leave Montgomery and divide her time between Baltimore and New York, where she freelanced for the Baltimore *Evening Sun*, the Virginia *Quarterly Review* and Mencken's *American Mercury*. Though Mencken still encouraged her, she was now well known in her own right. Her professional independence seemed to increase her deep reserve and Mencken mistakenly felt she did not fully care for him. During 1926 their letters became more distant, and with newspaper gossip linking his name with that of the Hollywood actress Aileen Pringle, their romance temporarily wavered.[4]

Zelda, beset with colitis, was now in worse health than Sara, which put a great strain on her marriage, already shaken by conflicts over Ernest. She was spared further hostile encounters with Hemingway after her decision in January to take the 'cure' at Salies-de-Béarn, a health resort in the Basses Pyrénées. In this drowsy spa town they stayed at the Bellevue, where the boarded-up windows were splashed with bird-droppings and the residents according to Scott were 'two goats and a paralytic'.[5] Scott took a photograph of Zelda while she painted, in one hand a brush, in the other the water-colour self-portrait she had begun in 1925. She scribbled underneath it: 'Portrait of the artist with portrait of the artist'. Several delightful photos show her and Scottie on banks of flowers and swinging in a play area.

During 1926 Zelda again tried vainly to conceive, for despite the rows between them she and Scott were still keen to have a second child. The idea that having more children might improve an ailing marriage is a popular though not necessarily accurate one, in which it seems the Fitzgeralds concurred. The failure to conceive that year was probably a consequence of previous abortions and her unsuccessful 1924 operation in Rome, but Zelda's distress became connected in her mind with what she deemed Scott's sexual inadequacies. Zelda would remain intensely emotionally attached to Scott, but sexually their problems were increasing. Scott had always exhibited a rigid Midwestern puritanism in the face of Zelda's Southern sexual openness. Wit and charm, but not virility, were his strong suits.[6]

Scott is reputed to have told Hemingway that Zelda had complained his penis was too small to give her satisfaction, a story that has all the hallmarks of an insecure male author's vivid invention.[7] Scott's apparent lack of imagination over alternative sexual pleasure, or his worsening alcoholism which may have caused occasional impotence, were more likely causes for Zelda's frustration.

It is worth looking at Hemingway's tale of Scott's complaints of rejection because it impacts cleverly on the impression Hemingway was trying to give of Zelda's unstable mental state.

Scott it seems first naïvely confessed to Hemingway: 'You know I never slept with anyone except Zelda.' Yet in Scott's account in *The Crack-Up* he admits that at Princeton in 1917 he slept with prostitutes; and Rosalinde Fuller's account of his sexual affair with her in 1919 convincingly throws doubt on the assertion that he had never slept with anyone except Zelda. According to Hemingway, Scott continued their conversation by saying: 'Zelda said that the way I was built I could never make anyone happy and that was what upset her.' Hemingway's account records that the two men go off to inspect Scott's penis in the toilet and are away a long time. At the end of the inspection Hemingway patronizingly reassures his friend: 'You're perfectly fine ... You are OK. There's nothing wrong with you.' In Hemingway's version Scott then asks pathetically: 'But why would she say it?' to which Hemingway responds: 'To put you out of business . . . Forget what Zelda said . . . Zelda is crazy . . . Zelda just wants to destroy you.'[8]

There is something curious here. Scott, a man who was extremely wary of intimacies with other men, was unlikely to have exposed and aroused his penis in front of a 'real man'. Yet without an erection Hemingway's calculations of penis size, which he terms for posterity 'A Matter of Measurements', is meaningless. It is far more likely, then, that the maliciously creative Ernest changed a lunch-table chat into a genital display in the toilets.

This 'matter' involves three major 'measurements'. The first is the magnification of Scott's confession from a small oral discussion to a mighty washroom performance. The second is the humiliating reduction of the size of Scott's penis in the minds of readers from what they might have thought of as a usual size (had they thought about it at all) to an image of a tiny childlike member. The third, and by far the most significant, measurement is that of the state of Zelda's mental health. What Hemingway was indisputably attempting to do was yet again to call Zelda's emotional stability into question.

In early March 1926, after their return to Paris from Salies-de-Béarn, the Fitzgeralds suddenly decided to go back to the Riviera. They lunched and dined with Hemingway who was returning from New York, where he had successfully – with Scott's help – negotiated a contract with Maxwell Perkins. He told them he was going to join Hadley and Bumby in Schruns, Austria, for a skiing break, but he did not go directly to see his family. Instead he started an affair in Paris with Sara Murphy's close friend, Pauline Pfeiffer.[9]

Pauline, a clever journalist with an original mind, was more intellectually compatible with Ernest than Hadley. After Pauline had praised Ernest's new book, *The Torrents of Spring*,[10] he decided she was also an excellent literary critic who fitted into the Fitzgerald-Hemingway circle, which included the Murphys, the MacLeishes and Dos Passos, better than Hadley, who had never felt at ease with them. Pauline also had private means,[11] much of which she used to tour and stay with the Hemingways, for Hadley saw Pauline as a good friend.[12]

Though Pauline, a practising Catholic who believed extra-marital sex was a sin, was terrified by the threat of pregnancy, she could not and did not resist Ernest. When Ernest, guilt-ridden, returned to Hadley in Schruns he did not confess nor did she ask any embarrassing questions. But Hadley and Ernest felt deep relief when Dos Passos and the Murphys arrived for a week's skiing and broke the tension.[13] The Murphys, becoming aware of the strained situation, did not overtly criticize Hemingway. Zelda, however, was incensed by Hemingway's treatment of Hadley, and told Sara Mayfield later she thought it shameful of Hemingway to plan to rejoin the Catholic Church in order to have his marriage to Hadley annulled so he could marry Pauline.[14]

The Fitzgeralds had arrived at Juan-les-Pins, where for two months from early March they rented the somewhat damp Villa Paquita. During that spring and summer Sara Murphy remembers Zelda as eternally 'fearless' in risk-taking swimming stunts. She felt that Zelda was 'much better than Scott at these things'.[15] At a farewell party in Juan for critic Alexander Woollcott Zelda went further in her display of fearless pranks. After the speeches had been made she said boldly: 'I have been so touched by all these kind words. But what are words? Nobody has offered our departing heroes any gifts to take with them. I'll start off.' Then daringly she stepped out of her black lace panties and threw them at the men.[16]

While Zelda was taking light-hearted risks, Hadley was going through black moments. In late spring, Pauline and her sister Jinnie invited Hadley to tour the Loire Valley. Pauline, patently uneasy, snapped at her nervously without explaining why. Hadley hesitantly asked Jinnie if Ernest was involved. When Jinnie replied that she thought the two were fond of each other, Hadley, shocked, retreated back to Paris, miserable and, like Bumby, suffering from a ferocious cough. She confronted Ernest who, enraged, indicated she shouldn't have forced the issue. Then he left for Spain to tour the bullfights.

The Murphys had invited both Hemingways to their guesthouse in the grounds of the Villa America in Antibes. Hadley arrived alone with her sick son, grateful for Zelda and Scott's company and that of the MacLeishes. Bumby was diagnosed with whooping cough and had to be quarantined. As Sara was terrified that her three children would catch it, the Fitzgeralds generously offered Hadley the last six weeks of their lease on Villa Paquita.

In May the Fitzgeralds found a larger, less damp residence, Villa St Louis, near Juan's casino and beach. It was set among orange and lemon groves with a garden overgrown with pink oleanders, scarlet bougainvillaea and purple clematis.

The Fitzgeralds gave four-year-old Scottie a party and invited Fanny Myers and Baoth, Patrick and Honoria Murphy. Zelda, who had formerly used her artistic skills to help Scott, now employed them to entertain her daughter. With Scott's help she creatively staged a mock crusaders' battle in the terraced rock garden of their villa. 'Zelda must have spent days making the intricate cardboard battlements and [papier mâché] castle,' Gerald said.[17] There were turrets, a tower, even a moat along which swam toy ducks. The princess with long blonde hair, wearing a white satin dress, stood at a tower window, her arms raised signalling distress. Was Zelda recreating Scott's fantasy of her as his princess carefully guarded in a castle? Scott lent his collection of two squadrons of lead soldiers, showed the children how the moats would have flooded during a siege, and captured a large black beetle which he cast as the dragon who guarded the fairy castle. Zelda, who had spent weeks sewing dresses for the princess, her lady-in-waiting and the witch, acted all three parts with verve. Honoria many decades later recalled it as a highlight of her childhood. 'Zelda and Scott had been going through hard times that summer but we had a beautiful day in their make-believe world. Zelda looked beautiful like a princess and we all cheered.'[18]

Zelda and Scott drove over to the Hôtel du Cap to bring Sara Mayfield, who was staying there, back to Villa St Louis. They told Sara that Hemingway, who had now arrived in Antibes with Pauline, had lent them his manuscript of *The Sun Also Rises*. When Sara asked what the novel was about, Zelda scoffed: 'Bullfighting, bullslinging, and bull[sh] . . . ' Scott cut her short: 'Zelda! Don't say things like that.' Zelda retorted: 'Why shouldn't I?' Scott, now very angry, growled: 'Say anything you please, but lay off Ernest.' Sara watched Zelda become increasingly furious: 'Try and make me!' she retorted.[19]

Zelda objected to the fact that since his arrival in Juan, Hemingway came daily to Villa St Louis, where Scott offered Ernest constructive criticisms on his manuscript while severely neglecting his own. During the last year Scott had sold only five stories and had made little progress on his novel. Sara Mayfield said 'Zelda blamed Hemingway for Scott's sprees in Paris as well as for interrupting his work in Juan-les-Pins.'[20]

When the Fitzgeralds' lease was up at Villa Paquita, which they had lent to Ernest and Hadley, Pauline came to the Hemingways' rescue by renting two rooms at the Hôtel de la Pineda in Juan and inviting Hadley and Ernest to be her guests. The intense trio became the focus of Zelda and Scott's gossip. Pauline, an early riser, dressed in tomboy pyjamas, would knock on the Hemingways' door and rush in, unconcerned that Hadley and Ernest slept only in pyjama tops. Pauline 'without her bottoms' soon tumbled into bed with them. Initially Hadley was distressed, but relaxed when Pauline gave equally affectionate embraces to her and Ernest. One day on the beach where the trio at Pauline's suggestion swam naked while Zelda and Scott swam in suits, Pauline told Hadley she was as much in love with her as with Ernest. She hoped the way the three of them were in bed could continue for ever. Desperate to save her marriage, Hadley suggested it to Ernest. To Hadley's surprise, though not to Zelda's, Ernest strongly declined. He reminded Hadley of Pauline's convent upbringing where girls unthinkingly indulged in displays of affection which meant nothing. They were a substitute until 'the real thing' came along. Ernest believed he was the real thing.[21]

In June Scott wrote to Perkins that they were making a quick trip to Paris to have Zelda's appendix removed on the 25th. Whether this was the precise nature of Zelda's operation is in dispute. According to Mayfield, who talked to Scott, 'having her appendix removed' was a 'euphemistic description of the operation' which she implied was another abortion.[22] At first glance Sara's belief does not appear to tally with the well-documented view that Zelda was extremely keen to become pregnant again. But Scott's Ledger for June 1926 states 'Operation' but not 'appendix', whereas an entry seven months later in January 1927 records 'appendix'. This would add to Sara's evidence that it was another abortion. One other entry is of interest. For many months Zelda had been under Dr Gros's care for her gynaecological problems, but in late May 1926 just before the operation, and for its purpose only, she switched to Dr Gluck, a new man, whom she never saw again.

During Zelda's stay at the American Hospital in Neuilly, Scott accidentally met Sara Mayfield in the ladies' bar of the Paris Ritz.[23] As soon as Scott saw the writer Michael Arlen with Sara he left his Princetonian companions and joined them. Aware that Arlen's book *The Green Hat* was currently outselling *The Great Gatsby*, Scott patronizingly told Arlen he would probably be his successor as the most popular novelist of the day. Arlen winced at the backhanded compliment, then made the mistake of criticizing Hemingway's *In Our Time*. Scott jumped angrily to Ernest's defence, called Arlen 'a finished second-rater that's jealous of a coming first-rater'. When Sara had calmed him down Scott insisted that she accompany him to visit Zelda in hospital because 'it would cheer her up to see someone from home'.[24]

However, before they reached the hospital Scott insisted they stopped at Harry's New Bar to check if Hemingway was back from Pamplona where he had taken the Murphys to the bullfighting fiesta. Unable to find a cab, Scott commandeered a hearse to take them to his apartment to rescue books for Zelda. He toured Sara around in the hearse, becoming steadily drunker and more argumentative until finally it was too late to visit Zelda.

In Pamplona the Murphys, watching bulls being gored, also watched an anxious Hadley and a tense Pauline move uncertainly in Ernest's wake. After the Spanish trip Hemingway made a decision and called on the Murphys at Villa America to tell them he had asked Hadley for a divorce.

Both Gerald and Sara, despite their traditional view of marriage for themselves, took Ernest's side. They even offered him Gerald's studio on rue Froidevaux in Paris. Sara thought Hadley had been wrong to confront Ernest as it had made him feel guilty. Gerald held the odd view that Hemingway's divorce decision was related to his artistic integrity. Scott told Ernest the news 'depressed and rather baffled me'.[25] Zelda, unlike the rest of their circle, was sympathetic to Hadley and told Sara Mayfield so.

After her operation Zelda's physical health improved but her mental well-being was shaken. From childhood Zelda had always taken enormous physical risks, but she had done so for fun. Now she took wildness to dangerous extremes in a desperate plea to be noticed.

Early one morning after a party Zelda threw herself down in front of their car and challenged Scott to drive over her.[26] During another late party evening at the casino with the Murphys an unforgettable incident occurred. Zelda rose from the table, lifted her skirt above her waist and began to dance. Scott sat motionless, staring at her. The orchestra began to play as she took her first dance steps. Gerald Murphy said: 'It was spectacular . . . She was dancing for herself; she didn't look left or right, or catch anyone's eyes . . . not even at Scott. I saw a mass of lace ruffles as she whirled – I'll never forget it. We were frozen. She had this tremendous natural dignity . . . so self-possessed, so absorbed in her dance . . . she was incapable of doing anything unladylike.'[27] Sara Murphy said: 'Her dignity was *never* lost in the midst of the wildest escapades – Even that time at the casino – at the end of an evening when she danced alone in the middle of the floor – she was cool and aloof; and unconscious of onlookers. No one ever took a liberty with Zelda.'[28] She later told Sara Mayfield that no matter what Zelda did, 'even the wildest, most terrifying things – she always managed to maintain her dignity. She was a good woman, and I've never thought she was bad for Scott, as other people have said.'[29]

Ada MacLeish confirmed that Zelda would 'do these things . . . But there was no mirth. No fun. "This is what we do and now I'll proceed to do it." Those were the Fitzgerald Evenings which we learned to avoid like the plague. They seemed intent upon living this lurid life; the ordinary evening wasn't enough.'[30]

Some nights Scott did not return home at all. Some evenings he filled their villa with strangers abhorrent to Zelda. Ada MacLeish said Zelda was not seen much on the beach and rarely with Scottie, who sat alone with her nanny on the sands.[31] Zelda later recalled: 'I wanted you [Scott] to swim with me at Juan-les-Pins but you liked it better . . . at the Garoupe with . . . the Murphys and the MacLeishes . . . You left me lots alone . . . I swam with Scottie except when I followed you, mostly unwillingly.'[32] Although Zelda's memory differs slightly from Ada's, one thing is clear: beneath the Fitzgeralds' vitality, misery formed the undercurrent.

Gerald described the Fitzgeralds as a 'pair of conspirators' who would stay out all night waiting for something to happen. 'Something had to happen, something extravagant. It was that they were in search of and they went for it alone.'[33]

During this summer, the most memorable quality was Zelda's eerie self-absorption. Ada recalled how distant she was, how often a strange small smile would flit over her face, how she displayed not a vestige of humour.[34]

If Zelda's aloof actions awed their friends, Scott's over-intimate actions irritated them. His worst habit of asking personal questions intensified. Ada MacLeish remembers an evening when suddenly Scott began to trail two young men round the dance floor asking if they were fairies. One of them was Ada's dance partner.[35]

Scott, who had once enchanted the Murphys, now annoyed them. He seemed incapable of leaving them alone, having a most particular absorption with Sara. He would stare at her across the dinner table, then if she momentarily ignored him would shout: 'Sara, look at me.'[36] One day in a taxi with Sara and Zelda he stuffed filthy hundred-franc bank notes into his mouth.[37] Even more obsessed with hygiene than Zelda, Sara, who washed coins before handing them to her children, was appalled.[38] Gerald was convinced Scott was 'in love with her. She fascinated him, her directness and frankness were something he'd never run into before in a woman.' Sara, not attracted by Scott's pretty, boyish looks, scoffed at the notion. 'He was in love with all women,' she told a friend years later. 'He was sort of a masher, you know, he'd try to kiss you in taxis . . . But what's a little kiss between friends?'[39]

Zelda observed that Scott seemed determined to behave at his worst before their friends. In June 1926 when the Murphys gave a stylish party for Hemingway, Scott became so jealous of the attention guests were paying to Ernest he threw ashtrays at other tables, roundly abused Gerald, then goaded him until their urbane host left his own party in disgust. At a dinner given by the Murphys to honour the Princess Chimay, Scott first threw a ripe fig down the back of the princess's décolletage, then began to throw Sara's delicate handblown Venetian glasses over the edge of their terraced garden. After the first two Gerald banished him, though not Zelda, from their villa for three weeks.

Finally the Murphys could bear no more of Scott's impertinent questions and crude scrutiny of their personal life. Sara wrote disapprovingly: 'you can't expect anyone to like or stand a *Continual* feeling of analysis + sub-analysis + criticism – on the whole unfriendly – Such as we have felt for quite a while. It is . . . quite unpleasant . . . + Gerald, for one, simply curls up at the edges . . . It's hardly likely that I should Explain Gerald, – or Gerald me – to you. If you don't know what people are like it's *your* loss.' Sara added acutely: 'it is more probably some theory you have, – (it *may* be something to do with the book). – But *you ought to know at your age* that you *Can't have Theories about friends* – If you Can't take friends largely, + without suspicion – then they are not friends at all –.' At their age and stage in life she and Gerald could not be bothered with Sophomoric situations. 'We are very simple people . . . and we are *literally* + actually fond of you both – (There is no reason for saying this that I know of – unless we meant it.)'[40]

Zelda, aware of Scott's appalling behaviour, did acknowledge the Murphys' deep affection. But her passionate loyalty to Scott in public never allowed her to side with the Murphys, whom she saw as their joint friends. Her private concerns about her own relationship with Scott were hinted at only to Rosalind or to *her* friend Sara Mayfield.

That summer was indisputably one of turmoil, yet when any of their circle rewrote that summer in their memoirs it became one of gaiety, entertainment and high-spirited dissipation. Even Zelda wrote to Perkins that it had been a fine season, filled with gay and decorative people who offered Antibes a 'sense of carnival', though she did add with honesty, 'and impending disaster'.[41]

After two and a half years abroad, the Fitzgeralds had saved no money; their domestic life had disintegrated; their daughter, though loved by them both, was not well parented; Scott had become an acknowledged alcoholic who had hardly written for over a year; Zelda had started purposefully to paint, but Scott saw this as frivolous. Zelda moreover still relied on Scott, the 'expert', to validate her work.

Sara Mayfeld said Zelda 'now realized clearly that her marriage was headed for the rocks . . . she was plainly tired of being a successful novelist's wife, who provided the copy for his stories and books . . . she wanted to make a life of her own, to achieve . . . intellectual and financial independence.'[42]

But Zelda was having more profound conflicts than Sara recognized. In an interview with a journalist Zelda remarked that she hoped Scottie would grow up to be a flapper, 'because flappers are brave and gay and beautiful', rather than a career woman, because careers call for 'hard work, intellectual pessimism and loneliness'.[43] This shows clearly the extent to which Zelda was still engaged with the destructive image created for her by Scott, which she tried to live up to at great cost to her self-identity.

These years, 1925 and 1926, were critical for Zelda's self-development despite a deteriorating marriage and constant ill-health. It is possible that the time she spent on her own *because* of these two factors allowed her an increased measure of artistic growth.

The Fitzgeralds had rushed away from the wild distractions of New York to seek refuge in Paris. Now they were returning to America to flee the profligacy and recklessness of France.

They sailed in December 1926 on the liner *Conte Biancamano* to discover that Ludlow Fowler and his young wife, Elsie Blatchford of Winnetka, Illinois, were fellow-passengers. Zelda took Ludlow aside and said gravely: 'Now Ludlow, take it from an old souse like me – don't let drinking get you in the position it's gotten Scott if you want your marriage to be any good.'[44] Only six years earlier Fowler had been best man at Zelda's wedding. Now he stood with her watching the waves and witnessing her disillusion. Zelda's later recollection was in line with her remark to Fowler: 'we were back in America – further apart than ever before.'[45] Not even Christmas in her beloved Montgomery could repair the damage.

PART IV

Creative Voices
January 1927–1929

CHAPTER 13

1927 started modestly. Though in an immodest place: Hollywood, home of stars, melodrama and if you were lucky, mighty big bucks.

It was the lure of the bucks that tempted Scott when United Artists invited him to Los Angeles to write an original flapper comedy for Constance Talmadge. They offered an advance of $3,500 and a further $12,000 if they accepted his script.

Zelda and Scott left Scottie and her nanny with Scott's parents, who now lived in Washington and were nearer than Zelda's parents. They travelled West on the Twentieth Century Limited train, where Zelda's painter's eye took in 'the red and purple streaks of a Western dark' and later described the landscape feather-stitching along the tracks. She saw 'a green and brown hill, a precipitate tunnel . . . an odd gate, a lamppost; and a little lead dog', trees and houses on green mountains that 'seemed on probation'.[1] Hollywood itself, as they approached, appeared provisional.

'We reached California in time for an earthquake . . .' she wrote. 'White roses swung luminous in the mist from a trellis outside the Ambassador windows; a bright exaggerated parrot droned incomprehensible shouts in an aquamarine pool . . . geraniums underscored the discipline of the California flora.'[2]

From their luxurious bungalow in the hotel's grounds Zelda wrote constantly to five-year-old Scottie, illustrating notes with drawings of Hollywood events or memories of her darling 'Boo Boo'.[3] Boo Boo bounces on her head in a tutu, legs high. Zelda's and Scottie's heads peep through a heart while the word love spirals the drawing. Boo Boo is lost in the woods, hanging soulfully on to a tree. Sometimes she draws 'love' with wings flying towards Scottie thousands of miles away.

Like her winged affection, Zelda's letters and drawings flowed.

January 1927: 'Dearest Darlingest Little Boo Boo . . . It is so hot here . . . even Daddy sleeps under one blanket . . . It is the most beautiful country . . . Eucalyptus and Poinsettias grow as tall as trees . . .

this is . . . the biggest and most beautiful hotel that I have ever seen
. . . John Barrymore lives next door and Pola Negri across the way.'
As well as the 'two leading vamps of the cinema', other neighbours
were Zelda's friend Carl Van Vechten and Scott's friend from Rome
Carmel Myers.

Late January 1927: 'Dear dearest Little Boo Boo, Mummy is sitting
out here without a coat in the most glorious sunshine . . . wishing
you were here . . . I would love to show you the lovely red and blue
parrot on the terrace . . . If you were here you would not like the little
pool because it's very shallow and not for people who can swim so
beautifully, like you. You and I could go in the big one.'

Hollywood, she told Scottie, 'is not gay like the magazines say but
very quiet. The stars almost never go out in public and every place
closes at midnight . . . Daddy let me buy a very very pretty black suit
that makes me look very proud and prosperous . . . [but] I am crazy
to get back East . . . I want so badly to see my Boo-Boo . . . write to
me, you old lazy bones.'

Scottie, however, did not write for several weeks. But still Zelda's
letters poured out. After mixing daily with film celebrities, among
whom Ronald Colman particularly impressed her, a wave of inferiority swept over her: 'Everybody here is very clever and can
nearly all dance and sing and play and I feel very stupid.'

Zelda became sceptical about Hollywood's improbability: 'At
first,' she told Scottie, 'it was very lovely and impressive, but . . .
everything is on the surface and we soon began to feel there was
nothing here but decorations . . . ' Hollywood was peddling fake fun
and implausible dreams but Zelda did not buy them. The more she
missed Scottie, the more unrealistically demanding became her
letters.

By February Zelda, having been 'properly moved by the fragility
of Lillian Gish', having 'dined at Pickfair to marvel at Mary
Pickford's dynamic subjugation of life',[4] still pined for Scottie's
answer. 'I am as cross as a bear and two elephants, a crocodile, a
lizard and a kangaroo with you for never writing to me – I do not
believe you know how to write.'

Zelda told Scottie Scott's movie about a prison was 'very good'
but that *The Great Gatsby* movie which they watched was 'ROTTEN
and awful and terrible.' Zelda was nostalgic for Paris in the spring.
'I am very homesick for the pink lights and the trees and the gay
streets . . . But most of all we are very lonesome for you.'

Scottie managed two letters to Zelda, who instantly responded:
'It was more fun to read them than eating or diving or having a new

dress . . . Lady Diana Manners . . . is out here now playing in the theatre . . . we are going to have dinner with her Saturday if Daddy ever ever ever finishes his work.' Scott was finding scriptwriting tougher than he'd imagined. It would take him two months to complete the assignment. '[Daddy] says he will never write another picture because it is too hard, but I do not think writers mean what they say about their work.'

Zelda worried about her daughter. 'Please, nanny, write me if everything is all right – if you and Scottie are comfortable and happy. I'm in a panic, I want to get home and start house-hunting so bad . . . I am crazy to own a house. I want you to have a lovely little Japanese room with pink cherry blossoms.'

Zelda filled a scrapbook with pictures of houses. But her panic did not solely arise from homesickness.

The Fitzgeralds had met Lois Moran, a seventeen-year-old actress, at a luncheon given for them by Douglas Fairbanks and Mary Pickford.[5] Scott was captivated immediately by Lois's innocence, intelligence, beauty and self-discipline. Zelda said sardonically that Lois's appeal to Scott was that of a 'young actress [who is] like a breakfast food that many men identified with whatever they missed from life'.[6]

Though Scott never visited Lois unless her mother was in attendance, nevertheless they met frequently. Zelda resented Scott's escalating admiration for Lois while Scott began to compare Zelda adversely with the starlet. Finally something in Scott burst and he told Zelda he respected Lois because at least she did something with herself which required effort as well as talent. Underneath her Southern courtesy to Lois, Zelda was furious. Had Scott not noticed her own efforts with her writing and painting? Had he not recognized how little space he gave her to concentrate her attention on her own work rather than his? She was acute enough to perceive that Scott's anger with her partly reflected his frustration that after two years abroad he had less money than when they set out and his novel was still unfinished.

One evening when Scott left to dine with Lois, Zelda, unable to contain her distress and fury, in a fit of violence burned in the bath all the clothes she had herself designed.[7] It was an extraordinary gesture, as self-destructive as those she had made the previous year on the Riviera, but this time she savaged something she had already achieved. Over the years this frenzied act of burning would gain in symbolic significance as it became merely the first of several acts of destruction by fire.

Zelda's jealous anger and Scott's barely-concealed resentment were the undercurrents to a series of wild pranks they engaged in. At a cocktail party to which Lois Moran invited them Scott collected the guests' watches, bangles and rings and boiled them in tomato soup. At a party given by Goldwyn to which nobody had invited them, Scott and Zelda gate-crashed, appearing at the street door on all fours barking like dogs. Once inside, Zelda, characteristically, stole upstairs to take a bath before joining the guests. When visiting William Randolph Hearst at San Simeon, Scott shocked his host by borrowing a brassière from Zelda to clothe one of Hearst's nude garden statues.

While writing his screenplay, 'Lipstick', Scott quarrelled with Constance Talmadge, which probably injured its chances, for when it was finished in March it was rejected. Scott had to face the fact that more than his $3,500 advance had already been used up. The Fitzgeralds slunk back East, barely surviving a quarrel over Lois Moran on their journey. In a newspaper article Moran had revealed she admired philosophers, adored bathing suits (as did Zelda) and her favourite authors were Frederick Nietzsche, Rupert Brooke and Scott Fitzgerald.[8] Patently Scott had spent time on his favourite pursuit: 're-educating' a young woman, giving her reading lists.

Zelda, accustomed to that ploy, was justifiably angry, more so when Scott revealed he had invited Lois to visit them. In a rage she threw her diamond and platinum watch, which Scott had given her in 1920, out of the train window. It was her most expensive sentimental keepsake, costing $600 in 1920, worth about $12,000 today.[9]

Moran had certainly left her mark on Scott. Though he met her only a few more times, she nestled securely in his fiction, first as the sixteen-year-old shop girl Jenny in 'Jacob's Ladder', then as eighteen-year-old ingenue Helen Avery in 'Magnetism', before her final transformation into Rosemary Hoyt in *Tender Is The Night*.[10]

For Zelda, who still found Scott's attentive fictionalization of herself in his novels flattering, it would have come as a shock to see him do something similar with Lois Moran.

Zelda's and Scott's autobiographical fiction had always held messages and warnings for each other, sometimes recriminations, occasionally prophecies. In 'Jacob's Ladder' the hero Jake, a failed tenor who has made a fortune in real estate, perceives himself, like Scott, as Pygmalion, and promotes young Jenny to Hollywood stardom. Scott made Zelda see what he saw in Lois: 'the face of a dark saint with tender, luminous eyes', the face of 'an intense little Madonna', a beautiful young woman who was 'somehow on the grand scale'. Initially the disillusioned older Jake neither finds her desirable nor sleeps with her, but finally he 'rode away in a mood of exultation, living more deeply in her youth and future than he had lived in himself for years'.[11] This was not a line calculated to increase Zelda's sense of security.

In 'Magnetism' George, a charismatic thirty-year-old film actor, is married to Kay, a former Ziegfeld *Follies* showgirl, now burdened with child and English nanny. They, like the Fitzgeralds, are seen as the ideal celebrity couple. But as George and Kay's marriage wears out George studies eighteen-year-old Helen. Helen staves off George's sexual passion with the light line 'O, we're such actors, George – you and I', a line echoed by Rosemary in *Tender Is The Night*. But just as it is hard for Kay to be content that her husband did not have a sexual encounter with Helen when he views Kay as 'one of those people who are famous beyond their actual achievement'[12], so it was for Zelda to take comfort from Scott's platonic dalliance with Lois, accompanied by the same bitter accusation.

Zelda would also use that Hollywood episode in 'A Millionaire's Girl', but she waited three years to retaliate. That too becomes a story of a young film actress, Caroline, who rises to stardom. But Zelda intends *her* heroine to be a more forceful character who achieves not merely movie star status but also marriage to a man with millions. Zelda's story ends with a description of the marriage three years on, when 'so far they have kept their quarrels out of the divorce courts, but . . . [they] can't go on forever protecting quarrels'.[13] What Zelda published in 1930 she already knew in 1927.

Zelda had begun dreaming repetitively about her daughter,[14] so it was with great relief that they went to collect her from Washington, stopping in Baltimore to see Mencken. Scott did not endear himself to the Sage by singing Hemingway's praises, then informing him Ernest was all set to beat him up. Nor did Scott endear himself to Sara Haardt and Sara Mayfield when he made 'scathing remarks' about Zelda.[15]

Sara Haardt's tuberculin infection had temporarily cleared and she had resettled into a room in Charles Street, Baltimore, writing and surviving her up-and-down romance with Mencken. Gossip columnists, having linked his name with actress Aileen Pringle, were now linking it with evangelist Aimee Semple McPherson and novelist Rebecca West. Angrily Sara Haardt told Mayfield that Mencken was now 'a closed chapter in my book'.[16] Mencken, however, continued to promote Sara's writing, and at Joseph Hergesheimer's literary party Zelda and Scott overheard Sara referred to as 'the future Mrs Mencken'.

Scott felt that in rural peace he could complete his novel so, after collecting Scottie, the Fitzgeralds stayed at the Du Pont in Wilmington, Delaware, while they house-hunted, helped by Scott's Princeton roommate John Biggs and his wife Anna.[17] In late March Biggs, now a Washington lawyer and writer, found them Ellerslie, a nineteenth-century colonial-style house at Edgemoor, near Wilmington, on the banks of the Delaware River. Zelda later described in detail the four Doric columns, the portico, the 'sombre horse chestnuts in the yard and a white pine bending as graciously as a Japanese brush drawing' which surrounded Ellerslie.[18] It was a house whose thirty rooms were so enormous that Zelda had to design outsize furniture, then have it especially made in Philadelphia. With characteristic flair she painted maps of France on the garden furniture and Scottie remembers her painting stars and flowers on wooden lawn chairs. Zelda planted hedges of her favourite tissue-paper white roses and trailed yellow climbing roses over fences. Her imagination was endless. Scottie recalled how 'she painted my bed with red and white stripes' and the bedroom walls with fairytale scenes.[19]

Zelda's first impression of Ellerslie was that the 'squareness of the rooms and the sweep of the columns were to bring us a judicious tranquility'.[20] *Ellerslie* became her earliest known oil on canvas, in which the tonal values she employs confidently convey that peace. She bathes the façade of the house in amber light against a strange green sky. There are no sharp lines; brushed soft colours give the house a moody atmosphere. The house in the top two-thirds of the canvas is warm and glowing, protected by its bright white columns and massive tree trunks which line the yard. But those trees cast ominous black shadows along the gritty path. The lingering impression is of a cosy secure home fringed by unpredictable terrors.

Zelda and Scott paid an incredibly low rent of $150 a month for eighteen months for this sprawling mansion which needed the attention of two black maids: Ella, who sang Deep South spirituals in the kitchen and sat like 'a dark ejection of the storm in the candlelight'; and Marie, 'a wonderful negro maid, high and gawky, who laughed and danced barefoot about the Christmas tree on the broken balls'.[21]

When the daughter of Scott's favourite cousin Ceci, twenty-two-year-old Cecilia Taylor, visited she noticed that Scott 'seemed to tell the several colored servants what to do. I think Zelda was perfectly capable of handling things but she seemed perfectly willing to let Scott do it.'[22]

Cecilia also observed Zelda had less control than Scott over Scottie's education and discipline. After Nanny left they hired Mademoiselle Delplangue, whom Zelda described as reeking of sachet, with large brown eyes that 'followed a person about like a mop'.[23] Zelda confessed to Van Vechten: 'She is a great trial, but . . . I am afraid to fire her.'[24]

Cecilia thought Zelda's immersion in her art led Scott to take domestic and parental responsibility: 'She was painting then. She had done a screen . . . [with] seashore scenes . . . and a lampshade of Alice-in-Wonderland characters for Scottie.'[25]

It is equally likely that Scott's control, which led to Zelda's renewed insecurities over both servants and child care, was a cause not a consequence of her working so hard at her art. Whatever the primary motive, and there must have been several intertwined in a complex network, Zelda's creative output remained steady. Scottie thought Ellerslie was where Zelda felt most imaginatively domestic. Zelda has been repeatedly criticized for her poor house management but, as Scottie always said, Zelda was a marvellously creative mother. 1927 was dedicated to artworks designed for Scottie. Zelda began what over many years would be several series of thick watercolour and gouache paper dolls with costume changes.[26]

She embarked on a series of accurate historical figures: the Courts of Louis XIV (the King, Cardinal Richelieu, courtiers and ladies), King Arthur's Round Table, and Joan of Arc. A second series of fairy tales included Red Riding Hood and Goldilocks, and in a third series of paper dolls Zelda, Scott and Scottie become witty lifelike paper people who display themselves in several changes of natty underwear. Another paper Scott has angel's wings, an umbrella and a satirical pink tie.

When Zelda's paper dolls or fairy-tale drawings are examined, a pencil sketch is visible beneath the layer of watercolour and gouache. Scottie remembered: 'These dolls had wardrobes of which Rumpelstiltskin could be proud. My mother and I had dresses of pleated wallpaper, and one party frock of mine had ruffles of real lace cut from a Belgian handkerchief . . . it was characteristic of my mother that these exquisite dolls, each one requiring hours of artistry, should have been created for the delectation of a six-year-old.'[27]

The paper dolls show Zelda's strong whimsical and sardonic illustrational skills. Her gifts flourished in this smaller scale, especially when her ideas were grounded in fantasy, myth or memory. Over the years she developed several noticeable features in these early paper dolls for use in her human figures and in her later paper-doll series. Most striking is their gender ambiguity. Both sexes have heavy muscles, exaggerated shoulders, bosomy chests, powerful thighs, massive feet and enlarged calves. Male courtiers with frothy clothes, high heels, red lips and feet in ballet poses could be women. This gender ambiguity is even more obvious in the fairy tales, where the big bad wolf sports a party dress, Papa Bear minces in a skirt, and Little Red Riding Hood has a male muscular body and large feet topped by golden hair like a transvestite's wig.

The doll-making allowed Zelda to feel young again. It was as if she was trying to repeat her childhood, but this time feminized in a way that her tomboy girlhood was not.[28]

This children's art, begun in 1927, became a lifelong preoccupation. Over the years she made several hundred paper dolls which, together with fairy-tale scenes, formed a quarter of her 1974 retrospective exhibition at the Montgomery Museum of Fine Arts. In 1927 she immersed herself in historical texts of each period she drew, while her knowledge of fairy-tale literature became prodigious. Her skill was to give it a nonconformist lift. Red Riding Hood, no longer inno-cent, becomes a sophisticated teenager while the wolf has several personae. One wolf wears a carnivorous red jumpsuit and an evil scowl. Another, in black hood and cape, menaces children with his arsenal of firearms. But Zelda turns the tables by showing his gentle side in flowing white party frock, elbow-length gloves and yellow wings. Wolf into angel becomes a counterpoint to Scott as writer into angel. Though Zelda is partly making children's art for Scottie, she is at the same time subverting the conventional childhood approach by using dolls to transgress male/female boundaries.

Critic Jane S. Livingston suggests Zelda was directly influenced by a certain strain of nineteenth- and twentieth-century French illustrational art. It is not surprising that a large part of Zelda's art belongs to the French culture she admired and understood.

Zelda used as a major source for her paper dolls two historical handbooks.[29] The first, *L'Histoire du Costume Feminin Français de l'an 1037 à l'an 1870* (compiled by Paul Louis de Giafferri), catalogues hundreds of costumes and accessories from capes to corsets, bodices to brollies from the Middle Ages through to the Victorian era. More interesting even than the historical material that informs Zelda's paper dolls are the changes her transforming imagination made to her models. Her figures are considerably more lifelike, have greater fluidity and are more inventive than the historical costume drawings she was consulting.[30]

If we compare the second book she used, another French volume from the 1920s, *L'Enfance de Becassine* (illustrated by J. Pinchon), it is clear that Zelda's dramatic flair and draughtsmanship have revitalized Pinchon's somewhat flat drawings.

One emotional reason that lay behind Zelda's early paper-doll drawings was that they offered her a special way to communicate with Scottie, from whom she felt increasingly distanced. Watercolour and gouache as an intimate medium may be particularly effective for communication with a child. The historical dolls were also an educational medium. And for Scottie they worked as such. 'Her [Zelda's] paper dolls were works of art,' she said, but 'the whole court of Louis XIV . . . weren't to play with'.[31]

During the year Zelda designed and built an elaborate dolls' house ostensibly for Scottie. But her little-girl's concentration made it seem as if she was also building herself a home. For months she worked on it secretly in a third-floor hideaway where she meticulously painted, papered and furnished the house with elegant furniture, stylish mirrors and glass windows. It was finished in November, ready for Scottie to unveil it at Christmas.

During the next two years Zelda also painted a series of extraordinary lampshades, some wittily depicting members of their family or friends, others illustrating fanciful fairy tales. The most famous lampshade shows Zelda, Scott, Scottie, servants and friends on a merry-go-round. Those who can be identified are George Jean Nathan on a lion, Tana the butler on a turtle, Scott on an elephant, Scottie on a horse, Zelda on a rooster, Nanny on a mouse, probably on the kangaroo one of their negro maids, on the pig Amy Rupert Thomas and on the goose their male servant Philippe.[32] Behind them are images of several places in America and Europe the Fitzgeralds had visited: Villa St Louis, Juan-les-Pins, White Bear Lake Yacht Club, Minnesota, Ellerslie, New York's Plaza Hotel, Capri, Villa Marie, St Raphaël, Rome's Spanish Steps, and the Westport cottage.

'I am painting again,' Zelda wrote to Carl, 'and will have to work if I am to turn two apples and a stick of gum into an affair of pyramids and angles and cosmic beauty before the fall.'[33] She attended regular art classes in Philadelphia, an extension of the formal tuition she had had in Capri.[34] She contemplated art as a profession but her bouts of eyestrain intensified, and because she refused to wear corrective eyeglasses a full-time painting career seemed questionable.

The Fitzgeralds' first large house party at Ellerslie took place the weekend of 21 May 1927. Guests included Scott's parents, Carl Van

Vechten, Ernest Boyd and Teddy Chanler, as well as Lois Moran on her much-heralded visit accompanied by her mother. Zelda behaved impeccably towards the starlet who noticed no hint of jealousy or distress. But Amy Thomas observed Zelda's efforts to feel like a star before Moran's arrival. Zelda placed 'at her dressing table, gold and silver stars leading up to the ceiling, ten feet high, like a milky way'.[35] Zelda's strongest memory was of Lois's appearance, recalled with irony. 'She had no definite characteristics . . . save a slight ebullient hysteria about romance. She walked in the moon by the river. Her hair was tight above her head and she was lush and like a milkmaid.'[36]

Private rivalries and tensions however were thrust aside as the news came that Lindbergh had landed at Le Bourget airport. Lois's strongest memory was of the houseguests, picnicking on the river bank, all looking upward towards the sky in great excitement.

Zelda's letters to Van Vechten suggest some emotional turmoil (probably about Lois) *did* accompany the weekend's drinking: 'From the depths of my polluted soul, I am sorry that the weekend was such a mess. Do forgive my iniquities and my putrid drunkness . . . it should have been a nice party if I had not explored my abyss in public. Anyhow, please realize that I am sorry and contrite and thoroughly miserable with the knowledge that it would be just the same again if I got so drunk.'[37]

Scott's Ledger offers no judgement on that weekend but records that he saw Lois again in May in New York.

Zelda's contrition appeared short-lived. A few days later she thanked Carl for his gift of a cocktail shaker in her usual droll vein: 'You were very sweet to make such a desirable contribution to the Fitzgerald household . . . It's such a nice one that I have been looking about to see what damage you must have done.'[38] Zelda kept up a running commentary on Ellerslie life for Carl's delectation. They had acquired Chat the cat and two dogs from the local pound. 'One of them is splotchy but mostly white with whiskers although he is sick now, so his name is Ezra Pound. The other is named Bouillabaisse or Muddy Water or Jerry. He doesn't answer to any of them so it doesn't matter.'[39]

Their notes were playful but Zelda's friendship with Carl remained sturdily platonic, unlike her more teasing friendship with Teddy Chanler, their friend from Paris days. During the Moran house-party weekend the Fitzgeralds took Teddy and the other guests to a local amusement park. Amy Thomas and Scott were photographed on one carousel horse while Teddy and Zelda took a ride on another. Zelda reported: 'He [Teddy] could understand why an amusement park is the best place to be amorous – it's something about the whitewashed trees and the smell of peanuts and the jogging of the infernal machines for riding.[40] Zelda's report of this incident is reminiscent of her Ferris wheel ride with Dos Passos.

Esther Murphy, a frequent visitor to Ellerslie, told Gerald and Sara how impressed she was with its grandeur. In early summer Zelda received a letter from Sara:

> your house – (according to Esther) – is palatial and then some – You keep, it appears, only 14 of the 27 bedrooms open + only 3 drawing rooms – and you + Scott have a system of calls + echoes to locate each other readily. Do you ever have a hankering for Villa St Louis? . . . Is Scott working? And how's the book coming on?[41]

Scott was making little progress with the novel that would become *Tender Is The Night* and had returned to short stories. Ironically, his income in 1927 was better than his negligible professional output would indicate. He earned $29,737, of which $15,300 came from stories for the *Saturday Evening Post*, which now paid him $3,500 per story. However, royalties from his published fiction totalled only $169, while his book earnings were $5,911.64, of which $5,752.06 was an advance against the novel he seemed incapable of moving forward. He cabled Ober every week for advances of $500 or $800 for projected stories he never actually delivered. Their Ellerslie expenses, already enormous, escalated with trips to New York, Virginia Beach, Princeton, Quebec, Norfolk (where Cousin Cecilia lived), and Long Island during the polo-playing season to visit Tommy Hitchcock. The figures – yet again – did not match up. It is no surprise that Scott began to have nervous attacks which in his Ledger he calls 'Stoppies'.[42]

Zelda, who had not written since 1924, began writing again, although despite the size of the house she did not have a study of her own. During 1927 she produced four more articles to which Scott gave cursory editorial supervision, three of which were published the following year. The first, 'The Changing Beauty of Park Avenue', which appeared in *Harper's Bazaar* in January 1928, was credited to Scott and Zelda, but in his Ledger Scott acknowledges Zelda alone wrote it. On the manuscript Scott wrote the title and both names, putting his first. The minor revisions he made on the manuscript were removed before publication and new revisions inserted, perhaps by the editor, possibly by Zelda.

Her unique, sensuous style with its lush physical description and fairy-tale references catch the elegance of the avenue that flows from 'the pool of glass that covers the Grand Central tracks' then smoothly through Manhattan. It is a street for satisfied eyes with 'crystalline shops, lying shallow against buildings, [which] exist on sufferance so long as they are decorative . . . It is full of nuances and suggestions of all New York, but they are shaped and molded into an etched pattern. There are disciplined, cool smells . . . of hot motors and gusty dust – of violets and brass buttons . . . gay awnings in the rarefied sunlight.' It is a street for strutting and in the centre 'floats, impermanently, a thin series of watercolor squares of grass – suggesting the Queen's Croquet Ground in *Alice in Wonderland*'.

Zelda makes some offbeat but accurate observations: 'this is a masculine avenue . . . subdued and subtle and solid and sophisticated in its understanding that avenues and squares should be a fitting and sympathetic background for the promenades of men', yet she sees it also as an international avenue, where tradespeople are accustomed to a clientele 'who need nothing, want nothing, and buy freely because they have large leisure and filled purses'.[43]

The second article, 'Looking Back Eight Years', which looks back to the postwar period then forward to the younger generation, appeared in *College Humor* in June 1928. Publicly attributed to Scott as well as Zelda, once more it is privately credited by Scott to Zelda. Artist James Montgomery Flagg drew two sketches of the Fitzgeralds which framed the feature. This article is more analytic than Zelda's previous writings. She dissects those feelings of frustration her peers have suffered from: how to survive youth and reach some kind of wisdom. 'It is not altogether the prosperity of the country and the consequent softness of life which have made them unstable . . . It is a great emotional disappointment resulting from the fact that life moved in poetic gestures when they were younger and has now settled back into buffoonery . . . sensitive young people are haunted and harassed by a sense of unfulfilled destiny.'[44]

The third article, 'Who Can Fall In Love After Thirty?', a cynical shot at romantic realism, also bought by *College Humor* (October 1928), was published as by Scott and Zelda, yet again shown in Scott's Ledger to have been written by Zelda.

Zelda told readers that after thirty the 'most vital contacts lay in a community of working interests', and that the mystery she once thought lay in other people was in fact one's own youthful wonder. She did not suggest youth's excitement and promise must necessarily be abandoned, but the 'whole varied glamour of existence can no longer be concentrated at will into another person'.[45]

The fourth feature, 'Paint and Powder', initially called 'Editorial on Youth', an amusing invective against the rouge pot and the marcel iron, was written solely by Zelda for *Photoplay* in 1927. It was bought not by *Photoplay* but by *The Smart Set*, which published it in May 1929 under Scott's name only.[46]

Most of Scott's biographers casually record these intellectual property thefts as being an inconsequential feature of marketing. 'Most of her work was published under the joint by-line . . . because the magazines insisted on using his name', runs a typical phrase.[47] These same biographers are fulsomely quick to point out that 'Fitzgerald punctiliously identified' Zelda's stories in his Ledger.[48] Scott himself assured Ober in a letter that 'My wife got $300 apiece for articles she wrote entirely herself for College Humor and Harpers Bazarre. The editors knew this but insisted my name go on them with her.'[49]

It is worth speculating how Scott might have felt if he alone had written one of those articles, if Zelda alone had been credited for it, and if she had punctiliously acknowledged his 'contribution' in her diary.

In contrast to Scott's poor productivity, Hemingway, still living in Gerald's Paris studio, was writing well. His book of short stories, *Men Without Women*, was due out with Scribner's in October. He reported to Scott that for the last two months he had been broke. He topped and tailed his letter with assurances that Scott was his 'devoted friend' and 'the best damn friend I have'.[50] Scott replied at once, sending him $100.

Scott generously sent Hemingway's book to Mencken for his approval, describing Hemingway as 'really a great writer . . . the best we have I think'.[51] Scott told Ernest that Zelda's favourite story was 'Hills Like White Elephants' and curiously, considering their mutual animosity, Zelda clipped a copy of Ernest's story to the back of one of her articles in her scrapbook.

Zelda and Scott did not find the tranquillity they needed in Ellerslie. Instead they plunged into new depths of dissipation and marital discord. Amy Thomas reported 'one party after another'.[52] One September weekend Scott organized a croquet-polo match for Fowler, Martin and yet more houseguests. A dance band was laid on for the evening; there was bootleg whiskey but no food. So hungry and fretful was Dos Passos that he rushed into Wilmington to buy sandwiches.

Van Vechten reported to Mencken that the Fitzgeralds were 'keeping a very wet house in Delaware'.[53] As James Thurber saw them, 'There were four or five Zeldas and at least eight Scotts so that their living room was forever tense with the presence of a dozen desperate personalities, even when they were alone in it.'[54] The constant quarrels with Scott, the entertaining and excess took their toll on Zelda. Dr Lewis 'Lefty' Flynn, their family physician there, recalled Zelda's frequent need of bed-rest, already showing signs of what he considered premature 'burn-out'.[55] One evening the doctor had to be summoned from Wilmington to give her a morphine injection for hysteria, the second time this had occurred. During parties not much attention was paid to Scottie who stood at doors or windows shyly observing.

Family members visited Ellerslie: Scott's mother in May; Zelda's sister Marjorie, Marjorie's daughter Noonie and Scott's sister Annabel in late July; Zelda's parents in August. Zelda took the Sayre contingent to Atlantic City, where the photo of them on the boardwalk shows Zelda in dark dress with white scalloped edges and a bleak look on her face. The grand house impressed her family more than Zelda's exhausted condition.

By September, when they entertained Perkins and Dos Passos to what guests described as a debauched chaotic house party for cousin Cecilia, Zelda was intermittently ill. She had developed a skin irritation which may have been her first attack of eczema.

At the house party was a New York lawyer, Dick Knight, who was to become increasingly attached to Zelda. Scott disliked him at once. Knight was considered odd, with a huge misshapen head and quirky manner. On his arrival he told Zelda and Cecilia he was late because he had been identifying his brother at the morgue. From his amused tone one would have thought he had just said something funny. Edmund Wilson believed that Knight was an unpredictable bounder – and at one Ellerslie party Knight threw a pot of mustard at the dining room door. Yet Zelda had a soft spot for him. On one trip to New York, when Scott met Lois Moran, Zelda spent several hours with Dick, seeing him again later at a party for Paul Morand, the French diplomat and writer. Scott was so jealous he forbade Zelda to see Dick again.[56]

Due to the disorderly chronicling of the Fitzgeralds' lives, it is not clear what first roused Scott's jealousy, but what is apparent is that he kept it up. Zelda herself wrote in an autobiographical sketch: 'I do not know why he [Dick Knight] is attractive . . . his head is too big for his body [but] [o]ne lost afternoon . . . we drank cocktails in a New York apartment and sat afterwards a long time on the stairway, oblivious with a kind of happy desperation.'[57]

Zelda grew more desperate. She and Scott visited New York later in September for the first time for several months, quarrelling incessantly and apologizing afterwards to Gilbert and Amanda Seldes, who were disgusted with their 'public brawl'.[58] In Manhattan they met and were each fascinated by socialite Emily Vanderbilt, who would make a significant impression on both their lives.[59]

As another bout of eyestrain led her away from the path of professional painting, Zelda determined to make dancing her career. By midsummer she had enrolled, with Scottie, in ballet classes with Catherine Littlefield, Director of the Philadelphia Opera Ballet Corps and former student of Madame Lubov Egorova. Although Zelda had not taken ballet lessons since she was a girl in Montgomery she was determined to be 'a Pavlova, nothing less'.[60] By November she was dancing three times a week and still painting daily. Anna Biggs went with her on a shopping trip to Philadelphia where Zelda purchased a large Victorian gilt mirror, which she hung in their front room. In front of it she installed a ballet bar where she practised to 'The March of the Toy Soldiers', playing the record over and over until Scott was wild with exasperation. She practised all the time. During meals, even when guests were there, she paused only to wipe away sweat or gulp some water. Scott worried that dancing was bad for her health as well as for his well-being.[61]

Scott saw her ballet as a vengeful act against him. Later he told a writer friend, Tony Buttitta, that he attributed Zelda's dancing ambition in 1927 not to the desire to compete with Lois Moran, but to a desire to 'replace Isadora Duncan now that she was dead, and outshine me at the same time'.[62]

Zelda cared little for his opinion. Only the opinions of those who danced now mattered to her. To a large extent she had created her own world, separate from Scott's world of drinking and debauchery. In a letter to Van Vechten she described her attempts to preserve her own spirit amidst the chaos: 'I joined the Philadelphia Opera Ballet,' she wrote, 'and everybody has been so drunk in this country lately that I am just finding enough chaos to pursue my own ends in, undisturbed.'[63]

After Zelda had restarted dancing, Sara Haardt visited her. Sara had followed the Fitzgeralds to Hollywood on *her* first stint as a screenwriter. While there Sara had spent several hours defending the Fitzgeralds from the bad reputation they had left behind. To one

Hollywood writer who criticized Scott's insulting manner Sara loyally protested: 'Scott's basically a sweet, nice person.' When that critic called Scott arrogant, Sara stood up for him: his arrogance, she said, was 'a kind of defense mechanism . . . He's trying to cover up a feeling of social inferiority he's always had. Underneath it, he's a nice, sensitive boy, who's pathetically eager to have people like him.'[64]

On Sara's return to Baltimore in late 1927, healthier and more financially secure, she resumed her relationship with Mencken who moved her into a new apartment;[65] they spent most evenings together there, while Sara wrote *The Diary of an Old Maid*.

In Ellerslie Zelda and Sara discussed Zelda's articles and Sara's projected series on wives of famous men. Then Zelda talked about ballet. The room they sat in with its tall ceilings, wide windows and pier glasses reminded Sara of the last place she had seen Zelda dance: 'The walls of this old house in Wilmington . . . fell away, and I was back in the ball-room of the Old Exchange Hotel in Montgomery.' Zelda told Sara she took four lessons a day. 'I thought Scottie had more time to do the work than I had,' Zelda said, 'and that I had better get it in!' She described the work as 'a highly artificial and enormously exacting science . . . so rigid and with such an elaborate technique that the artist is lost'. Zelda had already confessed she felt 'whatever women do is certain to be lost. They remind me of the Japanese beetle in their slow tedious processes – their endless exploitation of little instead of big things.' Yet Sara noticed that despite this attitude Zelda was now studying ballet with absolute absorption. 'She [Zelda] says . . . ballet dancers have the sensitivity of musicians and the savagery of acrobats, but . . . that kind of dancing is to self-expression in woman what violin and piano playing is to man.' Sara believed the dancing had given Zelda new self-esteem. Zelda had sounded confident: 'Of course, it requires youth, especially the resilience of youth – but I feel much younger than I did at sixteen, or any other age.' Sara saw them as brave words. 'With her bronze-gold hair and rose and ivory coloring, it seemed to me she looked as young too. She has changed . . . since 1918, of course; she is charming rather than glamorous, with all the deep sense of tragedy and beauty of the aristocratic South to which she was born – together with that fine ruthlessness the South has always had for the things it loved.'

Being with a Southern friend relaxed Zelda and before Sara left, she said dreamily: 'I'd like to have a pink villa high on a hill full of mirrors and done in black and white.'

Later, Sara wrote: 'Who but Zelda Fitzgerald could be so sure of her youth – so oblivious of a time when she would look fearfully and sadly past the haunting gleam of mirrors.'[66]

Zelda was in fact less sure than she sounded of her youth and less certain she had sufficient resilience for her belated ambitions. She told Amy Thomas, who remembers her in Wilmington as 'serious and cautious', that she already felt 'old' in her late twenties.[67]

What Zelda did was to pin her hopes on acquiring the two skills Scott had berated her for lacking: effort, mighty effort, and self-discipline, monumental self-discipline. Confident of her talent, now she determined to anchor it. No matter what the cost.

CHAPTER 14

As Zelda's self-discipline strengthened, Scott's grew weaker. He later recalled 1928 as the year he started drinking as a stimulant for his writing. Previously he drank when he wasn't working; now he drank to write. Zelda had no influence over him and he had no control over himself. Mixed loyalties beset her. In the eyes of her Deep South community and family, she had gone out on a limb to marry Scott. Her parents had never thought highly of him, but once he had made a name for himself as a novelist, Zelda felt her marriage was justified. At the time it had not occurred to her that she might justify her own existence. Although Scott, at present, could hardly be termed a successful novelist, their household still revolved around his role as 'the writer'.

Scott remained her closest friend, but as a friend he failed her daily. He had usurped her narrative, he took credit for her writing, now he resented her dedication to ballet. As much as she needed him, she needed also to get away from him. Living inside his orbit stifled her. Living with a drunk terrified her.[1] Her release she saw through ballet, which she practised ferociously; when not dancing she continued to paint, though at a steadier pace.

In his Ledger Scott misspelt (thereby characteristically devaluing) Zelda's dance teacher's name as 'Katherine' for Catherine (Littlefield), an act consistent with his misspelling of every name significant in their joint lives. Angry that Zelda chose to dance rather than join him in bars, Scott drank with men he hardly knew.

Scott's resentment of Zelda's productivity, a dark reminder of his own minimal progress with the novel, underlay their fierce rows. Better at inventing titles for the book than developing chapters, he swung through a variety: *Our Type*, *The World's Fair*, *The Melarky Case* (when its hero was Francis Melarky, a film technician who murders his mother) and one dreamed up by Zelda, *The Boy Who Killed His Mother*.

If Scottie was frightened by the severity of her parents' quarrels that year – and many children would have been – she never admitted it. She remembers instead her first formal education which took place at Ellerslie. 'Every week a packet would arrive from the Calvert School in Baltimore,[2] complete with wonderful stickers to be pasted in workbooks and red and gold stars to be dispensed when a poem was memorized or a dictation properly taken down. I had a tutor named Miss Miller, about whom I remember nothing except she was young and pretty.' She was one of the few household members with whom Zelda felt at ease but unfortunately she left in March 1928. The Calvert School, 'heavy on the temples of Cambodia and the jungles of Africa', enthused Scottie with a love of geography. 'I wanted to go everywhere that Calvert took me.'[3]

In February the Fitzgeralds left Scottie for a few days to go to Quebec as guests of the Canadian tourist office. Despite besieging six-year-old Pie with postcards, illustrated by Zelda, signed Easter Bunny, Jupiter and A. Rhinoscerous, they were unable to ease the tension between them. They stood shivering outside the Château Frontenac which Zelda described as 'built of toy stone arches, a tin soldier's castle'. She remembers their voices 'truncated by the heavy snow, [as] the stalactite icicles on the low roofs turned the town to a wintry cave'.[4] The photos of the couple also have an icy air. Zelda, in fur coat and hat, looks especially stern and gloomy.

On their return, Rosalind and Newman Smith visited them for a weekend in February which Scott's Ledger describes as a 'catastrophe'. Scott had been invited to speak at a Princeton Cottage Club dinner but was so drunk with nerves that after a few incoherent sentences he gave up. He returned home, hurt and humiliated, on a drunken crying jag. He picked a fight with Zelda in front of their guests, throwing a favourite blue vase of hers into the fireplace. When she retaliated by calling his father an Irish cop he hit her across the face. Her nose bled and she suffered a black eye. Newman intervened while Rosalind, shaken and appalled, decided that her sister's marriage was far worse than the family had suspected and advised her to leave Scott. Zelda's loyalty was severely tested: despite her ambivalence she still wanted to prove she had made a good marriage. She told Rosalind she and Scott chose to live in that manner and she would brook no family interference. The Newman Smiths, outraged, left the next day.

On 25 February Scott invited Thornton Wilder, one of his new literary heroes, who unfortunately had witnessed Scott's Princeton debacle, for the weekend. Scott also invited Wilson to the gathering he described as small but select. The selection included Esther

Murphy, Gilbert and Amanda Seldes, John and Anna Biggs and two actresses, Zoe Atkins and Laurette Taylor, in Wilmington for the try-outs of the play *The Furies*, plus some of their theatrical staff including a temperamental set designer. At dinner Wilson decided Zelda was at 'her iridescent best'.[5] But she then left the party to take a nap, and on re-emerging her iridescent best turned rapidly to her acid worst. When the moody stage designer told her to go away because he was thinking, Zelda's instant riposte, 'Oh, you're not really thinking, you're just being homogeneous!', upset him so much that he and his team departed in a huff. As Wilson later reported: 'The aftermath of a Fitzgerald evening was notoriously a painful experience.'[6]

Desperate about their life in the US, the Fitzgeralds decided to return to Europe, worrying as usual about the cost. In March, however, Scott suddenly produced a highly profitable short-story project based on the adventures of Basil Duke Lee, a bossy Midwestern boy who longs for a New York life. Harold Ober sold 'The Scandal Detectives', the first story in the series which follows Basil from fourteen-year-old stripling to Yale, for $3,500 to the *Saturday Evening Post*. Between March 1928 and the following February Scott wrote eight Basil Duke tales, which brought him $31,500 and financed their Paris trip.

Before they left Scott saw both Ober and Perkins, to whom he promised to deliver the new stories regularly. Secretly he hoped that Europe would work the same magic on his new novel as it had on *Gatsby*. Perkins reported to Hemingway (in Key West) that though Scott had got over his nervous 'Stoppies' he was very depressed. Hemingway, sympathetic about the nerves, was hardline about Scott's lack of progress. He felt because Scott was frightened he used defence mechanisms such as writing stories *only* to make money. Ernest felt Scott should have written three novels by now. Even if only one was *Gatsby* standard it would have been worth it.

On 21 April Zelda, Scottie and Scott sailed on the *Paris*. They hadn't much faith in travel, nor a great belief in a change of scene as a panacea for spiritual ills, but were simply glad to be going. In the photo taken on board ship, Scottie smiles as she cuddles a doll into her furry jacket, but Scott looks as though it would be too much effort to smile; he even holds his hat with a depressed gesture. As for Zelda, her photo is one of the harshest taken in the twenties: the scowling severity of her face matches the severe grey cloak and tight cloche hat restraining her ears.[7]

The Murphys eagerly awaited their arrival. Gerald had written to

Scott: 'We are very fond of you both . . . The fact that we don't always get on has nothing to do with it . . . To be able to talk to people after almost two years is the important thing.'[8] After the couples reconciled Scott wrote to Ernest: 'We are friends with the Murphys again. Talked about you a great deal.'[9]

Initially the Fitzgeralds stayed at the Hôtel de Palais, but the Murphys, who had taken one apartment on the quai des Grands-Augustins and a second at 14 rue Guynemer overlooking the Luxembourg Gardens, offered to lend them their second apartment while they were in Antibes that summer.[10] Zelda told her Montgomery friend Eleanor Browder that the décor reminded her of a setting for one of Madame Tussaud's gloomier figures.[11]

Scottie recalls her first school, the Cours Dieterlin. 'You went two days a week and the rest of the time you did your lessons at home with your "institutrice", in my case Mlle Serez to whom I was devoted.' Scottie's education was that of privileged French girls: mainly memorizing whole scenes from plays by Corneille or Racine. '[We also learnt] the names of not only the French kings but their wives . . . I have been trying to remember whether we also committed the names of the mistresses to mind.' Scottie said she had had a speaking acquaintance with Mme de Pompadour and Mme de Montespan long before she understood their professional proclivities.[12]

From Paris Zelda wrote to Eleanor Browder, recently married, apologizing for not sending a wedding present and describing her restlessness: 'We are vaguely floating about on the surface of a fancy French apartment . . . It looks as if we'll never stay anywhere long enough to see how we like it.'[13]

Scottie liked it at once, partly because she had a safe play area. 'When we were not in school,' she remembered, 'we would meet each other at the Luxembourg Gardens to sail the toy boats or ice skate at the Grande palace or roll hoops . . . under the Eiffel Tower . . . It was a delightful time.'[14]

Zelda liked it better when the Kalmans visited, and she confided in Sandy her new plan of becoming a professional dancer. She had told Gerald, who had deeper reservations than Sandy, feeling that at Zelda's age there were limits to her potential achievement. Nevertheless, impressed by her determination, he arranged for her to study with Madame Lubov Egorova, director of the Ballets Russes school, whom Zelda had already met. Egorova had previously taught Alexandra Danilova, Anton Dolin and James Joyce's schizophrenic daughter Lucia.

Zelda worked to Lubov's demanding schedule of eight to ten hours a day with absolute seriousness. As a Southern Belle, it had been a big leap for her to accept the idea that women's need for professional achievement rather than amateur 'self-expression' was essential if they were to have a healthy identity. But she had made it and the six stories she wrote that year and the next mirrored this very notion: that women need to work. The Murphys, who empathized with this view, resolved to support her despite their growing misgivings. Scott of course believed in the work-as-a-profession ethos, but for himself rather than for his wife. Some of their friends later thought he believed in it if necessary at the expense of his wife.

What Zelda had not told Gerald, doubtless because he was a joint friend, was that her desire to perfect this art was also rooted in the belief that it would release her from dependence on Scott. To this end, like Alabama in *Save Me The Waltz*, Zelda drove herself mercilessly, dancing to 'drive the devils that had driven her', believing that 'in proving herself, she would achieve that peace which she imagined went only in surety of one's self'. She felt 'that she would be able, through the medium of the dance, to command her emotions, to summon love or pity or happiness at will, having provided a channel through which they might flow.'[15]

One afternoon Zelda invited the Murphys to Egorova's studio to watch her dance. The studio floor was raked to resemble a stage so that spectators had to gaze upwards at the dancers, which was a most unflattering view. 'It made her [Zelda] seem taller, more awkward than she was. There was something dreadfully grotesque in her intensity – one could see the muscles individually stretch and pull; her legs looked muscular and ugly . . . One held one's breath until it was over. Thank God, she couldn't see what she looked like.'[16]

In fact Zelda knew exactly what she and the other practising dancers looked like and how they felt: exhausted. Streaming with sweat. Muscles bulging. Limp and drained. Yet withal on fire with the passion of the dance. Later in one of her most successful oil paintings, *Ballerinas Dressing*,[17] which she gave to Sandy Kalman, she attempted to draw precisely that experience, those emotions, that appearance. The limbs of the five naked ballet figures are again elongated in a quasi-mannerist style, feet are enlarged, big hands knotted with muscles, several heads sag with fatigue. This characteristic distortion of extremities is reminiscent of American artists Thomas Hart Benton or Paul Cadmus or, like her paper dolls, could have been influenced by the popular illustrator Maxfield Parrish.

When Zelda was asked why she painted her dancers, typically depicted as graceful and delicate, with alarmingly exaggerated limbs, she said 'Because that's how a ballet dancer feels after dancing.'[18] She believed strongly the depiction of the swollen physical flesh had to reveal psychological emotions, and by creating her forms in this way Zelda consciously rejected traditional feminine shapes. Her nude figures in this oil painting, as in many of her dance paintings, appear strong and asexual despite two figures with what look like stuck-on breasts. This could be related to Zelda's preoccupation with dance as work and may be trying to show that female dancers strive as hard professionally as men.

The close links between Zelda's visual and verbal arts are shown especially in the area of dance. In *Save Me The Waltz* she recreates in words the vision of *Ballerinas Dressing* and the experience which horrified Gerald Murphy. 'Alabama's work grew more and more difficult. In the mazes of the masterful fouetté her legs felt like dangling hams; in the swift elevation of the entrechat cinq she thought her breasts hung like old English dugs. It did not show in the mirror. She was nothing but sinew. To succeed had become an obsession. She worked till she felt like a gored horse in the bull ring, dragging its entrails.'[19]

Honoria Murphy recalls her parents 'were always very fond of her but that year when she started with Egorova they worried more about her. She was still very affectionate with that sense of magic that drew them to her . . . but suddenly she'd turn strangely silent. My father always blamed her breakdown on the dancing. I'll never forget his pacing up and down as he said: "She's overdoing it dammit! . . . In Russia they start at age seven and she's nearly thirty! She's killing herself."'[20]

Zelda's friends Dick and Alice Lee Myers felt the same. Fanny recalls her parents saying 'It was good for her to have an occupation of her own, but she took it too hard. She wanted to be a creative person in the public eye but she pushed too hard. She overdid it. She was so determined. Yes, she was driven.' Fanny believes Zelda 'was desperate to make up for the time she hadn't been dancing'.[21]

It became a summer of drinking, boredom and rows. Scott's anger about the ballet increased week by week. He wrote miserably: 'drinking and general unpleasantness', followed by: 'general aimlessness and boredom', which led to him landing in jail twice.[22] Later Zelda reproached him for his behaviour: 'You were constantly drunk. You didn't work and you were dragged home at night by taxi-drivers when you came home at all. You said it was my fault for dancing all day. What was I to do?'[23] Zelda confided to Sara Mayfield, who was at the Sorbonne: 'Scott and I had a row last week, and I haven't spoken to him since . . . When we meet in the hall, we walk around each other like a pair of stiff-legged terriers spoiling for a fight.'[24]

Scottie suffered from complete lack of parental attention and was left alone with her French governess Mlle Delplangue, whom Zelda disliked.

Scott had promised Perkins he would post two chapters a month, but when he did force himself to work it was not on his novel but on the Basil Duke stories. These stories reveal Scott had become much affected by remembrances of things past.[25] The first, 'The Scandal Detectives', was based on a club he had founded in St Paul where he and his schoolfriends had gathered in the magical Midwestern dusks. After the second story, 'The Freshest Boy', still attempting to recover the past, he tackled 'A Night at the Fair' in May, managing 'He Thinks He's Wonderful' in July and in September 'The Captured Shadow' to coincide with the publication of the first Duke tale. But he 'passionately hated [that work] and found [it] more and more difficult to do. The novel was like a dream, daily farther and farther away.'[26]

Zelda too made a shot at recapturing the past, but hers was rather more sinister. She and Sara Murphy attended a Paris luncheon together at which several people came up to them courteously. Zelda smiled, took their hands, then muttered under her breath 'I hope you die in the marble ring.' Sara recalled how charming and polite Zelda was. 'No one suspected that she was saying anything but the usual pleasantries; I heard her because I was standing right next to her.'[27] Previous biographers have failed to find any meaning in Zelda's statement; but in discussions with remaining Montgomery friends and family a reasonable suggestion emerged that this was a childhood taunt relating to the area of the State Capitol, where Zelda, Sara Mayfield and the others played in a ring around the marble rotunda circular staircase.

A great many friends in Paris that summer helped the Fitzgeralds escape their own desperation. They saw the three Murphys and Cole Porter constantly, and Zelda was thrilled when Sandy and Oscar Kalman returned. They spent time with Thornton Wilder, his companion Gene Tunney, and John and Margaret Bishop, in Paris while renovations were completed on their château in Orgeval. Margaret chattered more than ever; Scott and Zelda disliked her more than ever. She was not the only acquaintance to upset Scott, who found it hard to look as pleased as Zelda did when Dick Knight visited. Zelda recalled later that even when Scott himself was 'entangled sentimentally' he would forbid her to see Dick.[28]

At a dinner given by Sylvia Beach on 27 June[29] they met James Joyce, after which Scott hosted a dinner for him and his wife Nora at their apartment. Zelda, however, did not share her husband's adulation for Joyce which drove another wedge between them.

Unable to placate each other or find any harmony of spirit, they began to look around. Both began to notice and pay attention to Esther's exotic friend Emily Vanderbilt, who according to Scott's Ledger dallied with members of the Ballets Russes as well as with a number of 'fairies'.[30] The artistic homosexual set was unleashing Zelda's emotions. Although she continued to row with Scott about his sexual inadequacy, she was in fact coming slowly to terms with her own sexual loss of interest in him. Zelda's devotion to Egorova began in her mind to have a sexual component. Fantasies followed. In a letter to Scott in which she tried to unpick the summer patchwork that Scott called 'Ominous' (which he underlined three times)[32] she wrote:

> You made no advances towards me and complained that I was unresponsive. You were literally eternally drunk the whole summer. I got so I couldn't sleep and I had asthma again . . . it made you angry that I didn't care any more. I began to like Egorowa.[32]

At that point Scott denied the mounting importance of Egorova – or perhaps he simply didn't see it, being more concerned, as his birthday approached, with the fact that he had made 'no real progress in *any* way and *wrecked myself with dozens of people*'.[33]

Attempting to leave the wreckage behind them, the Fitzgeralds made a stormy crossing back to the US in September 1928 on the *Carmania*. During the boat trip Zelda, increasingly anxious, told Scott she was disturbed at the nature of her devotion to Egorova. 'I was afraid that there was something abnormal in the relationship and you laughed.'[34] He dismissed her remark, but they were taking the wreckage home with them.

CHAPTER 15

On their return to Ellerslie in September 1928, their lives in a mess, Scott took to drink . . . as was to be expected. Zelda took to her paintbrush and ballet bar . . . what else? Hemingway meanwhile took to blaming Zelda. Everyone was being predictable.

Hemingway wrote to Perkins that every stupid action Scott had taken had been influenced by Zelda. Scott might have been the world's best writer had he been married to someone else. Zelda was to blame for everything.

Perkins held a higher opinion of Zelda. '[She] is so able and intelligent,' he replied, 'and isn't she also quite a strong person? . . . I'm surprised she doesn't face the situation better, and show some sense about spending money.'[1] But Hemingway's critical attitude to Zelda had by now become obsessive. He was not prepared to recognize any evidence to the contrary, no matter which of their friends produced it.

Unaware equally of Hemingway's diatribe or Perkins' praise, Zelda mixed her paints thicker and thicker, and danced on the carpet, wearing it thinner and thinner, as if she could paint over or stamp out her turbulent thoughts. Scott may have shared some of his uneasy reflections with his new drinking companion, Philippe, a former French taxi-driver and boxer whom Scott had brought back to Ellerslie as a chauffeur/butler. Zelda, who found him stupid and insubordinate, despised him, Mademoiselle fell for him and Scott's tolerant lawyer friend John Biggs frequently bailed him and Scott out of jail.

Zelda, who had not seen Hemingway for two years, had not missed him, but Scott felt his friend's absence keenly and was delighted they were meeting in November. Pauline had given birth to baby Patrick, who according to Ernest was built like a brick shithouse, slept through the night and laughed constantly. Hemingway informed the Fitzgeralds he was available for hire as a sire of perfect children: a remark calculated to make Zelda and Scott feel inadequate. Though their sexual relationship was fast deteriorating and Zelda repeatedly told Scott he was a poor lover, both were still anxious to give Scottie a sibling. Hemingway, aware of the Fitzgeralds' marital problems, would have known his remark had a bitter edge. If Mayfield overstated the view that the terrible troubles that would crack the Fitzgeralds apart had their roots in quarrels with and over Hemingway, nevertheless Hemingway's methods of baiting and bad-mouthing Zelda, and undercutting Scott while still keeping him on a faithful string, accelerated the Fitzgeralds' vulnerability towards Hemingway and each other.[2]

The Fitzgerald–Hemingway reunion occurred on the 17th, the weekend of the Princeton–Yale game. Scott and Zelda were already ensconced at the Cottage Club when Ernest, Pauline and a painter friend, Henry Mike Strater,[3] arrived. Princeton won the game, Ernest was polite, Pauline friendly, and Zelda engaged the artist in conversation. Strater found Zelda 'a lovely person, a lovely, lovely person' who was having a tough time dealing with Scott's drinking, which in his view 'was out of control'.[4]

Zelda's easy relaxation with Strater was ruthlessly interrupted when trouble started on the post-game journey from Princeton to Philadelphia. Scott raced up and down the train asking vulgar questions of total strangers. To Zelda's embarrassment he accosted a passenger reading a medical book by shouting: 'Ernest I have found a clap doctor!' At Philadelphia they were met by Philippe, whom Scott forced to drive his overheating Buick without stopping for oil or water. As the Buick steamed so did Zelda. She and Scott rowed all the way to Ellerslie where they paused in their recriminations to offer Pauline and Ernest six bottles of excellent burgundy over dinner. Unfortunately Scott soon started a stream of insults aimed at their friendly black maid. 'Aren't you the best piece of tail I ever had?' he asked her repeatedly. 'Tell Mr Hemingway.'[5]

Another version of this dreadful Ellerslie weekend was given by Zelda to Sara Mayfield:

> To add to Zelda's troubles, the Hemingways arrived for a visit. Ernest was immensely pleased by his title for his new book, *Men Without Women*, because he thought it would sell well to the 'gay' boys and the old Vassar girls. His jokes with Scott about pederasty, anal eroticism, and other forms of perversion annoyed and frightened Zelda . . . . to judge from Ernest's unpublished letters to Scott, she had reason to be alarmed. Fitzgerald and Hemingway went on a bender, got in a fight . . .

landed in jail. Zelda was further outraged when she learnt that Ernest had borrowed a hundred dollars from Scott before he left.[6]

The subsequent publication of those letters indicates their indisputable vulgarity. Hemingway and Fitzgerald's favourite banter was about their book titles. One Hemingway riposte, 'The Sun Also Rises (like your cock if you have one)', provoked Fitzgerald's crude rejoinder: 'This tough talk is not really characteristic of me – it's the influence of All The Sad Young Men Without Women In Love . . . "Now I Lay Me" was a fine story – you ought to write a companion piece, "Now I Lay Her". Excuse my bawdiness but I'm oversexed.'[7] Scott's established reputation for the reverse suggests his puerile jokes were a defence.

When those two overgrown schoolboys continued their raunchy behaviour that weekend, Zelda, reared on Southern gentlemen's verbal courtesy, would have been shocked or disturbed. Her awareness of her growing emotions towards Egorova would have increased her sense of being threatened by Scott's and Ernest's lewd intimacy with each other.

Mike Strater, who felt that after the weekend he never wanted to see Fitzgerald or Hemingway again, spoke for all the guests. 'A bullfight is sedative in comparison . . . Those two . . . brought out the worst in each other.'[8]

Though Strater was referring to Ernest and Scott, the remark was equally apt in reference to Zelda and Scott. The Fitzgeralds still remembered the best in each other, but in 1928 they had lost the way to find it.

Bunny Wilson was also having marital problems. Admitting 'I had found it impossible to be married to an actress,'[9] he had separated from Mary Blair and was now subject to severe bouts of depression, though he still managed to start a book of essays, *Axel's Castle*, and a novel, *I Thought of Daisy*.[10] Wilson soon afterwards entered Clifton Springs Sanitarium for three months' treatment for a nervous breakdown, which made him highly sympathetic towards Zelda's depression. He was given hydrotherapy, electric shock and an addictive amount of paraldehyde.[11]

In November 1928 Scott had sent the first two chapters of his novel to Perkins, who enthusiastically replied that the first was 'excellent', the second contained 'some of the best writing you have ever done'. He eagerly awaited more.[12] He waited in vain. Scott stalled again, returning instead to his 'lousy Post stories' about Basil Duke Lee. He supplemented his income in other ways, too. During

1928 and 1929 he garnered $1,500 by lending his name to a soap beauty contest.[13] He also took out a life insurance policy for $60,000 which he found hard to maintain, but ultimately it constituted the majority of his estate.[14]

At Ellerslie, Christmas 1928 was cold in every sense. Scott's Ledger reported: 'Xmas night with family & Mlle & Phillipe. Coldness Amy. Car freezing. Mother there Xmas.' Even Amy Thomas, who had warmly tolerated Scott's drinking, had a chill air matched sadly by that of her host and hostess.

Zelda resumed both her painting and dance lessons in Philadelphia. She had a new dance instructor, thirty-six-year-old Alexandre Gavrilov, former dancer with Diaghilev's ballet, stand-in for Nijinsky and leader of New York's Ballet Moderne.[15] Again she threw herself into ballet with Gavrilov as she had with Egorova. Perhaps he was less protective of her (or of himself), for she once found herself in a potentially dangerous situation with him.[16] 'My dancing teacher was a protégé of Nijinsky. I ate lunch with him and went with him to his apartment. There was nothing in the commercial flat except the white spitz of his mistress and a beautiful collection of Léon Bakst. It was a cold afternoon. He asked me if I wanted him to kill me and said I would cry and [he] left me there. I ran to my lesson through the cold streets.'[17] Gavrilov and Zelda spoke French together so it is possible that the phrase 'if I wanted him to kill me' might refer to the French expression 'the little death', meaning orgasm.

Her description evokes a surreal film echoed in several paintings. At this stage she protested that her art was too personal to be shown in public but over the next three years, though her paintings continued blatantly autobiographical, she became as keen to exhibit as she was to publish.[18]

Using thick, turgid brush strokes she attempted highly emotional canvases, repetitiously returning to ballet themes. Her aim was to blast the viewer into an appreciation of the ballerina's physical-emotional reality, irrespective of its ugliness; so many canvases displayed hardworking ballerinas caught in a 'frozen movement' which became her particular trademark. This concept is also found consistently in modernist images. As the art critic Giles Neret pointed out: 'Artists transformed the notion of speed – particular to the decade – into a stereotype of "frozen movement".'[19] That element was frequently used by Léon Bakst, a painter Zelda met through the Murphys, who may have influenced her dance figures. Later Zelda told Henry Dan Piper: 'What I do is paint the basic,

fundamental principle so that everyone will be forced to realize
and experience it – I want to paint a ballet step so all will know
what it is – to get the fundamental essence into the painting.'[20] This
was highly significant because it was a huge departure from the
way most *male* artists of that period, influenced by Degas, portrayed the same subject. Their ballerinas hardly seemed to work
and were largely objects of exquisite femininity.[21]

As Zelda's dancers collapsed on the canvas, so she too began to
collapse as she held the brush hour after hour. She lost 15 lb in
weight, and her nerves stretched like elastic. Snapping point never
seemed far off. But despite her exhaustion from dancing and painting, that winter of 1928–9 she returned ferociously to writing, beginning a series of six stories about the lives of six young American
women. Initially all six were commissioned by H. N. Swanson of
College Humor magazine who bought five, though the sixth was ultimately sold to the *Saturday Evening Post*.

These stories were accompanied by new sketches and new ballet
routines. What is most striking about Zelda's three arts is that they
first come to fruition within a period of five years from 1929 to 1934
and these, the years of her most single-minded discipline, coincided
with the start of her mental breakdown and her initial hospitalization. It was as if she was living only through creative work and
everything else in her life was either on hold or dead. That included
her husband and daughter. Her relationship with seven-year-old
Scottie became even more distant, as though she was loving her
through a veil of muslin. Often Scottie was left in the charge of her
governess whom both her parents disliked. But though Scott's
November 1928 Ledger recorded 'Delplangue gets on our nerves',
the governess in fact lasted until the following April. This left Zelda
free to work on her six stories, which were united by a common
theme: women's failure to achieve a balance between work and
marriage.

Collectively, Zelda's fiction at that point makes a public statement
about women's need to work professionally if they are to survive.[22]
Privately, the stories may have conveyed to Scott the strength of her
aspirations and her anger over her frustrations.

The six tales concern a poor working girl, a girl liked by a prince,
a millionaire's girl, and three near to Zelda's heart: an original
Follies girl, a girl with talent as a dancer and a Southern girl.

Zelda began the first, 'The Original Follies Girl', that winter, finishing it by March 1929, the month their lease expired on Ellerslie.
By now the Fitzgeralds' restlessness had an almost pathological

quality and they were determined to set off with Scottie again for Europe. This time the reason they offered friends was that Zelda could continue ballet with Egorova and fit her writing and painting in between classes. Their plan was to see Genoa first, then move on to Nice before going to Paris in April.

They sailed on the *Conte Biancamano* where, Zelda recalled, Scott 'paid absolutely no attention of any kind to me'.[23] Scott did pay attention to other women and embarrassed Zelda by asking a woman passenger if women liked men's penises small or big. Zelda interrupted: 'Shut up, Scott, you fool,'[24] but her humiliating experiences were not over. In Genoa, perhaps fired by fears of his own impotence, he attempted sodomy. Zelda was disgusted and not a little afraid. 'I think the most humiliating and bestial thing that ever happened to me in my life is a scene that you probably don't remember even in Genoa . . . You were constantly drunk.'[25]

Scott himself, depressed at his inability to finish his novel, had written to Perkins before leaving that he was sneaking away just like a thief, failing yet again to give Perkins further chapters. He swore he would write them on the boat and he begged Max to trust him a little longer. Neither Max nor Scott could foresee that this trust would be forced to endure for several more years.

Despite Scott's novel-writing block he managed to produce seven short stories for the *Post* in 1929, dealing, inevitably, with marriage problems. They included three fine fictions: 'The Rough Crossing', 'The Swimmers' and 'Two Wrongs'. He did mail Perkins 'The Rough Crossing' in March from the Hôtel Beau Rivage, Nice. Almost certainly based on the Fitzgeralds' recent crossing on the *Conte Biancamano*, it involves a young couple, Eva and Adrian Smith, whose marriage disintegrates as they cross the Atlantic. Both playwright Adrian and his jealous wife have foolish affairs with people they despise whom they ditch by the end of the voyage. The woeful conclusion is that the Smiths agree to deny that anything sordid took place by pretending the affairs happened to two other Smiths. Unchanged by events, they are as ill at ease with each other as Zelda and Scott had been at the end of *their* voyage.

In Nice Zelda began ballet classes with the Russian dancer Nevalskaya, ballet coach at the Nice Opera, while Scott drank and gambled at the casino. Her productivity must have fired Scott with resentment, but they did not discuss the issue. It surfaces, though, in Zelda's newly-completed story 'The Original Follies Girl' with its focus on achievement.

Zelda's sad heroine, ironically named Gay, who receives $5,000 a year alimony from an ex-husband 'with a gift of fantasy',[26] has little need to work or marry, a state Zelda judges harshly. Without those two anchors that can lend women purpose or order, Gay drifts abroad as a New York showgirl, dreaming she can become a London theatre actress yet never settling to serious work. Instead she falls into aimless alcoholism and dies in childbirth. There is a sense of sin in Gay's highly decorated dilettantism and Zelda's heroine, like the style in which she is depicted, is evasive, elliptical and polished.

This story, like the others, is written in Zelda's characteristic associative 'spoken' language. There is a guarded singular tone predicated on alienation from the familiar. There is a sense in which all six heroines wear masks, as Zelda does. Never sufficiently plot-driven and rather impressionistic, the stories are distinguished by trademarks similar to those in her paintings: an overload of visual metaphors, fragmentation, descriptive non sequiturs, caustic observation and bubbling non-linear ideas. They leave the reader with more questions than they answer. Zelda's sensuous descriptions allow readers to smell the flowers in her writings, just as viewers can feel the texture of flesh in her paintings. Zelda never labelled herself a Southern writer in the way that she felt she was a Southern painter, yet in both arts her intensely Southern temperament focused on the dissolution of form into colour and the representation of emotion through colour.

There was already a startling congruence between Zelda's untamed paintings and her tumultuous ballet life. Then came her sudden determination to extend this verbally in stories with the same focus on appearances. In her six 'Girl' stories, as in her painting, she looked at people's souls through their appearance. 'The Original Follies Girl' is suffused with sounds, scents and scenery. Gay, a 'very kaleidoscopic' girl, who 'made the rest of the chorus look like bologna sausages', lived in a 'silver apartment with mulberry carpets and lots of billowing old-blue taffeta', which allowed the narrator and readers to 'see how bored she must have been with her Louis XVI tea service and her grand piano, the huge silver vase that must have calla lilies in it and the white bearskin rug'. When the narrator last glimpsed Gay before she died tragically, leaving a small baby and an empty blue velvet trunk plastered with hotel labels that symbolized the activity of isolation, 'she looked like a daffodil. She was taking a yellow linen sports thing for an airing and she reeked of a lemony perfume and Bacardi cocktails.'[27]

If the financial security in which Gay was embedded was one

impediment to fulfilling work, Zelda saw poverty as another. In 'Poor Working Girl', the second story to be written between winter 1928 and April 1929,[28] twenty-year-old Eloise lives in a newly industrialized community with which she is as out of touch as she is with solid rural values. The possessor of a downstate college education, a talent for the ukulele, a fumbling grasp of shorthand and a flawless skin, she yearns for a Broadway career.

As Zelda is consistently ironic throughout all six stories about acting careers, which she proposes as the goal only of shallow young women, it is hard not to view the irony in 'Poor Working Girl' as a barbed attack on Lois Moran.

Eloise works as a babysitter while saving up for drama school in New York but never earns enough for the financial independence she needs (and Zelda herself craves). Inevitably she gives up the job, fails to achieve stardom, and we leave her working as a 'pretty girl in the local power plant . . . [who] couldn't really imagine achieving anything'.[29]

In a third story, 'Southern Girl', Harriet, Zelda's heroine from Jeffersonville (modelled on Montgomery), is unique among Zelda's aspiring heroines in that she holds two authentic remunerative jobs: one as a schoolteacher, the other supervising her family's lodging house. Though single, she also has a more realistic appraisal of the compromises needed for marriage. Engaged to Dan, a laughing Northerner, she gives him up when she realizes, like Sally Carrol Happer in Scott's 'Ice Palace', that she can never fit into Northern society or live up to a life of 'leagues and organizations and societies for the prevention of things' stipulated by Dan's mother, a woman as formal and black and white as a printed page. But Zelda sees Harriet's return to her patchwork of mundane responsibilities in the vine-clad smouldering deep South as ultimately unfulfilling, because her determination about 'sticking to things' meant she never attempted to 'turn them into one bigger unit of a job'. When later Harriet meets Charles, a replica of Dan, she agrees to the compromise of a life 'working for leagues and societies' alongside Charles's black-taffeta-clad widowed mother.[30]

'Southern Girl' is remarkable for its sensuous description of long clay roads, straggling pines, isolated cabins in sand patches and 'far off in the distance the blue promise of hills.' The city where 'wistaria meets over the warm asphalt' is a young world that every evening moves out of doors, a world where 'telephones ring, and the lacy blackness under the trees disgorges young girls in white and pink, leaping over the squares of warm light toward the tinkling sound with an expectancy that people have only in places where any event is a pleasant one'.[31]

It is the world in which Zelda grew up, the world in which she flourished, the world of pink and white and organdie events, now a world rewritten from an entirely different place where many events have become unpleasant ones.

Zelda was not alone in trying to recapture Southern magic in her fiction. Both Scott and Sara Haardt had been attempting it.

In November 1928 Scott had written 'The Last of the Belles', set in Tarleton, his version of Montgomery. Like Zelda's 'Southern Girl' it has a nostalgic mood of loss. It offers a similar narrative of a popular Southern Belle jilted by a Northern soldier.[32]

That Scott might have felt anxious about Zelda following so closely on his heels is shown by a strange slip of his pen. In summer 1929, Ober asked Scott to choose one of his stories for a *Literary Digest* anthology. Scott, we assume inadvertently, suggested Zelda's 'Southern Girl'. Hastily he wrote again to Ober: 'When I suggested story for Lit Digest I accidentally said Southern Girl meaning Last of the Belles.'[33]

Sara Haardt's Southern fiction, which covered similar territory to Zelda's, had struggled into print while she combated illnesses even more serious than before. When Sara, who had missed Montgomery on a recent trip to Hollywood,[34] returned home she found Mencken had missed her.[35] They mended their temporary rift and she, like Scott and Zelda, began to recreate in her fiction the Southern homeland about which both she and Zelda felt so ambivalent. But in October 1928, before the Fitzgeralds had left for Europe, disease had once more shattered Sara's hopes. Mencken rushed her into Union Memorial Hospital, Baltimore, for emergency surgery for gynaecological problems exacerbated by appendicitis. In November, Scott, perhaps linking Sara's operation with Zelda's surgery in Paris, wrote Sara a curious note. He congratulated her as he often did, on her 'absolutely lyric' writing, and added: 'Terribly sorry to hear you're sick. Please get well. Name it after me. Yours with insatiable Passion. Old Hot Shot Fitzgerald.'[36] Sara did not get well. By July 1929 tuberculosis had infected her left kidney. There seemed no hope of total recovery. The doctors told Mencken she might live at best three years. Shocked and unutterably saddened, Mencken told Sara Mayfield he had vowed to marry his Sara as soon as she was strong enough, to make her last years the happiest of her life. He asked little Sara to be discreet; thus it was more than six months before Zelda and Scott or any Baltimore friends suspected they were engaged.

In hospital that summer, believing death was imminent, Sara repeated her final wish to be buried in Baltimore far from Alabama. Yet ironically, despite or perhaps because of her love-hate relationship with the sweet flowering tyrannical South, which only Zelda and Sara Mayfield fully understood, when she emerged from hospital in late 1929 she determined to rush out her Deep South novel *The Making of a Lady*.

The Fitzgeralds reached Paris in April 1929 and settled into an apartment on rue Mézières near St Sulpice, to be greeted by several old friends. Esther Murphy had a surprise for them. For some years Esther's sexual inclinations had led her towards women. Wickedly portrayed as the lesbian Bounding Bess in Djuna Barnes's chronicle *Ladies Almanack*,[37] she had been a rival for Natalie Barney's sexual affections with Dolly Wilde, and had ended up in bed with Barney.[38] But suddenly in March Esther had become engaged to the English economist and political writer John Strachey, and was eagerly planning her May wedding.

The Bishops now had an apartment in Paris as well as their Orgeval château, so the Fitzgeralds saw John as often and Margaret as little as possible, and met frequently with Townsend Martin. That spring Zelda met the English art critic Clive Bell whose avant-garde ideas impressed and influenced her. Sandy and Oscar Kalman were in Paris and Zelda instantly took them off to her ballet classes, where she had resumed rigorous group sessions in the mornings and a private class every afternoon with Egorova at the hot studio in rue Caumartin. 'I worked constantly and was terribly superstitious and moody about my work, full of presentiments,' she wrote. 'I lived in a quiet, ghostly, hypersensitized world of my own. Scott drank.'[39] Zelda saw herself as a priestess who had found an impersonal escape into a new world of self-expression.[40]

Egorova had become the focus of Zelda's life, for whom she practised every evening and most of Sunday. 'I had to work,' wrote Zelda later, 'because I couldn't exist in the world without it.'[41] Idealizing Egorova, seeing her as poor, pure and dedicated, she presented her daily with a symbolic bouquet of white gardenias. One evening in June, however, the intense Madame appeared to Zelda in a less pleasing light. The Fitzgeralds had taken her to dine at the luxurious George V restaurant. During dinner when Egorova responded with appreciation to Scott's flirtation, Zelda moved from shock to anger.

Pauline and Ernest were now living at 6 rue de Ferou, but Pauline had begun to disapprove of the Fitzgeralds and Hemingway had given Perkins strict instructions not to give Scott their address. The previous year Fitzgerald had insulted Ernest's landlord, pissed on their front porch, almost broken down their front door at 4 a.m. and finally got Hemingway evicted. Ernest was determined Scott should not get them thrown out of this new apartment. Scott's persistence persuaded Ernest to relent and invite them to dinner. Ernest and Zelda kept their mutual antagonism under wraps, but Scott registered a 'certain coldness' towards him from Ernest.[42] Hemingway was completing *A Farewell to Arms*, which Scott saw as another slight to his own slow progress.[43] When Scott finally read it he wrote an officious undiplomatic letter admitting it was a 'beautiful book' but suggesting more than fifty cuts and corrections.[44] Hemingway was furious. On the bottom of Scott's letter he wrote 'Kiss my ass. E.H.'[45]

Sara Mayfield, temporarily in Paris, stopped at the Deux Magots to find Zelda only just surviving a week-long party. 'Nobody knows where it started, when it'll end, or whose party it is,' Zelda told Sara. 'All of the people were white . . . But one of the women had slept with a Negro, a six-day bicycle racer, and a prizefighter that sniffs cocaine . . . Another one says she sleeps with men for money and women for fun.'[46]

Sara was disturbed at Zelda's appearance. 'There were triangular hollows under her cheek bones, and she was thin as a rail.' Had her friend stopped eating? 'No, I eat everything in sight,' Zelda said. 'But I work it off at the studio, straining and stretching and ending in nothing.' She ached to begin life over again. 'Really I do. I'd try so hard. Scott and I had it all – youth, love, money – and look how we've ended up, sitting around cafés, drinking and talking and quarreling with each other.' Sara saw Zelda as 'a soul lost in the mist on the moor'.[47]

Zelda admitted that most of their quarrels were about Hemingway. When Scott lurched over to join the women he told Sara that he and Ernest were quarrelling too, 'like a pair of jealous prima donnas', over the unsavoury machinations of Robert McAlmon.[48] Scott, highly disturbed, had written to Max Perkins: 'McAlmon is a bitter rat . . . Part of his quarrel with Ernest some years ago was because he assured Ernest I was a fairy – God knows he shows more creative imagination in his malice than in his work. Next he told Callaghan that Ernest was a fairy. He's a pretty good person to avoid.'[49]

Morley Callaghan was a twenty-six-year-old Canadian writer, now published by Scribner's, who with his wife met the Fitzgeralds that spring. Callaghan, insufficiently deferential to Fitzgerald, found him cold and Zelda watchful and depressed. At an early meeting Scott read Morley one passage that had impressed him from *A Farewell to Arms*. Morley, less impressed, said it was too deliberate, which annoyed Scott but pleased Zelda, who aired her view that Hemingway's prose was 'pretty damned Biblical'. Scott immediately told Zelda she was tired from dancing and sent her to bed, leaving the Callaghans startled at Zelda's meek acquiescence. Later the couples dined together and Zelda talked animatedly about her writing, saying she wrote well; Scott offered no comment, and she disconcerted them all by laughing to herself until Scott again sent her to bed. On another occasion with the Callaghans Zelda again talked about her writing before suggesting they all went roller skating, whereupon Scott grabbed Zelda's wrist and sent her home in a taxi. 'It was if she knew he had command over her,' Morley said, 'she agreed meekly . . . suddenly she had said good night like a small girl and was whisked away from us.' When Morley asked about Zelda's dancing, Scott explained edgily that Zelda wanted to 'have something for herself, be something herself'.[50]

Zelda ignored Scott's antipathy to her ballet classes and also worked on her remaining three stories, 'The Girl The Prince Liked', 'The Girl With Talent' and 'A Millionaire's Girl'. All three heroines possess talent or energetic driving ambition but still have not found appropriate outlets for a satisfying career.

Helena, heroine of 'The Girl The Prince Liked', has her father's ambition, mystic deep-set eyes and eight million dollars. This allows her to dominate her husband, two children, people of importance 'whom Helena wore like a string of glass beads' and a golf course at which she collects second prizes.[51] Ultimately she collects the Prince of Wales with whom she has an affair. Zelda satirizes England's most romantic hero to reveal Helena's triumphant story as essentially tragic. The Prince goes away, as princes do, leaving her a memory and a bracelet that she is acute enough to have valued. Inherently sharp, Helena realizes meaningful work, not money or contacts, might have given her life fulfilment.

Encouraged by the Murphys, the Fitzgeralds decided to leave Paris and spend the summer on the Riviera. From July till October they rented the Villa Fleur des Bois on boulevard Eugène Gazagnaive, in Cannes, where Zelda finished 'The Girl The Prince Liked' while studying under Nevalskaya. She also danced professionally in several engagements in Nice and Cannes.[52] Gerald, who constantly urged Zelda to meet prima ballerina Nemchinova in Antibes, reported Zelda looked haggard and had a strange laugh. On one occasion they went to see a documentary film about underwater life shot in an aquarium. When an octopus moved into view Zelda shrieked and threw herself against Gerald, screaming 'What is it? What is it!' Gerald saw nothing frightening and wondered whether Zelda saw it as a distortion of something horrific.[53] Zelda, unable to explain, seemed to be withdrawing into a private world. Yet she completed the 'Prince' story in late August.

On 23 September 1929 her ballet endeavours were rewarded. She received a formal invitation from Julie Sedowa to join the San Carlo Opera Ballet Company in Naples, Italy. Her *Aïda* debut at San Carlo, which Sedowa described as 'a very worthwhile solo number', would be followed by other solo performances as the season progressed. Sedowa wrote that if Zelda stayed for the whole season she would received a monthly salary. She told Zelda the theatre was magnificent, it would be useful experience to accept this offer, life in Naples was not expensive and she could have full board and lodging for 35 lire a day.[54]

It was the chance Zelda had been waiting for.

Inexplicably she turned it down. She had agonized over whether or not to accept. If she went to Naples she would go alone. The idea scared her, as did leaving Scottie, now almost eight, entirely in Scott's custody. Since girlhood she had been dependent on Scott. Could she live alone on a meagre salary and succeed without his backing? Could she face his anger? She had worked for months to reach this point, only to be suddenly assailed by self-doubt. Her sister Rosalind vividly recalled not only Zelda's ambivalence but also Scott's implacable disapproval. 'This frantic effort on Zelda's part, towards a professional career in the thing she did best, was motivated by the uncertainty of their situation . . . perhaps also by unhappiness, which she refused to admit . . . beneath an always brave front, and by her desire to put herself on her own. She told me that she received an offer from one of the Italian Opera companies as a première ballerina, but that Scott would not allow her to accept it.'[55] Only a few years earlier, Zelda would rebelliously have gone ahead and overruled Scott. Her strange passivity at this critical moment implies an emotional fatigue from many months of professional subservience to him.

Scott never acknowledged, at the time or later, not only how close Zelda had come to a serious ballet career but how he had stopped her.

1. Minnie Machen Sayre, born 1860, Zelda's mother: an avid reader

2. Judge Anthony Sayre, Zelda's father, in 1880. Zelda called him 'a living fortress'

3. The Church of the Holy Comforter, Montgomery, where Minnie Sayre played the organ and sang in the choir and Zelda was baptized

4. Marjorie Sayre, Zelda's eldest sister, born 1886: a frail nervous girl

5. Rosalind (Tootsie) Sayre, born 1889. Zelda's middle sister, stalwart and feisty

6. Clothilde (Tilde) Sayre, born 1891. Zelda's youngest sister, the model for Joan in *Save Me The Waltz*

7. Anthony Sayre Jnr, born 1894. Zelda's brother and rival. In *Caesar's Things* heroine Janno's brother was partly based on young Anthony

8. Zelda aged around eighteen in dance costume in her mother's garden in Montgomery

9. Katharine Elsberry Steiner, Zelda's Montgomery soulmate. She and Zelda looked alike, dressed alike, and often thought alike

10. Off for a picnic. Zelda (*second from right*) unsmiling, with Grace Gunter and their friends in regulation white middy blouses and black ties

11. Scott Fitzgerald, 1921–2, in Dellwood where he and Zelda enjoyed life in the resort on White Bear Lake

12. Zelda and Scott go swimming at Compo Beach, Westport Connecticut, July 1920

13. Zelda in white knickerbockers, her outrageous travelling outfit for the Fitzgeralds' auto trip south to Montgomery, 1920

14. Zelda and Scott pose for a *Hearst's International Magazine* photograph, 1923. Zelda called it her 'Elizabeth Arden face' and pasted it in her scrapbook

15. Marie Hersey, Scott's school chum and later confidante in his home town St Paul, Minnesota

16. Xandra Kalman, *c.* 1921: Zelda's closest, most supportive friend during her young motherhood days in St Paul

17. Sara Haardt, Zelda's frail writer friend from Montgomery who died aged 37 in 1935. Sara always received more encouragement for her writing from her husband H.L. Mencken than Zelda did from Scott

18. Critic H.L. Mencken, Scott's literary mentor. Mencken encouraged and published Haardt's fiction then after a long courtship married her in 1930, the year Zelda had her first breakdown

19. Annabel Fitzgerald, Scott's sister, 1919, aged eighteen. 'Scott advised his sister on conversation, couture and cosmetics and on how to listen to men'

20. The Fitzgerald family in the waves. Early happy years for Zelda, Scott and Scottie

21. Lubov Egorova, Zelda's beloved ballet teacher, autographed Paris 1928

22. Painter Romaine Brooks whom Zelda met on Capri, 1925

23. Parisian influences: writers Natalie Barney and Djuna Barnes, Nice, France 1928–30. Zelda frequented Barney's literary salon in rue Jacob, Paris

24. Emily Vanderbilt, who fascinated both Zelda and Scott and who committed suicide in May 1935

25. The beach at La Garoupe raked by Gerald Murphy, seen here under umbrellas with his wife Sara and Etienne and Edith de Beaumont, *c.* 1924. Zelda and Scott visited regularly from their villa at Juan-les-Pins

26. Ernest Hemingway, Zelda's enemy and Scott's hero, 1931. Hemingway's comic inscription to Scott on this photograph lewdly suggested he was the adventurous Princetonian travel writer Halliburton

27. Max Perkins, Scott's consistently generous publishing editor at Scribner's

28. Zelda Sayre in June 1918, as she looked when Scott first met her in Montgomery

29. (*below*) 'Birth of a Flapper': Zelda's earliest known drawing, crayon on paper, 1921: her book jacket design for Scott's *The Beautiful and Damned*

Opposite Page
30. (*top*) 'Family in Underwear', one of Zelda's earliest paper dolls featuring herself, her husband and child, *c.* 1927

31. (*bottom*) *Times Square New York* (gouache on paper, $13\frac{1}{2}''$ x $17\frac{5}{8}''$), *c.* 1944. One of the romantic cityscapes Zelda painted after Scott's death, as a memory of the places they had visited together

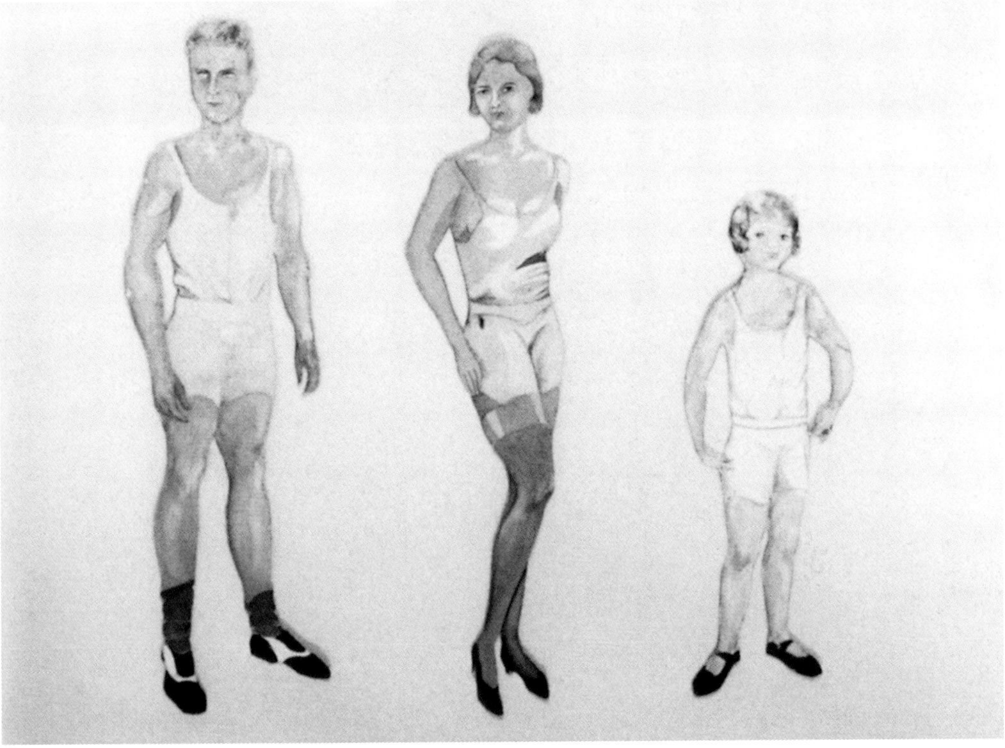

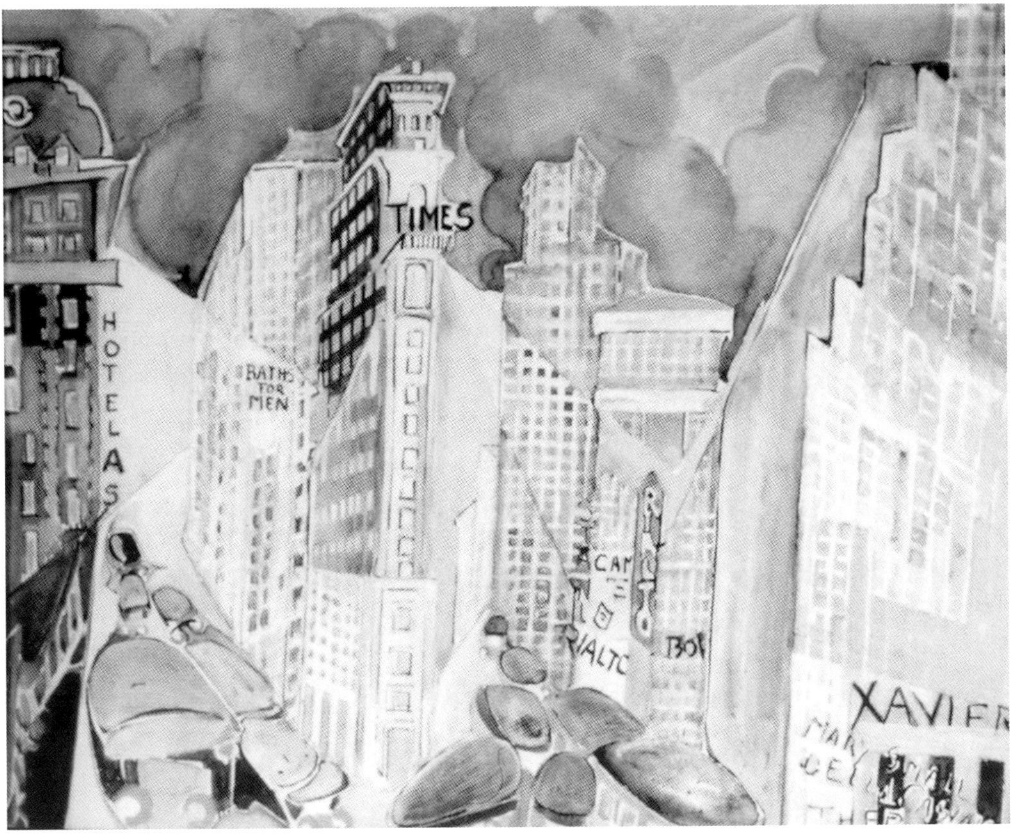
TIMES
HOTEL AS
BATHS FOR MEN

Recovered

32. (*above left*) Scott with three-year-old Scottie in Rome 1924

33. (*above*) The Fitzgeralds aboard ship leaving for France, 1928. Tension already shows on Zelda's face and in Scott's posture

34. (*left*) Zelda believing herself 'recovered' after her initial hospitalizations, 1931

35. (*above*) Scottie at her graduation, 1938. She did not want Zelda to attend the ceremony and ignored her when she arrived

36. (*above right*) Dr Irving Pine, Zelda's last psychiatrist, in 1990. He believed Zelda had been misdiagnosed and suffered as much from medical mistreatment as from her mental illness

37. (*right*) Zelda and her first grandson Tim, not long before her death in 1948

38. Zelda playing volley ball with her fellow patients during sports recreation at Highland Hospital, late 1930s. Photo taken by Mary Parker, Zelda's art therapist

39. The fire at Highland Hospital, 11 March 1948. Zelda, locked in an upstairs room, had died in the blaze

The scorn Zelda had shown towards Helena in 'The Girl The Prince Liked' for not making use of her ambitions and skills turned inward on herself for not having the courage to take the long-awaited opportunity. Zelda's guilt and confusion over rejecting the San Carlo offer are hinted at in 'The Girl With Talent', completed in October 1929 and sold only weeks later.

Lou, the dancer heroine, has genuine talent, a good job in New York, a rich successful husband, a baby. Like Zelda she is not domestic so the baby is largely cared for by the nanny. She is the one heroine of the six whose dreams of stardom in the dance field are attainable. So what does she do? In the middle of an 'unprecedented hit' she runs off to China with a tall blond Englishman with whom she has a second beautiful baby. Her dream *could* have come true, as could Zelda's. Only weeks before this event Lou told the narrator: 'I am going to work so hard that my spirit will be completely broken, and I am going to be a very fine dancer . . . I have a magnificent contract in a magnificent casino on the Côte d'Azur, and I am now on my way to work and make money magnificently.' The narrator did not believe her: 'those were excellent defense plans that would never be carried out because of lack of attack.' Is that what Zelda felt about her own self-destructive action? In the story Zelda makes one of her most characteristic comments: 'To my mind, people never change until they look different.'[56] Lou had looked exactly the same. The photos of Zelda in May 1929 and September 1929 also look much the same: tense and frozen-faced. But Zelda was a mistress of deceptive appearances and elusive effects.

Zelda's remorse over rejecting Sedowa's offer turned to raging grief when she learnt that Sergei Diaghilev had died in Venice. 'Diaghilev died,' wrote Zelda. 'The stuff of the great movement of the Ballets Russes lay rotting in a French law court . . . some of his dancers performed round the swimming pool of the Lido to please the drunk Americans . . . some . . . worked in music-hall ballets; the English went back to England. What's the use?'[57] For Zelda, whose dreams of dancing with the Ballets Russes had died with Diaghilev, nothing was of use.

That October, while Scott was driving along the Corniche, the most treacherous stretch of road in that locality, Zelda grabbed the steering wheel and attempted to force the car off the cliff. She almost killed herself and her husband. Later she said the car acted wildly on its own.

There is an obvious and illuminating connection, which has not previously been made, between these three events: firstly, Zelda's rejection of the ballet company offer; secondly, Diaghilev's death; and thirdly, the steering-wheel incident. One of Zelda's biographers, Milford, omits Diaghilev's death and even reverses the chronology of job offer and steering-wheel incident, so that no psychological sense can be made of it.[58] There is also the highly significant fact that all three events occurred during a period of enormous literary productivity for Zelda, every piece of which was published under Scott's name as well as hers or under Scott's name alone.

In October 1929 the Fitzgeralds returned to Paris where Zelda continued writing, working on her sixth story, 'The Millionaire's Girl', which would be sold in March 1930. The story, Zelda's witty answer to Scott's fictionalized treatment of the Lois Moran romance, is generally considered her best.[59]

Caroline, its heroine, is lower down the social register than her fiancé Barry. 'You could see that he was rich and that he liked her, and you could see that she was poor and that she knew he did.' But Barry's father likes her not, tries to buy her off. When Caroline accepts his cheque without realizing she is expected to break her engagement Barry, furious, does it for her, at which point Caroline decides to become a Hollywood superstar! Her reason, however, is not to find remunerative fulfilling work but to bring back the errant Barry. Though her first film is a big hit he doesn't return until she makes a dramatic suicide bid. As Zelda comments acidly: 'She married him, of course, and since she left the films on that occasion, they have both had much to reproach each other for.'[60] It sounded familiar even at the time.

Throughout the 'Girl' series the narrator has remained unidentified either by name or gender. But there is a nice touch in this sixth story: Caroline and Barry drive out to see their narrator friend on Long Island. On arrival Caroline asks: 'Is this Fitzgerald's roadhouse?', ensuring that readers now suspect that the narrator is either Zelda or Scott.[61] Rereading the series, particularly 'Southern Girl', it becomes obvious the narrator, too, is a Southern Girl: Zelda.

Zelda said she wrote these stories to pay for her dancing so that she would not be financially dependent on Scott. The money was good. But the deal organized by Scott on Zelda's behalf was not. Harold Ober recorded the transaction Scott made with *College Humor* for Zelda's stories. 'SF said that Z would do six articles for *College Humor*, that he would go over them . . . and that the articles would be signed with both their names.'[62]

Although *College Humor* had already bought two of Zelda's articles and considered her talented in her own right, five of the six stories were published with joint by-lines. Scott's justification for joint credits was not only that they would reap a higher fee, but that even if he didn't actually write the stories he might have done so at any moment! He assured Ober that most of the stories were 'pretty strong draughts on Zelda's and my common store of material. This [the heroine of 'The Girl With Talent'] is Mary Hay for instance + the "Girl The Prince Liked" was Josephine Ordway – both of whom I had in my notebook to use.'[63] He probably did. However, he did not in fact take Mary or Josephine out of his notebook and turn them into fiction, whereas Zelda took two role models out of her notebook and *did* turn them into stories.

'The Original Follies Girl' was sold in March 1929 to *College Humor* for $400. Published in July 1929, it was credited to Scott and Zelda. Scott had made no revisions. It was the cause of a fight between them. Zelda had finished it in the Philadelphia library, after which she celebrated with some women from the dance school, got drunk in an Italian restaurant and returned home to find Scott furious. Scott delivered it to Ober instead of a Basil story that was due. 'This is a poor substitute,' Scott wrote, 'tho it is a beautifully written thing.'[64] That story and the next four were highly praised by Swanson, the editor.

'Poor Working Girl' was sold to *College Humor* via Ober in April 1929 for $500. Published in January 1931, it was credited to Scott and Zelda, but written entirely by Zelda.

'Southern Girl' followed in June, was sold to *College Humor* for $500, published in October 1929, credited to Scott and Zelda but written entirely by Zelda.

'The Girl the Prince Liked' was sold to *College Humor* in September 1929 for $500, published in February 1930, credited to both Fitzgeralds but written entirely by Zelda. Scott asked Ober: 'Don't you think that Zelda's Girl-the-Prince-liked thing is good?'[65]

'The Girl With Talent' was sold to *College Humor* October 1929 for $800, published April 1930, credited to both Fitzgeralds but written by Zelda.

The credit surrounding 'A Millionaire's Girl' was even more contentious. Both Ober and Scott behaved in a shockingly high-handed manner. It was sold to the *Saturday Evening Post* in March 1930 for $4,000, and published on 17 May. Though it was entirely written by Zelda, the name under the story was F. Scott Fitzgerald alone. Scott's reason was that the *Post* had offered to pay $4,000 if Zelda's name was omitted. Ober later said that when he had received it he believed it to be one of Scott's and sent it off to the *Post*, which accepted it. On 5 March 1930 Ober wrote to Scott: 'Dear Scott, A Millionaires Girl has just come in and I have just finished reading it. I like it a lot and some of your lines about California are very amusing, indeed.'

As soon as the error was discovered Ober cabled Scott that the *Post* would only pay that amount if Zelda's name was dropped.[66] Scott agreed. Ober managed an apologetic line: 'I really felt a little guilty about dropping Zelda's name from that story . . . but I think she understood that using two names would have tied the story up with the *College Humor* stories and might have got us into trouble.' Ober insisted it was so good that it 'would have been recognized as your [Scott's] story no matter under what name it was published'. Attempting to placate Zelda, who might not have understood the Ober–Scott view that what mattered was the highest possible fee, Ober asked Scott to tell Zelda that it was 'a mighty good piece of work'.[67] By publication in mid-May 1930 Zelda was terribly ill, so Scott on her behalf told Ober: 'Zelda was delighted with your compliments about the Millionaires Girl!'[68]

Later, Scott confessed that the story 'appeared under my name but actually I had nothing to do with it except for suggesting a theme and working on the proof of the completed manuscript'. He also admitted to taking over the other material published 'under our joint names'. He said: 'I had nothing to do with the thing from start to finish except supplying my name.'[69]

One view of these events is that Scott lent his name to Zelda's work in order to help her, to reap more money for them as a couple, that Zelda did not mind, indeed was proud to be the recipient of such a famous name on her work, and that Scott had no hidden malevolent agenda. This is the view taken by most of Scott's male biographers.

The opposing view is that Scott ruthlessly took fraudulent credit for Zelda's work, partly instigated by his own insecurities due to his own procrastination over his novel *Tender Is The Night*. The events are seen as entirely selfish literary poaching.

There is a third view, to which this biographer subscribes. That Zelda was *not* surprised at the deal that had been struck, for when you live intimately with a famous artist you become accustomed to a life in the shadows. The only experience Zelda had to set against this prevalent attitude was that of her fellow writers Sara Haardt and H. L. Mencken. Though Mencken was better known than Sara he never at any point took credit for Sara's work and attempted constantly to get Sara a place in the sun. Zelda, perhaps because of this awareness, was resentful and frustrated. The original manuscripts of all six stories show her vigorous black handwriting scrawling out Scott's name on every by-line. Words like 'No!' and 'Me' are inserted where appropriate.

In this third view Scott did not act malevolently, because he had no need to. His actions fell within the gender expectations and conventions of the period, which gave full rein to his need to control their literary endeavours (and his wife) while allowing Zelda's reasonable resentments no outlet. That Scott acted with a strong self-focus is not in question. That he could *not* afford to act generously towards *this* fellow writer struggling to maintain her professional identity is interesting in view of his acknowledged generosity towards many other writers, including Sara Haardt whose work he praised. But Zelda was his wife, she was straying on to his territory, albeit often with his own muddled encouragement, and must be contained. The feminist framework that would have given Zelda the strength to resist was not in place in her circle, nor was it sufficiently acknowledged publicly in 1929 to give her a context for resistance.

By the time 'A Millionaire's Girl' was published under Scott's name, Zelda was in hospital. But previous biographies have made no link between the damage to Zelda's professional ambitions and her sudden breakdown. One lone literary voice in the years between 1928 and today has been that of Alice Hall Petry, who pointed out that Zelda's was a constant story of 'frustration and denial of thwarted ambitions and usurped achievements'.[70] In 1929 that story, that struggle to acquire both a coherent sense of her personal identity and to maintain a sense of her professional identity, was only just beginning and would be forced to continue inside a series of asylums.

There was another crucial incident before Zelda's collapse which she said helped to trigger it. Zelda and Scott's sexual problems had steadily worsened. Scott, jealous of Zelda's attentions to Egorova, saw the dance teacher and himself in a contest to dominate his wife. 'I've seen that everytime Zelda sees Egrova and me in contact, Egrova becomes gross to her. Apart, the opposite happens.'[71]

Zelda had become increasingly jealous of Scott's attentions towards Hemingway despite the sour note that had entered the men's relationship. Zelda's own sexual fears, as well as her disgust at the idea of her husband being homosexual, made McAlmon's taunts about the two men being 'fairies' more disturbing to her than she admitted.

The climax had occurred in Paris one night in June 1929 when Scott and Ernest had been out drinking without Zelda. Scott stumbled home drunk, crawled into bed, passed out, then in his sleep he muttered: 'No more baby'. Zelda took this as complete vindication of her suspicions that Scott and Ernest were having an affair.[72] Later she listed this event as among the causes of her breakdown. 'We came back to the rue Palatine and you, in a drunken stupor told me a lot of things that I only half-understood: but I understood the dinner we had at Ernests'. Only I didn't understand that it matterred.'[73]

Scott was shocked, perhaps terrified. She had forced him to wonder if there was any truth in her words. Later he admitted: 'The nearest I ever came to leaving you was when you told me you thot I was a fairy in the Rue Palatine.'[74]

It is plausible that Scott and Ernest at some level had sexual feelings about each other, but Ernest's hostility to his mother's lesbianism, and Scott's awareness of how other men found his appearance camp, would have been enough to make them back off. The McAlmon accusations had so disturbed Scott that when Morley Callaghan in Paris had offered his arm to Scott to cross a street Scott, believing that Morley had slightly resisted, drew back and said: 'You thought I was a fairy, didn't you?'[75] Scott and Ernest came from a generation hypersensitive about homosexuality to the point of paranoia. Gerald Murphy's lifelong fears about his own ambivalent nature, and the way that Fitzgerald, MacLeish and Hemingway talked about certain men as fairies, meant they all saw sexuality in absolute terms: either men were 'queer' or they were not.[76] If they were, it was a hideous matter.

In Scott's Notebooks, referring to Hemingway, he wrote wistfully: 'I really loved him, but of course it wore out like a love affair. The fairies have spoiled all that.'[77] But though McAlmon, in Scott's view Chief Fairy, asserted the two writers were homosexuals, he never made the leap from that to suggesting they were lovers. Zelda, who made that leap, continued to taunt Scott while he continued to neglect her. On two occasions Scott left her bed saying 'I can't. Don't you understand?'[78] But she didn't. During the summer he came into her room only once. But blindly involved with her dance teacher, she no longer minded. She knew if she looked around in Paris she could find actual or potential lovers. There were at least three other 'solutions' as well as 'the whole studio' who were all women.[79] 'In Paris again I saw a great deal of Nemchinova after classes, and my friend at the Opera.'[80] These women helped to stabilize her. As Scott recognized this he recalled the number of incidents relating to her women friends which had happened during 1929 leading up to their present point of hostility, then he began to throw Zelda's accusations of homosexuality back at her.

PART V

Other Voices
1929–1940

CHAPTER 16

Scott began to accumulate evidence.

He was convinced that the 'stinking allegations and insinuations' Zelda had thrown at him arose from her own loathsome behaviour.[1] Together they visited the studio of the lesbian artist Romaine Brooks. Scott noticed Zelda's interest in Romaine's portrait of Natalie Barney brandishing a whip and several portraits of women in male attire. That Zelda was intrigued by Romaine's *art* hardly registered with him. Zelda described the studio as 'a glass-enclosed square of heaven swung high above Paris'.[2] For Scott it was a disagreeable exposure to a distasteful underworld.

For some months Zelda had been attracting considerable attention from women. She became close to Lucienne, a fellow ballerina in Egorova's studio. 'Lucienne was sent away . . . I didn't know why there was something wrong. I just kept on going,' she recalled later.[3] Some time after this, at a dinner given by Nancy Hoyt, bisexual novelist and sister of poet Elinor Hoyt Wylie, Nancy 'offerred her services' but Zelda, who told Scott later 'there was nothing the matter with my head then', refused.[4] On other occasions Scott watched with fury Zelda's effect on the women at Barney's salon.

In the Parisian urban jungle, Zelda saw Barney's 300-year-old mansion, in particular its rambling garden, as an oasis of calm. A curtain of ivy blanketed the walls, in the cobbled courtyard a massive gnarled tree overhung the house.[5] Amidst the plants and flowers Zelda felt at peace with her turbulent new emotions which troubled her as much as they troubled Scott, though they did not cancel out her underlying bond with him.

Matters came to a head over Zelda's friendship with Oscar Wilde's exotic niece Dolly Wilde.[6] Born in 1895, three months after her uncle's notorious trials, she was fussed over by the Sitwells, photographed by Cecil Beaton, and in the artistic circles of Paris, London and Hollywood tales of her outrageous antics were discussed as indiscreetly as she discussed them herself. Dolly's

kohl-rimmed eyes, gold lamé scarves, vivid animation and dedication to drugs[7] initially fascinated both Fitzgeralds, who toured Paris
with her.

Together with Victor Cunard, Mercedes de Acosta, Radclyffe
Hall, Esther Murphy, Bettina Bergery and Djuna Barnes, they
danced till dawn, floated down the Seine in a luxurious houseboat
and tried strange cocktails at the Ritz.[8] Dolly's wit was sharp but her
actions were self-destructive. Her words flew out like soap bubbles,
she glittered for an entranced public, but alone at a table in Les Deux
Magots, waiting for a fix, a follower or a Fitzgerald, she sat with art-
fully posed pale hands and frightening apathy, reminiscent of her
Uncle Oscar just before his end in 1900, the year of Zelda's birth.

Dolly, lover of both Natalie and the journalist Janet Flanner,[9] constantly looked around for new women. One evening at the salon she
looked intently at Zelda. Zelda, very drunk, looking back, saw a
woman sculptured like a statue with two huge violets for eyes.[10]
The novelist Rosamund Harcourt-Smith described those eyes as
'grapes in a greenhouse before the blue bloom gets rubbed off.
When she was pleased they had a velvety lustre . . . when angry . . .
the blue grapes became splintered glass.'[11]

When Dolly made a pass at Zelda in front of Natalie and Scott, her
eyes were doubtless velvety at Zelda's intense response but splintered like glass as Scott furiously intervened.

Zelda felt that if Scott did not quite encourage her, he did at least
facilitate her behaviour. 'You introduced me to Nancy Hoyt and sat
me beside Dolly Wilde one moment,' she wrote later to him, 'and
the next disparaged and belittled the few friends I knew whose eyes
had gathered their softness at least from things I understood.'[12]

Scott's entry in his May 1929 Ledger is so terse it is as if he had his
emotions in a stranglehold. Before his relieved acknowledgement of
the bisexual 'Esther's Marriage' he wrote only the curt phrase:
'Zelda & Dolly Wilde'. For some insight into his feelings of wrath
and repulsion at lesbians generally, in particular Dolly Wilde, we
have the evidence of several cancelled episodes from two early
manuscript versions of *Tender Is The Night* where Scott fictionalizes
Dolly as Vivian Taube.[13]

The scene is a bar in Paris where Francis Melarky is to meet
Wanda, whom he had met and desired a few days earlier. She is
accompanied by three tall women in black tailored suits, with man-
nequin heads waving like venomous snakes' hoods. 'The handsomest girl swayed forward eagerly like a cobra's head.'[14] She was
Miss—— (Vivian Taube). The three tall rich American girls intimi-

date Francis with their height and critical gaze, Vivian most of all.
'To be a tall rich American girl can imply . . . an attitude towards
"this man's world" . . . It was increasingly apparent to him that the
bigger one was a lesbian.'[15] He is sexually attracted to Wanda but
alienated from those three women, 'who didn't like him any more
than he liked them'.[16] When Wanda informs him they will all dine
together, Francis, furious, 'contented himself with thinking that
they were witches'.[17] After dinner he tells Wanda he wants her, but
Wanda refuses to leave them: 'it was now apparent to him that
Miss—— the bitter one was a Lesbian.'[18] By using the terms 'bigger'
and 'bitter' Scott consciously draws on lesbian stereotypes operat-
ing in the Twenties, still prevalent today. Melarky continues to
watch Miss Taube.

> There was a flick of the lip somewhere, a bending of the smile, toward
> some indirection, a momentary lifting and dropping of the curtain over
> a hidden chamber. This was all he thought until an hour later he came
> out . . . to a taxi whither they had preceded him and found Wanda limp
> and drunk in Miss——'s arms. His first impulse was to think how sweet
> – then he was furious. Wanda was for him. 'What's the idea?' he
> demanded. Miss—— smiled at him . . . 'I love Wanda,' said Miss——.
> 'Vivian is a nice girl,' said Wanda.

Vivian urgently repeats she loves the girl. Melarky, rage escalating, insists she gets out of the cab. 'In answer Wanda drew the girl
close to her again.' In a spasm of fury Melarky pulls Vivian/Dolly
out of the taxi and heaves her on to the kerb. Angrily he then takes
Wanda to her disorderly apartment. He sits 'robbed and glowering':
'he had actually seen this thing in practise and it enfuriated him. He
knew it had spoiled some things for him, some quiet series of
human facts . . . as it had when he had first realized that about homosexuality some years before.'[19] In Wanda's apartment they row:
Wanda is furious he pulled Vivian out into 'the public gutter',
Francis confident 'it's where she belongs'. Wanda fires a pistol in the
bathroom, then says sneeringly she had wanted to see if she could
sleep with him, but she can't and won't. He is to get out. 'He hated
her for intangling him in this sordidness – it was unbelievable he
had ever desired a rotten hysterical Lesbian . . . He would have liked
to have hit her.' He leaves, thinking, 'God damn these women.'[20]
   In *A Moveable Feast* Hemingway suggested that Zelda threatened
Scott by having lesbian women friends as early as 1925, whilst biographer Mellow suggests that Zelda's reason was to make Scott

jealous by using women as she had formerly used men. This seems unlikely. Although jealousy was one possible *consequence* of Zelda's actions her motive was probably another attempt to do something for herself, to express new desires separate from Scott. That these tentative sexual expressions usually came only after she was drunk was because they were accompanied by anxiety.

In the Twenties lesbianism for some women was glamorized, for others stigmatized, for most risqué. An American survey in the late Twenties of 2,200 mainly middle-class women showed that more than half had experienced 'intense emotional relationships with women', and half again specified that these were sexual.[21] But most *out* of the public arena eventually married. Those in the public eye behaved differently. On Broadway Katherine Cornell and Eleonora Duse, and in Hollywood Joan Crawford, Marlene Dietrich, Barbara Stanwyck and Louise Brooks would later become lesbian icons. On Paris's Left Bank Gertrude Stein, Alice B. Toklas, Colette, Djuna Barnes and Natalie Barney took their sexuality more seriously, several holding feminist-lesbian views.

Compton Mackenzie, who had danced with them to Romaine Brooks's Decca portable on Capri, wrote a spoof, *Extraordinary Women*, which satirized their lesbianism as a wilfully chosen bizarre mindset.[22] But years later Mackenzie emphasized that in the Twenties lesbianism was as taboo as male homosexuality had been in Wilde's era.[23]

In 1928 Radclyffe Hall, another member of Barney's circle, found her outspoken lesbian novel *The Well of Loneliness* banned in Britain and initially, prior to appeal, in the USA.[24] Though Hall's literary career never recovered she, being monied, upper-class, eccentric, bold and British, outfaced prejudice and to some extent got away with it.[25] Women without those advantages did not. Zelda was American and, more significantly, she was from the Deep South, where lesbianism was an unspeakable word. Zelda, Sara Mayfield and Tallulah Bankhead, all bisexual at different stages in their lives, having been conditioned as Southern Belles confronted a special stigma.[26]

Camella Mayfield, Sara's cousin, explained:

In the Deep South in those days those kind of sexual proclivities and by that I mean homosexual or bisexual were seen as terrible . . . Zelda and Sara might have rebelled against what people thought was the right way for Southern Belles to behave but those attitudes of shaming oneself and one's family if you went off the correct path, were their foundation. No matter what they *did*, Sara and Zelda would know what people in the South thought. And it would have mattered to them.[27]

Previous researchers seem unaware that Sara Mayfield had an irregular but continuous correspondence for several years with both Zelda and Tallulah.[28] When Sara edited her papers in the late 1960s before donating them to the University of Alabama at Tuscaloosa, she destroyed Zelda's letters as well as many from Tallulah. She told the then university archivist and her cousin Camella, the Mayfield Collection's literary executor, that she was doing it to protect her friends' privacy, most especially Zelda's.[29]

Some critics in Montgomery believe that Sara, being a writer/researcher, would never have destroyed those letters, but both the current University of Alabama archivist and Camella Mayfield are convinced they were destroyed.[30] Camella, who read and typed the original manuscript of Sara's study of the Fitzgeralds, said firmly:

> It was 1959 when Sara told me about the letters from Zelda. They were of a deeply personal nature and may have included confidences about their troubled private lives which is why Sara destroyed them. There are two things in the Deep South which in that period would have been seen as deeply personal and shaming and would bring stigma on the family. One was anything sexual being homosexual or bisexual, the other was anything that could be construed as psychotic behaviour. Sara was not going to include any facts of that nature in the biographies of Zelda or Tallulah nor would she give Zelda's or Tallulah's letters to the University of Alabama.[31]

In her study of Zelda, Mayfield is at pains to say that neither Fitzgerald is homosexual 'in the exact meaning of the word'.[32] Camella offers a reason:

> From the start Sara cleaned up those biographies. She said the facts were 'too too personal' and it was from square one that she did her censoring . . . I typed the first draft and the final draft of Sara's *Exiles* about Scott and Zelda which . . . had been sanitized. She did clean up Zelda's character. Sara wanted to protect Zelda but she may have also wanted to protect herself.[33] [Camella added:] it was never confirmed publicly within the family that Sara had lesbian relationships though people had gotten a whiff of it from several places. If it had been known publicly that Sara had relationships with women it would have made her persona non grata in the South. It would have been the same for Zelda.[34]

This, then, was the context for Zelda's anxieties during 1929, in particular her complex feelings of desire and shame when Dolly made a pass at her, soon after which she transferred some of those emotions into an accusation about Scott and Ernest.

Later, when Zelda wrote to Scott about the attitudes of Barney's circle to their sexuality, she focused on Dolly Wilde and Emily Vanderbilt. Whereas several of Barney's set were at ease with their lifestyle 'Dolly Wilde was the only one who said she would do anything to be cured.'[35] Though Dolly had been born in London's Chelsea and Zelda in America's Deep South, they shared a sense of sexual shame which in Zelda's case was specifically *Southern*. Emily initially held a more autonomous attitude. Zelda recalled that Emily seemed 'to represent order and independance to me'. But Emily too began to waver and Zelda's view of her changed later that summer: 'I was sorry for her, she seemed so muddled and lost in the grist mill.' Zelda wrote to Scott that although she herself 'was much stronger mentally and physically and sensitively than Emily ... you said ... that she was too big a poisson for me'. Reasonably Zelda asked why. 'She couldn't dance a Brahm's waltz or write a story – she can only gossip and ride in the Bois and have pretty hair curling up instead of thinking – Please explain.'[36] Perhaps Scott couldn't explain that he felt competitive about the bisexual Emily with the pretty curling hair, who was too big a *poisson* for Zelda but perhaps not for him. He began to see Emily socially in Paris, for according to playwright Lillian Hellman Emily was a handsome woman seen at every literary cocktail party.[37]

Hellman, who remembered meeting Emily first after the opening night of her play *The Children's Hour*,[38] said: 'Emily ... was to marry Raoul Whitfield, a mystery story writer. A few years after the marriage she was murdered on a ranch they bought in New Mexico, and neither the mystery story expert nor the police ever found the murderer.'[39] Hellman slightly fictionalized these facts and got the date of their meeting wrong, for Emily killed herself with a pistol at Dead Horse Ranch on 24 May 1934.

Emily's violent death followed a life led with both men and women which was of such extraordinary fascination to both Fitzgeralds that after her dramatic suicide, each of them unbeknownst to the other cut out the newspaper reports about the tragedy and folded away the cuttings in their separate scrapbooks. During research for this biography the two aged yellow cuttings fell out on the desk. Neither Fitzgerald had forgotten the fish that got away.

Emily's ambivalent sexual desires may not have been as

'muddled' or 'lost' as Zelda perceived them, but they certainly contrasted with Natalie Barney's belief that coming to terms honestly
with your sexual feelings was a decided advantage. Zelda, who felt
in need of clarity, revealed to Scott how much Natalie influenced
her. She needed Scott's help to come to terms with her own sexual
feelings. She begged him to acknowledge 'the Beauty of homosexuality as our marital relationship'. God, she said, had willed it as a
means of requiting 'the second of our sexual functions . . . Thus there
will no longer be any necessity for the use of catatonic and homosexual controls which have sold too many of us into bondage.'[40]
Scott ignored all such pleas.

Rows about women, rows about Ernest, rows about Scott's drinking escalated. For Zelda every day seemed 'more barren and sterile
and hopeless'.[41] She still had problems with staff. She had disliked
intensely Mlle Bellois, the new governess, who had arrived in May
1929. If Scottie was with her Zelda consciously avoided them.
Scottie disliked her too, but as Zelda pointed out to Scott: 'You
wouldn't let me fire the nurse that both Scottie and I hated.'[42]
Thankfully, by fall 1929 Mlle Bellois had been replaced by the more
popular Mlle Serez.

Zelda still had problems with Scott's friendship with Ernest,
though at the time of her accusation about the two men Scott's relationship with Ernest was floundering. In June 1929 Scott, timekeep-
ing for a sparring match between Hemingway and Callaghan,
inadvertently allowed a round to run over time, during which
Morley knocked down Ernest. Both men were furious and the event
reaped great publicity, producing a major strain between
Hemingway and Fitzgerald. In August Scott wrote to Hemingway
that he was 'working like hell'.[43] Sceptically Hemingway responded
that it was just as likely that Scott was sending friends glowing
reports but not actually finishing his book.[44]

Though anxious and confused Zelda continued to be creative, with
bursts of dangerous energy. In Cannes that summer Scott tried to
match her productivity. By early fall he was able to report to Perkins
he had a new angle for his novel. He dropped the Melarky matricide
plot and used a film director and wife, Lew and Nicole Kelly, who
encounter Rosemary, a young actress, on board ship to Europe.[45]
Rosemary would be based on Zelda's bête noire, Lois Moran.

That September Ober left the Reynolds agency, struck out on his
own, and asked Scott to come with him. His bribe was that he would
'gladly make you advances when needed'.[46] After talking it over
with Zelda, Scott agreed.

They saw the Murphys frequently in Cannes and Zelda's relationship with them remained steady. But Scott's deteriorated into a series of rows. This could not have happened at a worse time for the Murphys, who desperately needed support from their friends. Their son Patrick was ill all summer with what would soon be diagnosed as tuberculosis. Scott's behaviour began to wear down their patience. Zelda recalled: 'You disgraced yourself at the Barry's party, on the yacht at Monte Carlo, at the casino with Gerald and Dotty.'[47] Scott, constantly tense and irritable, seemed unable to help himself. His anxiety over Zelda's sexuality made him even more obsessive about 'fairies' than he had been previously. In one of his Notes he said 'Fairies' represented 'Nature's attempt to get rid of soft boys by sterilizing them'.[48] This paranoid preoccupation with homosexuals daily infiltrated his writing and increased his anger towards Zelda. The strength of his obsession can be seen in several cancelled scenes from the early versions of *Tender Is The Night*.

The scene is Paris at night, a sleazy 'last call place in Montmartre', alive with hot American jazz: 'suddenly we were in a world of fairies – I never saw so many or such a variety together. There were tall gangling ones and little pert ones with round thin shoulders, and great broad ones with the faces of Nero and Oscar Wilde, and fat ones with sly smiles that twisted into horrible leers, and nervous ones who hitched and jerked . . . self-conscious ones who looked with eager politeness . . . satyrs whose lips curled horribly.'[49]

Sara Murphy felt Scott should forget fairies and concentrate on his wife and child. 'You don't even know what Zelda or Scottie are like –' she wrote '– in spite of your love for them. It seemed to us the other night (Gerald too) that all you thought and felt about them was in terms of *yourself* . . . I feel obliged in honesty of a friend to write you that the ability to know what another person feels in a given situation will make – or ruin lives.'[50]

Though Scott admitted that by now he was indifferent to Zelda,[51] he taxed her with precisely his own emotions. 'You were simply one of all the people who disliked me or were indifferent to me. I didn't like to think of you.'[52] He was probably correct. Their estrangement and hostility heightened. Zelda's health had become hazardous. She was creative in terrifying bursts of energy, followed instantly by bouts of reclusive fatigue, throughout the summer stay on the Riviera.

On 27 September 1929 Hemingway's *A Farewell to Arms* was published, which did not improve their tempers. Scott predicted it would sell about 50,000 copies but it did considerably better. The first printing of 30,000 sold out; two more printings of 10,000 each were run in October. Reviews were excellent. The book topped the bestseller lists. Then the stockmarket crashed, affecting all retail business including books. But Hemingway had become a highly desirable commodity. The fires of literary rivalry between Scott and Ernest were set to blaze.

When Zelda and Scott returned to 10 rue Pergolèse in Paris in October, Gertrude Stein stoked the coals with some maliciousness. In November[53] she asked Hemingway, then her particular protégé, to bring Scott and the Southern poet Allen Tate to one of her Wednesday literary evenings. Wives were also invited but would as usual be handed over to Alice B. Toklas to be entertained, whilst the men challenged each other intellectually and Stein adjudicated.

Zelda had already met Tate and his Southern novelist wife Caroline Gordon at a party given by the Bishops. She felt at home with her fellow Southerner, so despite her by now almost constant state of nerves she consented to go with Scott. Allen Tate found Zelda 'immensely attractive, with the Southern woman's gift for conversation that made people feel she must have known them for years', but found Scott – who at their first meeting asked him if he enjoyed sleeping with his wife – boorish.[54]

So on a December evening Zelda found herself sitting with Caroline Gordon, Pauline Hemingway and Margaret Bishop at Alice's tea table, whilst in a far corner of Stein's salon Scott, Ernest, Allen Tate, John Bishop and Ford Madox Ford listened to Stein lecture on American literature. Zelda found nothing worth concentrating on and sat, withdrawn and silent, for several hours while Gertrude traced the path of genius from Emerson through Henry James to herself. She told Ernest that *Farewell* was good when he invented but less so when he remembered. Ernest's literary 'flame' and Scott's 'flame', she said, were different. Zelda and Hemingway deduced that currently Stein preferred Fitzgerald's flame, yet Scott inexplicably converted this praise into a slighting remark, and en route home with Zelda and the Hemingways became aggressive towards Ernest. He behaved so badly that the next day, yet again, he was forced to tender apologies.[55]

Zelda's loneliness and confusion, presumably evident to the other guests at Stein's gathering, led her into another of her infatuations, this time with the first of two redheaded women she became attracted to.[56] Scott and Hemingway were united in their disgust. It seemed that everywhere the two men looked that year they found something from the fairy world to shock them, the most obvious centre being Stein's own.

Until now Hemingway had tolerated Gertrude and Alice's menage, which rather uncomfortably resembled a traditional role-ridden heterosexual marriage, because both he and Scott saw Stein as their mentor. But Stein began to repel Hemingway. First she lectured him: the male homosexual act was 'ugly and repugnant and afterwards they are disgusted with themselves'. Women lovers however did nothing disgusting or repulsive, 'and afterwards they are happy and can lead happy lives together'. Hemingway's education at 27 rue de Fleurus continued. One afternoon he arrived there to be told Miss Stein would be right down. He heard 'someone' (he doesn't name Alice) speaking 'as I had never heard one person speak to another; never, anywhere, ever'. Then Miss Stein's voice begged and pleaded: 'Don't, pussy. Don't. Don't, please don't. I'll do anything, pussy, but please don't do it. Please don't. Please don't, pussy.'[57] So appalled was Ernest that he decided to end his useful friendship with Stein. Scott, however, decided to act more strategically and maintain his friendship with Stein, despite Zelda's cold indifference to her.

In February 1930, resisting severe bronchitis and a high fever for two weeks, Zelda insisted on going to ballet classes. Only when dancing did she feel safe. She plied Madame with green silk for a dress, a bandanna filled with perfumes, and more bouquets: white lilacs, black tulips, carnivorous gladioli which she was also capturing on canvas.[58]

Unlike her gestures, there was nothing sentimental about Zelda's flower paintings. Her *Untitled* white flowers whose petals are like tentacles,[59] and her *White Flowers in a Vase*[60] whose blossoms spring from the vase to snake across the table, have writhing expressionistic forms similar to Van Gogh's. They appear mystical one moment, threatening the next. Zelda became aware of the parallels between her flowers and Van Gogh's: 'Those crawling flowers and venomous vindictive blossoms are the hallucinations of a mad-man – without organization or rhythm but with the power to sting and strangle . . . I loved them . . . They reassured me.'[61]

Despite exhaustion from illness, painting and dancing, Zelda grew restless. So Scott suggested a trip to North Africa in late February for them to recover. In her article 'Show Mr and Mrs F. to Number–' she later wrote: 'It was a trying winter and to forget bad times we went to Algiers. The Hôtel de l'Oasis was laced together by Moorish grills; and the bar was an outpost of civilization with people accentuating their eccentricities. Beggars in white sheets were propped against the walls, and the dash of colonial uniforms gave the cafés a desperate swashbuckling air.'[62]

She took her sketch pad but for once photographs offer greater insights. Study Zelda's eyes sharply. They seem caught in a remote iced-up expression, as if instead of seeing people she saw through them and trusted nobody.

In Biskra Scott photographed her on a camel, going up and up to visit the sculptor Clare Sheridan. Zelda is a tiny frail figure. Streets glare in the sun. Arabs sell 'poisonous pink' sweetmeats and cakes. There are two matching snapshots: Zelda forlorn in a vast empty desert which Scott captioned 'Lost in the Sahara', and Scott alone on another stretch of dunes peering into the horizon, labelled 'Looking for a Mirage'. The sad truth is that both figures look lost and lonely.[63] Zelda wrote letters to Madame, heard cries in the night, the bleak hills frightened her. She was desperate to return to dancing.

'Then we went to Africa and when we came back . . . You did not want me . . . when I wanted you to come home with me you told me to sleep with the coal man.'[64] They did not make love, they did not talk.

As Zelda recalled:

Then the world became embryonic in Africa – and there was no need for communication. The Arabs fermenting . . . the curious quality of their eyes and the smell of ants; a detachment as if I was on the other side of a black gauze – a fearless small feeling, and then the end at Easter.[65]

'The end' was her first nervous collapse, which took almost two months to reach breaking point. During those eight weeks after their return to rue Pergolèse in Paris her confidence slipped through her fingers. Her friends noticed. The Murphys arrived to take Zelda to an art exhibition and found Bishop and Scott outside the apartment trying to calm Zelda, who was wildly insisting the two men had been talking about her during a lunch the three had shared. Gerald was shocked. How could they have been discussing her without her knowledge? 'I mean, she was sitting right there with them!'[66] He and Sara, who soon had to return to Switzerland to be with Patrick, left deeply concerned about her.

On another occasion she threw herself at Egorova's feet after class. Egorova, disturbed by this display, felt Zelda's affection was becoming unhealthy.[67] Zelda was clear about her feelings. 'My attitude towards Egorova has always been one of intense love. I wanted

to help her in some way because she is a good woman . . . I wanted
to dance well so that she would be proud of me and have another
instrument for the symbols of beauty that passed in her head that I
understood.'[68]

Later, time in asylums and re-educative treatment would insist
Zelda's feelings were evil.

'Perhaps it is depraved,' she wrote later to Scott. 'I do not know,
but at home there was an incessant babbling . . . and you either
drinking or complaining because you had been. You blamed me
when the servants were bad, and expected me to instil into them a
proper respect for a man they saw morning after morning asleep in
his clothes.'[69]

In 1930 Edmund Wilson, now recovered from *his* nervous breakdown and married to Margaret Canby, asked solicitously after
Zelda's health. By this time at a flower market she had told Scott the
flowers were talking to her and she was hearing voices not available
to others.

Scott tried to hold *his* world together by writing a new series of
Post stories set during the First World War, about a Chicago debutante, Josephine Perry, based on Ginevra King. On 5 April 1930 'First
Blood', the first of his five tales, was published. The remaining four
('A Nice Quiet Place', 'A Woman with a Past', 'A Snobbish Story'
and 'Emotional Bankruptcy') followed.[70] The concept of emotional
bankruptcy, a financial metaphor close to Scott's heart and pocket,
became a key notion.

During 1930 Scott wrote eight stories altogether which secured
him $32,000, but yet again he had to borrow $3,700 from Scribner's
against his by now mythical novel. He blamed Zelda for ruining one
of his stories because she wanted them to take Madame out to dine.
He felt the apartment was foul, the maid stank and Zelda was
'going crazy and calling it genius – I was going to ruin and calling
it anything that came to hand'.[71]

When the Kalmans lunched at their apartment in March Zelda,
terrified she would miss her dance class, leapt from the table and
rushed out, followed by Oscar who took her in a cab. Increasingly
distressed, she changed into dancing clothes in the taxi, then when
stuck in traffic opened the door, hurled herself out and ran to the
studio. Oscar told Scott he thought Zelda was on the verge of a
breakdown.

In April Zelda, in great distress, burst into the flat where Scott was
drinking with Michael Arlen. She needed Scott but felt he preferred
drinking with the playwright. So distraught was she that Arlen sug-

gested she should try a clinic. She was in no state to resist. Nor could Scott resist the parallels between the narrative of his wife's life and that of her era. As Zelda succumbed to her first crack-up, Scott, noting the Wall Street crash, assiduously observed in his Ledger: 'The Crash! Zelda and America'.[72]

On 23 April 1930, Zelda entered the ominously named Malmaison Clinic near Paris. Predictably her first agitated words were about work: 'It's appalling, it's horrific, what's going to become of me, I have to work and I can't any more. I have to die, and yet I must work. I shall never be cured, let me go, I must go and see "Madame" . . . she gave me the greatest joy there can be, it is comparable to sunlight falling on a piece of crystal, to a symphony of scents.'[73] Professor Claude, who reported these words, said she was in such a state of anxiety she was unable to keep still.

On her admission, Zelda, slightly tipsy, told the doctors she found alcohol stimulated her dancing. The doctors saw drink as one cause for her anxiety attacks.[74]

Zelda's later letter to Scott recalled:

I went to Malmaison. You wouldn't help me – I don't blame you by now, but if you had explained I would have understood because all I wanted to do was to go on working. You had other things: drink and tennis, and we did not care about each other. You hated me for asking you not to drink . . . I still believed in love and I thought suddenly of Scottie and that you supported me.[75]

Professor Claude decided 'it is a matter of an anxious young woman exhausted by her work in the world of professional dancers. Some obsessive ideas, the main one being the fear of becoming homosexual. She believes she is in love with her dance teacher . . . She believes that in the past she has been in love with another woman.' The medical report mentioned 'Violent reactions, several suicide attempts, never carried through to the end . . .' and said her periods were regular, her blood pressure low, her pulse faint and she had a moderate appetite.

On 2 May, after ten days, she left Malmaison against her doctor's wishes.[76]

She returned to ballet, but within a fortnight was hallucinating, seeing horrific phantoms everywhere whether awake or asleep, and in terror tried to kill herself. Scott felt he could not leave her side – a sensible precaution but it increased Zelda's feelings of imprisonment. After she had collapsed into hospital, Scott's May 1930

Ledger records: 'Zelda weak and tired . . . Emily . . . Zelda every-day'. In June Mayfield reported that Scott's 'anxiety did not prevent him from beauing Emily Vanderbilt around Paris'.[77]

Zelda's friends Sara Mayfield and Sara Haardt in Montgomery had not been told about Zelda's breakdown. Ironically they were rejoicing that there was a temporary improvement in Sara Haardt's own health. She arrived in Montgomery to tell her father she was marrying Mencken,[78] then excitedly called Sara Mayfield in Tuscaloosa to say her novel *The Making of a Lady* had been accepted by Doubleday Doran for publication in 1931. By the time that Zelda's two friends heard about her illness Zelda had already entered Valmont Clinic, Glion, near Montreux, Switzerland, on 22 May 1930.

The clinic, recommended by friends, specifically handled gastro-intestinal ailments, so could do little for Zelda. She told the staff she was not sick, she did not want to be hospitalized, she had been brought there under duress. She also stated that ballet, her compen-sation for a miserable marriage, was her route to independence. She wrote to Scott later that 'at Valmont I was in tortue, and my head closed together. You gave me a flower and said it was "plus petite et moins etendue" – We were friends – Then you took it away and I grew sicker.'[79]

Scott took the French phrase away too, and re-used it in one of the sanatorium letters from his heroine Nicole in *Tender Is The Night*. 'One man was nice . . . he gave me a flower and said it was "plus petite et moins entendue". We were friends. Then he took it away. I grew sicker.'[80]

Zelda later described her entry to Valmont as 'practically volun-tarily but under enormous pressure . . . with the sole idea of getting back enough strenghth and health to continue my work in America as you had promised me. There, my head began to go wrong and the pristine nurse whom you accused me of attacking played almost constantly on the thing that I had assumed I was there to get over.'[81]

The doctors and Scott consistently emphasized that Zelda's lesbian desires were evil and would not be countenanced. But in Valmont she was unable to stop herself responding to a nurse who flirted with her constantly. In the clinic Dr H. W. Trutmann gave this report on her stay there from 22 May to 4 June:

> At the beginning Mrs Fitzgerald maintained that she had not been ill and that she had been taken forcibly to the nursing home[82] . . . she repeated that she wanted to return to Paris to continue with the ballet work in

which . . . she found her only satisfaction in life. Moreover, the patient described in a quite obscure way the physical sensations that she experienced and that she connected with her homosexuality. This represented another reason for returning to Paris. The husband's visits were often the occasion of violent quarrels provoked mainly by the husband's attempts to . . . refute the patient's insinuations that she suspected her husband of homosexuality. Mrs Fitzgerald would work herself into a very excited state at the thought that on the one hand she was losing precious time and on the other that people were trying to take away from her the things most dear to her: her work as a dancer and her lesbian leanings.

The doctor's version of the nurse incident differed from Zelda's: 'Some over-affectionate behaviour towards the nurse was repulsed by the latter, who fell into disgrace.'[83]

The doctors checked Zelda's agitation with Garderal every one to two hours. They induced sleep with Medinale and a sleeping drug. Trutmann said that when Zelda was calm she was aware she needed both to take care and be taken care of, but an hour later would insist on returning to Paris. He was clear that 'organically there was nothing to report, no signs of brain disorder'. But he felt a simple rest cure was insufficient, that she needed psychological treatment in a specialist nursing home.

It was evident that the relationship between the patient and her husband had long been weakened, and because of that the patient had not only tried to create a life for herself through the ballet (since family life and her duties towards her daughter were not enough to satisfy her ambition and her artistic leanings) but had also taken flight into homosexuality in order to distance herself from her husband.

When Trutmann asked her what role eight-year-old Scottie played in her life, she responded in English: 'That is done now, I want to do something else.'[84]

Nobody in either Malmaison or Valmont picked up on the effects that the consistent denial of her ambitions and exploitation of her talents might have had on her psyche. Uncovering and re-interpreting them would be left for the battery of psychiatrists who followed.

After two weeks Dr Trutmann called in Dr Oscar Forel of the Prangins Clinic, near Nyon, as a consultant. Forel said he would accept Zelda if she agreed to go there of her own free will and on condition of a temporary separation from Scott. Forel specified the treatment could only be psychotherapy based on analysis of causative factors in her case. On 3 June, the evening of the consultation,

Trutmann said: 'the patient herself said she felt very tired and ill and that she was in great need of being cared for. She gave the impression that she would agree to go to Prangins. The next day she was again . . . unapproachable. She is leaving the clinic with her husband.'[85]

Mayfield suggests that though Zelda initially agreed to go to Prangins, after a violent scene with Scott in Lausanne, in which she accused him of abusing, humiliating and breaking her, she refused to be re-hospitalized. Scott immediately sent for Zelda's brother-in-law Newman Smith, who with Rosalind was living in Brussels. Smith arrived the next day, helped to quiet Zelda, and persuaded her to put herself under Forel's care.[86] The Smiths continued to represent the Sayre family during Zelda's Swiss hospitalization. Rosalind, never fond of Scott, was convinced his drinking caused Zelda's breakdown. She wrote to him: 'I would almost rather she die now than escape only to go back to the mad world you and she have created for yourselves.'[87] Scott retaliated that the Sayres had a history of nervous illnesses, that Zelda had always been reckless and that she had long refused to take domestic responsibility. It is symptomatic of the period that a woman's domestic role as a symbol of sanity was so enshrined in popular culture that Scott felt entitled to use its lack as a symptom of Zelda's instability.

The doctors and Scott told the Smiths that Zelda's efforts to make a professional career as a writer and dancer were motivated by obsessive illness. Rosalind told Sara Mayfield her impression was, on the contrary, 'a clear-eyed realization of the financial uncertainties of her life with Scott and, perhaps, also by her unhappiness over their marital difficulties'. Rosalind believed Zelda had brilliant gifts, an unconquerable urge to express herself and a very sensible desire to earn a living. 'Unfortunately, according to Rosalind,' reported Sara, 'Scott refused to see it that way. He wanted her . . . to be dependent upon him, and he insisted upon treating her like a wayward child.'[88]

On 4 June Zelda entered Prangins, which resembled a country club in the midst of a 100-acre park on the shore of Lake Geneva. She would stay there for fifteen and a half months, until 15 September 1931. Later she described her journey to this expensive asylum:

> Our ride . . . was very sad . . . we did not have each other or anything else and it half-killed me to give up all the work I had done . . . I had wanted to destroy the picture of Egorova that I had lived with for four

years and give away my tou-tous and the suitcase full of shoes and free my mind from the thing . . . I had got to the end of my physical resources.[89]

In what is probably her first letter to Scott from Prangins she returned to their row in Lausanne:

Won't you please come and see me, since at least you know me and you could see, maybe, some assurance to give me that would counteract the abuse you piled on me at Lausanne when I was so sick. At any rate one thing has been achieved: I am thoroughly humiliated and broken if that was what you wanted.

Scott ruthlessly reproduced Zelda's sad phrases in *Tender Is The Night*, where Nicole writes to Dick Diver:

I am completely broken and humiliated, if that was what they wanted. I have had enough and it is simply ruining my health and wasting my time pretending that what is the matter with my head is curable.

Zelda, like the fictional Nicole, said she had a constant presentiment of disaster; that it was cruel that he would not explain to her what is the matter,

since you will not accept my explanation. As you know, I am a person, or was, of some capability . . . and if I could grasp the situation I would be much better able to handle it. Under existing conditions, I simply grovel about in the dark and since I can not concentrate either to read or write there does not seem to be any way of escape. I do not want to lose my mind.[90]

To the visitor, the external 'existing conditions' at Prangins had a resort atmosphere, with music rooms, billiard rooms, riding stables, winter gardens, hothouses, farms, tennis courts, a bathing beach and *ateliers* for occupational therapy. There were seven private villas, three occupied by the staff, four reserved for wealthy 'guests'. Scott assured the Sayres that the newly opened clinic was '*the best* in Europe', that Dr Oscar Forel's father Auguste Forel, Professor of Psychiatry at Zurich University, had 'an extraordinary reputation as a pioneer in the field of psychiatry', while Oscar was talented, versatile, and 'universally regarded as a man of intelligence and character'.[91] The tall, skinny, well-dressed Oscar, who was to have great influence on both Fitzgeralds, was born 1891, studied at the

Sorbonne and Lausanne's Faculty of Medicine and became a faculty member of Geneva University for twenty-five years. Though sensitive he had the dictator's qualities of crafty persuasion and an ability to impose his will on others.[92]

The 'existing conditions' maintained by the sensitive Oscar which the visitor did *not* see included the forcible restraint on Zelda for her first month. There were two types of control methods: the 'two-point restraint' which tied her wrists to the bed and the 'four-point restraint' which bound her ankles and wrists to the bed. Her hallucinations were treated with shots of chloral hydrate which completely tranquillized her.

The cost of Forel's clinic during that first year of the Depression was gigantic: $1,000 a month.[93] Scott, determined to spare no expense to provide the best for Zelda, and worried that the stock market crash would diminish his earning facilities, decided in June 1930 to invest $212 in a Northern Pacific Railway bond and an American Telephone and Telegraph debenture. Though Scott would make many grave errors during the next ten years over decisions regarding Zelda's hospitalization and treatment, and would put control of Zelda consistently ahead of understanding or releasing her, he never shirked his financial obligations to her and to Scottie.

For several weeks Zelda refused to partake in the activities provided and shunned contacts with other patients. Then she developed an intense emotional attachment to another woman patient and also – as at her previous hospital – became involved with several nurses.[94]

Mayfield satirically suggests that a 'puzzling' aspect of the case for Forel 'was that Zelda showed no erotic feeling for her husband'[95] while simultaneously Scott told the doctors he was extremely anxious to resume sexual relations. Dr Forel, however, forbade him to visit her until a treatment course which included a 're-education programme' had been maintained.

During Zelda's stay in Prangins Scott stayed in the nearby Swiss towns of Glion, Geneva, Lausanne, Montreux and Vevey. About four days a month he went to Paris, where Scottie lived with her governess at 21 rue des Marionniers and attended the Cours Dieterlin. Zelda was distressed Scottie had been left alone in Paris (she did not count the nurse), but Scott reported that she had already won a first prize at school[96] and Alice and Dick Myers would keep an eye on her.

During the Prangins incarceration Zelda and Scott exchanged

more than a hundred letters explaining themselves, offering recriminations, attributing blame. As they rarely dated letters establishing
a correct chronology is an enormous challenge, but a definite
pattern can be observed that runs parallel to Zelda's psychological
're-education' towards femininity, good mothering and the revalu-
ing of marriage and domesticity.

In mental hospitals of that period,[97] patients eventually learned
what was in their 'best interests' to say to staff or to write to intimates outside. By 'best interest', what most of them meant was their
interest in being judged sufficiently 'sane' to be released. All letters
were opened, in some hospitals censored, in every hospital
assessed. In Zelda's case the need to 're-educate' her into being 'a
good wife' was paramount. So her initial letters of anger, betrayal,
distrust, resentment, which were seen by the medical establishment
as signs of 'instability', ultimately gave way to more conciliatory,
affectionate letters which were viewed as signs of 'improvement'.

What strikes the reader at once is that in Prangins Zelda is aware
of how she *needs* to behave if she is to be relabelled stable. But as her
treatments intensify in four more clinics, she becomes as much a
victim of the treatments as of the illness, and this awareness – or any
written evidence of it – drops away.

If this were the only motive for the first discernible hostil-
ity/affection pattern, the letters would be simple to analyse. But
running parallel is a second motive. This is the alternating mixture
of genuine resentment Zelda held against Scott (and he against her)
and the memory (if not the current activity) of the strongest passion
and the deepest emotional bond either had ever found or would
ever find with anyone.

A second batch of letters, from Zelda to Scottie, shows Zelda's
constant devotion to her daughter, but with their increasing separation and her own wavering sense of self, the letters progressively
reveal a woman in retreat from, even terrified by, motherhood.

A third group of letters, from Fitzgerald to Zelda's psychiatrists,
shows how Fitzgerald was intimately involved in Zelda's treatment
and how important it was to him to see himself, and to be considered by the medical establishment, as a junior consultant almost on
a par with her doctors.

These letters tell the next stage of Zelda's story.

CHAPTER 17

The three main characters in the Prangins drama staked out their painful positions.

From inside Prangins, Zelda wrote to Scott:

> <u>Please</u> help me. Every day more of me dies with this bitter and incessant beating I'm taking. You can choose the conditions of our life and anything you want if I don't have to stay here miserable and sick at the mercy of people who have never even tried what its like . . . <u>I can't</u> live any more under these conditions, and anyway I'll always know that the door is tacticly locked – if it ever is . . . There's no justice . . . the longer I have to bear this the meaner and harder and sicker I get . . . Please, Please let me out now – Dear, you used to love me and I swear to you that this is no use . . . You said it was too good to spoil. What's spoiling is me, along with it and I don't see how anybody in the world has a right to do such a thing –.[1]

From outside Prangins, Scott wrote to Zelda, whose photo he held:

> When I saw the sadness of your face in that passport photo I felt as you can imagine . . . The photograph is all I have: it is with me from the morning when I wake up with a frantic half dream about you to the last moment when I think of you and of death at night. The rotten letters you write me I simply put away under Z in my file. My instinct is to write a public letter to the Paris Herald to see if any human being except yourself and Robert McAlmon has ever thought I was homosexual . . . if you choose to keep up your wrestling match with a pillar of air I would prefer to be not even in the audience . . . I will take my full share of responsibility for all this tragedy but I cannot spread beyond the limits of my reach and grasp. I can only bring you the little bit of hope I have and I don't know any other hope except my own . . . if I have failed you is it just barely possible that you have failed me . . .[2]

Scott the outsider wrote also to Dr Forel the insider:

When I last saw you I was almost as broken as my wife by months of horror. The only important thing in my life was that she should be saved from madness or death.[3]

At the heart of Prangins, its director Dr Forel wrote to Scott that he shared Scott's ordeal, that he appreciated Scott's co-operation, that his personal feelings were mixed with his professional role. Like Scott he wanted Zelda to become well.

Forel kept in close touch with Scott over Zelda's diagnosis, treatment and progress, allowing him to feel responsible in his new role as unofficial co-consultant.

Dr Forel saw Zelda as 'gay, playful, optimistic, artistic and independently minded' but also 'extremely irritable'.[4]

Zelda saw herself as terrified.

Forel catalogued her symptoms: bizarre reactions, strange interpretations, inadequate responses, autism, insomnia, daydreaming, and smiling without cause. She also heard things, was hysterical, and had an inclination towards homosexuality which she projected on to her husband.

Zelda, too, catalogued her symptoms. She accepted that she was in a state of 'continuous nervous horror'. She lived 'in some horrible subconscious dream'.[5] She had hours of terrible 'panic [which] settled into a persistent gloom punctuated by moments of bombastic hysteria'. Some days she wanted to die.[6]

Patient and doctor *did* agree about the hysteria. They did *not* agree about her homosexuality. The patient did not think it was a symptom of illness, rather an expression of desire. The patient, according to the doctor, was out of line, had not read the medical books, must be re-educated.

Zelda, a fast reactor, a woman of rapier wit, suddenly exhibited such slow psychological and verbal responses that Forel suspected she had a brain tumour. But he could discover no physical evidence.[7]

He considered schizophrenia, which in the Thirties had already been established as at least in part genetically transmitted. There appeared to be no history of schizophrenia in Zelda's family.[8] However, when the Sayres wrote to Forel in June, they did not furnish him with adequate information about the varied mental illnesses suffered by Zelda's family. Whether any of them *had* produced symptoms which a doctor at that time would have labelled schizophrenic is unknown.

The Sayres' reluctance to divulge information was based on the Deep South view of mental illness. As one Montgomery resident said: 'Every family in Montgomery has at least one mad person . . . But we never talk about it. Montgomery people didn't (and don't) talk about anyone's "unusual" sexuality though there is a lot of that in our families too. In Zelda's day sometimes they were said to be crazy when their families just couldn't handle their views or their behaviour. You could be shut away just for talking about it.'[9]

Forel felt Zelda's 'overweening inflated ambition' had caused serious exhaustion. He did not take sufficiently into account the terrifying strains Scott's alcoholism put on Zelda. He believed unspecified 'marital difficulties' had 'provoked a depression with suicidal tendencies and a strong propensity for drug taking, which has developed into definite schizophrenia'.[10]

This was a new term, meaning 'split mind', coined in 1911 by Eugen Bleuler, a Swiss psychiatrist educated at Zurich University who became medical director of Zurich's Burghölzli Hospital and Professor of Psychiatry. He redefined earlier views of madness by suggesting that dementia praecox, one form of insanity, could be expanded and renamed because its patients showed a split or loss of co-ordination between different psychic functions, such as intellect and emotions.[11] Bleuler was interested in Zelda's case because he believed that it was a discrepancy between high aspiration and moderate achievement which precipitated delusions.

Symptoms varied with individual patients, but even in 1930 there were certain observable core symptoms, some of which Forel felt Zelda exhibited. All his schizophrenic patients believed their mental processes were no longer under their own control. Some insisted that alien forces put thoughts into their minds. Others heard voices telling them what to do or threatening to kill them. The most acute suffered delusions or hallucinations. How did Zelda match up to that measuring scale?

When she entered Prangins, Zelda had 'imagined that there were corpses in the house, had thoughts of parricide, appeared to be sleepwalking';[12] before that, she had felt people were criticizing her and had been unable to face dressmakers, shopkeepers or servants.[13]

Forel informed Scott that key symptoms in the schizophrenic repertoire were vagueness of thought, illogicality and incomprehensible speech. Then they considered Zelda as a 'case'. Zelda certainly had shifting thought patterns and made complex connections, but these were characteristics she had exhibited since childhood when perfectly healthy. Another problem affecting her diagnosis, which Forel did not take into account, was that in Switzerland her doctors spoke little English and her French was mediated by a strong Deep Southern accent, complicated by her original turns of phrase, her non sequiturs and her extravagant hyperbole.

Most of Forel's schizophrenic patients had lost their drive, were unable to respond emotionally to others and had become isolated and apathetic.[14] In June 1930 this was *not* true of Zelda, although as she became institutionalized for years a terrible apathy consumed her.

The onset of schizophrenia is usually preceded by stressful events. In Zelda's case her sexual anxieties and artistic frustration had become overwhelming immediately before her breakdown. Yet these instances were reinterpreted by Forel. Her specific sexual fear was relabelled a joint marital conflict, her loss of identity due to mis-appropriation of artistic credit was renamed 'disappointed ambitions', and her illness seen as a reaction to feelings of inferiority, particularly towards Scott. In Thirties society where Scott was seen as the professional and Zelda as the amateur, his artistic superiority would automatically be validated, as much by the largely male medical profession as by the literary élite, therefore Zelda's resentful responses would be seen as inappropriate, even 'crazy'.

Forel thought Zelda needed routine, avoidance of drink and drugs, and a 'normal' marriage in which she oversaw her child's education. He felt Scottie should be put on her guard so that she did not seek to fulfil her mother's unsatisfied desires and ambitions. He outlined a treatment programme of systematic workshop activity, sports, entertainment and above all 'regular discipline'. His crucial recommendation was that Zelda should give up her 'inflated ambitions' and engage in 'activities appropriate to her talents and tastes'.[15]

Scott saw Zelda's state between 15 May and 15 July 1930 as a 'period of insanity obvious to any layman'. He characterized it as wild homosexuality, suicide threats, attempts at escape, delusions. But he admitted that Zelda was also writing and painting furiously.[16] She had told the doctors how eager she was to paint and Scott had obtained permission to send in art materials. But there were many days when she felt isolated and terrified. 'I can't read or sleep. Without hope or youth or money I sit constantly wishing I were dead –', she wrote.[17]

For a time Scott tried to play down the gravity of Zelda's condition. In May he had written to Ober: 'Zelda's been sick + not dangerously but seriously', but by June from Paris he wrote to his mother: 'Zelda has been desperately ill with a complete nervous breakdown and is in a sanitarium near here. She is better now but recovery will take a long time. I did not tell her parents the serious-ness of it so say nothing – the danger was to her sanity rather than her life.'[18] Scottie, who was still attending school at Paris's Cours Dieterlin, visiting Rosalind in Brussels and taking weekend trips to her tutor Mlle Serez's family home, was told *nothing* about her mother's condition. 'I knew she was ill,' she said later, 'but I didn't know why.'[19]

Scott, in residence at the Hotel Righi near Glion, still failed to tell the Sayres how seriously ill Zelda was. He described it as nervous exhaustion for which Zelda was taking a Swiss cure, but Minnie Sayre was not fooled. Zelda's regular weekly letters had suddenly stopped. Mamma Sayre, who had already nursed Marjorie and the Judge through mental breakdowns, was familiar with the patterns. Although frantic 'for news from my little baby', she wrote to Scott with Southern stoicism: 'we might just as well face facts for there is no dodging them.'[20] Rosalind, who held Scott responsible for Zelda's condition, insisted he was too irresponsible to oversee Scottie. She repeatedly suggested the child live with her and Newman. Scottie later wrote: '[Rosalind's] smouldering quarrel with my father broke out – she deemed him too unreliable to be in charge of me while my mother was in the hospital and demanded that he let her adopt me.'[21]

Scott refused, and in mid-June took Scottie to visit her mother for the first time. In an effort to seem normal Zelda became terrifyingly tense. After Scottie's departure Zelda suffered a virulent attack of eczema across her neck, shoulders and face, with unremitting pain. Scott, almost as appalled as Zelda herself, was deeply sympathetic but also made good use of her agony. In *Tender Is The Night* his description of an American mental patient runs: 'On her admittance she had been exceptionally pretty – now she was a living agonizing sore. All blood tests had failed to give a positive reaction and the trouble was unsatisfactorily catalogued as nervous eczema. For two months she had lain under it, as imprisoned as the Iron Maiden. She was coherent, even brilliant, within the limits of her special halluci-nations.' With some insight Scott has his Zelda-model say: 'I'm sharing the fate of the women of my time who challenged men to battle.'[22]

Zelda herself, still covered with sores, had been reading James Joyce but found 'it a night-mare in my present condition'. She told

Scott her concentration was failing, the pain so extreme that 'my head evaporates,' but she was still determined to read something 'upon which my head will be able to make no conjectures . . . something with ideas'. She fixed on the German philosopher Oswald Spengler. 'Will you send me "The Decline of the West" . . . so that I can put my sub-conscious, or whatever it is, back where it belongs and be left in peace to formulate and organize and absorb things that could find themselves a form afterwards?' She did not want anything in French because she was having sufficient difficulty with English 'and not Lawrence and not Virginia Wolf or anybody who writes by dipping the broken threads of their heads into the ink of literary history.'[23]

Scott sent the Spengler and some perfume, but by the time they arrived the eczema had escalated. Doctors injected her with calcium and morphine, administered X-rays, placed her on a strict diet which excluded cheese, preserves, cooked pork and *hors-d'oeuvre*, but to no avail.[24]

Despairingly she wrote: 'If you don't come take me out of this clinic I'm going crazy – swathed in embalming fluid all day and plastered with mud that decomposes and runs down my ears – I'd rather have hydro-phobia and all the plagues of the Holy Land and not be in captivity.'

With a wrenching return to satire she added: 'There's so little variety in eczema.'[25] In 1920 Zelda had written to Scott: 'I could never do without you if you hated me and were covered with sores like a leper.'[26] Which of them remembered it now?

One Sunday Zelda, taken for a walk by a *dame de compagnie*, suddenly broke away and fled.[27] It took three trained nurses to bring her back, whereupon she was immediately transferred to Villa Eglantine, a unit reserved for highly disturbed patients, where she was isolated, locked in and forcibly restrained.

In *Tender Is The Night* Scott uses the name Eglantine for a secure unit in the psychiatric clinic which housed 'those sunk into eternal darkness'. His fictional Eglantine, based on the hideous reality into which Zelda was confined, had the same exterior cheerfulness, the same concealed grilles, bars and immovable furniture where 'no uninstructed visitor would have dreamed that the light, graceful filagree work at a window was a strong, unyielding end of a tether'.[28]

In 1919 Scott had written repeatedly to Zelda how much he wished his princess was locked up in a tower. Now she was: confined by forcible bonds, the label madness, hearing other voices than his. Although Scott's Ledger entry records only the barest

summary: 'June 23rd Zelda confined Eglantine', it cannot have
made him feel good the way his 1919 fantasies had.

Although not legally committed, every time Zelda attempted to
leave Prangins she was forcibly brought back to Eglantine, where in
a blackened room she was administered morphine and bromides
rectally, preceded by an enema. These drugs induced a two-week-
long narcosis within twenty minutes.[29] Patients on this 'Swiss
Sleeping Cure' were aroused only to relieve bladder or bowel or for
minimal food. This narcotic procedure had several known side-
effects, one of which was eczema, by which Zelda was again tortured from 15 July onwards.

Zelda had already sent Scott desperate letters.

> I want you to let me leave here – You're wasting time and effort and
> money to take away the little we both have left. If you think you are pre-
> paring me for a return to Alabama you are mistaken, and also if you
> think I am going to spend the rest of my life roaming about without hap-
> piness or rest or work from one sanatorium to another . . . you are wrong
> . . . two sick horses might conceivably pull a heavier load than a well one
> alone. Of cource, if you prefer that I should spend six months of my life
> under prevailing conditions – my eyes are open and I will get something
> from that, too, I suppose, but they are tired and unhappy, and my head
> aches always. Won't you write me a comprehensible letter such as you
> might write to one of your friends? Every day it gets harder to think or
> live and I do not understand the object of wasting the dregs of me here,
> alone in a devasting bitterness.

Now deteriorating rapidly, she begged Scott to write Egorova 'a
friendly impersonal note to find out exactly where I stand as a
dancer'. In her postscript she repeated:

> Please write immediately to Paris about the dancing. I would do it but I
> think the report will be more accurate if it goes to you – just an opinion
> as to what value work is and to what point I could develop it before it is
> too late. Of cource, I would go to another school as I know Egorova
> would not want to be bothered with me.[30]

Forel, convinced that if she continued to dance Zelda would not
find stability, also wanted Scott to write to Egorova. He suggested that
Scott write asking Egorova to discourage her pupil, even if it meant
deceiving Zelda.[31] Forel felt that Zelda must be made to give up any
idea that ballet was her vocation. Scott was not prepared to play along
with Forel's fraudulent plan. He had written to Egorova on 22 June:

Zelda is still very ill. From time to time there is some improvement and then all of a sudden she commits some insane act . . . It is doubtful – though she is unaware of it – that she could ever return to her dancing school . . . doctors would like to know what her chances were, what her future was like as a dancer, when she fell ill . . . Her situation being critical, it is rather necessary that she should know the answer, despite all the disappointment it could cause her.[32]

Scott attached seven questions. Could Zelda achieve the level of a first-rate dancer; could she ever dance like Nikitina or Danilowa; how many years might that take if she could; if she couldn't become first rate could her charming face and beautiful body land her roles in ballets such as those produced by Massine in New York; were there students in Egorova's school better than Zelda; did she start too late to achieve good balance; was she working too hard for a woman her age; and if she had not fallen ill could she have satisfied both her ideal and her ambitions? On 9 July Egorova replied that Zelda had begun too late to become a first-rate dancer but she could become a very good dancer, capable of successfully dancing important roles in New York's Massine Ballet Company.

Scott and Forel saw this as positive, though they knew Zelda would be crushed.

Meanwhile in order to make sense of her illness Zelda wrote a series of analytic letters to Scott. The most remarkable was a forty-two-page summary of their marriage which displayed her extraordinary memory for precise colourful detail of places, people and emotions. She recalled their early days in New York with reporters, fur-smothered hotel lobbies, the impressiveness of the Fowlers, tea dances at the Plaza, her eccentric behaviour at Princeton, Townsend's blue eyes, the Biltmore's marshmallow odour. She raced through absinthe cocktails, roadhouses where they bought gin, her startling white knickers, Scott's affair with Gene Bankhead, their quarrels, their devilled ham, their trip to Europe where she was sick and he drank, Alabama's unbearable heat, St Paul's treacherous cold, the birth and wonder of Scottie. She dwelt on their adoration of the Kalmans, their dinners with Bunny, the intrusion of doctors, the encroaching disorder, the violent rows, her fantasy episode with Jozan, Scott's flagrantly sentimental relations with Moran, their attempts for another child, his indifference to her sickness, the pleasure the Murphys brought them and her cascading into the twin worlds of art and ballet. She conjured up their life of too many parties, too many people, too much noise, too little sanity.

In this rush through the years she paused at the problem with
Ernest, then at the counter-problem with Dolly, and concluded:

> I have just begun to realize that sex and sentiment have little to do with
> each other. When I came to you twice last winter and asked you to start
> over it was because I thought I was becoming seriously involved senti-
> mentally and preparing situations for which I was morally and practi-
> cly unfitted . . . I still know in my heart that it is a Godless, dirty game;
> that love is bitter and all there is, and that the rest is for the emotional
> beggars of the earth.[33]

Scott struck back with a seven-page memo called 'Written With
Zelda Gone To The Clinique', which he may not have sent but which
he kept for posterity. In it he tried to account for the interconnected
collapse of his career and destruction of their joy. He revisited Capri,
then Paris when he was a success, 'the biggest man in my profession
everybody admired me'. He was proud of his friendships with the
Murphys and Ernest, then deflated by the penalties of constant
drinking. He pondered the 'time of misery' when he dragged *The
Great Gatsby* out of the pit of his stomach, and described how he
woke up in Hollywood, 'no longer my egotistic, certain self but a
mixture of Ernest in fine clothes and Gerald with a career. . . .
Anybody that could make me believe that, like Lois Moran did, was
precious to me.' On reaching Ellerslie he was prepared to do anything to be liked, to make up from without for being under-
nourished from within. At rue Vaugirard when he needed
reassurance that he was a great man of the world, Zelda had
retreated. He felt exploited, not by her 'but by something I resented
terribly no happiness'. He remembered wondering why he kept
working to pay the bills for his desolate menage. Worst of all, his
novel was like a dream, further and further away. On the Riviera
Gerald and Sara cooled towards him, Ernest became irritable, he
drank to stave off his feelings of inferiority and Zelda had emotionally disappeared. 'I think everyone far enough away to see us
outside of our glib presentation of ourselves guessed at your almost
meglomaniacal selfishness and my insane indulgence in drink.
Toward the end nothing much mattered.'[34]

Yet even now the Fitzgeralds were offering presentations to each
other, some glib, some fanciful, many as honest as they could
manage. Their tearing need was to explain themselves to one
another.

In July Zelda reproached him for failing to guide her prior to her

illness: '. . . the obligation is, after all, with the people who understand, and the blind, of necessity, must be led'. As one of the blind,
she felt 'it is not astonishing that I should look on you with
unfriendly eyes'.[35]

Scott took the point. And the letter. It reappeared in *Tender Is The
Night* as a letter from Nicole: 'I kept waiting for some one to tell me.
It was the duty of some one who understood. The blind must be
led.'[36]

At that stage Zelda did not know that her husband was still
making literary use of her fractured life. She was busy looking for
causes: 'I have done nothing but turn over cause and effect in my
mind . . . your presentation of the situation is poetic even if it has no
bearing on the truth: your working to preserve the family and my
working to get away from it.' She felt he had given the 'absolute
minimum of effort both to your work and to our mutual welfare . . .
I envy you the mental processes which can so distort conditions into
a rectitude of attitude for you . . . so take whatever comfort you may
find in whatever self-justification you can construct.' Perhaps with
conscious irony, she added: 'This is not a treatise of recrimination,
but I would like you to understand clearly why, there are certain
scenes not only towards the end which could never be effaced from
my mind.'[37]

Scott felt a need both to defend himself yet also to accept responsibility for Zelda. What he failed to do was to accept any responsibility for the destructive effects on Zelda of his drinking. He also had
to protect Scottie from the worst effects of her mother's illness and
support them as a family by endlessly writing saleable stories.

He abhorred the psychiatrists' investigation into the hidden
places of their marital life and, as therapy revealed shaming aspects
of their past, he found Zelda's constant recriminations as unbearable as she found the reasons for them. Guilt and confusion left him
tormented, which in turn made him vacillate between deep sympathy and profound irritation. Scott blamed Zelda for not taking
responsibility for her own actions. He told Scottie that Zelda never
felt a sense of guilt even when she put other people's lives in jeop-
ardy. She felt – according to Scott – that other people subjugated her
or else situations beyond her control contrived against her. He felt
Zelda ignored ordinary moral standards and tried to solve ethical
problems independently. Years later he was still telling Scottie: 'The
insane are always mere guests on the earth, eternal strangers carrying around broken decalogues that they cannot read.'[38]

Zelda refused to feel guilty. 'Please don't write to me about blame.

I am tired of rummaging my head to understand a situation that would be difficult enough if I were completely lucid. I cannot arbitrarily accept blame now when I know that in the past I felt none. Anyway blame doesn't matter.'[39]

But despite her brave words, Zelda *did* blame Scott for the months he had spent drinking and ignoring her. They were squabbling like children. A deep weariness overcame them. Zelda managed to lift herself from depression to resignation:

> Anyhow, none of those things matter. I quite realize that you have done the best you can and I would like you to realize that so have I, in all the disorder. I do not know what is going to happen, but since I am in the hands of Doctor Forel and they are a great deal more powerful than yours or mine, it will probably be for the best. I want to work at something, but I can't seem to get well enough to be of any use in the world . . . Please send me Egorova's letter – Zelda.[40]

When Zelda read Egorova's verdict she was devastated. She had been confident she could achieve distinction of the first rank. Her professional ballet career was over.

CHAPTER 18

Zelda's resilience was uncanny. Fiction instantly replaced ballet as her primary ambition. She wrote like the wind. By July 1930 she had completed 'A Workman', 'The House' and 'The Drouth and the Flood'.[1] Scott, perhaps wanting to compensate Zelda for the loss of her ballet, offered all three stories to Ober for *Scribner's Magazine*. Subsequently they (and eight others) were lost; what survives is Scott's critique to Perkins: 'Zelda wrote [them] in the dark middle of her nervous breakdown . . . apart from the beauty & richness of the writing they have a strange haunting, evocative quality that is absolutely new . . . each of them is the story of her life when things . . . brought her to the edge of madness and despair. In my opinion they are literature.'[2] Max responded:

> I do think they show an astonishing power of expression . . . convey a curiously effective and strange quality. – But they are for a selected audience . . . the magazine thinks that on that account, they cannot use them . . . if she did enough more they might make a book . . . . I think one of the little magazines might use them. I wish we could.[3]

Scott, deeply disappointed, replied: 'Possibly they mean more to me than is implicit to the reader who doesn't know from what depths of misery and effort they sprang.' Then came his marvellous optimism: 'I think a book might be got together for next spring if Zelda can add a few more during winter.'[4]

Sadly his optimism was misplaced. Zelda's creative energy had sapped her strength to a 'childish, vacillating shell'.[5] She told Scott: 'I have forgotten what it's like to be alive with a functioning intelligence . . . I watch what attitude the nurse takes each day and then look up what symptom I have in Doctor Forel's book . . . why has my ignorance on a medical subject . . . reduced me to the mental status of a child?'[6] She said: 'I don't seem to know anything appropriate for a person of 30 . . . it's because of . . . straining so completely every fibre in that futile attempt to achieve with every factor against me –'.[7]

From that year onwards she was never free from the fear of mental illness nor, when released, from the greater fear of another asylum. That she wrote or painted at all when every factor *was* against her is a testament to her persistence and courage. But illness rattled her confidence: 'Do you mind my writing this way?' she asked Scott anxiously.

> Don't be afraid that I am a meglo-maniac again – I'm just searching and its easier with you – You'll have to re-educate me – But you used to like giving me books and telling me things. I never realized before how hideously dependent on you I was – Dr Forel says I won't be after. If I can have a clear intelligence I'm sure we can use it – I hope I will be different . . . I can't make head or tails out of all this dreary experience since I do not know how much was accidental and how much deliberate . . . but if such a thing as expiation exists it is taking place . . . [8]

When Scott told friends Zelda was still 'sick as hell',[9] Max and Wilson wrote sympathetically to Zelda. Max offered Scott hope: 'If she has made progress maybe it should become more rapid, and everything will come out right.'[10] Wilson, who had survived electric shock and hydrotherapy in a similar clinic, reassured Scott: 'these breakdowns when people go off their heads aren't necessarily serious'.[11]

To Perkins, Scott confided his financial anxiety: 'The psychiatrist . . . is an expensive proposition,' and he had been unable to write. It was 'terrible to be so in debt'. Zelda's Prangins bills alone were 70,561 Swiss francs, over $13,000, without counting the costs of Scottie's school, her Paris apartment and his own hotel. Worse still, Ober had refused him an advance. Could Max help him out? He'd promise him $3,000 from the next story. Little wonder Scott signed himself 'harrassed and anxious'.[12]

Support came from the Bishops, Townsend and the Murphys, whom Scott saw in Paris in July when visiting Scottie there. Dos Passos, who had married Katy Smith, Hadley's friend,[13] spoke for them all:

> Scott was meeting adversity with a consistency of purpose that I found admirable. He was trying to raise Scottie, to do the best possible thing for Zelda, to handle his drinking and to keep a flow of stories into the magazines to raise the enormous sums Zelda's illness cost. At the same time he was determined to continue writing first rate novels. With age

and experience his literary standards were rising. I never admired a man more.[14]

There were two flaws in Dos Passos's loyal statement. First, Scott was unwilling to handle his drinking; second, he was unable to touch his novel. Nevertheless his priority was to give Zelda excellent medical care and establish stability for Scottie. If Scott's horizons were limited and his fears of delving inside himself as great as Zelda's, he did the best he could at a time of despair and confusion.

Like the Fitzgeralds, the Murphys were haunted with might-have-beens. Sara would be admitted to the American hospital with a gallbladder disorder. Drained by Patrick's medical expenses and their three homes they decided to sell Villa America, where Patrick might never be sufficiently well to live.[15]

Dr Forel asked Zelda to write an autobiographical sketch.[16] Her mother she saw only in visual images: 'I can always see her sitting down in the opalescent sunlight of a warm morning, a black servant combing her long grey hair.' Her father, never visualized, was a man of 'great integrity', for whom she had 'enormous respect and some mistrust'. Significant emotional events were her marriage, after which 'I was in another world, one for which I was not prepared, because of my inadequate education'; her love for Jozan which 'lasted for five years', during which 'I was locked in my villa for one month to prevent me from seeing him'; and Lois Moran whom she dismissed as part of a superficial Hollywood society. 'I determined to find . . . a world in which I could express myself.' She found Egorova whom she loved 'more than anything else in the world . . . The brightness of a greek temple, the frustration of a mind searching for a place . . . all that I saw in her steps.'

Then the world stopped, and now she was 'where I cannot be anybody, full of vertigo . . . feeling the vibrations of everyone I meet. Broken down . . . I believed I was a Salamander and it seems I am nothing but an impediment.'[17]

That summer of 1930, Zelda's eczema grew worse. Doctors administered Flemings solution, grease and powder. But, she told Scott, they were useless to ward off the 'foul plague'. It ran, it made sores, it filled up the cavities at the back of her eyes with fire. It was like something that had rotted for centuries in the catacombs and poisoned the cellars of classic ruins.[18] Incredibly, her gift for language never left her any more than the poison did. In desperation she begged:

Please, out of charity write to Dr Forel to let me off this cure. I have been 5 months now, unable to step into a corridor alone. For a month and a week I've lived in my room under bandages, my head and neck on fire . . . The last two days I've had bromides and morphine but it doesn't do any good – All because nobody ever taught me to play tennis. When I'm most miserable there's your game to think of.

Scott had taken up tennis to forget his troubles. But Zelda reminded him of hers. She recalled their arguments over her homosexuality. 'You said you did not want to see me if I knew what I know. Well, I do know. I would have liked you to come to me, but there's no good telling lies.' Nothing could take away her clarity about the way she had felt and might feel again. 'If I have to stand much more to take away the thing in me that all the rest of you find so invaluable and superior when I get out I'm going to have Scottie at least.' Her threat was idle, because her 're-educative treatment' to retrain her into what the doctors saw as 'normal' behaviour included the *implied* intimidation that women with abnormal feelings were unsuitable as mothers. If she refused to suppress emotions the doctors saw as evil, they would refuse to release her. 'It's so hard for me to understand liking a feeling without liking the person that I suppose I will be eternally confined.'[19] Scott had already told Forel that over this issue, if necessary, he would abandon Zelda. 'In no sense am I asking her forgiveness, I have long determined for the sake of the future of my child and myself that if there is any renewal of homosexuality in her, or any suspicion of me . . . it is much better that we never meet again.'[20]

Scott did not answer Zelda's charges. He sent her gladioli. She painted them. Then she softened: 'Though I would have chosen some other accompaniment for my desequilibrium than this foul eczema . . . I am waiting impatiently for when you can come to see me . . . Do you still smell of pencils and sometimes of tweed? . . . It was much nicer a long time ago when we had each other and the space about the world was warm – Can't we get it back some-way – even by imagining? . . . it's desperate to be so alone – and you can't be very happy in a hotel room – We were awfully used to having each other about – Zelda.'

She added a tentative postscript: 'Dr Forel told me to ask you if you had stopped drinking – so I ask –.'[21]

Forel believed strongly that Scott's drinking was a major contri-bution to Zelda's illness, that he was in effect treating two people.

Scott must stop drinking if Zelda was to recover and live with him.
Scott refused to accept Forel's viewpoint.

During my young manhood for seven years I worked extremely hard . . .
bringing myself by tireless self-discipline to a position of unquestioned
preeminence among younger American writers; also by additional
'hack-work' for the cinema ect I gave my wife a comfortable and luxurious life My work is done on coffee, coffee and more coffee, never on
alcohol. At the end of five or six hours I get up from my desk white and
trembling and with a steady burn in my stomach, to go to dinner.

More justification ensued:

Two years ago in America, I noticed that when we stopped all drinking
for three weeks . . . I immediately had dark circles under my eyes, was
listless and disinclined to work . . . I found that a moderate amount of
wine . . . made all the difference in how I felt . . . the dark circles disappeared . . . I looked forward to my dinner [Scott's scarlet underlining]
. . . and life didn't seem a hopeless grind to support a woman whose
tastes were daily diverging from mine. She no longer read or thought or
knew anything or liked anyone except dancers and their cheap satel-
lites. People respected her . . . because of a certain complete fearlessness
and honesty that she has never lost, but she was becoming more and
more an egotist and a bore.

For Scott there was only room in their household for the one
egotist who did not bore him. Then came the crux:

Now when that old question comes up again as to which of two people
is worth preserving, I, thinking of my ambitions so nearly achieved of
being part of English literature, of my child, even of Zelda in the matter
of providing for her – must perforce consider myself first.[22]

Zelda's assessment that 'You have always told me that I have no
right to complain as long as I was materially cared for' was correct.[23]
He would always put himself first, but he would always provide for
her.
    And his intentions? 'To stop drinking entirely for six months and
see what happens . . . only a pig would refuse to do that. Give up
strong drink permanently I will. Bind myself to forswear wine
forever I cannot.'
    Was that childish? Stubborn? Without waiting for Forel's answer
he bowled into his most problematic remark: 'What I gave up for
Zelda was women and it wasn't easy in the position my success

gave me – what pleasure I got from comradeship she has pretty well ruined by dragging me of all people into her homosexual obsession.'

He of all people then asked Forel if there was not 'a certain disingenuousness in her wanting me to give up all alcohol? Would not that justify her conduct completely to herself and prove to her relatives and our friends <u>that it was my drinking that caused this</u> calamity, and that I thereby admitted it? [Scott's underlining].'24

Zelda accepted privation with dignity as Southern women were schooled to do. 'I am here,' she wrote, 'and since I have no choice, I will try to muster the grace to rest peacefully as I should, but our divergence is too great as you must realize for us to ever be anything except a hash to-gether.'25

Her resentment surfaced:

since we have never found either help or satisfaction in each other the best thing is to seek it separately. You might as well start whatever you start for a divorce immediately . . . You will have all the things you want without me, and I will find something. You will have some nice girl who will not care about the things that I cared about and you will be happier. For us, there is not the slightest use, even if we wanted to try which I assure you I do not – not even faintly. In listing your qualities I can not find even one on which to base any possible relationship except your good looks, and there are dozens of people with that: the head-waiter at the Plaza . . . my coiffeur in Paris.26

According to Sara Mayfield, though Zelda wanted a divorce she recognized that her dependence on Scott meant only reconciliation would procure her release. She told Sara the psychiatrists would keep her at the 'nut farm' as long as Scott paid them. 'Because her letters were censored she had no way of appealing to her family and friends; even if she could run away, she had no money and no means of earning any. The tone of her letters became more loving, and she showed more affection for him when they were together.'27

One letter among many similar illustrates this dependent tone:

Goofy, my darling . . . the sun was lying like a birth-day parcel . . . so I opened it up and so many happy things went fluttering into the air: love to Doo-do and the remembered feel of our skins cool against each other . . . And you 'phoned and said I had written something that pleased you and so I don't believe I've ever been so heavy with happiness . . . I walked on those telephone wires for two hours after holding your love like a parasol to balance me . . . Are you . . . looking rather reproachful that no melodrama comes to pass when your work is over . . . or are you just a darling little boy with a holiday on his hands . . . I love you – the way you always are.[28]

Scott was relieved. In August, after their long separation, he wrote, 'Husband finally sees her. She is still in bandages, shows lesbian tendencies and in spite of tenderness towards him makes irrational erotic remarks. But her violent feeling against him specifically has now abated.'[29] Zelda's doctors believed her recovery depended on a 'successful' marriage so they advised her against conflicts with Scott. In Forel's time doctors thought the propensity towards homosexuality and menstrual disturbances noted in female schizophrenics indicated endocrine or chemical imbalance. They gave Zelda endocrine treatments using ovarian extracts and dried thyroid gland powders. Patients were also injected with their own blood, and given potassium bromide and a serum made from the brain of a mentally stable person. Forel injected Zelda with morphine to induce sleep, belladonna for pain and luminal to sedate her constantly. She was also given purges of seidlitz water, wet packs and hydrotherapy.[30] The drugs alternately depressed and agitated her. Later Scott wrote to Forel about a hunch he had that Zelda's eczema was caused by lack of elimination of poison. He believed that some crucial physical element such as semen, salt or holy water was either absent or there was too much of it. It was a clever guess, for later discoveries confirmed that some mental illness can be caused by the body's chemical imbalance.[31]

Scott vacationed in Caux from 8 to 22 August, finishing the remarkable 'One Trip Abroad', based on his Kelly version of *Tender*.[32] Wealthy Nicole and Nelson Kelly travel to France to study painting and music, become dissipated, end up as patients in a Swiss clinic. 'Switzerland is a country where very few things begin, but many things end': a poignant description of a disintegrating marriage.[33]

While Scott, in Caux, was writing stories to explain the collapse of his life and career, Zelda's hospital letters glowed with romantic feeling. She drew a balcony lit by a moon with two upright chairs, each of which held a heart shaped cushion. 'Doodo's Balcon', she labelled it.

Dear balcony, where you walk absent-mindedly and drop a cigarette and stand poised in the morning sun, just an answering flash. Caux is so far away, but I love thinking of you there above the heat and smells

... O dear Doo-do ... I love you so ... I'm only happy when I'm doing what I think you're doing at the time ... You sometimes seem to be buttoning up yourself, slipping into you as if you were a freshly pressed suit, and your empty shoes lie expectantly on the floor as if they were waiting for Santa Claus.[34]

Her health improved.

Except for momentary retrogressions into a crazy defiance and complete lack of proportion I am better . . . . It's ghastly losing your mind . . . knowing you can't think and that nothing is right, not even your comprehension of concrete things like how old you are or what you look like.

Suddenly she noticed the asylum had stripped her of possessions.

Where are all my things? I used to have dozens of things and now there doesn't seem to be any clothes or anything personal in my trunk. I'd <u>love</u> the gramophone – What a disgraceful mess – but if it stops our drinking it is worth it – because then you can finish your novel and write a play and we can live somewhere and have a house with a room to paint and write ... with friends for Scottie and there will be Sundays and Mondays again which are different from each other ... my life won't lie up the back-stairs of music-halls and yours won't keep trailing down the gutters of Paris – if ... I can keep sane and not a bitter maniac.[35]

In Prangins Zelda found it impossible to write to Scottie. As her sense of self wavered, who she was as a mother became unclear. It was as if the free expression of her devotion to Scottie had closed down. There was little information inside an asylum that made good reading for a child.

In August Scottie made a four-day visit to Zelda. We cannot know which of them found it harder. They had little in common now, certainly no daily routines. Zelda's parental role had virtually disappeared and Scottie's anxiety to please made her behave unnaturally. Throughout the visit their pain was exacerbated by their awareness that soon they were again to be separated. Trying in her turn to please her daughter, Zelda wistfully urged Scottie to continue dancing. When she next visited New York she should go to Cappezio's on 44th Street to find some dance shoes. Zelda herself would like a pair of 'aesthete sandals size 5D'.[36]

On 27 August 1930 Sara Haardt married H. L. Mencken, but

Zelda was too ill even to pen a line to her friend. It was October before Scott could write: 'Dear Menk and Sarah: Excuse these belated congratulations, which is simply due to illness. Zelda and I were delighted to know you were being married and devoured every clipping sent from home. Please be happy. Ever Your Friend Scott (and Zelda) Fitzgerald.'[37]

In September Scott renewed his acquaintance with Thomas Wolfe, who would later use him in a novel.[38] Scott, who had assured Forel he had given up other women for Zelda while still seeing Emily Vanderbilt,[39] now started sleeping with Bijou O'Conor, whom he had met in the Twenties in Paris's Latin Quarter. Born in Bulgaria in 1896, English granddaughter of the second Earl of Minto, she had been widowed at twenty-eight, but preferred a scandalous reputation to remarriage.[40] Scott was attracted to this brilliant linguist whose reckless disposition, financial carelessness and independent spirit had the wildness of the young Zelda. Bijou, herself an alcoholic, led Scott into uncontrollable gin binges while he typed in her hotel room.[41] Bijou claimed she and Scott visited Zelda in Prangins, which if true was potentially destructive, for if Zelda had suspected they were lovers it could have precipitated a further breakdown.[42]

Fortunately in September came Zelda's first breakthrough. Forel decided to treat the eczema by hypnosis. In her trance Zelda recognized connections between the rash and her marital conflicts. The eczema virtually disappeared the next day, to return only intermittently. Yet not much else changed. She was still depressed; she still had infatuations – another in October, with 'the red headed girl' as Scott called her (the second of the two redheads), who resisted. Scott thought Zelda's 'initial shame . . . and the consequent struggle' caused a third attack of eczema. But when the eczema disappeared the infatuation continued. Scott recorded a second female infatuation in November which again did not produce eczema, but his appearances did.[43] Confused, his pride hurt, he reported: 'Eczema spasmodic. Lesbianism mild but constant – (they change the house of one girl after whom she tags, though now there are no more offences in that direction). Indifferent to husband. Appearance of unmotivated smile.'[44]

Scott had told Rosalind about Zelda's 'lesbian complex'. Rosalind, who immediately expressed the Southern horror of homosexuality, remembered that when Tallulah's lesbianism was mentioned at Ellerslie, her sister's reaction had 'made me think sex was preying on her mind'.[45] Rosalind thought it safer to send Zelda helpful suggestions about treating eczema. 'It's almost gone now,' Zelda replied, 'and, unfortunately, never was the sort that Cuticura Soap could help. The Brussels fire brigade might have skirted the edges.'[46]

But on 10 November another attack occurred and Forel, determined to discipline Zelda also for uncontrollable masturbating, moved her back to Eglantine. He told Scott they could not stop her wilful self-abuse unless she was locked up and observed. Scott's princess was strait-jacketed by facial bandages for eczema and bound hands so she could not touch herself. This merited Scott's terse line: 'Short confinement for refractoriousness'.[47] Forel, who found Zelda 'sneaky' because she tried hard to avoid discipline,[48] wrote to Scott: 'L'Eglantine is, from our point of view, a good thing . . . For too long your wife has taken advantage of our patience. For her health, for her treatment, L'Eglantine is indispensable, and I am happy, even, that the patient's conduct should have obliged us to try this . . . she sees that there are limits and that she must give in'.[49]

Zelda was administered insulin shock treatments which were continued for ten years.[50] Substantial evidence shows that more female than male patients were given insulin in that period, as much to realign their behaviour as to act as a therapy.

Zelda did not improve in Eglantine. Scott wrote to the Sayres: 'Zelda was acting badly and had to be transferred again to the house . . . reserved for people under restraint.'[51] He told them that dissatisfied with Zelda's progress, he had suggested calling in either Dr Blenler or Dr Jung, and Forel agreed.

Scott decided on Paul Eugen Bleuler, born 1857,[52] the psychiatrist who had named schizophrenia. Forel was keen on a second opinion because he had some hesitancy about his own diagnosis: 'The more I saw Zelda, the more I thought at the time: she is neither a pure neurosis (meaning psychogenic) nor a real psychosis – I considered her a constitutional, emotionally unbalanced psychopath – she may improve, never completely recover.'[53]

Interviewed later, Dr Forel acknowledged that over the years he had changed his original assessment. He had 'put aside' the schizophrenic diagnosis because 'apart from the clinical and classical forms . . . certain symptoms and behaviours or activities, are called schizoid and this does not mean that the person is schizophrenic.'[54]

Dr Irving Pine, Zelda's last psychiatrist, said he felt that Zelda had consistently been misdiagnosed. He disputed the label 'schizophrenia' and suggested that part of the failure of her psychiatrists was their failure to take her talents seriously. He believed much of her depression came from her family situation. As that accelerated, so did her depression. He and other doctors suggested that subsequently Zelda was treated for a psychosis, the treatment of which can cause patients to display some of the characteristics of schizophrenia when originally only severe depression was present. But by November 1930 Zelda was treading a path where she would become as much a victim of her treatment as of her illness.[55]

As Forel had already labelled her a 'difficult patient' he was glad to discuss her case with Bleuler,[56] who arrived on 22 November, charging Scott the exorbitant fee of $500.[57] For that amount he would spend an afternoon with Zelda and the evening with Scott and Forel.

Bleuler confirmed Forel's diagnosis of schizophrenia. He said the homosexuality was not constitutional, but merely a symptom which would disappear with continued treatment. He reassured Scott that marital conflict was not a contributory cause of illness. He found Zelda's emotional capacity impaired and advised against further dancing, since that 'passion is also engendered by the illness; just as Mme Aegorowa was the first lesbian passion after the onset of the illness'.[58]

Zelda was desperate to return to America but Bleuler forbade it. She must stay put, continue weaving, carpentry, and work in the greenhouses. She must rest but could make accompanied visits to shops, opera and theatre in Geneva and go skiing. He told Scott three out of four cases like Zelda's could be discharged as cured. One of those would resume 'perfect functioning' in the world; two would be delicate and slightly eccentric through life; the fourth would hurtle into 'total insanity'. To avoid that Zelda must submit to a master, who had to be a doctor. Scott asked if *he* should become more masterful but Bleuler replied: 'It is possible that a cast-iron character would be propitious but Mrs Fitzgerald loved and married the artist in Mr Fitzgerald.'[59]

Bleuler recommended Scott should not visit too often and Zelda should prepare presents for Scottie, write frequently but should not see her for several months as her child's first visit had proved 'her presence was undesirable'.[60] Neither doctor looked for the motives behind that disastrous visit, nor took into account the distressing effect separation would have on both mother and child.

Forel's re-education programme would, they hoped, check Zelda's 'incipient egomania'. Bleuler saw her as a woman competing publicly with her more famous husband in an inappropriate manner. That Zelda was also charged with ineptitude at housework, cooking and servant management was another example of pronounced gender implications in the way the label schizophrenia was constructed in the Thirties.[61] Bleuler insisted Zelda's re-entry into the world must be slowed down. That Scott was paying the clinic extravagant fees was not voiced as a factor. Bleuler said Scott could not have prevented Zelda's illness: 'This is something that began about five years ago . . . Stop blaming yourself. You might have retarded it but you couldn't have prevented it.'[62] Scott immediately told the Sayres 'because I know you despise certain weaknesses in my character' and he didn't want that to blur their belief in him 'as a man of integrity'.[63]

Zelda thought Bleuler 'a great imbecile', and refused to accept any of his recommendations. However, her despair deepened.

Dear Scott, You wrote you didn't want me to suffer any more. Please please come here and see for yourself. I'm sick and beaten . . . . If there's nobody in all this barren brothel who will look after me, I demand that I be allowed to go immediately to a hospital in France where there is enough human kindness to prevent the present slow butchery. Scott if you knew what this is like you would not dare in the eyes of God leave a person in it. Please help me.[64]

She wrote to her brother-in-law Newman Smith: 'I write to you because I do not want to worry Daddy but if you do not come to me I am going to write to him.'[65]

Newman did not come for her.

To Scott she admitted: 'now I am so frightened of the past that I am half afraid to think. There's so much conditioning to be done.'[66] This incredible piece of self-awareness did not effect her release. She even wrote to Forel:

please explain to me why I should spend five months of my life in sickness and suffering seeing nothing but optical illusions to devitalize something in me that you yourself have found indespensible and that my husband has found so agreeable as to neglect shamefully his wife during the last four years . . . if you do cure me what's going to happen to all the bitterness and unhappiness in my heart – It seems to me a sort of castration, but since I am powerless I suppose I will have to submit, though I am neither young enough nor credulous enough to think that you can manufacture out of nothing something to replace the song I had.[67]

Zelda's accusations shamed Scott. Her agony tortured him. But he did not ask Forel to free her. Instead, using those feelings, he wrote what was probably his best story, 'Babylon Revisited', a tale of emotional bankruptcy, in which he transferred some of that guilt on to Charlie Wales, a rich alcoholic American businessman. Charlie goes to Paris with his wife Helen and child Honoria,[68] then during a drunken row locks Helen out in the snow, after which she dies of heart disease. Scott's enemy Rosalind, fictionalized as Wales's sister-in-law Marion, had wished Zelda dead like Helen rather than see her return to dissipation. In 'Babylon' Marion's vengeful role as Honoria's guardian, because Charlie is too drunk to raise her, is based on Rosalind's suggestion that, feeling the same about Scott, she should adopt Scottie.[69] Rosalind's concern was understandable. Scottie saw her father intermittently and rarely heard from her mother. When Zelda *did* write, the once warm, unrestrained notes had become distant, hesitant, awkward: each letter filled with longing but hard for a child to respond to.

In early fall: 'Dear dear dear little Scottie, Mummy was so glad to get your sweet letter . . . it got to be the limit being sick for so long . . . I care dreadfully at your not being here with me. The times you spent with me in the summer were the happiest of the year.' Zelda had apparently forgotten how unhappy Scottie's August visit had been. 'It would give me so much pleasure to see you paddling in the waters of the lake.'

But that pleasure was not to be had.

In late fall:

Your card came with the pretty blowy lady on the back . . . when I don't get mail from you the days seem awfully long and dreary . . . It seems ages and ages and ages that I haven't seen you and I want dreadfully to be with you again and share your pleasures . . . What would you like Pere Noel to bring you? And are you going to have a tree like last time? Send me something from one of the branches to make you seem nearer, darling . . . I am awfully tired of the Swiss landscape and would like to be back in Paris with my baby girl.

Fall again:

Will your tiny apartment hold me for a little visit? Just a weekend, say, because if you can manage it I will slip away if I can get permission and come up and see you . . . With all the love in the heart of your Mummy.

But in Scottie's circle Mummies gave permission for treats, they did not seek it.

When Scottie and her governess moved outside Paris to Auteuil,

Zelda, feeling friendless, urged her daughter to remain friends with Fanny Myers. Go skating together. Have fun.[70] Zelda, pleased when Scottie saw Fanny regularly, wrote: 'The parents of Fanny are so agreeable that I knew she would be a companion that you would enjoy.'[71]

Zelda compensated for her lack of news with memories: Minnesota when Scottie was 'the size of a dime and crawling over the carpet in rose gingham'. Anna, the raw-boned Swede who kept Scottie sitting on a pot one whole afternoon while Zelda raved outside her door. 'Amuse yourself,' instructed Zelda, 'be sweet and obedient and a sensible child and I will be waiting anxiously and patiently to see to see you again in the spring . . . I do so hope you will be able to at least spend the night with me. With all my dearest love – Your delapidated Mother.'[72]

In spring 1931 Scottie appeared in a play. 'The theatre is nice and in your place with all those years before you I would keep it in my thoughts and become a star later on. That is why you should keep up your dancing lessons.' Zelda's own news was minute: 'We have had a [hospital] ball as well – I made myself a dress of paper to represent a lampshade.'[73]

Before their spring reunion there had been a disastrous Christmas visit. Zelda, unbearably keyed up, broke the ornaments on the tree, and made incoherent speeches. Scott hurried their daughter away to Gstaad to ski, recover and have some fun.

At the end of January 1931 Scott's seventy-seven-year-old father died of a heart attack in Washington. Zelda, distressed for him, hugged Scott tenderly, then 'she went into the other personality and was awful to me at lunch. After lunch she returned to the affectionate tender mood, utterly normal, so that with pressure I could have manoeuvred her into intercourse but the eczema was almost visibly increasing so I left early. Toward the very end she was back in the schizophrania.'[74] Scott had tried for nine months to persuade Zelda to resume a sexual life with him, but when she saw him for any length of time he felt she still slipped in and out of 'madness'. His insistence distressed her; her behaviour and her appearance repelled him.

On board the *New York* on his way to his father's funeral, Scott met a dark dramatic professional card sharp, Bert Barr, born Bertha Weinberg in a Brooklyn slum. Fascinated by her cleverness, he saw her again in New York and Paris, even suggested they collaborate on some stories, although nothing came of it.[75]

At Edward Fitzgerald's funeral in Rockville, Maryland, Scott, standing at the graveside, suddenly recognized that in his mind his father was linked irrevocably to his American past. In a draft of an essay, 'The Death of My Father', Scott assessed his influence: 'I loved my father – always deep in my subconscious I have referred judgments back to him.'[76]

Scott hoped for an immediate letter of condolence from Ernest but initially nothing arrived. The Hemingways had bought a house in Key West[77] and Scott and Ernest, now on the same continent, had talked of getting together, but it remained talk. Their once blooming friendship was reduced to memories. Scott later wrote sadly: 'Four times in 11 years (1924–1940). Not really friends since '26.'[78] Ernest finally wrote in April sending also deepest regrets about Zelda's 'rotten time'. He advised Scott to make good literary use of his father's death. Acknowledging that authors' parents only die once Ernest suggested that Scott should write it for a novel, not a magazine. The event was too valuable to be 'pooped' away. Hemingway's warning was right on target, for Scott *had* tried to poop his feelings into the indifferent 'On Your Own' which Ober was unable to sell. Scott did however resurrect his best phrase: 'Good-by, my father – good-by, all my fathers' in *Tender Is The Night*, where Dick Diver, like Scott, returns to the USA for his father's funeral and there in the cemetery speaks his farewell to his past.[79]

Scott went to Montgomery to see Zelda's parents, expecting their sympathy for his bereavement, but found instead deep hostility. They blamed him entirely for Zelda's illness, seeing him not Zelda as insane. They accused him of placing her in an asylum to get rid of her. To the end of her days Minnie Sayre believed that Scott 'was not good for my daughter . . . He was a selfish man. What he wanted always came first.'[80] Rosalind, who had already exchanged acrimonious letters with Scott holding him responsible for Zelda's breakdown, was more accusatory. Incensed, he had written (but had not sent) a vituperative letter in which he told her she packed under her 'suave exterior' such a 'minor quantity of humanity' that he demanded she 'never communicate with me again in any form and I will try to resist the temptation to pass you down to posterity for what you are'.[81]

In Scott's absence Zelda made an astonishing improvement. Her concentration sharpened. Her mind focused. Forel wrote patronizingly to Scott: 'Mrs Fitzgerald takes her meals regularly from the set menu, and behaves well. She has begun skiing at St Cergues and is delighted with it.'[82] Yet not one doctor or nurse linked her unexpected progress with Scott's departure. By his return, Zelda was skiing daily and was translating Arthur Rimbaud's 'Une Saison en

Enfer'. Scott's optimistic assessment ran: 'Forel hopeful . . . Good behaviour. Intermittent eczema, but hope – gradually fixing itself on husband and child . . . Becomes popular in clinic – no more homo-sexuality. Loves sports. Is somehow "good". Unmotivated smile disappearing and normal relations with husband renewed at end of this period.'[83]

In April, Zelda was allowed trips to Geneva and Montreux with Scott, with Rosalind, even with some patients: 'I went to Geneva all by myself with a fellow maniac,' she reported wittily.[84] She sent Scott 'kisses splattering you[r] balcony tonight from a lady who was once, in three separate letters, a princess in a high white tower and who has never forgotten her elevated station in life and who is waiting once more for her royal darling.'[85]

During the spring the re-education programme deleted and rewrote her past. She was 'waved and manicured to a chic and elegant turn' for Scott's visit, she had a 'more feminine' room in a new villa which lacked corners like 'a phrase without adjectives or a woman without a past'.[86]

The Fitzgeralds saw each other more often. Zelda also began to see Scottie more frequently. She found her 'such an amusing person', reflected 'it's rare to find the appropriate emotion going toward the appropriate object'.[87] Scottie 'was darling . . . not a bit boyish'. They'd had a good picnic. 'She is a dear girl close to my heart – so close.'[88]

Although Zelda let slip she was still angry because 'people wont let me be insane',[89] most of her letters to Scott reached new heights of outrageous dependency. One of Scott's biographers takes a typical line, 'I realize more completely than ever how much I live in you and how sweet and good and kind you are to such a dependent appendage', and suggests that Zelda had 'burned out her bitterness and achieved new insight . . . accepted rather than resented her inev-itable dependence on Scott, and expressed gratitude for his sacrifice and support'.[90] This simplistic view fails to acknowledge that Zelda had pragmatic reasons for reconciliation which certainly allowed Scott to become contrite, devoted and to send flowers.

Together they planned Zelda's first long trip, an idyllic two weeks in July with Scottie in Annecy. They stayed first at the Hôtel Beau Rivage, garlanded in roses, on Lake Annecy's Western shore. Then they moved to Menthon on the east bank, where Zelda recalled long cool shadows shelving the precipice of the Hôtel Palace. They fished, played tennis, danced Viennese waltzes, ate in a café lit by Japanese lanterns and celebrated Zelda's thirty-first birthday. Zelda wrote happily to her father: 'It is as peaceful inside its scalloped mountains as a soup-ladel full of the sky.'[91] It was a rare moment in the Fitzgerald family history of happiness, relaxation, peace. The time they spent there was so perfect they decided they would never return, because no other time could ever match it.

News from the Murphys was better. Patrick was considered sufficiently well for them to leave the US in July and move into Ramgut, a hunting lodge in Bad Aussee in the Austrian Alps. Earlier that year when Zelda was permitted visitors, the first person she had asked to see was Gerald. Though 'absolutely terrified', he had gone to Prangins and made elegant small talk about the basket Zelda was weaving. 'I said that all my life I had wanted to make baskets like hers, great heavy, stout baskets.'[92] It mattered little that their conversation was desultory, for underneath lurked a bond based on a shared sense of black demons, of unreality, of an awareness that they had both been haunted by feelings of otherness, of difference, some sexual, some social, many personal, few expressed.[93] Gerald once tried to explain himself: 'For me only the invented part of life is satisfying, the unrealistic part . . . sickness, birth, Zelda in Lausanne, Patrick in the sanatorium . . . these things were realistic . . . [I] accepted them but I didn't feel they were the important things . . . the *invented* part, for me, is what has meaning.'[94] Scott made a good shot at understanding Gerald, but with Zelda Gerald did not need to list 'real' versus invented events; like him she fictionalized even her emotions.

In August Scott suggested he and Zelda should visit the Murphys. On arrival, as Scott told their good friend Alice Lee Myers, 'Scotty + the little Murphys begin to glare as soon as they're in a radius of a hundred yards from each other,'[95] but only one incident literally clouded the waters, taking place, inevitably, in a bathroom. The children's nurse put bath salts in Scottie's bath water. Scottie, thinking it had been used to bathe all the Murphy children, complained to her parents. Scott, fearing Patrick had used it, made a scene, which he used later in *Tender*. Zelda, however, found the Murphys' ambience healing.

On 15 September 1931 Zelda was released from Prangins. Her case was summarized as a 'reaction to her feelings of inferiority (primarily towards her husband)'. She was said to have had ambitions which were 'self-deceptions' and 'caused difficulties between the couple'. Her prognosis was favourable as long as all conflicts could be avoided.[96] Scott summarized his thirty-fourth year: 'A Year in Lausanne. Waiting. From Darkness to Hope.'[97]

Excitedly they drove to Paris, then, after four and a half years
abroad, they returned to America permanently. A photo of Zelda on
board the *Aquitania*, ironically labelled 'Recovered', shows her as
tense, coarse-skinned and ugly. She looks ten years older than
thirty-one.

Briefly they paused in Washington, saw Ring in New York and
then headed for Montgomery. They began a new sleepy Southern
life of tennis, golf, old friends and house-hunting.[98] They settled on
819 Felder Avenue in the prestigious Cloverdale district. The house
was half-shingled, with a rose garden at the side and in the front
yard an exquisitely scented magnolia tree, whose pink blossoms
still bloomed seventy years later when their house became the Scott
and Zelda Museum. They acquired a bloodhound called Trouble, a
white Persian called Chopin, a black couple called Freeman and
Julia to cook and clean, and sent Scottie, now almost ten, to the
Margaret Booth School. By October Scott was bored; even Zelda felt
out of place amongst Southern women with small horizons. She
gave one friend Faulkner's new novel *Sanctuary* to wake her up.

What they did most of the time was write. Scott worked furiously
on *Tender*, hardly noticing that Zelda, intent on new stories, was also
planning a novel. She was about to move into his professional territory.

CHAPTER 19

That fall Judge Sayre's health failed. No one doubted the gravity of the situation. Minnie, outwardly stoical, daily more anxious, relied on Marjorie, Clothilde, Anthony and now Zelda, a difficult role for the frail haggard-looking Sayre 'baby'. Scott's attitude towards Zelda 'was that of an anxious parent toward a sick child. He sent her to bed at 9.30.'[1] Slowly Zelda recovered in safe Southern territory perfumed by magnolias and tea-olives. Livye Hart, glad to see her again, commented: 'She seemed to love everybody and they loved her right back.'[2]

In November 1931 death stalked another of Zelda's friends. Gerald's father, Patrick Murphy, died before his son could reach him. Gerald and Esther were each left half the wealthy Mark Cross Company, but control went to their father's longterm mistress.[3] Though Gerald had left the company a decade ago he couldn't stand his position of subservience, so he resigned as Vice President and sailed back to France. His mother wished he had stayed to look after Esther, whose marriage to John Strachey was foundering. Zelda wished he had stayed, for he was one of the few friends who understood her.

Sadly she watched over *her* father, helped her family, felt remote. The Sayres' disapproval of Scott weighed on her. The Judge advised her to divorce him. It was impossible for her to make a good life with 'a fella like that', he pointed out. But as Zelda told Sara Mayfield, she and Scottie were economically dependent, her father was dying, and though her health was broken her psychic bond with Scott was not.[4]

As she already had a small public literary reputation she decided to build on that professionally; hoping, though not entirely trusting, that Scott would support her endeavours.

Then Scott broke the news that Hollywood's MGM had offered him $1,200 a week for six weeks to rewrite the screenplay *Red-Headed Woman*, to be directed by Irving Thalberg, Norma Shearer's husband, as a vehicle for Jean Harlow. The movie industry had changed drastically since Scott's last trip. Al Jolson had appeared in *The Jazz Singer* with synchronized sound effects, music, even dialogue. Marlene Dietrich and Gary Cooper in *Morocco* were heading for stardom. Greta Garbo too had made the transition from silent films to talkies. Scriptwriters now had to write credible-sounding dialogue.

He would be home by Christmas, Scott reassured Zelda. Before he left he knelt by the Judge's bed and begged him to say he believed in him. 'I think you'll always pay your bills, Scott,' said the Judge wearily.[5]

Zelda felt bereft. Scott had become her anchor, a translator between her and the world outside. It was his optimism, his confident presence she missed. She regretted their quarrel before his departure. 'It makes me so sad to sit at your desk . . . Your cane is still on your bed. It's unbearable to think that I was mean to you . . . Scottie cried all the way home because she said she knew we were quarrelling. Goofo *please* love me . . . I want you back – You can choose your own terms.'[6] In Scott's absence she worked in Minnie's garden, composed a fugue and a nocturne à la Bach and Chopin and played tennis with Noonie, her niece.[7]

She re-established her lost rapport with Scott by reading one of his stories every night, admiring their consummate skill, learning fresh ways to construct her fiction. She was engaged on seven new stories, one revision, a children's play and her novel. Though she set only two tales in the Deep South – locating the rest in the smart societies of Europe and New York – the sexual frustrations, violence and aberrations which accompanied her car crashes, shootings and attempted incest had a passionate macabre Southern feel. Reading Faulkner had intensified the heat of her prose.

While writing fast with great professionalism, simultaneously Zelda sent Scott more than thirty letters filled with low self-esteem about her fiction. Interrupting her work on 'All About the Downs Case' and 'Crime Passionnel',[8] she wailed: ' "Home to Babylon" is a fine and moving story . . . I want to write like you some day.' She told him she could feel him in every place, feel his cheek, hear his feet on the stairs, every time a car drew up she could see him standing there saying 'Well I'm going to Hollywood'.[9] She finished another story: 'It is another flop I'm afraid. I do not believe I can write.'[10] She read his 'Absolution'. It was one of the best stories she'd ever read; his 'Baby Party' too was wonderful; she would 'never be able to write like that. Help, Deo'.[11] Deo, however, was not around to help, so briskly (and significantly) without showing Scott her stories, she mailed them to Ober.

None of her unpublished stories survive in manuscript; only Ober's summaries offer clues to their content. His memo on 'All About The Downs Case' reads: 'Difficult – cleverly written but doesn't get anywhere. Reminiscent of Nixon-Nordlinger case. Woman married to very rich man who gives her everything but treats her as part of his possessions. She and a musician fall in love and he sees them kiss each other. He takes her to Europe and won't let her speak to anyone. She shoots him in the end. Strong language on p. 20.'[12] Zelda's strong language may have been related to her fierce feelings about men who treat their women as possessions.

At high speed she finished 'Cotton Belt', 'Sweet Chariot', 'Getting Away from it All', 'Gods and Little Fishes' and 'The Story Thus Far'.[13] Ober cabled: 'Sweet Chariot is beautifully written. I am immensely pleased with it.'[14]

No one recognized that her extraordinary productivity might prove dangerous to her health. At the end of November she told Scott 'Cotton Belt' was fine, as was her Southern story 'à la Faulkner'. Then, re-assessing her progress, she lamented: 'With some ruinous facility junk just flows and is utterly worthless.' She reworked 'One And, Two And' and 'Duck Supper', while another woebegone note said 'It's so gloomy that my story should be no good.' This she followed up with '[I] can't write a line' and 'I do not believe I can write' while battling with 'There's A Myth in a Moral', which she probably rewrote as 'A Couple of Nuts'.[15]

The previous November Scott had urged Ober to submit a batch of Zelda's stories under the title 'Stories from a Swiss Clinique' to *Century* magazine or to Edmund Wilson at *The New Republic*. On 6 January 1931 Wilson had agreed to keep the stories for possible use. Now, however, Ober was unable to place any of Zelda's fiction except her two finest, 'A Couple of Nuts' and 'Miss Bessie', later retitled for publication 'Miss Ella', both of which had been drafted in Prangins.

Perkins declined the first version of 'Nuts', asking Zelda to revise it, telling Fitzgerald: 'I think there is no doubt that Zelda has a great deal of talent, and of a very colorful, almost poetic kind.'[16]

Zelda revised it quickly; Perkins praised its metaphorical freshness and the way the career of the American cabaret entertainers, Lola and Larry, cleverly represented their time and viewpoint. It was published in *Scribner's Magazine* in August 1932. Several critics assessed it as Zelda's most accomplished short story.[17] A St Paul reviewer likened it to *Gatsby*, suggesting that a dual egotism sustained the protagonists in both Zelda's story and Scott's novel.[18]

The story line is simple. Lola and Larry star in French decadent café society in the Twenties, then become corrupted. Lola sabotages their marriage by an affair with their wealthy amoral promoter Jeff Daugherty. Larry takes a mistress, Daugherty's former wife, with whom he drowns in a yachting accident. Having started out believing life was a romantic adventure, they finish as dissipated adventurers.

Once again Zelda uses an unnamed female narrator-participant, who moves in the same world as the Nuts and watches their metamorphosis from innocence to dissolution. The atmosphere is sinister. Romance is illusory, magic destroyed at the touch of a predator. Zelda sustains an ominous air of loss and destruction. Like the Fitzgeralds, the young couple had 'possessed something precious that most of us never have: a jaunty confidence in life and in each other'.[19] For the real as well as the fictional Nuts those dreams had been crushed. With bitter irony Zelda replaced her former themes of love, success and beauty with destruction.

Waste and devastation, of the kind imaginable only in the Deep South, also haunt Miss Ella, a faded Victorian spinster, whose story 'like all women's stories was a love story and like most love stories took place in the past'. As a young belle she jilted her respectable fiancé Mr Hendrix in favour of Andy Bronson, a Southern scoundrel, who roused her sexually by lighting a firecracker which set fire to her dress, then gallantly smothering the flames with his hands. Images of fire, the noise of gunshot flare through this tale of sound and fury as the discarded Hendrix malevolently shoots himself in her grounds on the day of her proposed nuptials to Bronson. Hendrix's brains splatter the earth in a bloody mess. As Miss Ella mournfully cancels her wedding, in effect she cancels her happiness. 'Years passed but Miss Ella had no more hope for love.' She exists only as a burnt-out case. Now 'bitter things dried behind the eyes of Miss Ella like garlic on a string before an open fire'. Her memories have 'acrid fumes'.[20] Reduced to guilt and despair, she rocks in her hammock, rides in a carriage with her elderly aunt, knowing she has thrown away her life merely because a trigger-happy beau threw away his.

Suicides and stifled sexuality were the backdrop to Zelda's youth. Miss Ella, foreshadowing the memorable characters of Carson McCullers and Eudora Welty, sprang from the same roots as did the fictional heroines of Zelda's Southern contemporaries, novelists

Caroline Gordon and Sara Haardt. Zelda's recent reading of fiction by that other Southerner William Faulkner, as well as some psychological studies in repression, informs her story of Miss Ella. Her antagonistic-affectionate conflict with her own Southernness is remarkably similar to Faulkner's, whose Quentin Compson cries: 'I don't hate the South.'[21]

Her technique in 'Miss Ella', as in her *College Humor* stories – little dialogue, much description, the point-of-view focused through an observer-participant – is similar to Scott's style in *Gatsby* and 'The Rich Boy'. Zelda's narrator, though genderless and ageless, is suggestive of a young girl, receptive to Miss Ella's tragic past yet intimate with her in the present. What makes this story work is the impassioned sense of sympathy, even identity, between the narrator and Miss Ella. The narrator makes the reader feel she *is* Miss Ella, she too is repressed, she too is suffused with guilt, she too is riddled with self-denial.

Perkins told Scott Zelda had achieved 'a very complete strong sense of a character in this Southern old maid. It was moving in that way, but it had another quality that was still more moving . . . it made the reader share the feelings of the young girl through whose eyes Miss Bessie was seen, so that she was not only real, and in some degree was not real, but was as the young girl saw her.'[22]

The control of her narrative viewpoint meant the structural problem Zelda had formerly encountered – her insouciant intolerance of plots for instance – was solved. In 'Miss Ella' she strictly disciplined her material of carnage and sacrifice. Written in the clinic, grounded in her own misery, it sounded the note of ruin currently characterizing the lives of both Fitzgeralds.

Scribner's accepted it for the December 1931 issue for $150 dollars, provided Zelda revised what Max called her 'too numerous', 'too remote' similes. Perkins believed Zelda would accept these revisions as she 'probably knows just as much about writing as anybody hereabouts, but few writers can get sufficiently away from their own work to know how it will strike a reader'.[23]

Despite her two successes, Ober's failure with her other stories rankled. '*Please* tell me your *frank* opinion . . . I wish we could sell something. Can't we *give* them away?' she moped.[24]

Her depression rendered her letters to Scott more childlike: 'Without you I can't weigh and balance and be intellectually curious: I'm too afraid I might discover the truth all alone . . . Aren't you scared of such an utterly dependent Baby?'[25] Those baby letters were written in a small less well-formed childish scrawl.

She called herself Scott's 'stupid wife' and added an ironic post-script: 'Excuse me for being so intellectual. I know you would prefer something nice and feminine and affectionate.'[26]

To celebrate Thanksgiving, Scott sent her a recording of his voice. 'Dearest that is the sweetest loveliest voice I ever heard. It made me feel all safe in the centre of things again and important.' His voice, she said, filled the house with assurance, vitality, excitement and love. Then nervously she added: 'You are *sure* you are my own, aren't you? Because when anyone is perfect other people have to be very careful.'[27] That day, putting nerves aside, she wrote a thousand words, assuring him she would finish another two stories before his return. Her next letter recorded: 'I have finished my one-act play and got all the rest of my things off to Ober.' But still she fretted: 'I will never be so foolish as to think I can get on without you again . . . I will let you play with my pistol and you can win every golf game . . . you can always be the one that's perfect.'[28] Then she added: 'I want to write like you some day.'[29]

What are we to make of these letters which reek of overstated dependency and affection? How can we account for the fact that Scott said later this period was the happiest of his and Zelda's life?[30] Were those notes Zelda's intellectual attempts at supreme irony? Or were they written in another private code which amused them both yet neither took seriously? Was the language of passivity Zelda's determination to be seen as sane, using dependency as the measuring stick? Or did acting passive make her feel more feminine, therefore more likeable?

The letters do *not* sound as if they were written for fun, as Zelda was becoming more apprehensive about her father's illness and more insecure in Scott's absence. Zelda told Sara Mayfield that she would never forgive Scott for immuring her in Prangins, that she still didn't know whether Scott had called in psychiatrists to help her or to protect himself. Sara Mayfield believed the dependent letters were 'obvious flattery' as a means of temporary survival, while Zelda's stories were an effort to overcome her financial dependence and gain her release. This is a reasonable view, but it omits the complexity of Zelda's love–hate feelings for Scott, which mirrored precisely her love–hate feelings for the South.

There was another curious and contradictory aspect. At the same time as writing Scott such exaggerated lines as 'we are like a lot of minor characters at table waiting for the entrance of the star', Zelda *was* investigating divorce. She went to see Peyton Mathis, who had recently persuaded the husband of a friend of Zelda's to give her an uncontested divorce. Peyton, though willing to help, pointed out that Scott would never allow the public humiliation of losing Scottie. He would fight for custody, and on the basis of the Prangins report would claim she was mentally unfit as a mother. Zelda's family had already sampled the vengeance Scott could reap with 'Babylon Revisited'. What neither Zelda nor Peyton knew was that after refusing to allow Scottie to live with Rosalind in Brussels, Scott had written to his cousin Ceci that if anything happened to him while Zelda was still deemed 'sick', she was to take care of Scottie.[31]

Seeing no solution, Zelda concentrated her energies on her daughter, to whom in Scott's absence she had become closer. She told Scottie she was 'safer here [in Montgomery] than you've ever been in your life'.[32] Although Scott did not want Scottie educated in the South, or to acquire any of Zelda's effete Southern attributes which he felt were partly responsible for her breakdown, Zelda had insisted Scottie attend Margaret Booth's, where she was doing well.

The Judge, charmed by ten-year-old Scottie's shy manners and French, Yankee and Confederate patois, frequently asked to see her. Then came a change: 'Daddy is . . . as oblivious to his surroundings as he always was when he is himself,' Zelda reported, 'and when he is not he is tormented by imaginary prisons.'[33]

On 17 November Judge Sayre died. On 18 November Zelda sent Scott a reassuring telegram: 'DADDY DIED LAST NIGHT DO NOT WORRY ABOUT US LOVE ZELDA', which the same day she followed with: 'YOU CANNOT ARRIVE FOR FUNERAL DO NOT WORRY ABOUT US WITH DEAREST LOVE ZELDA.' Initially, though sad and lonely, she accepted her father's death with great self-control.

Her letter on the 19th told Scott: 'Daddy seemed so elegant and concise. I have never seen anything so beautiful. The Capitol flag is flying at half-mast and old grayheaded men seem terribly sad. But Daddy seems young and beautiful and somehow master of every-thing. He looks very little in his clothes.'[34] The entrance to the Supreme Court chambers was hung with black crepe. Miss Minnie wore mourning with a widow's veil around her black hat. Zelda did not take Scottie to the funeral but reported her mother was 'abso-lutely amazingly courageous'. The State of Alabama sent a large wreath while the Capitol employees sent all the roses from the grounds. Zelda bought a blanket of flowers for the coffin, and decided that she and Scott should pay most of it, about $50, as Marjorie was crying because she could not afford a black dress and Anthony was very poor. 'I knew how you felt towards Daddy and that you would have wanted us to.'[35]

As the sun set behind the Capitol dome, on a bleak November
day, her father was buried under an ancient oak in Oakwood
Cemetery, where the young Zelda had taken the young Scott to
show him the Confederate graves, their iron crosses now overgrown with clematis. Zelda stood by the low wall crumbling under
faded roses and ancient ivy and realized her father, who had guided
her life, had left her no final word. She had searched through his
papers in his Capitol office but there was nothing personal except
the first three nickels he had earned, stuffed into a mildewed purse.
'He must', she told Sara sadly, 'have forgot to leave the message.'[36]

She drove out frequently to sit by her father's grave, recalling his
good name, his high principles and intellectual doubts. She told
Sara Mayfield she'd never entirely thrown those off despite her
decadent life. She was a carrier, she said, a Typhoid Mary of
Confederate tradition.[37]

She snuggled into a small world with Scottie and her family,
telling Scott they were not afraid, but felt so lonely without him they
seemed like wet paper dolls. In Prangins during the summer Zelda
had drawn and painted more paper dolls of the Fitzgerald family,
giving Scott 'doggy green socks' to match his eyes.[38] Now she
closely observed her child's similarities to Scott. She told him that
Scottie had a 'coating of moon-light for a skin and I watch her and
think of you'.[39]

Scott sent news of Hollywood stars. Zelda did not want to hear
about them. She wanted Scott in Montgomery. She wanted 'for us
to have a son and lots of vital things we own'. After a shopping trip
with Scottie when they saw some 'sweet baby dolls', she instantly
wrote: 'Deo, we really do need a baby.'

Suddenly ominous symptoms recurred. Zelda suffered bad
insomnia, then renewed asthma attacks. Against Scott's advice she
decided to go to Florida to escape the damp, finally compromising
by taking along a trained nurse.

On her return, slightly better, 'Miss Ella' was published in
December. Montgomery residents read it enthusiastically. 'My story
made quite a sensation. People seem to like it,' she wrote Scott.
Though she had sent a copy to Dr Forel 'from sheer vanity', she
added self-deprecatingly: 'I do not dare read the story. Knowing it
is not first rate, I don't want to be discouraged – I wish you could
teach me to write.' Dick Knight, Scott's bête noire who constantly
charmed Zelda, sent her a wildly appreciative telegram. Though
she lost the cable she paraphrased its contents for Scott: '"Am
moanin' low over your story. You are the swellest short-story writer

living as I have just found out from Scribner –" words to that effect – I was very tickled about the story, naturally.'[40]

One of her survival techniques after her father's death was to prepare a Christmas surprise for Scottie. The huge historical panorama that greeted her daughter made it a Christmas she never forgot: 'Weeks before Christmas the sun porch of our house was shut off. When it was opened on Christmas Eve the tree stood in the center of the room and around it my mother had constructed the whole history of mankind, with a little electric train that started its journey in Egypt and went on to Greece, Rome, the Crusades, the War of the Roses.'[41]

Scott returned for Christmas. His screenplay had not been used.[42] Apart from making an exhibition of himself at one of Thalberg's parties where he sang a foolish sophomore song about a dog, he had behaved well and had not been fired as he later claimed. Never one to waste a degrading experience, he turned his doggerel behaviour into the central episode of an excellent story, 'Crazy Sunday', about the marital problems of a Hollywood movie director. It was published by Mencken in *American Mercury* in 1932.[43]

Scott had earned $6,000 which he hoped would buy him time to work on the novel. By the end of 1931 he had sold nine stories, but the *Post* complained to Ober they were not up to Fitzgerald's usual standard.[44] Scott immersed himself in what was now a painful novel focusing on Dick and Nicole Diver's troubled marriage, the apparently charmed life of the rich on the Riviera and Swiss psychiatric sanatoriums. He utilized every scrap of what he had learnt about Zelda's mental breakdowns, remorselessly pilfering her letters, her fears, her punishments. Her madness became his new material. It was, and is, of course not unusual for writers to exploit family and friendship sources for their fictions. However, what *is* reprehensible is Scott's high disregard for Zelda's mental frailty or the possible psychological consequences.

Scott's Ledger recorded the arrival of Rosalind after Zelda's asthma worsened and he had decided to take his wife first on a trip to the Gulf Coast, and from there to the empty Don Ce-Sar hotel in St Petersburg, Florida. She was still writing her novel, while Scott worked what he saw as Zelda's madness into his new version of *Tender*. His habit was to read material aloud to Zelda, and Zelda would have heard and read that version in Montgomery as well as in Florida. It was one thing to have your husband turn you into a flapper, quite another to have him display your mental illness as the *raison d'être* of his main female character. Zelda's shock and consequent emotions can only be surmised, as we have no evidence of any conversation between Zelda and Scott about this appropriation of the most vulnerable part of her life. What we do know is that the Fitzgeralds had a violent conflict, that soon after their arrival in Florida in January 1932 a spot of eczema appeared on Zelda's neck, that another spot appeared, that she was terrified. She was away from her family, there were no other witnesses to the events that followed. Scott reported that on their way back to Montgomery she drank the contents of his flask, that she believed terrible things were being done to her with his knowledge, that she insisted on being hospitalized.

Scott informed Forel, who suggested readmitting Zelda to Prangins which was out of the question. Forel then recommended Dr Adolf Meyer of Phipps Clinic at Johns Hopkins Hospital, Baltimore, another leading authority on schizophrenia.[45] Scared that Zelda would again turn against him, Scott hurried her in to Phipps. On 12 February 1932, only five months after her release from Prangins, Zelda started her second breakdown in her fourth clinic.

Scott did not get on with Meyer, a man of distinguished appearance, heavy moustache and white goatee beard, who refused to treat him as co-consultant and who implicated him in Zelda's breakdown by diagnosing it as a *folie à deux*, a dual case. Dr Meyer infuriated Scott by insisting he should submit to psychoanalysis. Scott, who resisted any such treatment by asserting psychotherapy would ruin his creativity, returned to Montgomery. He spent the winter with Scottie, teaching her chess and reading her *Great Expectations*.

Zelda also found Dr Meyer's heavy Germanic ruminations distinctly off-putting but established a close relationship with her first woman doctor, Mildred Squires. Squires, trained at Pennsylvania Medical School, thirty years younger than Meyer and only four years older than Zelda, admired her talent and found her easy to talk to as long as they did not discuss the patient's medical problems. Zelda resolutely refused to talk about her illness. Though she still smiled uncontrollably, she slept well, and was comfortable with the routine, which allowed her two hours a day to write and paint as part of her therapy. It is of considerable significance that this medical endorsement and validation of Zelda's two arts led to a particularly intense period of creativity from 1932 to 1934. In Phipps Zelda achieved a novel, a play and a great many paintings.

She read numerous theoretical art books, and began to employ a variety of visual styles. Hungry for experiment, her artistic aesthetic became increasingly more sophisticated. 'When I was nineteen,' she told a Baltimore news reporter, 'I thought Botticelli was unbeautiful because the women in the Primavera did not look like the girls in the Follies. But now I don't expect Ann Pennington to hold the same charm for me as a Matisse odalisque.'[46]

Her artistic development was stimulated by art therapy with Dr Frederick Wertham, a special consultant on Zelda's case. Eleven paintings attributed to Zelda were acquired by Wertham in the two years he worked with Zelda.[47] Wertham had developed the mosaic test, in which patients assembled small multicoloured wooden pieces into free-form patterns from which psychiatrists could evaluate patients' ego organizations. Zelda utilized Wertham's diagnostic techniques in her watercolours.[48] The constant exposure to unorthodox colour patterning enabled her to explore colour properties in her compositions, as she did in two watercolours over graphite, *Rams* and *Le Sport*. Both display an unusual use of colour in the background. *Rams* depicts two rams placed against a dazzling multicoloured patchwork like a rainbow jigsaw, the background shades so hectic that they overwhelm the central image. In the more muted *Le Sport*, areas of background colour fuse into one another around tennis rackets and golf clubs battling for priority. Zelda leaves a clear white space round the central figure, a sportsman with typically large curling fingers and feet. The curious element in these paintings is that unlike her previous emotionally expressive, thickly painted canvases these are linear, even in some cases minimalist. Their sharp lines encouraged Scott to suggest she might consider a career as a commercial artist.[49]

But while Zelda was purposefully increasing her painting skills, in terms of a career she was still bent on writing. Mildred Squires' active encouragement led Zelda to feel for the first time appreciated as an artist. It is hardly surprising that eventually she dedicated *Save Me The Waltz* to Squires.[50]

Zelda wrote to Scott that she loved and was lonely for him, that she felt there was 'nothing so sordid as being shut up', but that she was reading contemporary French painting texts and particularly admired flower painters who could make blossoms seem malevolent like the hallucinations of the dead.[51] She did not mention her novel.

Scott, who communicated regularly with the clinic, learnt she was writing at an enviable speed. Zelda asked Dr Squires to read a section of her novel, after which Squires wrote to Scott describing it as vivid and charming, though it occasionally broke off abruptly. Squires found the style similar to 'Miss Ella' and believed once

Zelda revised her draft it would be excellent. By 2 March Squires reported Zelda's anxiety had decreased, her second chapter was finished, success was predicted. Nearing completion, Zelda wrote to Scott: 'I am proud of my novel, but I can hardly restrain myself enough to get it written. You will like it – It is distinctly École Fitzgerald, though more ecstatic than yours . . . Being unable . . . to avoid the reiterant "said" I have emphasized it a la Ernest much to my sorrow. He is a very determined writer, but I shall also die with my boots on.'[52]

Scott, sadly, had removed his own boots, halted his work on *Tender* and when the lease on the Montgomery house expired, trudged to Baltimore to find new accommodation nearer to Zelda. His Ledger reveals: 'depression . . . Scotty and her friends, becomes a racket . . . Rosalind still there . . . Scotty sick, me sick, Mrs Sayre playing the fool . . . everything worser and worser.'[53]

He had, however, become curiouser and curiouser about Zelda's novel. On 8 March he wrote authoritatively to Squires that Zelda was not a '"natural story-teller" in the sense that I am, and unless a story comes to her fully developed and crying to be told she's liable to flounder around rather unsuccessfully among problems of construction.' But Zelda was not floundering around unsuccessfully. To Scott's amazement, Squires wrote back on 9 March that Zelda had just completed her fiction.

Zelda did not mail her manuscript to Scott for advice or guidance. Instead she sent it at once, deceiving the hospital by switching addresses, to Max Perkins. It arrived at Scribner's with this note: 'Scott, being absorbed in his own [novel], has not seen it, so I am completely in the dark as to its possible merits, but naturally, terribly anxious that you should like it . . . As soon as I hear that you have safely received the copy, I want to mail the ms to Scott, so could you wire?'[54]

Zelda wrote to Scott that she was sure Scribner's would reject it, but still she held back the manuscript. Then a trifle apprehensively she posted it. How right she was to have apprehensions.

When Scott finally received it on 14 March his rage was boundless.

CHAPTER 20

Scott felt that this time Zelda had gone too far. Zelda felt that this time she had gone some way in asserting herself.

Scott believed she had 'poached' what he admitted were their *joint* life experiences for her now completed novel which he had intended to use for his work-in-progress. Although today it would seem at the very least problematic, Scott was able to justify his term 'poaching' because of his entrenched belief that his wife was expected to be 'a complementary intelligence' concerned exclusively with his interests and ambitions.[1] Zelda's life he saw as his raw material. Zelda's writings he saw as his literary property.

Despite suffering self-doubt, diminished self-respect and loss of identity through Scott's treatment of her, Zelda still felt that she had a perfect right to use her experiences for own literary source material. But the fact that she furtively sent the manuscript to Perkins indicated she knew how much Scott would resent it.

Neither Fitzgerald spoke directly to the other. A dialogue of blame, resentment, anger and defence was passed to Dr Squires, who diplomatically mediated. On 14 March a furious Fitzgerald told Mildred Squires that after four years' work on his novel, from spring 1930 he had 'been unable to proceed because of the necessity of keeping Zelda in sanitariums'. His letters reveal how much it rankled that her book was finished so swiftly while his was still being developed: 'about fifty thousand words exist and this Zelda has heard and literally one whole section of her novel is an imitation of it, of its rhythm materials even statements and speeches'. He acknowledged Squires might think 'the experiences which two people have undergone in common is common property – one transmutes the same scene through different temperaments and it "comes out different"'. He emphasized 'there are only two episodes, both of which <u>she</u> has reduced to anecdotes <u>but upon which whole sections of my book turn</u>, that I have asked her to cut'. As for Zelda's dancing, her love for Jozan, her observations about

Americans in Paris, 'the fine passages about the death of her father', his criticisms, he said, would be impersonal and professional. But he would not tolerate Zelda naming her central character Amory Blaine, the name of his autobiographical hero in *This Side of Paradise*.

> Do you think that his turning up in a novel signed by my wife as a some-what anemic portrait painter with a few ideas lifted from Clive Bell, Leger, ect. could pass unnoticed? . . . it puts me in an absurd and Zelda in a rediculous position . . . this mixture of fact and fiction is simply cal-culated to ruin us both or what is left of us and I can't let it stand. Using the name of a character I invented to put intimate facts in the hands of [our] friends and enemies . . . My God, my books made her a legend and her single intention . . . is to make me a non-entity.[2]

The technique of mixing fact and fiction which so incensed him was, of course, one he himself used extensively. He was disturbed that her public portrayal of him did not coincide with the way he wished to be seen. Not only had she betrayed him, she had also exploited him by writing in time he paid for through selling stories that took him away from *his* novel. He overlooked his plundering of Zelda's diaries, letters and ideas in order to offer up *her* character for public inspection.

On 16 March he wired Perkins: 'PLEASE DO NOT JUDGE OR IF NOT ALREADY DONE EVEN CONSIDER ZELDAS BOOK UNTIL YOU GET REVISED VERSION LETTER FOLLOWS.'[3] To pacify Scott, Zelda wrote:

> Dr Squires tells me that you are hurt that I did not send my book to you before I mailed it to Max. Purposely I didn't – knowing that you were working . . . honestly feeling that I had no right to interrupt you to ask for a serious opinion . . . I was in my usual rush to get it off my hands – You know how I hate brooding over things once they are finished: so I mailed it post haste, hoping to have yours + Scribner's criticisms to use for revising.

Scott scrawled red pencil marks over her first paragraph and angrily noted in the margin, 'This is an evasion. All this reasoning is specious.'

Zelda tried placation: 'Scott, I love you more than anything on earth and if you were offended I am miserable. We have always shared everything but it seems to me I no longer have the right to inflict every desire and necessity of mine on you.' She skirted round the most crucial point: 'I was also afraid we might have touched on the same material.' Then a retreat into humility: 'feeling it to be a dubious production due to my own instability I did not want a scathing criticism such as you have mercilessly – if for my own good given my last stories, poor things . . . So, Dear, my own, please realize that it was not from any sense of not turning first to you – but just time and other ill-regulated elements that made me so bombastic about Max.

'Goofo, please love me – life is very confusing – but I love you.'[4]

Scott was not buying her version of events. Enraged at Zelda's temerity, he determined to use every available culturally constructed tool to impose and to justify his literary restrictions upon his wife. The first restriction was to insist that Scribner's should cut hefty sections of her novel, cuts to be decided by him, before he would countenance publication. The second was to insist that if Scribner's published it they should not praise it to Zelda, as it might damage her mental health or give rise to what he termed her incipient egomania. His third restriction was to insist on a contractual clause stipulating that one half of the royalties earned by Zelda would be retained by Scribner's, to be credited against *his* debts to them until a total of $5,000 had been repaid.

Scott's letter to Zelda demanding specific cuts, like so many other Fitzgerald materials, has 'gone missing'. Retained is Zelda's initial submissive response: 'Of cource, I glad[ly] submit to anything you want about the book or anything else. I felt myself the thing was too crammed with material upon which I had not time to dwell. Shall I wire Max to send it back? . . . The Pershing incident which you accuse me of stealing occupies just one line and will not be missed. I willingly relinquish it.'[5]

Reluctantly on 27 March Zelda cabled Max: 'ACTING ON SCOTTS ADVICE WILL YOU RETURN MANUSCRIPT PHIPPS CLINIC JOHNS HOPKINS WITH MANY THANKS REGRETS AND REGARDS VELDA [*sic*] FITZGERALD.'[6]

Max cabled back: he had 'READ ABOUT 60 PAGES WITH GREAT INTEREST STOP VERY LIVE AND MOVING STOP HOPE YOU WILL RETURN IT STOP AFFECTIONATE REGARDS.'[7]

Zelda, wishing to return it, refused to give in to all Scott's demands.

I would like you to thoroughly understand that my revision will be made on an aesthetic basis: that the other material which I will elect is nevertheless legitimate stuff which has cost me a pretty emotional penny to amass and which I intend to use when I can get the tranquility of spirit necessary to write the story of myself versus myself. That is the book I really want to write . . . With dearest love, I am your irritated Zelda.[8]

She was more than irritated. She was fuming. A nurse at Phipps overheard her saying to herself: 'I have always done whatever I wanted to do, whenever I could possibly manage it. My book is none of my husband's Goddamned business.'[9]

She held back her fury while explaining to Scott how lonely and friendless she felt: 'all our associates have always taken me for granted, sought your stimulus and fame, eaten my dinners and invited "The Fitzgeralds" place[s].' She reminded him he had always been the one person with whom she had felt the need to communicate intimately.[10]

Scott was unmoved by her plea. He felt as misused as she had felt in the past. His telegrams to Perkins spoke of mood changes and irrationality. One said Zelda's novel needed only small but necessary changes. Another said it was a fine novel. A new cable insisted the hero's name and the book title be changed. Scott's next telegram screamed that the whole middle section must be drastically redrafted. Finally, at the end of March he went to Baltimore to work with Zelda on revisions. Yet again the original manuscript and Zelda's first draft revisions have been 'mislaid'. We are left with a printer's copy of the typed manuscript, two consecutive sets of much-revised galley proofs and a set of pristine page proofs.[11] This means we cannot know what deletions Scott insisted on that first time. We know Scott was satisfied at the extensive changes because he wrote to Perkins, 'Zelda's novel is now good, improved in every way. It is new. She has largely eliminated the speakeasy-nights-and-our-trip-to-Paris atmosphere. You'll like it. It should reach you in ten days. I am too close to judge it but it may be even better than I think.' However, he again begged Perkins not to praise Zelda or imply she might achieve money or success.[12] Two weeks later Scott sent the manuscript to Perkins: it was 'a good novel now, perhaps a very good novel'. He likened it to Wolfe's *Look Homeward, Angel*, was sure it would interest the many thousand dance enthusiasts, felt it was 'absolutely new, and should sell'. He forbade Perkins to mention the novel to Hemingway, whose new book was to be published that same season, not because of 'conflict between the books' but because of the hostility between Hemingway and Zelda. And he finally gave Perkins permission to write directly to Zelda about her book.[13]

Perkins sent Zelda the same gracious telegram one assumes he would have sent without such a cavalier instruction. 'HAD A GRAND SUNDAY READING YOUR NOVEL STOP THINK IT VERY UNUSUAL AND AT TIMES DEEPLY MOVING PARTICULARLY DANCING PART STOP DELIGHTED TO PUBLISH

STOP WRITING STOP MAXWELL PERKINS.'[14] His written comments suggested that the New York and Westport parts were not as good as the Alabama state sections, which were 'very good indeed'. The 'best part' was when her heroine Alabama takes up dancing.[15]

On 19 May Zelda, overjoyed, replied: 'To catalogue my various excitements and satisfactions that you liked my book would be an old story to you – It seems so amazing that you are going to actually publish it . . . My God! Maybe the ink will fade, maybe you'll discover that it doesn't make sense! It couldn't be possible that I was an author!

'Of cource, I will gladly change the questionable parts. I, too, felt the New York part was weak, though I liked the Paris party.' Then with her characteristic thoughtfulness which has been little remarked on, she asked after his sick daughter. 'Scott told me your daughter had been ill. I am beginning to feel qualified to make suggestion about the Invalid Racket: John's-Hopkin's is an awfully good place with very competent nurses and entirely lacking the general air of negligence that pervades most places where people are going to be sick a long time. We were dreadfully distressed – and I hope she will soon be well again. I know how worried you and Louise must be. Those nervous maladies are always alarming . . . it's worse always on the people who care than on the person who's ill.'[16]

She had complied with Scott's request to change the novel's title and hero's name. Zelda found *Save Me The Waltz* from a Victor record catalogue. A superficial sweetness is implied in the old-fashioned dance request, but the bitterness of its frequent shortening to 'Save Me' blasts the sweetness apart.

If the irony of using Amory Blaine, Scott's fictional hero's name, for her own portrait of Scott did not appeal to her husband, the greater irony of substituting the name David Knight displeased him almost as much. Her hero's new first name was probably taken from Van Vechten's novel *Parties*, where Scott appears as the volatile, jealous David Westlake. Using the name of Scott's enemy Dick Knight for her hero's surname might be a neat revenge for the way Scott was dealing with her writing.[17] Zelda had already mentioned Scott's dislike of Knight to her doctors at Phipps. Later that year Scott displayed his jealousy when, after an unpleasant meeting at which he had called Knight a fairy, he tetchily apologized: 'I have never in my wildest imaginings supposed you were a fairy . . . It is a lousy word to anyone not a member of the species.' Scott did acknowledge how Knight's encouragement of Zelda's achievements had helped her. 'That was swell praise you gave Zelda and needless to say delighted her and set her up enormously. She revised the book so much that she lost contact with it and yours is the first word that gives it public existence.' But Scott couldn't leave it at that. He acknowledged: 'the sincerity of your feeling toward her shouldn't offend anybody except the most stupid and churlish of husbands ... [but] ... [w]hen you city fellows come down you can't put ideas in the heads of our farm girls, without expecting resistance.'[18]

Though Scott sharply scrutinized Zelda's novel for features which might damage his public image, he allowed it to be printed without decreasing the convoluted metaphors or correcting the grammatical errors, typographical mistakes and misspellings which litter the text. Scott, a notoriously bad speller, may not have recognized these flaws but that Perkins allowed the book to be published in this woeful state did Zelda ill-service.

Save Me The Waltz is a searing portrayal of a woman's search for identity within a tangled marriage, both a particular woman and any woman. Because of its deeply autobiographical links, it is often read as a companion piece to *Tender Is The Night*. The critic Dan Piper suggested that 'together, these two chronicles of the same marriage seen from the wife's and husband's viewpoints, form one of the most unusual pairs of novels in recent literary history'.[19] But in its own terms, this moving novel has the hallmarks of Zelda's best and worst stylistic points. There are her characteristic wit, her skill in making unexpected connections between ideas, and her idiosyncratic metaphoric descriptions with their sensual illumination of small details. Inanimate objects spring into life with a menacing air. Severed parts of the body abound: ears, eyes, limbs. When Alabama Beggs, her autobiographical heroine, falls in love with blond lieutenant David Knight, Alabama focuses on David's ear:

> She felt herself very small and ecstatic. Alabama was in love.
> She crawled into the friendly cave of his ear. The area inside was gray and ghostly classic as she stared about the deep trenches of the cerebellum ... she set out following the creases. Before long she was lost. Like a mystic maze, the folds and ridges rose in desolation; there was nothing to indicate one way from another. She stumbled on ... Vast tortuous indentations led her round and round. Hysterically, she began to run. David, distracted by a tickling sensation at the head of his spine, lifted his lips from hers.
> 'I'll see your father,' he said, 'about when we can be married.'[20]

An ear is a mundane object. But this is a fantastic journey into and out of it. Zelda is not writing an ordinary romantic description. For

Alabama and David's relationship will be no ordinary romance. She has piled up, like cars hurtling into each other behind one that has crashed, a series of crazy dissimilar elements in order to achieve an an unforgettable richness. It works here because she stops the sur-realistic method in time and brings readers down to earth with David's sudden decision to marry the girl.

Throughout the book Zelda offers the material of myth, where many of the narrative connections are deliberately cut. Diametrically opposed to Scott's shaped orderliness, some sections have the nightmare quality of Angela Carter's fiction. Others, lush and associative, reach into the unconscious, and read like a dis-tinctly Modernist novel. When David asks Alabama to say she loves him and Alabama replies: 'I never say anything to anybody. Don't talk',[21] Zelda points to her stylistic intention: to express what cannot be expressed.

Where Zelda's work is flawed is where she fails to heed her own red light. She overloads the prose and it races out of control. Take this: 'A shooting star, ectoplasmic arrow, sped through the nebulous hypothesis like a wanton hummingbird. From Venus to Mars to Neptune it trailed the ghost of comprehension, illuminating far horizons over the pale battlefields of reality.'[22] The reader is stranded amongst muddy lines encrusted with too many images.

The plot, in four sections, has overwhelming similarities to Zelda's life.[23] It faithfully captures, in the first section, Alabama's Southern family home, pinpointing the influential authority of Alabama's father Judge Beggs, the devotion of her mother Millie, the affection of her older sisters, Dixie (who resembles Rosalind and like her is society editor of the town newspaper) and Joan, blessed with 'an unattainable hue of beauty'.[24] We watch Alabama's rebel-lious girlhood, and her marriage to David Knight (a painter not a writer) whom she met during World War One.

The second section follows David's early celebrity in New York, the birth of Bonnie/Scottie, their Riviera trip, Alabama's infatua-tion[25] for French naval aviator Jacques Chevre-Feuille, who discou-rages her from leaving David, their move to Paris where David has a retaliatory romance with movie actress Gabrielle Gibbs of the blancmange breasts and blue veins. 'David opened and closed his personality over Miss Gibbs like the tentacles of a carnivorous mar-itime plant.'[26] After this revelation Alabama determines on a ballet career to bring order into her chaotic lonely existence.

The third section recreates the Paris ballet years, where Madame usurps the central place in Alabama's life. In the final section

Alabama accepts the role with the San Carlos Opera Ballet Company, Naples, which Zelda had turned down, and briefly and successfully lives in Italy without her husband and daughter, which Zelda never managed to do. But Alabama too is forced to give up her dance career. Blood poisoning from an infected foot necessitates an operation that will sever her tendons and make dancing impossible. David, with renewed devotion, comes to the hospital. Together they return to the Deep South, where she sees her father die. She is left with David, dumping ashtrays, as their guests depart. When David scolds her for starting her chores before the guests have vanished, she says: 'It's very expressive of myself. I just lump everything in a great heap which I have labeled "the past," and, having thus emptied this deep reservoir that was once myself, I am ready to continue.'[27]

Though all psychiatric episodes and all mention of homosexuality have been expunged, the novel is a transparent reworking of the Fitzgeralds' early years.

The establishment of the interior lives of her characters, as well as the atmosphere of the places they visit, is achieved partially through a suffusion of flower images. Zelda was also painting daily, and while imprisoned in this Baltimore clinic she recreated on canvas the same wild Montgomery blossoms that flourished in her novel. Whether in print or oils, plants explode with emotion. In the paintings geometric, angular flowers allow the viewer to feel Zelda's spikiness, while curled, layered flowers are uncontrollably sensuous. Most flowers are magnified so that, impossible to ignore, they startle the viewer. The mounds and buds have both the fragile beauty of those Zelda picked as a girl, but also the iron strength she had drawn on during the previous two years. There was a cyclical process between the flowers she gathered in armfuls, the flowers that hurtled from her paintbrush on to canvas and the flowers in her richly descriptive prose which synthesized the senses.

In chapter 3, in Paris, dancer Alabama's fatigued feet are too sore to wear new shoes which she would have liked to buy, nor does she feel comfortable purchasing new dresses, so in a moment of wild extravagance she spends every cent of the hundred franc notes in her purse on flowers. Most of them are for Madame. As Alabama endows the flowers with the qualities of the material possessions she might have bought, Zelda pours out a rich surrealistic litany whose metaphors would ambush the most jaded reader.

> Yellow roses she bought with her money like Empire satin brocade, and white lilacs and pink tulips like molded confectioner's frosting, and

deep-red roses like a Villon poem, black and velvety as an insect wing
... malignant parrot tulips scratching the air with their jagged barbs ...
She gave Madame gardenias like white kid gloves ... threatening sprays
of gladioli, and the soft, even purr of black tulips. She bought flowers
like salads and flowers like fruits, jonquils and narcissus, poppies and
ragged robins, and flowers with the brilliant carnivorous qualities of
Van Gogh.[28]

During April, a month when Scott described Zelda as 'strange',[29]
he wrote a decidedly fictional response to the crisis over Zelda's
novel in the guise of a *Post* story, 'What A Handsome Pair'.[30] The
protagonists are a young sporting couple who become bitter rivals,
counterbalanced by a second couple where the man is a musician
and his wife 'merely' a homemaker. Scott posits the idea that for a
creative man to enjoy a good marriage he needs a non-competitive,
unambitious wife. Scott does not deal with the needs of a creative
woman.

He wrote two more stories that year, but the *Post* cut his fees from
$4,000, first to $3,500, then to $3,000, then to $2,500, his 1925 rate.
Again the *Post* complained about the low level of his stories to Ober,
who subsequently found it impossible to sell 'Nightmare', set in an
insane asylum, to any reputable magazine. That year Scott's earnings dropped to $15,832.40, his lowest annual total since 1919.

In mid-April Scott visited Zelda daily at Phipps, where they quarrelled constantly. Often their rows were rooted in Zelda's refusal to
show him her latest story. Scott retaliated by providing her psychiatrists with his views on Zelda's breakdown, focusing particularly
on what he considered her detrimental relationship with Minnie
Sayre. He saw mother and daughter unhealthily attached by a silver
cord. Zelda objected to her husband trying to play Dr Fitzgerald.
Scott objected to the patient continuing to write.[31]

Dr Meyer, meanwhile, was having severe problems communicating with Zelda, who still refused to moderate her desire to work
('My work is not a strain. All I ask to do is to work'[32]), and getting
Scott to see that his drinking and dictatorial attitude was further
damaging Zelda.

On 20 May 1932 Scott, who had been house-hunting from his base
at the Rennert hotel, rented La Paix, a house set in 28 acres on the
Bayard Turnbull estate in Towson, Baltimore, where the Fitzgeralds
lived until November 1933. Zelda told Max the house was soft and
shady like 'a paintless playhouse abandoned when the family grew
up ... surrounded by apologetic trees and meadows and creaking

insects.[33] Sara Mayfield described the 'fantastic exterior' as a veritable Mad Hatter's Castle, rusty grey, with gingerbread arches, bays thrown at random and a porch decorated with jigsaw scrollwork. Scott, said Sara, 'had outdone himself this time'. Zelda remarked wittily to Sara that had she named the house she would have called it 'Calvin Coolidge, Jnr because it was so mute'.[34]

Initially Zelda spent mornings there, returning to Phipps after lunch. Scott was determined that when Zelda rejoined them full-time she would follow a disciplined schedule, ordered by the doctors but controlled by him. He believed a strict routine would tire her less, but he also felt that as he would be blamed for any mistakes he 'should be able to dictate the conditions'.[35] Zelda wrote to Bishop:

> We are more alone than ever before while the psychiatres patch up my nervous system . . . they present you with a piece of bric-a-brac of their own forging which falls to the pavement on your way out of the clinic and luckily smashes to bits . . . Don't *ever* fall into the hands of brain and nerve specialists unless you are feeling very Faustian. Scott reads Marx – I read the Cosmological philosophers. The brightest moments of our day are when we get them mixed up.[36]

Zelda startled visitors by floating through La Paix in a tutu, for she still practised ballet regularly. Eleven-year-old Andrew Turnbull (later Scott's biographer) saw Zelda, biting her lip, picking at her face, dancing round the living-room table to the tune of her gramophone. He felt she was not quite wholesome. Though Scott's drinking bothered the teetotal Turnbulls, Mrs Margaret Turnbull affectionately recalls the patience he exercised with her three children, Eleanor, Frances and Andrew, who became firm playmates of Scottie's. Scottie also made another local friend, Margaret 'Peaches' Finney, daughter of Scott's Princeton classmate Eben Finney. Peaches and Scottie both attended Calvert School, then became day students at Bryn Mawr. Whenever tension arose in the Fitzgerald household Scottie would stay with the Finneys.

Margaret Turnbull thought Scott felt guilty about Zelda, needed her approval, talked warmly of her charm, brilliance and appeal to men. But, said Mrs Turnbull, 'she was his invalid', and it was as an invalid Margaret viewed her. 'She struck one like a broken clock.'[37]

At La Paix Zelda's relationship with Scottie worsened as Scott tightened his hold on his daughter's education and social routines. Though fiercely authoritarian he gave Scottie a great deal of atten-

tion, thereby cutting Zelda out of the family picture while upbraid-
ing her for her lack of interest in Scottie's progress. By treating Zelda
as 'sick', Scott effectively prevented Scottie from turning to her
mother for help or advice.

A new young doctor, Thomas Rennie, with whom Zelda felt some
rapport, had taken charge of her case. Zelda confessed to Rennie she
feared her child was growing away from her. 'I can't help her at all
. . . I'm like a stranger in the house.' She admitted she was unable to
control temper outbursts against Scottie. 'I lose my temper when I
get up. It's awfully unfair to my husband and child.'[38]

In May, Scott hired his first fulltime secretary, Isabel Owens (who
worked for him until 1938), for $12 a week. She quickly became a
surrogate mother to Scottie and a companion to Zelda. She chauf-
feured them everywhere, swam with them, bought Zelda's art
materials and, carefully chosen by Scott as the kind of woman with
whom he would not fall in love, she never became embroiled in the
Fitzgeralds' emotional tangles.

On 26 June Zelda was discharged from Phipps to join the family.
As Squires, Meyer and Rennie did not see her as cured, both she and
Scott attended regular sessions at the clinic. Despite Zelda's release
from hospital disciplines, to her chagrin Scott predictably began to
wield authority over her. Aided by Meyer, who had angered Scott
by encouraging Zelda's creativity, Scott also put restraints on her
writing. He feared Zelda would write about psychiatry which he
intended to keep for exclusive use in *Tender*. He had dropped both
the Melarky matricide and the Kelly shipboard plot and had constructed a draft centred on the ruination of an American psychiatrist
by his marriage to a rich mental patient. Entwined with this plot
were his recent emotions of loss and damage.[39]

Zelda *had* begun a new novel with insanity as its theme. She
divulged to Rennie that she wanted to create a view of madness so
close to normality that readers would not see the difference. The
clever plot shows a married couple driven to a mental clinic by their
scheming daughter, but not till the conclusion do readers discover
that the couple are already patients inside the asylum. Later Zelda
refocused the novel on the schizophrenia of Vaslav Nijinsky,
Diaghilev's lover and main male dancer with his Ballets Russes.[40]

Determined that Zelda should not proceed with this book, Scott
encouraged her to paint. It was at La Paix that Zelda had her first
professional painting studio, where many of her strongest ballet
paintings were done between 1932 and 1934.

Sara Mayfield and Sara Haardt, who visited La Paix, were

shocked both by their friends' appearances and by Zelda's paintings. 'Both Scott and Zelda had lost the fresh, well-scrubbed look
that marked them in their youth,' said the younger Sara. '[Scott had]
developed flabby arms and a fat pot . . . Zelda was immaculate . . .
[but] [h]er once lustrous blond hair had taken on a dull red-gold
tint; her skin, a grayish pallor.' Zelda found it hard to converse with
her friends. 'Beyond an exchange of Confederate amenities with
Sara and me and an occasional inquiry about her family and friends
in Montgomery, Zelda's conversation was confined almost wholly
to her painting. A corner of her eye twitched, and her mouth twisted
from nervous strain when she spoke,' said young Sara:

> as she showed us her canvases, I gathered that Scott must be cavilling
> that she was now becoming as obsessed by her painting as she had been
> by her dancing . . . . Among the sketches of New York, of Paris, of ballet
> dancers, and dream gardens stacked against the wall there were two
> crucifixions. The face on the cross in one of them was unmistakably
> Zelda's. As Scott saw that Sara and I recognized the likeness, he turned
> abruptly and walked out of the room. If he could not face it, I could not
> forget it.[41]

Both Saras felt that to see the Fitzgeralds at La Paix while remembering early days in Montgomery was 'like reading a palimpsest on
which a stark Greek tragedy had been written over the faint traces
of a romantic comedy . . . it was not the way to spend a pleasant
afternoon.'[42]

Scott later sold two of Zelda's paintings from this period to Sara
Haardt on Zelda's behalf. Though Sara Mayfield later saw the
receipt, dated 1932, amongst Sara Haardt's papers, the paintings
were never recovered. Whether Zelda knew is not clear. Judging by
her generous gifts to other friends, including the Murphys and
Sandy Kalman, she would have been more likely to have *given* them
to Sara.

Zelda's most important oil painting to date, the mannerist *Ballet
Figures*, was to be shown at New York's Anderson Galleries for the
American Art Association's Spring Salon in May 1933: the first
known public showing of her art. That afternoon, when Zelda was
excitedly telling her friends about the event, Scott interrupted them,
and asked Sara Haardt to look over his manuscript of *Tender* (currently called 'Dr Diver's Holiday'). Sara Mayfield remembers him
pounding on the table as he shouted: 'And it's good, good, good!'
She said he spoke 'as if he were whistling in a cemetery to bolster

his own morale . . . . As if to reassure himself, he said, "It *is* good, isn't it, Zelda?" ' Scott's thoughtlessness in inviting praise for fiction centred on Zelda's mental condition became obvious to her friends only later. At the time they heard Zelda's peal of irrelevant, mirthless laughter. 'For a moment,' recalled Sara Mayfield, 'I thought Scott was going to slap her. Their eyes met and locked in a conflict that had rent them both . . . Anger flashed in the dead silence between them and then paled into inward desolation and despair.' Scott, worried that Zelda's friends would be embarrassed, said huskily: 'She's mad,' then seeing their shocked faces, he quickly added: 'Schizophrenia, the doctors say.'[43]

Driving the women back to town, he attempted to justify himself. 'He began by disparaging Zelda. Then he blamed her illness on her family, whom he taxed with bringing her up to be spoiled, selfish, and dependent . . . We tried half a dozen times to change the subject, but it was impossible to stop his scathing criticisms of Zelda and her family.'[44]

In Baltimore Scott had taken to bursting in on Sara and Mencken at 704 Cathedral Street. Because of Sara's operation they were not able to have children but, deeply in love, they had settled quietly into an affectionate routine. Mencken rose early and breakfasted alone at eight, believing that breakfasting with one's spouse imposed an unnecessary hazard on marriage. Then they both wrote in separate rooms, Sara writing articles for *Country Life*, before lunching together, after which Sara napped. Early evening provided them with what Mencken called 'philosophical belching' before dinner. Sara Mayfield said that they never exchanged a cross word. If an argument seemed imminent, they each retreated in silence to a separate room until calm could be restored.[45] Nothing could be more different from the Fitzgeralds' row-riven lives.

Though Scott's noisy drunken visits began to irritate the Menckens, as they had the Murphys and Hemingways, his alcoholic ravages concerned them.[46] Mencken managed to interest a doctor friend, Benjamin Baker, who tried to stop Scott drinking. Initially Scott entered Johns Hopkins in August 1932 with a tentative diagnosis of typhoid fever,[47] but between 1933 and 1937 he was re-hospitalized eight times for alcoholism and for suspected inactive fibroid tuberculosis.

In September 1932 Scott summed up the year as a 'strange year of Work & Drink. Increasingly unhappy – Zelda up and down. 1st draft of novel complete Ominous!'

While Scottie started a new dancing school in the fall, Zelda, waiting anxiously for the publication of *Save Me The Waltz*, worked on a lighthearted farce called *Scandalabra*, turning to it in relief when either her new novel or Scott's criticisms became too heavy.

On 7 October *Save Me The Waltz* was published at $2 with a minimum of publicity, printed on cheap paper, bound in green linen, with a tiny print run of 3,010 copies. The poor proofreading formed the bulk of the *New York Times*'s negative criticism among mixed reviews.[48]

Dorothea Brande in *The Bookman* enlarged on this: 'It is not only that her publishers have not seen fit to curb an almost ludicrous lushness of writing . . . but they have not given the book the elementary services of a literate proofreader.' Brande said if one persisted past the mistakes one came upon an earnest, honest, good story of a girl trying desperately to make a character for herself which will carry her through life. In the Judge Zelda had 'drawn with loving care as fine a man as we have had in fiction for many a month'.[49]

Several critics, ignoring the proofreading defects, gave it good reviews. William McFee in the New York *Sun* told readers: 'here is a peculiar talent, and connoisseurs of style will have a wonderful time . . . there is the promise of a new and vigorous personality in fiction'. McFee, whose review Zelda considered 'the only intelligible (to me) criticism of the book', suggested that the effect of the accumulated fantastic metaphors was fascination. 'Veteran word-mongers will read [it], with envy and a kind of dizzy delight . . . the book [has] an almost alcoholic vitality. Mrs Fitzgerald's next novel will be an interesting event.' Like most reviewers McFee thought the ballet sections towered above the rest, whilst the character of Alabama was insufficiently developed, resembling rather 'an insane child'.[50]

Some critics saw the novel as the last will and testament of a departed era that began as a bar-room ballad and ended as a funeral oration. The *New York Herald Tribune* perceived Alabama as a heroine who 'somersaults through the pages' with a hardboiled experimentalist surface concealing an uncompromising sentimentalist. The *Tribune* suggested 'the writing has a masculinity that is unusual: it is always vibrant and always sensitive'.[51]

The subhead above a review that amused Zelda immensely ran 'Mrs Fitzgerald's First Novel Places Her On Scott's Level',[52] but amusement was curtailed by a realistic appraisal of the book's finances. Fitzgerald's contractual clause stipulating that half Zelda's royalties up to $5,000 were to be credited against his publishing debt did him little good, for the novel sold fewer than 1,400 copies. Its earnings totalled a mere $120.73, for Zelda had to pay expensive proof revision costs. When Max sent Zelda the cheque he wrote: 'Maybe I ought to have warned you about corrections for they came to a great deal. I knew they would, when the proofs began coming back, but I knew you wanted to get the book the way you thought it ought to be.' This was a slight slip of the truth, for most of the revisions were incurred because Scott wanted to get the book the way *he* thought it ought to be. Max realized Zelda was sad: 'The result won't be encouraging to you, and I have not liked to ask you whether you were writing any more . . . but I do think the last part of the book in particular, was very fine; and that if we had not been in the depths of a depression, the result would have been quite different.'[53]

Some of their established writer friends thought highly of the book. Malcolm Cowley wrote to Scott: 'It moves me a lot: she has something there that nobody got into words before. The women who write novels are usually the sort who live spiritually in Beloit, Wisconsin.'[54]

Despite this praise, the overall financial failure of the book sent Zelda spiralling down again. She locked herself in her room and drove Scott mad with fury as she threw herself into her new novel, based on her own asylum experiences. Angrily Scott wrote to Dr Rennie that Zelda had negated her promise not to write any more fiction until he had finished his novel.

He drank instead of writing. She wrote instead of submitting, locking up her manuscript after every day's work. They were building towards their biggest confrontation yet.

CHAPTER 21

Fall came. The leaves drifted, so did Zelda, anxiously waiting as several New York producers rejected *Scandalabra*.[1] She hid in her roof-top eyrie, writing, dancing and painting. Down below, Scott, nerves frayed, endlessly redrafted *Tender Is The Night*.[2] Isabel Owens recalled him in 1932 slouching in his smoke-filled study wrapped in an ancient towelling robe, clutching his gin bottle like a security blanket. Zelda and Scott, who both craved privacy and peace, could not leave each other alone. They trawled from room to room, rowing, repenting, screaming, making up. Mrs Owens remembers: 'She took a lot from him . . . and I never remember her criticizing him. Of course she had no say.' Zelda didn't want him in her workplace but never refused her help. Scott, who protected her from drink and visitors, never understood that she also needed protection from *him*. 'He would go up to her room and ask advice about things they had done together, conversations they had.' Scott, Mrs Owens said, 'couldn't write about anything he didn't know . . . Zelda's memory was good.'[3] In an interview in the *Saturday Evening Post* Scott admitted that, though highly professional, he now experienced feelings of 'utter helplessness'. Where were his fresh themes or new plots? 'We have two or three great moving experiences in our lives. Then we learn our trade . . . and we tell our two or three stories – each time in a new guise . . . as long as people will listen.'[4] That year he feared people had stopped listening.

The New Year of 1933 rang in with sadness and continued miserably through to September. January brought 'Quarrels' with Scottie,[5] February saw a severe quarrel with Ernest, but neither proved as depressing to Scott as Ring Lardner's death in September which he told Max was 'a terrible blow'.[6] Earlier in the year, looking for cheer, Scott met Lois Moran in New York. It was but a temporary palliative. He turned to luminal and drink which necessitated further treatment at Johns Hopkins. Dr Meyer told Forel that Scott's alcoholic deterioration was ruining Zelda's slight improvement.

Weekly for six months the Fitzgeralds had visited Phipps for discussions with Doctors Rennie and Meyer. Scott, who found Meyer's attitude disagreeable, decided these conferences were futile. Initially, Scott said, the Phipps discussions had worked because Zelda was 'still close to the threat of force and more acutely under the spell of your [Meyer's] personality'. Once again Scott needed the authority to control her. He wanted the 'power of an ordinary nurse . . . over a child; to be able to say "If you don't do this I shall punish you."' Meyer should authorize him to tell Zelda 'when she is persistently refactory to pack her bag' and return to hospital. Scott accepted that possibly Zelda 'would have been a genius if we had never met', but felt 'In actuality she is now hurting me and through me hurting all of us'. Her Iowa schoolgirl ambitions to write made her think 'her work's success will give her some sort of divine irresponsibility backed by unlimited gold'. The gold was provided by him, while she worked 'under a greenhouse which is my money and my name and my love . . . . she . . . feels she can reach up and knock a piece of glass out of the roof at any moment, yet she is shrewd to cringe when I open the door of the greenhouse and tell her to behave or go'. Scott knew 'the picture of Zelda painting things that show a distinct talent, or Zelda trying faithfully to learn how to write is much more sympathetic and, superficially, more solid than the vision of me making myself iller with drink as I finish up the work of four years'. Eventually, he fantasized, he might 'be carried off . . . by four strong guards shrieking manicly that after all I was right and she was wrong, while Zelda is followed home by an adoring crowd in an automobile banked with flowers, and offered a vaudeville contract'. But was Zelda more worth saving than he was? As the wage-earner he must be worth more. Zelda had merely the 'frail equipment of a sick mind and a beserk determination', whereas he 'was integrated – integrated in spite of everything, in spite of the fact that I might have two counts against me to her one'.

Scott believed a point had been reached where he would have to 'resort to legal means to save myself, my child and the three of us in toto'. If Meyer didn't agree that Zelda should be told she had exhausted everyone's patience, that Meyer would not always be there as a prop for Zelda to lean on, then the Fitzgeralds would go 'out in the storm, each one for himself, and I'm afraid Scotty and I will weather it better than she'.[7]

Meyer, too, felt their conversations were futile. He pointed out that Zelda was not merely a patient as far as he was concerned and that Scott too was a potential patient, albeit an unwilling one. This opener did not

go down well with Scott. Nor did Meyer's line: 'The question of authority is simple. We have decided to relieve you of having to be the boss
... But you have the right to say when things are to be referred to us ...
That saves you from having to be boss and psychiatrist.' Meyer reassured Scott he was not trying to emasculate him; nevertheless his
'instability with the alcohol' prevented them from handing Zelda over
to Scott. For progress there must be 'a conjoint surrender of the alcohol'.[8]

Incensed that drinking had contributed to his poor image with
Zelda's doctors, Scott in an undated pencil draft raged at Meyer's
suggestion of 'a dual case'. Until recently he had the strong drink
matter in hand; he still needed no help; if Meyer checked with their
friends and business associates he would find that though a good
percentage liked Zelda better than they liked him, 'on the question
of integrity, responsibility, conscience, sense of duty, judgement,
will-power ... 95% of that group of ghosts would be as decided [in
Scott's favour] as Solomon pronouncing upon the two mothers'.
Scott acknowledged his note was his 'old plea to let me sit apon the
bench with you instead of being kept down with the potential
accomplices on the charge of criminal associations'.[9]

The Fitzgeralds and their doctors were at an impasse.

Finally, on 28 May 1933, Zelda and Scott decided to hold a discussion at La Paix with a stenographer and Dr Rennie as a moderator
to try to reach the root of their troubles. The transcript runs to 114
pages.[10] They began to talk at 2.30 on Sunday. Darkness fell before
they had finished wounding each other.

Scott aimed the first shot. At seventeen Zelda was merely boy-
crazy whereas at seventeen Scott wrote the Princeton Triangle
shows. The whole equipment of *his* life was to be a novelist. He
struggled. He sacrificed. He achieved. From age ten his life was a
professional line towards writing. This made him artistically different from Zelda. 'Her theory is that anything is possible, and that a
girl has just got to get along, and so she has the right, therefore to
destroy me completely in order to satisfy herself.'

Zelda, appalled, interrupted: 'Dr Rennie, that is completely
unfair and it is not my theory. And I have never done anything
against you, I have absolutely nothing to reproach myself with. And
as far as destroying you is concerned I have considered you first in
everything I have tried to do in my life.'

Ignoring her, Scott dismissed her writing as a few 'nice little
sketches' but as for being a novelist, 'Did she have anything to say?
No, she has not anything to say. She has certain experiences to
report, but she has nothing essentially to say.'

Defensive about his own eight-year publishing delay – swiftly reduced to 'seven years – six years' – he blamed Zelda. 'Three of those years were directly because of a sickness of hers, and two years before that . . . for which she was partly responsible, in that she wanted to be a ballet dancer; and I backed her in that.'

Zelda quietly interjected: 'You mean you were drinking constantly . . . It is just one of the reasons why I wanted to be a ballet dancer, because I had nothing else.'

Any mention of drink infuriated Scott. 'She wanted to be a ballet dancer because when we went out to Hollywood . . . I got interested in a girl . . . [who] seemed to me to be more honest and direct than Zelda, who . . . was trying to be just an average flirt, standing in my way every way she could . . . I never drank till I was 16 years old. The first time I met her I saw she was a drunkard.'

Scott accused Zelda of egotism, self-love, and feeling responsible only to herself: 'the mentality of a very cheap prostitute'.

The transcript does not read like a 'discussion' between two people trying to work out their problems but as a trial, with Zelda as defendant. Scott allotted himself the role of prosecuting lawyer, using terms like 'admission' or 'I have the documents'. Zelda in defence was forced to say: 'Dr Rennie, I will have to interrupt that', then wait for Rennie's agreement.

Zelda explained Scott had restricted her mothering role. 'He made it impossible for me to communicate with the child . . . [he refused] to take any of my judgments or opinions of people who were in charge of her . . . there was nothing in my life except my work.' Later, when Scott said, 'you know that Scotty relies on me utterly and completely,' Zelda responded: 'She has got nobody else to rely on. You alienated her affections from me years ago . . . [by] refusing to allow me authority on the job.'

Zelda, appalled at Scott's accusation that she had called out nearly a hundred doctors to administer morphine injections, pointed out he was lying. Scott said: 'I am trying to tell the truth. What you say does not happen to come in my story.' Zelda's perceptive response, 'Oh, I see, you say the truth is your story,' was lost on her husband.

The focus of their quarrel became Zelda's novel. Scott considered it 'plagiaristic, unwise in every way . . . should not have been written, because I have a certain public weight'. When Zelda asked: 'Didn't you want me to be a writer?', first he said flatly 'No', then aggressively: 'I do not care whether you were a writer or not, if you were any good . . . [but] You are a third-rate writer and a third-rate ballet dancer.'

Quietly Zelda said: 'You have told me that before.' Though Scott admitted 'You may be a good painter', he invoked Hemingway to attack her fiction: 'But as far as writing is concerned, if I told you the opinion that Ernest Hemingway had . . .' Zelda did not care a damn what Hemingway thought. By now Scott was beyond curbing his arrogant vitriol. 'If you want to write modest things, you may be able to turn out one collection of short stories . . . [but] you as compared to me is just like comparing – well, there is just not any comparison. I am a professional writer, with a huge following. I am the highest paid short story writer in the world.'

Zelda, feelings concealed, said: 'It seems to me that you are making a rather violent attack on a third-rate talent then . . . Why in the hell you are so jealous, I don't know. If I thought that about anybody, I would not care what they wrote.'

Scott's violence stemmed from his belief that because he supported Zelda, her entire life belonged to him for literary purposes.

'If you ruin me, what becomes of you?' he shouted. 'You could not sell a story . . . You could not make 50 dollars on your writing . . . You are just a useless society woman.'

'That', said Zelda, 'is what you want me to be.' But what Scott wanted was more than that. He was after complete capitulation. 'I want you to do what I say. That is exactly what I want you to do, and you know it.' Zelda did know it. 'I have done that often enough, it seems to me,' she said.

Scott fumed over the forty-thousand-word manuscript on Nijinsky and insanity she had been 'sneakingly writing' for months.[11] 'You have tried to take every sneaking advantage of me, always, working behind my back.' To Zelda it was almost laughable. 'Oh, Scott I cannot accept that. That is silly.' Scott stubbornly said he didn't care whether or not she accepted it. 'You damned well do care, it seems to me.'

Scott had indeed cared sufficiently to 'sneakingly' read parts of her new novel which he handed to Dr Rennie. 'I have not opened it or read it, except just enough to check what you are writing about . . . I don't want you . . . to write a novel about insanity, because you know there is certain psychiatric stuff in my books, and if you publish a book before me, or even at the same time, in which the subject of psychiatry is taken up, and people see "Fitzgerald", why, that is Scott Fitzgerald's wife, they read that, and that spoils the whole central point of being a novelist, which is being yourself. You pick up the crumbs I drop at the dinner table and stick them in books.'

Zelda, icily calm, retorted: 'you have picked up crumbs I have dropped for ten years, too.' But Scott was reluctant to acknowledge that Zelda had been his muse or his own writing difficulties related to her decline in that role. He needed to possess everything they had shared. Maybe experiences Zelda had used creatively would have her magic touch or give him back his.

Scott's ill-health, alcoholism and waning confidence heightened his desperation. He boasted to Rennie that Zelda did not understand concepts of human justice or morality that professional writers use. 'Hers is just automatic writing.' To Zelda he said: 'You have one power. You can ruin us. To make us or help us, you have not got that power. I am the only person in the world that can make us. And I can share with you the honor and the glory that I make, and the money.'

That, said Zelda courteously, is not what I want. She wanted to live by her writing, not least because Scott had reproached her all year for draining his resources. 'When you have that thrown in your face constantly, day after day, naturally there is some impetus to try to do something about it.' She determined to write about her asylum experiences because they had consumed her. It was what she knew about. Scott, boiling like a cauldron, shouted: 'She does not know anything about it. I have a dozen books on psychiatry.' Zelda appealed to the moderator. 'Dr Rennie, it is what I want to write. It is a very emotional novel, and that is the whole purpose of the thing, and the reason for it . . . I had to lay it there because I never had the material for laying it any place else.'

Scott could not contain himself. 'So you are taking my material, is that right?'

'Is that your material?' Zelda asked. The asylums? The madness? The terrors? Were they yours? Funny, she hadn't noticed.

'Everything we have done is mine. If we make a trip . . . and you and I go around – I am the professional novelist, and I am supporting you. That is all my material. None of it is your material.'

Rennie did not make a good job of impartiality. There could be no more secrecy on Zelda's part. No more attempts at independence. No more dabbling with psychiatric material. 'If in the future you attempt to bring out a novel, it ought to go through his [Scott's] hands.' How, he asked her, did she rate herself in comparison with Scott? 'I do not rate myself as anything compared to him, Dr Rennie, but I certainly want to write.' Rennie replied: 'If you believe that, you have got to grant him the first opportunity.' 'I have never argued about it,' said Zelda. 'That is what I cannot understand, why he is making such a stew about it. If I can write the story at all I want to write it as a story of defeat . . . [but] I cannot get the thing in print if he does not want it published.'

Scott could not stand her repeated use of the first person. 'Can't you stop your "I"s? Who are you? You are a person of six or seven different parts. Now, why don't you integrate yourself? . . . you [have] let yourself become such a mess.'

Zelda burst out: 'Listen, Scott, I am so God damned sick of your abuse that honestly I don't know what I will do . . . It is terrible. One reason why I have to do things behind your back is because you are so absolutely unjust and abusive and unfair, that to go to you and ask you anything would be like pulling a thunderbolt down on my head.'

As the terms of this marital contest became increasingly embittered, the state of Zelda's mental health became increasingly endangered. Scott suffered blows to his ego while Zelda's fragile identity was further stripped.

'What is your life now?' Scott asked her. 'Are you a dead person?' Without a pause she said: 'I suppose I am. I would rather be dead.' She reminded him that the previous fall he had said she'd ruined his life. 'You were drunk . . . you did not love me and you were sick of me and wished you could get away . . . that is the kind of life I am expected to live with you, and make whatever adjustment I can . . . It is impossible to live with you. I would rather be in an insane asylum, where you would like to put me.' She told Rennie that Scott's drinking was the root of their troubles. To Scott she said: 'You are a rotten neurasthenic about two-thirds of the time . . . I may be crazy, but . . . I certainly am sane to more people than you.' Scott refuted the accusation by saying their child didn't think Zelda was sane. Zelda was bitter. 'You said to that child, twelve years old, "Your mother is crazy, and you are bad, and I wish I was dead, and I may kill myself."' Zelda insisted she had been close to Scottie in Paris, but after Scott had described her as crazy she could not make the child do anything she wanted.

Scott was keener to battle out their literary problems than to argue about parenthood. 'I am asking her to give up the idea of writing on nervous energy . . . she should not write more than two hours a day . . . she should not take any long work . . . She should not attempt anything bigger than her strength. Who is the judge of what is bigger than her strength but me, who has to live here and see it.' Rennie suggested Zelda put aside her novel. 'Dr. Rennie, I am perfectly willing to put aside the novel, but I will not have any agreements or arrangements because I will not submit to Scott's neurasthenic condition, and be subjected to these tortures . . . I cannot live in this kind of world. And I would rather live in an insane asylum. That is my ultimatum.' Zelda claimed the right to go to an asylum because she would rather live anywhere on earth than the way she was living now. Then surprisingly, Scott revealed: 'I was told by the doctors they did not want you to go into an asylum because you were not insane . . . Sometimes I am inclined to think you do these things because you are psychotic, and other times . . . because you are just wicked. But I know that the woman that hates her child and does things behind her husband's back is either crazy or a criminal . . . Either you are sick . . . or you are responsible.'

Zelda said she was responsible. If that was so, Scott said, if she was interested in the future then there were two choices: 'here are the alternatives, either you be committed to a sanitarium, which is a scandal, a trouble and an expense, or you do differently.'

The threat of committal was real yet, only ten pages earlier in the transcript, Scott had admitted the doctors did not believe she was insane. Her first sane task, said Scott, was to be kinder to him. 'I have tried to be kind to you,' she said, 'and you have mistreated me continuously. There has not been one day since I have been in this house that you have not done something unpleasant to me.' 'I have supported you,' he repeated like a robot. 'Yes, you have supported me, and you have been reproaching me for that,' Zelda retorted in the same mechanical manner. 'Don't you think,' Scott asked, 'that a woman's place is with the man who supports her, that her duty is to the man who supports her? . . . I would like you to think of my interests. That is your primary concern, because I am the one to steer the course, and the pilot . . . I am just the captain of this ship, and as long as you watch with the captain the ship goes, and as soon as you stab the captain in the back the ship goes down, and you go down with it.'

It was an issue they would never resolve. She too needed him to be different. He should either finance her with good grace or cease to do so. Neither were options Scott could countenance. He tried another tack. Until recently, he suggested, 'Our sexual relations were very pleasant'. Ironically Zelda retorted, 'I am glad you considered them satisfactory.'

'You did not?'

'No.'

The possibility that he might have been a poor lover provoked another outburst.

'When did you cease to enjoy them? You did not act as if you did not. Oh, you are lying . . . It is just like talking to a circus clown . . . What the hell, you can't live without some kind of sexual life. At least I can not, and you can not.'

'Well, I can very well.'

She asked him if it meant anything to him that her life had been so miserable that she would rather be in an asylum. 'It does not mean a blessed thing,' he said curtly.

Shocked, she said: 'What would you like me to do?'

'I want you to stop writing fiction . . . Whether you write or not does not seem to be of any great importance.'

'I know, nothing I do seems to be of any great importance.'

'Why don't you drop it then?'

'Because I don't want to live with you. Because I want to live some place that I can be my own self.'

'Would you go to law about it?' Scott asked.

'Yes, I would . . . I am quite sure that I can not live with a person to whom neither my well-being or anything else makes the slightest bit of difference, and who has told me repeatedly that you don't care anything about me, in spite of any efforts I have made to re-establish whatever little affection there was between us before.' After a few minutes she said: 'I think honestly the only thing is to get a divorce, because there is nothing except ill-will on your part and suspicion.'

Zelda pointed out sadly that though she preferred an institutional life to one with him, they both knew she wouldn't be able to write in an asylum.

Dr Rennie intervened to suggest Scott only became aggressive when drunk. When Zelda wearily reminded him Scott was always drunk, Rennie said: 'You have to discount that when he is drunk.' Scott admitted that he was awfully sick of drinking, but 'if I ever stopped drinking, her family and herself would always think there was an acknowledgment that I was responsible for her insanity, which is not so . . . I would rather die fighting until that selfish egotism comes out of her . . . Zelda is a selfish egotist.'

Zelda suggested they put all their disagreements aside until he had finished his novel, after which they could institute a formal arrangement. Dr Rennie was pleased but surprised: 'That means a complete abnegation of yourself, until this paramount thing is over. . . . You are willing to do that?' She said she was. Rennie suggested she confine herself to a play until *Tender* was finished. But this still wasn't enough for Scott. 'It has got to be unconditional surrender on her part . . . Otherwise, I would rather go to law, because I don't trust her . . . it is necessary for her to give up the idea of writing anything . . . she must only write when under competent medical assistance I say that she can write . . . it is the only way I can ever organize my life again.'

Rennie asked Zelda which was paramount in her life: to create or to be married? There was a lapse of over a minute during which no one spoke. Then Zelda said: 'I want to write, and I am going to write; I am going to be a writer, but I am not going to do it at Scott's expense if I can possibly avoid it, so I agree not to do anything that he does not want, a complete negation of myself, until that book is out of the way, because the thing is driving me crazy . . . if he can not adjust it, and let me do what I want to do, and live with me after that, I would rather do what I want to do. I am really sorry.'

Both Scott and Rennie constantly belittled Zelda's ambitions, using the word negatively when applied to her writing, positively when applied to Scott's. His literary ambitions were reasonable or good, Zelda's insane or aggressive. Rennie told Zelda that if she could not write masterpieces then her ambitions would continue to depress her. 'I will always be unhappy, then,' she said, adding, 'I was a good deal more unhappy when I did not want to write.'

She tried to explain her motives. 'I have always felt some necessity for us to be on a more equal footing . . . because I cannot possibly . . . live in a world that is completely dependent on Scott . . . I don't want to be dependent just in every way . . . I just don't want to be dependent on him.' When Rennie inquired if she meant financial dependence Zelda, thoroughly exasperated, acknowledged that it was the great humiliation of her life that she couldn't support herself but reiterated that she needed independence in *every* way. 'I want to be able to say, when he says something that is not so, then I want to do something so good, that I can say, "That is a God damned lie" and have something to back it up.'

Scott interrupted: 'Now, we have found rock bottom.' Rennie agreed. Zelda pressed on, telling them it was better to shut herself up in an institution than take Scott's judgement on everything. She was determined to be a functioning unit with her own stamina and ability. 'I don't want to be a complementary intelligence.' Scott, who had suggested that might suit her, said the discussion had been reduced to its fundamentals. 'It is the simple issue of the wholly Amazonian and the Lesbian personality, when she expresses it that way.'

Miserably they returned to the subject of their marriage, holding painfully different versions. Zelda saw it as hollow. 'It has been nothing but a long battle ever since I can remember.' Scott refuted it. 'We were about the most envied couple in about 1921, in America.' Zelda with bitter accuracy said: 'We were awfully good showmen.' The years had brought her one certainty: 'I can not live under the conditions we are living under.'

Scott, however, had not finished with her. He had more conditions to impose. 'If you write a play, it can not be a play about psychiatry, and it can not be a play laid on the Riviera, and it can not be a play laid in Switzerland; and whatever the idea is, it will have to be submitted to me.'

What they were left with was nothing less than a battle for survival. If Scott came out as victor, Zelda *could* sink back into a delusionary state. If Zelda won back her sanity through fiction that used their joint raw material Scott, suffering delusions himself, feared his creative source would be cut off. 'I am just fighting for my life,' he confessed. 'I want my own way. I earned the right to my own way.' Zelda, too, demanded the right to her own way. '[Y]ou cannot have it without breaking me,' Scott told her '. . . I have to sacrifice myself for you and you have got to sacrifice yourself for me, and no more writing of fiction.'

'Sacrifice' was one of three key words Scott used repetitively. He had sacrificed himself financially, she should sacrifice her spirit and talent. 'Egotistic' was the second word which Scott applied detrimentally to Zelda, but productively to himself. The third word, 'logic', held the most significance. In his view Zelda was incapable of logic, she could not follow an argument. Those differences in their speech and thought patterns echoed differences in their writing. Scott's syntax and language was linear, logical, formal and shaped. Zelda's was enigmatic, associative, fragmentary and modernist. Because Scott prioritized the linear as aesthetically superior it is no surprise that he failed to see the merits in Zelda's writing.

After the line about 'sacrifice', Zelda seemed too strained to fight any longer. 'Scott, you can go on and have your way about this thing and do anything until you finish the book. And when you finish the book I think we better get a divorce, and any decision you choose to make with regard to me is all right, because I can not live on those terms, and I can not accept them.'

Despite Rennie's view that nothing more could be achieved, Zelda made two further points. After the publication of *Tender*, she would no longer countenance Scott reserving the right to dictate the entire terms and attitude towards life for them both. She would make her own 'honest attack' on life.

'I cannot give up the way I think,' she said. 'That is the one thing he wants me to give up.'

Her second point refocused their central issue. 'I have a feeling for prose, and I have something to say . . . I am perfectly sure I can write, and he knows that, too, or he would not be raising so much hell about it.'

Scott, apoplectic, had the last line: 'Well, that is all, you need not write any more.'

Several features stand out in this transcript. Scott set the frame of the discussion which made it hard for Zelda to bring up new material. Scott used a patronizing tone throughout, as if Zelda were his child: for instance, he often called Zelda's novel 'the thing' or 'that thing'. (Rennie and even Zelda followed his use of the word.) As 'things' are worthless, Scott's novel was never called a thing. Scott's own vehement display of insecurity, both extraordinary and unnecessary, illustrated how threatening Zelda's writing was to him.

Though Scott's identity was intricately tied into 'being himself', he was opposed to any suggestion that Zelda might create her own identity. That placed him in a strange position from which he railed against Zelda for being 'irresponsible' yet refused to allow her to undertake certain responsibilities.

Zelda's biggest challenge was that she had bought into the notion of Scott as professional genius and herself as gifted amateur.[12] Against that context she had to set her own needs. According to Scott's theory any unacceptable behaviour on his part could be excused in the cause of his art, which allowed him to operate a double standard.

Though Zelda resisted Scott's assumption that his earnings gave him rights of control over her health and her writing, at no point did Rennie support her, or even remain neutral. Rennie's acquiescence to Scott's view that all the psychiatric material belonged to him was not merely outrageous in literary terms but could have been dangerous to Zelda, his patient. Though Rennie and Meyer agreed that Scott's alcoholism endangered Zelda's health, when she called into question not only his obsessional drinking but *his* sanity, again she received no medical backing.

Throughout the conference, both Scott and Rennie saw Zelda as competing artistically with Scott. Zelda believed she was doing something for herself. To some extent their disagreement lay in prevailing cultural notions that married women doing something artistic for themselves might be seen as infringing on male-owned territory.

What were the consequences of this three-way conference?

For the first time Scott seriously considered divorce. He consulted a Baltimore lawyer, his former Princeton friend Edgar Allan Poe Jnr.[13] Poe assured him that if he resided in Nevada state for six weeks he could speedily gain a divorce. Scott decided against it and continued to live on the battlefield that had become their marital terrain.[14]

Zelda instigated something more dramatic. A few days after the conference, she systematically burnt her old clothes in an upstairs fireplace at La Paix.[15] While she returned to her typewriter to revise *Scandalabra* (finally to be produced locally the following week), the fire spread swiftly through the house. Several top-floor rooms were ruined. Many of Scott's valuable books and manuscripts were damaged, many of Zelda's paintings were destroyed. The local newspaper, unaware of the conflict preceding the fire, ran a romantic story. 'Mr Fitzgerald dashed to save his wife's manuscripts and paintings, while her first thought was for his manuscript. After leading their eleven year old daughter, Frances, to safety, the couple carried out several valuable pieces of furniture.' Scott discreetly told reporters faulty wiring had short-circuited the system and caused the 'accident'. News photographs show the Fitzgeralds on the lawn surrounded by books and furniture saved from the blaze, looking brave.[16]

It was a good story. A clever photo. As Zelda had pointed out, they were good showmen. But La Paix had lost its charm. Scott told Andrew Turnbull they were moving into Baltimore as 'Zelda needed to be near her art school'.[17] The truth was, neither of them wished to stay longer in a house with burnt and gloomy edges. By November their residence would be a townhouse at 1307 Park Avenue.

Zelda's hopes were pinned to the Baltimore production of *Scandalabra* from 26 June to 1 July by the Vagabond Junior Players, and on the acting of Zack Maccubbin playing the hero Andrew Messogony, whose name was Zelda's play on the words misogyny and misogamy.[18] The farce was a comic inversion of *The Beautiful and Damned*. In Scott's novel, Grandfather Patch refuses to will his wealth to his nephew Anthony and his wife Gloria because they are dissipated and extravagant. In Zelda's play, her hero will inherit his uncle's millions so long as he lives a life of wicked debauchery. The idea was zany, some lines were witty, but the sets, some designed by Zelda, were considerably more exciting than the play, whose exhausting length and hectic style reflected the current turbulence of their marriage and of Zelda's mind.[19]

Zelda's determination not to let Scott view her work meant he did not see it until the dress rehearsal, which ran from 8.15 p.m. till 1.00 a.m. Obviously the play could not open in that state at that length. Scott assembled the cast, worked them through the night, drastically revised and cut the script – to no avail. It lacked action, said some reviewers. Highly confusing, muttered others. 'Much credit' went to the director, Mrs Nicholas Penniman. No credit went to the playwright.[20]

On 31 July Minnie Sayre wrote to Zelda that her beloved brother Anthony, who had recently lost his job and was already in debt, was desperately ill with depression. Edith, Anthony's young wife, always deemed 'unsuitable' by the Sayres, took him to the coast near Charleston, but neither this nor the nerve specialist in Asheville who advised rest and no visitors helped.[21] Minnie told Zelda instability was the curse of their family's bloodline. She felt the family *should* visit, so she and their cousin Dr Chilton Thorington, who knew Anthony's 'constitution better than strange doctors', were going to North Carolina.[22] Anthony begged Thorington to let him go to Johns Hopkins, where Zelda was still an outpatient. But in August he was hospitalized in Mobile where a nerve specialist, Dr Eugene Bondurant, Judge Sayre's friend, treated him for toxic poisoning caused by bile and malaria, but did not treat his depression.[23] Edith, sick with strain herself, suddenly gave up on Anthony, and went to Rome to stay with her mother.[24] Thorington wrote to Scott that Anthony's condition had been diagnosed as 'neuro-psychosis – possibly familial'. Anthony's symptoms were of the 'melancholic type, with obsessions of suicidal and homicidal inclinations, however, I do not believe he would actually do acts of violence'.[25] The doctor was wrong. Anthony, suffering from recurrent nightmares of killing his mother, decided to kill himself. In an indisputable act of violence he leapt out of a hospital window to his death. The Sayres concealed most of the horrific facts about his suicide from the Fitzgeralds.[26]

Zelda, dazed with miserable disbelief, threw herself into her painting. In October she exhibited a strange and powerful still life at the Independent Artists Exhibition at Baltimore's Museum of

Art.[27] The oil, *Tiger Lilies*, is now missing, but a black and white photograph still exists. The way in which the brushstrokes are ruled by a massive emotional energy rather than by detached construction resembles Van Gogh's *Four Cut Sunflowers*. Zelda deliberately chose a peaceful plant then painted it like a creature ready to devour anyone foolish enough to pick it. Newspaper photographers took photos of Zelda at her easel.

Malcolm Cowley visited Zelda's studio. He remembered those paintings years later: 'They had freshness, imagination, rhythm, and a rather grotesque vigor, but they were flawed . . . by the lack of proportion and craftsmanship.' Cowley was shocked at Zelda's appearance. Deep lines above her mouth fell into unhappy shapes. Her face was emaciated and twitched as she spoke, reflecting her recent suffering.[28]

Within a few months she had experienced three intense blows: emotional destruction during the conference, the failure of *Scandalabra*, and now her beloved brother's death. She held on courageously, but would be unable to sustain further strain. At her side Scott was preparing *Tender Is The Night* for its January serialization in *Scribner's Magazine*. He had sold *Scribner's* the serial rights for $10,000 (for four instalments, January to April 1934). Zelda knew the heroine was largely based on herself. She knew the source for Nicole Diver's behaviour was what Scott saw as her own insanity. But she had no idea of the further shock concealed in Scott's fiction.

CHAPTER 22

Scott was staking everything on *Tender Is The Night*. That he might be staking Zelda's well-being was probably not part of his calculations. His 1933 income of $12,000 was his lowest since the start of his career. Existing on borrowed money, he needed a commercial success.[1]

By November 1933, having corrected the January/February serialization proofs, he took Zelda to Bermuda where it rained continuously. Scott caught pleurisy but Zelda, fresh from Baltimore's Fine Art School, sat on the rain-soaked beach sketching shipyard workers, ballerinas, and women by a banyan tree, using new figurative techniques.

Though she and Scott exhumed their old affection, a sepulchral sadness persisted. 'For years we had wanted to go to Bermuda,' Zelda wrote wistfully in an *Esquire* article. 'We went. The Elbow Beach hotel was full of honeymooners, who scintillated so persistently in each other's eyes that we cynically moved.' Perhaps she had a premonition, for she wrote: 'Maybe this would be the last trip for a long while.'[2]

On their return to Baltimore the galleys of *Tender* arrived, followed by the first two serialized instalments. Zelda read them, deeply shocked. She collapsed. On 12 February 1934 she re-entered Phipps Clinic for the start of her third breakdown. It would last until 1940.

As a measure of self-protection Scott informed John Palmer, Clothilde's husband, 'merely as a matter of record and not with any idea of alarming any member of Zelda's family'. Zelda had suffered a 'slight relapse', he assured them. Scott asked John not to tell Minnie, Marjorie or even Clothilde as it would take five years off Minnie's life, for she would immediately link Zelda's collapse to Anthony's troubles.[3]

Scott's optimism was misplaced. Far from 'slight', Zelda's relapse was serious. Initially under constant observation for fear of suicide,

she lost a further 15 lb, looked malnourished, was given daily sedatives and restricted to total bedrest, and silently eluded medical
ministrations.

Mayfield believed that reading the first half of Scott's novel
ripped open the wound inflicted by the synopsis Zelda had scanned
in Florida. Certainly it was the first time Zelda had seen her
husband's merciless use of her most despairing hospital letters.
Now everyone could read her profoundly private thoughts. Scott
did not merely paraphrase Zelda's anguished epistles, he efficiently
pasted her phrases together with his stylish prose glue.

Zelda, attempting grim humour, had written to Scott: 'The farcicle element of this situation is too apparent for even a person as
hopeless and debilitated as I am.' Scott rewrote it for *Tender*: 'it
seems to me if this farcicle situation is apparent to one as sick as me
it should be apparent to you.'[4] After months with no progress and
little hope, Zelda had written to Scott: 'I will more than gladly
welcome any alienist you may suggest.' Scott hardly changed this:
'I would gladly welcome any alienist you might suggest.'[5] Zelda
admitted to Scott she was 'completely humiliated and broken',
Nicole, scripted by Scott, was also 'completely broken and humiliated'.[6]

Zelda's first encounter with Scott's explosive Dr Diver material
disturbed her even more. Initially Nicole Diver has Sara Murphy's
lyrical glow, but as the novel progresses and Scott draws on Zelda,
we learn that as a child Nicole was raped by her father.

Scott's sketch for Nicole, the rich mental patient, stated that the
rape occurred at fifteen

> under peculiar circumstances . . . She collapses, goes to the clinic and
> there at sixteen meets the young doctor hero who is ten years older. Only
> her transference to him saves her – when it is not working she reverts to
> homicidal mania and tries to kill men. She is an innocent, widely read
> but with no experience and no orientation except that he supplies her.
> Portrait of Zelda – that is, a part of Zelda.[7]

Scott 'authenticated' his novel by using direct quotes from
Bleuler's diagnosis of Zelda.[8] Moreover, under the heading
'Classification of the Material on Sickness', he included reports from
Malmaison, Valmont and Prangins.[9]

Zelda, in bed at Phipps, admitted she was 'a little upset about it
[*Tender*]', then said bitterly: 'What made me mad was he made the
girl so awful and kept on reiterating how she had ruined his life and

I couldn't help identifying myself with her because she had so many of my experiences.' Loyally she insisted any author had the 'right to interpret . . . it really doesn't matter'. Then, unable to deal with the material, she began to cry: 'It was a chronological distortion . . . I don't think it's true – I don't think it's really what happened.'[10] Despite her distress she never referred directly to the effect on her of the fictionalized father-daughter rape, for which there is *no* biographical evidence, merely a series of rumours.'[11] Her eerie passivity over this character violation may have been related to her constant sedation. Zelda was of course aware that Scott knew about the childhood sexual violence on which she based her fictionalized abuse of Janno by the Magnetic Twins in *Caesar's Things*.

Whether Scott borrowed and extended a known event in childhood or later, or whether he invented Nicole's traumatic rape, he must have been aware it would cause Zelda intense pain. Although he knew he risked increasing Zelda's instability he did not see himself as heartless. He always cared for her, even though care had largely degenerated into financing her hospitalization. He kept his novel from her for as long as possible, he warned her against projecting too much of herself into it. He saw the book as melancholy, even haunted, but he saw it also as something they could put behind them before they moved on.[12] But at Phipps Zelda was not moving anywhere. Sobbing uncontrollably, she told the nurses: 'I can't get on with my husband and I can't live away from him – materially impossible . . . I'm so tired of compromises. Shaving off one part of oneself after another until there is nothing left.'[13]

She behaved as if she was indeed invisible. Her silences grew palpable. She shivered in the heat, she laughed when most sad, she kept her distance from everyone, including Scottie.

> She is about as far away from me as anyone can be . . . She's just like her father, she's a cerebral type . . . she rather looks down on me . . . I've never interfered [in her education] . . . because I realized that eventually Scott and I would have to separate and she is his child . . . It would just be the undoing of him to take her away from him.[14]

Still she dwelt on separation. Mayfield, who understood this, said: 'many people who know the circumstances under which Scott labored over it [*Tender*] found that its chief flaw lay in the fact that it was written with one eye on the Book-of-the-Month Club and the other on the divorce court.' Sara, invariably Zelda's partisan, felt that either the writing stood as a psychological defence should

Zelda make good her threat of divorce, or the offensive passages were written as self-justification.[15] It is possible that Scott wrote the most wounding parts in retaliation for those sections in *Save Me The Waltz* which had disturbed him, but it is more probable artistically that Diver, the psychiatrist-hero, *had* to deal with explosive material. Scott needed a spoiled priest, a man replacing idealism and talent with drink and dissipation. As both husband and psychiatrist Dick fails to maintain professional perspective. By sharing Nicole's family's wealth, his commitment to medicine is finally eroded. When Nicole recovers her sanity and independence and leaves him for Tommy Barban, a French/American soldier of fortune, Dick dwindles into a corrupted small-town doctor.[16]

Ironically, despite the authentic psychiatric source material, Edmund Wilson, who read the serialization, thought that though Scott had achieved something 'real' in his protagonists' marital relationship, he had failed to establish Diver's professional credibility.[17] Scott himself acknowledged he must be 'careful not to reveal basic ignorance of psychiatric and medical training yet not [be] glib'.[18] Diver, of course, plays the role Scott had tried to play: fellow-psychiatrist and husband. In *Tender*, Scott tried to resolve in literary terms the issues remaining unresolved in his life.

The earliest reactions came from kind friends who had read either the serialization or an inscribed pre-publication copy. Bishop assured him: 'The first installment of the novel confirms what I have long thought, that your gifts as a novelist surpass those of any of us.'[19] Robert Benchley said: 'I would have given my two expensivly-filled [*sic*] eye-teeth to have written just one page of the book . . . it is a beautiful piece of work, not only technically, but emotionally.'[20] Tom Wolfe offered cautious praise: 'It seems to me you've gone deeper in this book than in anything you ever wrote,'[21] while Archie MacLeish threw caution away: 'Great God Scott you can write. You can write better than ever. You are a fine writer. Believe it. Believe it – not me.'[22] Scott needed to believe this in the light of later criticisms.

Zelda, feeling better at Phipps, demanded to be released. As she was not committed, theoretically she could leave when she wished, but in practice could not depart without money. Scott, busy with his galleys, was not prepared to cope with a sick wife. He transferred Zelda to Craig House, Beacon, where she stayed from 8 March to 19 May. In upstate New York, two hours by train from Manhattan, on the Hudson River, the sanatorium was recommended by Forel, who was a friend of the director, Dr Clarence Slocum.[23] The resort-like grandeur of Prangins was repeated in a golf course, tennis courts, bowling green, two swimming pools, bridge, backgammon and table-tennis games rooms. An emphasis on patients' freedom, no locks and keys, and a private nurse for each patient meant attendant heavy costs of more than $750 a month. Scott, already $12,000 in debt, plunged still further.

Initially Zelda treated Craig as a country club. She dug holes in golf greens, almost uprooted a gigantic oak with what used to be a chip-shot, worked on a piece for the *New Yorker* about hotels they had visited[24] and played bridge.

Her surroundings had charm: 'The ground is shiverring with snow-drops and gentians . . . I wish you could [rest] for a while in the cool apple-green of my room. The curtains are like those in John Bishop's poem to Elspeth and beyond the lawn never ends . . . we walk . . . [to] where tumbling villages prop themselves on the beams of the afternoon sun. We have tea, and many such functions to fulfill.' She added irritably: '*Please* send the book.'[25]

The costs distressed her: 'You can imagine how I feel sitting here in this lovely place when I realize the worry and effort it is costing you . . . I feel very guilty: as if maybe I could have conformed more satisfactorily at home.'

Then suddenly her money and most activities were restricted.

On 12 March Scott had written to Slocum that Zelda had absolutely no sense of money, so he felt that every extra expense should be curtailed. Scott told Slocum that Zelda's artistic materials alone came to about $50 a month without her typing costs. With her basic fees Scott estimated this at four-fifths of the household income. Slocum agreed to limit Zelda's expenses, but reported that after he'd read aloud to her Scott's letter Zelda had a 'hysterical outbreak'.[27]

Scott informed Slocum that the 'nervous strain' of creative work meant Zelda's writing must be restricted. Zelda, he said, had an 'extraordinary talent' for metaphor and simile, was markedly successful with short character studies, might contribute regularly to the *New Yorker*, but her nervous system could not stand criticism. Slocum agreed Zelda was 'doing too much in her literary efforts'. He assured Scott he had made her promise after she had finished her latest story 'to desist until we feel that it is wise for her to re-enter this field again'.[27]

Zelda countered with another request: 'Please ask Mrs Owens to rush my paints. I want them very badly. It's such expensive equipment, I don't want to buy another.' She needed pastels to try sketching covers for the *Post*. Would Scott retrieve her oil paints and the Dante, still at Phipps?[28] When Slocum, deciding her flower paintings were 'recreational', relented, Zelda designed a floral watercolour Easter card with 'Easter Greetings Scott and Zelda

Fitzgerald' looped inside. But she no longer felt part of the contented couple who sent friends home-made cards.

Later that March Slocum told Scott that though 'prohibiting Mrs Fitzgerald's writing has been helpful', it was a struggle getting Zelda to breakfast in bed, or rest after her 11 a.m. massage. She was determined 'to be as active as possible in her work'.

Slocum gave permission for Scottie to spend a day and night with Zelda before going with Scott to the Adirondacks for Easter.[29] 'She will like it here with the pool and the tennis,' Zelda wrote excitedly to Scott, 'and I will be awfully glad to have her . . . I wish I were well, and you could get something more out of life for all you put into it than bills, and more bills.' It was unfair he 'should have to shoulder the heavy debts necessary to reconstitute a member of a disintigrated family'.[30]

To cheer up Zelda and raise some funds, Scott became enthusiastic about arranging an exhibition of her paintings. Gallery owner Cary Ross, whom the Fitzgeralds had met in Europe, had been trying for two years to find a New York dealer to exhibit Zelda's paintings. Ross had asked the photographer-art dealer Alfred Steiglitz to show Zelda's drawings to his wife, Georgia O'Keeffe, but 'except for Picasso, Marin and herself, I think she is not interested in any living artists,' Ross wrote disappointedly to Scott.[31] So Ross decided to exhibit Zelda's work at his own gallery at 525 East 86th Street.

Though ill, Zelda painted assiduously. 'Please ask Mrs Owens to hurry with my paints. There are so many winter trees exhibiting irresistible intricacies . . . and there are gracious expanses of snow and the brooding quality of a gray and heavy sky, all of which makes me want terribly to paint,' she wrote Scott. 'I have a little room to paint in with a window higher than my head . . . [I] feel like Faust in his den.'[32]

Scott, who routinely agonized over his own art in similar terms, felt when Zelda did so she was obsessional. They quarrelled. Was it out of fear for herself or to offer him reassurance that she wrote:

Dear: I am not trying to make myself into a great artist or a great anything. Though you persist in thinking that an exaggerated ambition is the fundamental cause of my collapse . . . I cannot agree with you . . . I do the things I can do and that interest me and if you'd like me to give up everything I like to do I will do so willingly if it will advance matters any. I . . . do not like existing entirely at other peoples expense . . . If you feel that it is an imposition on Cary to have the exhibition, the pictures can wait. I believe in them and in Emerson's theory about good-workman-ship. If they are good, they will come to light some day.[33]

But they quarrelled again when Scott took over all the exhibition arrangements. Utterly frustrated, Zelda went to bed and refused to get up.[34] Ross, however, ensured that Zelda's work came to light from 29 March to 30 April 1934.

The exhibition ran jointly with a photographic collection by Marion Hines.[35] There was a smaller supplementary show at the Algonquin Hotel. The exhibition brochure, entitled *Parfois La Folie Est La Sagesse* (Sometimes Madness is Wisdom),[36] emphasized Zelda's knowledge of the Diaghilev tradition.

Scott asked Slocum's permission for a nurse to take Zelda to New York to 'hand her over to me'.[37] On opening day Perkins gave a luncheon for Zelda. Afterwards she went to the Georgia O'Keeffe exhibition. 'They . . . excited me so that I felt quite sick afterwards. I loved the rhythmic white trees winding in visceral choreography about the deeper green ones, and I loved the voluptuous columnar tree trunk with a very pathetic blue flame-shaped flower growing arbitrarily beneath it. And there was a swell rhythmic abstraction done in blue and green and heart-breaking aspiration . . . She is the most moving and comprehensible painter I've ever seen.' In another article she recalled: 'We saw Georgia O'Keeffe's pictures and it was a deep emotional experience to abandon oneself to that majestic aspiration so adequately fitted into eloquent abstract forms.'[38]

O'Keeffe had significantly influenced Zelda's flower paintings for four years. In Zelda's recent *Untitled* dogwood blossoms, the compositional arrangement of two single flowers isolated from their surroundings was washed over with O'Keeffe's atmospheric water-colour.[39] Both artists magnified single flowers from several angles to emphasize organic curves, so there exists a relationship between Zelda's watercolour *Antheriums* and O'Keeffe's 1928 *Calla Lilies with Red Anemone*. Zelda employed O'Keeffe's swaying impasto brush-strokes for her *White Anemones*, *Red Poppies* and *White Roses*, all shown at Ross's exhibition.[40]

Zelda's exhibition brochure listed thirteen paintings and fifteen drawings, but four additional paintings and three additional drawings were included.[41]

Zelda sat silently watching her good friends the Murphys, Max Perkins, Dorothy Parker, H. L. Mencken, Dos Passos, Edmund Wilson, Malcolm Cowley and Gilbert Seldes, who comprised many of the purchasers. Scott had also invited Dr Rennie and Dr Squires.

Ross himself bought two oils, *Laurel* ($150) and *Russian Stable* ($175), and a drawing, *Diving Platform* ($15), of a swimmer on a ladder.[42] Mencken purchased two drawings for Sara Haardt, sadly again in hospital. Mabel Dodge Luhan bought the drawing *Red Death* for her New Mexico collection.[43] Gilbert Seldes had already purchased two paintings but had promised Scott to put them on exhibition any time Zelda or Scott requested it during the next twenty years.[44]

Sara Murphy paid $200 for *Chinese Theater*, which Gerald said depicted 'monstrous, hideous men, all red with swollen intertwining legs. They were obscene . . . figures out of a nightmare, monstrous and morbid.'[45] *Time* magazine more soberly described it as 'a gnarled mass of acrobats'. Zelda, aware the oil was stylistically opposed to Gerald's own cool precision, later wrote to Scott: 'I am going to paint a picture for the Murphy's . . . as those acrobats seem somehow, singularly inappropriate to them and I would like them to have one they liked . . . I don't see why they would like that Buddhistic suspension of mass and form and I will try to paint some mood that their garden has conveyed.'[46]

Honoria Murphy said, 'There was no Zelda painting in our house. We would certainly have preserved it. It would have been just like my father Gerald to have left it behind in the gallery.'[47] More probably Zelda retrieved it after her decision to paint them a substitute.

Apart from Sara's painting most prices were pitifully low. Scott's friends from St Paul, Frances and Tom Daniels,[48] paid only $15 for the drawing *La Nature*, polo player Tommy Hitchcock acquired the drawing *Au Claire de la Lune* and Muriel Draper the *Red Devil* drawing for the same low price; New Yorker Adele Lovett bought the drawing *Ferns* for $16.25, while Max Perkins's wife paid $32.50 for two drawings, *The Plaid Shirt* and *Spring in the Country*, a verdant scene geometrically laced with telephone wires. Scott *gave away* several of Zelda's pictures, including the drawing *Two Figures* to Dick and Alice Myers.[49]

Dorothy Parker, who found Zelda's work tortured, loyally bought two watercolour drawings for a mere $30. Feeling sorry for Zelda, she insisted on paying an extra $5 for the frames. *Etude Arabesque* was a self-portrait of Zelda as a ballerina, *The Cornet Player* a portrait of Scott.[50] '[S]he had talent,' Parker recalled. 'Arabesque . . . [had] a striking resemblance to Zelda. I bought the portrait of Scott . . . because I thought it the best she did. But I couldn't have stood having them hang in the house. There was that blood red color she used and the painful, miserable quality of emotion behind the paintings.'[51] Ironically, Parker's portrait of Scott was destroyed in a fire.

John Biggs was struck by a second portrait of Scott wearing a crown of thorns. 'Yes, it was good. The eyelashes were feathers; it was astonishing really – looked like him, and then those mad, lovely, long feathery eyelashes.' Biggs found the eyes arresting. 'Very cold blue eyes – almost green – they were as cold as the Irish Sea.'[52]

James Thurber, who accidentally met Scott in a bar, said later *Scott in Thorns* was 'a sharp, warm, ironic study of her husband's handsome and sensitive profile'. The two men drank till 3 a.m., then Scott asked Thurber if he knew a good girl they could call. Scott passed the rest of the night talking to an actress Thurber knew, showering her with dozens of Zelda's catalogues. Thurber recalled that year as one when 'Fitzgerald made several pathetically futile attempts to interest himself in other women, in an effort to survive the mental and emotional strain of Zelda's recurring psychotic states.'[53]

One of those women was Dorothy Parker, with whom Scott had a brief involvement, he out of despair, she out of compassion. Parker, who had herself attempted suicide over a broken affair, felt she understood both Scott's and Zelda's confused miseries.[54]

Despite high-profile reviews Zelda felt critics did not take her work seriously. *Time* magazine understood her intentions in *Football*: 'an impression of a Dartmouth football game [which] made the stadium look like portals of a theatre, the players like dancers', but apart from a brief discussion of the paintings both it and the *New York Post* concentrated on Zelda as former Jazz Age Priestess and Famous Writer's Wife. *Time* saw the show as 'the work of a brilliant introvert . . . vividly painted, intensely rhythmic', but headed the review 'Work of a Wife' and concluded that Zelda Fitzgerald hoped her pictures would gratify her great ambition – to earn her own living.[55]

The *New York Post*'s 'Jazz Age Priestess Brings Forth Paintings' was more interested in Zelda's response to Georgia O'Keeffe's exhibition and her relationship with Scott. Having taken the words right out of Scott's mouth with her novel last year, they wrote, this year 'she trumps all his aces' with her art.[56]

Scott reported to Slocum that Zelda's exhibition was a weird event. At times there were crowds of visitors yet there were lengthy spells when Zelda and the curator waited quite alone for someone to walk in. Scott said he could not speculate over Zelda's feelings but she seemed to him to have retreated inwards.

When Zelda returned to Craig House, Scott remained at the Algonquin for the publication of *Tender*.[57] On Easter Day, 1 April, Zelda recalled their parting:

> I was so sorry to see you so sad when you said good-bye and I wish the time would come when you could be free to rest for a little while . . . I watch the book section for the first opinions on Tender Is The Night. You forgot to send me a copy. Please do. Or shall I order it from Scribners? . . . You and Cary were awfully kind about the pictures – and I hope it hasn't cost too much.[58]

On 8 April, four days before *Tender*'s publication, Scott suggested to Slocum that Zelda again be 're-educated', with the most 'desirable aims' placed in their proper relation to each other. As this relied on the adult's 'proper respect for her mentor' Scott was unsure whether they would succeed with his wife. Slocum replied that despite the hospital's efforts Zelda still had 'a distinct craving to be productive', therefore was not up to re-education. He would keep prescribing rest and 'eliminate a certain amount of her intellectual efforts'.[59]

Zelda's agitation about not receiving a copy of *Tender* increased: 'Since you have not sent me a copy of the book, I have not bought one.' But she *had* acquired one. 'I watch the papers and no reviews. I can hardly wait to know what the critics will say of those "excursions into the frontiers of a *social* consciousness". No matter what they say, it's exquisite prose and a trip into unexploited fields so far as the material is concerned.' In another generous letter she said: 'I certainly hope the sales move as smoothly as the prose. The beginning is lyric and breath-taking and the end is tragic and ominous and it is a good book. So don't mind if there are critics who have sought solace in gin rather than poetry and who like reading matter that can be discussed between the yapping of Dorothy Parker's dog.'[60]

Though Scott had been prepared to sacrifice everyone to achieve a piece of flawless fiction, the later critics saw it as flawed. It failed to achieve a single strong effect. It failed to make clear the causes of Diver's destruction. Some thought the story rambled, others that the style became commonplace, many felt the central characters had shifting identities. Scott phoned Zelda in a state of anxiety. She responded at once in shaky handwriting. 'Dearest: You sounded so all-in over the telephone. Please *dont* – Your book is a beautiful and moving story of a man's disillusionment and its relative values against the social back-ground in which he counts most.'[61]

But more biting criticism focused on *Tender'*s lack of social-political relevance. To achieve a background in which the leisure class at play on the Riviera was at its most brilliant, Scott drew on the Murphys' lifestyle. But his ambivalence towards that class evoked censure. From Malcolm Cowley came this line: 'It is as if he had a double personality. Part of him is a guest at the ball given by the people in the big house; part of him has been a little boy peeping in through the window and being thrilled by the music and beautifully dressed women.'[62] Philip Rahv's review in the *Daily Worker* was harsher. *Tender* was a 'fearful indictment of the moneyed aristocracy' which Fitzgerald himself, taken in by its false glamour, had not quite recognized.[63]

The Murphys, who represented the Divers' dazzling side before their tragic fall, were negative in their response. Nor did they appreciate the dedication: 'To Gerald and Sara Many Fêtes'. Sara was outraged about Scott's portrayal. 'I hated the book when I first read it,' she said, 'and even more on rereading. I reject categorically any resemblance to ourselves or to anyone we know.'[64]

More than twenty-five years later Sara was still furious. Was she angry because Scott had misread their characters and lives, or was it because he touched on truths she did not want aired? There were obvious visual parallels between the Divers and the Murphys. Dick, moving 'gravely about with a rake, ostensibly removing gravel' from their strip of beach; Nicole with 'her bathing suit . . . pulled off her shoulders . . . set off by a string of creamy pearls': these are precise verbal photographs of Gerald and Sara. The stimulating conversations in the Divers' exquisite villa probably took place in Villa America. It was more likely that what upset Sara was Nicole's decision to leave Dick for an adventurer like Ernest Hemingway, whom Sara adored, to whom Sara was sexually attracted, but for whom she would never have left Gerald. In the light of Gerald's later determination to give up painting for ever, Dick's renunciation of his family and his life's work would have been equally frightening.[65]

Sara wrote bitterly to Scott that 'consideration for other people's feelings, opinions or even time is *completely* left out of your make-up – I have always told you you haven't the faintest idea what anybody but yourself is like.' In that same irritated letter she spoke warmly about Zelda. 'Please don't think that Zelda's condition is not very near to our hearts – and that all your misfortunes are not, in part, ours too.'[66]

Scott told Gerald the book 'was inspired by Sara and you, and the way I feel about you both and the way you live, and the last part of it is Zelda and me because you and Sara are the same people as Zelda and me.' Nothing could have been further from the truth, as Gerald pointed out. Scott 'never did really understand our life'.[67]

Yet in December 1935, when Gerald's life had been torn apart, he changed his mind. 'I know now that what you said in *Tender Is The Night* is true. Only the invented part of our life – the unreal part – has had any scheme any beauty. Life itself has stepped in now and blundered, scarred and destroyed.'[68]

Scott was even more anxious about Hemingway's response. A month after publication Scott wrote fretfully: 'Did you like the book? For God's sake drop me a line and tell me one way or another. You can't hurt my feelings. I just want to get a few intelligent slants at it to get some of the reviewers jargon out of my head.'[69] Ernest had already told Max he disapproved of *Tender* because the Divers acted in ways the Murphys never would. Ernest said that Scott could not invent real characters because he knew very little about people: 'he has so lousy much talent and . . . has destroyed himself and destroyed Zelda, though never as much as she has tried to destroy him.'[70] Hemingway finally sent Scott a three-page letter assuring him the writing was brilliant but the distortion of the Murphys had invalidated the novel: 'faked case histories' and 'silly compromises' as well as Scott's use of the Murphys for the Divers' glamour, and of himself and Zelda for the traumatized aspects, violated the book's integrity.

Hemingway scolded him: ignore your emotional traumas. You're not a drama queen. You, like me, are just a writer. What writers do is write. You lack focus. An encouraging wife could have helped your self-discipline. Instead you chose Zelda: a jealous, competitive, destructive woman.[71]

A week before *Tender* appeared the Menckens returned from a Mediterranean cruise. Sara, feverish with an infection she had picked up in Algeria, read *Tender* in hospital. She admired its prose but told Sara Mayfield how angry she was on behalf of Zelda and the Sayres.

Scott, meanwhile, leant on Mencken for consolation. On 26 April Mencken told him not to fret over 'a few silly reviews . . . The quality of book reviewing in the American newspapers is really appalling. Reviews are printed by imbeciles that know nothing about the process of writing and hence miss the author's intentions completely. I think your scheme is a capital one, and that you have carried it out very effectively . . . Please remember me to Zelda. I surely hope that she is making good progress.'[72]

But she was not.

By May 1934 her condition had become critical. She was not responding to medication, she was not responding to the doctors. Though Scott told Mencken that Zelda was 'katatonic', the only supporting evidence is her submission to the medical profession's treatment of her. Occasionally she was hysterical, and often despairing about her hospital costs. 'I cannot see why I should sit in luxury when you are having such a struggle. Since there seems to be no way I can hasten my recovery, maybe it would be wise to try a cheaper place . . . I will not be discouraged by any such change you might make and, of cource, will do the best I can, anywhere.' The following month she wrote: 'I do not see how you can reasonably expect me to go on unworriedly spending god-knows-how-much-a-day when we haven't got it to spend . . .'[73]

On her better days she had been trying to improve their finances by writing two autobiographical articles for *Esquire*, 'Show Mr and Mrs F. to Number–', published May-June, and 'Auction – Model 1934', published July.

Those essays were a farewell to her life with Scott. 'Show Mr and Mrs F. –' was a nostalgic travelogue of hotel rooms they had shared from 1920 until Bermuda in 1933.

Scott edited 'Show Mr and Mrs F. –'. His most striking amendment was to cut Zelda's use of 'I', changing every first person pronoun to 'we'. This not only weakened her style but also recalled his angry interjection in their discussion with Rennie: 'Can't you stop your "I"s'? Who are you?'

Scott did no editorial work on 'Auction – Model 1934', Zelda's inventory of the few possessions they had collected over those years to be sold at a mock auction. Most objects were broken, dirty, flawed, useless. Only the memories were intact and precious. The Fitzgeralds open their packing cases, look over their heirlooms, and ultimately decide that 'the tangible remnant of the four hundred thousand we made from hard words and spent with easy ones' should be kept in their attic.[74]

Both articles again, though written by Zelda, were published under joint names.

On 19 May Scott transferred Zelda to Sheppard and Enoch Pratt, a cheaper hospital in Baltimore, where she would spend the next two years.[75] The primary reason was not medical but financial. Although his novel had been on the *Publishers Weekly* April and May bestseller lists, Scott could no longer afford Craig House fees.

Zelda wrote in a shaky hand to console him: 'D.O. you know that I do not feel as you do about state institutions – . . . many excellent doctors did their early training there. You will have to conceal as much of this from Scottie as you can, anyway. So, in the words of Ernest Hemmingway, <u>save yourself</u> . . . I am so glad your book is on the list of best sellers . . . Devotedly Zelda.'

She had already assured him: 'Ill as I am, one place is not very different from another . . . I would appreciate your making whatever adjustments would render your life less difficult.'[76]

However, this place was tragically different from Craig, or Phipps, or Prangins.

Mayfield described her first visit: 'Zelda had a horror of the place – a sinister-looking sanitarium with enclosed passageways joining its buildings, barred windows, locked doors, and dismal rooms that appeared to have been done by a decorator with a depressive psychosis.'

Zelda's first shock was her reception. There was a rough search of her body. Her money, make-up and cigarettes were confiscated. She told Sara that attendants callously took away her clothes then doused her in a disinfectant bath. She realized immediately her hopeless situation: 'locked in a bare ward', Sara recalled, 'with no means of communicating with her family and friends – literally buried alive in a strange place – [it] was too much for her. This time there was no doubt about it; she had broken down – or, perhaps, more accurately, after four years between the upper and nether millstones, she had been ground down.'[77]

In addition to a balanced diet and much sleep her new physician, Dr Chapman, tried out new drug therapies. Zelda received morphine for sedation, stramonium for mania, digitalis for depression and tranquillizers including the first synthetic sedative, chloral hydrate, and the new discovery, sodium amytal. During her incarceration at Sheppard Pratt the hospital experimented with insulin shocks and Metrazol convulsive treatment, which produced shocks akin to epilepsy seizures. Dr Oscar Schwoerer, hired to oversee this process, had trained in the use of insulin coma therapy with Manfred Sakel whose most noteworthy patient was the dancer Nijinsky. Twice a week patients – including Zelda – were injected with a 10 per cent aqueous solution of Metrazol. Within seconds a thirty- to sixty-second violent seizure would follow. Some patients had to be held down for fear of hipbone, jaw or spinal fractures. After an explosion in the head Zelda and other patients would be given intravenous injections of sodium pentothal to counteract sensory fears.[78]

Zelda wrote to Scott: 'The Sheppard-Pratt hospital is located somewhere in the hinterlands of the human consciousness and I can be located there any time between the dawn of consciousness and the beginning of old age. Darling: life is difficult. There are so many problems. 1) The problem of how to stay here and 2) The problem of how to get out.' She concluded with a sketch of Scott in Guatemala and a request for him to take her there.[79]

The hospital grounds adjoined La Paix's, which Zelda found difficult to bear. 'Yesterday', she wrote to Scott, 'we took a long ride around familiar roads and it seemed so unreal not to be going home to La Paix.' In June she walked under the tulip trees by the dank little bridge which made her homesick. 'Will we be close again and will I feel the mossy-feeling back of your head and will I share those little regulations by which you keep your life in order: the measured drinks, the neatly piled papers.' Her letters were desolate. 'Darling I feel very disoriented and lonely. I love you, dear heart. Please try to love me some in spite of these stultifying years of sickness.' Then not knowing that he had long stopped being faithful, she added, 'I will compensate you some way for your love and faithfullness.'[80]

Zelda began hallucinating. She heard Scott's voice over and over. Sometimes he repeated her name. Sometimes he said, 'O, I have killed her!' Other times he cried, 'I have lost the woman I put in my book.' Zelda told the doctors she was terrified of Scott because he interpreted life for her. Dr William Elgin, one of her current physicians, initially forbade Scott to visit her.[81]

For weeks she became incoherent with despair; once she tried to strangle herself. With what little was left of her spirit Zelda hated Elgin, while he found Zelda inaccessible and stony.

Guilt suffused her: 'I am heart broken that I should have trailed this disaster through your life. Scottie writes me vague notes sometimes. I am so sorry for her. She has always been so brave and made her effort in spite of an inevitable sense that all was not as it might have been . . . There is an irrelevant, though welcome sunshine.'[82]

Most things, not merely the sun, became irrelevant. Zelda's letters were despatches from the edge of the abyss. She wrote as if she was searching for something she had left behind on the outermost fringes of life. The meaning of her communications resided in the interstices. She now suffered from severe loss of memory and an apathetic personality due to constant shock therapies.[83]

She had nothing but her shared memories with Scott to cling to. She recalled boathouses in Atlanta, pinewoods in Alabama, blistering bath-houses, dead moons, relics from the Deep South, mementoes from the Riviera, phantoms and conspiracies from past times they would never recapture. She coded even those memories as if she was an informant taking material across the border.

Scott urged the doctors to let him visit. He bargained that he could raise her spirits. Zelda seemed keen. 'Darling: I want so to see you. Maybe . . . before very long I will be well enough to meet you under the gracious shadows of these trees and we can look out on the distant fields to-gather. And I will be getting better.'[84]

But she wasn't. Once when he was allowed to visit, they strolled along a local railroad track separating the grounds of La Paix from the hospital. As a train approached she broke away from Scott and dashed towards the rails. He managed to drag her back seconds before the train rushed by. This was one of several suicide attempts. She had given up hope of recovery. Her means of survival was religion and she read the Bible hour after hour. 'It's my only strength – my only strength . . . And I have to pray to – to live,' she told Sara Mayfield.[85]

Scott too was in despair: 'I left my capacity for hoping on the little roads that led to Zelda's sanitarium.'[86] Frustration heightened Scott's bouts of bad behaviour. John O'Hara remembered an occasion when he drove Zelda back to Pratt from Baltimore. 'I had Scott and Zelda in my car and I wanted to kill him. *Kill.* We were taking her back to her Institution and he kept making passes at her that could not possibly be consummated . . . I wanted to kill him for what he was doing to that crazy woman who kept telling me she had to be locked up before the moon came up.'[87]

Then a younger doctor, Harry Murdoch, made a small breakthrough and persuaded Zelda to talk to him.[88] She told him she intended to kill herself, a remark that returned her to twenty-four-hour observation. Finally a glimmer of improvement occurred in her self-confidence, and she was allowed home some weekends. She saw Scottie, now twelve, who was preparing for summer camp. 'When I kissed her good-bye the little school-child scent of her neck and her funny little hesitant smile broke my heart. Be good to her Do-Do.'[89]

Scott had thought that lifting the ban on Zelda's writing might help her. While working on a film script of *Tender* he wrote to Elgin, saying he had been mistaken about not allowing Zelda to write serious fiction. Now he recognized that Zelda 'grew better in the three months at Hopkins where it was allowed'.[90]

Zelda begged to be allowed to write another novel. Scott, still uneasy, tried instead to persuade Perkins to accept a proposal for a book of Zelda's short stories and essays.[91] Excitedly Zelda planned the book jacket then, without warning, suffered another collapse, became inaccessible, unco-operative, occasionally violent. There was no question of her writing.

In July Rosalind suggested Scott consult Minnie Sayre and the family about Zelda. On 19 July Scott angrily responded, marking the letter 'Not to be mailed. File only': 'I am not going to call your mother into consultation nor have I ever called anybody into consultation on this problem except trained technicians who are dealing with it.' When he had telephoned Rosalind and Newman from Switzerland it was merely to have a family member aware of his actions. To suggest his conclusions were influenced by drink was as absurd as to think that Grant's campaigns were influenced by the fact that he used stimulant. 'Whenever I handle the case by myself it goes well; whenever I . . . tell you about it I run into that same old Puritanism that makes drinking unmoral, that makes all thinking done with the help of a drink invalidated and I am put down to a level of a person whose opinion can't be trusted and that reaches the doctors . . . they get confused . . . it all has to start over again.'

Scott insisted, 'Mrs Sayre is an old woman . . . you are irreparably prejudiced against me. . . It must all be left to me.'[92] His job was to 'reconstruct a broken egg shell' that was Zelda's mind; he had Scottie to think of, and he consistently ran up against obsolete family prides such as were shown over Anthony's death when the real facts were concealed from him. He appreciated Rosalind's help with Scottie but 'on the problem of Zelda you are completely blinded, even I accuse you of being purposely blinded'.[93]

Scott's relationship with the Sayres never recovered from that summer's series of confrontational letters. His bad mood infected Zelda, who occasionally rebelled. Bill Warren, a Baltimore friend who had worked with Scott on the *Tender* film script, recalled a scene at Pratt when Scott refused to play tennis with Zelda and asked him to substitute. Zelda acted as if Scott 'were backing out of the honeymoon', said Bill. Scott ignored her and climbed into the high referee's chair, so Zelda retaliated by stripping as she played. 'After the first point, Zelda took off her sweater . . . after the second point, she . . . unhooked her bra and tossed it away. Still Scott remained silent. After the third point, Zelda's short white tennis skirt dropped like a hoop at her feet. After the fourth she freed herself from her panties. I was playing with a stark naked woman.'[94] Warren said when you play tennis with a naked woman while her husband watches coolly, you try not to look at her! Scott never intervened, even when hospital attendants arrived, bound her in a cold wet-pack and carried her off, screaming hysterically.

Christmas 1934, spent with Scott and Scottie, was one of Zelda's unhappiest. On Christmas Eve Gertrude Stein and Alice B. Toklas visited the Fitzgeralds. Scott insisted that Zelda show Stein her paintings then, without consulting his wife, invited Stein to choose what she would like. Stein chose two oils already promised by Zelda to her doctor. Though Scott tried to persuade Zelda that her art would become famous if hung on the rue de Fleurus apartment walls, Zelda would not budge. Stein was forced to select *Tulips*, an oil, and *Crossing Roses*, a drawing. A few days later Scott wrote to Stein: 'It meant so much to Zelda giving her a tangible sense of her own existence, for you to have liked two of her pictures enough to want to own them.'[95] There was no truth in this: being compelled to give, not even sell, two paintings to a woman she disliked meant nothing but frustration to Zelda. This interchange with Scott's friends in Baltimore set Zelda back. On her return to Pratt in the new year her condition was so grave she was again placed in isolation.

Throughout 1935 her condition was designated as suicidal. She took in almost no news from the outside world. But news there was. While the Murphys' son younger Patrick was still gravely ill, suddenly in March their other son, fifteen-year-old Baoth, died of spinal meningitis.[96] At the end of his memorial service at St Bartholomew's in Manhattan, Sara Murphy rushed out of the church cursing God. She never fully recovered.

Two months later Mencken wrote: 'My dear Scott, Poor Sara, I fear, is now gravely ill – in fact, the chances that she will recover seem to be very remote. After all her long and gallant struggles she has developed meningitis, and the doctors tell me that the outlook is virtually hopeless. You can imagine my state of mind.'[97] Zelda's Montgomery friend and fellow writer Sara Haardt, who had been typing throughout fevers and sickness all spring, died in Johns Hopkins on 31 May, leaving Mencken bereft and Zelda one less Southern ally. Two terrible deaths had occurred in Zelda's close circle, but she neither noticed nor responded.

CHAPTER 23

Zelda was under a stone. She hardly spoke. That Scott's health had been poor during the winter and spring passed her by. That he had left Baltimore for Tryon, Hendersonville and North Carolina several times was of little consequence.[1] To his letter asking her what she needed, Zelda replied: 'I don't need anything at all except hope, which I can't find by looking either backwards or forwards, so I suppose the thing is to shut my eyes.'[2] Visiting her was like visiting a ghost. Half-remembering his world, she wrote: 'I want you to be happy again with Scottie – some place where it is bright . . . and you can have some of the things you have worked so hard for . . . Please get well and love Scottie and find something to fill up your life –.'[3] But by midsummer she no longer wrote to him.

Scott had tried to fill up his life with new companions and desultory affairs. During summer 1935 in North Carolina he met Laura Guthrie Hearne, a Columbia Journalism School graduate and amateur psychic who told fortunes to guests at Asheville's George Vanderbilt Hotel. Hired as Scott's part-time secretary, she also became go-between and recorder of his affair with Beatrice Dance, a rich Texan, who like Scott was staying at the Grove Park Inn.[4] Beatrice fell histrionically in love with Scott, who rapidly finished the affair by telling Dance that he was unable to abandon Zelda.[5] Scott, ever self-serving, accustomed to purloining Zelda's intimate letters, now sent Beatrice one of Zelda's saddest to justify his ruthless rejection of her.

Dearest and always
Dearest Scott:
    I am sorry too that there should be nothing to greet you but an empty shell. The thought of the effort you have made over me, the suffering this <u>nothing</u> has cost would be unendurable to any save a completely vacuous mechanism. Had I any feelings they would all be bent in gratitude to you and in sorrow that of all my life there should not even be

the smallest relic of the love and beauty that we started with to offer you at the end.

You have been so good to me – and all I can say is that there was always that deeper current running through my heart: my life – you.

You remember the roses in Kinneys yard . . . we crossed the street and said we loved the south. I thought of the south . . . thought I was part of the south . . . We were gold and happy all the way home.

Now that there isn't any more happiness and home is gone and there isn't even any past and no emotions but those that were yours . . . – it is a shame that we should have met in harshness and coldness where there was once so much tenderness and so many dreams . . . I love you anyway – even if there isn't any me or any love or even any life . . .

Oh, Do-Do

Do-Do – Zelda.[6]

Scott spelt out the implications for Dance: 'There are emotions just as important as ours running concurrently with them – and there is literally no standard in life other than a sense of duty.'[7]

The rejected Beatrice was hospitalized with distress while Scott, lungs already inflamed by tuberculosis, went on an alcoholic bender until Dr Paul Ringer admitted him to hospital in Asheville as, in Rosalind's words, a 'floundering wreck'. Rosalind added later: 'Poor devil! I always was sorry for him even while detesting him.'[8] Minnie Sayre told Rosalind she was so crushed by Zelda's hopelessness that she had to '[philosophize] herself into keeping cheerful'. After Rosalind had comforted the Sayres, she visited Zelda, who 'was dressed in white and seemed very ethereal, somehow, like somebody not of this world'. Rosalind told Scott: 'Most of the time . . . she was reproaching herself for having wrecked your life and having brought Scottie into the world . . . Her present condition was a great shock to me . . . and I feel discouraged about her.' Zelda begged Rosalind to take her for a ride, but when Rosalind asked Dr Elgin he said Zelda was so dangerously ill he could not allow her out in a car for fear she would escape. 'I pray', wrote Rosalind, 'that she will soon be quiet enough to have this little diversion from that horrible atmosphere in which she lives.'[9]

Scott's own diversions to avoid that 'horrible atmosphere' included a new friendship with twenty-nine-year-old writer Tony Buttitta, proprietor of Asheville's Intimate Book Shop in the George Vanderbilt Hotel arcade. One night Buttitta heard a knock at his door.

Standing outside was a tall blond chap in grey flannels who reminded me of a photo on a book jacket. 'Where's the Men's Room?' the guy said. 'Why, upstairs', I answered. 'Well it's loaded. Downstairs is loaded too. Find me one that isn't loaded!' I led him through the hotel garden, he tripped unsteadily through magnolias, jasmine and mimosa where he did his business. Then he stood under the moonlight and I knew. 'You're Scott Fitzgerald', I said. 'You have a romantic profile.' He liked that. He'd crashed, been beaten down, so if someone recognized him, especially a fellow writer, he liked that. I told him I'd sold half a dozen of his books but I hadn't sold hardly any. He didn't believe he was important any more, but he needed other people to believe it.

That summer, Buttitta, trying to restore Scott's self-esteem, introduced him to prostitute Lottie Stephens: a poor idea, for she complained about Scott's lack of virility while Fitzgerald fretted about contracting syphilis.

Buttitta recalled how Scott would suddenly start sobbing: 'He always sobbed about Zelda. He'd cry out: "We meant so much to each other in our early life. But Zelda wanted to be a star. She didn't feel what I did was important to her."' Buttitta felt 'Scott had to be the star. Scott wanted Zelda in the audience. He kept saying "I feel responsible because now she's gone batty."'[10]

What Scott saw as battiness was Zelda's retreat from suicide into religious despair. 'God has evolved us,' she wrote to him, 'that we may ennoble our souls until they shall have attained a spiritual stature.'

She had reverted to her preoccupation with homosexuality, with God on her side. 'Since Eden, man has been endowed with a double sexual impulse. Complete sexual fulfillment between man and wife is homosexuality. It is God's word that this is so.' She knew Scott's negative view of 'fairies', but hoped he would accept homosexual *practices* as part of their marital contract because God did. 'God's promise to man is emotional fulfillment . . . that is sucking the genital organs of your mate . . .' Zelda hoped these 'beautiful and honourable' practices might stop married couples becoming homosexual, which she knew from her experience was always punished.[11]

Scott had returned, debt-ridden and depressed, from Asheville to Baltimore's Cambridge Arms where Isabel Owens was caring for Scottie. By November, finances and spirits sunk, he had moved them to cheaper accommodation at 3300 St Paul Avenue, where he wrote a series of mediocre stories about a widowed father and his teenage daughter Gwen; only two were sold. He gave Scottie ten dollars, left her with Mrs Owens and the Finneys and headed for Hendersonville, North Carolina, where he rented a tawdry room at Skylands Hotel. Later he had to borrow $7,500 from Oscar Kalman.[12]

Only weeks into his fortieth year, suffering his own nervous breakdown, he wrote three wretchedly honest confessional essays: 'The Crack-Up', 'Pasting It Together' and 'Handle With Care'. Ironically they were brilliant pieces of writing about a writer who can no longer write because he can no longer care. Scott felt they were creative attempts at examining his emotional and spiritual bankruptcy. Perkins saw them as disgusting exercises in self-pity which would further ruin Scott's disintegrating reputation. Hemingway saw them as shameful and cowardly. Only Sara Murphy understood Scott:

> You have been cheated . . . but to have Zelda's wisdom taken away – which would have meant *everything* to you, is crueller even than death. She would have felt all the right things through the bad times – and found the words to help. For you, & for her real friends – I miss her too – You have had a horrible time – worse than any of us, I think – and it has gone on for so long . . . your spirit & courage are an example to us all.[13]

At Christmas 1935, Scott tried to cheer up fourteen-year-old Scottie by organizing a theatre party for her, Peaches Finney and friends, but his gloom disoriented them.

During the spring when Arnold Gingrich made Scott's self-revelatory articles public in *Esquire*, Scott's health worsened[14] as Zelda's religious fervour increased. Rosalind, visiting Zelda in April, was horrified. 'I found her at Sheppard Pratt weighing only 89 pounds and fast going downhill.' Through regular conversations with God, Zelda believed she was in direct communication with Christ, Apollo and William the Conqueror. Dressed in white, she either prayed by her bed day and night or, convinced the end of the world was approaching, hastily wrote and distributed God's word to their friends. On Rosalind's insistence Scott removed Zelda from Pratt on 7 April 1936 and entered her into Highland Hospital, Asheville, the following day. 'One of the saddest memories I have', recalled Rosalind, 'is of going through her trunk in Baltimore . . . to see what there was she might want to take with her. What I found was a bit of old clothing, a brass candlestick, and a musical powder-box with a Pierrot on top that turned with the tune.'[15]

Scott had told the Murphys he now felt Zelda was his child, and that he acted as Zelda's 'great reality, often the only liason agent who could make the world tangible to her'.[16] The hospital director, Robert Carroll, thought differently. After two weeks at Highland, during which Scott offered Zelda his version of reality, Carroll suggested Scott return to Baltimore. 'You are her emotional disorganizer . . . We did not . . . organize her treatment until after you left.'[17]

The treatment was controversial, fierce and frightening. That it eventually reduced some of Zelda's symptoms, many of which were the product of earlier treatments, did not outweigh new devastating side-effects. Carroll was pioneering injections of placental blood, honey and hypertonic solutions, and of horse blood, into patients' cerebrospinal fluid. Horse serum caused aseptic meningitis with vomiting, fever and head pains, but Carroll used it on Zelda because it could induce long spells of lucidity. He also regularly gave Zelda the now standard electro-shock and insulin shock treatments, disregarding their known effects of memory loss.[18] Dr Irving Pine (Zelda's last psychiatrist) said she was given between thirty and ninety insulin shocks, producing convulsions followed by comas that lasted up to an hour.[19] Mary Parker, assistant to Highland's psychotherapist (later Zelda's art therapist), though reluctant to discuss insulin treatment, admitted that 'insulin was only supposed to be given to "difficult" patients because it shocked their brains so that they couldn't be left on their own afterwards without a nurse. Though most recovered there *were* bad aftereffects.'[20]

Theorizing that toxic substances caused mental illness, Carroll placed patients on strict diets and regimented exercise routines. Every morning Zelda had outdoor gymnastics, then wholewheat peanut butter sandwiches, followed by occupational therapy (in her case painting), with a five-mile walk every afternoon. Parker recalled how well the schedule suited Zelda's athletic nature. 'Dr Carroll believed healthy bodies meant healthy minds, he wanted patients occupied so they couldn't sit and mope. Zelda played medicine ball and volley ball. After the regulation five miles Zelda would climb a hill. Sometimes she'd have to climb the hill ten times! If she got a few minutes freedom she'd turn a dance step.' But Carroll held more questionable views: the same questionable views as Forel and Slocum had held before him. 'He believed in re-education for women patients,' said Parker, 'which meant redirecting them into wholesome normal values. It was taken for granted women would want to be good wives and mothers in a wholesome way.'[21]

Highland's wholesome programme cost $1,200 a quarter but Scott, pleading poverty, paid only $240 a month plus extra for day trips, concerts, movies and art materials. Scott also sent $100 a month for Zelda's personal expenses: chewing gum, flowers, fruit, clothes, dentistry and occasional telegrams. He paid for dance lessons and Zelda danced to the point of exhaustion unless monitored by nurses. Later she choreographed ballets for hospital events.[22]

Scott, increasingly pressured by debts, closed up the Baltimore house and moved to Asheville.[23] Despite the Fitzgeralds' geographical proximity they met seldom. Occasionally they lunched at the Inn where, removed from other guests, Zelda nibbled a cucumber salad. Although physically healthier, she told Scott the restrictions stifled her soul. Looking back, she wrote:

> Friendship, conviviality, the right of choice, the right of resentment, anger, impetuosities; all these are as much a part of life as obedience, submission, obligation and necessity. In . . . Highland Hospital, these manifestations of the human temperament are subject to reprimand and regarded as illness. Knowing this, patients (mostly) suppress themselves as much as possible, endure, and hope to get out.[24]

It is worth noting there is nothing incoherent in Zelda's analysis.

That summer was exceptionally sad for them both. Gerald wrote grimly that young Patrick's health had worsened. Hemingway attacked Scott publicly in 'The Snows of Kilimanjaro' in August's *Esquire*. Then on 2 September Scott's mother died of a cerebral haemorrhage. Unexpectedly moved, Scott told Oscar Kalman: 'A most surprising thing in the death of a parent is not how little it affects you, but how much . . . there is a sense of being deserted.'[25] To Beatrice Dance he went further: 'She was a defiant old woman, defiant in her love for me in spite of my neglect of her.'[26]

Scott hoped his mother's loan to him of $6,000 would not be deducted from his share of her $42,000 estate, but this provoked a bitter quarrel with Annabel. Her two daughters recalled: 'Mother [told] us that the dispute and hard feelings . . . stemmed from F. Scott Fitzgerald's desire that the money he had earlier borrowed periodically from Grandmother not be deducted from his inheritance. Daddy felt this was unfair to Mother.'[27] The unfairness, rectified in Annabel's favour, meant that Scott received only $5,000.

He spent some money taking Scottie regularly to see Zelda. Sticking to Carroll's guidelines for 'normal' family life, they would shop in Asheville then dine out. Earlier, on Zelda's birthday he had intended driving her to a swimming lake but injured his shoulder diving the previous day. Subsequent arthritis encouraged him to hire nurse Pauline 'Phil' Brownell who, with her husband George, frequently drove Scott to Zelda's hospital. In appreciation Zelda gave Phil a watercolour of Alabama lilies enclosed in a religious motif. Zelda kept an Easter lily plant in her hospital room, which she painted. In her notebook she described its demise. 'My lillies died; they just plain died, so I can only paint the memory of white desirability – of so much beauty.'[28]

For Scottie's education Gerald had highly recommended the Ethel Walker School in Simsbury, Connecticut, but for her entrance in September 1936 Scott had to borrow even the reduced amount of the $2,200 tuition fees from Ober and Perkins. Scottie later speculated: 'he would have hated it if I hadn't been at a "chic" school, but no sooner was I there than he started worrying about its bad influence on me . . . daddy was torn between trying to make up for my lack of stability at home with the sense of belonging that comes from being a member of a club and his own instinctive lack of respect for the values of that club.'[29] Scott told Sara Mayfield he feared Scottie, now almost fifteen, would wear out young like her parents, so he lectured her constantly on the dangers of petting, drinking and joy-riding.[30]

Because Scottie's school was close to the Obers' Scarsdale home Scott asked Harold and Anne who, with two sons, already loved Scottie as a daughter, to act as foster parents. For years they paid for Scottie's summer camps, ski trips, visited her at school and gave her a home.

In terms of stability, the Fitzgeralds began to reverse their roles. Scott was subjected to a cruel interview in his Grove Park Inn room on 25 September, his fortieth birthday, by Michel Mok, a *New York Post* journalist who portrayed him as a broken drunk; he reacted by taking a morphine overdose which he then, humiliatingly, vomited up.

Zelda meanwhile was gallantly coming to terms with her final sanatorium. It had tennis courts and a swimming pool and stood in eighty acres of land, encircled by the Great Smoky and Blue Ridge mountains, close to the banks of the Swannanoa and French Broad rivers. The mountains were familiar to Zelda from Saluda childhood holidays. As her religious fervour decreased she spent hours outside, painting the lush greens and rich browns of the pine-filled backdrop.[31] Most of Zelda's paintings are complex layered works imbued with past autobiographical associations. These are not. No humans with tangled emotions intrude on Zelda's mountains or trees. Landscapes are simple, uncluttered, with a luminosity crafted by the paper's whiteness shining through watercolour washes. An oriental influence suggests an infinity of space, while her triangular mountain peaks speak of Cézanne. The vegetation does not writhe, the paintings do not disturb viewers. But their very calmness upset the staff's stereotyped attitudes about artist-patients. Parker was more comfortable with Zelda's art therapy paintings. 'They were more powerful. I can still see her hands at work stroking on the paint, using the brush repetitively. I felt she was going over and over stuff that worried her inside.'[32]

Although Zelda's art *could* demonstrate connections to her instabilities by visualizing her deepest emotions, the Highland classes were considered therapeutic simply because they were recreational, unlike those under Wertham at Phipps which were used for diagnostic purposes. The success of the art work and the exercise regime permitted Zelda more freedom. 'She was allowed to walk into Asheville alone,' Parker recalled. 'Once she searched everywhere for a special material to make herself a circular skirt to save Scott money.'[33] Then Carroll allowed Zelda to visit her mother, vacationing in Saluda, and Rosalind in Manhattan; both were astonished at the change: 'Zelda bloomed again,' said Rosalind. '. . . [She] was almost like her old self, beautiful once more, still interested in music, the theatre and art, but toned down to an almost normal rhythm.'[34]

Parker, who got to know Zelda well, never believed she was schizophrenic.

I knew her history. I knew she'd broken down. I knew the reports from Johns Hopkins . . . but I saw *no signs* of *that* mental illness. I saw no signs of schizophrenia. I saw or heard no hallucinations. She had none of those symptoms. As for her speech it was *not* incoherent. She was absolutely lucid . . . She merely spoke in an unusual way. When *she* talked you certainly listened. She was interesting, intelligent, a compelling woman to talk to. She had a very good mind that wasn't being stretched. Her character was clear like her speech. I had a lot of regard for Zelda. I saw nothing wild or mad about her.[35]

Dr Irving Pine agreed. He believed that Zelda had been both misdiagnosed and misunderstood.[36]

By December 1936 Zelda was indisputably acting more sanely

than Scott. In Baltimore he gave a tea dance for Scottie, then embarrassed his daughter by getting piggishly drunk, insisting on dancing with her girlfriends and boorishly ordering them to leave. 'After the ghastly tea dance,' wrote a mortified Scottie, 'Peaches Finney and I went back to her house in a state of semi-hysteria.' To deal with the episode Scottie used her standard denial tactics: 'I was busy surviving and what I couldn't ignore . . . I would put in the emotional attic . . . if I'd allowed myself to care I couldn't have stood it.'[37] The day after Christmas Scott was back at Johns Hopkins till 3 January, drying out.[38] Scottie, relieved of paternal embarrassment, celebrated Christmas with Zelda at Highland where they had an unusually calm time.

The New Year, which would see Amelia Earhart disappear on a Pacific flight, the Duke of Windsor marry Wallis Simpson, and George Gershwin, two years younger than Scott, die, brought another tragedy to the Fitzgeralds. On 30 January 1937 a telegram came from the Murphys: 'PATRICK DIED PEACEFULLY THIS MORNING.'[39] Scott replied at once:

> the whole afternoon was sad with thoughts of you and the past and the happy times we had once. Another link binding you to life is broken and with such insensate cruelty that it is hard to say which of the two blows was conceived with more malice . . . it would take words like Lincoln's in his letter to the mother who had lost four sons in the war to write you anything fitting at the moment. The golden bowl is broken indeed but it *was* golden; nothing can ever take those boys away from you now.[40]

One effect of the two Murphy boys' deaths was to increase Scott's anxieties over Scottie; yet curiously later, in June 1938, he did not attend her graduation from Ethel Walker. Zelda, however, managed it in style. Anne Ober drove Zelda and Rosalind to Connecticut where Zelda, elegant and proud of her daughter, chatted graciously to Scottie's friends and teachers. Later she and Rosalind attended two Broadway shows, then Zelda took a carriage ride through New York's Central Park. Suffused with nostalgia, she paused by the Plaza fountain into which she and Scott had dived years before. Perhaps past memories comfortingly clouded a present in which Scottie had been discomforted by her attendance. 'I didn't want my mother at graduation because it wasn't the big deal daddy was trying to make it, and she *was* crazy.'[41]

But in 1937 there were ongoing signs that Zelda was far from crazy. The problem was that years of alienation from Scottie meant

Zelda was now her mother in little more than name. When Scottie started at Vassar, it would again be Anne Ober who would act as her surrogate mother. 'It is an important relationship to me,' Anne wrote to Scott '. . . I think it is to Scottie too. *Please* let me know what I can do and *when* to expect my child.'[42]

If Zelda felt a failure as a mother, Scott was swamped by his failure as a writer. On 4 June 1937 he had met Hemingway at the second American Writers' Congress in New York.[43] As he watched Ernest's anti-Fascist speech fire up the 3,500-strong audience, the difference between Ernest's fame and his own sliding career overwhelmed him. That afternoon, in front of the Algonquin, Carl Van Vechten photographed Scott in a checked jacket and knitted club tie. His hair was thinning, his smile nervous, his eyes held a desolate look. He was only forty.

In Hollywood that July, on a six-month writing assignment for MGM arranged by Ober, to whom along with Perkins and Scribner's he was $22,000 in debt, Scott's first job was to rewrite *A Yank at Oxford* before he was allowed to script *Three Comrades*.[44] He needed Hollywood more than it needed him. He had sacrificed Zelda's and Scottie's future security by reducing his life insurance policy to $30,000. He was behind in payments to Highland. He could only allow himself $400 and Zelda $30 a week from a hefty pay-check of $1,000.[45] The rest was apportioned between regular debt repayments, Zelda's fees and Scottie's tuition. He saved by sharing a $300 a month unit with scriptwriter Eddie Mayer in Hollywood's Garden of Allah, a compound for film artistes at 8152 Sunset Boulevard.

Determined to avoid alcohol and drinking buddies like Don Ogden Stewart, Dorothy Parker and Robert Benchley,[46] he appeared subdued, but was seen as sullen, aloof, even arrogant. His diffidence increased after his next meeting with Hemingway, who swung into Hollywood hero-style to screen his and Hellman's film *The Spanish Earth*, fund-raising for Spanish loyalists.[47] Scott was invited to Fredric March's home on 12 July to watch the movie. Scott and Ernest did not exchange a word. The next day Scott wired Ernest: 'THE PICTURE WAS BEYOND PRAISE AND SO WAS YOUR ATTITUDE = SCOTT.'[48] Their intimacy was over. In his notebook Scott admitted: 'I talk with the authority of failure – Ernest with the authority of success. We could never sit across the table again.'[49] They did not, for it was their last meeting.

There is a neat irony in the fact that two days after the death of his friendship with a man he always considered first class, Scott met the

Hollywood gossip columnist Sheilah Graham, a woman he learnt to love but always secretly considered third class. It was at Robert Benchley's Garden of Allah party that Scott suddenly spotted this twenty-eight-year-old English girl, who looked uncannily like his youthful Zelda. In *The Last Tycoon*, his final unfinished Hollywood novel, Scott romanticized their initial encounter in the first meeting between film producer Monroe Stahr and young Kathleen, who resembles his dead wife Mina. 'Smiling faintly at him from not four feet away was the face of his dead wife, identical even to the expression.'[50]

But the resemblance between Zelda and Sheilah was more fancied than real. Sheilah had a streak of vulgarity and a line in lies that would have appalled Zelda. Born Lily Shiel in London's East End, she lived with a washerwoman in a slum that smelt of boiled potatoes and laundry soap. Sent as a child to an orphanage, Lily then worked as a parlourmaid and clerk before secretly marrying, then divorcing, an elderly English major. Determined to become famous, she changed her name to Sheilah Graham when Charles Cochran hired her for his Young Ladies chorus line. It is possible that part of Scott's interest in Sheilah, who had become a successful musical comedy star before arriving in New York, was that she reminded him also of his old love, the musical actress Rosalinde Fuller. More significant however were the punishing effects of his TB, alcoholism, debts and Zelda's illness, which had weakened him sufficiently to need Sheila's disciplined working methods and down-to-earth appreciation of him. He embarked on the affair with speed.

Though he saw through Sheilah's glittering façade to her shallow, ignorant nature, he found her spunky and sustaining. Pragmatic Scottie, who arrived to see her father on 2 August, understood those virtues. 'He had a wife who couldn't live with him. It was an unbelievable emotional and financial drain . . . [he] needed someone who was eminently practical, someone with her feet on the ground . . . someone perhaps like Sheilah Graham.'[51]

If the word 'perhaps' was a give-away to Scottie's underlying feelings, she kept them to herself. During the visit Sheilah saw a less attractive side to Scott: a greying fretful father who irrationally scolded his daughter; but Sheilah was already too much in love to retreat. Scottie shook off familiar paternal corrections: 'The first Hollywood visit was fabulous. Daddy was on the wagon and he took me everywhere with him. I had a room at the Beverly Hills Hotel and Helen Hayes was supposed to be my "chaperone".'[52]

Hayes felt Sheilah offered Scott emotional support but because 'she represented . . . the second-rate he had fallen into' he treated her badly.[53] Indeed he did. When drunk he struck Sheilah, abused her, recalled her hidden origins, even denigrated her as his 'paramour'. In December 1937 Scott wrote to the Murphys that he hoped they would welcome Sheilah when she visited New York in late January. Sara refused, partly because it was the anniversary of Patrick's death and partly because her fierce loyalty to Zelda saw that as a betrayal of friendship.[54] When Perkins and Ober met Sheilah later, like the Murphys they thought her materialistic and banal, but hoped she would be a good influence on Scott's alcoholism. Wilson, now married to writer Mary McCarthy, considered Sheilah had given Scott a new sobriety. Sheilah, they thought, was less interesting than Zelda but kept Scott in better order.

Although Scott painstakingly told Sheilah that Zelda and Scottie would remain his priorities, she never quite recognized the interwoven complexities of the Fitzgeralds' relationship. 'I now realize', she later admitted, 'that during the time I knew Scott, he was leading a sort of double life. I knew he looked after Zelda, and I understood that he must. But I didn't know that he was still . . . writing her love letters.'[55] But those letters did *not* include any information about Miss Graham, which Scott had insisted Scottie hide from Zelda.

Nevertheless her mother had already sensed a change in Scott's letters. He never gave her his precise address. 'What is your actual address?' she asked. 'Spose I wanted to 'phone you – or do something unprecedented like that?' Another letter repeated: 'What would I do if I should have a bad dream or an inspiration? It's much more conventional to know where your husband [is] when you've got one.'[56]

Zelda strongly suspected a liaison but, like Scott, felt it wiser to maintain the pretence. Only after *The Last Tycoon* was published posthumously did Zelda write to Margaret Turnbull of her dislike for Scott's protagonist Kathleen, the only heroine to be based on Sheilah. 'She seemed the sort of person who knows too well how to capitalize on the unwelcome advances of the iceman who smells a little of the rubber shields in her dress.'[57] It would be characteristic of Zelda's acid wit to use the pun 'shields' for Sheilah's real name 'Shiel', thus acknowledging enigmatically that she knew Scott's secret.

Perhaps Scott's conscience drove him to take Zelda and Scottie to Charleston and Myrtle Beach in September 1937, and after

Christmas fly with Zelda to Miami and Palm Beach before they visited Montgomery. After Charleston Scott told Sara Murphy Zelda 'held up well enough but there is always a gradual slipping. I've become hard there and don't feel the grief I did once – except sometimes at night or when I catch myself in some spiritual betrayal of the past.'[58] After Miami, he told Scottie her mother was much better than expected, only his tiredness spoilt their fun. But when Zelda wanted to return to Hollywood with him Scott's relationship with Sheilah coloured his reply. As long as she needed medical care, he said firmly, they would have to live apart.

At the end of March 1938, his MGM contract safely renewed,[59] Fitzgerald took Zelda and Scottie for their last trip as a family, first to Virginia Beach then to see cousins in Norfolk. During a golf lesson Zelda picked a fight with Scottie; Scott got drunk, then became so violent that Zelda reported him to the Cavalier Hotel's manager. Simultaneously they recognized they could no longer tolerate each other's behaviour. Zelda, in tears, fled back to Dr Carroll's office. Scott had already told Carroll he had become the worst person for Zelda rather than the best. 'Certainly the outworn pretence that we can ever come together again is better for being shed. There is simply too much of the past between us ... The mainsprings are gone.' Yet he could not quite relinquish their bond. 'So long as she is helpless, I'd never leave her or ever let her have a sense that she was deserted.'[60]

The episode set them both back. Scott, ill at ease on the wagon, tumbled off completely when on his return to Hollywood he met Ginevra King, now a divorcée, for lunch for the first time in two decades. Then he quarrelled with Scottie, now nearly seventeen, who joined him on Malibu Beach before she prepared for her Vassar entry. Scottie, after several distressing scenes when her father 'had entered a phase in his drinking in which his personality changed from Jekyll to Hyde',[61] was glad to leave Hollywood that summer and tour Europe with Fanny Myers and their friends under Alice Lee Myers' auspices.

While Zelda steadily improved, Scott's luck ran out. His contract was not renewed when it expired at the end of January 1939, so from March 1939 to October 1940 he freelanced for Paramount, Universal, Twentieth Century Fox, Goldwyn and Columbia Studios.[62]

Despite this, with characteristic financial generosity he sent extra money to Highland for Zelda to accompany the Carrolls to Sarasota, Florida, where for three weeks she took classes in life drawing and costume design at the Ringling School of Art.[63] The hospital had begun at last to take her painting seriously. During the next two years she kept her first consistent artist's notebook; began exploring the possibilities of sculptures; and exhibited at Mrs Maude King's Art School Sketch Club, then with the Asheville Artists' Guild at the Rhododendron Festival.[64]

Dr Carroll arranged another trip, this time to Cuba, but because Scott delayed giving his approval Zelda was left behind. Philosophically she wrote: 'Havannah is probably a substantial sort of place and may well be there till next time . . . Let me see you fly East. We can go to Cuba ourselves . . .'[65] To everyone's surprise Scott agreed. In April 1939 they set off, Zelda nervous, for Scott had arrived drunk and exhausted following a quarrel with Sheilah and a script cancelled by Paramount. On arrival at Club Kawama, Varadero, Scott went on a sustained bender, got into a fight, and Zelda was forced to get them both back to New York City. She managed it with extraordinary equilibrium and had him admitted to hospital. Zelda returned alone to Asheville, telling no one how Scott had deteriorated or how stable she had remained under crisis. Back in California Scott, guilty and apologetic, wrote to her:

> You were a peach throughout the whole trip and there isn't a minute of it when I don't think of you with all the old tenderness . . . You are the finest, loveliest, tenderest, most beautiful person I have ever known, but even that is an understatement because the length that you went to there at the end would have tried anybody beyond endurance.[66]

Zelda and Scott would never see each other again.

CHAPTER 24

Minnie Sayre, convinced that Scott had wrecked her daughter's mind, started a series of strong petitions to Dr Carroll to release Zelda into her care. Angry notes flew in all directions.

The Sayre sisters wrote to Zelda assuring her she was well enough to come home; the family wrote to Scott urging him to provide his wife with an allowance to live in Montgomery. Zelda, feeling recovered, wrote to Scott begging for freedom. Scott wrote to everybody informing them Carroll would not sanction Zelda's release and if she left against his advice would not take her back. Then Scott wrote to Carroll to confirm this *was* the position to which they would both hold.

Subsequently Carroll wrote to Minnie to say that no matter how normal Zelda's behaviour appeared, her psyche was shattered: she was mentally damaged goods. She would always live in a house of thinly spun glass.[1] Scott and Minnie just about managed to keep their correspondence cordial, but Scott's fury and Zelda's desperation broke out time and time again.

With Zelda confused, Scott enraged, the Sayres frustrated and Carroll implacable, the battle continued for months. Studying some of the battle-ground communiqués reveals the state of emotions on both sides.

War had started slowly in 1938.

26 April: Minnie wrote to Scott: 'I am not trying to combat the doctors. I'm thinking of my child's happiness . . . I feel that contact with those she loves is good for her and gives her a sense of protection . . . If Zelda can live here with me I am not afraid to try it.'

27 May: Scott replied, but to Rosalind: 'I want more trial of Zelda's capacities but I will not override Carroll . . . the idea of your mother assuming responsibility is, of course, fantastic – it would simply mean turning Zelda loose.'

29 May: Rosalind disregarded Scott's reported prescription from Carroll, that the best life for Zelda would be 'attractive quarters' in

hospital and 'frequent travel for diversion'. As a luxury Scott could no longer afford, 'it can be dismissed from consideration'. The Sayres wanted a 'practicable plan whereby she could live outside the hospital relieving you of the expense of her staying there and allowing her a chance to re-establish herself'. Rosalind outlined the cheapest alternative. 'If you cannot afford an attendant for her . . . I feel she is entitled to it [release] under the only other arrangement open to her, which is sharing Mama's roof . . . denying her this without offering her something better would be condemning her arbitrarily to permanent hospitalization without giving her a trial, and neither you nor the rest of us would be willing to do that.'

Rosalind fired her 'final word' to Scott: 'As you wrote Dr Carroll, you realize the time has gone when you can undertake Zelda's supervision, and you must now find another way for her. Why not give her back to us, with allowance enough for normal support, and let us do the best we can for her.'[2]

18 September 1938: Rosalind informed Scott that Zelda wished to experiment in the new year in an Asheville apartment with a companion. The Sayres felt that as Zelda had not once slipped during the summer, 'continued hospitalization, against her will, will be detrimental'.[3] Scott, furious, ignored Rosalind's letters.

7 December: Rosalind wrote again. Scott, who had asked for her advice, had neither acknowledged nor taken it. 'We want something done about re-establishing Zelda in the world, and would appreciate your co-operation.'

21 December: Scott finally picked up his pen.

You seem to believe that the business of 're-establishing Zelda' consists of signing a lease on a house in Asheville! . . . never for a moment did he [Carroll] take [your suggestion] seriously . . . what he told me is . . . 1) that Zelda is incurable though her disease is arrested for the present . . . 2) that she will never be able to live alone . . . 3) that her condition will inevitably move downward . . . . [if] Zelda comes into the world [with] no governing force upon her – with her damaged equipment she faces . . . not one chance in 10,000 – in order that Mrs Sayre can pass her last years in peace! . . . Imagine Zelda running amuk in Montgomery! I saw your mother when Zelda had the public masturbation illusion – she went very quickly home . . .

Scott told Rosalind the Sayres' personal charm and tea-table ideas would not talk away dementia praecox. 'Cure her I cannot and simply saying she's cured must make the Gods laugh.'

When the Sayres refused to reduce their pressure Scott wrote to

Marjorie, as 'the only member of your family that has ever treated this business with ordinary human decency'.

'I have taken the whole thing pretty well from Rosalind's first accusation in 1930 that I "drove Zelda crazy" through your mother's accusation that I sent her to Johns Hopkins in 1932 for ulterior motives.' He reminded Marjorie it was Minnie's 'rotten care' that allowed John Sellers to seduce Zelda at fifteen. 'Your mother is a sort of typhoid Mary projecting her own defeated egotism . . . [it is a] preposterous idea that Zelda's sanity can be bought with a one way ticket to Montgomery . . . You have nothing to offer. Why don't you, for god's sake, shut up! Any further communication from any of you will be returned unopened.' Minnie's long-distance thrusts would drive Zelda to suicide. She was behaving like the wicked mother in the Judgement of Solomon: 'better the baby dead than not the baby at all'.[4]

Some remnant of sense made Scott file that letter instead of mailing it. But that same week he wrote Rosalind a sarcastic appreciation of her sanctimonious advice; then told her that if she wanted him to resist the temptation to pass her down to posterity for what she was, she should never communicate with him again. On top of the letter he scrawled: 'When you people stink you certainly stink.'[5]

There is something deeply dispiriting about a bunch of well-meaning people, each genuinely concerned about the welfare of one of their number, quarrelling over treatment methods and release time. The possessiveness shown by both the Sayres and Scott over the rights to Zelda's recovery is akin to the controlling way families sometimes behave over a dying member.

Not even Scottie was excluded from battle. In July 1939, after an appendix operation in Asheville when she was spending recovery time with her mother, who now appeared stable, seventeen-year-old Scottie entered the fray on the Montgomery side.

Scott immediately asked Carroll's deputy, Dr Suitt, to inform Scottie that though her mother might hold up for short periods she would never be able to operate in the world without guidance. Suitt was to stress the onset of menopause was likely to cause Zelda derangement. Scott, determined to control his family's relationships, warned Dr Suitt that Scottie's new attitude towards Zelda could affect 'my whole future relation with my daughter'.[6]

When Scottie asked Scott if she could join him in California that summer, her positive attitude towards Zelda's release made him hesitate. 'She is a dominant little girl in a polite way and to have her appear here now as a sort of ambassador of . . . the Montgomery point of view ... would be much more than upsetting.'[7] So Scott told Scottie he was depressed and nervous. He would rather not see her 'than see you without loving you'. She must now realize that her home was Vassar.[8] Scottie, distressed, showed Zelda the letter.

Zelda wanted Scott to understand that his note might have further endangered Scottie's sense of safety. 'She is such a particularly brave and self-reliant child that it would be lamentable to allow a sense of the absence of stability to twist her mind with neuroses.'[9]

On 27 September 1939, after two months' illness, Scott wrote to Carroll saying he had run out of funds. Would Highland credit him for another month without depriving Zelda of necessities? Carroll agreed to trust Scott and not to release Zelda to her family. Harold Ober, who for years had generously lent Scott money, was less gracious, and finally refused. Scott, believing Ober had lost faith in his talents, broke with him. This had severe repercussions on Scottie's relationship with the Obers, who had acted as her most immediate kin since she first went to the Ethel Walker School. Firing Ober also made Scott financially worse off in October. 'I am almost penniless,' he told Zelda, informing her that their friends were helping to pay for Scottie's return to Vassar. 'Scottie has got to survive and this is the most important year of her life.' Zelda must stop harassing him with requests for freedom and must leave him in peace with his haemorrhages and his hopes. He had a new novel to write and a child to rear.[10]

Zelda wrote back reasonably:

your letter somewhat hurt me ... you do not give a thought to the fact that this hospital regimentation, while most excellent for whipping into shape, is very gruelling ... Mamma would be happy to have me: if any trouble arose I could and would return here ... I cant see any legitimization of keeping me under hospitalization much longer .... There is every reason to believe that I am more able to observe the social dictats than yourself – on the evidence of our 'vacations' from the hospital – which have been ... a dread affair of doctors and drink and confirmation of the impossibility of any equitable reunion. Although you know this – and that the probabilities are much against our ever having any life to-gether again – you are persistent in not letting me have a chance to exist alone at least in comfort – in Alabama and make my own orientation. Or even in Ashville, I might be able to get a job ... Won't you, in fairness, please consider this letter from some other basis than that I am your possible enemy and that your first obligation is self-defensive.[11]

Furiously he retorted that only if they were divorced would he agree to her request, as that way he would have no further responsibility for her. His anger escalated in a nine-page aggressive letter which a moment's diplomacy stopped him from mailing.

That a fifty dollar ticket to Montgomery would in some way purchase your eternal mental health is a proposition I will not debate. I won't even debate it with Dr Carroll . . . Do you think she [your mother] cares or ever has cared about you . . . ? Do you think she would ever quarrel with you for your impersonal good? She constructed herself on a heroic romantic model as a girl and you were to be the stuffed dummy . . . She chose me – and she did – and you submitted at the moment of our marriage when your passion for me was at as low ebb as mine for you – because she thought romanticly that her projection of herself in you could best be shown thru me. I never wanted the Zelda I married. I didn't love you again till after you became pregnant . . . This is the very questionable element I bought and your mother asks to be given back . . . I'd like to discover the faintest basis for your family's accusation that I drove you crazy . . . that old witch drove you crazy. You were 'crazy' in the ordinary sense before I met you. I rationalized your eccentricities and made a sort of creation of you . . . If it hadn't been you perhaps I would have worked with more stable material. My talent and my decline is the norm. Your degeneracy is the deviation.[12]

Under considerable pressure and unusually nervous, in October 1939 Scott began to draft *The Last Tycoon*, in which his protagonist Monroe Stahr was based on director Irving Thalberg.[13] When John and Belle O'Hara visited him for Sunday lunch that fall at Belly Acres in the San Fernando Valley, Scott showed O'Hara his manuscript: 'Promise you won't tell anyone about it,' he said. 'Don't tell them what it's about, or anything about the people . . . [don't] even tell anyone I'm writing another book.' While John read with a deadpan expression Scott sat tortured. Eventually his friend said: 'Scott, don't take any more movie jobs until you've finished this. You work so slowly and this is so good, you've got to finish it. It's real Fitzgerald.'[14]

Heartened, he carried on with a taxing schedule against failing health. By contrast, Zelda's health was holding up well.

During the fall she shopped alone in Asheville, directed gym classes, worked with other patients in athletics and art therapy. Her Southern flower painting *Hope* is characteristically not all that it seems. It might be a spiralling mass of soft blue bubbles or a hymn in praise of foetal unfurlings.[15] Her paintings in two recent exhibitions had received good reviews: 'There is an arresting and imaginative quality about this painter's use of vivid color and abstract circular design to portray pure emotion that sticks in the observer's mind . . . And there is a velvety effect about her handling of oil paint which suggests the visions one conjures up by pressing the palms of the hands over the eyeballs in a dark room.'[16]

This success was followed that winter by an invitation from Dr Carroll to paint floral scenes on large window screens for the new assembly building. She would be paid, her materials provided by Carroll, and when Duke University eventually took over Highland, her work would reach a wider audience. Though excited she feared professional exploitation. 'I sent word', she wrote Scott, 'that I ultimately would not subscribe to the commandering of a professional talent. The fact that an artist is temporarily incapacitate ought not to make him fair game to anybody who is able. My talent has cost a lot in heart-ache and paint-bills; and I don't want to compromise myself.'[17]

Her fear of exploitation was realized when she discovered the screens would be used not in the hall but in the patients' bedrooms. Feeling betrayed, she wrote to Scott: 'To waste a professional talent, the cumulate result of years of effort, aspiration and heartbreak on a venture which will never see the light of day but most probably will be maltreated by every manifestation of psychosis is, to me, an abuse of the soul, human faith, and metier that is almost beyond my capacity to envisage.'[18]

Even the payment for her work would be offset against her hospital bills, just as her royalties from *Save Me The Waltz* had been offset against Scott's debt to Scribner's. She felt strongly payment of hospital fees was Scott's responsibility. 'I dont want to pay these bills', she told him, 'because I do not need what they buy.' She was, however, frightened that if she refused the art job she would be relabelled psychotic.

By Christmas she had been well enough to travel alone to Montgomery, where she remained absolutely stable throughout the vacation. On her return she wrote to Scott determinedly: 'There isn't forever left for either of us . . . I have a home to turn to while I organize an existence . . . I ask you to acknowledge not only on the basis of your obligation to me – as your wife – but also on the terms of your social obligation.'[19]

Scott, occupied with his new Pat Hobby stories about an ex-Hollywood gag writer, ignored her.[20]

However, something *was* changing, even though Scott's mind

was not. For the first time since her initial hospitalization ten years ago, Zelda was able to send and receive uncensored mail.[21] In February Carroll agreed to a compromise over the screens which were to be decorative only, so that as she explained with relief to Scott, her 'best and most exacting talents [were not] being buried within the confines of psychotic morass'.[22] She was convinced Carroll was on the point of letting her out. Scott treated her hunch as fantasy until suddenly he received a letter from Carroll, dated 4 March 1940, informing him Zelda had held to her routine in Montgomery and could be trusted to be self-sufficient, and suggesting she be released from Highland.

Scott, astonished, responded: 'Your letter was a complete surprise, but of course I am delighted.'[23] He gave Zelda the long-awaited news immediately: 'It is wonderful to be able to write you this. Dr Carroll has for the first time and at long last agreed that perhaps you shall try to make a place for yourself in the world . . . you can go to Montgomery the first of April and remain there indefinitely or as long as you seem able to carry on under your own esteem . . . I can share your joy.'[24] Simultaneously he wrote to Minnie: 'This is a complete about-face for him [Carroll], but I do not think that his suggestion comes from any but the most sincere grounds.'[25]

Scott seemed more confused by the news than Zelda. It is not clear whether he had been exaggerating the hospital's position to the Sayres in 1939 or whether Carroll had suddenly reversed his attitude. If so, why? It is possible that Zelda knew more about the reasons than she let on, and even – judging from a later event – might not have been above a bit of blackmail to secure her release.

During Zelda's last months at Highland, Carroll had been involved in a rape case with one of his patients. There is strong evidence that the patient in question was not the only one subjected to sexual abuse, and that Zelda herself may have been an unfortunate victim of Dr Carroll's mistreatment. Dr Irving Pine, Carroll's colleague, said many years after Zelda's release but without equivocation: 'Dr Carroll treated his women patients badly including Zelda.' Pine went further: 'Dr Carroll took advantage of several women patients including Zelda.'[26] This traumatic incident could have given a bright patient like Zelda a certain leverage.

That Zelda was prepared to use this advantage later when, out of hospital, she received a staggeringly expensive Highland bill, is shown in a letter she wrote to John Biggs, who had taken over the management of her financial affairs after Scott's death.

My own attitude towards the hospital was one of complete compliance until August [1939] – after which time I resorted to my own discretion; having received no recognition of an impeccable record for two years. The proprietor [Carroll] has been implicated in a rape case (which could no doubt be substantiated from legal records) and might be willing to compromise; if I am in a position to protest this bill.[27]

In the event, it seems she had protested sufficiently to be allowed to leave Highland. At last Scott would be free of hospital bills. At last Zelda would be free. Scott, however, had made two provisions: one that she be paroled into her mother's care; the other that if she became ill she could be readmitted to Highland. He asked Carroll for a written statement that would absolve him of any responsibility if Zelda relapsed. Carroll agreed and wrote a warning letter.

Mrs Fitzgerald's history shows a definite cyclic tendency and we must look forward with apprehension to her inability to meet emotional situations, to face infections, or to indulge in alcohol, tobacco or drugs without a rapid return to her maniacal irresponsibility. Let it be known that Mrs Fitzgerald is capable of being absolutely irresponsible and intensely suicidal. Her present condition, however, is one of gentleness, reasonable capacity for cooperation and yet with definitely reduced judgment maturity.[28]

On previous departures from hospitals, Scott had fetched her in a car. Either he transferred her to another institution or he took her home, where Scottie awaited her. This time, on 15 April 1940, when after four years she left Highland it was entirely on her own. She climbed on an early morning bus to Montgomery, clutching not her husband's hand but his cool letter which made it chillingly clear she was not welcome in Hollywood. 'I do hope this goes well. I wish you were going to brighter surroundings but this is certainly not the time to come to me and I can think of nowhere else for you to go in this dark and bloody world . . . So Bon Voyage and Stay well.'[29]

On Zelda's arrival in Montgomery the oak-vaulted streets were garlanded with purple and white wisteria, the gardens blazed with hydrangeas, azaleas and flowering quinces, and pink primroses clothed the fields.

During the early months Zelda worked in Minnie's garden, building a patio where she could listen to the white doves while she painted flowers which she saw as a spiritual expression of turmoil and hope. She hired a bicycle and rode regularly through town, attracting attention in new exotic coloured clothes, for Scott provided her with a small board and dress allowance of $30 a week. She restarted dance lessons, resumed her regime of long walks, invited her old friends Livye Hart and Julia Garland to join her on excursions. Evenings she spent with her mother quietly reading, cooking or at the movies. But the tranquillity of this limited life was insufficient to throw off the effects of ten years' institutionalization. Initially she wrote to Scott: 'I don't write; and I dont paint: largely because it requires most of my resources to keep out of hospital . . . making the social adjustment is more difficult tha[n] I had supposed.' Though Zelda acknowledged the challenge: 'I am conversant with the difficulties which probably confront me: middle aged, untrained, graduate of half-a-dozen mental Institutes', she was not prepared for its toughness.[30]

Setbacks occurred in June when according to Minnie, shocked at the severity of Zelda's suffering, her daughter suffered a 'toxic attack'.[31] Scott urged Scottie to spend part of her summer with Zelda. But on the morning of 18 June Zelda telegraphed Scott: 'I wont be able to stick this out. Will you wire money immediately that I may return Friday to Ashville. Will see Scottie there. Devotedly Regretfully Gratefully – Zelda.' However, in a renewed burst of optimism that afternoon, she wired again: 'Disregard telegram am fine again. Happy to see Scottie.'

When Scottie arrived on 20 June both mother and daughter were determined to make the visit a success. Scottie reported to Scott that she had been an angel and they had 'really gotten along rather well'. But Scottie had been unprepared for her mother's elaborately worded ideas and lack of energy. She saw Zelda as a 'fish out of water'.[32] Whereas Zelda was in truth a patient who'd swum out of a hospital tank and was in danger of drowning in the sea. Scottie knew too little to take into consideration how a decade of insulin shocks had altered her mother's personality.

What the hospital had failed to tell the Sayres, what even Scott had failed to take into account, were the side-effects of her electroshock therapy, which were evident in Scott's description to the Murphys of Zelda's changed persona. 'Zelda is home . . . She has a poor pitiful life, reading the Bible in the old fashioned manner walking tight lipped and correct through a world she can no longer understand . . . Part of her mind is washed clean + she is no one I ever knew.'[33]

But part of Zelda's mind was still functioning well, if not consistently. She was determined that with God's help she would regain a hold on a normal, if much more ordinary, existence. After a few months she began exhibiting art works locally, and made a serious sustained attempt at her last novel with its ironic title *Caesar's Things*.

When Sara Mayfield saw her in late summer Zelda confessed how devastating it was to have returned to Montgomery as a semi-invalid. She told Sara that most weekdays she sat 'in peace and serenity' in St John's Episcopal Church because there was 'no place else to go and think unless I take a streetcar and ride to the end of the line and back'. On Sundays she went to the Church of the Holy Comforter where, watched by old friends, she would make notes for her novel, with its religious theme. Religious convictions had become increasingly a source of strength for Zelda.

She drew strength also from the regular correspondence with Scott which, with the safety of thousands of miles between them, had again become affectionate. Scott however still avoided two subjects: his mistress, Sheilah Graham, and his worsening health. To deny illness to Zelda perhaps allowed him to deny it to himself.

Scott's first heart spasm took place in January 1940, while opening a jammed window in his Belly Acres cottage. Dr Clarence Nelson scared him with warnings of worse to come, so Scott moved back to a city apartment on North Laurel Avenue, West Hollywood, just one block from Sheilah. He still kept his address hidden from Zelda. In March 1940, on a flight to Tucson, he felt sick, panicked and asked for a doctor, nurse and ambulance to meet him at the airport. When they landed he had miraculously recovered. But his illness was not merely a fantasy. At Dorothy Parker's cocktail party in September 1940, playwright Clifford Odets observed 'Fitzgerald, pale, unhealthy, as if the tension of life had been wrenched out of him'.[34] Forty-eight drops of digitalis to keep his heart working properly, as well as potentially dangerous doses of barbiturates, became insufficient.

On 28 November at Schwab's drugstore on Sunset Boulevard he suffered his first serious attack of angina pectoris.[35] He was ordered bedrest and wrote on a lap-board. He told Zelda the cardiogram showed his heart was repairing itself, and that by writing 1,750 words a day he hoped to finish the first draft of *The Last Tycoon* by 15 January.

He was weaving the tale of his romance with Sheilah into the novel, but like his protagonist Stahr, Scott was in love with the memory of his wife – though by now only with the memory. He was also half in love with death. It haunted his thoughts, for he felt more fragile than he admitted. He wrote to Scottie: 'You have two beautiful bad examples for parents. Just do everything we didn't do and you will be perfectly safe. But be sweet to your mother at Xmas . . . Her letters are tragically brilliant in all matters except those of central importance.' Remember, he told Scottie, 'the insane are always mere guests on earth, eternal strangers carrying around broken decalogues that they cannot read'.[36]

At the same time as his reflection about Zelda, only one week before his own death, Scott was still ruminating over his friendship with Emily Vanderbilt. He wrote two letters mentioning how well Tom Wolfe had captured Emily's character in his novel *You Can't Go Home Again*. 'I've read . . . most of Tom Wolfe's [novel]', he wrote to Perkins. 'The portraits of the Jacks . . . [and] Emily Vanderbilt are magnificent.' Two days later he wrote to Scottie: 'I am still not through Tom Wolfe's novel & can't finally report it but the picture of "Amy Carlton" (Emily Davies Vanderbilt who used to come to our appartment in Paris – do you remember?) with the cracked grey eyes and the exactly reproduced speech, is just simply perfect. She tried hard to make Tom – *sans succes* – and finally ended by her own hand in Montana . . . in a lonely ranch house.'[37]

Then he put his will in order and instructed his executor to destroy all documents relating to Zelda's illness unless she proved still to be ill, in which case they must be handed to a responsible doctor and kept out of Scottie's reach. In December, recurrent dizziness made him vacate his second floor apartment and move into Sheilah's ground floor flat on North Hayworth. Again he reassured Zelda: 'I'm quite able to work, etc., if I do not overtire myself.'[38]

However, on Friday 20 December, while he and Sheilah were leaving the Pantages Theatre after seeing a film, dizziness turned into a second heart attack, and he stumbled to the car. The following day at three o'clock in the afternoon he suffered his third, this time fatal, attack. He was propped up on Sheilah's green armchair, munching a chocolate bar as he worked on a feature for the Princeton *Alumni Weekly*. Suddenly he jerked like a puppet out of the chair, fell against the mantelpiece, clutching at it in terror, then silently slumped on to the floor. Though Sheilah summoned medical aid it arrived too late to save him.[39] He died of occlusive coronary arteriosclerosis, aged forty-four, with 44,000 words of his last novel written.

John Biggs, Scott's executor, asked Frances Kroll, Scott's young secretary, to call a Los Angeles mortician to take Scott's body to the Pierce Brothers Mortuary in a seedy part of town at 720 West Washington Boulevard. A cosmetic mortician did his worst and

Scott, with rouged cheeks and flushed temples, was put on view in the William Wordsworth room. A visitor recalled he was laid out to look like a cross between a floor-walker and a wax dummy. 'Except for one bouquet of flowers and a few empty chairs, there was nothing to keep him company except his casket.' Dorothy Parker, one of the few friends present, ironically quoted Owl-eyes' comment on Gatsby: 'The poor son-of-a-bitch.'[40]

Ober called Zelda to tell her that Scott had died, but she was out walking with Julia Garland. It was Minnie who broke the devastating news when she returned. Zelda found the idea of a world without Scott Fitzgerald inconceivable. According to Gerald Murphy, she 'seized upon his death as the only reality that had pierced the membrane since they separated . . . [she] gave weird orders for the disposition of the body . . . then collapsed. She is not allowed to come to the funeral.'[41]

Scottie, staying with the Obers over the Christmas vacation, was at a dance in Poughkeepsie so Harold sent his son Dick to tell her. How did nineteen-year-old Scottie react? Fanny Myers was shocked to discover that on the day her father died Scottie also went to the opera. At the time Fanny felt this was insensitive, but in conversation many years later she and Honoria Murphy concluded that Scottie's lifelong habit of distraction and denial had operated at this most severe crisis of her young life.[42] Certainly, the day before the funeral, Gerald Murphy reported that 'Little Scottie is tragic and bewildered tho' she says that she has thought for so long that *every* day he would die for some reason.'[43]

The decision to send the body east was made by Zelda, in telephone discussions with Biggs, who felt Scott would like to be buried where his father was buried.

An official at Baltimore Diocese refused permission for a Catholic funeral service and burial at St Mary's Church, Rockville, Maryland, because Scott had not been a practising Catholic at his death. Instead the burial was at Rockville Union Cemetery, on 27 December, following an Episcopal service at the Pumphrey Funeral Home in Bethseda. Although too ill to attend, Zelda was involved in all the arrangements and asked her brother-in-law Newman Smith to act in her place. Sheilah Graham was asked not to attend out of respect for Zelda. About twenty loyal friends supported Scottie. They included Sara and Gerald Murphy, Louise and Max Perkins, Anna and John Biggs, Anne and Harold Ober, Ludlow Fowler and the Turnbulls. Cousin Cecilia Taylor and her four daughters came, so did Newman Smith but not Rosalind, and, most curiously, Dick Knight, the man Scott had detested. Max Perkins thought of telegraphing Hemingway in Cuba but instead wrote to him after the funeral: 'it didn't seem as if there were any use in it, and I shrank from doing it.'[44]

Zelda, who wanted the occasion filled with flowers, sent a basket of pink gladioli, which exactly matched Ludlow Fowler's spray. The Sayres sent red roses, the Bishops white chrysanthemums, the Turnbulls a white rose wreath, Honoria Murphy a mixed rose wreath, the Princeton Class of 1917 provided yellow roses and John and Anna Biggs showered the room with snapdragons, red roses and Zelda's favourite lilies.

The newspaper obituaries and articles recalled Scott as the symbol of the Jazz Age. The *New York Times*, acknowledging that Fitzgerald had 'invented a generation', said Fitzgerald was 'better than he knew'. The *New York Herald Tribune* called up the glamorous world of Fitzgerald novels before the Depression: 'the penthouses, the long weekend drunks . . . the vacuous conversations, the lush intoxication of easy money'.[45] Budd Schulberg wrote: 'He was not meant, temperamentally, to be a cynic . . . But Scott made cynicism beautiful, poetic, almost an ideal.'[46] Edmund Wilson edited tributes by Scott's friends, who included John O'Hara, Dos Passos, Glenway Westcott and John Peale Bishop, for two issues of *The New Republic*.[47]

John O'Hara wrote: 'He was professionally one of the most generous artists I've ever known . . . He kept his integrity . . . And he kept it in death . . . F. Scott Fitzgerald was a right writer . . . the people were right, the talk was right, the clothes, the cars were real, and the mysticism was a kind of challenge . . . the man could do no wrong.' O'Hara recalled telling Dorothy Parker: 'The guy just can't write a bad piece,' and Parker replying: 'No. He can write a bad piece but he can't write badly.'[48]

Scott wrote his own accurate epitaph in a conversation he had in Hollywood with Budd Schulberg Jnr.

I used to have a beautiful talent once, Baby. It used to be a wonderful feeling to know it was there, and it isn't all gone yet . . . I have enough left to stretch out over two more novels . . . maybe they won't be as good as the best things I've done. But they won't be completely bad either, because nothing I ever write can ever be completely bad.[49]

Nor can it.

For Zelda, in the dark night of her soul, it was always three o'clock in the morning. Some of her emotions were shared by John

Peale Bishop in his obituary poem 'The Hours':

All day, knowing you dead,
I have sat in this long-windowed room,
Looking upon the sea and, dismayed
By mortal sadness, thought without thought to resume
Those hours which you and I have known –
Hours when youth like an insurgent sun
Showered ambition on an aimless air,
Hours foreboding disillusion,
Hours which now there is none to share.
Since you are dead, I live them all alone.[50]

Did she fill those hours with memories of him as a wild child or a scapegrace wit, did she momentarily put aside his dissipations, his wasteful despairs, did she recall all he did and all he might have done before undone by death?

It seems she did, for what she wrote to Scottie, with forgivable exaggeration, was: 'Daddy was the key-note and prophet of his generation and deserves remembrance as such since he dramatized the last post-war era + gave the real signifigance to those gala and so-tragicly fated days.'[51]

Before the funeral Zelda wrote to Ober: 'In retrospect, it seems as if he was always planning happinesses for Scottie, and for me. Books to read – places to go. Life seemed so promisory always when he was around: and I always believed that he could take care of anything. It seems so useless and purposeless that I wont be able to tell him about all this. Although we were not close any more, Scott was the best friend a person could have [been] to me.'[52]

Her best friend who was also her worst friend was dead. His voice might continue to sound in her head but if she herself was not to remain silent she had at last to fill those unshared hours with sounds of her own. She started by looking back on the years she had shared with Scott. She recalled New York and Paris. Her love for both had been evident in *Save Me The Waltz* but she had never visualized it. Grieving for Scott, she saw dreamy flashbacks through cobwebs to a remembered (or newly reconstructed) happy past. But as Gatsby discovered, you can't repeat the past. If a future was to be created out of her solitary present, if she was to earn a solo credit, she had to write and paint in her own voice.

PART VI

In Her Own Voice
1941–March 1948

CHAPTER 25

Most descriptions of Zelda after Scott's death see her as frail, forgotten, hopelessly unproductive, constantly ill and a religious maniac. She is shown spending her last eight years in and out of Highland Hospital or dragging through Montgomery's sultry streets, lugging her Bible on a one-woman mission to convert the residents.

This overwhelmingly powerful myth sets her up as the left-over widow of the more famous Fitzgerald: pathetic, irrelevant, an insignificant epilogue to Scott's life. Her first biographer suggested: 'With Scott dead her life would become largely a matter of recollecting.'[1] Thereafter, 'broken' and 'past' became the two most popular epithets applied to her. She becomes the 'once dazzling beauty, who . . . returned to Montgomery in a broken and pitiful state'.[2] We are told old Southern friends were kind to her with the kindness reserved 'for the broken and helpless'.[3] Her life is condemned 'rather like the marquee on a theatre that has closed down; the main attraction . . . a thing of the past.'[4]

Many facts however do not support this myth. Nor do they support its attendant thesis that Zelda continued to wander in the borderlands between hysteria and insanity.[5] If we deconstruct the myth's three central components: Zelda's religious zeal as a symptom of madness, her invalidism and her creative stasis, we find evidence of clarity, healthy activity, above all enormous creative output.

During 1940–48 Zelda's art and writing both flourished. After Scott's death she produced a cycle of romantic watercolour cityscapes of New York and Paris to commemorate places they had visited together. By 1944, in seventeen nostalgic scenes, she immortalized New York's Fifth Avenue, Grand Central Station, Grant's Tomb, Times Square, Washington Square, the Big Apple and the New York Skyline. Her Parisian visualizations spanned the Arc de Triomphe, Notre Dame, the Pantheon, Luxembourg Gardens, Place de l'Opéra and aperitifs in the Madeleine.[6] These landmarks are arguably her most coherent and delicately assembled paintings. Yet amid the magic lurk two unsettling features: her beloved Paris completely lacks people, while busy Manhattan scenes show people with disconcertingly depressed faces. Is Zelda remembering a vacuum, acknowledging the cracks that showed through even their carefree times?

In the later 1940s, her mood strikingly different, Zelda embarked on her Biblical Tableaux, monumental in their brooding tragedy. Several, one critic suggested, displayed a quality bordering on magnificence through the sheer doggedness of their optical effect.[7] Glaring lemon, blood red and royal blue paintings interpret the Commandments, or offer Zelda's version of Christ's miracles and martyrdom. They are both layered and laboured as if the artist is insisting the viewer grapples with some arduous truth.

Bearing injunctions like 'Love One Another' and 'Do Not Steal', Zelda devotedly designed them as moral tracts for her first grandchild,[8] but their fierceness expresses Zelda's own dislocations of spirit. Fortunately her most tormented scenes are infused with reassuring symbols of hope: a trinity of white doves and a scattering of heavenly butterflies.[9] Autobiographical themes filter through religious references. Though it is too neat to see the Fitzgeralds as Eve and Adam, eyeing up temptation in the form of juicy red apples fallen at their feet, Zelda frequently indicated their marital tragedies were the consequences of their materialistic glossy lives.

These two significant series – cityscapes and religious renderings – marked the beginning and end of Zelda's most artistically productive eight-year period. In between she created another set of historical paper dolls, made an imaginative foray into nursery rhyme illustrations and invented a fairy tale cycle.

During the 1940s, four exhibitions of her work were held in Montgomery. In August 1941 the Late Paper Dolls were shown at the Museum of Fine Arts. They were in no way ordinary paper dolls, said the *Montgomery Advertiser*, but 'paintings after the manner of modern French painters, which Mrs Fitzgerald believes is the best way to introduce children to the trends in contemporary painting'.[10] These paintings, based on Arthurian legends which conveyed moral values, Zelda later sent to her grandchild as a way of staking a place in Scottie's family life.[11]

In May 1942 the Museum exhibited a selection of twenty-six paintings and drawings, which garnered a review saying there had never been 'seen in Montgomery a collection . . . showing a more exquisite feeling for color and design. She has evolved a style which is a mixture of Surrealism, Abstraction and her own originality.' Though several were portraits, Zelda did not attempt to produce likenesses, but turned her sitters into Surrealistic dreams.[12] The Museum hosted a reception for Zelda. She wrote excitedly to Biggs who, officially Scott's executor and Zelda's financial administrator, unofficially became her chief correspondent and confidant: 'My exhibit was a great success . . . 300 people came to the tea.'[13]

That November the Museum put on a third exhibition, followed in December by a show of watercolours and drawings at the Women's Club, Montgomery, where Zelda's new Chinese style dominated her flower sketches. The two most controversial paintings were a self-portrait, in which her intense strained gaze stares out stiffly, and an emerald green portrait of Scott with a cat slithering over his shoulder.

Wit took over when Zelda moved to fairy tales, using her trademark manneristic figures. Little Red Riding Hood loses her innocence to become an American Barbie with well developed breasts.[14] Liberating her characters from convention meant she transformed Wolf 1 with a screaming red jumpsuit and an aggressive scowl, while dressing Wolf 2 in menacing black hood and cape, with an arsenal of firearms. But Wolf 2 also owns a white flowing party frock, dainty elbow-length gloves and golden angel's wings. Like Hansel, in a strawberry-pink dress, Wolf is typically bisexual, as are all Zelda's male fairytale figures.

Her Three Piglets prance in front of a vista of three sweeping hills which are different shades of green so they recede shade by shade. There is nothing logical about Zelda's perspective so large daisies, the same size as small flowers in the foreground, bounce around on faraway hilltops.[15] At the topsy-turvy heart of Zelda's art lie the tragi-comic Alice-in-Wonderland illustrations she drew in her last years. Six watercolour and gouache works depict *The Pool of Tears*, *Advice from a Caterpillar*, *A Mad Tea-Party*, *The Queen's Croquet Ground*, *The Lobster Quadrille*, and *Who Stole The Tarts?* which, wildly theatrical like an improbable stage set, flaunts reckless reds and yellows. Absurd birds and beasts dare viewers to take them seriously.

It is a striking coincidence that Alice's creator and Zelda's nemesis were both named Carroll. Her children's art faithfully reflects the crazy nature of the adult's hospital life.[16]

That Zelda's last eight years were far from passive is shown most significantly in her paintings. Fairy tales and nursery rhymes are whimsical romps. These late paintings cavort, tumble and topple, though in a strictly disciplined fashion.

Zelda even ventured into painting and decorating bowls, trays and baskets which she was able to sell as a small source of income.[17] Acknowledging that many artists were even poorer than she, in 1942 she donated a substantial number of paintings to the Federal Art Project of Alabama to be given to artists in need of painting materials. Curiously, she insisted the artists clean her canvases and paint over them: an exceptional act of spiritual generosity.[18]

Despite Zelda's publicly acknowledged talent, her mother and her daughter privately refused to accept her paintings. Scottie felt she had talent but no eye for the market place. She constantly urged Zelda to paint more commercial pictures or produce more bowls so that she could sell them. Minnie Sayre saw *no* merit in Zelda's art, she quite simply hated the paintings. They were sick, tormented, ugly. She could not bear to hang them on her walls and would not go and see them displayed.[19]

Zelda had another clash with Minnie. She remained grateful towards her mother but no longer found her compatible to live with. Part of their incompatibility was due to Minnie's dislike of Zelda's paintings which were her most precious works of art. By 1942 she desperately resented living in Minnie's house. What would happen when Minnie, then eighty-three, died? Mama Sayre possessed only $15,000 plus her house, which would be divided between the the four remaining siblings. Worried that she would be made homeless, Zelda urged Biggs to let her buy a 'shelter' in North Carolina. Instead of her regular monthly sum could the estate turn over to her between $1,000 and $2,500?[20] When he pointed out the impracticality, she began a relentless campaign to leave Sayre Street.

In October 1943 she told Biggs she did not believe 'that my presence here is a very equitable arrangement and I can pay Mrs Wolff $3.50 for a room in Ashville and stay up there . . . My mother . . . has her way of life arranged and I am sick some and not absorbable. The arrangement is not compatible . . . . Since my presence is . . . a burden . . . since I cannot keep from resenting the air of surveillance with which I am surrounded and since this evokes hostility . . . if it lies with[in] the realm of possibility, I want to go. I am too grateful to her and far too much in her debt to forward unpleasantness, if there is any means of doing it otherwise.' She might get a job at one of the mills in Asheville 'and eventually straighten out this morass of expensive malady, regrettable social exigence and general malheur'. She implored Biggs: 'Won't you answer?'[21]

She even fretted over having no money for a burial fund for herself.

Feeling most urgently that my presence here is neither profitable nor pleasurable to my mother any longer, I write in half-desperation to ask if I may have a last $50 from the estate? With this sum I could pay bus-fare and float the extra ten dollars a month more than I have which it takes me to live and perhaps rehabilitate my shattered health . . . under the less personal . . . heavens of Ashville . . . How soon, if ever, will [Scott's] books be sold and will that money be available at any immediate or reasonable date?[22]

Biggs wrote back on 27 November: 'I think it would be very much better for you to stay with your mother through Christmas and then go up to Asheville . . . I know from my own experience that family matters are often very disturbing, but that if one acts suddenly one never feels right about it thereafter.' Zelda had no choice but to stay.

Zelda's writing ran parallel to her painting. She worked continuously on her novel *Caesar's Things*, so that by the time of her death she left a 40,000-word manuscript, in need of as much revision and a great deal more ordering and interpreting than Scott's *The Last Tycoon* had needed at his death. During summer 1942 she told Biggs: 'I am writing a book about the social structure being only manifestations of the Christian precepts to show how *every* deed we do is included within some principle of Christ. It is not anywhere near as formidable as it sounds.'[23]

But it *was* formidable, for two reasons. One was the lack of discipline and incoherence in part of the book, which showed the disastrous effects of insulin shock more obviously than did her paintings. The other was the complex layering of texts. For her ambitious design was to match a reworking of her initial autobiographical theme of childhood-marriage-aviator romance with a secondary theme of insanity (on which she had been working since 1933), then overlay both with a third theme of religious purpose.

Zelda saw her novel as heroic, with heroine Janno moving swiftly through events that closely mirrored the times the Fitzgeralds lived in. Childhood escapades, in a town most certainly modelled on Montgomery, are often violent and take place near a mental asylum which mends and punishes its residents. Under its brooding shadow, doom hangs latent in the air, while everyone waits for cataclysmic situations to develop. Janno grows up counselled by inner voices who urge her to obey authority figures. The child's faith is constantly broken and courageously renewed. When she meets Jacob (modelled on Scott), momentarily the scenes in Paris and the

Riviera lighten until the incident with Jacques (Jozanesque hero) plunges them into dark power struggles.

The twin tools Zelda uses to reinvent the familiar narrative are religious parables and the vision of the sane through the eyes of those labelled insane. The silencing of Zelda's fiction and the attempted murder of her literary creativity are repetitively pointed up in the novel. When Zelda handwrites the word 'writing' it comes out as 'muting' and when she uses the word 'aspirations' it is usually preceded by 'lost' or 'truncate[d]'. The book asks a great deal of readers but it is possible to 'read' the text as a journey from sanity (childhood and Jozan days) through 'madness' (hospital days) to rehabilitation (religious days).

When not engaged on the novel, Zelda gave editorial advice about several publications of Scott's work, and urged Wilson to edit *The Last Tycoon* and Max Perkins to publish it until finally, in October 1941, it appeared in print. She gave seminars about Scott's writings to English literature students at Huntington College,[24] lectured on religion and led a spiritual discussion at the Bluestockings,[25] took ballet lessons from Amelia Harper Rosenberg, a former pupil of George Balanchine, and (under John Biggs's auspices) began to dabble in stocks and shares on the New York Stock Exchange.[26]

That she was intensely preoccupied with religion is indisputable. She spent hours writing religious tracts for family and friends or sending concerned spiritual messages, some of which verged on the apocalyptic.[27]

Baffled biographers have used Zelda's evangelical approach as a synonym for insanity. Even Minnie Sayre thought her daughter had 'gone off the deep end about religion', due to Zelda's studious interest in the Book of Revelation and to her increased use of imagist and metaphorical language.

Her religious preoccupations, however, can be viewed *not* as a symptom of mental illness but as a way of optimistically dealing with the tragedies of the previous decade. The scholar Kirk Curnutt points out that Zelda's doctrinaire faith, far from being a manifestation of madness, was something that relieved the psychological instability she had long suffered.[28] Rosalind would have agreed. Zelda, she said, had become 'a person of the utmost rectitude who spent her time at her art and in trying bravely to rehabilitate herself and in doing good for others'.[29]

When Zelda used religious symbolism in her *Biblical Tableaux* and throughout *Caesar's Things*, she was attempting something akin to

Scott's purpose and methodology in *The Crack-Up* essays. Curnutt suggests that her fundamentalism or conversion was an experiment to achieve a similar 'clean break' from her past.[30] Like Scott, she wanted to burn away traumas and start anew. That she was able to make so productive a start whilst still facing recurrences of ill-health is because, as Rosalind rigorously emphasized, Zelda was *not* an invalid. 'I find the description of her as "frail" unfitting. She had great physical endurance and energy. And even in her last years at our mother's here, she walked miles every day and worked the garden . . . She was too vital to appear delicate.'[31]

Yet, in order to present Zelda systematically both as 'an invalid' and as 'invalid', biographers have stated that she returned to Highland several times for very long periods each time. Hospital bills and correspondence between Zelda and John Biggs show conclusively that those dates are inaccurate and the stated lengths of internment false.

Zelda's first return to the Asheville hospital is reputed to be August 1943 to end of February 1944: a six-month sojourn. Zelda *did* spend part of that August in Asheville, but she stayed with Tom Wolfe's mother at 48 Spruce Street, from where she wrote regularly to Biggs, telling him she had run into former hospital 'cell-mates' on the street. She picnicked, swam, and would have stayed longer, 'but the house is so dirty I think it best to go before atrification sets in. It seems remarkable that the vitality and inclusive metaphor and will-to-live of Wolff's prose should have known these origins.'[32] Back at Minnie's house, her letters to Biggs until Christmas 1943 show she did *not* enter hospital until the new year 1944, when she stayed only eight weeks.

Her second hospitalization is generally held to be from early 1946 to late summer/early fall: this would have been another eight-month incarceration, again suggesting serious illness. However her correspondence with Biggs throughout winter, spring and summer 1946, written from and received at 322 Sayre Street, Montgomery, shows otherwise. She did not re-enter hospital until the start of July 1946 and she left 23 September: a period of only twelve weeks.[33]

Rosalind's assessment of Zelda's health is more realistic: 'She remained a highly nervous person and *occasionally* had to return to the hospital to get herself under control, but she also had many long good periods when she was able to follow her interests, keep up with her friends, and live a fairly normal life.'[34]

Let us scrutinize Zelda's last seven years to see how she fared before her third, final, hospitalization.

We find her in January 1941 still living at the Rabbit Run, her mother's small white bungalow at 322 Sayre Street. Zelda's old upright piano and rocking chairs offered a place for repose in the chintzy sitting room. Zelda divided her time between her sister Marjorie next door, her mother, old friends like Livye and a young disabled girl she befriended.

Her years at Sayre Street were years of struggle.

Her first battle was with encroaching poverty.

Although Biggs remarked that Scott left the estate of a pauper and the will of a millionaire,[35] Fitzgerald was not quite as destitute as legend suggests. His 1940 earnings had been $14,570. He left $738.16 in the bank, $486.34 in cash and his personal possessions. Those apart, the bulk of his estate was a mere $44,225.15, the reduced value of his insurance policy.[36] He died owing $4,067.14 to Highland, $5,456 to Scribner's, more than $1,500 to Perkins, and $802 to Ober who waived nearly $3,000 in accumulated interest on loans. Those debts were paid out of the estate. Biggs used the remaining amount of less than $35,000 from the insurance policy to set up a trust for Zelda and Scottie for the next seven years.[37] An annuity purchased for Zelda gave her just under $50 a month and she qualified for a $35 monthly pension as a veteran's widow.[38] When Biggs reassured her that Scott had left enough to take care of her on the same basis as before, she replied stoutly: 'The idea of poverty is not a new one and I am well-conversant with its exigence.'[39]

She confessed to Biggs that 'to encompass the fact that he [Scott] wont be getting off the train any more bringing the promise of happiness and the possibilities of new purposes makes my heart-break. His pockets were always full of good times and his heart full of silly songs about what wonderful things there were to do, and I will miss him.'[40]

She missed Scott particularly for his protective role towards her, so Biggs took over that function too. In January 1941, Zelda, worried that there was insufficient money to keep Scottie at Vassar, told Biggs 'she can start looking around for a job – or maybe Max could find her something to do at Scribners. She is intelligent and beautiful and there must be some way of supporting the youth when they are as deserving as herself.' Biggs immediately organized Ober, Perkins and Murphy to pay jointly for Scottie to finish college.

Anna Biggs also became Zelda's good friend, often inviting her to their gracious Wilmington house with its 'haunted terrace and bounteous windows'.[41] John, however, let Zelda down in two significant ways. When his secretary, who posted Zelda's regular monthly cheques, was on holiday, he would frequently forget to post them himself. Biggs, as a wealthy lawyer soon to be Senior Circuit Judge of the 3rd Circuit,[42] could not comprehend that the poor live from hand to mouth without reserves to draw upon.[43] Many times Zelda was forced to endure the humiliation of reminding him. Though her correspondence shows a new businesslike competence (she even dates some letters) there is still the familiar undertone of the housewife-dependent who is 'devoted and grateful'.

When she accumulated debts her letters became wittier: 'Dear John, Scottie tells me that the streets in Heaven only are paved with gold: a matter which really should receive more attention from the local civic authorities. However, she says that you most generously will take care of a staggering and involved array of debts which I have, unsuspectingly, accrued.' Among debts to Minnie for board ($20), to a jewellery store for a wedding gift ($10), to a dressmaker for what in Scottie's eyes was an 'acceptable' suit-kimona ($30) and to the bank to replace some pension back-pay she had 'borrowed' ($100) lurked a highly intriguing 'spiritual debt' of $42 which she owed the Lord.[44] On that occasion Biggs, not wishing Zelda to fall out with God, took care of the debts; but he wrote a typically admonishing letter warning Zelda to live within her means.[45] The problem for Zelda was that the means were insufficient to live within, despite the fact that she rarely went to the hairdresser or movies, did not drink, smoked six cigarettes at most a day, had four friends whom she seldom saw, bought only one Victrola album a month ($5), a mere $5 worth of paints a month, and went to bed at nine to save electricity.[46]

Biggs's second failure was in not recognizing how much Zelda's art meant to her. In January 1941 Zelda asked him to send to Montgomery her paintings which were stored with Scott's possessions.[47] It was the first of many similar requests for fifteen months during which Biggs ignored the issue. Only in January 1942, when the Montgomery Museum of Fine Arts wanted to give Zelda a show, did he deal with the matter. Even then she did not receive the paintings until 18 March.[48]

Though surrounded by family, Zelda struggled with a particular kind of loneliness. She missed the stimulation of old friends but was unsure how to preserve them in the light of her new spiritual ideas and her medically dampened-down personality.

Gerald and Sara, saddened at her absence from Scott's funeral, had told her of its grace. In reply she sent them a poignant letter: 'Those tragic ecstatic years when the pockets of the world were filled with pleasant surprizes and people still thought of life in terms of their right to a good time are now about to wane . . . That he won't be there to arrange nice things and tell us what to do is grievous to envisage.'[49]

But beneath the overt text, it is as if Zelda was saying farewell not only to Scott but to the Fitzgeralds' fifteen-year friendship with the Murphys.

Ernest, who had dumped Pauline in favour of the journalist Martha Gellhorn, now his third wife, also said an appreciative farewell to the Fitzgerald-Murphy friendship, indicating it had hinged on Scott: 'Poor Scott,' he wrote to Sara. 'No one could ever help Scott but you and Gerald did more than anyone.'[50]

That year, however, the Murphys were having their own share of personal problems. The deaths of their two sons had left them struggling with complex griefs. Sara turned to no one. Gerald, in 1940, turned to a young homosexual Rhodes scholar, Alan Jarvis, a sculptor and art historian. Gerald, who shared the blond youth's passion for Manley Hopkins and Bach, initially became his mentor, then his beloved soulmate. Their relationship may not have been physical but on Gerald's side was intense and consuming. Though Sara noticed and became edgy the strength of their marriage, unlike the Fitzgeralds' under a similar tension, was able to accommodate this.[51]

When Zelda visited the Murphys in New York, both she and they were less at ease than they had been when Scott was alive. Perhaps it was because the Murphys had access to information about Scott's last years in Hollywood with Sheilah that Zelda only suspected. Or perhaps the Murphys' emotional difficulties made them defensive. The bonds, still there, were rooted now in memories.

As Zelda turned the Murphys into her wealthy fictional couple, the Cornings, in *Caesar's Things*, she cast a cooler satirical glance at her friends than their old affection warranted. The Cornings, who offer Janno and her husband Jacob (the Zelda and Scott characters) Bacardi cocktails before brilliant dinners for 'the stars . . . migratory Americans and . . . French people of consequence', have a treasure-house in St-Cloud which Zelda with her new anti-materialistic stance found disturbing.

Van Vechten, her former ribald buddy, was another who came under her axe for over-indulgences. 'There is much need of faith and charity in this aching world where there is so much spiritual destitution,' she admonished him.[52]

Zelda found it easier to keep in regular contact with Perkins, firstly because they focused on publishing Scott's posthumous writings, and secondly because he became her consultant in 1941 when she made serious plans to publish a book of her paper dolls.[53]

Zelda was more able to deal with new acquaintances, for brief periods, because they had fewer preconceived ideas about her. She enjoyed meeting Alabama University student Paul McLendon, who visited regularly in the early Forties to discuss literature. Later a Princeton undergraduate, Henry Dan Piper, arrived in Montgomery to conduct several interviews with Zelda about her life with Scott. Piper recalls Zelda itemizing her four most traumatic life events: her broken relationship with Lubov Egorova; her brother Anthony's suicide; her own suicide attempts at Sheppard Pratt; and her marriage breakdown. It is interesting, in the light of her continuous fictional reworking in *Caesar's Things* of the unconsummated romance with Jozan, that he does not get a mention. For both Fitzgeralds it seems the Jozan incident was significant solely in literary terms. Perhaps it was another example of Gerald's comment to Scott that only the *invented* parts of life were meaningful.

Zelda showed Piper her manuscript, took him to the Montgomery Museum of Fine Art to see her paintings, then to honour their new friendship gave him a self-portrait. Nor was he the only recipient of her paintings. She sent oils to the Kalmans, painted the Montgomery Capitol on a compact for Sara Mayfield, decorated a cocktail tray for Anna Biggs, gave Lawton Campbell a watercolour of a rhododendron in bloom and painted bowls with scenes of Great Neck, St Raphaël, Ellerslie, La Paix and Felder Avenue for Scottie.

In December 1941 the United States entered World War Two. Virginia Cody, sister of Zelda's old beau Dan, who was organizing an élite Red Cross unit, asked Zelda to attend first aid classes then work for the unit.

The war, with its inevitable death toll of young people, made Zelda more conscious of her role as sole parent to Scottie, who in 1942 had graduated from Vassar to become a journalist on the temporary staff of the *New Yorker*. After that she took a fulltime post at Radio City Hall as a publicist but lasted only ten weeks. Despite her ignorance about sports she braved a *Time* magazine job as sports reporter. After abysmal coverage of baseball, boxing, tennis, golf and harness racing she moved speedily to *Time*'s radio news programme, followed later by a spell on *Fortune* magazine.

Throughout her daughter's ever-changing career Zelda struggled to establish an acceptable mother-role. She loved Scottie, she admired her, but she never quite got it right.

She begged Scottie to say her prayers, but in case she didn't, she prayed for her. Tentatively she offered housekeeping advice: 'In choosing arrangements, decide first on a theme . . . grandeur, simplicity, casualness or some studied harmony. These qualities are spiritual . . . Choose cheap Platonic concepts of furniture: split bottom chairs, kitchen chairs and wicker rather than imitation decorators items. A pewter pot or an earthenware crock is more appropriate to garden roses . . . Lamps are a major item: one should be able to see by them.'[54] All highly sound, but in Scottie's view out of date and unasked for!

In 1942 they argued about Scott's library (largely contemporary fiction), bequeathed to Zelda in his will. Zelda, impecunious, did not want 'this testimonial of our generation to be moth eaten and worn away fruitlessly when it might be serving some purpose' and wished to sell it to Princeton University Library. Scottie disagreed furiously. 'Even millionaires are disposing of their goods,' Zelda wrote in exasperation to Biggs. 'When Christ taught "Store not up for yourselves treasures on earth" – He was not just making pretty phrases by giving us a way of salvation. He said: "Go sell everything and follow me" and that is what He meant.'[55] Scottie now had the Lord against her as well; and within days John Biggs also. He thought that Scott's own papers should be sold to give Zelda sorely-needed funds as well as to provide a permanent memorial to Scott. Such an idea, he said, would have given Scott no end of a kick![56] Zelda, who agreed, generously asked John to send Scottie half the money.[57]

Their relationship improved after Scottie married Ensign Samuel Jackson (Jack) Lanahan, whom she had dated since she was at Vassar and he at Princeton. Son of a wealthy stockbroker, like Scott a graduate of St Paul Academy, he was serving on the USS *Card* in the Atlantic as assistant navigator. During his leave, their wedding took place at the Church of St Ignatius Loyola, New York, on 13 February 1943. The Obers planned both the wedding, for which Anne bought Scottie's dress and at which Harold gave Scottie away, and the reception at the Barclay Hotel. Shortly after the wedding Jack returned to overseas duty.

Although the wedding announcement, embossed with the Fitzgerald coat of arms, read: 'Mrs Francis Scott Fitzgerald has the honor of announcing the marriage of her daughter . . .' Zelda was conspicuously absent. Most biographers write off her non-attendance as another sick episode. The truth is more complex. Scottie failed to invite her early enough. 'I felt guilty', Scottie wrote later, 'about having left notifying my mother until it was too late for her to plan to come, but she was not well enough at the time and I feared that if she was in one of her eccentric phases it would cast a pall over the affair.'[58] It must have seemed to Zelda like a rerun of Scottie's graduation where she was made to feel unwelcome, or even her own wedding. This was worse.

Zelda wrote one sad letter to Anne Ober thanking her for the wedding cake, which she had shared with Dos Passos who had briefly called on her in Montgomery. Zelda said how sorry she was 'she couldn't be of any service' at her daughter's wedding.[59]

Then with great fortitude Zelda returned to forgiving her spirited daughter.[60] The hospital experiences Zelda had endured would have made many people bitter but astonishingly Zelda seemed to have become more compassionate. In June 1943 she asked Biggs to burn all the hospital correspondence, Scott's copies of which were then in the estate files, as she thought they would upset her daughter. Her own distress at reading not only the medical reports but also Scott's private letters about her condition can be imagined, but she never revealed it to Scottie.

To compensate for the wedding debacle, Scottie invited Zelda to Scarsdale, New York, for a week during summer 1943. Zelda had to ask Biggs for $100 for the trip. She said she felt 'very selfish at asking vacation while the Belgians die of starvation and degradation stifles the French and the British hang on by shell-shock and delusions of grandeur.'[61]

When Scottie accepted another reporting job at the New Yorker in February 1944, Zelda frequently sent her watercolours which Scottie showed to staff writer Brendan Gill. Though Gill tried to get them published, their 'nonrepresentational diagonal slashes, triangles and other geometric forms . . . the expression of a violent, undischarged rage . . . [were] works radically unsuited to the New Yorker.'[62]

Scottie herself suited the magazine very well. Gill described her as 'exceptional in energy and in her sunny good nature – none of the series of misfortunes that had dogged her parents appeared to have cast the least shadow over her.'[63]

Shadows that *did* lurk between mother and daughter were swept into the background by the news of Scottie's pregnancy. On 26 April 1946, when Thomas Addison Lanahan was born, Zelda wrote:

'Scottie darling, I am so <u>happy</u> about the baby; So glad he is a little boy and so rejoiced that you are well + going to be happy with a family + love + happiness which you deserve. It's <u>wonderful</u> to be a grandmother. I haven't been so beaming in years and I can't wait to hold him and see how he works etc . . . isn't it swell to have a grandson? I can't think of anything more to the point and I am so full of happiness for you and all the love a heart can hold.'[64] She wrote proudly to Ludlow Fowler to announce her grandson's arrival, reminding him of the excited telegrams they had exchanged at Scottie's birth. Entirely positive about her new role, she decided that 'without small children now one seems out of tempo with the world as human relationships seem to have survived the more pressingly than the impersonal aspects of civilization.'[65] In May she wrote to Biggs: 'I long to see my grandchild who is surely miraculous and will try to get to New York this summer . . . human relationships mean more than they did.'[66]

Before Zelda was able to see her grandson, again she grappled with ill health. During her hospitalization from 1 July to 23 September 1946, Zelda wrote to Biggs to say she was folk dancing and hiking outdoors while silver throated birds flew in protest over the mountains. 'I will bend all my resources,' she said stoutly, 'to conforming and try to get off the debit-side as soon as I can.'[67] Her optimism increased when John sent her money from the movie rights of *Tender Is The Night* and when Scottie sent her 'darling pictures of the baby'. Highland told Scottie Zelda had adjusted well and 'at no time [had they] had any trouble with her'.[68]

They suggested it would be unwise for Zelda to live alone, but she should not be supervised so closely that she was unable to express her own personality.[69] After leaving hospital, Zelda stayed on in Asheville whence she wrote to Biggs that she was now 'in wonderful physical shape' and was sketching and played tennis with two entertaining friends.[70]

On 3 October she visited Scottie at 310 West 94th Street, New York, and was so delighted with baby Tim that they arranged for Scottie and Jack to bring the baby to Montgomery the following June, when Zelda would give a party for them and twenty guests at the Blue Moon restaurant.

After seeing Scottie, on 10 October 1946 Zelda visited the Biggs family. During an otherwise agreeable visit there were two discomfiting moments. When Anna placed a bowl of fresh berries on the table Zelda said their thorns reminded her of Christ's crown of thorns. Anna placatingly threw them out. Then John became worried that Zelda would be late for her train back to Montgomery, and momentarily Zelda thought Scott was by her side reassuring her she wouldn't miss it. She told John, and he anxiously hurried her off the premises.

A few months later, on 24 April 1947, Zelda confessed to Biggs something she had been holding back for years.

Dear John . . . For five years I have been desperately in love with a Russian General. Our love is sent by God and hallowed of Him and means more to me than marriage. You may not feel that your very great magnamity is au fait under such circumstance; since – of course – you assumed the obligation in fidelity to Scott . . . I . . . pray that you will forgive my not having told you before; which last is as incomprehensible to myself as it must be to you.[71]

The next typed letter from Biggs, on 6 May, totally ignores the reference to Zelda's romance. Either he did not take the remark seriously or he felt it wiser not to discuss it, but it is possible that he hand-wrote her an answer between 25 April and 5 May unseen by his secretary.[72] If so, Zelda destroyed it as she did most of her correspondence in the Forties.

Earlier clues offer evidence that this confession could have been rooted in reality. Zelda's fascination with Russia began with her love for Egorova, after which she painted a *Russian Stable* and at least two *Portraits of Russians*, one of which is now missing. In her last years she wrote an unfinished sketch about the Russian ballet and an unfinished story about a Russian officer. In 1942 she met a number of the militia stationed in Montgomery, among whom might have been a Russian General. Most significantly, six months before her confession she told John that she wanted to ask him something that he might find 'ridiculously unrealizable':

For some years now, I have longed to go to Russia: anyway, I have a spiritual mission in Russia. Of course I would never be able to save enough to get there . . . Therefore would you consider giving me my part of the proceeds of Tender Is The Night to this end & I will . . . write to Archie MacLeish and see if he will help me get a pass-port. I want to spend the summer there, going from Moscow to Sachi for nude bathing in the Black Sea, and visit the resorts of the Caucasus . . . I know that Russia is a big big country where bears eat people who stray off the highway; however, neuro-psychotic hospitals . . . are also soul-consuming; so it would probably come out about even. Won't you seriously consider what I so prayerfully ask: the world probably isn't going on much longer. Maybe you + Anna would also like to go to Russia.[73]

No money was available for such a trip, but Zelda refused to drop the idea. In January she wrote: 'Did you consider the idea of going to Russia about which I wrote you? This is probably the moment for cataclysmic action, if ever, now that the old order is done and the new one yet unasserted . . . maybe we had better go now.'[74]

Zelda's depression over the failed trip to Russia increased when tragedy struck several old friends that year. In June, Perkins died. 'I can't imagine why Max should die,' she wrote to John Biggs. 'He was so decorous + punctilious about keeping life in hand – It is so sad.'[75]

In September 1947 a worse event befell Katy and John Dos Passos. On 12 September, driving from Cape Cod to Connecticut, Dos, blinded for a second by the setting sun, collided with a truck. Dos lost an eye, but also his wife. Katy's head was sheared off by the windshield; she died instantly.

The smell of fear, illness, death and political paranoia was every-where. 1947 was the year the Un-American Activities Committee of the House of Representatives held their Hollywood hearings in which the Hollywood Ten (artists and writers) were all blacklisted. Dorothy Parker, Lillian Hellman, Don Ogden Stewart, now victims of the McCarthy regime, could no longer find work.

Zelda's third hospitalization, intermittent from 7 November 1947,[76] was not entirely with her agreement but at Scottie's repeated urgent requests. On 3 November Zelda wrote to Biggs: 'Scottie (as of course you know) wants me to go to Highlands for a while. [Though] glad of a chance to straighten up again . . . I hope I won't have to stay too long.' Admitted for deep shock insulin and another 'rehabilitation and re-education' programme, she stayed only a few weeks before returning to Montgomery. During late fall her sadness increased. She knelt with her mother by her bed, praying as they had done when Zelda was a child. Nothing lifted her spirits. She told Rosalind: 'I have tried so hard and prayed so earnestly and faithfully asking God to help me . . . I cannot understand why he leaves me in suffering.'[77]

After Zelda suffered a severe attack of asthma Mrs Sayre, believing she was close to collapse, called Scottie who convinced Zelda to take the train back to hospital. Her mother, her sister Marjorie and Livye Hart gathered on the porch of the Rabbit Run. Livye told Sara Mayfield that after they had said goodbye to Zelda, who began walking towards the taxi, she felt Zelda had a premonition. She ran back to the porch, threw her arms round Minnie and said: 'Mamma, don't worry, I'm not afraid to die.'[78]

In January 1948 Dr Pine, as her attending physician,[79] ordered a three-month electro-shock and insulin programme. The insulin further damaged her memory and increased her weight by 20 lb to 130 lb, which upset her. Whatever she had forgotten she could no longer remember. But she held on to the idea of herself as a painter and worked steadily on her Biblical paintings.

Her spirits improved dramatically when on 25 January her first granddaughter Eleanor Lanahan was born. On 9 March she wrote to Scottie:

> There is promise of spring in the air . . . I urgently long to see the new baby and know that you must be engrossed in the affairs of your increased family. Here we bat the volley ball through the promisory afternoon . . . I go into Ashville every now and then to sense the tempo of the traffic and see what new aspirations are engrossing the people . . . I am having insulin treatment which is extremely disconcerting; however it is almost over – I will be most grateful to be leaving . . . with dearest love Mamma.

She wrote cheerful letters to the Sayres saying how much she was looking forward to her spring return. She felt positive, her mind lucid. The night of her death, a friend of Sara Mayfield's from Selma visited the hospital:

> I was with Zelda in Asheville, NC, about an hour before her death. We had been to a hospital dance and, really, all of us had a wonderful time . . . At the time of her death her mind, to me, was as clear as a bell. She was attractive, gracious, and charming . . . When she found out . . . that we had mutual friends and acquaintances, she was overjoyed . . . She did not talk too much about Scott, but when she did, there did not appear to be any bitterness. I believe she was at peace with herself.[80]

Throughout this stay Zelda, treated as a voluntary patient, had been in an unlocked room and had gone into Asheville alone or with a companion. But that night, her bedroom was on the top fifth floor in Central Building, where she was locked in, and given sedatives by Nurse Doris Jane Anderson.[81] At 11.30 p.m. Anderson smelt smoke and reached the diet kitchen five minutes later, where she saw a five-foot wooden table with galvanized top burning like a hoop of fire. Terrified by the flames, Anderson made no attempt to put out the fire, but hurried to wake patients and unlock doors on the lower floors. Before calling the fire department she telephoned the Men's Building, Oak Lodge, as instructed by her supervisor,

Nurse Willie May Hall, who later denied at the inquest she had ever given such instructions. Anderson, told that internal lines were disconnected, finally telephoned the Fire Department at 11.44. By this point the fire had spread up a dumb-waiter shaft leading to the roof, spurting flames on every landing. There was no automatic fire alarm, no sprinkler system, stairways were cut off, wooden external fire escapes caught fire, blaze engulfed the building. When firemen arrived, it had been on fire three-quarters of an hour. Despite all their efforts, by 4 a.m. the building was reduced to rubble. Though twenty-two patients on lower floors in Central Building had been saved, no one had reached the fifth floor where Zelda lay. The Fire Chief, ironically named J.C. Fitzgerald, claimed if the alarm had been given thirty minutes earlier no lives would have been lost.[82]

Dr Pine said: 'Had she not been asleep, Zelda ought to have been well enough to have escaped and walked away from the top floor where she was trapped.'[83] A very different version appeared in the New York Herald Tribune on 12 March. Zelda's escape was impossible, they said, because all patients on her floor had been locked in their rooms, the windows were shackled with massive chains and padlocks, and of the ten women imprisoned in those top rooms only one managed to break the window and leap to safety. The report said journalists at the scene heard harrowing cries of victims in the top rooms. Dr Wylie D. Lewis later stated that all top floor victims were asphyxiated by smoke inhalation at about 11.45 p.m.[84] This would suggest that Zelda and the eight other women were already dead.

It took until 12 March to identify Zelda's remains by their location, her dental records and a single charred slipper beneath her burnt body.[85]

Rosalind, outraged at the accident, fired off an angry letter to Highland demanding that Minnie Sayre be spared all details. She had told Minnie Zelda was overcome by smoke when sleeping and not burned. 'She believes the body is intact and takes some comfort in the thought.'[86]

Three weeks after the fire, the night supervisor, Willie May Hall, surrendered herself to the city jail asking to be locked up, because she had had a compulsion to burn Oak Lodge and thought she might have set off the fire on 10 March. She claimed she had wanted to start a 'little trouble' to show up the night watchman, who had spurned her advances and would get the blame. Psychiatrists claimed Hall was suffering from delusions and dismissed her, but rumours persisted that the fire was arson and Highland employees were forbidden to discuss it.

All the victims' families sued Highland and were each awarded $3,000 compensation damages. Except for Zelda's. Questions remain. Why did the Sayres not ask for or receive compensation?[87] How could a modern hospital be so lacking in interior safety? Why was Zelda so fearful of returning to Highland? Why did she make that prophetic statement to her family about not being afraid to die? Why was she locked in a room on a top floor?

Zelda's ashes[88] were sent to the same Bethseda mortician who had directed Scott's funeral, and the same Episcopalian minister, Raymond P. Black, officiated at Zelda's memorial. Minnie Sayre was not well enough to attend, but Rosalind and Clothilde with husbands Newman Smith and John Palmer were there, as were Scottie, Jack Lanahan, John and Anna Biggs, the Obers, Peaches Finney, Margaret Turnbull and other friends.[89] After the service they drove out to the graveside in the Rockville Union Cemetery, Maryland, where Scott's original burial plot had been extended into a double vault for Zelda, and placed bunches of spring flowers on her grave. Margaret Turnbull laid two wreaths of pansies from La Paix over Zelda and Scott.

Two days later, Scottie wrote to her grandmother: 'Seeing them buried there together gave the tragedy of their lives a sort of classic unity . . . it was . . . reassuring to think of their two high-flying and generous spirits being at peace together at last. I have simply put out of my mind all their troubles and sorrows and think of them only as they must have been when they were young.'[90]

Despite Scottie's affectionate words, when she came to write her own memoir she did not mention Zelda's death at all. Zelda would not have been surprised.

At the time of her mother's death Scottie begged her grandmother to see Zelda's demise, as she herself did, as part of a pattern, as inevitable as day and night. But the pattern of Zelda's life and the mode of Zelda's death evoked terrible bitterness as well as distress in Minnie Sayre. Zelda's work, like Zelda's body, must be consumed by fire. Minnie instructed Marjorie to take every one of Zelda's paintings that were stored in the garage and burn them one by one in the yard.[91]

As a woman of her time Zelda had connived in literary and social self-sacrifice. She had learnt she could neither commission nor control desire but would accept its consequences. She had understood passion, both human and the Passion of Christ, in the Latinate sense of suffering. But she did not suffer meekly. Sara Haardt believed Zelda possessed 'a great deal more than the audacity or the

indestructibility of those war generations . . . she had super courage
– the courage that is not so much defiance as a forgetfulness of
danger, or barriers.'[92] Like her heroine Gay, Zelda 'was very courageous – braver than the things that happened to her, always.'[93]

In her last years, Zelda's voice was the voice of struggle: poverty,
obligation, loneliness and, in relation to her mother Minnie and her
daughter Scottie, loyalty and resentment.

From 1940 to 1948 Zelda's voice was also the voice of aspiration,
a word she used over and over in her last novel and throughout her
art and fiction notebook. Her most creative voice was the voice of
spiritual quest. But *every* voice she used was the voice of the South.
Although she was buried in the North with Scott rather than in the
grey gullied, grey stone Montgomery cemetery, Zelda's reconciliation was with the Deep South. Today 322 Sayre Street is burnt down.
A blistered waste ground encourages children to chase each other.
But outside 819 Felder Avenue Zelda's magnolia tree still blooms.
Paper-white narcissi blow in the breeze. Confederate jasmine perfumes the night air.

NOTES

The following abbreviations have been used:

FSF   Francis Scott Fitzgerald
ZSF   Zelda Sayre Fitzgerald
EH   Ernest Hemingway
MP   Max Perkins
PUL   Princeton University Library

1. Collections held in the Manuscripts Division, Department of Rare Books and Special Collections, Princeton University Library, are identified in the endnotes as follows:
    Zelda Fitzgerald Papers: CO183
    F. Scott Fitzgerald Papers: CO187
    F. Scott Fitzgerald Additional Papers: CO188
    John Biggs Collection of F. Scott Fitzgerald Estate Papers: CO628
    Craig House Collection: CO745
    Charles Scribner's Sons Author Files: CO101

2. When the author read all Zelda Fitzgerald's letters in the PUL archives only a few had been published (in *Life in Letters* and *Zelda Fitzgerald: Collected Writings*). When she wrote the biography the bulk of those letters were still unpublished. As this book goes to print some letters are being published in *Dear Scott, Dearest Zelda. The Love Letters of F. Scott and Zelda Fitzgerald*, which will alter their status.

3. The author took the decision to retain the idiosyncratic spelling of both Zelda and Scott Fitzgerald in passages quoted from their writings.

INTRODUCTION

1 Though Scott took the credit, H. L. Mencken coined the term flapper fifteen years before *This Side of Paradise*. He said it originated in England and described adolescent girls who *flapped* awkwardly while walking. British shops sold flapper dresses with long straight lines to hide such gracelessness.

2 Ironically, Zelda's daughter Scottie most cogently expressed this view: 'in defining genius as one percent inspiration and ninety-nine percent perspiration, Edison surely meant in one direction not in three. It was my mother's misfortune to be born with the ability to write, to dance and to paint, and then never to have acquired the discipline to make her talent work for, rather than against, her.' Scottie Fitzgerald Smith, *Zelda Fitzgerald: The Collected Writings*, ed. Matthew J. Bruccoli, Abacus, Little, Brown, London, 1993, p. vi. (Prefatory comments based on Scottie's Introduction to the exhibition catalogue for the Montgomery Museum of Fine Arts 1974 exhibition of Zelda Fitzgerald's paintings.)

3 I have followed the example of several contemporary art critics including Jane S. Livingston and Carolyn Shafer who have divided Zelda's art by theme or subject, i.e. landscapes, cityscapes, paper dolls, figurative paintings, Biblical allegories, flowers, fairy tales etc. Some themes do fall into specific time periods. The romantic hazy watercolour cityscapes of Paris and New York were painted in the 1940s after Scott's death to

commemorate their visits together. Some nursery tales were painted during Scottie's childhood; a further set were painted in Zelda's last eight years, some for her grandchild Thomas Addison Lanahan.

4 Eleanor Lanahan, Zelda's artist granddaughter, pointed out to me in our first conversation that all Zelda's paintings illustrate the idea of 'no ground beneath our feet'. Scott himself used a similar phrase earlier when he wrote in his September 1922 Ledger that life though comfortable was 'dangerous and deteriorating. No ground under our feet'. Scott's Ledger was the 14½" by 9½" business ledger in which he methodically recorded his professional and personal activities. He maintained this record until the end of 1936. It divides into five sections: 1. 'Record of Published Fiction' (sixteen columns giving the publication history of each work); 2. 'Money Earned by Writing since Leaving Army'; 3. 'Published Miscelani for which I was Paid' (including movies); 4. 'Zelda's Earnings': 5. 'Outline Chart of My Life' (a month by month chronology beginning with the day of his birth, partly in the third person). He probably began the Ledger late in 1919 or early 1920, though he may have started it in 1922 when he wrote to his agent that he was 'getting up a record of all my work'.

5 At the time Rebecca West noticed there was something 'frightening' about Zelda, 'not that one was frightened from one's own point of view, only from hers'. West to Nancy Milford, 10 Aug. 1963, Milford, *Zelda*, Harper & Row, New York, 1970, p. 99.

6 Elaine Showalter in *The Female Malady: Women, Madness and English Culture, 1830–1980* (Penguin, 1985) shows explicitly and at length how this worked during the period of Zelda's various hospital sojourns.

7 Henry Phipps Psychiatric Clinic of Johns Hopkins University Hospital, Baltimore.

8 I saw Zelda's problem (relating to the contentious issues of the rightful distribution of credits and who-owns-whose autobiographical material) as similar to the one Radclyffe Hall faced when she wrote the controversial lesbian novel *The Well of Loneliness*, which was taken to trial and banned as obscene. (Ironically, in America Scott Fitzgerald was among the impressive list of writers who came to the book's defence.) Hall's sensational martyrdom to a cause meant that a spotlight focused on one significant area of her life and rendered the rest unimportant by comparison.

9 Xandra Kalman gave this file to St Paul historical researcher Lloyd Hackl who generously made it available to me.

10 Ten years later Nancy Milford wrote in an essay about her experience with the biography: 'before publication, when I was done writing, I had sent the Fitzgeralds' daughter my manuscript and waited. She could not bear to read it, she said. She threatened suicide. I didn't know what to do, for I could not have done without what she had given me. She turned upon me as if I had stolen her past.' *The Writer on Her Work*, ed. Janet Sternburg, W. W. Norton & Co., New York, London, 1980, p. 35.

11 This batch at PUL included some records which could not be photocopied, but I was able to read everything and take accurate notes. Zelda Fitzgerald Papers, CO183: Box 6 III, Miscellaneous Notes and related material; Folder 18; F. Scott Fitzgerald Papers, CO187: Box 39, Folder 45; Box 40, Folder 4; Box 43; Box 49, Folders 2A, 6A; Box 51, Folders 7A, 10A, unmarked folder; Box 53 II, Folders 3A, 14A, unmarked folder; Box 54, Folder 10A; Craig House Medical Records, CO745: Box 1, Folders 1, 2, 3, 6A.

12 Dr Irving Pine.

CHAPTER 1

1 Sara Mayfield, *Exiles from Paradise: Zelda and Scott Fitzgerald*, Dell Publishing, New York, 1971, p. 11.

2 Jeffrey Meyers, *Scott Fitzgerald*, Papermac, Macmillan, London, 1995, p. 43.

3 ZSF, 'The Original Follies Girl', *Collected Writings*, ed. Bruccoli, p. 293.

4 Sara Mayfield, *The Constant Circle: H. L. Mencken and his Friends*, Delacorte Press, New York, 1968, p. 21.

5 Scottie Fitzgerald Smith, Memoir (holder Cecilia Ross). Also Eleanor Lanahan, *Scottie the Daughter of . . . : The Life of Frances Scott Fitzgerald Lanahan Smith*, HarperCollins, New York, 1995, p. 20.

6 Union General Tecumseh Sherman is remembered for his 'total war' technique, an unprecedented assault on non-military targets. His Atlanta campaign was known as the 'March to the Sea'. In Atlanta he defeated Confederate General John B. Hood in September 1864. Sherman's capture of the Confederate capital Richmond, Virginia, on 3 April 1965 was a decisive turning point in the war; four days later Confederate General Robert E. Lee surrendered to General Grant.

7 Most young women in Montgomery in the early part of the twentieth century recognized this aspect of their heritage. Zelda's Montgomery friend Sara Haardt wrote before her death aged 37 on 31 May 1935: 'Well, death, a full tropical death at the moment of greater promise, was the peculiar heritage of the South, and of all Southerners. I was merely coming into my own.' Sara Haardt, 'Dear Life', *Southern Souvenirs*, p. 310. ('Dear Life' originally published as 'Story', *Southern Album*, Sep. 1934.)

8 Scottie Fitzgerald Smith, 'The Maryland Ancestors of Zelda Sayre Fitzgerald', *Maryland Historical Magazine* 78:3, fall 1983, p. 217.

9 Thomas was known as 'The Big Spoon' by Indian friends because he fed them so well and as 'The Rattlesnake Colonel' by the British who came to fight the French.

10 Oldtown was later renamed Cresaptown.

11 Scottie Fitzgerald Smith, 'Maryland Ancestors', p. 217.

12 A revolt of corngrowers and distillers against excise tax on whiskey.

13 Sarah inherited her bravery from her great-great-grandfather the infamous John Coode, leader of the 1689 Maryland Revolution.

14 It was of course a severe case of rigor mortis but it scared the wits out of poor widowed Sarah. However she 'soon remarried, to a Mr Cobb'. Scottie Fitzgerald Smith, 'Maryland Ancestors', p. 227.

15 Ibid. Another version of this incident is given in a letter from Zelda to Scottie, *c.* 1947, quoted in Matthew J. Bruccoli, Scottie Fitzgerald Smith and Joan P. Kerr, eds., *The Romantic Egoists*, Charles Scribner's Sons, New York, 1974, p. 39.

16 Mayfield, *Exiles*, p. 4.

17 This ensured that both Anthony Sayre and Minnie Machen had Chilton cousins and were therefore distantly related.

18 He was elected both by soldiers in the field and by residents in his district.

19 In Zelda's first novel *Save Me The Waltz* she uses Willis's last fatal adventure. Alabama asks her mother about her grandfather. '"He was thrown from a race cart when he was eighty-three years old, in Kentucky."' This means something special to the young girl. 'That her mother's father had a graphic life of his own to dramatize was promising to Alabama. There was a show to join.' (ZSF, *Save Me The Waltz*, *Zelda Fitzgerald: Collected Writings*, p. 24). For Zelda there was always a show to join. Like Willis she had trouble picking which one. Though Willis the showman died seven years before Zelda's birth, she remembered him gazing down at her from his portrait on the sitting room wall. She swore he was twinkling. Zelda gave the Adventurer's portrait to Scottie, who hung it on her sitting-room wall until she died.

20 ZSF, *Waltz*, pp. 12, 9.

21 Zelda Sayre to FSF, late fall 1919, CO187, Box 42, Folder 27, PUL.

22 Scottie Fitzgerald Smith, Memoir.

23 Ibid.

24 Anthony D. Sayre graduated as valedictorian of his class. So excellent was his Greek that the previous year the College had awarded him a Maltese Cross, which his granddaughter Scottie kept for years under a towel in the guest room (Scottie Fitzgerald Smith, Memoir).

25 Helen Blackshear, 'Mama Sayre, Scott Fitzgerald's Mother-in-Law', *Georgia Review*, Winter 1965. Helen Blackshear was a close friend of Minnie's granddaughter Marjorie and knew Minnie well for ten years.

26 Ibid.

27 ZSF, *Waltz*, p. 10.

28 ZSF, *Caesar's Things*, ch. I, CO183, Box 2A, Folder 2, PUL. Zelda uses Scott Fitzgerald as well as Tony for her characterization of 'Monsieur'.

29 Blackshear, 'Mama Sayre'.

30 ZSF, *Waltz*, p.10.

31 Mayfield, *Exiles*, p. 15.

32 ZSF, *Waltz*, pp. 32, 21.

33 Given the Judge's icy calm, this only seems possible if the visit had occurred at the time of the Judge's nervous breakdown in 1918. The story originated with Gerald Murphy who had been told it by the Fitzgeralds as a racy part of their courtship.

34 Scottie Fitzgerald Smith, Memoir. Also Lanahan, *Scottie . . .* p. 19.

35 ZSF, *Waltz*, p. 10.

36 Records kept by Dr Oscar Forel (trans. Mme Claude Amiel) during Zelda's stay at Les Rives de Prangins clinic, Switzerland, 5 June 1930–15 Sep. 1931, p. 8. (Subsequently referred to as 'Prangins records'.)

37 ZSF, *Waltz*, p. 10.

38 Ibid., p. 12.

39 Ann Henley, Introduction, *Southern Souvenirs: Selected Stories and Essays of Sara Haardt*, ed. Henley, University of Alabama Press, Tuscaloosa, 1999, p. 27.

40 Anne Goodwyn Jones, *Tomorrow Is Another Day: The Woman Writer in the South, 1859–1936*, Louisiana State University Press, Baton Rouge, 1981, pp. 14–15.

41 There is a wonderful description of the town in Zelda's story 'Southern Girl', *Collected Writings*, p. 299.

42 Ann Henley, Introduction, *Southern Souvenirs*, 1999, pp. 2–3.

43 Sara Haardt, 'Southern Souvenir' (short story), *Southern Souvenirs*, p. 298.

44 Sara Haardt interview with ZSF at Ellerslie, Delaware, 1928, accepted but unpublished by *Good Housekeeping*. According to H. L. Mencken this was because of editor W. F. Bigelow's rage on discovering that Haardt was almost engaged to Mencken.

45 It was many years before Zelda's sister Rosalind and Scott and Zelda were all able to live in the prestigious Cloverdale area. Rosalind later bought a house in Perry Street. Scott and Zelda rented 819 Felder Avenue in 1931.

46 Koula Svokos Hartnett, *Zelda Fitzgerald and the Failure of the American Dream for Women*, Peter Lang, New York, 1991, p. 10. See also Eddie Pattillo, 'Last of the Belles: A Remembrance', *Montgomery*, July 1994. Both Pattillo and Hartnett (p. 10) report that Zelda and Katharine Clitherall Elsberry Perkins Steiner May Haxton considered themselves soulmates. Zelda's uncle Calvin Sayre married Katharine's great-aunt Kate Elsbury (the name is spelt several different ways, the two most frequent being Elsberry and Elsbury).

47 Zelda Sayre to FSF, Feb. or Mar. 1919, CO187, Box 42, Folder 13, PUL.

48 Conversations between Ida Haardt McCulloch (Zelda's classmate) and Janie Wall, and between Janie Wall and the author, June 1999, Montgomery.

49 Scottie Fitzgerald Smith, Memoir; also quoted in Lanahan, *Scottie . . .*, p. 19.

50 Scottie Fitzgerald Smith, Memoir.

51 ZSF, *Waltz*, p. 32.

52 Prangins records.

53 Sara Mayfield, *Constant Circle*, Delacorte Press, New York, 1968, ch. 2.

54 Tallulah's mother, Adelaide, died of blood poisoning three weeks after Tallulah's birth. Tallulah and her sister Eugenia were taken by their father, attorney and Congressman William Brockman Bankhead, to his parents in Fayetteville, Alabama. Tallulah, who always perceived herself as chubby and went on a lifelong series of diets, felt overshadowed in her youth by Gene's good looks and well-proportioned body. Though Zelda saw herself as Tallulah's rival in childhood, it was Gene who later attracted Scott.

55 Zelda found the Capitol's green slopes, known locally as Goat Hill, more fascinating than the fairground, the zoo at Oak Park, or even the gypsy palmist at Pickett Springs whom Zelda and Sara Haardt occasionally consulted. Mayfield, *Constant Circle*, ch. 2.

56 Ibid.; also author's conversations with Camella Mayfield, Tuscaloosa, June, July, Aug. 1999.

57 ZSF, *Waltz*, p. 56.

58 Prangins records.

59 Ibid.

60 The 1900s was an era when even the vote the blacks had gained in the Civil War was exercised under duress and in stringently reduced numbers after white supremacy had been restored. 'Reconstruction', which officially transformed slaves to citizens, left liberated

slaves landless, powerless, impoverished and with nothing but their 'freedom'. By 1900 the strict social boundaries between blacks and whites in the South were still in force and would only gradually be eroded. These divisions helped to establish the American convention that the South was another land.

61 ZSF, *Caesar*, ch. I, CO183, Box 2A, Folder 2, PUL.

62 Prangins records.

63 The school, later known as the Sayre Street Grammar School, was named after her great-uncle William Parish Chilton of Tennessee, twice brother-in-law of Zelda's paternal grandmother Musidora Morgan. First he married Musidora's eldest sister Mary Catherine. Then two years after Mary died in Talladeega in 1845, William married Musidora's younger sister Elvira Frances, known as Ella, sixth in their family of ten children. The Chiltons like the Sayres, their cousins, were a distinguished family with insufficient funds so Miss Chilton founded the school to find employment.

64 Mayfield, *Exiles*, p. 5.

65 Minnie Sayre had suckled Zelda until she was four and old enough to bite through a chicken bone.

66 Mayfield, *Exiles*, p. 13.

67 ZSF, 'The Original Follies Girl', *Collected Writings*, p. 295.

68 Prangins records.

69 Sara Haardt's mother told her: 'No Southerner has lengthened his life or his fame for a day by writing his memoirs. The South, my dear, wants to forget.' Sara Haardt, 'Southern Souvenir', *Southern Souvenirs*, p. 299.

70 William Faulkner, *Requiem for a Nun* (1951), Act I.

71 Lanahan, *Scottie . . .*, p. 159.

72 Minnie Sayre to ZSF, 31 July 1933, CO183, Box 5, Folder 21, PUL.

73 Conversation between Katharine Elsberry Steiner and Eddie Pattillo, reported to the author by Eddie Pattillo.

74 Minnie Sayre to ZSF, 31 July 1933, CO183, Box 5, Folder 21, PUL.

75 He was named for both their parents, Daniel Sayre and Musidora Morgan.

76 The author suggests that the stonemason confused Daniel Morgan with his father Daniel, who did indeed die in 1888.

77 John Reid Stonewall's birth is a curious statistical mystery. The tombstone records 8th April 1862, the Family Bible offers 1842 in Tuskegee, but as the Sayres did not move to Tuskegee until late that year the most probable date is 1852.

78 She taught both at home and at the Classical and Scientific Institute.

79 Musidora's eldest child Lucille, born Montgomery 16 May 1837, died aged eight within two days of the death of the second daughter Catherine Viola, born 1841, who was only four. Musidora's strength sapped when her third daughter May, born 1847, died aged seven, followed by Ella, eighth child, who died at a mere two years old. Two more children died in young adulthood: Daniel Jnr, second child, from bilious fever at twenty-three, and daughter Gem, seventh, born in 1853, at eighteen.

80 Calvin was born 13 Nov. 1844 in Talladeega and died 12 Jan. 1909.

81 Although John Tyler Morgan had only three years of formal schooling his scholarship was outstanding. At nine he 'had already read *Historiae Sacrae*, the first six books of *Caesar*, the *Georgics*, the *Bucolics*, and the *Aeneid*. He had also dipped into Sallust and Horace.' A brigadier general in the Confederate army, he served as a US Senator from 1876 to 1907, introducing several progressive measures. Mayfield, *Exiles*, p. 5.

82 Lanahan, *Scottie . . .*, p. 159.

83 Mayfield, *Exiles*, p. 9.

84 Conversations between Katharine Elsberry Steiner, Eddie Pattillo and the author.

85 Janie Wall in interview with the author, Montgomery, June 1999.

CHAPTER 2

1 FSF, *The Great Gatsby*, ed. Matthew J. Bruccoli, Abacus, 1992, p. 6.

2 ZSF in conversation with Sara Haardt, Ellerslie, Delaware, 1928 (unpublished interview).

3 Sidney Lanier High School, now known as the Baldwin High School, is still in

Montgomery. Judge Sayre did not allow Zelda to attend Miss Margaret Booth's private girls' finishing school at Miss Booth's home at 117 Sayre Street with Sara Haardt.

4 FSF, *Paradise*, p. 156.

5 ZSF, 'The Original Follies Girl', *Collected Writings*, p. 293.

6 She was in fact a couple of inches shorter than Scott's five foot seven, which on his passport he elevated to five foot eight and a half.

7 Sara Haardt/ZSF interview, 1928.

8 In 1917.

9 Sara Haardt/ZSF interview, 1928.

10 Livye Hart Ridgeway, 'A Profile of Zelda', original manuscript, Sara Mayfield Collection, University of Alabama, Tuscaloosa.

11 Bruccoli *et al.*, eds., *Romantic Egoists*, p. 43.

12 ZSF, 'The Original Follies Girl', p. 293.

13 Scottie Fitzgerald Smith, Memoir, p. 62.

14 Grace Gunter Lane to the author, June 1999, Montgomery. Middy outfits were a skirt and blouse with a tie.

15 Zelda Sayre to FSF, spring 1919, CO187, Box 42, Folder 2, PUL.

16 She was following the 'custom' that if women teachers married they would resign. In 1889 in Washington two married teachers caused a sensation by refusing to follow the custom and the Columbia District School Board trustees attempted to turn a custom into a rule to prevent married teachers from working. The School Board Trustees finally stepped down. Harold Evans, *The American Century*, Jonathan Cape, 1998, p. xxii.

17 This lifelong love of flowers made Scottie say later that its intensity was surely as Southern as Zelda's strong feelings for tradition and colour. Scottie Fitzgerald Smith, Memoir.

18 Sometimes the whole Sayre family went to Alabama's cooler Mountain Creek for the summer with Judge Sayre joining them at weekends.

19 Sara Mayfield thought she looked like one of Modigliani's better models. *Exiles*, p. 19.

20 Conversations between Grace Gunter Lane and the author, Montgomery, June 1999.

21 Sara Haardt/ZSF interview, 1928.

22 Later the Belles attended the dances Zelda fictionalized at the Country Club or the auditorium over the old City Hall.

23 Sara Haardt/ZSF interview, 1928.

24 Virginia Foster Durr, *Outside the Magic Circle*, Tuscaloosa, Alabama, 1985, p. 64; interview with Virginia Durr, 1992, in Meyers, *Scott Fitzgerald*, pp. 44–5. Her acid tone might be due to the fact that Virginia's husband-to-be, Clifford Durr, was for several months one of Zelda's beaux.

25 Rosalind Sayre to Sara Mayfield, Mayfield Collection, University of Alabama, Tuscaloosa. Quoted in Hartnett, *Zelda Fitzgerald*, p. 25.

26 Grace Gunter Lane to the author, Montgomery, June 1999.

27 Conversations between Ida Haardt McCulloch and Janie Wall, and Janie Wall and the author, Montgomery, June 1999.

28 John P. Kohn to Sara Mayfield, quoted in Hartnett, *Zelda Fitzgerald*, p. 19.

29 Grace Gunter Lane to the author, Montgomery, June 1999.

30 Mayfield, *Constant Circle*, p. 22.

31 Ibid., p 25.

32 After the Academy of the Sacred Heart Tallulah and Gene went to Mary Baldwin Academy, Staunton, Virginia, then to Fairmont Seminar , Washington DC.

33 Information from Marie Bankhead's cousin Sara Mayfield. Mayfield, *Constant Circle*, p. 25.

34 Tallulah Bankhead confided this intimate fact to Sara Mayfield. Ibid., p. 26.

35 Bruccoli, *et al.*, eds., *Romantic Egoists*, p. 43.

36 Sara Haardt graduated from the Margaret Booth School on 24 May 1916.

37 Quoted by Ann Henley, Introduction, *Southern Souvenirs*, p. 28.

38 Grace Gunter Lane to the author, Montgomery, June 1999.

39 Ironically one of the writers she most admired who encouraged her early stories was Scott Fitzgerald.

40 ZSF, 'The Original Follies Girl', p. 294.

41 John Sellers' family belonged to the Twenty Twos, the Montgomery equivalent of New York's Four Hundred. His father was a wealthy cotton broker. John was later trained to class and staple cotton in his father's firm.

42 Scott would appropriate Dan Cody's name for *The Great Gatsby*.

43 FSF to ZSF, unsent letter, late 1939, CO187, Box 41, PUL.

44 FSF to Marjorie Sayre Brinson, Dec. 1938, CO187, Box 38, Folder Marjorie Brinson (Sayre), PUL.

45 The Act was the Mann Act. According to Camella Mayfield, Sara Mayfield's cousin and literary executor of the Mayfield Collection at the University of Alabama, Tuscaloosa, a confidential letter in the divorce records confirms this violation of the code of sexual behaviour.

46 ZSF, *Caesar*, ch. I, CO183, Box 2A, Folder 2, PUL.

47 Ibid., ch. IV, CO183, Box 2A, Folder 5, PUL.

48 Zelda's childhood reading in her father's library included Aristotle and Aeschylus (see above, ch. 1). In a letter to Scott (written after 13 June 1934) she wrote: 'You talk of the function of art. I wonder if anybody has ever got nearer the truth than Aristotle: he said that all emotions and all experience were common property – that the transposition of these into form was individual and art.'

49 ZSF, *Caesar*, ch. IV, CO183, Box 2A, Folder 5, PUL.

50 Ginevra King, Scott's idealized first love, behaved similarly to Zelda. In an interview after Scott's death she said that Scott had been one of a 'string', that later she was engaged to two other men. 'That was very easy during the war because you'd never get caught. It was just covering yourself in case of loss.' Meyers, *Scott Fitzgerald*, p. 29. During the war women set less store on their men than the men did on them, Scott for instance kept every letter sent by both Ginevra and Zelda. Each of them lost his or destroyed them.

51 Sara Haardt/ZSF interview, 1928.

52 ZSF. 'Southern Girl', *Collected Writings*, pp. 299–300.

53 Sara Haardt/ZSF interview, 1928.

54 ZSF, *Waltz*, p. 37.

55 ZSF, *Caesar*, ch. IV, CO183, Box 2A, Folder 5, PUL.

56 Eddie Pattillo, 'The Last of the Belles', *Montgomery*, July 1994.

57 ZSF, 'Southern Girl', p. 302.

58 Sara Haardt/ZSF interview, 1928.

59 Sara Haardt/ZSF interview, 1928.

CHAPTER 3

1 ZSF, *Waltz, Collected Writings*, p. 37.

2 Mayfield, *Exiles*, p. 2.

3 FSF, *This Side of Paradise*, Penguin, 1963, p. 156. Rosalind Connage was based on a combination of Zelda Sayre and Beatrice Normandy from H. G. Wells' *Tono-Bungay*, 1909.

4 Dorothy Parker to Nancy Milford, interview 26 Aug. 1964, quoted in Milford, *Zelda*, p. 68.

5 Zelda Sayre to FSF, spring 1919, CO187, Box 42, Folder 3, PUL.

6 FSF to Scottie Fitzgerald, summer 1935.

7 Zelda Sayre to FSF after receiving from Scott a gift of Compton MacKenzie's book *Plashers Mead*, which she hated.

8 FSF, Notebooks 938.

9 Completed in an amazing three months' work at weekends only.

10 FSF, 'The Romantic Egotist', unpublished MS, ch. 1, pp. 33–4, CO187, Box 17, PUL.

11 Quoted in Laura Guthrie Hearne, 'A Summer with F. Scott Fitzgerald', *Esquire* 62, Dec. 1964, p. 258.

12 Zelda Sayre to FSF, Feb. or Mar. 1919, CO187, Box 42, Folder 13, PUL.

13 Zelda Sayre to FSF, ibid.

14 Janis L. Magin, 'Montgomery Recalls High-Living Zelda', *Atlanta Journal and Atlanta Constitution*, 6 Nov. 1993. The author was also told this by Eddie Pattillo and Janie Wall, Montgomery, 1999.

15 When Scott was ordered to Camp Sheridan he had written to Lawton Campbell, a fellow

Princetonian who came from Montgomery, to ask for the names of the prettiest girls in Montgomery. Lawton sent back three. These did not include Zelda because she had grown up after he left. Scott had already dated all three who were busy that night so he went on his own to the dance.

16 Mayfield, *Exiles*, p. 3.
17 Ibid.
18 Arthur Mizener, *The Far Side of Paradise*, Heinemann, 1969, p. 23.
19 FSF, Notebooks No. 1378.
20 ZSF, *Waltz*, p. 34.
21 Zelda illustrates this in her story 'The Original Follies Girl' when Gay, asked why she had suddenly become serious about taking the veil, retorts 'Because I've never done *that*' (ZSF, 'The Original Follies Girl', *Collected Writings*, p. 294).
22 ZSF, *Waltz*, p. 36. This is similar to Daisy Buchanan's response in *The Great Gatsby* (1925) when she too smashes up people then retreats back into her money and her 'vast carelessness', FSF, *Gatsby*, p. 167.
23 Mayfield, *Exiles*, p. 3.
24 ZSF, *Waltz*, p. 39.
25 Zelda Sayre to FSF, spring 1919, CO187, Box 42, Folder 17, PUL.
26 FSF, *Paradise*, p. 156.
27 ZSF, *Caesar*, ch. IV, CO183, Box 2A, Folder 5, PUL.
28 FSF, *Gatsby*, pp. 138–9.
29 FSF, Notebooks Nos. 466 and 765.
30 ZSF, 'The Original Follies Girl', p. 293.
31 FSF, Notebooks No. 938.
32 FSF to John O'Hara, 18 July 1933, CO187, Box 51, PUL.
33 Mayfield, *Constant Circle*, p. 31. Scott Fitzgerald and Francis Scott Key were related as second cousins three times removed: Philip Key, founder of the Maryland family and Francis Scott Key's great-grandfather, was Scott's great-great-great-great-grandfather. Matthew J. Bruccoli, *Some Sort of Epic Grandeur*, Sphere Books, London, 1991, p. 16.
34 Mizener, *Far Side of Paradise*, p. 2.
35 He became a benefactor of St Paul's Catholic church, founder of the McQuillan Block of buildings and streets and owner of an impressive Victorian mansion complete with cupola.
36 Richard Washington to Arthur Mizener, quoted in Mizener, *Far Side of Paradise*, p. 2.
37 FSF, 'Author's House', in *Afternoon of an Author*, ed. Arthur Mizener, Princeton University Library, 1957, p. 184.
38 Meyers, *Scott Fitzgerald*, p. 5.
39 FSF, 'The Romantic Egotist', p. 4, CO187, Box 17, PUL.
40 The American Rattan and Willow Works.
41 The Fitzgeralds moved to Syracuse, New York (Jan. 1901) and back to Buffalo (Sep. 1901).
42 Interview by Michel Mok of the *New York Post* on 24 Sep. 1936, Scott's fortieth birthday.
43 Lloyd Hackl to the author, St Paul, July 1999.
44 FSF, 'A Debt of Honor', *St Paul Academy Now and Then*, Mar. 1910.
45 Mizener enlarges on this (*Far Side of Paradise*, p. 29).
46 Scott would immortalize him as Monsignor Thayer Darcy in *This Side of Paradise*.
47 FSF, *Paradise*, p. 46.
48 As editor of the *Nassau Lit* Wilson published the first of Scott's contributions.
49 Alfred Kazin, *F. Scott Fitzgerald: The Man and His Work*, World, Cleveland, 1951, p. 47. Scott himself wrote: 'I discussed books voluminously, books I had read, books I had read about, and books I had never heard of.' 'The Romantic Egotist', ch. V, p. 33, CO187, Box 17, PUL.
50 Edmund Wilson, *A Prelude*, Farrar, Straus & Giroux, New York, 1967, p. 148.
51 *The Apprentice Fiction of F. Scott Fitzgerald*, ed. John Kuehl, Rutgers University Press, 1965, p. 136.
52 He joined Cottage with Sap Donahoe but Alex McKaig, Townsend Martin, Ludlow Fowler and John Peale Bishop all joined the more literary club, Quadrangle.
53 FSF, 'Handle with Care', *The Crack-Up*, Penguin, Harmondsworth, 1965, p 47.
54 FSF, *Gatsby*, p. 103.

55 Ibid., p. 113.
56 FSF to Annabel Fitzgerald, *c.* 1915, *F. Scott Fitzgerald: A Life in Letters*, ed. Matthew J. Bruccoli, Touchstone, New York, 1995, p. 7.
57 Mitchell was an instructor at the naval air station in Key West, Florida, as well as an aviator. He may also have been the 'beautiful Billy Mitchell' whom Scott met with Ginevra at Lake Forest (Aug. 1916). James R. Mellow, *Invented Lives*, Houghton Mifflin, Boston, 1984, p. 53.
58 Shane Leslie to Charles Scribner, 6 May 1918, PUL.
59 FSF to Zelda Sayre, *c.* 1918, Bruccoli *et al.*, eds., *Romantic Egoists*, p. 47.
60 Scott saved the wedding invitation and a piece of Ginevra's handkerchief in his scrapbook with the note: 'The end of a once poignant story'.

CHAPTER 4

1 Zelda Sayre to FSF, 1919, CO187, Box 42, Folders 18, 11, 10, PUL.
2 Zelda Sayre to FSF, early 1919, CO187, Box 42, Folder 31, PUL.
3 Ibid.
4 ZSF, *Waltz, Collected Writings*, p. 29.
5 For war benefits.
6 Sara Haardt/ZSF interview, 1928, unpublished.
7 Recalled years later by Zelda. ZSF to FSF, 13 Feb. 1940, *Romantic Egotists*, p. 225.
8 FSF, Notebook G, 'Descriptions of Girls'.
9 Rosalind Sayre to Sara Mayfield, Mayfield Collection, University of Alabama, Tuscaloosa.
10 Zelda Sayre to FSF, 1919, CO187, Box 42, Folder 11, PUL.
11 FSF, 'Handle with Care', *Crack-Up*, p. 47.
12 Mayfield, *Exiles*, p. 44. Scott was given the post of aide-de-camp to General J. A. Ryan. He was discharged Feb. 1919.
13 Meyers, *Scott Fitzgerald*, p. 49.
14 FSF to Scottie Fitzgerald, 7 July 1938, *The Letters of F. Scott Fitzgerald*, ed. Andrew Turnbull, Penguin, 1968, p. 48.
15 Zelda and Eleanor also ran the street-car all day until they got fired.
16 FSF to Ruth Sturtevant, 4 Dec. 1918, *Letters of F. Scott Fitzgerald*, ed. Turnbull, p. 474. Turnbull (p. 474) says that Scott had made Ruth Sturtevant of Washington a confidante in his romance with Zelda. Later (in 1920) it was Ruth Sturtevant who organized somewhere for Scott and Zelda to stay on the shores of Lake Champlain before they settled on the Wakeman house in Westport, Connecticut. André Le Vot, *F. Scott Fitzgerald*, Allen Lane, London, 1984, p. 86.
17 FSF, Ledger, 1918 (Scott's Sep. summary of the year).
18 Milford does; Mayfield doesn't.
19 FSF, Notebook G, 'Descriptions of Girls'. Scott compared Zelda's fearlessness and indiscretion with that of Beatrice Dance and Nora Flynn, two other 'spoiled babies' with whom he had brief affairs. He knew Beatrice Dance in Asheville in 1935. Nora Flynn was a friend of his in Tryon NC, wife of former Yale football star and movie actor Lefty Flynn.
20 Milford, Zelda's first biographer, follows Scott's line by saying that by Christmas 1918 Zelda was sexually incautious and, enchanted by him, she moved into a 'passionate attachment' (Milford, *Zelda*, p. 35). But Scott's memory, therefore Milford's version, is faulty. Scott's biographer Matthew J. Bruccoli also thinks they might have had sex before Scott's unit went north on 26 Oct. 1918, using as his fictional evidence Gatsby's line about Daisy: 'He felt married to her, that was all' (Bruccoli, *Epic Grandeur*, 1991, p. 105), but factual evidence does not support this.
21 Biographer Jeffrey Meyers, who sees Zelda as an 'impulsive yet calculating' woman who will sleep with Scott yet won't marry him before he is a financial success, also believes April to be the probable date. Meyers bases his theory on Scott's own view when he revises his portrait of Rosalind in *This Side of Paradise*, so that he can reveal Rosalind/Zelda's desire to remain young and irresponsible but have wealth to comfort and protect her. Meyers, *Scott Fitzgerald*, p. 48.

22 He lived at 200 Claremont Avenue. His trips to Montgomery were in April, May and June 1919.
23 Zelda Sayre to FSF, *c.* spring 1919, quoted in Meyers, *Scott Fitzgerald*, p.48.
24 FSF to Isabel Amorous Palmer, 26 Feb. 1920.
25 Zelda Sayre to FSF, spring 1919, CO187, Box 42, Folder 14, PUL. From this experience she would consistently paint dancers' feet as monstrously swollen with exercise.
26 Zelda Sayre to FSF, Apr. 1919, CO187, Box 42, PUL.
27 Zelda Sayre to FSF, possibly spring 1920 (or a year earlier) CO187, Box 42, Folder 6, PUL.
28 In Alabama Katharine dated John Durr but his strait-laced family wouldn't countenance a divorced woman, so she married the more liberal Harvard-educated Robert E. Steiner and had two more children. Eddie Pattillo, 'Last of the Belles', 1994; also conversations between Pattillo and the author, June 1999.
29 Harry T. Baker invited Mencken to adjudicate the students' short stories. It was at the 1923 Goucher College adjudication, the year Sara Mayfield won the contest, that Mencken first met Sara Haardt.
30 Subtitled 'A Magazine of Cleverness'.
31 Zelda Sayre to FSF, 1919, CO187, Box 42, Folder 12, PUL.
32 Zelda's letters suggest both gifts came at this time. Scott's 'Early Success' states that the $30 he earned from *The Smart Set* in spring 1919 was spent on 'a magenta feather fan for a girl in Alabama'. But in 'Auction – Model 1934' Zelda says the money was used to buy Fitzgerald's flannels and the fan was 'paid for out of the first *Saturday Evening Post* story' – 'Head and Shoulders', written fall 1919.
33 Zelda Sayre to FSF, 1919, CO187, Box 42, Folder 13, PUL.
34 Zelda Sayre to FSF, spring 1919, ZSF, *Collected Writings*, p. 446.
35 FSF, *Paradise*, p. 253.
36 Misspelled by Scott as 'dairy' in his December 1918 Ledger entry.
37 Mayfield, *Constant Circle*, pp. 35, 36.
38 Mayfield, *Exiles*, pp. 50–51.
39 Mellow, *Invented Lives*, p. 74.
40 FSF to Maxwell Perkins, *c.* 21 Feb. 1920, *Dear Scott/Dear Max: The Fitzgerald–Perkins Correspondence*, ed. John Kuehl and Jackson R. Bryer, Charles Scribner's Sons, New York, 1971, p. 29.
41 Two years later than previous versions.
42 George Jean Nathan, 'Memories of Fitzgerald, Lewis and Dreiser', *Esquire*, Oct. 1958, pp. 158–9.
43 Meyers, *Scott Fitzgerald*, p 49.
44 The early draft of Zelda's first novel and Scott's angry letter demanding cuts and revisions were also 'mislaid'.
45 Zelda Sayre to FSF, late fall 1919, CO187, Box 42, Folder 27, PUL.
46 Zelda Sayre to FSF, Dec. 1919, CO187, Box 42, Folder 29, PUL.
47 Zelda Sayre to FSF, late Mar. 1919, CO187, Box 42, Folder 14, PUL.
48 Mayfield, *Exiles*, p. 48.
49 Zelda Sayre to FSF, *c.* Apr. 1919, CO187, Box 42, Folder 18, PUL.
50 Ibid.
51 'I used to wonder why they locked princesses in towers': FSF, Ledger, Apr. 1919.
52 Zelda Sayre to FSF, *c.* Apr. 1919, CO187, Box 42, PUL.
53 Zelda Sayre to FSF, *c.* early June 1919, CO187, Box 42, Folder 24, PUL.
54 Zelda Sayre to FSF, 1919, CO187, Box 42, Folder 3, PUL.
55 Zelda Sayre to FSF, Apr. 1919, CO187, Box 42, Folder 19, PUL.
56 Helen Dent appears in FSF's Ledger in fall 1919.
57 Mellow, *Invented Lives*, p. 83. In Rosalinde Fuller's diary she describes riding through the city like Emma Bovary and Leon Dupuis in a closed carriage that aroused their sexual appetites.
58 Hartnett, *Zelda Fitzgerald*, p. 35; Edwin McDowell, 'Fitzgerald-Fuller Affair Recounted', *New York Times*, 9 Nov. 1984.
59 Mellow, *Invented Lives*, p. 83.
60 Zelda Sayre to FSF, *c.* Apr. 1919, CO187, Box 42, Folder 19, PUL.
61 Scott inflated the story by saying Zelda had sent him a photograph of herself affection-

ately inscribed to Bobbie Jones, a world famous sports champion. Even in his June 1919 Ledger he wrote: 'Zelda's mistake about the pictures'. But Jones had never met Zelda much less dated her.

62 Scott lived with his parents at 599 Summit Avenue.
63 FSF to MP, *c.* 1 June 1925, *Life in Letters*, p. 121.
64 FSF, 'The Sensible Thing', *F. Scott Fitzgerald: The Collected Short Stories*, Penguin, 1986, pp. 384–97.
65 Bruccoli and Bryer, eds., *Fitzgerald In His Own Time*, p. 251.
66 FSF to MP, 18 Sep. 1919, *Life in Letters*, p. 32.
67 Wilson said that despite Compton Mackenzie's obvious influence and its hero Amory Blaine being 'a fake of the first water', he had read it with 'riotous mirth'. Edmund Wilson to FSF, 21 Nov. 1919, *Letters on Literature and Politics, 1912–1972*, ed. Elena Wilson, Farrar, Straus & Giroux, New York, 1977, pp. 45–6.
68 Zelda Sayre to FSF, Oct. 1919, CO187, Box 42, Folder 28, PUL.
69 Zelda Sayre to FSF, May 1919, CO187, Box 42, Folder 22, PUL.
70 'Head and Shoulders' was about a prodigy who marries a chorus girl and exchanges roles with her to become a trapeze artist while she becomes a success.
71 FSF, 'The Sensible Thing', p. 397.
72 Mayfield, *Exiles*, p. 47.
73 Zelda Sayre to FSF, Dec. 1919, CO187, Box 42, Folder 29, PUL.
74 Zelda Sayre to FSF, Dec. 1919, CO187, Box 42, Folder 30, PUL.
75 He spent a month in a New Orleans boarding house, 2900 Prytania Street.
76 Quoted in Meyers, *Scott Fitzgerald*, p. 54.
77 Zelda had asked him to 'write to my Daddy' having wished that she was detached – 'sorter without relatives. I'm not exactly scared of 'em, but they could be so unpleasant about what I'm going to do.' He did write but sent it to her. 'I'm slowly mustering courage to deliver it – He's so blind, it'll probably be a terrible shock to him.'
78 Zelda Sayre to FSF, 1919, CO187, Box 42, Folder 3, PUL.
79 Zelda Sayre to FSF, Feb. 1920, ZSF, *Collected Writings*, p. 447.
80 FSF to Isabel Amorous Palmer, 26 Feb. 1920.
81 Zelda Sayre to FSF, Feb. 1920, CO187, Box 42, PUL.
82 According to Mayfield Mencken did not acknowledge the book or review it until after Nathan introduced him to Scott and Zelda the following summer.
83 Mayfield, *Constant Circle*, p. 33.
84 Zelda Sayre to FSF, *c.* Mar. 1920, ZSF, *Collected Writings*, pp. 447–8.
85 Mayfield, *Exiles*, p. 54.
86 Ibid.
87 At 43rd Street and Vanderbilt Avenue.
88 Ludlow Fowler to Arthur Mizener, quoted in Mizener, *Far Side of Paradise*, p. 119.
89 Rosalind Sayre Smith, unpublished documentation on Zelda Fitzgerald, Sara Mayfield Collection, W. W. Hoole Special Collections Library, University of Alabama, Tuscaloosa
90 FSF, 'Handle with Care', *Crack-Up*, p. 47.

CHAPTER 5

1 ZSF, *Waltz, Collected Writings*, p. 49.
2 Mizener, *Far Side of Paradise*, p. 118.
3 ZSF, 'Auction – Model 1934', *Collected Writings*, p. 436. First appeared in *Esquire*, July 1934, published as by F. Scott and Zelda Fitzgerald but credited to Zelda in Scott's Ledger.
4 John Dos Passos, *The Best Times. An Informal Memoir*, The New American Library, 1966, p. 128.
5 ZSF, 'A Millionaire's Girl', *Collected Writings*, p. 327. First appeared in *Saturday Evening Post*, 7 May 1930. Published as by Scott but written by Zelda.
6 Ibid. In 1932 she still hadn't forgotten the experience and revamped her impressions for her first novel (see *Save Me The Waltz*, p. 47).
7 ZSF, 'A Millionaire's Girl', p. 327.

8 Winzola McLendon, 'Interview: Frances Scott Fitzgerald to Winzola McLendon', *Ladies Home Journal*, Nov. 1974, pp. 59–60, 62.

9 Best descriptions in ZSF, 'Miss Ella', *Collected Writings*, pp. 343–9.

10 ZSF, *Waltz*, p. 41.

11 ZSF, 'The Changing Beauty of Park Avenue', *Collected Writings*, p. 403.

12 ZSF, *Waltz*, p. 48.

13 Ibid., p. 49.

14 ZSF, 'Southern Girl', *Collected Writings*, p. 301. First appeared in *College Humor*, July 1929 published as by F. Scott and Zelda Fitzgerald but written solely by Zelda.

15 Later still she decorated wooden bowls with oils of the same scenes. Fiction 1930s, paintings early 1940s, wooden bowls late 1940s. ZSF's Album of Slides and Art, CO183, Box 8, PUL.

16 ZSF, 'A Millionaire's Girl', p. 327.

17 'Vincent Youmans wrote the music for those twilights just after the war. They were wonderful. They hung above the city like an indigo wash, forming themselves from asphalt dust and sooty shadows under the cornices and limp gusts of air exhaled from closing windows. They lay above the streets like a white fog off a swamp.' ZSF, *Waltz*, p. 47.

18 James Mellow directed me to this idea.

19 Curiously, during Zelda and Scott's first year in New York Ina Claire was appearing at the Lyceum in the comedy *The Gold Diggers*.

20 Mellow, *Invented Lives*, pp. 91, 506. In the PUL MS (CO187, Box 17) of 'The Romantic Egotist', ch. 2, Fitzgerald describes the ferry ride as occurring when he was thirteen on a journey from Manhattan to boarding school. See also *The Crack-Up, with Other Uncollected Pieces, Note-Books and Unpublished Letters*, ed. Edmund Wilson, New York, New Directions, paperback, 1945, 1956, pp. 23, 24.

21 FSF, Notebooks No. 158.

22 Biographer Henry Dan Piper pointed out this image had only just begun to emerge as the symbol of the most sophisticated cosmopolitan aspects of the national culture. Piper, *F. Scott Fitzgerald*, Bodley Head, London, 1965, pp. 61, 62.

23 FSF, *Crack-Up*, p. 14.

24 Piper, *F. Scott Fitzgerald*, p. 62. Also FSF, *Crack-Up*, pp. 26–7.

25 FSF, *Crack-Up*, pp. 26–7.

26 ZSF, *Waltz*, p. 49.

27 Mayfield, *Exiles*, p. 55.

28 Edmund Wilson, *The Twenties: From the Notebooks and Diaries of the Period*, ed. with introduction by Leon Edel, Farrar, Straus & Giroux, New York, 1975, p. 53; Jeffrey Meyers, *Edmund Wilson: A Biography*, Houghton Mifflin, New York, 1995, p. 109.

29 Milford, *Zelda*, p. 47.

30 ZSF, *Caesar*, ch. IV, CO183, Box 2A, Folder 5, PUL.

31 Alexander McKaig, Diary, 12 Apr. 1920.

32 Mayfield, *Exiles*, p. 62.

33 Wilson, *Letters on Literature and Politics*, p. 478.

34 Meyers, *Edmund Wilson*, p. 109; *The Portable Edmund Wilson*, ed. Lewis M. Dabney, Viking Press, New York, 1983, p. 191.

35 Wilson, *Letters*, p. 478.

36 Lawton Campbell to Milford, 19 Sep. 1965, quoted in Milford, *Zelda*, p. 78.

37 Scott Donaldson, *Fool for Love: A Biography of F. Scott Fitzgerald*, Delta, New York, 1983, pp. 28, 29.

38 FSF to Marie Hersey, May 1920, CO188, Box 4, Folder 25, PUL. The occasion was 25 Apr. 1920. The following week without Zelda to witness his renewed humiliation Scott drove back to Princeton with Bishop and Wilson for a banquet for former *Nassau Lit* editors. Attired in a foolish costume of halo and wings and carrying a lyre, Scott was ejected from a rear window and told he was suspended from the Cottage Club.

39 The New York press reported their infamous acts just the way the *Montgomery Advertiser* had reported Zelda's youthful exploits.

40 ZSF, *Waltz*, p. 51.

41 Dos Passos, *Best Times*, p. 128. He was describing his time with Zelda and Scott in 1922.

42 On this he paid $1,444.25 federal tax.

43 Zelda said later that her two highly autobiographical novels accurately reflected her feelings about their time in New York in the early Twenties. In *Save Me The Waltz* David wakes up in the Biltmore groaning over their fame in the newspapers. Alabama says it is nice. David shouts 'Nice! But it says we're in a sanitarium for wickedness. What'll our parents think . . .?' Alabama, still 'glad we're famous anyway', dances riotously and thinks up ways to spend money. *Save Me The Waltz*, p. 45.

44 Fowler's affluence so deeply affected Scott that five years later he based Anson Hunter on Ludlow in 'The Rich Boy'.

45 McKaig, Diary, 15 Sep. 1920.

46 Ibid., 13 Oct. 1920.

47 Mayfield, *Exiles*, p. 62. Wilson, who also recognized Zelda's usefulness to Scott in the early Twenties, was the first of Scott's friends to respect Zelda's independent artistic talent as the decade wore on. Years later, when corresponding with Scott's biographer, Wilson urged him to 'make clear that even when her mind was going, the writing and painting she did had her curious personal quality of imaginative iridescence and showed something of real talent' (Meyers, *Edmund Wilson*, pp. 109–10).

48 Meyers, *Scott Fitzgerald*, p. 72.

49 Wilson, *The Twenties*, p. 55.

50 Wilson wished to marry Millay, who had already gone through eighteen love affairs. McKaig called her 'a modem Sappho'.

51 Wilson, *The Twenties*, p. 214.

52 Wilson to Arthur Mizener, 27 Jan. 1950, Yale University.

53 Ibid.

54 Later Wilson wrote to Scottie about these incidents that it was smart in the Twenties for attractive young married women to hold levees in their bathrooms. Wilson reassured Scottie that though Zelda did do this she always did it casually and only with good friends of Scott's.

55 ZSF to FSF, c. late summer/early fall 1930, *Life in Letters*, p. 190.

56 Eugenia and Morton married in August possibly during her affair with Scott, and were to divorce and remarry three times. On one stormy ocean crossing with Eugenia the depressed Morton jumped overboard in an attempt to kill himself. Scott, always on the lookout for material, used that aborted death leap in several early versions of *Tender Is The Night*, and even after finally expunging it, he retained the name Hoyt for young Rosemary who poses the threat to Nicole and Dick Diver's marriage.

57 ZSF, *Caesar*, 'She Had A Right To It' (ch. VI in author's new edited structure), CO183, Box 2A, Folder 6, PUL.

58 ZSF, *Waltz*, p. 44.

59 ZSF, *Caesar*, ch. VI, CO183, Box 2A, Folder 6, PUL.

60 According to Scott, those healing conversations continued until their trip to Europe in the late Twenties.

61 FSF to Ruth Sturtevant, 14 May 1920.

62 The mill's speciality was grinding kiln-dried corn for shipment to the West Indies. The house was later known as the Switch House because it was where the trolleys switched tracks to go on to Compo beach. Eve Potts, *Westport – A Special Place*, Westport Historical Society, 1985, p. 113.

63 ZSF to Ludlow Fowler, 9 May 1920, CO183, Box 5, Folder 4, PUL.

64 Wilson, *The Twenties*, p. 59.

65 Wilson to H. L. Mencken, 12 May 1922, *Letters*, p. 82.

66 ZSF to FSF, c. late summer/early fall 1930, *Life in Letters*, p. 190.

67 Mayfield, *Exiles*, p. 57. Gotham is a suburb of New York.

CHAPTER 6

1 They were so financially unprepared for motor bills that Scott had to send Bunny Wilson an emergency letter asking him to wire money ahead of them.

2 ZSF to Ludlow Fowler, 16 Aug. 1920, CO183, Box 5, Folder 4, PUL.

3 In Greensboro they stayed at the O. Henry Hotel.

4 FSF, 'The Cruise of the Rolling Junk', *Motor*, Feb. 1924.

5 Mayfield, *Exiles*, p. 61.

6 Eleanor Lanahan, *Scottie . . .*, p. 410.

7 Eleanor Lanahan, *Scottie . . .*, p. 411. The Montgomery friend was Julia Garland, who was with Zelda the day Scott died.

8 In Zelda's story 'Southern Girl' Harriet, like her creator, sees bathing as an invitation to love. Wrapped only in a bath towel, she answers the front door to an unknown man who becomes her lover. When he eventually throws her over, again wrapped in a bath towel she throws open her front door, this time more effectively to a stranger who becomes her husband.

9 This would become *The Beautiful and Damned*.

10 FSF, *The Beautiful and Damned*, Penguin, 1966, p. 155.

11 Ibid., p. 111.

12 ZSF to Ludlow Fowler, postmarked 16 Aug. 1920, CO183, Box 5, Folder 4, PUL.

13 Sara Mayfield says that the incident is portrayed in *Save Me The Waltz* exactly in the way Zelda described it to her (*Exiles*, p. 57).

14 ZSF, *Waltz*, p. 51.

15 Mayfield, *Exiles*, p. 59.

16 Mellow, *Invented Lives*, p. 100.

17 Wilson, *The Twenties*, p. 20.

18 'I had lost my job in a Dayton, Ohio bank', Stewart told Zelda's friend Sara Mayfield, 'and that is how I became a writer instead of a banker.' Mayfield, *Exiles*, p. 65.

19 During the next few years when Scott met Ring Lardner, journalist and humorous writer, and Ernest Hemingway, he would go to even greater lengths than he had with Stewart to promote *their* talents.

20 Mellow, *Invented Lives*, p. 450.

21 Anderson's stories and character sketches became *Winesburg, Ohio* (1919), preceded by *Windy MacPherson's Son* (1916), *Marching Men* (1917) and two others. His best writing occurs in several volumes of short stories, including *Horses and Men* (1923).

22 At the height of his career Dreiser wrote *An American Tragedy* (1925), for which he was ultimately paid $90,000 for the film rights.

23 Mellow, *Invented Lives*, p. 183 and original sources in endnotes.

24 James Drawbell, *An Autobiography*, Pantheon Books, New York 1964, p. 173.

25 Members sometimes also met for Saturday evening poker games. This group was known as Thanatopsis Literary and Inside Straight Club.

26 Wilson, *The Twenties*, p. 45.

27 Marion Meade, *Dorothy Parker: What Fresh Hell Is This?*, Minerva, London, 1991, p. 90.

28 Wilson, *The Twenties*, p. 45.

29 Ibid.

30 Wilson, *The Twenties*, p. 33.

31 FSF, Notebooks No. 314.

32 Marion Meade in correspondence with the author, Oct. 2000.

33 Dorothy Parker to Milford, 26 Aug. 1964, Milford, *Zelda*, p. 68.

34 Mayfield, *Exiles*, pp. 59–60.

35 Wilson, *The Twenties*, pp. 79–80.

36 ZSF, Autobiographical Sketch written 16 Mar. 1932 while in Phipps Clinic, Johns Hopkins Hospital.

37 Carl Van Vechten to Milford, 17 Apr. 1963, Milford, *Zelda*, pp. 98–9.

38 Carl Van Vechten, *Parties*, 1930, p. 224. Arthur Mizener is useful on Zelda's distress when Scott was lionized (*Far Side of Paradise*, p. 133).

39 Van Vechten, *Parties*, p. 78. Jeffrey Meyers makes an interesting comment (*Scott Fitzgerald*, p. 102).

40 Wilson, *The Twenties*, p. 52.

41 McKaig, Diary, 15 Sep. 1920.

42 Mayfield, *Exiles*, pp. 62–3.

43 McKaig, Diary, 15 Sep. 1920.

44 ZSF to FSF, undated *c*. 1920, CO187, Box 42, Folder 32, PUL.

45 Gloria, miserable and lonesome, writes to Anthony Patch: 'I can almost look down the tracks

and see you going but without you, dearest, dearest, I can't see or hear or feel or think. Being apart – whatever has happened or will happen to us – is like begging for mercy from a storm, Anthony; it's like growing old. I want to kiss you so – in the back of your neck where your old black hair starts. Because I love you and whatever we do or say to each other, or have done, or have said, you've got to feel how much I do, how inanimate I am when you're gone. I can't even hate the damnable presence of PEOPLE, those people in the station who haven't any right to live – I can't resent them even though they're dirtying up our world because I'm engrossed in wanting you so. If you hated me, if you were covered with sores like a leper, if you ran away with another woman or starved me or beat me – how absurd this sounds – I'd still want you, I'd still love you, I KNOW my darling.' FSF, *Beautiful and Damned*, p. 293.

46 ZSF, *Caesar*, ch. V, CO183, Box 2A, Folder 6, PUL.
47 Mellow, *Invented Lives*, p. 113.
48 George Jean Nathan to ZSF: 'Fair Zelda', 12 July 1920; 'Prisoner', undated, 1920, CO183, Box 5, Folder 18, PUL. Both Arthur Mizener and Kendall Taylor suggest Zelda's relationship with Nathan was sexual. This author finds insufficient evidence for this.
49 Nathan to ZSF, *c.* Sep. 1920, CO183, Box 5, Folder 18, PUL.
50 ZSF to Ludlow Fowler, 16 Aug. 1920, CO183, Box 5, Folder 4, PUL.
51 This film was so popular that six silent versions preceded the successful talkie.
52 Nathan to ZSF, 13 Sep. 1920, CO183, Box 5, Folder 18, PUL.
53 'Beginnings of coldness' he records in his Ledger, Oct. 1920.
54 FSF to Mr and Mrs Philip McQuillan, 28 Dec. 1920.
55 Mayfield, *Exiles*, p. 64.
56 Marion Elizabeth Rodgers, *Mencken and Sara: A Life in Letters*, McGraw-Hill, New York, 1987, p. 4.
57 One evening the Fitzgeralds drove to have dinner with Mencken and Nathan at the Plaza, but by the end of the evening were far too drunk to drive their car. Their anxious friends suggested they sleep at the hotel but Scott refused. Mencken thought they would never reach home alive. To his surprise Scott telephoned next day to report they were recovered and whole.
58 This quotation is from the 'Sententiae' section of *A Mencken Chrestomathy*, Alfred A. Knopf, New York, 1949, pp. 619–21, quoted in Rodgers, *Mencken and Sara*, p. 1.
59 *Sherwood Anderson's Memoirs. A Critical Edition*, ed. Ray Lewis White, University of North Carolina Press, 1969, p. 369.
60 The stories in *Flappers and Philosophers* had all been previously published in magazines so it seemed like extra money. They were: 'The Offshore Pirate'; 'The Ice Palace'; 'Head and Shoulders'; 'The Cut Glass Bowl'; 'Bernice Bobs Her Hair'; 'Benediction'; 'Dalyrimple Goes Wrong'; 'The Four Fists'.
61 Reviews were a mixed bunch, some critics finding it a letdown after *This Side of Paradise*.
62 Six printings (total 15,325 copies) by November 1922.
63 Mencken's review called it 'a sandwich made up of two thick and tasteless chunks of *Kriegsbrot* with a couple of excellent sardines between'. *The Smart Set* XLIII, Dec. 1920.
64 H. L. Mencken to James Branch Cabell, Mar. 1922, *Between Friends: Letters of James Branch Cabell and Others*, ed. Padraic Colum and Margaret Freeman Cabell, Harcourt Brace & World, New York, 1962, p. 25.
65 *Metropolitan Magazine* took 'The Jelly Bean', 'His Russet Witch', Two For a Cent' and 'Winter Dreams' between 1920 and 1922.
66 To repay an advance for an unwritten story.
67 Mayfield, *Exiles*, p. 65.
68 They would not be due to him till January 1921.
69 Mayfield, *Exiles*, p. 65.
70 André Le Vot, *F. Scott Fitzgerald*, Warner Books, New York, 1984, p. 90.
71 Fitzgerald, Ledger, July and Nov. 1920.
72 ZSF to James Branch Cabell, Dec. 1920, CO183, Box 5, Folder 2, PUL.
73 McKaig, Diary, 17 and 12 Oct. 1920.
74 FSF to Scottie Fitzgerald, 15 June 1940, *Letters*, ed. Turnbull, p. 97.
75 FSF to Ober (received 2 Feb. 1928), *As Ever, Scott Fitz-: Letters Between F. Scott Fitzgerald and His Agent Harold Ober, 1919–1940*, ed. Matthew J. Bruccoli, Woburn Press, London, 1973, p. 109. 'The Jelly Bean', written May 1920, *Metropolitan Magazine* 52, Oct. 1920.

76 'The Lees of Happiness', written July 1920, *Chicago Sunday Tribune*, 12 Dec. 1920, Blue Ribbon Fiction Section.
77 FSF, *Beautiful and Damned*, p. 343.
78 In his Ledger Scott summarized the year that brought him both Zelda and literary recognition as: 'Revelry and Marriage. The rewards of the year before. The happiest year since I was 18.'
79 It contains what he himself called 'a touch of disaster'. FSF, 'Early Success', *The Crack-Up*, New Directions, New York, 1945, p. 87.
80 Lawton Campbell, 'The Fitzgeralds Were My Friends', unpublished Memoir.
81 McKaig, Diary, 12 Oct. 1920.
82 Zelda in *Caesar's Things* established Jacob as a 'pouting' Scott figure who says mildly: 'I want to be totally unpredictable but I never can prevent wondering . . . what should be done about the suit at the cleaners.'
83 ZSF, *Caesar*, ch. IV, CO183, Box 2A, Folder 5, PUL.
84 FSF to Perkins, 10 Nov. 1920, *Dear Scott/Dear Max*, p. 32.
85 Le Vot makes this point strongly. He says McKaig fell 'hopelessly' in love. *F. Scott Fitzgerald*, p. 91.
86 McKaig, Diary, 27 Nov., 4 Dec. 1920.
87 Ibid., 4 Dec. 1920.
88 Zelda recalls the bathroom incident and hurt eye during a winter of dissipation, probably Nov./Dec. 1920, in a letter to Scott, late summer/early fall 1930. Scott writes up the incident in his Ledger, Jan. 1921.
89 McKaig, Diary, 11 Dec. 1920.
90 Ibid., 18 Dec. 1920.
91 ZSF, *Caesar*, ch. V, CO183, Box 2A, Folder 6, PUL.
92 Lawton Campbell, Memoir.
93 ZSF, *Waltz*, pp. 47–8.
94 ZSF to FSF, late summer/early fall 1930, *Life in Letters*, p. 190.
95 Mayfield, *Exiles*, p. 67.
96 At Grove Lodge.
97 Mellow, *Invented Lives*, pp. 136, 137. The other two writers were Conrad and Anatole France.
98 FSF to Shane Leslie, 24 May 1921, CO188, Box 4, Folders 33–4, PUL.
99 Wilson, *The Twenties*, p. 94.
100 FSF to J. F. Carter, spring 1922, *Correspondence of F. Scott Fitzgerald*, ed. Matthew J. Bruccoli and Margaret M. Duggan, Random House, New York, 1980, p. 99.
101 FSF to Edmund Wilson, quoted in Mellow, *Invented Lives*, p. 138.
102 Bruccoli *et al.*, eds., *Romantic Egoists*, pp. 84–5.
103 H. L. Mencken, *My Life as Author and Editor*, Alfred A. Knopf, New York, 1993, p. 258.
104 I am indebted to Koula Svokos Hartnett for the notion of an odyssey. Even in Zelda's decade of hospitalization she would be moved nine times, never to have the benefit of continuity and familiarity of one particular setting such as she had experienced in Montgomery. Hartnett, *Zelda Fitzgerald*, p. 78.
105 Katharine Elsberry Haxton tells Scottie the story in Lanahan, *Scottie . . .*, p. 410.
106 Lanahan, *Scottie . . .*, p. 21.
107 Mayfield, *Exiles*, p. 71.

CHAPTER 7

1 ZSF to FSF, late summer/early fall 1930, *Life in Letters*, p. 191.
2 St Paul itself, the state capital, known as 'the last city of the east', which housed many Fitzgerald residencies, was originally called Pig's Eye after a shifty French-Canadian fur trader who sold whiskey at a Mississippi river landing in the 1840s.
3 Scott wrote the story in 1919 before Zelda visited St Paul. FSF, *The Ice Palace, Babylon Revisited and Other Stories*, Charles Scribner's Sons, New York, 1971, p. 10.
4 FSF to Marie Hersey Hamm, 28 Oct. 1936, CO187, Box 49, PUL.
5 Owned by Mackey J. Thompson.

6 ZSF, 'The Girl The Prince Liked', *Collected Writings*, ed. Bruccoli, pp. 311–12.

7 Held at Ramaley Hall on Grand Avenue. Scott had joined in 1908.

8 Xandra Kalman to Lloyd Hackl; Hackl to the author, 1999.

9 Born in Pictou, Nova Scotia, 13 May 1813, Daniel A. Robertson became an editor and a US Marshal in Ohio. In Minnesota he founded the Horticultural Society, was editor of the Minnesota *Democrat* and served as a member of the Minnesota legislature 1859–60.

10 481 Laurel Ave: Scott's birthplace. 623 Summit Ave: Scott's grandmother Louisa McQuillan's home. Scott visited for one month in summer 1899. 294 Laurel Ave: Louisa McQuillan's next home. Scott and Annabel stayed there in 1908 when the family moved back to St Paul. Their parents stayed at the home of John A. Fulton at 239 Summit Ave. 514 Holly Avenue: Scott and family moved there September 1909. 509 Holly Ave: Scott and family moved to this rowhouse September 1910. 499 Holly Ave: Scott and family moved there in late 1911 and stayed until 1915. Between 1915 and 1922 the Edward Fitzgeralds lived at 593 Summit Ave and 599 Summit Ave.

11 FSF to Sinclair Lewis, 26 Jan. 1921, *Letters of F. Scott Fitzgerald*, ed. Turnbull, p. 487; to Burton Rascoe, Dec. 1920, *Correspondence of F. Scott Fitzgerald*, ed. Bruccoli and Duggan, p. 73.

12 ZSF to MP, 1921, Scribner's Author Files, CO101, Box 53, Folder Zelda Fitzgerald 1921–1944, PUL.

13 This phrase, used by Minnesotans about their key characteristic of kindness, was explained by Lloyd Hackl to the author.

14 Mizener, *Far Side of Paradise*, p. 150.

15 David Knight calls Alabama this in *Save Me The Waltz*. ZSF, *Collected Writings*, p. 39.

16 Once Zelda began painting seriously in 1925 she gave Xandra many of her favourite paintings.

17 Xandra Kalman to Lloyd C. Hackl, St Paul, as reported by Hackl to the author, St Paul, 1999. Hackl uses this in 'Fitzgerald in St Paul: An Oral History Portrait', Minnesota Historical Society.

18 In the early days of their marriage Zelda affectionately called Scott Goofo or Goofy. In later letters she called him Deo, or D.O. or Do-Do possibly from the Latin word for God.

19 FSF, *The Great Gatsby*, Abacus, London, 1992, p. 20.

20 Lanahan, *Scottie . . .*, p. 22.

21 ZSF to Ludlow Fowler, winter 1921, CO183, Box 5, Folder 4, PUL.

22 Bruccoli *et al.*, eds., *Romantic Egoists*, p. 87.

23 ZSF, *Waltz, Collected Writings*, p. 57.

24 ZSF to FSF, late summer/early fall 1930, *Life in Letters*, p. 191.

25 Mizener, *Far Side of Paradise*, p. 151.

26 Bruccoli *et al.*, eds., *Romantic Egoists*, p. 92.

27 Until June 1922. The street was named after Aaron Goodrich, Xandra's great-grandfather. St Paul historical researcher Lloyd C. Hackl calls it Goodrich *Street* in his '*Still Home to Me': F. Scott Fitzgerald and St Paul*, Adventure Publications, Cambridge, Minnesota, p. 52.

28 This is curious because before Scottie's birth, as they drove past the Catholic Church, Scott had muttered to himself: 'God damn the Catholic Church: God damn the Church; God damn God.' Reported by Scott's friend Arthur Hartwell to Mizener (Mizener, *Far Side of Paradise*, p. 151) and to Mayfield (Mayfield, *Exiles*, p. 74).

29 Barron had always encouraged Scott's writing and had engaged with him in philosophical discussions.

30 Her family nickname was Scottie. The Fitzgeralds had initially thought of calling the baby Patricia and on a few occasions Zelda called her Pat but it never stuck.

31 Author's conversations with Lloyd Hackl, 1998, 1999.

32 Hackl, *F. Scott Fitzgerald and St Paul*, p. 13.

33 ZSF, 'The Girl The Prince Liked', *Collected Writings*, p. 313.

34 ZSF to Ludlow Fowler, winter 1921, CO183, Box 5, Folder 4, PUL.

35 Hergesheimer had become suddenly famous for *Cytherea*.

36 Mayfield, *Exiles*, pp. 77–8.

37 FSF, 'The Ice Palace', written Dec. 1919, published *Saturday Evening Post*, 22 May 1920; *Flappers and Philosophers*, Charles Scribner's Sons, New York, Sep. 1920.

38 The novel was initially called 'The Demon Lover' (1919), then 'Darling Heart' (1920), then 'The Flight of the Rocket' (Aug. 1920), then at Christmas 1920 'The Beautiful Lady Without Mercy' and finally (Feb. 1921) *The Beautiful and Damned*. An abridged version in seven instalments was published in *Metropolitan Magazine* (Sep. 1921 to Mar. 1922). *The Smart Set* bought an excerpt from Book 2 ch. 2 (Feb. 1922).

39 MP to FSF, 27 Dec. 1921, *Dear Scott/Dear Max*, pp. 49–50. Due to Zelda's suggestions the book ends on a sardonic note as the broken hero whispers to himself: '"I showed them . . . It was a hard fight, but I didn't give up and I came through!"' *The Beautiful and Damned*, p. 364.

40 FSF to Charles Scribner II, 12 Aug. 1920, *Life in Letters*, p. 41.

41 Mary Gordon, Introduction, *Zelda Fitzgerald: The Collected Writings*, p. xxiv, is very perceptive on this point.

42 Mizener, *Far Side of Paradise*, p. 112.

43 Alexander McKaig, Diary, 17 Apr. 1921. Years later Zelda revealed in her letters the intellectual detachment Scott had depended upon: 'Nobody has ever been able to experience what they have thoroughly understood – or understand what they have experienced until they have achieved a detachment that renders them incapable of repeating that experience.' ZSF to FSF, Mar. 1932, PUL.

44 FSF to MP, *c.* 31 Jan. 1922, *Dear Scott/Dear Max*, p. 52.

45 Carolyn Shafer compares Zelda's crayon sketch thematically and in terms of its composition to Botticelli's 1482 *The Birth of Venus*. Each work celebrates a particular era's emerging female image. But whereas Botticelli's Renaissance goddess rises from sea foam, nude but modest, hands held gracefully over breasts and vagina, Zelda's naked Flapper figure rises from champagne bubbles, bold and brazen.

46 FSF to Charles Scribner II, 12 Aug. 1920, *Life in Letters*, p. 41.

47 H. L. Mencken, 'Fitzgerald and Others', *The Smart Set*, vol. XLVII, Apr. 1922, pp. 140–1.

48 He had called in at St Paul to see them during her pregnancy.

49 Wilson to Stanley Dell, 19 Feb. 1921, *Letters on Literature and Politics*, p. 56.

50 FSF, *Beautiful and Damned*, p. 132.

51 Ibid., p. 300.

52 Montgomery relatives and friends to the author, 1999.

53 FSF, *Beautiful and Damned*, pp. 175, 149.

54 FSF to Phyllis Duganne Parker, fall 1920, *Correspondence of F. Scott Fitzgerald*, p. 71.

55 FSF to ZSF, 'Written with Zelda gone to the Clinique', *c.* summer 1930, *Life in Letters*, p. 189. He may not have sent this letter.

56 John Peale Bishop, 'Three Brilliant Young Novelists', *Collected Essays of John Peale Bishop*, Charles Scribner's Sons, New York, 1948, pp. 229–30.

57 Mayfield, *Exiles*, p. 62.

58 Wilson was preparing an essay about Fitzgerald for *The Bookman*.

59 FSF to Wilson, Jan. 1922, Yale University.

60 Critic André Le Vot suggests 'there are the passages directly *inspired by* Zelda's letters, which are attributed to Gloria [author's italics]'. Le Vot, *F. Scott Fitzgerald*, p. 98.

61 FSF to Perkins, *c.* 21 Feb. 1920, *Dear Scott/Dear Max*, p. 29.

62 FSF, *Beautiful and Damned*, p. 111. Scott used a parody of Minnie Sayre's belief in theosophy, a religion based on reincarnation, but reinvented it as 'bilphism' so as not to hurt her feelings.

63 FSF, *Beautiful and Damned*, pp. 121–5.

64 ZSF, 'Friend Husband's Latest', *New York Tribune*, 2 Apr. 1922, section 5, p. 11; *Collected Writings*, pp. 387–9.

65 Bruccoli, *Epic Grandeur*, p. 192.

66 Wilson to FSF, 26 May 1922, Wilson, *Letters*, p. 85.

67 There is no mention of this piece in FSF's Ledger.

68 ZSF, 'What Became of the Flappers?', *McCall's*, Oct. 1925; *Collected Writings*, pp. 397–9.

69 ZSF, 'Eulogy on the Flapper', *Metropolitan Magazine*, June 1922; *Collected Writings*, pp. 391–2.

CHAPTER 8

1 Scott hoped Nathan would read his *Vegetable* script while they were there.
2 ZSF, 'Show Mr and Mrs F. to Number –', *Collected Writings*, p. 420. First Published *Esquire*, May–June 1934, as by F. Scott and Zelda Fitzgerald but credited to ZSF in Scott's Ledger.
3 Wilson, *Letters on Literature and Politics*, pp. 78–9.
4 FSF to Wilson, *c.* Mar. 1922.
5 ZSF to FSF, late summer/early fall 1930, *Life in Letters*, p. 191.
6 Mayfield, *Exiles*, p. 80. Mayfield later also told her cousin Camella this.
7 FSF, Notebooks No. 1564.
8 This would confirm the notion of several abortions about which Camella Mayfield, who typed her cousin Sara's manuscript of the Fitzgeralds, is both convinced and convincing. Mayfield, *Exiles*, p. 80; Camella Mayfield, Tuscaloosa, USA, to the author, series of conversations, 1999 and 2000.
9 FSF, *Beautiful and Damned*, p. 169.
10 FSF, *Beautiful and Damned*, earlier MS version, CO187, Box 3, PUL.
11 Xandra Kalman to Milford, Sep. 1964, Milford, *Zelda*, p. 93.
12 Conversations between Xandra Kalman and Lloyd Hackl; between Hackl and the author, 1999.
13 Lloyd Hackl's oral portrait of Fitzgerald in St Paul based on interviews with Xandra Kalman; Lloyd Hackl to the author, Minnesota, 1999.
14 Wilson to FSF, 26 May 1922, Wilson, *Letters*, p. 85. Margaret eventually purchased for Bishop and herself the Château de Tressancourt at Orgeval, Seine-et-Oise.
15 FSF to Wilson, postmarked 30 May 1922, Yale University.
16 Xandra Kalman to Milford, Sep. 1964, Milford, *Zelda*, pp. 92–3.
17 ZSF to Oscar Kalman, 1940, author's collection and Minnesota Historical Society.
18 Xandra Kalman to Milford, Sep. 1964, Milford, *Zelda*, p. 93.
19 Ibid.
20 Xandra Kalman to Hackl, Sep. 1975; Hackl to the author, 1999.
21 The three friends were Sara Mayfield, Sara Haardt and Sara Murphy. It was Sara Murphy who pointed out Zelda s pronunciation of the name, as did the late Honoria Murphy Donnelly in interviews with the author, 1997 and 1998.
22 Xandra Kalman to Hackl and conversations between Hackl and the author, 1999.
23 A possible reason why the official history of the club has not listed their names.
24 Lloyd Hackl, *F. Scott Fitzgerald and St Paul*, p. 56.
25 Probably because of its serialization.
26 *Tales of the Jazz Age* included: Stories: My Last Flappers: 'The Jelly Bean', 'The Camel's Back', 'May Day', 'Porcelain and Pink'; Fantasies: 'The Diamond as Big as the Ritz', 'The Curious Case of Benjamin Button', 'Tarquin of Cheapside', 'O Russet Witch!'; Unclassified Masterpieces: 'The Lees of Happiness', 'Mr Icky', 'Jemina'.
27 The film starred Marie Prevost and Kenneth Harlan.
28 Wilson to Bishop, 22 Sep. 1922, Wilson, *Letters*, p. 96.
29 At the Plaza (Sep. 1922): Sara Mayfield was en route back from Europe.
30 Mayfield, *Exiles*, p. 82.
31 Gilbert Seldes to Milford, 27 May 1965, Milford, *Zelda*, p. 97.
32 ZSF, *Waltz*, *Collected Writings*, p. 47.
33 Dos Passos was the illegitimate son of a Portuguese-American corporation lawyer.
34 Dos Passos, *Best Times*, p. 127.
35 Bishop to Wilson, 1921, Yale University.
36 Dos Passos told Bishop that the only two reviews he cared for were the ones by Bishop and Fitzgerald, Mellow, *Invented Lives*, p. 162.
37 Dos Passos, *Best Times*, pp. 128, 130.
38 Ibid., p. 128.
39 Dos Passos to Milford, 17 Oct. 1963, Milford, *Zelda*, p. 93.
40 Dos Passos, *Best Times*, p. 128.
41 Lardner, formerly a sports columnist and wit for the *Chicago Tribune*, had moved to Long Island to write a syndicated column and comic strip based on his successful short story collection *You Know Me Al* (1916).

42 Dos Passos, *Best Times*, p. 129.
43 Mellow, *Invented Lives*, p. 165.
44 Dos Passos, *Best Times*, p. 130.
45 Dos Passos to Milford, 17 Oct. 1963, Milford, *Zelda*, pp. 93–4.
46 Dos Passos, *Best Times*, p. 130.
47 ZSF to Xandra Kalman, *c.* 13 Oct. 1922, author's collection and Minnesota Historical Society.
48 ZSF to FSF, late summer/early fall 1930, *Life in Letters*, p. 191.
49 ZSF to Xandra Kalman, *c.* Oct. 1922, author's collection and Minnesota Historical Society.
50 FSF to Wilson, letter postmarked 13 July 1922.
51 19 Nov. 1923.
52 Mayfield, *Exiles*, p. 87.
53 FSF, *Afternoon of an Author*, ed. Mizener, pp. 93, 94. The disastrous one-week run in November left the Fitzgeralds in deeper debt. Help came through Townsend Martin, now a partner in the Film Guild. Scott wrote a script for $2,000 from which the Clara Bow film *Grit* was made.
54 FSF and ZSF to Xandra and Oscar Kalman, after 17 Nov. 1923.
55 Ring Lardner Jnr to the author, June 1999.
56 ZSF to the Kalmans, undated, author's collection and CO183, Box 5, Folder 5, PUL.
57 ZSF to FSF, late summer/early fall 1930, *Life in Letters*, p. 191.
58 ZSF to the Kalmans, Oct. 1922, CO183, Box 5, Folder 5, PUL.
59 Scott Donaldson, *Fool for Love*, p. 53.
60 ZSF to FSF, late summer/early fall 1930, *Life in Letters*, p. 191.
61 Ibid.
62 FSF to Thomas Boyd, *Correspondence of F. Scott Fitzgerald*, p. 138.
63 Quoted in Mellow, *Invented Lives*, p. 272. Forty years later when Zelda had been labelled Scott's mad wife, West produced a description of Zelda's appearance quite unlike anyone else's: 'my impression [was] that she was very plain . . . I would almost go so far as to say that her face had a certain craggy homeliness. There was a curious unevenness about it, such as one sees in Géricault's pictures of the insane . . . We got on quite well . . . There was something very appealing about her. But frightening' (West to Milford, 10 Aug. 1963, Milford, *Zelda*, p. 99).
64 Ring Lardner, *What Of It?*, Charles Scribner's Sons, New York, 1925, pp. 18, 59. In return Zelda drew a dinner party place card for Ring on which a redheaded nude wearing a grey fedora kicks her scarlet slipper towards his name.
65 ZSF, Scrapbook, CO183, Box 7, PUL.
66 ZSF to the Kalmans, Oct. 1922, author's collection and CO183, Box 5, Folder 5, PUL.
67 'What a "Flapper Novelist" Thinks Of His Wife', *Baltimore Evening Sun*, 7 Oct. 1923, section 5, p. 2. This interview was syndicated to the *Louisville Courier-Journal*, 30 Sep. 1923. Reproduced in *Romantic Egoists*, p. 112. See also Milford, *Zelda*, pp. 100–1.
68 FSF, Ledger, summary of the year to Sep. 1922.
69 Anita Loos, *Kiss Hollywood Good-by*, Viking Press, New York, 1974, pp. 121, 122. Another version of the anecdote is in Turnbull, *Scott Fitzgerald*, p. 130.
70 FSF, Ledger, Apr. 1923. Zelda confirmed 'We drank always' (ZSF to FSF, late summer/early fall 1930, *Life in Letters*, p. 191).
71 Scott often watched Tommy play championship polo matches at Meadow Brook Club on Long Island. Like Jay Gatsby Hitchcock had done two terms at Oxford. He married a steel heiress and became a successful banker.
72 ZSF to Xandra Kalman, summer 1923, CO183, Box 5, Folder 5, PUL. Scott had long been haunted by the lure of the flesh versus Catholic ruminations on sexual abstinence and the idea of 'the dark celibacy of greatness' appealed. See also Wilson's letter to Bishop, 22 Sept. 1922 about 'seminal juice' (note 28 above).
73 Milford, *Zelda*, p. 100.
74 Sara was also taking an advanced degree in psychology at Johns Hopkins.
75 Mayfield, *Constant Circle*, p. 3; Ann Henley, Introduction, *Southern Souvenirs*, p. 8.
76 Mayfield, *Constant Circle*, pp. 5, 56.
77 Rodgers, *Mencken and Sara*, p. 1.
78 Sara Haardt, 'Joe Moore and Callie Balsingame', *Smart Set*, Oct. 1923.

79 ZSF, 'Our Own Movie Queen', *Collected Writings*, pp. 273–292. The story is set in Minnesota where dull watery people 'grew mushrooms and made incompetent whiskey'. Minnesota has several significant Swedish-American communities.

80 Seen and recorded by this author in the Princeton archives.

81 Wayne J. Flynt, *Montgomery: An Illustrated History*, Windsor Publications, Woodland Hills, California, 1980, p. 69.

82 Mayfield, *Constant Circle*, p. 25.

83 To discover the constant editorial assistance Zelda rendered him, one has to read in detail his letters to editor and agent and check his notebooks.

84 FSF to MP, *c.* 10 Apr. 1924, *Life in Letters*, p. 67. That year Zelda offered criticism on *The Vegetable* and insisted Scott keep the title *Tales of the Jazz Age*.

85 Wilson to Bishop, 15 Jan. 1924, Wilson, *Letters*, pp. 118–19.

86 Wilson, *The Twenties*, p. 95.

87 FSF, Ledger, summing up 1923.

88 Ring sent Zelda a farewell poem. Part of it ran: 'Zelda, fair queen of Alabam',/ Across the waves I kiss you! /You think I am a stone, a clam; / You think that I don't care a damn, /But God! How I will miss you!/ . . ./ So, dearie, when your tender heart / Of all his coarseness tires, / Just cable me and I will start / Immediately for Hyères' (ZSF, Scrapbook, CO183, Box 7, PUL).

CHAPTER 9

1 Gertrude Stein in Calvin Tomkins, *Living Well Is the Best Revenge: Two Americans in Paris 1921–1933*, André Deutsch, 1972, p. 25. Also quoted in Amanda Vaill, *Everybody was So Young: Gerald and Sara Murphy. A Lost Generation Love Story*, Little, Brown, 1998, p. 134.

2 ZSF to Perkins, May 1924, CO101, Box 53, Folder Zelda Fitzgerald, 1921–1944, PUL.

3 Lawton Campbell to Milford, 19 Sep. 1965, quoted in Milford, *Zelda*, p. 104.

4 FSF to Wilson, postmarked 7 Oct. 1924, Yale University.

5 Scott also owed Scribner's $700 because they had purchased a set of the *Encyclopaedia Britannica* for their trip. In 1923 Scott reported in his article 'How To Live On $36000 a Year' that they spent $296 dollars a month on servants. That year at Great Neck he earned $28,759.78.

6 ZSF to MP, May 1924, Scribner's Author Files, CO101, Box 53, Folder Zelda Fitzgerald, 1921–1944, PUL.

7 ZSF, 'Nanny, A British Nurse', unpublished, CO183, Box 3, Folder 15, PUL.

8 ZSF, *Caesar*, ch. V, CO183, Box 2A, Folder 6, PUL.

9 The Murphys together with the Fitzgeralds themselves became models for Scott's protagonists in *Tender Is The Night*.

10 ZSF, *Caesar*, ch. VI, CO183, Box 2A, Folder 7, PUL.

11 Quoted in Tomkins, *Living Well*, p. 10.

12 It was worth $2 million when Gerald inherited it in 1931.

13 Tomkins, *Living Well*, p. 11.

14 Sara Murphy to Calvin Tomkins, 'Living Well Is The Best Revenge', *New Yorker*, 28 July 1962, p. 50.

15 The MacLeishes summed up the Murphys' success: 'English, French, American, everybody – met them and came away saying that these people really are masters in the art of living.' Tomkins, *Living Well*, pp. 6, 7.

16 Gertrude Stein (1874–1946) used the phrase 'you are all a lost generation' in talking about some of the young who served in the First World War. She borrowed the phrase in translation from a French garage mechanic whom she heard address it disparagingly to an incompetent apprentice. Ernest Hemingway subsequently took it as his epigraph to *The Sun Also Rises* (1926).

17 Archibald MacLeish, *Riders On The Earth*, Houghton Mifflin, Boston, 1978, p. 79.

18 It would become *The Seven Lively Arts*.

19 Donald Ogden Stewart, *By a Stroke of Luck! An Autobiography*, Paddington Press/ Two Continents, New York, 1975, p. 117.

20 Dos Passos confessed himself 'eternally grateful'. Dos Passos, *Best Times*, p. 140.

21 Ibid., p. 146.
22 Hemingway was then correspondent for the *Toronto Star*.
23 Tomkins, *Living Well*, p. 6.
24 Dos Passos, *Best Times*, pp. 145, 146.
25 Ibid., p. 146.
26 Tomkins, *Living Well*, p. 6.
27 ZSF, *Caesar*, ch. VI, CO183, Box 2A, Folder 7, PUL.
28 Gerald Murphy to FSF and ZSF, 19 Sep. 1925, CO187, Box 51, Folder 13, PUL.
29 Gerald Murphy also said: 'Her beauty was not legitimate at all.' Murphy to Milford, interview, 26 Apr. 1963, Milford, *Zelda*, p. 124.
30 Sara Murphy to Milford, interview, 2 Mar. 1964, ibid.
31 Gerald Murphy to Milford, 2 Mar. 1964, Milford, *Zelda*, p. 107.
32 Sara Murphy to FSF, 20 Aug. 1934 or 1935, CO187, Box 51, Folder 15, PUL.
33 ZSF to Scottie Fitzgerald Lanahan, *c.* 1944, CO183, Box 4, PUL.
34 Zelda's first painting lessons took place in Capri in early 1925.
35 FSF, *Tender*, p. 11.
36 In *Tender Is The Night*. The architects were Hale Walker and Harold Heller.
37 ZSF to MP, May 1924, CO101, Box 53, Folder Zelda Fitzgerald, 1921–1944, PUL.
38 ZSF, Show Mr and Mrs F. to Number –', *Collected Writings*, p. 421.
39 ZSF, *Waltz*, *Collected Writings*, pp. 71–2.
40 Fanny Myers Brennan to the author, New York, 1998. She gave the author a copy of the inscription. The Stopes book was published in 1928.
41 Scottie Fitzgerald Lanahan to her daughter Eleanor Lanahan; Lanahan to the author, Vermont, 1998.
42 ZSF, *Waltz*, p. 82; FSF, Ledger, June 1924.
43 FSF, Ledger, June 1924.
44 ZSF, *Waltz*, pp. 81–2.
45 ZSF, *Caesar*, ch. VII, CO183, Box 2A, Folder 8, PUL.
46 Edouard Jozan to Milford, interview 11 Jan. 1967, Milford, *Zelda*, p. 108.
47 ZSF, *Waltz*, pp. 80, 81, 82.
48 Mayfield said that almost half a century after Zelda's flirtation with him Jozan was still 'unusually charming and handsome'. Mayfield, *Exiles*, p. 96.
49 Ibid.
50 Jozan to Milford, 11 Jan. 1967, Milford, *Zelda*, p. 109.
51 Mayfield, *Exiles*, pp. 96–7.
52 Jozan to Milford, 11 Jan. 1967, Milford, *Zelda*, p. 109.
53 Scott constantly misspells the name as Josanne. FSF, Ledger, June 1924.
54 Gerald and Sara Murphy to Milford, 2 Mar. 1964, Milford, *Zelda*, p. 110.
55 Jozan's view, many years later, was 'one day the Fitzgeralds left and their friends scattered, each to his own destiny'. Jozan to Milford, 11 Jan. 1967, Milford, *Zelda*, p. 109.
56 ZSF, *Waltz*, pp. 86, 89.
57 Ibid., p. 94.
58 ZSF, *Caesar*. ch. VII, CO183, Box 2A, Folder 8, PUL.
59 FSF, Ledger, July 1924.
60 Gerald Murphy, quoted in Tomkins, *Living Well*, p. 102.
61 Tomkins, *Living Well*, p. 42.
62 Jozan to Milford, 11 Jan. 1967, Milford, *Zelda*, p. 112.
63 ZSF, *Caesar*, ch. VII, CO183, Box 2A, Folder 8, PUL.
64 Sheilah Graham, *The Real F. Scott Fitzgerald*, Grosset & Dunlap, New York, 1976, p. 61.
65 Mayfield, *Exiles*, pp. 96–7.
66 Jozan to Milford, 11 Jan. 1967, Milford, *Zelda*, p. 112.
67 Hadley Hemingway (Mrs Paul Scott Mowrer) to Nancy Milford, 25 July 1964, Milford, *Zelda*, p. 114.
68 Mayfield, *Exiles*, pp. 96–7.
69 Janno also says: 'Love is a funny thing: it says so in the advertisements, in the popular songs, on the radio and in the moving-pictures. Though it seldom says what to do about it. It always shows the havocs wrought.' ZSF, *Caesar*, ch. VII, CO183, Box 2A, Folder 8, PUL.
70 Calvin Tomkins to Milford, 4 Jan. 1964, Milford, *Zelda*, p. 111.

71 Mayfield, *Exiles*, p. 97.
72 Vaill follows a suggestion by Calvin Tomkins. Vaill, *So Young*, p. 147.
73 Honoria Murphy Donnelly to the author, New York, 1998.
74 The article appeared 20 Sep. 1924.
75 I am indebted to the perceptive James R. Mellow for this insight.
76 Meyers, *Scott Fitzgerald*, pp. 116, 117.
77 ZSF, *Caesar*, ch. VII, CO183, Box 2A, Folder 8, PUL.
78 FSF, Notebooks no. 839.
79 ZSF to FSF, late summer/early fall 1930, *Life in Letters*, p. 191.
80 FSF to MP, 27 Aug. 1924, *Life in Letters*, p. 79.
81 An apt piece of awareness occurs in *Save Me The Waltz* (p. 79): 'David worked on his frescoes; Alabama was much alone. "What'll we *do*, David", she asked, "with ourselves?" David said she couldn't always be a child and have things provided for her to do.'

CHAPTER 10

1 ZSF 'Show Mr and Mrs F. to Number –', *Collected Writings*, p. 422.
2 ZSF to MP, undated fragment, *c.* fall/winter 1924, CO101, Box 53, Folder Zelda Fitzgerald, 1921–1944, PUL.
3 ZSF to MP, 11 Nov. 1924, ibid.
4 ZSF to FSF, late summer/early fall 1930, *Life in Letters*, p. 192.
5 Honoria Murphy Donnelly to the author, series of telephone conversations and interviews, New York, 1998. Mayfield, *Exiles*, consistently confirms this.
6 ZSF, 'Show Mr and Mrs F. to Number –', p. 422.
7 Ibid.
8 MP to FSF, 20 Nov. 1924, *Dear Scott/Dear Max*, p. 83. In October Scott had sent the novel to Perkins who responded (18 Nov.): 'I think the novel is a wonder . . . it has vitality to an extraordinary degree, and *glamour*, and a great deal of underlying thought of unusual quality . . . as for sheer writing it's astonishing.'
9 FSF to MP, *c.* 1 Dec. 1924, *Dear Scott/Dear Max*, p. 85.
10 FSF to MP, *c.* 20 Dec. 1924, ibid., p. 89.
11 FSF to MP, *c.* 1 Dec. 1924, ibid., p. 85.
12 FSF to MP, *c.* 20 Dec. 1924, ibid., p. 88.
13 'The Adjuster', *Redbook Magazine*, Sep. 1925; 'Not In The Guidebook', *Woman's Home Companion*, Nov. 1925.
14 'The Adjuster', *All The Sad Young Men*, Charles Scribner's Sons, New York, 1926, pp. 189–90.
15 Wilson, *The Twenties*, p. 298.
16 Scottie in later years looked back on all her Christmases as decorative occasions and times of excitement.
17 Scott drew on the discarded *Gatsby* section for his romantically disposed hero, Rudolph Miller. Miller's background was initially intended to represent Gatsby's early life.
18 Sara Mayfield had looked after her during 1923.
19 It was published 24 July 1924. Fifteen years later, after Sara's early death, Mencken confessed 'to my shame' that he had failed to recognize its 'solid maturity' (Ann Henley, Introduction, *Southern Souvenirs*, p. 9).
20 Mayfield, *Exiles*, p. 126. The conversation took place in 1928.
21 FSF, Ledger, Feb. 1925.
22 FSF to John Peale Bishop, *c.* Apr. 1925, *Life in Letters*, p. 104.
23 ZSF, 'Show Mr and Mrs F. to Number –', p. 422.
24 Aunt Annabel had travelled to Rome for the Holy Year observances.
25 Wilson, quoting Fitzgerald, to Arthur Mizener, 10 Nov. 1949, *Letters on Literature and Politics*, pp. 562–3; Mellow, *Invented Lives*, p. 229.
26 Through Mackenzie the Fitzgeralds also met Francis Brett Young, Mary Roberts Rinehart and Axel Munthe, who was working on what would become his bestselling *The Story of San Michele*.
27 His biographer James Mellow pointed out that though Scott was always edgy and boorish in the company of 'fairies', as he disparagingly called them, he developed an

ever-increasing curiosity about their habits. Scott's contorted complex relationship to this sexual issue was yet another of his remarkable resemblances to Zelda.

28 FSF to MP, 31 Mar. 1925, Turnbull, *Letters*, p. 197.
29 James Mellow is interesting on this matter. *Invented Lives*, p. 229.
30 FSF to Wilson, 7 Oct. 1924.
31 FSF to Wilson, 10 Jan. 1918; Mellow, *Invented Lives*, p. 229.
32 Kendall Taylor, *Sometimes Madness Is Wisdom. Zelda and Scott Fitzgerald: A Marriage*, Ballantine Books, New York, 2001, p. 143.
33 Art critic Carolyn Shafer to the author, Feb./Mar. 2001.
34 Documentation of Zelda's artistic work in Europe is particularly lacking. Shafer holds the view that as Europe was where Zelda first began to paint, she may have taken art lessons on more than one occasion in more than one European city. She may also have had exhibitions during her frequent visits to Europe of which both Shafer and this biographer are unaware.
35 The painting is both unfinished and painted over.
36 Shafer, 'To Spread a Human Aspiration: The Art of Zelda Sayre Fitzgerald', unpublished MA thesis, University of South Carolina, 1994, pp. 28, 19.
37 Jane S. Livingston is one critic who takes this view.
38 Shafer believes Picasso had a substantial influence on Zelda. Other critics disagree.
39 Sara Murphy to Mizener, 17 Jan. 1950; letter lent to this author by Honoria Murphy Donnelly.
40 Winzola McLendon, 'Interview: Frances Scott Fitzgerald to Winzola McLendon', *Ladies Home Journal*, Nov. 1974. Nasturtiums were always on the table set for the lunches *en famille* Zelda organized during that period.
41 Shafer, 'To Spread a Human Aspiration', pp. 101, 102.
42 Eddie Pattillo to the author, Feb./Mar. 2001 and in discussions with the author, Montgomery, 1999, 2000.
43 Shafer to the author, Feb./Mar. 2001.
44 Calvin Tomkins, *Living Well*, p. 42.
45 Memories of Ginevra's wedding provided Scott with details for Daisy's marriage to Tom Buchanan.
46 FSF, *Gatsby*, Abacus, p. 124.
47 Whereas in 'The Sensible Thing' George O'Kelly accepts love's mutability: 'There are all kinds of love in the world but never the same love twice', Gatsby believes that one can recapture the past. 'Can't repeat the past? . . . Why of course you can!': FSF, 'The Sensible Thing', *All The Sad Young Men*, pp. 237–8; *The Great Gatsby*, p. 104.
48 Baker may also have been based on a champion golfer called Jordan, a classmate of Ginevra, the other woman Scott considered 'disloyal'. However Scott told Perkins that Jordan was Edith Cummings, another golfing schoolfriend of Ginevra's. FSF to MP, *c.* 20 Dec. 1924, *Dear Scott/Dear Max*, p. 90.
49 FSF to Annabel Fitzgerald, *c.* 1915, *Life in Letters*, p. 9.
50 Taylor, *Sometimes Madness*, p. 145.
51 Ruth Hale, Brooklyn *Daily Eagle*, reproduced in *Romantic Egoists*, p. 125.
52 *F. Scott Fitzgerald In His Own Time*, p. 345.
53 Ibid., p. 347.
54 Lardner to FSF, Mar. 1925, CO187, Box 50, PUL.
55 Wilson to FSF, 11 Apr. 1925, Wilson, *Letters*, p. 121.
56 Mencken to FSF, 16 Apr. 1925, *Correspondence of F. Scott Fitzgerald*, p. 158.
57 Seldes, 'Spring Flight', *The Dial*, Aug. 1925, p. 162.
58 T. S. Eliot to FSF, 31 Dec. 1925, *Romantic Egoists*, p. 135.
59 FSF quoted in Scott Donaldson, *Hemingway vs. Fitzgerald: The Rise and Fall of a Literary Friendship*, John Murray, London, 2000, p. 60.
60 On the 102nd anniversary of Scott's birth, novelist Alan Gurganus called *Gatsby* a 'work of pure protein genius, the most disciplined and prophetic novel of its decade'. Gurganus, 'Sacrificial Couples, the Splendor of our Failures and Scott and Zelda Fitzgerald', paper commissioned by the F. Scott Fitzgerald Society, delivered at the Fitzgeralds' 1930s haunt, Grove Park Inn, Asheville, North Carolina, 24 Sep. 1998. Lent to the author by Gurganus.
61 Scott learned this in June 1925.

62 This would after many name changes become *Tender Is The Night*.
63 These were raw studies for his masterpiece the *Demoiselles d'Avignon*.
64 ZSF to FSF, undated, CO187, Box 44, Folder 15, PUL.
65 Gertrude Stein to FSF, 22 May 1925, *Crack-Up*, New Directions, 1945, p. 308.
66 FSF to Stein, June 1925, *The Flowers of Friendship: Letters Written to Gertrude Stein*, ed. Donald Gallup, Alfred A. Knopf, New York, 1953, p. 174; *Life in Letters*, p. 115.
67 Mayfield, *Exiles*, p. 220.
68 Scottie Fitzgerald Smith, Memoir.
69 As Stein reported to Sherwood Anderson, who had introduced Hemingway to her. Donaldson, *Hemingway vs. Fitzgerald*, p. 62.
70 James R. Mellow points out that Hemingway's meeting with Zelda seems to have taken place before, not after, his trip to Lyons with Scott in May. It is clear from a letter to Van Vechten that Stein and Toklas left for Belley on 18 May 1925; the date of this letter to them from Hemingway should therefore be mid-May. Mellow, *Hemingway: A Life Without Consequences*, Hodder & Stoughton, London, Sydney, Auckland, 1992, p. 290.
71 He had been alerted by Edmund Wilson to Hemingway's writings in the *Transatlantic Review*.
72 EH, *Moveable Feast*, p. 147.
73 It is worth noting that *Moveable Feast* warns: 'If the reader prefers, this book may be regarded as fiction. But there is always the chance that such a book of fiction may throw some light on what has been written as fact.' Hemingway's statements about the Fitzgeralds are often unreliable. In *Moveable Feast* he says Fitzgerald came to the Dingo with Princetonian Duncan Chaplin, thus providing another witness to Scott's bad behaviour, but Chaplin was not in Europe in 1925.
74 EH to MP, 9 June 1925, EH *Selected Letters*, ed. Carlos Baker, Charles Scribner's Sons, New York, 1981, pp. 162–3.
75 Scott Donaldson, *Hemingway vs. Fitzgerald*, p. 61.
76 FSF to Stein, June 1925, *Flowers of Friendship*, p. 174; *Life in Letters*, p. 115.
77 FSF to MP, *c.* 10 Oct. 1924, *Dear Scott/Dear Max*, p. 78.
78 Mayfield, *Exiles*, pp. 136–7.
79 Gerald Murphy to Milford, 26 Apr 1963, Milford, *Zelda*, p. 117. Scribner's did not publish Hemingway's savage attack on both the Fitzgeralds and the Murphys in *Moveable Feast* until 1964, the year Murphy died. Nearly forty years later additional research on Hemingway as the 'real thing' has shown just how much insight Zelda had about Hemingway and how intelligent Murphy was to remain cautious.

CHAPTER 11

1 EH, 'Hawks Do Not Share', *Moveable Feast*.
2 Zelda herself told Sara that 'it smelled like a church chancery and was furnished with genuine Louis XV from the Galeries Lafayette'. Mayfield, *Exiles*, p. 110.
3 Mellow, *Hemingway: A Life Without Consequences*, p. 291.
4 Ibid.
5 EH to FSF, 1 July, 15 Dec. 1925, EH, *Selected Letters*, pp. 165, 177.
6 Honoria Murphy Donnelly with Richard N. Billings, *Sara and Gerald*, Holt, Rinehart & Winston, New York, 1982, p. 21.
7 Mayfield, *Exiles*, p. 137; ZSF to MP, 1926, CO101, Box 53, Folder Zelda Fitzgerald, 1921–1944, PUL.
8 Mayfield, *Exiles*, pp. 137, 113.
9 Ibid., p. 141.
10 Mellow, *Hemingway*, p. 290.
11 Quoted by Richard N. Billings, Donnelly and Billings, *Sara and Gerald*, p. 21.
12 EH to FSF, 28 May 1934, EH, *Selected Letters*, p. 408.
13 Mayfield, *Exiles*, p. 141.
14 Matthew J. Bruccoli, *Scott and Ernest: The Authority of Failure and the Authority of Success*, Random House, New York, 1978, p. 22.
15 Honoria Murphy Donnelly to the author, New York, 1998.

16 Mayfield, *Exiles*, p. 115.
17 Mizener, *Far Side of Paradise*, p. 220.
18 They even had identical toys: cuddly baby dolls, china tea sets and miniature air rifles.
19 Mellow, *Hemingway*, p. 104.
20 Ibid., p. 20.
21 Hemingway's father committed suicide in 1928. In later years Hemingway said 'I hate her guts and she hates mine. She forced my father to suicide.' Ibid., p. 565.
22 Ibid., p. 297.
23 Mayfield, *Exiles*, pp. 141, 140.
24 Mellow, *Hemingway*, p. 294. Later Hemingway claimed that Jinnie had tried to convert Pauline (then his second wife) to the lesbian cause.
25 Mayfield, *Exiles*, p. 106.
26 This draft was possibly for use in *Moveable Feast*.
27 Mayfield, *Exiles*, 107.
28 Ibid., pp. 138–9.
29 Hadley Hemingway (Mrs Paul Scott Mowrer) to Milford, 25 July 1964, Milford, *Zelda*, p. 115.
30 Ibid.
31 Hadley fell from a second storey window and her damaged back required months of bed-rest.
32 Bernice Kert, *The Hemingway Women*, W. W. Norton, New York, 1983, p. 86.
33 Ibid., pp. 94, 96.
34 Her mother had left her a modest amount and her grandmother had left her a capital account that yielded an income of $2,500 a year.
35 Hadley Hemingway to Milford, 25 July 1964, Milford, *Zelda*, p. 116.
36 Hadley like Hemingway felt this led Zelda into flirtations to attract Scott's notice.
37 EH, *Moveable Feast*, pp. 181–3.
38 Hadley Hemingway to Milford, 25 July 1964, Milford, *Zelda*, p. 117.
39 Artist Kitty Cannell, girlfriend of Harold Loeb, who introduced Pauline and Jinnie Pfeiffer to the Hemingways, quoted in Mellow, *Hemingway*, pp. 295, 296.
40 Noel Murphy's other reason was that she had formed an attachment to Natalie's friend Janet Flanner, the *New Yorker* correspondent. Amanda Vaill, *So Young*, p. 157.
41 Though Zelda later worked in oils on canvas, much of her surviving artwork is in this smaller medium at which she excelled. One problem was that its fragile nature limited the time those works could be on display, and there existed in the 1920s, and still exists today, an unspoken hierarchy in the art world which privileges paintings on canvas over works on paper. Carolyn Shafer, Introduction, 'To Spread a Human Aspiration', 1994.
42 Larionov had been painting in Paris since 1914. He designed the set for *The Merchants Garden*, 1921, and a sketch for the curtain of *Chout*, 1921. Shafer is interesting on the connection between his work and Zelda's in the mid-1920s. 'To Spread a Human Aspiration', p. 23.
43 Shafer expounds this point.
44 Murphy, *Razor*, 32" × 36". Exhibited: Salon des Indépendants 1923: Berheim Jeune 1936; Dallas Museum for Contemporary Arts 1960, Collection of Dallas Museum for Contemporary Arts.
45 Mayfield, *Exiles*, pp. 104–5.
46 Sara Murphy to Mizener, 17 Jan. 1950.
47 In fall 1925 Scott lent Hemingway $400, the following April he sent him $100 in a letter telling Ernest that Hollywood had just purchased the rights to *Gatsby* for $15,000. Because of Hadley's modest income the Hemingways were not dependent on Ernest's income from stories or journalism.
48 Mayfield, *Exiles*, p. 112.
49 Though Hemingway had many male friends, in almost every case he later broke off those friendships. He resented and never forgave friends like the Murphys and Fitzgerald who had helped him financially. Hadley said: 'Once he took a dislike to someone you could absolutely never get him back [to them]. If he took exception to anyone, that was it; there was no reasoning with him about it. He eventually turned on almost everyone we knew, all his old friends.' Hadley Hemingway to Milford, 25 July 1964, Milford, *Zelda*, p. 116.

50 Donaldson, *Hemingway vs. Fitzgerald*, p. 61.

51 It was published in *Redbook Magazine* Jan., Feb. 1926.

52 FSF to Ludlow Fowler, *c.* Mar. 1925, CO188, Box 4, Folders 22–3, PUL.

53 FSF, *All The Sad Young Men*, pp. 1–2.

54 FSF mentions this twice (Ledger, June and July 1925). Among the people they met that summer were Edith Wharton, Theodore Chanler, Robert McAlmon, Sylvia Beach, William L. Shirer, Harold Stearns, James Thurber, Deems Taylor.

55 FSF to ZSF, *c.* summer 1930, *Life in Letters*, p. 187.

56 Fanny Myers Brennan to the author, New York, 1998.

57 Mayfield, *Exiles*, p. 113.

58 Ellen Barry interview, Vaill, *So Young*, p. 155.

59 Scott even got Gerald to demonstrate how to do handstands then walk the length of a room upside down, a trick he had learned from his father.

60 Sara Murphy to Mizener, 17 Jan. 1950.

61 Donaldson, *Hemingway vs. Fitzgerald*, p. 88.

62 Gerald felt that Ernest's desire to strip away ornamentation in his writing and produce a honed simple language reflected a similar goal in his own paintings.

63 Donnelly and Billings, *Sara and Gerald*, p. 21.

64 Scott's discipline broke down however if Scottie did something he approved of. One day he had told her to go to bed as a punishment. When he walked in to check, she was reading: 'he took the book away and started reading it himself. He decided it was good literature, and gave it back to me to finish.' Scottie to Honoria Murphy Donnelly; Donnelly to the author, 1997 and 1998.

65 Sara Murphy to Mizener, 17 Jan. 1950.

66 Mayfield, *Exiles*, p. 118.

67 Sara Murphy to Mizener, 17 Jan. 1950.

68 Ibid.

69 Nathan thought it was a hangover from Scott's undergraduate days when 'he sent out questionnaires to prospective feminine dates as to 1) whether they had their hair washed during the day, and 2) how many baths they had taken.' Nathan, 'Memories of Fitzgerald, Lewis and Dreiser', *Esquire*, Oct. 1958.

70 FSF to MP, 28 Aug. 1925, *Dear Scott/Dear Max*, p. 120. In 1924 University of Chicago students Nathan Leopold and Richard Loeb kidnapped and slew fourteen-year-old Robert Franks. After they confessed they were defended by Clarence Darrow and said in court they had done it for the exhilaration of planning and executing the 'perfect crime'. Scott admired this as an 'intellectual murder'.

71 FSF to Bishop, postmarked 21 Sep. 1925, *Life in Letters*, p. 126.

72 Eleanor Lanahan to the author in conversations 1997, 1998, 1999, Vermont and Asheville, North Carolina.

73 Winzola McLendon, 'Interview: Frances Scott Fitzgerald to Winzola McLendon', *Ladies Home Journal*, New York, Nov. 1974.

74 Eleanor Lanahan to the author in conversations 1997, 1998, 1999.

75 Gerald Murphy to Milford, 26 Apr. 1963, Milford, *Zelda*, pp. 117–18. Several years later when Zelda wrote about the scene she completely transformed her own part in it. She wrote that she was able to steal two glass automobiles for salt and pepper from the café in St Paul. 'Nobody was looking because Isadora Duncan was giving one of her last parties at the next table. She had got too old and fat to care whether people accepted her theories of life and art, and she gallantly toasted the world's obliviousness in lukewarm champagne.' ZSF, 'Auction – Model 1934', *Collected Writings*, p. 434.

76 Mayfield, *Exiles*, p. 117.

77 Gerald Murphy to Milford, 26 Apr. 1963, Milford, *Zelda*, p. 118.

78 Gerald Murphy to FSF, 19 Sep. 1925, CO187, Box 51, Folder 13, PUL.

79 ZSF to Madeleine Boyd, wife of the critic Ernest Boyd, 18 Dec. 1925, CO183, Box 5, Folder 1, PUL.

80 They also attended parties given by Tallulah's friend the Marchioness of Milford Haven and the Mountbattens.

81 ZSF to Scottie Fitzgerald, 1939, CO183, Box 4, PUL.

82 ZSF to Madeleine Boyd, 18 Dec. 1925, CO183, Box 5, Folder 1, PUL.

83 FSF to EH, 30 Nov. 1925, John F. Kennedy Library.
84 Published 26 Feb.

CHAPTER 12

1 Mayfield, *Exiles*, p. 108.
2 EH to Harold Loeb, 5 Jan. 1925, EH, *Selected Letters*, p. 143.
3 Mencken, *My Life as Author and Editor*, p. 261.
4 Rodgers (ed.), Introduction, *Mencken and Sara*, pp. 8–9.
5 FSF to Henry Albert Phillips, winter 1926.
6 As a Southern woman friend from West Virginia said: 'I'm afraid Scott just wasn't a very lively male animal,' comparing him unfavourably with her more physically satisfying Southern beaux. Elizabeth Beckwith MacKie, 'My Friend Scott Fitzgerald', *Fitzgerald-Hemingway Annual* 2 (1970), pp. 20–21.
7 In 1935 Scott told an Asheville prostitute that he had once discussed his penis size with Hemingway.
8 EH, *Moveable Feast*, pp. 188–9. These points offer clear evidence that Hemingway's account teems with inaccuracies and misalignments.
9 Initially Ernest had been attracted to Pauline's sister Jinnie with her rapier wit and aristocratic means. Jinnie was amused at Ernest's attention but her own was already turned towards women.
10 *Torrents* ironically is a satire about a man hesitantly trying to change an older woman for a more vital younger one.
11 Pauline's father, who had made a fortune on the St Louis grain exchange and was one of the wealthiest landowners in north-eastern Arkansas, gave her an income to travel freely.
12 Hadley invited Pauline to spend Christmas at Schruns with her and Ernest.
13 When Gerald Murphy confessed to the athletic Ernest that he had been scared up the slopes, Hemingway famously explained that Gerald had exhibited true courage: 'grace under pressure'. Later Gerald told his daughter Honoria that like their friends who basked in Ernest's approval he had felt childishly elated (Honoria Murphy Donnelly to the author, 1998; Honoria Murphy Donnelly with Richard N. Billings, *Sara and Gerald*, p. 22). The events surrounding this oft-quoted phrase, 'grace under pressure', may be different from Honoria and Gerald's story. A second version is that Scott heard it first from Hemingway and retold it to Murphy when they discussed Hemingway's passion for bullfighting. Hemingway said that he had not been referring to courage but to something he called 'grace under pressure'. A third version is that Hemingway used the phrase when Dorothy Parker asked him what he meant by 'guts' in an interview for the *New Yorker* (30 Nov. 1929). This could merely add up to the fact that Hemingway re-used a good phrase as often as possible.
14 Mayfield, *Exiles*, p. 113.
15 Sara Murphy to Arthur Mizener, 17 Jan. 1950. Letter lent to the author by Honoria Murphy Donnelly.
16 Meyers, *Scott Fitzgerald*, p. 161.
17 Honoria Murphy Donnelly and Fanny Myers Brennan described the incident to the author in New York in 1998 and 1999. Earlier Gerald Murphy had described it to Nancy Milford, 2 Mar. 1964, Milford, *Zelda*, p. 106.
18 Honoria Murphy Donnelly to the author, summer 1998.
19 Mayfield, *Exiles*, p. 112.
20 Ibid., p. 113.
21 Peter Griffin, *Less Than A Treason: Hemingway in Paris*, Oxford University Press, New York, 1990, pp. 142, 144.
22 Mayfield, *Exiles*, p. 109.
23 Mayfield was having cocktails with René Herrera, son of the Spanish ambassador to the US, and Michael Arlen, the fashionable British writer of *The Green Hat*, the play Zelda had seen and mocked in London.
24 Mayfield, *Exiles*, p. 109.
25 FSF to EH, fall 1926, John F. Kennedy Library.

26 Mayfield, *Exiles*, p. 116.
27 Gerald Murphy to Milford, 26 Apr. 1963, Milford, *Zelda*, p. 120.
28 Mayfield to Mizener, 17 Jan. 1950.
29 Mayfield, *Exiles*, p. 115.
30 Ada MacLeish to Milford, 11 Mar. 1965, Milford, *Zelda*, p. 121.
31 Ibid., p. 120.
32 ZSF to FSF, late summer/early fall, 1930, *Life in Letters*, pp. 192–3.
33 Gerald Murphy to Milford, 26 Apr. 1963, Milford, *Zelda*, p. 121.
34 Ada MacLeish to Milford, 11 Mar. 1965, Milford, *Zelda*, pp. 120–1.
35 Ibid., p. 120.
36 Honoria Murphy Donnelly to the author, 1998; Calvin Tomkins' notes, Honoria Murphy Donnelly Collection.
37 Calvin Tomkins, *Living Well*, p. 101.
38 Vaill, *So Young*, p. 155.
39 Gerald and Sara Murphy to Calvin Tomkins, 1961, Tomkins interview tapes, Honoria Murphy Donnelly Collection; also Honoria Murphy Donnelly to the author, 1998.
40 Sara Murphy to FSF, June 1926, CO187, Box 51, Folder 15, PUL.
41 ZSF to MP, *c.* Nov. 1926, CO101, Box 53, Folder Zelda Fitzgerald, 1921–1944, PUL.
42 Mayfield, *Exiles*, pp. 117–18.
43 Milford, *Zelda*, pp. 125–6.
44 Turnbull, *Scott Fitzgerald*, p. 168.
45 ZSF to FSF, late summer/early fall 1930, *Life in Letters*, p. 193.

CHAPTER 13

1 ZSF, 'A Millionaire's Girl', *Collected Writings*, pp. 331–2.
2 ZSF, 'Show Mr and Mrs F. To Number –', *Collected Writings*, p. 424.
3 'Boo Boo' was Zelda's new name for Scottie. All these letters are from Ambassadors Hotel, Los Angeles, CO183, Box 4, Folders 4–13, PUL.
4 ZSF, 'Show Mr and Mrs F. To Number –', p. 424.
5 Lois Moran joined the Paris Opera as a ballerina aged only fourteen. At fifteen she acted in her first (French) film. She made her US debut in 1925 in Goldwyn's *Stella Dallas*.
6 ZSF, 'Autobiographical Sketch', 16 Mar. 1932, written at Phipps Clinic, Johns Hopkins Hospital, for her psychiatrists, in particular Dr Mildred T. Squires.
7 As an expert seamstress she had designed her own clothes for years following Manhattan fashions.
8 Radie Harris, 'Movie Monotypes', reproduced in Bruccoli *et al.*, eds., *Romantic Egoists*, p. 150.
9 This is the version given by Bruccoli (*Epic Grandeur*, pp. 300–1) and Milford (*Zelda*, p. 131). There are other versions. In Fitzgerald's Ledger he makes the enigmatic note 'The watch' in January, when they were in fact still in Hollywood, and in July: 'Rows. New watch'. These sparse notations suggest there was a watch incident two months earlier than the train journey, and a loss that involved a renewal purchase, though no indication as to whether the loss was accidental or deliberate. Zelda's friend Livye Hart recalled: 'Zelda was very careless with her personal effects, clothes, jewelry etc. and so very thoughtlessly she laid the watch on the commode in the bathroom, from where it was accidentally brushed and flushed. Zelda caring very little for jewelry, most casually informed me of what had happened' (Livye Hart Ridgeway, 'A Profile of Zelda', Sara Mayfield Collection, University of Alabama, Tuscaloosa). This version is adopted by Koula Hartnett (*Zelda Fitzgerald*, p. 123). Livye also told Mayfield she never knew Zelda to deny any story about herself no matter how absurd or damaging, so Zelda may have given credence to the train window disposal story (Mayfield, *Exiles*, p. 122). It may even have been true. Certainly the deliberate disposal of the watch is psychologically in line with Zelda's other 1926–28 destructive actions against things she considered of value. That it was her *wristwatch* Zelda threw away may have much to do with the fact that Moran's hobby was collecting wristwatches because she kept breaking them (Radie Harris, 'Movie Monotypes').
10 'Jacob's Ladder', *Saturday Evening Post*, 20 Aug. 1927; 'Magnetism', ibid., 3 Mar. 1928. In

Tender Is The Night many of the words and much of the content from 'Jacob's Ladder' are repeated. For instance lines relating to the 'grand scale' and to the older man 'chilled by the innocence of her kiss' are repeated almost verbatim. *Tender Is The Night* (first published 1934), Penguin, 1986 (first edition with emendations), p. 74.

11 FSF, 'Jacob's Ladder', *Bits of Paradise*, Penguin Books, 1982, pp. 145, 147, 149, 153.
12 *The Stories of F. Scott Fitzgerald*, ed. with introduction by Malcolm Cowley, Charles Scribner's Sons, New York, 1952, p. 226.
13 ZSF, 'A Millionaire's Girl', *Collected Writings*, p. 336.
14 Scottie had sent Zelda a cross and in Hollywood Zelda had begun obsessively kissing it.
15 Mayfield, *Exiles*, p. 119.
16 Ann Henley, 'Sara Haardt and "The Sweet Flowering South"', *Alabama Heritage* 31, Winter 1994, p. 16.
17 John had married Anna Rupert, a childhood neighbour and the daughter of a successful manufacturer, in 1925.
18 ZSF, 'Show Mr and Mrs F. to Number –', *Collected Writings*, p. 425.
19 Frances Fitzgerald Smith in Carolyn Shafer, 'To Spread a Human Aspiration', p. 36.
20 ZSF, 'Show Mr and Mrs F. to Number –', *Collected Writings*, p. 425.
21 ZSF, 'Autobiographical Sketch', 16 Mar. 1932.
22 Cecilia Taylor to Milford, 10 Aug. 1965, Milford, *Zelda*, pp. 136–7.
23 ZSF, 'Autobiographical Sketch', 16 Mar. 1932.
24 ZSF to Van Vechten, 6 Sep. 1927, Beinecke Library, Yale Collection of American Literature.
25 Cecilia Taylor to Milford, 10 Aug. 1965, Milford, *Zelda*, p. 137.
26 In Montgomery where 'paper dolls . . . were homemade and a tradition', Zelda as a child had made and designed them for other children. Catalogue, Retrospective Exhibition, Montgomery, 1974, p. 7.
27 Scottie Fitzgerald Smith, Foreword to *Bits of Paradise*, pp. 8–9.
28 I am indebted to Rebecca Stott's suggestion that Zelda's dancing and doll-making are reminiscent of Sylvia Plath's feminization of her childhood: ballet, piano, sewing – women's accomplishments.
29 Zelda eventually left these books to Scottie, who handed them on to her painter daughter Eleanor Lanahan who still owns them.
30 Jane S. Livingston has a full discussion of this point, *Zelda: An Illustrated Life*, ed. Eleanor Lanahan, Harry N. Abrams, Inc., New York, 1996, p. 84.
31 Winzola McLendon, 'Scott and Zelda', *Ladies Home Journal* 91, Nov. 1974, p. 60.
32 Kendall Taylor suggests that it is Amy Thomas on the goose. This author however feels it is unlikely that Amy wore a butcher's apron, trousers or moustache.
33 ZSF to Carl Van Vechten, 6 Sep. 1927.
34 Carolyn Shafer to the author, Mar. 2001.
35 Amy Thomas to Koula Hartnett, 23 Dec. 1981, Hartnett, *Zelda Fitzgerald*, p. 148.
36 ZSF, 'Autobiographical Sketch'.
37 ZSF to Van Vechten, 27 May 1927.
38 ZSF to Van Vechten, 29 May 1927.
39 ZSF to Van Vechten, 14 June 1927.
40 ZSF, 'Autobiographical Sketch'.
41 Sara Murphy to ZSF, 28 June 1927, CO183, Box 5, Folder 17, PUL.
42 'Stoppies' mentioned in Ledger for August and September in the context of rows and little writing.
43 ZSF, 'The Changing Beauty of Park Avenue', *Collected Writings*, pp. 403–5.
44 ZSF, 'Looking Back Eight Years', *Collected Writings*, p. 409.
45 ZSF, 'Who Can Fall in Love After Thirty?', *Collected Writings*, pp. 412–13.
46 Scott's alleged reason was that in order to get *Photoplay* magazine to pay up he wrote to Paul Reynolds at the Reynolds agency claiming that Zelda's article was his. He further claimed that the reason he hadn't asked his agent to handle it for him was it was too small a matter. When Harold Ober later placed the article he too did not want to reveal Zelda was the author.
47 Bruccoli, *Epic Grandeur*, p. 304.
48 Ibid.
49 FSF to Ober, received 2 Feb. 1928, *As Ever*, p. 94.

50 Quoted in Donaldson, *Hemingway vs. Fitzgerald*, p. 111.
51 Ibid., p. 112.
52 Hartnett, *Zelda Fitzgerald*, p. 122. John and Anna Biggs, Ernest Boyd, Edmund Wilson, Thornton Wilder, Gilbert Seldes, Zoe Atkins, Joseph Hergesheimer were among regular visitors in 1927.
53 Mayfield, *Exiles*, p. 119.
54 James Thurber, *Credos and Curios*, Harper & Row, New York, 1962, p. 154.
55 Hartnett, *Zelda Fitzgerald*, p. 148.
56 Mellow, *Invented Lives*, p. 305.
57 ZSF, 'Autobiographical Sketch'.
58 FSF to Gilbert Seldes, fall 1927. In New York they saw George Jean Nathan, Teddy Chanler, Charles Angoff, Tommy Hitchcock and H. L. Mencken.
59 FSF, Ledger, Sep. 1927.
60 Calvin Tomkins, *Living Well*, pp. 25–6.
61 In a later letter to one of Zelda's doctors Scott wrote: 'Began dancing at age 27 and had two severe attacks of facial eczema cured by electric ray treatment' (FSF to Dr Oscar Forel, 29 Jan. 1931, *Life in Letters*, p. 204). There is no corroboration for this statement, but if Zelda's skin was her vulnerable feature there was already sufficient trauma in her life to produce a skin disease without locating the cause in her ballet classes.
62 Quoted in Hartnett, *Zelda Fitzgerald*, p. 123.
63 ZSF to Van Vechten, 14 Oct. 1927.
64 Mayfield, *Exiles*, p. 120.
65 16 West Read Street, Baltimore.
66 Conversation between ZSF and Sara Haardt at Ellerslie which Sara turned into an article, submitted in 1928 to *Good Housekeeping* which bought but never published it.
67 Amy Thomas to Koula Hartnett, Hartnett, *Zelda Fitzgerald*, p. 164.

CHAPTER 14

1 She told Sara Mayfield this on several occasions. It emerged during discussions with Montgomery residents, including relatives of the Haardt family, and in conversation with Camella Mayfield.
2 The school was aimed primarily at children of Americans overseas.
3 Scottie Fitzgerald Smith, Memoir, written for her daughters and owned by Cecilia Ross, p. 24.
4 ZSF, 'Show Mr and Mrs F. To Number –', *Collected Writings*, p. 425.
5 Edmund Wilson, *The Shores of Light*, New York, Farrar, Straus & Young, 1952, p. 379.
6 Ibid., p. 382.
7 Fitzgeralds' photo album, PUL. Reproduced in Bruccoli *et al.*, eds., *Romantic Egoists*, p. 160.
8 Gerald Murphy to FSF, May 1928, CO187, Box 51, Folder 13, PUL.
9 FSF to EH, July 1928, Hemingway Collection, John F. Kennedy Library.
10 Vaill, *So Young*, p. 195. The apartment's address was also 58 rue de Vaugirard as it was on the corner of Vaugirard.
11 Milford quotes Zelda as saying 'Madame Tausand's' which is patently a mistranscription or printer's error. Milford, *Zelda*, p. 140.
12 Scottie recalls she was placed in 'the equivalent of third and fourth grade'. Scottie Fitzgerald Smith, Memoir, p. 24.
13 ZSF to Eleanor Browder Addison, postmarked 29 May 1928.
14 Scottie Fitzgerald Smith, Memoir, p. 25.
15 ZSF, *Waltz, Collected Writings*, p. 118.
16 Gerald Murphy to Nancy Milford, interview, 2 Mar. 1964, Milford, *Zelda*, p. 141.
17 *Ballerinas Dressing*, c. 1941 though it could be much earlier, oil on canvas, 42″ × 30″. Xandra Kalman had it on show in her St Paul house for many years. Owned by Kristina Kalman Fares; also CO183, Box 8, Fg. 23, PUL.
18 Jerry and Robbie Tillotson, 'Zelda Fitzgerald Still Lives', *The Feminist Art Journal*, spring 1975, p. 32.
19 ZSF, *Waltz*, p. 144.

20 Honoria Murphy Donnelly to the author, New York, 1999.
21 Fanny Myers Brennan to the author, New York, 1999.
22 FSF, Ledger, July, Aug. 1928.
23 ZSF to FSF, late summer/early fall 1930, *Life in Letters*, p. 193.
24 Mayfield, *Exiles*, p. 131.
25 He had been reading Proust. FSF, Ledger, Mar. 1928.
26 FSF to ZSF, summer? 1930, *Life in Letters*, p. 188.
27 Sara Murphy to Milford in 1963, Milford, *Zelda*, p. 142; to Calvin Tomkins who was writing a memoir of the Murphys.
28 ZSF to FSF, late summer/early fall 1930, *Life in Letters*, p. 193.
29 Other guests were Nora Joyce, Adrienne Monnier (proprietor of bookstore La Maison des Amis des Livres and Sylvia Beach's lover) and André and Lucie Chamson.
30 FSF, Ledger, June 1928.
31 FSF, Ledger, summary of year Sep. 1927–Sep. 1928.
32 ZSF to FSF, late summer/early fall 1930, *Life in Letters*, p. 193.
33 FSF, Ledger, summary of year Sep. 1927–Sep. 1928.
34 ZSF to FSF, late summer/early fall 1930, *Life in Letters*, p. 193.

CHAPTER 15

1 MP to EH, 2 Oct. 1928, *The Only Thing That Counts: The Ernest Hemingway/Max Perkins Correspondence 1925–1947*, ed. Matthew J. Bruccoli, Charles Scribner's Sons, New York, 1996, p. 81.
2 Mayfield, *Exiles*, p. 142. Mayfield was referring especially to quarrels that year and the following year.
3 Strater, an early Princeton hero of Scott's, is the role model for Burne Holiday, the campus radical, in *This Side of Paradise*. Strater and Father Fay had been very impressed with each other when Fitzgerald introduced them.
4 Robert Taylor, 'A Strater Retrospective: No Faces of Fame', *Boston Globe Magazine*, 6 Aug. 1981, pp. 22–4.
5 A. E. Hotchner, *Papa Hemingway*, Random House, New York, 1966, p. 121.
6 Mayfield, *Exiles*, p. 133. There is another version: on 6 Dec. 1928 Hemingway was suddenly informed his father had died. He wired Scott and also Perkins for money so that he could go West. Most reports say Scott delivered the money in person in December. Scott's Ledger says he delivered it in January.
7 'The Sun Also Rises': EH to FSF, c. 24 Nov. 1926, EH, *Selected Letters*, p. 231; 'This tough talk': FSF to EH, Dec. 1927, *The Letters of F. Scott Fitzgerald*, pp. 302–3.
8 Quoted in Donaldson, *Hemingway vs. Fitzgerald*, p. 122.
9 Wilson, *The Twenties*, p. 354.
10 The Daisy novel would be published by Scribner's the following year.
11 Wilson entered the sanatorium in 1929. On leaving he went to live on Cape Cod for the summer; there he became involved with Margaret Canby, who had been the lover of Ted Paramore in the early Twenties when Wilson and Paramore had shared a flat on Lexington Avenue, New York, and Wilson had courted Edna St Vincent Millay. Mellow, *Invented Lives*, pp. 100, 372.
12 MP to FSF, 13 Nov. 1928, *Dear Scott/Dear Max*, p. 154.
13 Together with co-judges Cornelius Vanderbilt Jnr and John Barrymore.
14 Scott took out the policy in Feb. 1929.
15 Gavrilov had graduated from the Maryinsky School in 1911 and left the Imperial Ballet that year to join Diaghilev's Ballets Russes, where he understudied Nijinsky and alternated several roles with him.
16 Zelda ate with him at Reuben's lunch bar then returned to the apartment he shared with his mistress at 5–20 Chestnut Street.
17 ZSF, 'Autobiographical Sketch', 16 Mar. 1932, Johns Hopkins Hospital records. In Zelda's address book (CO183, Box 6, Folder 1, PUL) there is a listing for Gavrilov at the Cortissoz studios in Philadelphia.

18 Carolyn Shafer, 'To Spread a Human Aspiration', p. 45, and author's correspondence with Shafer, 2001.
19 Giles Neret, *The Arts of the Twenties*, Rizzoli, New York, 1986, p. 14.
20 Interview between ZSF and Henry Dan Piper, 1947. See also Shafer, 'To Spread a Human Aspiration', p. 96.
21 Degas admitted that he had painted dance classes without ever having attended one. Shafer, 'To Spread a Human Aspiration', p. 98.
22 Alice Hall Petry makes a fascinating case along these lines in her article 'Women's Work: The Case of Zelda Fitzgerald', *Literature-Interpretation-Theory*, vol. 1, Gordon and Breach Science Publishers S.A., USA, 1989, pp. 69–83.
23 ZSF to FSF, late summer/early fall, 1930, *Life in Letters*, p. 193.
24 Diary of Geneva Porter, Buffalo and Erie County Public Library.
25 ZSF to FSF, late summer/early fall, 1930, *Life in Letters*, p. 193.
26 ZSF, 'The Original Follies Girl', *Collected Writings*, p. 294.
27 Ibid., pp. 294, 296.
28 It was however the last to be published (Jan. 1931).
29 ZSF, 'Poor Working Girl', *Collected Writings*, p. 342.
30 ZSF, 'Southern Girl', *Collected Writings*, pp. 305, 304, 301, 307.
31 Ibid., p. 299.
32 It was published in March 1929, four months before Zelda's story.
33 FSF to Ober, *c*. Aug. 1929, *As Ever, Scott Fitz–*, ed. Bruccoli with Jennifer McCabe Atkinson, p. 142.
34 Sara had been in Hollywood in 1927. On her return she began work as Joseph Hergesheimer's researcher on his Southern novel *Swords and Roses*.
35 Rodgers, *Mencken and Sara*, and Carl Bode, *Mencken*, Southern Illinois University Press, Carbondale and Edwardsville, 1969, both discuss this in detail.
36 FSF to Haardt, 6 Nov. 1928, PUL, copy lent to the author by Vincent Fitzpatrick, Curator, H. L. Mencken Collection, Enoch Pratt Free Library, Baltimore.
37 Djuna Barnes, *Ladies Almanack* (1928), Dalkey Archive Press, Illinois, 1992.
38 Barney called Esther a 'brilliant, didactic' woman. Joan Schenkar, *Truly Wilde*, Virago, London, 2000, pp. 158, 353.
39 ZSF, Autobiographical Sketch, 16 Mar. 1932, Johns Hopkins Hospital Records.
40 Mellow, *Invented Lives*, p. 337.
41 ZSF to FSF, late summer/early fall 1930, *Life in Letters*, p. 194.
42 FSF, Ledger, June 1929.
43 Scott felt snubbed that Hemingway did not show it to him before it was in galley proofs ready for serialization in *Scribner's Magazine*.
44 FSF to EH, June 1929, John F. Kennedy Library.
45 Ibid. More than 20 years later Hemingway was still angry. In 1951 he told Scott's biographer Arthur Mizener that Scott's letter was 'one of the worst damned documents I have ever read and I would give it to no one' (EH to Mizener, 11 Jan. 1951).
46 Mayfield, *Exiles*, p. 138.
47 Ibid., p. 139.
48 Ibid., p. 140. McAlmon was married to British heiress Winifred Ellerman who wrote under the name Bryher. It was a marriage of convenience, as Bryher was bisexual and wanted freedom from her upper-class family and McAlmon was homosexual. McAlmon used his father-in-law's wealth to set up Contact Editions, a vanguard publishing company in Paris, which published among others Djuna Barnes, William Carlos Williams and Nathaniel West.
49 FSF to MP, *c*. 15 Nov. 1929, *Dear Scott/Dear Max*, pp. 158–9. Though McAlmon had published Hemingway's first book *Three Stories and Ten Poems*, its author agreed with Scott that McAlmon was a poisonous piece of body fungus.
50 Morley Callaghan, *That Summer in Paris*, Coward-McCann, New York, 1963, pp. 152, 160–3.
51 ZSF, 'The Girl The Prince Liked', *Collected Writings*, pp. 309–10.
52 FSF, Ledger, July 1929.
53 Gerald Murphy to Milford, 26 Apr. 1963, Milford, *Zelda*, p. 155.
54 Julie Sedowa, Naples, to ZSF, 13 Sep. 1929, CO183, Box 5, Folder 22, PUL.

55 Rosalind Smith, unpublished documentation on ZSF, Mayfield Collection, University of Alabama, Tuscaloosa.

56 ZSF, 'The Girl With Talent', *Collected Writings*, pp. 324, 325.

57 Quoted in Petry, 'Women's Work: The Case of Zelda Fitzgerald', p. 82.

58 Milford, *Zelda*, p. 156.

59 Some of Scott's biographers considered 'A Millionaire's Girl' a story that approached Fitzgerald's standard. Mellow, *Invented Lives*, p. 340.

60 ZSF, 'A Millionaire's Girl', *Collected Writings*, pp. 328, 336.

61 Ibid., p. 329.

62 Ober's notes on Scott's deal with *College Humor* stated that 'as he remembered, they paid $200 for one article that Zelda did and $250 for another. He said we had better leave the price until they did the first article . . . I should think they ought to pay $500 for them, if they are 4 or 5 thousand words in length.' 14 Feb. 1929, *As Ever*, p. 127. (Ober often uses the term 'article' both for features and for stories.)

63 FSF to Ober, received 8 Oct. 1929, *As Ever*, pp. 146–7.

64 FSF to Ober, received 2 Mar. 1929, *As Ever*, p. 130.

65 FSF to Ober, c. Aug. 1929, *As Ever*, p. 142.

66 A wire from New York told Scott: 'Millionaires Girl can sell Post four thousand without Zeldas name cable confirmation', 12 Mar. 1930.

67 Ober to FSF, 8 Apr. 1930, *As Ever*, p. 166.

68 FSF to Ober, received 13 May 1930, ibid., p. 167.

69 FSF to ZSF, 13 June 1934, CO187, Box 41, PUL.

70 Petry, 'Women's Work: The Case of Zelda Fitzgerald', p. 69.

71 FSF, Notebooks, No. 1293.

72 Mellow, *Invented Lives*, p. 359.

73 ZSF to FSF, late summer/early fall 1930, *Life in Letters*, p. 194.

74 FSF to ZSF, c. summer 1930, *Life in Letters*, p. 189.

75 Callaghan, *That Summer in Paris*, p. 207. Callaghan and the bisexual writer Robert McAlmon had each been challenged to write stories about two homosexuals for *This Quarter*. Callaghan's entry, 'Now that April's Here', dealt with a gay man leaving his lover for a woman. This commission may have made Scott over-sensitive.

76 Vaill, *So Young*, p. 228.

77 FSF, Notebooks No. 62.

78 ZSF to FSF, late summer/early fall 1930, *Life in Letters*, p. 194.

79 Ibid., p. 195.

80 ZSF, 'Autobiographical Sketch', 16 Mar. 1932.

CHAPTER 16

1 FSF to ZSF, summer? 1930, *Life in Letters*, p. 198. Scott was now worried that people, even if unaware of his youthful cross-dressings, might believe those stinking accusations because when acquaintances told him he looked like someone else, that 'someone else' usually turned out to be homosexual. Donaldson, *Hemingway vs. Fitzgerald*, p. 159.

2 ZSF, 'Show Mr and Mrs F. To Number –', *Collected Writings*, p. 427.

3 ZSF to FSF, late summer/early fall 1930, *Life in Letters*, pp. 194–5. Scott's Ledger May 1929 mentions 'Lucien again' – probably another reference to Lucienne.

4 ZSF to FSF, late summer/early fall 1930, *Life in Letters*, p. 194. Scott's Ledger dates the Nancy Hoyt dinner as 30 March 1930. Subsequently Elinor became a close friend of Dos Passos. Elinor Hoyt Wylie and Nancy Hoyt were sisters of Morton Hoyt who was married to Eugenia Bankhead, Tallulah's elder sister, with whom Scott had an affair. In 1922 Wilson continued his flirtation with Elinor Wylie but she became more seriously involved with John Peale Bishop. At Bishop's wedding to Margaret Hutchins the bride's father tried to rape Elinor Wylie. Mellow, *Invented Lives*, p. 157.

5 Natalie had lived at 20 rue Jacob, Paris, since 1909. She told Zelda she staged *tableaux vivants* and held pacifist meetings in the garden where Racine was supposed to have strolled with his mistress La Champsmesle. A tiny Doric temple fronted a disused well

which led to an underground cave below which was a passage under the Seine to the Louvre.

6 Dolly (Dorothy Ierne Wilde) was the daughter of Oscar's elder improvident brother Willie who died in 1899, the year before Oscar. She was born 11 July 1895 in Oakley Street, Chelsea, London.

7 The drugs included cocaine and morphine. See Joan Schenkar, *Truly Wilde*, Virago Press, London, 2000.

8 Bettina Bergery (1902–1993) was one of the three beautiful American Jones girls for whom the phrase 'keeping up with the Joneses' was invented. She worked for Schiaparelli and was one of Paris's finest raconteuses. Victor Cunard (1898–1960), writer Nancy Cunard's witty cousin, was the London *Times* correspondent in Venice, at twenty had an affair with Harold Nicolson, Vita Sackville West's husband, and was one of Dolly's closest friends.

9 Janet Flanner (1892–1978) wrote the *New Yorker*'s bi-monthly 'Letter from Paris' column under the *nom de plume* Genêt.

10 Schenkar, *Truly Wilde*, p. 116.

11 Rosamund Harcourt-Smith in Natalie Barney, ed., *In Memory of Dorothy Ierne Wilde*, Darentière, Dijon, 1951, pp. 28–9, quoted in Schenkar, *Truly Wilde*, p. 117.

12 ZSF to FSF, probably June or July 1930, CO187, Box 42, Folder 53. Nancy Milford (*Zelda*, p. 138) suggests this letter was in answer to one from Scott headed 'Written with Zelda gone to the Clinique'; the handwriting, notepaper, style and content are similar to correspondence dated early June/July. The reference to Scottie having finished school and the heat of the city would fit this author's dating.

13 The two versions are: cancelled drafts of early versions of *Tender Is The Night*, 'The Melarky Case' (MS versions), chs III to IV, CO187, Box 10, Folder 7, PUL; and *The Melarky and Kelly Versions. A Facsimile Edition of F. Scott Fitzgerald Manuscripts*, ed. Matthew J. Bruccoli, associate ed. Alan Marjolies, A Garland Series, Garland Publishers, New York and London, 1990 (based on MSS in PUL).

14 'Melarky Case' MS version.

15 Ibid.

16 Melarky/Kelly facsimile version.

17 Ibid.

18 Ibid.

19 Ibid. Scott crossed out that sentence and substituted: 'The sight of this legendary aberration in action had spoiled some quiet series of human facts for him as it had when he had first become aware of its other face some years before.'

20 Ibid.

21 Diana McLellan, *The Girls: Sappho Goes to Hollywood*, Robson Books, 2001.

22 Compton Mackenzie, *Extraordinary Women: Theme and Variations*, Martin Secker, London, 1928. On Capri the circle included Radclyffe Hall, Una Troubridge, Gertrude Stein, Alice B. Toklas, Janet Flanner, Djuna Barnes. When the circle regrouped in Paris it included Dolly Wilde, Elisabeth, Duchess of Clermont-Tonnerre, Esther Murphy, Emily Vanderbilt and Zelda Fitzgerald. Mackenzie's view of the women was a mild form of late Victorian patriarchal superiority.

23 Mackenzie to Meryle Secrest. Secrest, *Between Me and Life: A Biography of Romaine Brooks*, Macdonald & Jane's, London, 1976, p. 302.

24 Radclyffe Hall, *The Well of Loneliness*, Jonathan Cape, London, 1928.

25 Hall became known as a one-book polemicist.

26 When Tallulah came to London in the Twenties, although she was said to have seduced half a dozen Eton boys who had then been expelled, a damaging Scotland Yard report said there were rumours about her sexual perversion with her own sex. Another informant wrote to Scotland Yard that 'she is both a lesbian and immoral with men'. The informant reported she 'keeps a girl in London' as formerly it had been suggested that before she came to the UK in 1925 she 'kept a negress in USA'.

27 Camella Mayfield, series of conversations and taped interviews with the author, Princeton, Tuscaloosa, Montgomery and from the UK, 1999, 2000, 2001.

28 Mayfield also wrote a biography about Tallulah Bankhead.

29 Author's conversations with Camella Mayfield and with Rebecca Roberts, Public and

Outreach Services Coordinator, W. S. Hoole Special Collections Library, University of Alabama, Tuscaloosa, 1999, 2000.

30 Rebecca Roberts said the fact that 'Sara Mayfield destroyed all of her correspondence with Zelda in order to protect Zelda's privacy is an honorable act, but a great loss for researchers'. (Letter to author, 18 May 1999, and in several conversations with the author 1999.) Roberts said the university received Sara Mayfield's materials in 1955, but between 1955 and 1965 they were allowed only to house them, not to offer access to them. Papers arrived piecemeal, were edited in the late 1950s and early 1960s and officially 'given' to them in 1980.

31 Camella spent a summer typing the first draft of Mayfield's biography of Tallulah, 'but when the publishers asked Sara to make it spicier she refused. She would not put in new facts that she was aware of, she would only put in was what already acknowledged. Sara did know new negative things but she refused to use them.' Camella Mayfield to the author as before.

32 Mayfield, *Exiles*, p. 151.

33 Camella Mayfield to the author. Sara's self-protection may have included her relationships with Montgomery women Elizabeth Thigren Hill (who looked after Rosalind Sayre in the latter's last years) and Wilda Malloy Williams, both women from highly reputable well-established families. These two affairs appear to be 'common knowledge' among locals in Montgomery. Several residents talked to the author openly about them.

34 Camella Mayfield to the author.

35 ZSF to FSF, summer 1930, CO187, Box 42, Folder 51, PUL. Same blue squared paper, emotional tone and continuance of ideas as letters the author has dated June and July. Author's suggested date for this letter is July.

36 Ibid.

37 Interestingly, in about 1930 when Scott listed those people who had responded to his bad behaviour by snubbing him, Emily Vanderbilt featured on his list. Also on the snub list were Tallulah Bankhead, Ada MacLeish, Bijou O'Conor, John Barrymore, Tommy Hitchcock, Ruth Vallombrosa and the Murphys. Donaldson, *Hemingway vs. Fitzgerald*, pp. 321–2.

38 In Nov. 1934.

39 Lillian Hellman, *Pentimento*, written 1973, Macmillan, London, 1974.

40 ZSF to FSF, no date, CO187, Box 44, Folder 27, PUL.

41 ZSF to FSF, late summer 1930, CO187, Box 42, Folder 52, PUL.

42 ZSF to FSF, late summer/early fall 1930, *Life in Letters*, p. 194.

43 FSF to EH, 23 Aug. 1929.

44 EH to FSF, 4 Sep. 1929, EH, *Selected Letters*, Swallow Press, Chicago, 1975, pp. 304–5. Part of Scott's trouble, Hemingway thought, was that Scott believed because of *Gatsby*'s reviews he must write a masterpiece. However 'nobody but Fairies' could write masterpieces, Hemingway intoned, the rest of their crowd 'can only write as well as they can'.

45 The Kellys would finally be deleted from the novel but would become the main characters in his story 'One Trip Abroad'. Rosemary however would be kept for *Tender Is The Night*.

46 Ober to FSF, telegram, 21 Sep. 1929, *As Ever, Scott Fitz–*, ed. Bruccoli with Jennifer McCabe Atkinson, p. 146.

47 ZSF to FSF, late summer/early fall 1930, *Life in Letters*, p. 194. The yacht was the Murphys' *Honoria*; Dotty was Dorothy Parker.

48 Quoted in Donaldson, *Hemingway vs. Fitzgerald*, p. 159.

49 'Melarky Case' MS version (CO187, Box 10, Folder 7, PUL). The phrase 'satyrs whose lips curled horribly' is scored through. In another version of the same scene Francis Melarky looks around this fairy world with 'an angry shocked expression'. '"Is this real?" he demanded. "Or a sort of show?"' He is assured by a character called Horseprotection that it *is* real, and that Horseprotection will show him how the scene works. 'He got up and spoke to a man painted, bewigged and attired in a woman's evening dress at the next table. The man fluttered and presently they were dancing together . . ., Horseprotection winking at us over the man's shoulder. Francis got up saying "Let's get out of this dump!"' (Melarky/Kelly facsimile version).

50 Sara Murphy to FSF, no date, CO187, Box 51, Folder 15, PUL.

51 FSF, Ledger, Sep. 1929.

52 FSF to ZSF, summer? 1930, *Life in Letters*, p. 189.

53 This biographer dates this as late November; as do Mellow and Donaldson. Allen Tate dates it early December. Previous biographers dated it as October but internal evidence rules out October.

54 Allen Tate, *Memoirs and Opinions 1926–1974*, Swallow Press, Chicago, 1975, p. 62. Tate told Scott to mind his own business.

55 In response Hemingway repeated that Stein had been admiring of Scott's work which he himself continued to admire, but added sensibly that comparison of hypothetical flames was 'pure horseshit'. EH to FSF, *c.* 5 or 12 Dec. 1929, EH, *Selected Letters*, pp. 309–11.

56 In his Ledger Scott left the first redheaded woman anonymous but the second was a nurse in Zelda's first hospital.

57 EH, *Moveable Feast*, quoted in Donaldson, *Hemingway vs. Fitzgerald*, p. 153.

58 ZSF fictionalized the flowers as having 'the brilliant carnivorous qualities of Van Gogh'. *Save Me The Waltz*, *Collected Writings*, p. 130.

59 Painting undated but *c.* 1929 (author's dating).

60 Undated oil on canvas, *c.* 1929/1930 (author's dating).

61 ZSF to FSF, 1932 (no date), CO187, Box 44, Folder 15. Zelda had been reading Jan Gordon's book *Modern French Painters* (J. Lane, London, 1923). As well as a chapter on Van Gogh there were chapters on Impressionism, Neo-Impressionism, Cézanne, Renoir, Gauguin, Art and the New Civilization, the Designing Instinct, Rousseau and Utrillo, Savage Art and Modigliani, 'Space' and 'Life' in Painting, the Value of Art, Derain and Vlaminck, Cubism, the Modern Realists, the Women Painters, and the Slavonic Influence. Art historian Carolyn Shafer believes Zelda was very familiar with Van Gogh's art which she probably encountered first while in France. In June 1943 Zelda renewed this acquaintance at a major travelling exhibition of Van Gogh paintings in the Montgomery Museum of Fine Arts (*Montgomery Advertiser*, 7 June 1943).

62 ZSF, 'Show Mr and Mrs F. to Number –', *Collected Writings*, p. 428.

63 Another snap of Zelda huddled inside a huge fur coat at the top of a slope, labelled 'Have I got to go down?', is meant to be witty but Zelda's frozen gaze belies any humour.

64 ZSF to FSF, late summer/early fall 1930, *Life in Letters*, p. 194.

65 ZSF to FSF, late summer 1930, CO187, Box 42, Folder 52, PUL.

66 Vaill, *So Young*, p. 219.

67 Milford to the author, New York, 1998.

68 ZSF to FSF, *c.* July 1930 (author's dating), CO187, Box 42, Folder 57, PUL.

69 Ibid.

70 Scott's five-story series appeared in the *Saturday Evening Post* between 5 Apr. 1930 and 15 Aug. 1931.

71 FSF to ZSF, summer? 1930, *Life in Letters*, p. 189.

72 Scott's Ledger summary of the year Sep. 1929–Sep. 1930.

73 Doctor's report, Malmaison, n.d., 1930. (Original in French; translation by author and Rosemary Smith). CO187, Box 51, Folder 7A, PUL.

74 Ibid.

75 ZSF to FSF, late summer/early fall 1930, *Life in Letters*, p. 195.

76 Malmaison report.

77 Mayfield, *Exiles*, p. 155.

78 Her trip to Montgomery was April 1930.

79 ZSF to FSF, late summer/early fall 1930, *Life in Letters*, p. 195.

80 FSF, *Tender*, 1986, p. 137.

81 ZSF to FSF, *c.* July 1930, CO187, Box 42, Folder 57, PUL. This letter also includes the significant line: 'Finally by constant references to . . . pronounced and vulgar symbollism [*sic*] I at last began to believe that there was but one cure for me: the one I had refused three times in Paris.'

82 In a later letter to Dr Forel Zelda wrote: 'My husband forced me to go to Valmont. I am here with you, in a situation where I can not be anybody.'

83 Report on ZSF by Dr H. W. Trutmann, June 1930, CO187, Box 54, Folder 10A, PUL. (Translation from French by the author and Rosemary Smith.)

84 Ibid.
85 Ibid.
86 Mayfield, *Exiles*, pp. 152–3.
87 Rosalind Sayre Smith to FSF, 8 June 1930, CO187, Box 53, Folder 14A, PUL.
88 Mayfield, *Exiles*, pp. 151–2.
89 ZSF, 'Autobiographical Sketch', 16 Mar. 1932, Johns Hopkins Hospital records.
90 ZSF to FSF, *c.* June 1930, CO187, Box 42, Folder 50, PUL.
91 FSF to Judge and Mrs A. D. Sayre, 1 Dec. 1930, *Life in Letters*, p. 202.
92 Forel saw religion as incompatible with science and was a highly cultured man fascinated by literature, art and music.
93 During 1930–31 Zelda's treatment cost 70,561 Swiss francs, the equivalent of $13,000.
94 Mayfield, *Exiles*, p. 153.
95 Ibid., p. 154.
96 Ibid., p. 158.
97 Also still in many today.

CHAPTER 17

1 ZSF to FSF, *c.* late Aug. 1930 (author's dating), CO187, Box 42, Folder 58, PUL.
2 FSF to ZSF, summer? 1930, *Life in Letters*, p. 198.
3 FSF to Dr Oscar Forel, summer? 1930, *Life in Letters*, p. 196.
4 Forel, psychiatric report on Zelda's temperament, 15 Sep. 1931. Original French, translated by Marion Callen in conjunction with the author. CO745, Box 1, Folder 2, PUL.
5 Psychiatric evaluation, patient's temperament before marriage, Craig House medical records, ibid., PUL.
6 ZSF to FSF, summer 1930 (author suggests late June), CO187, Box 42, Folder 64, PUL. Zelda began to alternate between three different states. The first one was of quiet depression in which she still had hopes on recovery for her future career; the second wild hysteria in which she blamed other people for her breakdown; the third less hysterical but her problems seemed insoluble and her only wish was to die.
7 Forel, psychiatric report, 15 Sep. 1931, CO745, Box 1, Folder 2, PUL.
8 Mayfield, *Exiles*, p. 153. Several studies in Europe and North America show the illness runs in families and the concordance rate is higher in identical than non-identical twins. It has also been established since the 1950s that two drugs often used to increase the release of brain dopamine (amphetamines and levodopa) may worsen schizophrenia. Amphetamines have been known to produce in previously healthy volunteers a condition that is indistinguishable from acute paranoid schizophrenia. *Oxford Companion to the Mind*, ed. Richard L. Gregory with the assistance of O. L. Zangwill, Oxford University Press, 1998, pp. 698–9.
9 Janie Wall to the author, Montgomery, 1999.
10 Forel, psychiatric report, 15 Sep. 1931, CO745, Box 1, Folder 2, PUL.
11 At the time of Zelda's birth, psychiatrist Emil Kraepelin had suggested that most forms of insanity were manifestations of two major disorders: dementia praecox and manic depressive insanity. Bleuler expanded and renamed Kraepelin's dementia praecox.
12 Forel, psychiatric report, 15 Sep. 1931, CO745, Box 1, Folder 2, PUL.
13 Psychiatric evaluation: patient's temperament before marriage, ibid.
14 Generally schizophrenic patients retain intelligence and memory but their personality as a whole seems affected. In 1930 environmental and emotional factors, which today play a large part in understanding schizophrenia, were seen as less significant. Because the causes of schizophrenia, despite extensive research, remain elusive, in more recent years the syndrome has engendered alternative theories. Psychiatrist R. D. Laing saw it as a rational response to an insane world and located it within the family; to many post-1960s sociologists it was merely a convenient label used by society to control troublesome deviants; and psychiatrist Thomas Szasz in the late 1970s came up with the groundbreaking notion that the illness simply didn't exist. There could have been useful elements for Zelda's case in some of these theories had they been available.
15 Forel, psychiatric report, 15 Sep. 1931, CO745, Box 1, Folder 2, PUL.

16 FSF, Five Year Consultation Record (from middle of 7th year of marriage), Craig House Medical Records, ibid., PUL. FSF wrote this assessment of Zelda's state to help the doctors who also wrote an assessment of Zelda's state. Although Forel had not allowed Scott to send Zelda a story she had started in Valmont on the grounds that she was too ill to concentrate, Zelda actually began to write a ballet libretto.

17 ZSF to FSF, c. Sep. (author's dating) 1930, CO187, Box 42, Folder 67, PUL.

18 FSF to Ober, received 13 May 1930, Lilly Library; to Mollie McQuillan Fitzgerald, June 1930, *Life in Letters*, pp. 183, 184.

19 Lanahan, *Scottie . . .*, p. 48.

20 Mrs Sayre to FSF, 14 and 16 July 1930, CO187, Box 53, PUL.

21 Lanahan, *Scottie . . .*, p. 45.

22 FSF, *Tender*, 1986, pp. 202, 203.

23 ZSF to FSF, 1930 (author's dating on grounds of internal evidence), CO187, Box 43, Folder 4, PUL.

24 Forel, psychiatric report, 15 Sep. 1931, CO745, Box 1, Folder 2, PUL. Scott had written to his mother: 'Zelda's recovery is slow. Now she has terrible ecxema – one of those mild but terrible diseases that don't worry relations but are a living hell for the patient. If all goes well . . . we will be home by Thanksgiving.' But they were not. FSF to Mollie McQuillan Fitzgerald, June 1930, *Life in Letters*, p. 184.

25 ZSF to FSF, summer 1930, CO187, Box 42, Folder 55, PUL.

26 ZSF to FSF, n.d. 1920, CO187, Box 42, Folder 32, PUL.

27 The Sunday of the week before 23 June 1930.

28 FSF, *Tender*, pp. 200, 201.

29 The formula for inducing lengthy narcosis was Cloetta's Mixture. This contained chloral hydrate, alcohol, digitalin, amylene hydrate, paraldehyde, barbituric acid and ephedrine hydrochloride. The mixture was diluted with water.

30 ZSF to FSF, n.d., c. June 1930, ZSF, *Collected Writings*, p. 449.

31 Forel to FSF at Hotel Righi Vaudois, Glion, 23 June 1930, CO187, Box 49, Folder 2A, PUL.

32 FSF to Madame Lubov Egorova, 22 June 1930, CO187, Box 40, Folder 1A (in French); Eng. trans., *Life in Letters*, pp. 185–6, PUL.

33 ZSF to FSF, late summer/early fall 1930, *Life in Letters*, pp. 189–195, PUL.

34 FSF to ZSF, summer? 1930, ibid., p. 189.

35 ZSF to FSF, July? 1930, CO187, Box 42, Folder 57, PUL.

36 FSF, *Tender*, p. 137.

37 ZSF to FSF, c. June/July (author's dating) 1930, CO187, Box 42, Folder 53, PUL.

38 FSF to Scottie Fitzgerald, c. 15 Dec. 1940, *Life in Letters*, p. 475. Broken decalogues meant in this case moral laws.

39 ZSF to FSF, after June 1930, ZSF, *Collected Writings*, p. 450.

40 ZSF to FSF, c. July (after 9 July), 1930, CO187, Box 42, Folder 57, PUL.

CHAPTER 18

1 These three stories were among the set of Zelda's stories submitted to Ober that were subsequently lost. 'Drouth' is sometimes spelt 'Drought'.

2 FSF to MP, c. 8 July 1930, *Dear Scott/Dear Max*, p. 166.

3 MP to FSF, 5 Aug. 1930, ibid., p. 168.

4 FSF to MP, c. 1 Sep. 1930, ibid., p. 169.

5 ZSF to FSF, late summer 1930, CO187, Box 42, Folder 52, PUL.

6 ZSF to FSF, Aug./Sep. 1930, CO187, Box 42, Folder 60, PUL.

7 ZSF to FSF, late summer 1930, CO187, Box 42, Folder 52, PUL.

8 Ibid.

9 FSF to MP, c. 20 July 1930, *Life in Letters*, p. 186.

10 MP to FSF, 5 Aug. 1930, *Dear Scott/Dear Max*, p. 168.

11 Wilson to FSF, 8 Aug. 1930, Wilson, *Letters*, pp. 201–2.

12 FSF to MP, c. 20 July 1930, *Life in Letters*, p. 186.

13 Katy Smith had introduced Hadley to Hemingway. Katy became a close friend of Pauline Hemingway too.

14 Dos Passos, *Best Times*, pp. 209–10.
15 They also gave up their Paris apartment and sold their boat *Honoria*. However, in October Zelda heard that with Murphian style they had built a new seagoing schooner 27 metres long to use as a floating villa and Mediterranean classroom for their children.
16 Zelda wrote seven pages in French. The following quotations are from the translation used in Nancy Milford, *Zelda*, pp. 174–6.
17 Zelda's reference to the salamander, the domestic deity that Plato said could pass unscathed through fire, is an allusion to Owen Johnson's 1914 bestseller *The Salamander* which Zelda read. The play based on it, starring Nathan's girlfriend Ruth Findlay (which opened at the Harris Theatre, New York, 23 Oct. 1914), came to Montgomery when Zelda was in her junior year at Sidney Lanier High School. The heroine, Dore Baxter, sees herself as an extraordinary woman who like Zelda adores precipices, danger and the forbidden and has a desire to experience everything. For a useful account see Taylor, *Sometimes Madness*, p. 5.
18 ZSF to FSF, Sep. 1930, CO187, Box 42, Folder 66, PUL.
19 ZSF to FSF, *c.* Sep. 1930 (author's dating), CO187, Box 42, Folder 67, PUL.
20 FSF to Dr Oscar Forel, *c.* summer 1930 (author's dating), CO187, Box 49, Folder 2A, PUL.
21 ZSF to FSF, *c.* July 1930 (author's dating), CO187, Box 42, Folder 64, PUL.
22 FSF to Forel, summer? 1930, *Life in Letters*, pp. 196–7.
23 ZSF to FSF, June/July? 1930, CO187, Box 42, Folder 53, PUL.
24 FSF to Forel, summer? 1930, *Life in Letters*, p. 197.
25 She had seen her mother accept poverty and family illnesses with stoicism. Her adult resignation is the more interesting because as an adolescent Zelda had rebelled against the Southern female training that was a crash course in self-denial.
26 ZSF to FSF, *c.* July 1930 (author's dating on grounds of handwriting, notepaper, internal evidence), CO187, Box 42, Folder 53, PUL.
27 Mayfield, *Exiles*, pp. 161–2.
28 ZSF to FSF, n.d., *c.* summer/fall 1930, ZSF, *Collected Writings*, pp. 458–9.
29 FSF, Five Year Consultation Record (from middle of 7th year of marriage), Craig House medical records, CO745, Box 1, Folder 2, PUL.
30 Wet packs involved patients being tightly rolled in wet cold sheets. Wrapped over these was a blanket to reduce loss of body heat. This treatment aimed to calm 'uncooperative' patients. Edmund Wilson told Zelda he had only just survived hydrotherapy and nearly became addicted to paraldehyde in Clifton Springs sanatorium. Spinal douches or hydrotherapy, introduced by Jacques Charcot, had been used since 1890 in French hospitals for hysteria. Cold water jets violently applied to the spine to agitate the neurovascular structure often caused tissue damage.
31 The drug lithium which has salt as one component is a good example, for it is used to control manic depression cycles by correcting chemical imbalance.
32 He also finished 'A Snobbish Story'.
33 'One Trip Abroad', *Afternoon of An Author*, ed. Mizener, p. 161.
34 ZSF to FSF, *c.* Aug./Sep. 1930, CO187, Box 43, Folder 19, PUL.
35 ZSF to FSF, probably mid-Aug. possibly early Sep. 1930, CO187, Box 42, Folder 59, PUL.
36 ZSF to Scottie, *c.* summer 1930, CO183, Box 4, Folder 14, PUL.
37 FSF to Haardt and Mencken, 18 Oct. 1930, PUL, copy lent by Enoch Pratt Free Library, Baltimore.
38 Scott had already met Wolfe in July. In September they met in Montreux, Vevey and Geneva. Scott also took a trip to Paris in fall 1930 to meet Wolfe after his 1929 success, *Look Homeward Angel*. Wolfe turned Scott into Hunt Convoy in *You Can't Go Home Again*. Scott liked Wolfe but Wolfe was suspicious of Scott.
39 FSF, Ledger, Aug. 1930. Bruccoli (*Epic Grandeur*, p. 364) suggests that Scott started sleeping with other women to counter Zelda's accusations of homosexuality. As it was Zelda he wished to convince of his heterosexuality, and as he never told Zelda about his affairs, this seems unlikely. But Scott provoked Zelda's anger by admitting he took Emily Vanderbilt out in Paris. Rebecca West saw Scott and Emily at Armenonville. West said Scott 'was leaning towards her, sometimes caressing her hands.' Donaldson, *Fool for Love*, p. 56.
40 Bijou's real name was Violet Marie. A French nurse gave her the nickname. The daugh-

ter of a Calvinist Scot, Sir Francis Elliot, in 1920 she married Lieut. Edmund O'Conor, a professional naval officer from Dunleer, County Louth, Ireland. She accompanied him to China, learnt Chinese expertly, stayed with him until he contracted TB and died of disease in 1924. She had one son Michael whom she abandoned.

41 Scott deluded himself the binges were a way of escaping his pain.
42 Bijou O'Conor, taped interview, *Bijou O'Conor Remembers Scott Fitzgerald*, Audio Arts, London, 1975.
43 FSF to Forel, 29 Jan. 1931, *Life in Letters*, pp. 205–6.
44 FSF, report on Zelda's mental state Oct. 1930 – Feb. 1931, Five Year Consultation Record, CO745, Box 1, Folder 2, PUL.
45 Rosalind Sayre Smith to FSF, 21 Nov. 1930, CO187, Box 53, Folder 14A, PUL.
46 ZSF to Rosalind, *c.* summer 1930, CO183, Box 5, Folder 11, PUL.
47 FSF, Five Year Consultation Record, CO745, Box 1, Folder 2, PUL.
48 Forel, 15 Oct. 1930, quoted in Milford, *Zelda*, p. 179.
49 Forel to FSF, 16 Nov. 1930, CO187, Box 49, Folder 2A, PUL (orig. in French, translated by Marion Callen and the author).
50 Dr Irving Pine to the author, 1998, 1999.
51 FSF to Judge and Mrs A. D. Sayre, 1 Dec. 1930, *Life in Letters*, p. 202.
52 He died in 1939.
53 Forel to Milford, 6 May 1966, Milford, *Zelda*, p. 179.
54 On 9 March 1966 Forel told Milford that schizophrenia had been his original assessment. But on 18 May that same year he acknowledged to Milford that privately he had later changed his diagnosis (Milford, *Zelda*, p. 161n.). Sara Mayfield, who also later talked to Forel, said that the doctor had been reluctant to diagnose Zelda as schizophrenic because she did not manifest enough of the stereotyped schizophrenic thoughts and actions (*Exiles*, p. 153).
55 Dr Irving Pine to the author 1998, 1999. Some doctors have thought that had Zelda been treated twenty years later her diagnosis might have been 'manic depression'. Others have felt that even if the diagnosis had been schizophrenia, the tranquillizing effects of certain drugs might have been beneficial in controlling acute illness or preventing relapses.
56 Forel to Milford, 6 May 1966, Milford, *Zelda*, p. 179.
57 In 1930–31 FSF sold seventeen stories. In 1931 he earned $37,599.
58 Résumé of the consultation with Professor Bleuler and Doctor Forel, 22 Nov. 1930. Craig House medical records, CO745, Box 1, Folder 2, PUL. Translated from French by Marion Callen in conjunction with author.
59 Ibid.
60 Ibid.
61 It was the first of two similar programmes on which Zelda was placed in two hospitals aimed at changing 'inappropriate' feminine behaviour into something nearer the conventional wifely model of the era. Like other women of her time including Vivien Haigh-Wood (wife of T. S. Eliot), Jane Bowles, Sylvia Plath, and her friend Sara Mayfield, Zelda's failure to live up to a traditional feminine role was to some extent buried within a diagnosis of mental disorder. Many women like Zelda, who were artists or married to artists, who were unwilling or unable to conform, whose behaviour or speech did not fit approved family patterns, were administered remedies or 'cures' in mental asylums that were often a method of containing them for long periods of time.
62 Résumé of Bleuler/Forel consultation, 22 Nov. 1930, CO745, Box 1, Folder 2, PUL.
63 FSF to Judge and Mrs A. D. Sayre, 1 Dec. 1930, *Life in Letters*, p. 203.
64 ZSF to FSF, fall 1930, CO187, Box 42, Folder 65, PUL.
65 ZSF to Newman Smith, late summer 1930 (author's dating), CO187, Box 43, Folder 21, PUL.
66 ZSF to FSF, Nov. 1930 (author's dating), CO187, Box 43, Folder 10, PUL.
67 ZSF to Forel, *c.* Nov. 1930, CO183, Box 5, Folder 3, PUL.
68 Named after the Murphys' daughter.
69 In later life Scottie herself, always close to Rosalind, had admitted she would have liked it but Scott never countenanced it.
70 ZSF to Scottie, Oct/Nov.? 1930 (author's dating), CO183, Box 4, Folder 10, PUL.
71 ZSF to Scottie, spring 1931, CO183, Box 4, Folder 17, PUL.

72 ZSF to Scottie, Oct./Nov.? 1930 (author's dating), CO183, Box 4, Folder 10, PUL.
73 ZSF to Scottie, spring 1931, CO183, Box 4, Folder 17, PUL.
74 FSF to Forel, 29 Jan. 1931, *Life in Letters*, p. 207.
75 She was sister to Sidney Weinberg, a wealthy Wall Street investment banker. She married prominent Brooklyn judge Louis Goldstein. Scott portrayed her as Evelyn, a girl burning with vitality, in his story 'On Your Own' (1931).
76 *The Apprentice Fiction of F. Scott Fitzgerald*, ed. John Kuehl, Rutgers University Press, New Brunswick, NJ, 1965, p. 178.
77 In January 1931. They spent winters and springs in Florida and warmer months in the West, a pattern which enabled Hemingway to hunt, fish and finish his books.
78 FSF, autobiographical note, 1940, PUL. During the 1930s he and Hemingway met only four times: once in 1931, once in 1933, twice in 1937.
79 FSF, *Tender*, 1986, p. 224.
80 Helen Blackshear, 'Mama Sayre, Scott Fitzgerald's mother-in-law', *Georgia Review*, winter 1965, p. 467.
81 FSF to Rosalind Sayre Smith, n.d. (*c.* June 1930), CO187, Box 53, Folder 14, PUL.
82 Forel to FSF, 7 Feb. 1931, CO187, Box 49, Folder 2A, PUL. Translated from French by Marion Callen in conjunction with author.
83 FSF, Five Year Consultation Record, CO745, Box 1, Folder 2, PUL. The period referred to is 1 Feb. – 1 Mar. 1931.
84 ZSF to FSF in Lausanne, early spring? 1931, CO187, Box 43, Folder 8, PUL.
85 ZSF to FSF, *c.* early spring 1931, ibid.
86 ZSF to FSF, *c.* spring 1931, CO187, Box 43, Folder 11, PUL.
87 ZSF to FSF, late summer? 1931, CO187, Box 43, Folder 13, PUL.
88 ZSF to FSF, early or late summer 1931, CO187, Box 43, Folder 15, PUL.
89 ZSF to FSF, late summer? 1931, CO187, Box 43, Folder 13, PUL.
90 Meyers, *Scott Fitzgerald*, p. 200.
91 ZSF to Judge A. D. Sayre, *c.* July 1931, *Romantic Egoists*, ed. Bruccoli *et al.*, p. 180.
92 Vaill, *So Young*, p. 232.
93 See Vaill's analysis, *So Young*, pp. 221–6, which includes Gerald's letter to Archie MacLeish, 23 Jan. 1929, with his detailed expression of his sense of unreality.
94 Gerald Murphy/Calvin Tomkins interview notes, Honoria Murphy Donnelly Collection, quoted in ibid., p. 226. Murphy is here recalling his letter to FSF of 31 Dec. 1935.
95 Vaill, *So Young*, p. 232.
96 Forel, report, 15 Sep. 1931, CO745, Box 1, Folder 2, PUL.
97 FSF, Ledger, summary of year Sep. 1930–Sep. 1931.
98 While house-hunting they stayed downtown at Jefferson Davis Hotel.

CHAPTER 19

1 Mrs George Mark Wood, Montgomery, Alabama.
2 Mayfield, *Exiles*, p. 166.
3 Mark Cross Company assets were $2,000,000. Their sister Anna was already provided for. The mistress was Lillian Ramsgate.
4 ZSF to Mayfield, *Exiles*, p. 173.
5 Ibid., p. 174.
6 ZSF to FSF, early Nov. 1931, CO187, Box 43, Folder 31, PUL.
7 Her sister Marjorie's daughter.
8 She later amalgamated these into one tale.
9 ZSF to FSF, early Nov. 1931 (author's dating), CO187, Box 43, Folder 47, PUL.
10 ZSF to FSF, late Nov./early Dec. 1931, CO187, Box 43, Folder 43, PUL.
11 ZSF to FSF, *c.* 13 Nov. 1931, CO187, Box 43, Folder 49, PUL.
12 Only in Ober's note does 'Downs' have no apostrophe; where it occurs elsewhere it has one. The story was rejected by *Harper's Bazaar*, *College Humor* and *The Delineator*.
13 Ober's memos on 'Cotton Belt' and 'One And, Two And' were dated 1932. Ober received some stories in 1931, some in 1932. Some had been written at Prangins and rewritten after Zelda left there.

14 Zelda reported this in a letter to FSF, fall 1931, CO187, Box 43, Folder 64, PUL.
15 All the above quotations are from Zelda's letters to FSF, fall 1931, CO187, Box 43, Folders 37, 28, 25, 26, 43, 42, PUL. 'Nuts' may have been started or almost fully written in Prangins as Perkins was sent it by mid-Oct. 1931.
16 MP to FSF, 21 Oct. 1931, *Dear Scott/Dear Max*, p. 172.
17 W. R. Anderson said the story 'displayed Mrs Fitzgerald's mastery of irony as a device for control', 'Rivalry and Partnership: The Short Fiction of Zelda Sayre Fitzgerald', *Fitzgerald/Hemingway Annual 1977*, ed. Margaret M. Duggan and Richard Layman. A Bruccoli Clark Book, Gale Research Co., Book Tower, Detroit, Michigan, USA, p. 38. Bruccoli said it was 'Zelda Fitzgerald's best effort . . . closer to a real story than any of the others', Preface, F. Scott and Zelda Fitzgerald, *Bits of Paradise*, ed. Bruccoli, p. 17. Milford said in this story 'Zelda was in control of her talent', *Zelda*, p. 194.
18 James Gray, 'St Paul Family of Writers Have Almost Scribner's Monopoly', *St Paul Dispatch*, no date, clipping in Zelda's album, CO183, Box 2, Folder 6, PUL.
19 ZSF, 'A Couple of Nuts', *Scribner's Magazine*, Aug. 1932, pp. 80, 82, 84.
20 ZSF, 'Miss Ella', *Collected Writings*, pp. 345, 348, 343.
21 Zelda's use of this idea and setting is highly reminiscent of Faulkner; his setting for his Sartoris novels is called Jefferson, Zelda calls her Southern setting Jeffersonville. Quentin Compson first appears in Faulkner's 1929 *Sartoris*, the start of a series describing decline of the Compson and Sartoris families who like Zelda's Miss Ella's family represented the Old South. Faulkner's 1929 *The Sound and the Fury*, which illustrates the decline of the South through Benjy Compson's eyes, has a similar context and Southern philosophy to Zelda's work.
22 MP to FSF, 12 Nov. 1930, *Dear Scott/Dear Max*, p. 170. Zelda's original name for Miss Ella was Miss Bessie.
23 Ibid.
24 ZSF to Ober, 21 Dec. 1931.
25 ZSF to FSF, fall 1931, CO187, Box 43, Folder 27, PUL.
26 ZSF to FSF, c. fall 1931, CO187, Box 43, Folder 25, PUL.
27 ZSF to FSF, c. 25 Nov. 1931 (author's dating), CO187, Box 43, Folder 59, PUL.
28 Her play was an untitled one-act play for children. ZSF to FSF, Nov. 1931, CO187, Box 43, Folder 42, PUL.
29 ZSF to FSF, c. Nov./Dec. 1931, CO187, Box 43, Folder 47, PUL.
30 Mayfield's comment on this line of Scott's was that from Zelda's viewpoint it 'was as far from truth as hypocrisy is from holiness', *Exiles*, p. 181.
31 Scott wrote from on board SS *Olympic* returning from his father's funeral, Feb. 1931.
32 Mayfield, *Exiles*, p. 165.
33 ZSF to FSF, early Nov. 1931, CO187, Box 43, Folder 35, PUL.
34 ZSF to FSF, undated (author's dating 19 Nov. 1931), CO187, Box 43, Folder 56, PUL.
35 ZSF to FSF, c. 20 Nov. 1931, CO187, Box 43, Folder 57, PUL.
36 ZSF to Mayfield, Nov. 1931, *Exiles*, p. 176. She repeats this in *Save Me The Waltz* when her fictional Judge Beggs dies. '"He must have forgot," Alabama said, "to leave the message"' (*Collected Writings*, p. 188).
37 Mayfield, *Exiles*, p. 177.
38 ZSF to FSF, summer 1931, CO187, Box 43, Folder 12, PUL.
39 ZSF to FSF, early Nov. 1931, CO187, Box 43, Folder 35, PUL.
40 ZSF to FSF. c. Dec. 1931, CO187, Box 43, Folder 24, PUL.
41 Winzola McLendon, 'Scott and Zelda', *Ladies Home Journal* 91 (Nov. 1974), p. 62. Scott's Christmas present initially was going to be a one-act play Zelda wrote for five of Scottie's friends. She rented the Little Theatre, planned egg nog and cake for the twenty-strong proposed audience, and she'd sewn half the costumes. Then her father died and plans had to be abandoned.
42 To his chagrin Anita Loos later wrote a script instead.
43 In 'Crazy Sunday' Scott combined himself with screenwriter Dwight Taylor and exaggerated his humiliation at Thalberg's party. The story was rejected by the *Post* as too sexually frank.
44 The *Post* even rejected one called 'Six of One' which Ober sold to *Redbook*.
45 Meyer, born in Zurich, trained there as a neurologist/pathologist with Oscar Forel's

father Auguste. From 1892 in the USA Meyer worked as a pathologist at Kankakee Hospital, Illinois, taught at the University of Chicago and Clark University and worked at Worcester Hospital, Massachusetts. After a stint at the New York State Hospital he became director of Johns Hopkins Medical School and the esteemed dean of US psychiatry.

46 Quoted in Carolyn Shafer, 'To Spread a Human Aspiration', p. 32.

47 Wertham had come from Europe in 1922 to work with Dr Meyer. The eleven paintings of Zelda's he acquired are now in the Frederick Wertham Collection, Fogg Art Museum, Harvard University. How they came into Wertham's possession is unclear.

48 Shafer, 'To Spread a Human Aspiration', p. 42.

49 The Wertham paintings are undated and the authorship of some is disputed. The reason for the dispute is that larger La Paix canvases differ from the Wertham clinical drawings with their ambiguous subject matter and cleanly drawn outlines. That Scott suggested their suitability for commerce supports the Zelda-as-artist theory. A strong case can be made in favour of Zelda as artist of *Rams* and *Le Sport*, because Zelda worked closely with Wertham and was directly exposed to his mosaic test. *Rams* has a similar fantasy feel to her fairy-tale paintings and *Le Sport* has the characteristic elongated extremities.

50 To express her appreciation Zelda also designed a Christmas card for Squires in black ink and white gouache on grey card. The card depicted a woman holding a lighted candle and wreath. On the card Zelda wrote 'Mildred Squires wishes you A Merry Christmas'.

51 ZSF to FSF, c. Feb. 1932, CO187, Box 44, Folder 15, PUL. She referred specifically to Van Gogh who had long been a favourite.

52 ZSF to FSF, c. end Feb./beginning Mar. 1932.

53 FSF, Ledger, Feb., Mar. 1932.

54 ZSF to MP, postmarked 12 Mar. 1932, CO101, Box 53, Folder Zelda Fitzgerald 1921–1944, PUL.

CHAPTER 20

1 Jacqueline Tavernier-Courbin, 'Art as Woman's Response and Search: Zelda Fitzgerald's Save Me The Waltz', *Southern Literary Journal*, vol. XI, No. 2, spring 1979, Department of English, University of North Carolina, p. 23. The phrase 'complementary intelligence' is a quotation from the three-way conference between ZSF, FSF and Dr Rennie, 28 May 1933.

2 FSF to Dr Mildred Squires, 14 Mar. 1932, Johns Hopkins Hospital records, *Life in Letters*, p. 209.

3 FSF to MP, 16 Mar. 1932, PUL.

4 ZSF to FSF, Mar. 1932, ZSF, *Collected Writings*, pp. 466–8.

5 ZSF to FSF, c. Mar. 1932, ibid., p. 468. In *Tender Is The Night* the Pershing incident, where Scott's character Abe North stands in the lobby of the Paris Ritz pretending to be General Pershing, was also one line, and would not have been missed either.

6 ZSF to MP, 27 Mar. 1932, CO101, Box 53, Folder Zelda Fitzgerald 1921–1944, PUL.

7 MP to ZSF, 28 Mar. 1932, ibid., PUL.

8 ZSF to FSF, c. Mar. 1932, ZSF, *Collected Writings*, pp. 468–9.

9 Milford, *Zelda*, p. 253.

10 ZSF to FSF, c. Mar. 1932, ZSF, *Collected Writings*, p. 468.

11 Each of the two galleys has a duplicate worked over in Zelda's handwriting.

12 FSF to MP, end Apr./early May 1932, *Life in Letters*, p. 217.

13 FSF to MP, c. 14 May 1932, ibid., pp. 218–19.

14 MP to ZSF, telegram, 16 May 1932, CO101, Box 53, Folder Zelda Fitzgerald 1921–1944, PUL.

15 MP to ZSF, letter, 16 May 1932, ibid., PUL.

16 ZSF to MP, c. 19 May 1932, ibid., PUL.

17 James R. Mellow certainly holds this view. *Invented Lives*, p. 401.

18 FSF to Richard Knight, 29 Sep. 1932, quoted in ibid.

19 Henry Dan Piper, *F. Scott Fitzgerald*, p. 192.

20 ZSF, *Waltz, Collected Writings*, p. 40.

21 Ibid.

22 Ibid., p. 67.

23 It is in four chapters each subdivided into three sections.

24 ZSF, *Waltz*, p. 23.

25 This is definitely not a sexual affair.

26 ZSF, *Waltz*, p. 105.

27 Ibid., p. 196.

28 Ibid., p. 130.

29 FSF, Ledger, Apr. 1932.

30 During April–May 1932 he also wrote for the *Post* 'Family in the Wind' and 'The Rubber Check'.

31 In an unpublished sketch he blatantly discloses his resentment. A professional dancer Nikitma, about to create a major role La Chatte in London, has delayed her performance in order to support her sick sister, a less experienced ballet dancer who has secretly been rehearsing the same role. Nikitma is livid: Nikitma: 'That's out . . . Rehearse anything else and I'll back you but not that. If your London performance comes before mine, with the name I've made I'm done . . .' Sister: 'But I want to express myself.' Nikitma: 'Nevertheless that's out.' Sister: 'But I saw the script the same day you did.' Nikitma: 'But I chose it and bought it and paid for it.' Sister: 'But I would if I could.' Nikitma: 'But I did.' . . . Sister: 'I've seen you rehearse so many times I think I could do it nearly as well as you.' Nikitma: 'When I've tried it you can try it. Not till then.' Sister: 'But I'm going on rehearsing.' Nikitma: 'Not on this stage. Not with these lights and this music.' . . . Sister: 'But I want to express myself.' Nikitma: 'All right. Whatever that means. But you can't exploit your relation to me to do me harm.' Scott called this revealing trifle 'Analogy'. Unpublished MS, PUL.

32 Quoted in Milford, *Zelda*, p. 257.

33 ZSF to MP, undated, 1932, CO101, Box 53, Folder Zelda Fitzgerald 1921–1944, PUL.

34 Mayfield, *Exiles*, pp. 193, 194.

35 FSF to Dr Squires, 20 May 1932, quoted in Milford, *Zelda*, p. 257.

36 ZSF to John Peale Bishop, undated, *c.* summer 1932, John Peale Bishop Papers, CO138, Box 21, Folder 4, PUL.

37 Mrs Bayard Turnbull to Milford, 12 Oct. 1963, Milford, *Zelda*, p. 259.

38 Quoted in Milford, *Zelda*, p. 265.

39 By August 1932 Scott was able to note in his Ledger: 'The novel now plotted & planned never more to be permanently interrupted.'

40 All MS drafts of this contentious novel have disappeared. Kendall Taylor suggests that the novel on which Zelda was working in 1932 was *Caesar's Things* but this author has found no supporting evidence for this early date.

41 Mayfield, *Exiles*, p. 195. Carolyn Shafer says the crucifixion painting has never been found.

42 Ibid., pp. 195–6.

43 Ibid., p. 196.

44 Ibid., p. 197.

45 Mayfield, *Constant Circle*, p. 179.

46 Though Mencken and Sara were highly sympathetic to Scott's unannounced drunken visits to discuss Zelda's plight their patience gradually wore thin until one evening in fall 1933 Scott disgraced himself at the home of Mencken's friend Joseph Hergesheimer. Drunk as usual he dropped his trousers publicly at the dinner table, after which Mencken told Sara to stop seeing him.

47 He utilized his stay to write a doctor-nurse love story called 'One Interne'.

48 'Of the Jazz Age', *New York Times*, reproduced in *Romantic Egoists*, ed. Bruccoli *et al.*, p. 190.

49 Dorothea Brande, *The Bookman*, ibid., p. 189.

50 William McFee, 'During the Jazz Age', New York *Sun*, 8 Oct. 1932.

51 *New York Herald Tribune* review, reproduced in *Romantic Egoists*, ed. Bruccoli *et al.*, p 189.

52 Review in a Baltimore paper, reproduced in ibid., p. 190.

53 MP to ZSF, 2 Aug. 1933, CO101, Box 53, Folder Zelda Fitzgerald 1921–1944, PUL.

54 Malcolm Cowley to FSF, 22 May 1933, CO187, Box 39, PUL.

CHAPTER 21

1 Ober submitted it October 1932.
2 Isabel Owens typed three final versions this year.
3 Isabel Owens to Milford, 12 Oct. 1963, Milford, *Zelda*, pp. 268, 267.
4 FSF, 'One Hundred False Starts', *Saturday Evening Post*, 4 Mar. 1933.
5 FSF, Ledger, Jan. 1933.
6 FSF to MP, 29 Sep. 1933, *Life in Letters*, p. 239.
7 FSF to Meyer, 10 Apr. 1933, CO187, Box 51, Folder 10A, PUL. Scott believed that whereas Forel held an admirable 'teutonic idea of marriage', Meyer's more liberal stance encouraged Zelda to negate all her marital duties.
8 Meyer to FSF, 18 Apr. 1933, CO187, Box 51, Folder 10A, PUL.
9 FSF to Meyer, undated pencil draft, probably Apr. 1933, ibid.
10 In his Ledger Scott lists 'The typescript of Zelda conversation' in June.
11 Every one of those 40,000 words has been 'lost'.
12 This notion has subsequently been echoed by most Fitzgerald critics.
13 Poe had helped Scott find La Paix.
14 Though Scott did not pursue Poe's plan for divorce, in his Notebook he outlined a divorce strategy should Zelda continue to write fiction. 'Attack on all grounds: Play (suppress), novel (delay), pictures (suppress), character (showers), child (detach), schedule (disorient to cause trouble), no typing. Probable result – new breakdown.' Quoted in Donaldson, *Fool for Love*, p. 86.
15 I am indebted to writer Rebecca Stott for discussions on this point. Again there is a strong similarity between Zelda's actions and those of Sylvia Plath, who also sloughed off a former self in order for a new self to rise from the ashes.
16 Report and photograph, *Baltimore News*, reproduced in *Romantic Egoists*, ed. Bruccoli *et al.*, p. 192.
17 Shafer, 'To Spread a Human Aspiration', p. 47; Turnbull, *Scott Fitzgerald*, p. 242. André le Vot also mentions that Zelda was improving her painting technique at 'the Fine Art School' in Baltimore (Le Vot, *F. Scott Fitzgerald*, p. 275).
18 Zelda had met Maccubbin in spring 1933, walking near the grounds of La Paix, and had persuaded him to suggest the play to his company. Maccubbin was 'consistently the best performer'.
19 The uncut version runs to 91 pages while the shorter version is still 61 pages. The undated 61-page version is at PUL (CO183, Box 3, Folder 33); the 91-page typescript was deposited for copyright on 31 Oct. 1932. Both have a prologue and three-act structure.
20 Scrapbook of reviews of *Scandalabra*, CO183, Box 2, Folder 6, PUL.
21 Anthony was first taken to Edith's brother-in-law's coastal house, then to a sanatorium on Black Mountain.
22 Minnie Sayre to ZSF, 31 July 1933, CO183, Box 5, Folder 21, PUL.
23 Minnie Sayre to ZSF, 1 Aug. and 6 Aug. 1933, ibid. She could not afford to move Anthony to Baltimore.
24 As Edith gave up her apartment in Memphis, Tennessee, before leaving it seemed unlikely she would return. After Anthony's death she disappeared and was never mentioned again by the family.
25 Dr Chilton Thorington to FSF, 11 Aug. 1933, CO745, Box 1, Folder 1, PUL.
26 The Sayres told people Anthony had died from malaria contracted when surveying a swamp at Mobile as a civil engineer. They said in his delirium he rushed out of bed thinking he was playing football and accidentally fell through an open window.
27 The Society of Baltimore Independent Artists fourth annual no-jury exhibition, Baltimore Museum of Art.
28 Malcolm Cowley, 'A Ghost Story of the Jazz Age', *Saturday Review* XLVII, 25 Jan. 1964. pp. 20–21.

CHAPTER 22

1 Scott had loans from his mother, a loan from Scribner's at 5 per cent against possible screen rights, advances from Ober. Without another generous boost – a $4,000 Scribner's

advance on the hardcover – his finances would have been shakier still. $6,000 of his year's income was withheld to pay off some of his debts to his publishers. The rest was given to Ober who gave Scott money as and when needed.

2 ZSF, 'Show Mr and Mrs F. to Number –', *Collected Writings*, p. 431.

3 FSF to John Palmer, 12 Feb. 1934, CO187, Box 51, Folder John Palmer, PUL.

4 ZSF to FSF, no date, CO187, Box 42, Folder 63, PUL; FSF, *Tender*, p. 138.

5 ZSF to FSF, no date, CO187, Box 42, Folder 63, PUL; FSF, *Tender*, p. 139.

6 ZSF to FSF, no date, CO187, Box 42, Folder 50, PUL; FSF, *Tender*, p. 138.

7 FSF, General Plan and Sketch for *Tender*, CO187, Boxes 9–10, PUL.

8 Bleuler's report of 22 Nov. 1930, CO745, Box 1, Folder 2, PUL.

9 In his General Plan and Sketch FSF lists: 'A. Accounts B. Baltimore C. Clinics and clipping. D. Dancing and 1st Diagnoses E. Early Prangins – to Feb. 1931 F. From Forel (include Bleuler Consultation) H. Hollywood L. Late Prangins M. My own letters and comments R. Rosalind and Sayre Family S. Squires and Schedule V. Varia'.

10 ZSF, Phipps Clinic, Feb.–Mar. 1934, quoted in Milford, *Zelda*, p. 286.

11 Virginia Durr said that in later years Minnie Sayre confided to her that the Judge came to her bedroom and she locked him out. Some researchers have taken this as evidence that he might have turned to one of his daughters if he was refused sexual relations by his wife. This, together with Fitzgerald's creation of a heroine based partly on Zelda who is raped by her father, accounts for a flurry of incest rumours. But this author found no definite supporting evidence for this allegation and many interviewees in Montgomery refuted the idea.

12 FSF to ZSF, 26 Apr. 1934, *Life in Letters*, pp. 256–7.

13 ZSF, Phipps Clinic, Feb.–Mar. 1934, Milford, *Zelda*, p. 286.

14 Ibid.

15 As in 'Babylon Revisited'. Mayfield, *Exiles*, pp. 211–12.

16 It is the image of his father as moral touchstone which Scott uses for the 'honor, courtesy and courage' by which Dick Diver holds himself together until he is forced to realize he has betrayed those very qualities.

17 Wilson to Malcolm Cowley, 1951, Wilson, *Letters on Literature and Politics*, p. 254.

18 FSF, General Plan and Sketch for *Tender Is The Night*.

19 John Peale Bishop to FSF, Dec. 1933/Jan. 1934, PUL.

20 Robert Benchley to FSF, 29 Apr. 1934, reproduced in *Romantic Egoists*, ed. Bruccoli *et al.*, p. 201.

21 Thomas Wolfe to FSF, Mar. 1934, reproduced in ibid., p. 201.

22 Archie MacLeish to FSF, reproduced in ibid., p. 200.

23 Dr C. J. Slocum, born Rhode Island 1873, trained at Albany.

24 This became 'Show Mr and Mrs F. to Number –', published in *Esquire*, May–June 1934.

25 The book was of course *Tender Is The Night*. ZSF to FSF, two letters, c. Mar. (author's dating) 1934.

26 Slocum to FSF, 19 Mar. 1934, CO745, Box 1, Folder 1, PUL.

27 FSF to Slocum, 22 Mar. 1934; Slocum to FSF, 19 Mar. 1934, ibid.

28 ZSF to FSF, c. Mar. (author's dating) 1934, CO187, Box 44, Folder 34, PUL; telegram, 12 Mar. 1934.

29 Slocum to FSF, 26 Mar. 1934, CO745, Box 1, Folder 1, PUL. Zelda's schedule had been: 7.30 bath; 8.00 breakfast; 9.00–10.00 writing; 10.30–1.00 craft-painting; 1.00–1.30 lunch; 1.30–5.30 outdoor activities – golf, tennis, swimming, riding; 5.30–6.00 prepare for dinner; 6.00–6.30 dinner; 6.30–7.00 rest; 7.00–7.30 bridge, drawing, painting, reading; 9.30–10.00 room and bed (schedule not followed Saturday or Sunday). Slocum insisted on inserting rest periods instead of mental activities.

30 ZSF to FSF, Mar. 1934; Apr. (author's dating) 1934, CO187, Box 44, Folders 35, 24, PUL.

31 Cary Ross to FSF, 26 Aug. 1932, CO187, Box 53, Folder 9, PUL. Ross, a Yale graduate and would-be poet whom Fitzgerald had mentored, had stayed with Stieglitz at Lake George in 1932.

32 ZSF to FSF, c. early Mar. 1934.

33 ZSF to FSF, Mar. 1934, ZSF, *Collected Writings*, p. 470.

34 Mayfield, *Exiles*, p. 208.

35 Hines was Associate Professor of Anatomy at Johns Hopkins Medical School.

36 I agree with Kendall Taylor's suggestion that Zelda's retreat into madness was the way she enabled herself to 'breathe freely'. *Sometimes Madness*, p. 13.

37 FSF to Slocum, 22 Mar. 1934, CO745, Box 1, Folder 1, PUL.

38 Zelda recalled Diaghilev's theory that art should shock the emotions. 'A person certainly could not walk about that exhibition and maintain any dormant feelings.' ZSF, letter about the O'Keeffe exhibition at An American Place, Feb./Mar. 1934, CO183, Box 6, Folder 6, PUL; ZSF. 'Show Mr and Mrs F. to Number –', *Collected Writings*, p. 431.

39 It is possible also to link the way Zelda filled the picture plane with luminous water-colour washes, which seem to float freely through her pictures without defining lines, to her comment about Paris when she was already ill but had not recognized it: 'there was a new signifigance to everything: stations and streets and façades of buildings – colors were infinite, part of the air, and not restricted by the lines that encompassed them and lines were free of the masses they held'. ZSF to FSF, late summer 1930, CO187, Box 42, Folder 52, PUL.

40 *Antheriums* was probably painted the year before her exhibition. Zelda had written Dr Rennie a series of letters from Craig House decorated with writhing swelling flower shapes, in colours of decayed flesh. They too showed the anthropomorphic potent aura of O'Keeffe's flowers. Montgomery art dealer Louise Brooks later described Zelda's *Japanese Magnolias*, drawn at this time, with its bubbles and foetus shapes as looking 'like an abortion' (Brooks to Carolyn Shafer, interview, 27 Aug. 1993). Impasto is paint applied thickly so that the brush marks are evident. One of Zelda's nurses at Highland Hospital, Mary Parker, saw this kind of brushwork as an extension of her illness. She said it was like a visual interpretation of the term 'ruminating' in psychiatry. 'It's going over and over things in your head. Her painting was like that to me – using the brush over and over' (Parker to Shafer, interview, 15 July 1993). Shafer is very informative about the relationship between O'Keeffe and Zelda as painters. Shafer, 'To Spread a Human Aspiration', 1994.

41 Original list of paintings: 1. *White Anemones* (priced at $250); 2. *Red Poppies* ($200); 3. *White Roses* ($200); 4. *Laurel* ($150); 5. *Vestibule* ($300); 6. *Dancer* ($175); 7. *Chinese Theater* ($200); 8. *Spectacle* ($300); 9. *Football* ($250); 10. *Chopin* ($125); 11. *Afternoon* ($175); 12. *Portrait in Thorns* ($200); 13. *Portrait of a Russian* ($200). Additional paintings: 14. *Nude* ($300); 15. *Russian Stable* ($175); 16. *Tulips*; 17. *Ballet Figures* ($250). Original list of drawings: 1. *Spring in the Country* ($15); 2. *The Plaid Shirt* ($15); 3. *The Cornet Player* ($15); 4. *Ferns* ($15); 5. *Au Claire [sic] de la Lune* ($15); 6. *Forest Fire*; 7. *Girl on a Flying Trapeze* ($ 15); 8. *Two Figures* ($ 15); 9. *Red Death* ($ 15); 10. *La Nature* ($ 15); 11. *Etude Arabesque*; 12. *Two People* ($25); 13. *Feuété* ($25); 14. *Pallas Athene* ($50); 15. *Study of Figures* (pencil, $12). Additional drawings: 16. *Crossing Roses*; 17. *Diving Platform* ($15); 18. *Red Devil* ($15). The additional paintings and drawings may have been those shown separately at the Algonquin.

42 *Diving Platform* is sometimes called *Swimmer on a Ladder*.

43 Mabel Dodge Luhan sent Ross from New Mexico a bid for *Portrait in Thorns*, but when her offer was refused because Zelda had said earlier she did not want to sell it, she bought *Red Death*. Though Scott and Ross could have done with another large sale, *Portrait in Thorns* was never sold. Cary Ross to FSF, 4 May 1934, CO187, Box 53, Folder 9, PUL.

44 Seldes, typed note, 12 Sep. 1933.

45 Gerald Murphy to Milford, 2 Mar. 1964, Milford, *Zelda*, p. 290. *Chinese Theater* is also known as *Chinese Acrobats*.

46 ZSF to FSF, *c.* Apr. 1934.

47 Honoria Murphy Donnelly, conversations with the author, summer 1998 and 1999. When Dick Knight visited Zelda in Montgomery in 1940 he was able to buy it. James K. Moody, current owner of the painting, believes it was left in the gallery and was later shipped to Montgomery. According to Moody, when Knight died of alcohol poisoning in 1948 his ex-wife, from whom he was divorced in 1940, put his possessions in storage. After her death her two daughters gave the painting to her executor godson Claude Kemper, who sold the painting to Sotheby's, New York. They sold it to Moody. Kemper told Moody that Knight's wife knew how enamoured Richard was of Zelda and that on several occasions he broke away to go and see her (James Moody in conversation with the author, 28 Nov. 1999 and 27 Aug. 2001).

48 Tom Daniels lived near Scott in St Paul, gave him rides to St Paul Academy and attended

the Baker dancing classes with him. He carried the manuscript of *This Side of Paradise* to Scribner's.

49 Jane O'Connell and Mr A. K. Mills, who had helped put the exhibition together, received two drawings, each valued at $25: *Two People* and *Feuété* (which is possibly a pun on the ballet term Fouetté).

50 *Arabesque* is listed in 1942 at Zelda's exhibition of watercolours and drawings at Montgomery Women's Club.

51 Dorothy Parker to Milford, 26 Aug. 1964, Milford, *Zelda*, pp. 290–1.

52 John Biggs Jnr to Milford, 9 June 1963, ibid., p. 291.

53 James Thurber, 'Scott in Thorns', *The Reporter*, 17 Apr. 1951.

54 Parker attempted suicide when her affair with Charles MacArthur broke up.

55 *Time*, 9 Apr. 1934.

56 *New York Post*, 3 Apr. 1934.

57 On 30 April Zelda was allowed to return to New York with a nurse to see the last day of her exhibition.

58 ZSF to FSF, *c.* 1 Apr. (author's dating) 1934, CO187, Box 44, Folder 29, PUL. She reminded him of the mass of stuff she had written and wondered if *Esquire* might take some of it. Even though his own novel was due out 12 April he was still nervous about her writing.

59 FSF to Slocum, 8 Apr. 1934; Slocum to FSF, 11 Apr. 1934, CO745, Box 1, Folder 1, PUL.

60 ZSF to FSF, two letters, Apr. 1934 (author's dating), CO187, Box 44, Folders 24, 41, PUL.

61 ZSF to FSF, Apr./May 1934, CO187, Box 44, Folder 46, PUL.

62 Malcolm Cowley, review of *Tender*, *The New Republic*, 6 June 1934.

63 Quoted in Mellow, *Invented Lives*, p. 418.

64 Donnelly and Billings, *Sara and Gerald*, p. 38. Scott used other friends as models for the Divers' circle. Ring Lardner and Charlie MacArthur became Abe North. Nicole's acid sister Baby Warren was based on Scott's disapproving sister-in-law Rosalind Smith and Sara Murphy's sharp-tongued sister Hoytie, while Rosemary Hoyt, the naïve young actress who is infatuated by Dick, was based on Lois Moran and possibly also on Mary Hay. According to Scott's notes for the novel Barban was based on a combination of Edouard Jozan, Mario Braggiotti, Tommy Hitchcock and two Princetonians, Percy Pyne and Denny Holden. Bruccoli and other critics believe Barban was also based on Ernest Hemingway though Scott did not list him.

65 Murphy finally gave up all painting after the deaths of both his sons.

66 Sara Murphy to FSF, 1934, CO187, Box 51, Folder 15, PUL.

67 Donnelly and Billings, *Sara and Gerald*, p. 43.

68 Gerald Murphy to FSF, 31 Dec. 1935, CO187, Box 51, Folder 13, PUL.

69 FSF to EH, 10 May 1934, J. F. Kennedy Library.

70 EH to MP, 30 Apr. 1934, *The Only Thing That Counts*.

71 Hemingway later thought *Tender Is The Night* was excellent, of a higher standard than anything Scott had written before. He did wonder however whether Scott's writing career might be over. He sent via Perkins affectionate greetings to Scott with the assurance that the novel was threateningly good.

72 FSF to Mencken, 23 Apr. 1934, PUL, lent by Enoch Pratt Free Library; Mencken to FSF, 26 Apr. 1934.

73 ZSF to FSF, Apr. 1934; May 1934 (author's dating), CO187, Box 44, Folders 41, 46, PUL.

74 ZSF, 'Auction – Model 1934', *Collected Writings*, p. 438.

75 Sheppard Pratt, founded as Sheppard Asylum in 1853, was given an influx of funds five years later by Enoch Pratt, a rich railroad and steamship owner. It was one of the USA's oldest mental hospitals, housing 500 patients in 1934. In 1931 6 per cent of its patients were hospitalized free; in 1932 198 of its 271 patients paid less than the full fees, which averaged $38 per week. Most full-fee-paying patients came from the South like Zelda because the Deep South had few private mental hospitals.

76 ZSF to FSF, *c.* Apr. 1934 (author's dating); *c.* Apr./May 1934 (author's dating), CO187, Box 44, Folders 42, 46, PUL.

77 Mayfield, *Exiles*, p. 214. Mayfield was herself a patient there later and her own descriptions of the hospital and her experiences (Mayfield Collection, University of Alabama, Tuscaloosa) precisely match the horror of Zelda's. Mayfield believed Zelda had been

'ground down by Scott and the doctors', that if she had been allowed to leave, to write and paint, she could have survived mentally.

78 Taylor, *Sometimes Madness*, p. 197.

79 ZSF to FSF, *c*. Oct. 1934.

80 ZSF to FSF, summer 1934: *c*. June (author's dating) 1934; *c*. June (author's dating) 1934, CO187, Box 44, Folders 49, 26, 47, PUL.

81 ZSF to Dr Elgin and other medical staff, Sheppard Pratt, 1934. Dr William Elgin was born in Cincinnati in 1905, graduated from Washington and Lee University in Virginia, and took his medical degree at Johns Hopkins.

82 ZSF to FSF, undated fragment (author's dating summer 1934), CO187, Box 41, Folder 42, PUL.

83 Taylor, *Sometimes Madness*, p. 300.

84 ZSF to FSF, late May/June 1934, CO187, Box 44, Folder 47, PUL.

85 Mayfield, *Exiles*, p. 275.

86 FSF, Notebooks, No. 1362.

87 Quoted in Mellow, *Invented Lives*, p. 429.

88 Dr Murdoch (Mayfield gives his name as Kenneth Murdock), a graduate of Nebraska Medical School and a Commonwealth Fellow in Psychiatry at Colorado Psychopathic Hospital, joined Sheppard Pratt in 1930 and soon became its third director. He also taught psychiatry at the University of Maryland.

89 ZSF to FSF, late May 1934, CO187, Box 44, Folder 47, PUL.

90 FSF to Elgin, 21 May 1934, CO187, Box 40, Folder 4, PUL.

91 FSF to MP, 13 June 1934. His proposed table of contents began with a 500-word introduction by him. The first section, 'Eight Women', would contain Zelda's stories (26,250 words). The second section, 'Three Fables' (5,000 words), would include 'The Drought and the Flood', 'A Workman' and 'The House'. The third section, 'Recapitulation' (5,000 words), would include 'Show Mr and Mrs F. –' and 'Auction –' Model 1934' (total approximately 50,000 words).

92 FSF to Rosalind Sayre Smith, 19 July 1934, CO187, Box 53, Folder 14A, PUL.

93 FSF to Rosalind Sayre Smith, 16 Aug. 1934, ibid.

94 Quoted in Aaron Latham, *Crazy Sundays: F. Scott Fitzgerald in Hollywood*, Viking Press, New York, 1971, p. 183.

95 FSF to Stein, 29 Dec. 1934, Yale University. Isabel Owens was there when Zelda refused to hand over her paintings. Owens said 'She made it stick too.'

96 17 Mar. 1935 at Massachusetts General Hospital.

97 Mencken to FSF, 30 May 1935, CO187, Box 51, PUL.

CHAPTER 23

1 Afraid of a resurgence of tuberculosis, Scott took Scottie out of school for two weeks in February 1935, and went to Tryon's health resort (which offered a tuberculosis centre) in Blue Ridge mountains, where his wealthy friends Lefty (Zelda's former physician at Ellerslie) and Nora Flynn lived. (Nora, the youngest of the five beautiful Langhorne sisters, was said by Edmund Wilson to have had an affair with Scott. Nora's daughter by her first marriage was the actress Joyce Grenfell. Nora's sister Nancy married Viscount Astor and succeeded him as Conservative MP, the first woman in parliament. Another sister, Irene Langhorne, was the original Gibson Girl.) On Scott's return to Baltimore in late March X-rays revealed he had further lung damage. He spent part of the spring in Hendersonville, then when Scottie went to camp he resided at Grove Park Inn, Asheville, while lung specialist Dr Paul Ringer treated him. In September he again returned to Baltimore, where he took an apartment at Cambridge Arms, Charles Street.

2 ZSF to FSF, *c*. 1935 (author's dating), CO187, Box 45, Folder 14, PUL.

3 ZSF to FSF, no date, author's dating spring 1935, CO187, Box 45, Folder 5, PUL.

4 Scott daily confided details of his affair to Hearne who recorded them in her journal.

5 Mellow has an engaging witty account of the Dance–Fitzgerald affair, Mellow, *Invented Lives*, pp. 433–7.

6 ZSF to FSF, *c.* June 1935, ZSF, *Collected Writings*, p. 477. Earlier FSF had sent this exact letter also to Ober as evidence of his tragic relationship.

7 FSF to Beatrice Dance, early Sep. 1935, CO188, Box 4, Folder 16, PUL.

8 Letter from Rosalind Sayre Smith to Kendall Taylor, 3 Dec. 1964, quoted in Taylor, *Sometimes Madness*, p. 305.

9 Rosalind Sayre Smith to FSF, 4 June 1935, CO187, Box 53, Folder 14A, PUL. From March 1935 Rosalind had sent Scott a series of friendly letters containing material about the Sayre Cresap ancestry for a family history Scott was compiling for Scottie. When *Taps at Reveille* was published Rosalind sent him good reviews and generous praise.

10 Tony Buttitta, interview with the author, Sep. 1998, New York, and conversations and letters throughout 1998 and spring 1999. In 1935 Buttitta was a struggling writer who wrote his account of that summer in *The Lost Summer. A Personal Memoir of F. Scott Fitzgerald*, Robson Books, London, 1987.

11 ZSF to FSF, undated, CO187, Box 44, Folder 27, PUL. Zelda actually spelt 'genital' as 'genitile'.

12 Oct. 1936.

13 Sara Murphy to FSF, 3 Apr. 1936, CO187, Box 51, Folder 15, PUL.

14 The articles were published Feb., Mar. and Apr. 1936. Scott was again in Johns Hopkins Hospital 14–17 Jan. and 13–15 Feb. 1936.

15 Rosalind Sayre Smith, unpublished documentation on ZSF, Mayfield Collection, University of Alabama.

16 FSF to Sara and Gerald Murphy, 30 Mar. 1936, Honoria Murphy Donnelly Collection.

17 Carroll to FSF, 25 June 1936, CO187, Box 49, Folder 26A, PUL. Carroll, born 1869 in Cooperstown, Pennsylvania, graduated in medicine from Marion Sims College and had further psychiatric training at Rush Medical College Chicago. With his wife he founded Highland Hospital of Nervous Diseases in 1904.

18 There is a good discussion of these therapies in Kendall Taylor, *Sometimes Madness*, p. 311.

19 Dr Pine felt these treatments were savage by today's standards. Interviews with the author, 1998, 1999.

20 Mary Parker to the author, interview 12 Sep. 1998 and conversations winter 1998 and spring 1999.

21 Ibid.

22 In January 1937 at the New Year costume ball, Zelda danced the solo role of angel in the ballet she had choreographed.

23 In 1934 Scott earned $20,000. In 1935 he could still earn $3,000 for a story but with reduced productivity his income fell to $17,000. His expenses included Zelda's Highland costs and Scottie's fees for Ethel Walker School, Connecticut (which together totalled $3,000). In 1935 he had borrowed $2,000 from Scribner's, by summer 1936 he owed Scribner's $9,000 and Ober $ 11,000. In 1936 his earnings fell to $10,180.97.

24 ZSF to FSF, *c.* Christmas 1939, CO187, Box 48, Folder 1, PUL.

25 FSF to Oscar Kalman, quoted in Meyers, *Scott Fitzgerald*, p. 276.

26 FSF to Beatrice Dance, 15 Sep. 1936, CO188, Box 4, Folder 16, PUL.

27 Annabel's daughters (Pat Sprague Reneau and Courtney Sprague Vaughan) sent the author their privately published memoir of their father Clifton Sprague, *Remembered and Honored* (1992), with their accompanying notes and comments.

28 One of several painted at Highland. ZSF, Art and Religious Notebook, CO183, Box 6, Folder 4, PUL. The painting, *Easter*, has disappeared.

29 Scottie Fitzgerald, quoted in Lanahan, *Scottie . . .*, p. 89.

30 Mayfield, *Exiles*, p. 229.

31 She never used the variegated fall hues of amber or orange. Watercolours and gouaches on paper include: *Mountains, North Carolina, Untitled 1, Untitled 2, Great Smoky Mountains, Hospital Slope*. Sketches for some were done in Highland, others completed in North Carolina in the 1940s.

32 Mary Parker to the author, interview 12 Sep. 1998.

33 Ibid.

34 Rosalind Sayre Smith, unpublished documentation on ZSF, Mayfield Collection, University of Alabama.

35 Mary Parker to the author, 12 Sep. 1998 and subsequent conversations.

36 Dr Pine thought if Zelda were alive today her depression would probably have responded well to drugs such as lithium. Irving Pine to the author, interviews 1998, 1999.
37 Scottie Fitzgerald, Introduction, *Letters to his Daughter*, ed. Andrew Turnbull, Charles Scribner's Sons, New York, 1963, p. xii.
38 Scott was at Johns Hopkins again 11–14 Jan. 1937.
39 Sara and Gerald Murphy to FSF, 30 Jan. 1937, CO187, Box 51, Folder 13, PUL.
40 FSF to Sara and Gerald Murphy, 30 Jan. 1937, *Letters*, ed. Turnbull, pp. 446–7.
41 Lanahan, *Scottie . . .*, p. 89.
42 Anne Ober to FSF, undated, PUL.
43 Presided over by Donald Ogden Stewart.
44 On the strength of the contract Ober loaned Scott more money to pay a percentage on his bills and take Zelda on a trip to Myrtle Beach in September. From Sep. 1937 to Jan. 1938 Scott worked on *Three Comrades*, which became his only screen credit.
45 The contract stipulated $1,000 a week for six months, extended to Jan. 1938 if it went well, then $1,250 weekly in the second year.
46 Benchley and Parker were both living at the Garden of Allah, Parker with her husband Alan Campbell.
47 The film was co-written by Lillian Hellman, Archibald MacLeish, Ernest Hemingway and Joris Ivens.
48 FSF to EH, telegram, 13 July 1937, J. F. Kennedy Library.
49 FSF, Notebooks, No. 1915.
50 FSF, *The Last Tycoon*, Charles Scribner's Sons, New York, 1941, p. 26.
51 Lanahan, *Scottie . . .*, p. 92.
52 Ibid., pp. 83–4.
53 Taylor, *Sometimes Madness*, p. 326.
54 Vaill, *So Young*, p. 288.
55 Sheilah Graham, *The Real F. Scott Fitzgerald*, p. 50.
56 ZSF to FSF, mid-Dec. 1938; c. Jan. 1939, CO187, Box 46, Folder 51; Box 47, Folder 1, PUL.
57 Quoted in Kendall Taylor, *Sometimes Madness*, p. 329.
58 FSF to Sara Murphy, 27 Nov. 1937.
59 The MGM contract had been renewed Dec. 1937 for one year at $1,250 a week. Scott worked on scripts for 'Infidelity', 'Marie Antoinette', *The Women* and *Madame Curie*.
60 FSF to Dr Robert Carroll, 4 Mar. 1938, CO187, Box 39, Folder 45, PUL.
61 Lanahan, *Scottie*, p. 92.
62 In January 1939, after a trip with Budd Schulberg to Dartmouth College to work on *Winter Carnival*, Scott was fired for drinking and seriously damaged his reputation.
63 Feb. 1939.
64 These two exhibitions took place in spring and summer 1939.
65 ZSF to FSF, late Jan. 1939, CO187, Box 47, Folder 4, PUL.
66 FSF to ZSF, 6 May 1939, *Life in Letters*, p. 391.

CHAPTER 24

1 The spun glass phrase was used by Scott reporting Carroll's words to Minnie Sayre, 3 Jan. 1939, CO187, Box 53, Folder 13, PUL.
2 The idea that Zelda should live with a companion near her family was impractical as a companion's fee was beyond anyone's means; that Zelda should reside alone in a Montgomery cottage to give her a sense of responsibility was equally impractical because Zelda was an undomesticated artist.
3 Rosalind also reported Dr Carroll's view that a trained nurse was unnecessary.
4 FSF to Marjorie Brinson, c. end Dec. 1938, CO187, Box 53, Folder Marjorie Brinson (Sayre), PUL. The letter is marked in pen 'unsent'.
5 FSF to Rosalind Sayre Smith, c. end Dec. 1938, CO187, Box 53, Folder 14, PUL.
6 FSF to Dr R. Burke Suitt, 5 July 1939, CO187, Box 53, Folder Burke Suitt, PUL. Scott wrote this *after* he had registered Minnie Sayre's comment that though Zelda's 'visit came at the time of the month that is most trying (I mean menstruation) . . . there was no undue nervousness' (Minnie Sayre to FSF, 26 Apr. 1938, CO187, Box 53, unnumbered folder, PUL).

7 FSF to Suitt, 27 July 1939, CO187, Box 53, Folder Burke Suitt, PUL.

8 FSF to Scottie Fitzgerald, July 1939, CO187, Box 40, PUL.

9 ZSF to FSF, July 1939, CO187, Box 47, Folder 48, PUL.

10 FSF to ZSF, 6 Oct. 1939, *Life in Letters*, pp. 412–13.

11 ZSF to FSF, Oct. 1939, CO187, Box 47, Folder 70, PUL.

12 FSF to ZSF, unsent letter, *c.* late 1939, PUL.

13 Thalberg had died in 1936.

14 John O'Hara, 'In Memory of Scott Fitzgerald: II', *The New Republic*, 3 Mar. 1941.

15 Zelda's Montgomery friend and biographer Sara Mayfield saw it simply as a study in blue and white of a planter's cotton bolls.

16 Quoted in Koula Hartnett, 'Zelda Fitzgerald and the Failure of the American Dream', paper presented at Southern Atlantic Modern Language Association Annual Meeting, 1981, p. 142.

17 ZSF to FSF, *c.* winter 1939–40 (author's dating), CO187, Box 48, Folder 10, PUL.

18 ZSF to FSF, *c.* Jan./Feb. 1940 (author's dating), CO187, Box 48, Folder 7, PUL.

19 ZSF to FSF, 31 Dec. 1939, CO187, Box 48, Folder 4, PUL.

20 'Pat Hobby's Christmas Wish', the first of seventeen stories, was published in *Esquire*, Jan. 1940.

21 'Meantime: it is good to be able to receive uncensored mail.' ZSF to FSF, 31 Dec. 1939, CO187, Box 48, Folder 4, PUL.

22 ZSF to FSF. *c.* mid–late Feb. 1940 (author's dating), CO187, Box 48, Folder 17, PUL.

23 FSF to Dr Robert Carroll, 8 Mar. 1940, CO187, Box 39, Folder 45, PUL.

24 FSF to ZSF, 8 Mar. 1940, *Life in Letters*, p. 438.

25 FSF to Minnie Sayre, 8 Mar. 1940, CO187, Box 53, Folder 13, PUL.

26 Dr Irving Pine to the author in two conversations, 1998 and 1999. Further confirmation comes from the fact that Dr Pine used virtually the same phrase to describe Carroll's mistreatment of patients to a previous biographer, who did not use the quote in her study of the Fitzgeralds but repeated it to this author.

27 ZSF to John Biggs Jnr, 29 Jan. 1941, CO628, Box 2, Folder 11, PUL. The bill for 1 May 1939 to 14 Apr. 1940 was $4,017.14 for professional services; plus incidental expenses of $50 (shampoo and shoe repairs) and $18.80 (special attendance, special medication). The bill was submitted several times and not paid until 15 Jan. 1942.

28 Dr Robert Carroll's statement on ZSF's condition, 6 Apr. 1940, CO187, Box 49, Folder 26A, PUL.

29 FSF to ZSF, 11 Apr. 1940, *Life in Letters*, p. 442.

30 ZSF to FSF, early summer 1940 (author's dating); *c.* Mar./early Apr. 1940 (author's dating), CO187, Box 48, Folders 39, 23, PUL.

31 FSF wrote to Scottie 6 June 1940 to tell her, *Life in Letters*, p. 449.

32 Lanahan, *Scottie . . .*, p. 127.

33 FSF to Gerald and Sara Murphy, early summer 1940, Honoria Murphy Donnelly Collection.

34 *The Time Is Ripe: The 1940 Journal of Clifford Odets*, New York 1988, p. 293.

35 Many alcoholics suffer alcoholic cardiomyopathy, enlargement of heart chambers.

36 FSF to Scottie Fitzgerald, *c.* 15 Dec. 1940, *Life in Letters*, p. 475.

37 FSF to MP, 13 Dec. 1940, *Dear Scott/Dear Max*, p. 268; to Scottie Fitzgerald, 15 Dec. 1940, *Life in Letters*, pp. 474, 475.

38 FSF to ZSF, 6 Dec. 1940, *Life in Letters*, pp. 473–4.

39 Sheilah Graham characteristically gives two different versions of Fitzgerald's death. In *Beloved Infidel* (1958) she says he was still breathing when he hit the floor (p. 251). In *The Real Scott Fitzgerald* (1976) she said he died instantly (p. 15). Meyers, *Scott Fitzgerald*, follows version one. Edmund Wilson in his letters and Mizener, *The Far Side of Paradise*, follow version two.

40 Quoted in Meyers, *Scott Fitzgerald*, p. 334.

41 Ibid.

42 Fanny Myers Brennan and Honoria Murphy Donnelly in conversation with the author.

43 Meyers, *Scott Fitzgerald*, p. 334.

44 MP to EH, 28 Dec. 1940, PUL.

45 Reproduced in *Romantic Egoists*, p. 230.

46 Budd Schulberg Jnr, 'In Hollywood', *The New Republic*.

47 Issues of 17 Feb./3 Mar. 1941.
48 O'Hara, 'In memory of Scott Fitzgerald: II', *The New Republic*.
49 Schulberg, 'In Hollywood'.
50 John Peale Bishop, 'The Hours', *The New Republic*.
51 ZSF to Scottie Fitzgerald, undated (author's dating *c.* June 1945), CO183, Box 4, Folder 36, PUL.
52 ZSF to Ober, 24 Dec. 1940, *As Ever*, p. 424.

CHAPTER 25

1 Milford, *Zelda*, p. 352.
2 Meyers, *Scott Fitzgerald*, p. 340.
3 Bruccoli, *Epic Grandeur*, p 586.
4 Mellow, *Invented Lives*, p. 489.
5 This view is promulgated by Meyers, *Scott Fitzgerald*, p. 341.
6 The cityscapes were pale coloured, suffused with a grey cloud-like wash, each one imbued with nostalgia and light. Scenes steeped in shades of grey ran the risk of dissolving into obscurity but Zelda punctuated the predominant hue with single bolts of vivid red or electric yellow. A dark skyline is edged with champagne corks blazing golden, grey horses have lips and ears of red, glowing pink street lamps flare on a dark grey street.
7 Jane S. Livingston, 'On the Art of Zelda Fitzgerald', in Lanahan, ed., *Zelda: An Illustrated Life*, p. 81.
8 On 12 April 1946 Zelda told Biggs she was painting an album of Bible pictures for her grandchild 'which gives me great pleasure as they are academic in execution but with a sense of satire. It will be gratifying and I trust edifying to be a grandmother.'
9 The Biblical Tableaux are watercolour and gouache on paper, some started in the late 1930s, most produced between 1946 and 1948. Zelda used theatrical Diaghilev devices familiar from her ballet paintings. Zelda's fixation with ethics is obvious from the titles of these mainly moral tales from Old and New Testaments: *Do Not Commit Adultery, Let Him Who Is Without Sin Cast the First Stone, The Parable of the Vineyard, Honor Thy Father and Mother, Do Not Steal*. Others, *Adam and Eve, Untitled (Deposition), The Nativity* and *The Marriage at Cana*, also incorporated precepts to live life well.
10 'Zelda Fitzgerald Exhibits Dolls', *Montgomery Advertiser*, Aug. 1941.
11 They include: King Arthur, Merlin, Queen Guinevere, Queen Elaine, Sir Launcelot, Sir Gawain, Sir Percival, Sir Galahad, Sir Erwaine. Like the Early Paper Dolls they are watercolour and gouache on paper. Each doll is different, drawn and coloured on heavy cardboard-stock paper, the character's identity written in pencil on the top right corner. Most had two costumes drawn and coloured on thinner lighter paper. No doll is cut out.
12 'Zelda Sayre Fitzgerald's Pictures On View At Museum', undated, no newspaper credit, Biggs Papers, CO628, Box 2, Folder 12, PUL. Figures in the ballet and circus paintings were typically elongated and neutralized to blend into the design instead of dominating the picture.
13 ZSF to Biggs, May 1942, CO628, Box 2, Folder 12, PUL. It is interesting that Biggs became Zelda's confidant because when they first met Biggs felt Zelda disliked him. He wrote later: 'Zelda was wildly jealous of both men and women who liked Scotty [Scott]. I don't think she liked me.' John Biggs quoted in Toll, *An Uncommon Judge*, p. 102, referred to in Taylor, *Sometimes Madness*, p. 123.
14 The version with the traditional red boots, hood and dress was captioned 'Red Riding Hood in academic vein'.
15 The Piglets are typical of her fairy tales which are as much an exercise in composition as in fantasy, with spatial relationships determined not only by conventional perspective lines but also by gaudy colours. The dolls and fairytale scenes which constitute a large part of Zelda's surviving work formed a quarter of the 1974 Retrospective Exhibition of her art at the Montgomery Museum of Fine Arts.
16 Zelda had painted some scenes from *Alice* for Scottie during the 1920s but the significant paintings begin in the 1940s. Faithful to Carroll's story, she mixes this with striking inno-

vative ideas of her own. They are complex and detailed and carry autobiographical meanings as well as literary references.

17 On 10 March 1947 Zelda wrote to a friend that she was painting 'trays and trays and trays' which offered her another medium to express religious feelings. On an oil on metal tole tray and an oil on metal dough rising tin she painted scarlet pomegranates, symbols of Christian Resurrection. One of her painted bowls is adorned with blazing poppies, portents of death.

18 Other critics are divided as to motives. Some think Zelda suffered a sudden bout of low self-esteem regarding her own work. Carolyn Shafer suggests wild mood swings drove her to extremes.

19 People in Montgomery, even today, recall Minnie's horror and hatred. They are not surprised she ordered them to be burnt after Zelda's death.

20 ZSF to Biggs, 26 May 1943, CO628, Box 2, Folder 13, PUL.

21 ZSF to Biggs, undated 1943, author's dating between 6 and 11 Oct., ibid.

22 ZSF to Biggs, undated 1943, author's dating mid-Nov., ibid. She hoped, vainly, that she might receive cash from the sale of Scott's books for this venture.

23 ZSF to Biggs, July/Aug. 1942 (ZSF's emphasis), CO628, Box 2, Folder 18, PUL.

24 ZSF to Biggs, 12 Apr. 1946, CO628, Box 2, Folder 16, PUL.

25 Mayfield, *Exiles*, p. 282.

26 ZSF–Biggs correspondence, 8 and 12 Apr. 1946, CO628, Box 2, Folder 16, PUL. Zelda through Biggs (via Laird Blassell and Meeds of Wilmington) purchased 35 shares in Panhandle Eastern Pipeline common stock at 51¼. On 3 May 1946 she purchased 20 shares in Lane Wells at the cost of $377.55.

27 In April 1941 Zelda sent religious essays to Anna Biggs and Perkins. Once she had a revelation that Biggs would die next year. 'Won't you pray and thank God for his blessings and don't die?', she wrote anxiously (1 Sep. 1947). John Biggs lived (longer than Zelda). When his mother died Zelda consoled him: 'Dear John, I am so sorry about your mother . . . The only peace now lies on the other side; many people are tired of struggling with these ungrateful horizons' (9 Feb. 1943), CO628, Box 2, Folders 18, 17, 13, PUL. To Perkins she wrote comfortingly: 'I brood about my friends; about their Christian virtues and their aspirational purposes and want them to find salvation. You have done so much for people and so endeared yourself . . . that, of course the Lord takes care of you' (undated), CO101, Box 53, Folder Zelda Fitzgerald 1921–1944, PUL.

28 Dr Kirk Curnutt, Associate Professor of English, Troy State University, Montgomery, 'Zelda's Last Years: Fundamentalism and Madness', lent to the author July 2000.

29 Rosalind Sayre Smith, quoted in Lanahan, *Scottie . . .*, p. 185.

30 Curnutt to the author, 7 July 2001 and subsequent communications.

31 Rosalind Sayre Smith to Kendall Taylor, 3 Dec. 1964.

32 ZSF to Biggs, late Aug. 1943, CO628, Box 2, Folder 13, PUL. She wrote from Mrs Wolfe's in Asheville where she had a room with two windows for $3.50 a week and where 'the plumbing bears an outward semblance to modernity'. She said 'The hospital is filling up with the old contingent of my heyday there . . . Also have been to the flower-show with an inmate head-nurse who was my friend.'

33 Zelda's first letter from Highland is 13 July 1946. Five days earlier Biggs had sent Highland a cheque for $275 to cover only four weeks hospitalization. A second bill for $205.71 covered four weeks from 1 August. Biggs paid the final bill of $275. CO628, Box 2, Folder 16; Box 3, Folder 7, PUL.

34 Lanahan, *Scottie . . .*, p. 185 (author's emphasis).

35 Quoted in Bruccoli *et al.*, eds., *Romantic Egoists*, dedication; also quoted in Mellow, *Invented Lives*, p. 488.

36 The State of California valued his unfinished manuscript of *The Last Tycoon* at $5,000 and all other manuscripts at $1,000.

37 In his 1937 will FSF appointed John Biggs and Harold Ober as executors, but on 10 Nov. 1940 he crossed out Ober's name and substituted Perkins. As this raised legal problems Perkins and Ober withdrew as executors in favour of Biggs but all three worked together to administer Scott's literary affairs and Zelda's and Scottie's finances. On 12 Apr. 1941 Biggs sent Zelda her monthly interest on Scott's life insurance policy. He had collected the amount of the policy and would invest half in Government Bonds which would bring

in a small income for Zelda and Scottie. He had also stipulated that income from writings would be held in trust for them.

38 On 30 July 1941 Court of California awarded Zelda $50 a month plus $250 back-pay for the previous 5 months. On 7 Apr. 1941 Zelda efficiently wrote to Biggs to say she was applying for a war veteran's widow's pension. CO628, Box 2, Folder 11, PUL

39 Biggs to ZSF, 31 Dec. 1940; ZSF to Biggs, Dec. 1940, CO628, Box 2, Folder 10, PUL.

40 ZSF to Biggs, Jan. 1941, CO628, Box 2, Folder 11, PUL. Biggs advised her about Scott's headstone. She had wanted one engraved with Scott's name, dates of birth and death, his college and profession, costing no more than $50. Biggs disagreed. He thought it should only say: 'Francis Scott Key Fitzgerald September 24, 1896 December 21, 1940 "Come unto me all ye that labour and are heavy laden and I will give you rest".'

41 ZSF to Biggs, 15 Aug. 1947, CO628, Box 2, Folder 17, PUL.

42 Biggs still harboured a secret desire to be a writer, but had been on the Bench for three years. He had Chambers in Federal Buildings, Wilmington. The 3rd Circuit ran from Pennsylvania to the Virgin Islands.

43 On 7 July 1943 for instance Biggs forgot to send her July cheque. His court cases had intervened. CO628, Box 2, Folder 13, PUL.

44 ZSF to Biggs, 23 Jan. 1947, CO628, Box 2, Folder 17, PUL.

45 The typical Biggs admonishment ran: 'I want to make it perfectly clear that the sending of this amount cannot act as a precedent and you will have to live on your income. The previous paragraph sounds very severe. It is not meant to be.' 25 Jan. 1947, ibid.

46 ZSF to Biggs, 23 Jan. 1947, ibid.

47 ZSF to Biggs, 4 or 5 Jan. 1941, CO628, Box 2, Folder 11, PUL. She also asked him to send her rare *History of the Dance* and her treasured books on music and ballet. Svetlov's *History of the Dance* had cost Zelda $40 in Paris.

48 Curiously, she told Biggs to send the paintings by the cheapest freight possible and uninsured (8 Jan. 1941). It took until 1943 for Biggs to send Zelda a box containing her costume jewellery and a steel file containing her ballet materials and camera.

49 ZSF to Sara and Gerald Murphy, Dec. 1940/Jan. 1941, Honoria Murphy Donnelly Collection.

50 EH to Sara Murphy, Dec. 1940, Honoria Murphy Donnelly Collection. Zelda did not hear directly from her old enemy Ernest Hemingway, but during the war she learnt of his exploits from Sara Murphy. Hemingway had been covering the closing days of battle in Europe as a Colliers correspondent when he wrote to Sara that he and Martha Gellhorn had broken up. 'I need a wife in bed and not just in even the most widely circulated magazines.' He was marrying someone else, 'a girl named Mary Welsh . . . [who] is a great believer in bed' (EH to Sara Murphy, 5 May 1945, Honoria Murphy Donnelly Collection). Mary, another writer, would be the first of Hemingway's wives to stay the course.

51 For a full discussion see Vaill, *So Young*, pp. 314–17.

52 Zelda sent Van Vechten a mimeographed religious essay, 13 Nov. 1944, Beinecke Library, Yale University.

53 'I have painted . . . King Arthur's round-table. Jeanne d'Arc and coterie, Louis XIV and court, Robin Hood are under way,' she wrote Max. 'The dolls are charming: there isn't any reason why children shouldn't learn while having a good time. Would you be kind enough to advise me what publishers could make such "literature", and how to approach?' 31 Mar. 1941, CO101, Box 53, Folder Zelda Fitzgerald 1921–1944, PUL. Perkins responded enthusiastically with several publishers' names (3 Apr. 1941). But the paper dolls did not see publication until *Esquire* published some in 1960; then in 1996 Zelda's granddaughter Eleanor Lanahan put them into book form.

54 ZSF to Scottie, undated, CO183, Box 4, Folder 63, PUL.

55 ZSF to Biggs, 9 May 1942, CO628, Box 2, Folder 12, PUL.

56 Biggs to ZSF, 19 May 1942. The Princeton University Library librarians had offered a preliminary figure of $1,000 for all Scott's manuscripts, library files and letters from literary people. The interchange about the sale of Scott's books and papers dragged on for months as California Counsel advised against it until the estate had been distributed. On 5 Feb. 1943 Biggs wrote that he was about to crate Scott's library and manuscripts to send to PUL, which was not prepared to purchase them at that point but would almost certainly

make Zelda an offer for them; 14 Oct. 1943 Biggs wrote that Princeton would probably pay $2,000. As far as the rest of Scott's estate was concerned, Zelda wanted the silver sent to her for domestic use and Francis Scott Key's table (which the Museum would keep in trust for Scottie). She instructed that everything else should be sold or given to the poor. CO628, Box 2, Folders 12, 13, PUL.

57 ZSF to Biggs, 21 May 1942, CO628, Box 2, Folder 12, PUL.

58 Lanahan, *Scottie . . .*, p. 150.

59 ZSF to Anne Ober, postmarked 22 Feb. 1943. Scottie and Jack Lanahan were divorced 20 years later.They had four children, Tim, Eleanor, Jack Jnr and Cecilia. Scottie's next partner was Clayton Fritchey, after whom she married C. Grove Smith in 1967. They divorced in 1980. Scottie died in Montgomery 15 June 1986. She was buried like her parents in Rockville, Maryland.

60 Zelda told friends that she saw Scottie as the Spirit of Truth. 'If the dearth of hair-pins, A L Lewis' fantasies, the eccentricities of H. L. Menken, sugartickets and the presence [of] Satan break your heart or spoil your digestion, call up Scottie.' ZSF to Biggs, undated, 1943, CO628, Box 2, Folder 13, PUL.

61 ZSF to Biggs, 21 May 1943, ibid.

62 Brendan Gill, *A New York Life*, Poseidon Press, New York, 1990, p. 315.

63 Ibid.

64 ZSF to Scottie Lanahan, 26 Apr. 1946, CO183, Box 4, Folder 52, PUL. Previous biographers have intimated that Zelda was in hospital when her grandson (always called Tim) was born. This is incorrect. The Zelda–Biggs correspondence shows she was resident in Montgomery.

65 ZSF to Ludlow Fowler, undated, 1946, CO183, Box 5, Folder 4, PUL.

66 ZSF to Biggs, 8 May 1946, CO628, Box 2, Folder 16, PUL. Tim later shot and killed himself on 18 Oct. 1973 at Diamond Head Park, Honolulu.

67 ZSF to Biggs, 13 July 1946. On 22 July she wrote to Biggs again saying there wasn't any time because 'in the hospital, one follows an inexorable schedule calculated to rehabilitate the most battered of morales + the weariest of skepticisms'. She hoped to emerge better able to observe her social obligations than before she went in. Ibid.

68 Woodrow W. Burgess, Highland Hospital, to Scottie Lanahan at 310 West 94th Street, New York, 25 July 1946. On 1 August Biggs wrote to Zelda that the California Court would allow him to spend only $250 out of corpus for her benefit every month, so as the Highland charges were about $275 a month he would have to retain her annuity cheque of $50 a month if she stayed longer than four weeks. Zelda never received that letter: the hospital intercepted it as they had been instructed by Scottie not to tell Zelda what the hospital cost her. On 17 August Biggs replied to the hospital saying it was better Zelda knew she was not getting annuity cheques but he had no objection to the hospital withholding his letter. Yet again Zelda's post was being tampered with and censored. CO628, Box 3, Folder 7; Box 2, Folder 16, PUL.

69 Burgess to Scottie Lanahan, 13 Sep. 1946, CO628, Box 3, Folder 7, PUL.

70 ZSF at 58 Grove Street, Asheville, to Biggs, 25 Sep. 1946, CO628, Box 2, Folder 16, PUL.

71 ZSF to Biggs, 24 Apr. 1947, CO628, Box 2, Folder 17, PUL.

72 Most extant Biggs–Zelda letters are carbons of letters typed by his secretary.

73 ZSF to Biggs, 25 Nov. 1946, CO628, Box 2, Folder 16, PUL.

74 ZSF to Biggs, 26 or 27 Jan. 1947, CO628, Box 2, Folder 17, PUL.

75 ZSF to Biggs, 28 June 1947, ibid.

76 Earlier biographers date the start inaccurately as 2 Nov. and make it a continuous stay until her death.

77 ZSF to Rosalind Sayre Smith, quoted in Taylor, *Sometimes Madness*, p. 356.

78 Mayfield, *Exiles*, p. 285.

79 Dr Carroll had retired two years earlier leaving Dr Basil Bennett as medical director. Highland was now operated by Duke University.

80 Mayfield, *Exiles*, p. 285.

81 Early biographers say Zelda's room was on the third floor. Ted Mitchell who has done excellent scholarly research into Zelda's death is clear it was the fifth. The author has been to Highland and verified this. Previous biographers have also accepted that insulin patients needed to be locked in. This was questioned at the inquest.

82 Ted Mitchell, 'I'm Not Afraid to Die', talk given at Fitzgerald Conference, 24–27 September 1998, and in conversation with the author, 1998 and 1999.

83 Dr Bennett said firmly Zelda had been asphyxiated by noxious fumes before the flames reached her. Bennett to Kendall Taylor, 1963 and 1964; Dr Pine to Koula Hartnett, 1991.

84 Zelda's death certificate states death by asphyxiation trapped in a burning building.

85 Dentist Dr Eugene Shapiro used X-rays of previous dental work.

86 Rosalind Sayre Smith to Highland Hospital, 14 Mar. 1948.

87 Ted Mitchell suggests that Scottie and the Sayres were too stunned to sue Highland. He confirms that Rosalind told Mrs Sayre that Zelda died in her sleep, which if asphyxiation can be considered sleep is correct. Ted Mitchell to the author, 13 Nov. 1998 and in several subsequent conversations.

88 Or the ashes believed to be hers.

89 Many of Zelda's friends wrote to Mrs Sayre including H. L. Mencken: 'I needn't tell you that all of Zelda's old Baltimore friends have been greatly shocked by her tragic death. She is *verywell* [sic] remembered here, and very pleasantly. My utmost sympathy to you.' The obituaries reclaimed her as Scott's wife or amanuensis. *Time* magazine described her as 'the brilliant counterpart of the [Fitzgerald] heroines.' The *Montgomery Advertiser* pointed out 'Mrs Fitzgerald had collaborated with her husband on some of his books.'

90 Scottie Lanahan to Mrs Sayre, 19 Mar. 1948.

91 Edward Pattillo, Introduction, 'Zelda: Zelda Sayre Fitzgerald Retrospective', Montgomery Museum of Fine Arts, 1974, p. 10.

92 ZSF/Sara Haardt interview, Ellerslie, 1928.

93 ZSF, 'The Original Follies Girl', *Collected Writings*, p. 297.

BIBLIOGRAPHY

ARCHIVE MATERIAL

Princeton University Library, Manuscripts Division, Department of Rare Books and Special
Collections:
    Zelda Fitzgerald Collection (CO183)
    F. Scott Fitzgerald Collection (CO187)
    F. Scott Fitzgerald Additional Papers (CO188)
    John Biggs Collection of F. Scott Fitzgerald Estate papers (CO628)
    Craig House Collection (CO745)
    Charles Scribner's Sons Author Files (CO101)
Eleanor Lanahan Art Archive Collection, Vermont
Cecilia Ross Collection, Pennsylvania
Sprague Family Collection, California
Scott and Zelda Fitzgerald Museum Archives, Montgomery, Alabama
Sara Mayfield Collection, University of Alabama, Tuscaloosa
H. L. and Sara Haardt Mencken Collection, Julia Rogers Library, Goucher College, Baltimore
Honoria Murphy Donnelly Collection, New York
Fanny Myers Brennan Collection, New York
Lloyd Hackl Collection, Center City, Minnesota
H. L. Mencken Collection, Enoch Pratt Free Library, Baltimore
John F. Kennedy Library, Boston, Massachusetts
Yale Collection of American Literature, Beinecke Library, Yale University

WORKS BY ZELDA SAYRE FITZGERALD

PUBLISHED WORKS

Collections
Zelda Fitzgerald: The Collected Writings, ed. Matthew J. Bruccoli, introduction by Mary Gordon,
    Charles Scribner's Sons, New York, 1991; Abacus, Little, Brown & Co., London, 1993;
    University of Alabama Press, Tuscaloosa, 1997

Novels
Save Me the Waltz, Charles Scribner's Sons, New York, 1932

Short stories
'Other Names for Roses', Collected Writings, 1991
'A Couple of Nuts', Scribner's Magazine XCII, Aug. 1932
'The Continental Angle', New Yorker VIII, 4 June 1932
'Miss Ella', Scribner's Magazine XC, Dec. 1931
'Poor Working Girl', College Humor 85, Jan. 1931
'A Millionaire's Girl', Saturday Evening Post CCII, 17 May 1930
'The Girl with Talent', College Humor 76, Apr. 1930
'The Girl the Prince Liked', College Humor 74, Feb. 1930

'Southern Girl', *College Humor* XVIII, Oct. 1929
'The Original Follies Girl', *College Humor* XVII, July 1929
'Our Own Movie Queen', *Chicago Sunday Tribune*, 7 June 1925

Plays
Scandalabra, Bruccoli Clark, Bloomfield Hills MI and Columbia SC, 1980

Articles and essays
'On F. Scott Fitzgerald', *Fitzgerald/Hemingway Annual*, 1974
'Auction – Model 1934', *Esquire* II, July 1934
'Show Mr and Mrs F. to Number –', *Esquire* I–11, May–June 1934
'Paint and Powder', *The Smart Set* LXXXIV, May 1929 (originally written as 'Editorial on Youth' for *Photoplay*, 1927, but not published there)
'Who Can Fall in Love after Thirty?', *College Humor* XV, Oct. 1928
'Looking Back Eight Years', *College Humor* XIV, June 1928
'The Changing Beauty of Park Avenue', *Harper's Bazaar* LXII, Jan. 1928
'Breakfast', *Favorite Recipes of Famous Women*, Harper & Brothers, New York and London, 1925
'Does a Moment of Revolt Come Sometime to Every Married Man?', *McCall's* LI, Mar. 1924
'Eulogy on the Flapper', *Metropolitan Magazine* LV, June 1922
'Friend Husband's Latest', *New York Tribune*, 2 Apr. 1922

UNPUBLISHED WORKS

Novel
Caesar's Things

Short stories
'Garden of Eden' (fragment)
'Here's the True Story' (story/letter)
'Lilian Rich' (fragment)
'Nanny, a British Nurse'

Articles and essays
'Autobiographical Sketch' (written for her psychiatrists), Phipps Clinic, Johns Hopkins Hospital, 1932
'Choreography of an Idea' (also a second version, 'A Good Idea')
'Circus Day'
'Technically in August'
'This Time of Year'
'Travel/Touring/Moving About'
'Unembellish'
''The World Angered God'

WORKS ABOUT ZELDA SAYRE FITZGERALD

Books
Going, William, T., *Zelda Sayre Fitzgerald and Sara Haardt Mencken*, University of Alabama Press, Alabama, 1975
Hartnett, Koula Svokos, *Zelda Fitzgerald and the Failure of the American Dream for Women*, Peter Lang Publishing Inc., New York, 1991
Lanahan, Eleanor, *Zelda, an Illustrated Life: The Private World of Zelda Fitzgerald*, Harry N. Abrams Inc., New York, 1996
McDonough, Kaye, *Zelda: Frontier Life in America. A Fantasy in Three Parts*, City Lights Books, San Francisco, 1978
Milford, Nancy, *Zelda: A Biography*, Harper & Row, New York, Evanston, London, 1970; Bodley Head, London, Sydney, Toronto, 1970; Avon Books, New York, 1971; HarperCollins, New York, 2001

Articles, theses, journals, magazines

Anderson, W. R., 'Rivalry and Partnership: The Short Fiction of Zelda Sayre Fitzgerald', *Fitzgerald/Hemingway Annual*, 1977

Brinson, Claudia Smith, 'Zelda more than an appendage of Fitzgerald', *The State*, Columbia, South Carolina, 27 Oct. 1991

Brisick, William C., 'Artistic promise unfulfilled', *Los Angeles Daily News*, 25 Aug. 1991

Bruccoli, Matthew J., 'Zelda Fitzgerald's Lost Stories', *Fitzgerald/Hemingway Annual*, 1979

Bullock, Heidi Kunz, 'The Art of Zelda Fitzgerald: Alice in Wonderland and Other Fairy Tales', introduction to exhibition brochure, Maier Museum of Art, Randolph-Macon Woman's College, 22 Oct.–23 Dec. 1998

Cary, Meredith, '*Save Me The Waltz* as a Novel', *Fitzgerald/Hemingway Annual*, 1977

Cooper, Douglas Marshall, 'Form and Fiction: The Writing Style of Zelda Sayre Fitzgerald', unpublished dissertation, University of Michigan, 1979

——'Portraits of Zelda', unpublished MA thesis, Department of English, Wagner College, New York, 1970

Coughlin, Ruth Pollack, 'Zelda Fitzgerald's collected writings tell a sad tale of promise unfulfilled', *Detroit News*, 7 Aug. 1991

Cowley, Malcolm, 'A Ghost Story of the Jazz Age', *Saturday Review* XLVII, 25 Jan. 1964

Curnutt, Kirk, 'Zelda's Last Years: Fundamentalism and Madness', paper given at F. Scott Fitzgerald Conference, Nice, 27 June–4 July 2000

Donaldson, Scott, 'Zelda Fitzgerald, thoughts gathered', *USA Today*, 9 Aug. 1991

Fitzgerald Smith, Scottie, 'The Maryland Ancestors of Zelda Sayre Fitzgerald', *Maryland Historical Magazine* 78:3, fall 1983

Franklin, Rebecca, 'Zelda Fitzgerald, Tallulah the Most?', *Birmingham News*, 17 June 1956

Frost, Laura, 'Zelda, in Her Own Words', *San Francisco Chronicle*, 4 Aug. 1991

Going, William, T., 'Two Alabama Writers: Zelda Sayre Fitzgerald and Sara Haardt Mencken', *Alabama Review* XXIII, Jan. 1970

Greenhaw, Wayne, 'The Spirit Tree', Montgomery, 1997

——Two reviews of *Collected Writings*, *Alabama Journal*, 5 and 12 Aug. 1991

Hartnett, Koula Svokos, 'Zelda Fitzgerald and the Failure of the American Dream', paper presented at Southern Atlantic Modern Language Association Annual Meeting, 1981

Hudgins, Andrew, 'Zelda Sayre in Montgomery' (poem), *Southern Review* 20:4, 1984

Kakutani, Michiko, 'That Other Fitzgerald Could Turn a Word, Too', *New York Times*, 20 Aug. 1991

Kramer, Peter D., 'How Crazy was Zelda?', *New York Times Magazine*, 1 Dec. 1996

Laurence, Charles, 'My Secret Legacy from Zelda', *Daily Telegraph*, 20 Aug. 1996

MacDonald, Marianne, 'Zelda Fitzgerald's art makes a novel return', *Independent*, 26 July 1996

Magin, Janis L., 'Montgomery recalls high-living Zelda', *Atlanta Journal/Atlanta Constitution*, 6 Nov. 1993

Marvel, Mark, 'The Collected Writings of Zelda Fitzgerald', *Vogue*, Aug. 1991

Mitchell, Ted, '"I'm Not Afraid To Die": The Death of Zelda Fitzgerald', paper given at International F. Scott Fitzgerald Conference, Asheville, North Carolina, 24–27 Sept. 1998

Mizener, Arthur, 'The Good Gone Times', *New York Times Book Review*, 13 Aug. 1967

O'Brien, Sharon, 'More Than Just a Crazy Flapper', *New York Times*, 1 Sept. 1991

Petry, Alice Hall, 'Women's Work: The Case of Zelda Fitzgerald', *Literature-Interpretation-Theory*, vol. 1, Gordon and Breach Science Publishers SA, 1989

Ridgeway, Livye Hart, 'A Profile of Zelda', Sara Mayfield Collection, University of Alabama, Tuscaloosa

Rubin, Merle, 'The Other Fitzgerald', *Christian Science Monitor*, 23 Sept. 1991

See, Carolyn, 'Cautionary Tale From the Other Fitzgerald', *Los Angeles Times*, 18 Aug. 1991

Shafer, Carolyn, 'To Spread a Human Aspiration: The Art of Zelda Sayre Fitzgerald', unpublished MA thesis, University of South Carolina, 1994

Tavernier-Courbin, Jacqueline, 'Art as Woman's Response and Search: Zelda Fitzgerald's Save Me the Waltz', *Southern Literary Journal* XI.2, spring 1979

Tillotson, Jerry and Robbie, 'Zelda Fitzgerald Still Lives', *Feminist Art Journal*, spring 1975

Upchurch, Michael, 'Zelda's intense, original work surpasses F. Scott's', *Atlanta Journal/Atlanta Constitution*, 25 Aug. 1991

White, Ray Lewis, 'Zelda Fitzgerald's *Save Me The Waltz*: A Collection of Reviews from 1932–1933', *Fitzgerald/Hemingway Annual*, 1979

Yorke, Lane, 'Zelda: A Worksheet', *The Paris Review*, fall 1983
'Zelda's side of paradise', editorial, *San Francisco Examiner*, 28 Aug. 1991

Newspaper reports
'Asheville Nurse Questioned', *Raleigh News and Observer*, 15 Apr. 1948
'Asheville Nurse Tells Cops "I Could Have Started Fire"', *Raleigh News and Observer*, 14 Apr. 1948
'Bodies of Two More Victims of Fire Found', *Asheville Citizen*, 13 Mar. 1948
'Central Building Destroyed', *Asheville Citizen*, 13 Mar. 1948
'Coroner's Jury Hears Ten at Fire Inquest', *Asheville Citizen*, 30 Mar. 1948
'Doctor To Make Psychiatric Test of Hospital Head', *Greensboro Daily News*, 14 Apr. 1948
Erxleben, Al, 'Fire Caused Confusion', *Asheville Citizen*, 12 Mar. 1948
'Fire-Death Record Set by Blaze at Hospital', *Asheville Citizen*, 12 Mar. 1948
'Five Bodies Still Sought in Wreckage', *Asheville Citizen*, 12 Mar. 1948
'Hospital Staff Members and 2 Youths Praised', *Asheville Citizen*, 12 Mar. 1948
'Hospitalized', *Raleigh News and Observer*, 17 Apr. 1948
'Mental Hospital Nurse Put Under Observation', *Raleigh News and Observer*, 16 Apr. 1948
Miller, I. P., 'Strange Human Stories Come From Big Fire', *Asheville Citizen*, 12 Mar. 1948
'Nurse Testifies She Discovered Hospital Fire', *Asheville Citizen*, 27 Mar. 1948
'Psychiatrist Says Nurse Did Not Start Fire', *Greensboro Daily News*, 15 Apr. 1948
'Toll in Fire at Asheville Reaches Nine', *Greensboro Daily News*, 12 Mar. 1948
'Two More Bodies Found in Debris', *Greensboro Daily News*, 13 Mar. 1948

SELECTED WORKS BY F. SCOTT FITZGERALD

PUBLISHED WORKS

Letters, Ledgers, Notebooks
F. Scott Fitzgerald: A Life in Letters, ed. Matthew J. Bruccoli, Charles Scribner's Sons, New York, 1994; Touchstone, Simon & Schuster, New York, 1995
Correspondence of F. Scott Fitzgerald, ed. Matthew J. Bruccoli and Margaret M. Duggan, Random House, New York, 1980
The Notebooks of F. Scott Fitzgerald, ed. Matthew J. Bruccoli, Harcourt Brace Jovanovich/Bruccoli Clark, New York, London, 1978
As Ever, Scott Fitz-: Letters Between F. Scott Fitzgerald and His Literary Agent. Harold Ober 1919–1940, ed. Matthew J. Bruccoli with the assistance of Jennifer McCabe Atkinson, J. B. Lippincott, Philadelphia and New York, 1972; Woburn Press, London, 1973
F. Scott Fitzgerald's Ledger: A Facsimile, ed. Matthew J. Bruccoli, Bruccoli Clark/NCR Microcard Books, Washington DC, 1972
Dear Scott/Dear Max: The Fitzgerald–Perkins Correspondence, ed. John Kuehl and Jackson R. Bryer, Charles Scribner's Sons, New York, 1971; Cassell, London, 1973
The Letters of F. Scott Fitzgerald, ed. Andrew Turnbull, Charles Scribner's Sons, New York, 1963; Bodley Head, London, 1964; Penguin, Harmondsworth, 1968

General collections
F. Scott Fitzgerald: The Princeton Years. Selected Writings, ed. Chip Deffaa, Cypress House Press, Fort Bragg, 1996
F. Scott Fitzgerald Manuscripts (Facsimiles), ed. Matthew J. Bruccoli: *This Side of Paradise, The Beautiful and Damned, The Great Gatsby* galleys, *Tender Is The Night, The Vegetable*, Stories and Articles, 18 vols., Garland, New York and London, 1990–1991
Afternoon of an Author, ed. Arthur Mizener, Princeton University Library, Princeton NJ, 1957; Charles Scribner's Sons, New York, 1958; Bodley Head, London, 1958
The Crack-up With Other Uncollected Pieces. Note-Books and Unpublished Letters, ed. Edmund Wilson, New Directions, New York, 1945, 1956; *The Crack-Up: With Other Pieces and Stories*, Penguin, Harmondsworth, 1965

Short story collections
The Jazz Age, New Directions, New York, 1996
The Diamond as Big as The Ritz and Other Stories, Wordsworth Editions, Ware, 1994
The Fantasy and Mystery Stories of F. Scott Fitzgerald, Robert Hale, London, 1991
The Short Stories of F. Scott Fitzgerald, Charles Scribner's Sons, New York, 1989
The Collected Short Stories of F. Scott Fitzgerald, Penguin Books, London, 1986
The Price was High: Fifty Uncollected Stories by F. Scott Fitzgerald, ed. Matthew J. Bruccoli, Harcourt Brace Jovanovich/Bruccoli Clark, New York, 1979
The Basil and Josephine Stories, ed. Jackson R. Bryer and John Kuehl, Charles Scribner's Sons, New York, 1973
The Ice Palace, Babylon Revisited and Other Stories, Charles Scribner's Sons, New York, 1971
The Apprentice Fiction of F. Scott Fitzgerald, ed. John Kuehl, Rutgers University Press, New Brunswick NJ, 1965
Six Tales of the Jazz Age and Other Stories, Charles Scribner's Sons, New York, 1960
The Stories of F. Scott Fitzgerald, ed. Malcolm Cowley, Charles Scribner's Sons, New York, 1951
Taps at Reveille, Charles Scribner's Sons, New York, 1935
All the Sad Young Men, Charles Scribner's Sons, New York, 1926
Tales of the Jazz Age, Charles Scribner's Sons, New York, 1922; Collins, London, 1923
Flappers and Philosophers, Charles Scribner's Sons, New York, 1920; Collins, London, 1922

Novels
The Love of the Last Tycoon: A Western, ed. with introduction by Matthew J. Bruccoli, Abacus, London, 1995
The Last Tycoon, Charles Scribner's Sons, New York, 1941, 1969; Penguin Books, 1960
Tender Is The Night, Charles Scribner's Sons, New York, 1934, 1962; Penguin, Harmondsworth, 1955, 1986
The Great Gatsby, Charles Scribner's Sons, New York, 1925, 1969; ed. Matthew J. Bruccoli, Abacus, London, 1992; Penguin, Harmondsworth, 1994; Oxford University Press, Oxford and New York, 1998
The Beautiful and Damned, Charles Scribner's Sons, New York, 1922; Grey Walls Press, London, 1950; Penguin, Harmondsworth, 1966
This Side of Paradise, Charles Scribner's Sons, New York, 1920, 1970; Penguin, Harmondsworth, 1963

Plays and screenplays
Babylon Revisited: The Screenplay, Carroll & Graf Publishers, New York, 1993
The Vegetable, Charles Scribner's Sons, New York, 1923, 1976

Articles and essays
The Cruise of the Rolling Junk, Bruccoli Clark, Bloomfield Hills Ml and Columbia SC, 1976

UNPUBLISHED WORKS

'Analogy'
'The Romantic Egotist'

WORKS ABOUT F. SCOTT FITZGERALD

Books
Allen, M. Joan, *Candles and Carnival Lights: The Catholic Sensibility of F. Scott Fitzgerald*, New York University Press, New York, 1978
Bruccoli, Matthew J., *Fitzgerald and Hemingway: A Dangerous Friendship*, André Deutsch, London, 1995
——*Some Sort of Epic Grandeur*, Harcourt Brace Jovanovich, 1981; Hodder & Stoughton, London, 1981; Sphere Books, London, 1991
——*Supplement to F. Scott Fitzgerald: A Descriptive Bibliography*, University of Pittsburgh Press, Pittsburgh, 1980

——*Scott and Ernest: The Authority of Failure and the Authority of Success*, Random House, New York, 1978

——*'The Last of the Novelists': F. Scott Fitzgerald and The Last Tycoon*, Southern Illinois University Press, Carbondale and Edwardsville, 1977

——*Apparatus for F. Scott Fitzgerald's The Great Gatsby*, University of South Carolina Press, Columbia, 1974

——*F. Scott Fitzgerald: A Descriptive Bibliography*, University of Pittsburgh Press, Pittsburgh, 1972

——*The Composition of Tender Is The Night*, University of Pittsburgh Press, Pittsburgh, 1963

——comp., *Profile of F. Scott Fitzgerald*, Charles E. Merrill Publishing Company, Columbus, Ohio, 1971

——and Bryer, Jackson R., eds., *F. Scott Fitzgerald in His Own Time*, Popular Library, New York, 1971

Bryer, Jackson R., *The Critical Reputation of F. Scott Fitzgerald*, Archon, Hamden CT, 1967

——ed., *The Short Stories of F. Scott Fitzgerald: New Approaches in Criticism*, University of Wisconsin Press, Madison, Wisconsin, 1982

——ed., *F. Scott Fitzgerald: The Critical Reception*, Burt Franklin, New York, 1978

Buttitta, Tony, *After the Good Gay Times*, Viking Press, New York, 1974; republished as *The Lost Summer: A Personal Memoir of F. Scott Fitzgerald*, Robson Books, London, 1987

Chambers, John B., *The Novels of F. Scott Fitzgerald*, Macmillan, London/St Martin's Press, New York, 1989

Cross, K. G. W., *F. Scott Fitzgerald*, Grove, New York, 1964

Donaldson, Scott, *Hemingway vs. Fitzgerald: The Rise and Fall of a Literary Friendship*, Overlook Press, New York, 1999; John Murray, London, 2000

——*Fool For Love: A Biography of F. Scott Fitzgerald*, Delta, New York, 1983

Eble, Kenneth E., *F. Scott Fitzgerald*, Twayne Publishers Inc., New York, 1963

Fryer, Sarah Beebe, *Fitzgerald's New Women: Harbingers of Change*, UMI, Ann Arbor MI, 1988

Goldhurst, William, *F. Scott Fitzgerald and His Contemporaries*, World, Cleveland and New York, 1963

Graham, Sheilah, *The Real F. Scott Fitzgerald*, Grosset & Dunlap, New York, 1976

——*College of One*, Viking, New York, 1967

——and Frank, Gerold, *Beloved Infidel*, Holt, Rinehart & Wilson, New York, 1958

Hackl, Lloyd C., *'Still Home to Me': F. Scott Fitzgerald and St. Paul*, Adventure Publications, Cambridge, Minnesota, 1996

——*Fitzgerald's Life in His Works*, College for Working Adults, Minneapolis, 1983

Higgins, John A., *F. Scott Fitzgerald: A Study of the Stories*, St. John's University Press, New York, 1971

Hook, Andrew, *F. Scott Fitzgerald*, Edward Arnold, London, New York, Melbourne, Auckland, 1992

Kazin, Alfred, ed., *F. Scott Fitzgerald: The Man and His Work*, World, Cleveland, 1951; Collier Books, New York, 1974

Koblas, John and Page, David, *F. Scott Fitzgerald in Minnesota: Toward the Summit*, North Star Press of St Cloud, Inc., St Cloud, Minnesota, 1996

Latham, Aaron, *Crazy Sundays: F. Scott Fitzgerald in Hollywood*, Viking Press, New York, 1971

Lehan, Richard D., *F. Scott Fitzgerald: The Man and His Works*, Forum House, Toronto, London, Sydney, 1969

——*F. Scott Fitzgerald and the Craft of Fiction*, Southern Illinois University Press, Carbondale, 1966

Le Vot, André, *F. Scott Fitzgerald: A Biography*, Doubleday & Co. Inc., New York, 1983; Warner Books, Inc., 1984; Allen Lane, London 1984

Long, Robert E., *The Achieving of The Great Gatsby*, Bucknell University Press, Lewisburg PA, 1979

Meyers, Jeffrey, *Scott Fitzgerald: A Biography*, HarperCollins, New York, 1994; Macmillan, London, 1994; Papermac, London, 1995

Miller, James E., *F. Scott Fitzgerald: His Art and His Technique*, New York University Press, New York, 1964

Mizener, Arthur, *Scott Fitzgerald and His World*, Thames & Hudson, London, 1972

——*The Far Side of Paradise: A Biography of F. Scott Fitzgerald*, Houghton Mifflin, Boston, 1951; Heinemann, London, Melbourne, Toronto, Johannesburg, Auckland, 1969

O'Conor, Bijou, *Bijou O'Conor Remembers Scott Fitzgerald*, Audio Arts, London, 1975

Piper, Henry Dan, *Fitzgerald's The Great Gatsby: The Novel, The Critics, The Background*, Charles Scribner's Sons, New York, 1970

——*F. Scott Fitzgerald: A Critical Portrait*, Bodley Head, London, 1965

Ring, Frances Kroll, *Against The Current: As I Remember F. Scott Fitzgerald*, Donald S. Ellis Publisher/Creative Arts Book Company, San Francisco, 1985

Shain, Charles E., *F. Scott Fitzgerald*, University of Minnesota Press, Minneapolis, 1961

Sklar, Robert, *F. Scott Fitzgerald: The Last Laocoön*, Oxford University Press, New York, 1967

Stern, Milton R., ed., *Critical Essays on F. Scott Fitzgerald's Tender Is The Night*, Hall, Boston, 1986

Tredell, Nicolas, *F. Scott Fitzgerald: The Great Gatsby*, Icon Critical Guides, Icon Books, Cambridge, 1997

Turnbull, Andrew, *Scott Fitzgerald*, Charles Scribner's Sons, New York, 1962; Bodley Head, London, 1962; Mayflower-Dell, London, 1964

Way, Brian, *F. Scott Fitzgerald and the Art of Social Fiction*, Edward Arnold, London, 1980

Westbrook, Robert, *Intimate Lies: F. Scott Fitzgerald and Sheilah Graham*, HarperCollins, New York, 1995; Little, Brown & Co., London, 1995; Abacus, London, 1995

Articles, journals, magazines, newspapers

Allen, Brooke, 'The Other Sides of Paradise', *New York Times*, 1995

Bruccoli, Matthew J., ed., *Fitzgerald Newsletter 1958–1968*, NCR Microcard Books, Washington, 1969

Fitzgerald: A Commemorative Publication, Primarius Limited Publishing, Minneapolis MN, Sept. 1996

'F. Scott Fitzgerald Dies at 44; Chronicler of "Lost Generation"', *New York Herald Tribune*, 22 Dec. 1940

F. Scott Fitzgerald Society *Newsletter*, 1991; 1992; 1994; 1995; 1996; 1997; 1998; 1999

Goodwin, Dr Donald W., 'The Alcoholism of F. Scott Fitzgerald', *Journal of the American Medical Association*, 212: 1, 6 Apr. 1970

Hackl, Lloyd C., 'Fitzgerald in St. Paul: An Oral History Portrait', *Fitzgerald/Hemingway Annual*, 1976

Hearne, Laura Guthrie, 'A Summer with F. Scott Fitzgerald', *Esquire*, Dec. 1964

Kerr, Frances, 'Some Terrible Abnormality: Gothic Tendencies in "The Rich Boy"', paper given at F. Scott Fitzgerald Conference, Nice, 27 June–4 July 2000

MacKie, Elizabeth Beckwith, 'My Friend, Scott Fitzgerald', *Fitzgerald/Hemingway Annual* 2, 1970

Mencken, H. L., 'Fitzgerald and Others', *The Smart Set* XLVII, Apr. 1922

Mok, Michel, 'The Other Side of Paradise. Scott Fitzgerald, 40, Engulfed in Despair', *New York Post*, 25 Sep. 1936

Nason, Thelma, 'Afternoon (And Evening) Of An Author', *Johns Hopkins Magazine*, Feb. 1970

Nathan, George Jean, 'Memories of Fitzgerald, Lewis and Dreiser', *Esquire*, Oct. 1958

Norman, Philip, 'Great Scott', *Sunday Times Magazine*, 26 Oct. 1997

Prigozy, Ruth, 'A Matter of Measurement', *Commonweal* XCV:5, 29 Oct. 1971

Renalls, Candice, 'F. Scott's Pal Jackson Reminisces', *Highland Paper*, 10 Nov. 1982

Rompalske, Dorothy, 'From Dazzle to Despair: The Short, Brilliant Life of F. Scott Fitzgerald', *Biography*, Mar. 1999

Schulberg, Budd, 'No Second Acts', *New Choices*, June 1998

'What a "Flapper Novelist" Thinks of his Wife' (interview), *Detroit News*, 30 Sept. 1923

'Writing Histories', *CCUE News* 14, winter 2001

Radio programmes and videos

BBC Radio 3, 'The Authority of Failure: The Life and Work of F. Scott Fitzgerald', presented by Julian Evans, produced by Noah Richler, 1 Sept. 1996

Brennan, Fanny Myers and Donnelly, Honoria Murphy, 'F. Scott Fitzgerald: Memories of Fitzgerald, I' (video), F. Scott Fitzgerald Society Conference, Hofstra University, New York, 1992

WORKS BY ZELDA SAYRE FITZGERALD AND F. SCOTT FITZGERALD

Dear Scott, Dearest Zelda. The Love Letters of F. Scott and Zelda Fitzgerald, ed. Jackson R. Bryer and Cathy W. Barks, St Martin's Press, New York, 2002

Bits of Paradise: Twenty-one Uncollected Stories by F. Scott and Zelda Fitzgerald, Bodley Head, London, 1973; Charles Scribner's Sons, New York, 1974; Penguin, Harmondsworth, 1976, 1982

'What Became of Our Flappers and Our Sheiks?'(two separate articles, one by each author), *McCall's*, Oct. 1925

WORKS ABOUT ZELDA SAYRE FITZGERALD AND F. SCOTT FITZGERALD

Books

Bruccoli, Matthew J., ed., *Fitzgerald/Hemingway Annual*, Gale Research, Detroit, 1977–1979; Information Handling Services, Englewood CO, 1974–1976; NCR Microcard Books, Washington, 1969–1973

——, Smith, Scottie Fitzgerald and Kerr, Joan P., eds., *The Romantic Egoists: A Pictorial Autobiography from the Scrapbooks and Albums of F. Scott and Zelda Fitzgerald*, Charles Scribner's Sons, New York, 1974

Lanahan, Eleanor, *Scottie The Daughter Of . . .: The Life of Frances Scott Fitzgerald Lanahan Smith*, HarperCollins, New York, 1995

Mayfield, Sara, *Exiles from Paradise: Zelda and Scott Fitzgerald*, Dell Publishing Co. Inc., New York, 1971

Mellow, R. James, *Invented Lives: F. Scott and Zelda Fitzgerald*, Houghton Mifflin, Boston, 1984

Tate, Mary Jo, *F. Scott Fitzgerald A to Z: The Essential Reference to His Life and Work*, Facts on File, Inc., New York, 1998

Taylor, Kendall, *Sometimes Madness Is Wisdom. Zelda and Scott Fitzgerald: A Marriage*, Ballantine Books, New York, 2001

Articles, journals, magazines, newspapers

Flanagan, Barbara, 'Daughter of F. Scott Fitzgerald Visits Author's St. Paul Haunts', *Minneapolis Tribune*, 1964

Gurganus, Allan, 'Sacrificial Couples, the Splendor of our Failures and Scott and Zelda Fitzgerald', draft of paper given at International F. Scott Fitzgerald Society Conference, Asheville, North Carolina, 24–27 Sep. 1998, lent to the author

McLendon, Winzola, 'Interview: Frances Scott Fitzgerald to Winzola McLendon', *Ladies Home Journal*, Nov. 1974

——'Scott and Zelda', *Ladies Home Journal*, Nov. 1974

Norman, Philip, 'They'd dance half naked and were obsessed with luxury. Meet the first Posh and Becks', *Daily Mail*, 21 Dec. 2000

Sinclair, Gail D., 'Disparaging a Source: Scott and Zelda Fitzgerald's Creative Indebtedness', paper given at International F. Scott Fitzgerald Society Conference, Asheville, North Carolina, 245–7 Sep. 1998

Unpublished memoirs

Campbell, C. Lawton, 'The Fitzgeralds Were My Friends'

Smith, Scottie Fitzgerald, Memoir, Cecilia Ross Collection, 1985

GENERAL READING

Books

Aaron, Daniel, *Writers on the Left: Episodes in American Literary Communism*, Harcourt, Brace & World, New York, 1961

Adie, Kate (foreword), *The Twentieth Century Year by Year*, Marshall Editions, London, 1998

Algren, Nelson, *Nonconformity: Writing On Writing*, Seven Stories Press, New York, 1996

Anderson, Sherwood, *France and Sherwood Anderson: Paris Notebook 1921*, Louisiana State University Press, Baton Rouge, 1976
——*Sherwood Anderson's Memoirs. A Critical Edition*, ed. Ray Lewis White, University of North Carolina Press, 1969
Angoff, Charles, *Mencken: A Portrait from Memory*, Yoseloff, New York, 1956
Arlen, Michael, J., *Exiles*, Farrar, Straus & Giroux, 1970
Baker, Carlos, *Ernest Hemingway: A Life Story*, Charles Scribner's Sons, New York, 1969
—— ed., *Hemingway and His Critics*, Hill & Wang, 1961
Bankhead, Tallulah, *Tallulah: My Autobiography*, Victor Gollancz, London, 1952
Barnes, Djuna, *Ladies Almanack: showing their Signs and their tides; their Moons and their Changes; the Seasons as it is with them: their Eclipses and Equinoxes; as well as a full Record of diurnal and nocturnal Distempers* (originally published 1928), Harper & Row, New York, 1972; Dalkey Archive Press, Illinois, 1992
Barney, Natalie, ed., *In Memory of Dorothy Ierne Wilde*, Darentière, Dijon, 1951
Baughman, Judith S., ed., *American Decades: 1920–1929*, Manly/Gale, Detroit, 1995
Benchley, Robert, *The Best of Robert Benchley*, Wing Books, New York, 1995
Berg, A. Scott, *Max Perkins: Editor of Genius*, Hamish Hamilton, London, 1979
Betterton, Rosemary, *An Intimate Distance*, Routledge, London and New York, 1996
Bishop, John Peale, *The Collected Essays*, Charles Scribner's Sons, New York, 1948
Bode, Carl, *Mencken*, Southern Illinois University Press, Carbondale and Edwardsville, Illinois, 1969
——*The New Mencken Letters*, The Dial Press, New York, 1977
Borzello, Frances, *Seeing Ourselves: Women's Self-Portraits*, Thames & Hudson, London, 1998
——*A World of Our Own: Women as Artists*, Thames & Hudson, London, 2000
Bradbury, Malcolm, *Dangerous Pilgrimages: Transatlantic Mythologies and The Novel*, Penguin Books, London, 1995
——*The Modern American Novel*, 2nd edn, Oxford University Press, Oxford, New York, 1992
——ed., *The Atlas of Literature*, De Agostoni Editions, London, 1996
Bressler, Karen W. *et al.*, *Lingerie: Icons of Style in the Twentieth Century*, Apple Press, London, 1998
Brown, Dorothy M., *Setting a Course: American Women in the 1920s*, Twayne Publishers, Boston, 1987
Bruccoli, Matthew J., ed., *The Only Thing That Counts: The Ernest Hemingway/Maxwell Perkins Correspondence 1925–1947*, Charles Scribner's Sons, New York, 1996
Buck, Claire, ed., *Women's Literature A–Z*, Bloomsbury, London, 1992
Burrows, Terry, ed., *ITV Visual History of the Twentieth Century*, Carlton Books, London, 1999
Busfield, Joan, *Men, Women and Madness: Understanding Gender and Mental Disorder*, Macmillan Press, 1996
Cabell, James Branch, *Between Friends: Letters of James Branch Cabell and Others*, ed. Padraic Colum and Margaret Freeman Cabell, Harcourt Brace & World, 1962
Callaghan, Morley, *That Summer in Paris: Memories of Tangled Friends*, Coward-McCann Inc., New York, 1963
Carr, Virginia Spencer, *Dos Passos: A Life*, Doubleday, Garden City, New York, 1984
Cash, W. J., *The Mind of the South*, Vintage Books, New York, 1960
Chesler, Phyllis, *Women and Madness*, Avon Books, New York, 1972
Cline, Sally, *Couples: Scene from the Inside*, Little, Brown & Co., London, 1998; Overlook Press, New York, 1999
——*Radclyffe Hall: A Woman Called John. A Biography*, John Murray, London, 1997; Overlook Press, New York, 1998; paperback, John Murray, 1998
——*Lifting the Taboo: Women, Death and Dying*, Little, Brown & Co., London, 1995; Abacus, London 1996; Gustav Lübbe Verlag, Germany,1997
——*Women, Celibacy and Passion*, André Deutsch, London, 1993; Carol Southern Books, New York, 1993; Ediciones Temas de Hoy, Spain, 1993; Optima, London, 1994
Cowley, Malcolm, *And I Worked at the Writer's Trade*, Viking Press, New York, 1973
——*Unshaken Friend: A Profile of Maxwell Perkins*, Roberts Rinehart, Inc., Colorado, 1972
——*Exile's Return: A Literary Odyssey of the 1920s*, Viking Press, New York, 1951
Crosby, Harry, *Shadows of the Sun: The Diaries of Harry Crosby*, Black Sparrow Press, Santa Barbara, 1977

Dabney, Lewis M., ed., *The Portable Edmund Wilson*, Viking Press, New York, 1983

Dau's New York Blue Book: Containing the Names and Addresses of Thirty Thousand Prominent Residents Arranged Alphabetically, Dau, New York, 1914

Donaldson, Scott, *Archibald MacLeish: An American Life*, Houghton Mifflin, Boston, 1992

Donnelly, Honoria Murphy with Billings, Richard N., *Sara and Gerald: Villa America and After*, New American Library, New York, 1982; Holt, Rinehart & Wilson, New York, 1984

Dos Passos, John, *The Best Times: An Informal Memoir*, New American Library, New York, 1966

Drawbell, James, *An Autobiography*, Pantheon Books, New York, 1964

Durr, Virginia Foster, *Outside the Magic Circle: The Autobiography of Virginia Foster Durr*, University of Alabama Press, Tuscaloosa, 1985

Elder, Donald, *Ring Lardner*, Doubleday, Garden City, 1956

Ellmann, Richard, *James Joyce*, Oxford University Press, New York, 1982

Empson, Donald, *The Street Where You Live*, Witsend Press, St Paul, Minnesota, 1975

Evans, Harold, *The American Century*, Jonathan Cape, London, 1998

Fallaize, Elizabeth, ed., *Simone de Beauvoir: A Critical Reader*, Routledge, London, New York, 1998

Faulkner, William, *Go Down Moses and Other Stories*, Penguin Books, London, 1942

Fecher, Charles A., ed., *The Diary of H. L. Mencken*, Alfred A. Knopf, New York, 1989

Fetterley, Judith, *The Resisting Reader: A Feminist Approach to American Literature*, Indiana University Press, Bloomington, 1978

Flanner, Janet, *Paris Was Yesterday*, Viking Press, New York, 1972

Flynt, Wayne J., *Montgomery: An Illustrated History*, Windsor Publications, Woodland Hills CA, 1980

Forkner, Ben and Samway, Patrick, eds., *Stories of the Modern South*, Penguin Books, London, 1986

Gallup, Donald, ed., *The Flowers of Friendship: Letters Written to Gertrude Stein*, Alfred A. Knopf, New York, 1953

Gilbert, Martin, *A History of the Twentieth Century*, vol. I: *1900–1933*, HarperCollins, London, 1997; vol. II: *1933–1951*, HarperCollins, London, 1998; vol. III: *1952–1999*, HarperCollins, London, 1999

Gill, Brendan, *A New York Life*, Poseidon Press, New York, London, Toronto, Sydney, Tokyo, Singapore, 1990

Goodwyn Jones, Anne, *Tomorrow is Another Day: The Woman Writer in the South 1859–1903*, Louisiana State University Press, 1981

Gordon, Jan, *Modern French Painters*, J. Lane, London, 1923

Gregory, Richard L., ed., *The Oxford Companion to the Mind*, Oxford University Press, Oxford, 1987

Griffin, Peter, *Less Than A Treason: Hemingway in Paris*, Oxford University Press, New York, Oxford, 1990

Grun, Bernard, *The Timetables of History: A Horizontal Linkage of People and Events*, Simon & Schuster, New York, London, Toronto, Sydney, Tokyo, Singapore, 1975

Haardt, Sara, *Southern Souvenirs*, ed. Ann Henley, University of Alabama Press, Tuscaloosa, London, 1999

——*Southern Album*, Doubleday, Doran & Co. Inc., New York, 1936

Hackl, Lloyd C., *The Wooden Shoe People: The Story of the Real Karl Oskar and Kristina*, Minnesota Treasures, Center City, Minnesota, 1986

Hall, Radclyffe, *The Well of Loneliness*, Jonathan Cape, London, 1928

Hardwick, Elizabeth, *Seduction and Betrayal: Women and Literature*, Random House, New York, 1970

Haskell, Barbara, *The American Century: Art and Culture 1900–2000*, W. W. Norton & Co., New York, London, 1999

Heilbrun, Carolyn G., *Writing, A Woman's Life*, The Women's Press, London, 1988

Hellman, Lillian, *An Unfinished Woman*, Bantam Books, New York, 1980

——*Pentimento*, Macmillan, London, 1974

Hemingway, Ernest, *The Collected Stories*, David Campbell Publishers, London, 1995

——*Selected Letters*, ed. Carlos Baker, Charles Scribner's Sons, New York, 1981; Granada, London, 1981

——*The Old Man and the Sea*, Collins Publishing Group, London, 1976

——*Selected Letters*, Swallow Press, Chicago, 1975

——*The Torrents of Spring*, Charles Scribner's Sons, New York, 1972
——*Death in the Afternoon*, Penguin Books, London, 1966
——*A Moveable Feast*, Charles Scribner's Sons, New York, 1964; Penguin Books, London, 1964; Bantam Books, New York, 1969
——*The Essential Hemingway*, Penguin Books, London, 1947
——*For Whom the Bell Tolls*, Jonathan Cape, London, 1941
——*The Short Stories of Ernest Hemingway*, Modern Library, Random House, New York, 1938
——*The Sun Also Rises*, Modern Library, Random House, New York, 1930
Hickman, Tom, *The Sexual Century*, Carlton Books, London, 1999
Hobsbawm, Eric, *Age of Extremes: The Short Twentieth Century 1914–1991*, Abacus, London, 1994
Hoffer, Abram and Osmond, Humphrey, *How to Live with Schizophrenia*, University Books, New York, 1966
Holland, Jack, *New York: The Rough Guide*, Rough Guides, 1993
Hotchner, A. E., *Papa Hemingway*, Random House, New York, 1966
Jamison, Kay Redfield, *An Unquiet Mind: A Memoir of Moods and Madness*, Picador, London, 1995
——*Touched with Fire: Manic-Depressive Illness and the Artistic Temperament*, Free Press Paperbacks, New York, 1993
Kaplan, E. Ann, ed., *Psychoanalysis and Cinema*, Routledge, New York and London
Kert, Bernice, *The Hemingway Women*, W. W. Norton & Co., New York, London, 1983
Klehr, Harvey, *The Heyday of American Communism: The Depression Decade*, Basic Books Inc., New York, 1984
Lardner, Ring, *Some Champions*, Charles Scribner's Sons, New York, 1976
——*What of It?*, Charles Scribner's Sons, New York, 1925
Lee, Israel, *Miss Tallulah Bankhead*, G. P. Putnam's Sons, New York, 1972
Lifar, Serge, *Serge Diaghilev: His Life, His Work, His Legend: An Intimate Biography*, G. P. Putnam's Sons, New York, 1940
Loos, Anita, *Kiss Hollywood Good-by*, Viking Press, New York, 1974
Ludington, Townsend, *John Dos Passos: A Twentieth Century Odyssey*, E. P. Dutton, New York, 1980
——*The Fourteenth Chronicle: Letters and Diaries of John Dos Passos*, Gambit Inc., Boston, 1973
Lunbeck, Elizabeth, *The Psychiatric Persuasion*, Princeton University Press, Princeton, 1994
Mackenzie, Compton, *Extraordinary Women: Theme and Variations*, Martin Secker, London, 1928
MacLeish, Archibald, *Letters*, Houghton Mifflin, Boston, 1983
——*Riders on the Earth: Essays and Recollections*, Houghton Mifflin, Boston, 1978
——*Collected Poems*, Houghton Mifflin, Boston, 1962
Manchester, William, *Mencken: Disturber of the Peace*, Collier Books, New York, 1967
Mankiller, Wilma *et al.*, eds., *The Reader's Companion to U.S. Women's History*, Houghton Mifflin, New York, 1998
Mayfield, Sara, *The Constant Circle: H. L. Mencken and His Friends*, Delacorte Press, New York, 1968
McLellan, Diana, *The Girls: Sappho Goes to Hollywood*, Robson Books, London, 2001
McLendon, James, *Papa. Hemingway in Key West 1928–1940*, Popular Library, New York, 1972
Meade, Marion, *Dorothy Parker. What Fresh Hell is This?*, Minerva, London, 1991
Mellow, James R., *Hemingway: A Life Without Consequences*, Houghton Mifflin, Boston, 1992; Hodder & Stoughton, London, Sydney, Auckland, 1992
——*Charmed Circle: Gertrude Stein and Company*, Praeger Publishers, New York, 1972
Mencken, H. L., *My Life as Author and Editor*, edited with introduction by Jonathan Yardley, Alfred A. Knopf, New York, 1993
——*In Defense of Women*, Time-Life Books Inc., Alexandria, 1982
Meyers, Jeffrey, *Edmund Wilson: A Biography*, Houghton Mifflin, Boston, New York, 1995
Miller, Linda Patterson, ed., *Letters from the Lost Generation: Gerald and Sara Murphy and Friends*, Rutgers University Press, New Brunswick NJ, London, 1991
Minsky, Rosalind, ed., *Psychoanalysis*, Routledge, London & New York, 1996
Neret, Giles, *The Arts of the Twenties*, Rizzoli, New York, 1986
Odets, Clifford, *The Time Is Ripe: The 1940 Journal of Clifford Odets*, New York, 1988

O'Hara, John, *Selected Letters*, Random House, New York, 1978

Olsen, Kirsten, *Remember the Ladies*, Main Street Press, Pittstown, 1988

Patmore, Brigit, *My Friends When Young: The Memoirs of Brigit Patmore*, Heinemann, London, 1968

Perkins, Maxwell E., *Editor to Author: The Letters of Maxwell E. Perkins*, Charles Scribner's Sons, New York, 1979

Porter, Roy, ed., *The Faber Book of Madness*, Faber & Faber, London, Boston, 1991

Potts, Eve, comp., *Westport: A Special Place*, Westport Historical Society, Westport CT, 1985

Rascoe, Burton, *We Were Interrupted*, Doubleday & Co., Garden City, 1947

Rees, A. L. and Borzello, Frances, eds., *The New Art History*, Camden Press, London, 1986

Reynolds, Michael, *Hemingway: The 1930s*, W. W. Norton & Co., New York, London, 1997

——*Hemingway: The American Homecoming*, Blackwell Publishers, Cambridge MA, 1992

——*Hemingway: The Paris Years*, Basil Blackwell, Cambridge MA, 1989

——*The Young Hemingway*, Basil Blackwell, Oxford, 1986

Robinson, Roxana, *Georgia O'Keeffe: A Life*, Bloomsbury, London, 1997

Rodgers, Marion Elizabeth, ed., *Mencken and Sara: A Life in Letters: The Correspondence of H. L. Mencken and Sara Haardt*, McGraw-Hill, New York, 1987; Anchor Books, Doubleday, 1992

Rose, Barbara, *American Art Since 1900*, Praeger Publishers, New York, 1975

Rubin, William, *The Paintings of Gerald Murphy*, Museum of Modern Art, New York, 1974

Sampson, Harold *et al.*, *Schizophrenic Women: Studies in Marital Crisis*, Atherton Press, New York, 1964

Sandler, Irving, *The Triumph of American Painting*, Harper & Row Publishers, New York, Hagerstown, San Francisco, London, 1970

Scammell, William, *All Set to Fall Off the Edge of the World*, Flambard Press, Hexham, 1998

Schenkar, Joan, *Truly Wilde: The Unsettling Story of Dolly Wilde, Oscar's Unusual Niece*, Virago, London, 2000

Schulberg, Budd, *The Disenchanted*, Random House, New York, 1950

Secrest, Meryle, *Between Me and Life: A Biography of Romaine Brooks*, Macdonald & Jane's, London, 1976

Showalter, Elaine, *Hystories: Hysterical Epidemics and Modern Culture*, Picador, London 1997

——*The Female Malady: Women, Madness and English Culture 1830–1980*, Penguin, Harmondsworth, 1985

Silvano, Airieti, MD, *Interpretation of Schizophrenia*, Basic Books Inc., New York, 1955

Stann, Kap, Marshall, Diane and Edge, John T., *Deep South*, Lonely Planet Publications, 1998

Stenerson, Douglas C., *H. L. Mencken, Iconoclast from Baltimore*, University of Chicago Press, Chicago, 1971

Sternburg, Janet, ed., *The Writer on Her Work*, W. W. Norton & Co., New York, London, 1980

Stewart, Donald Ogden, *By a Stroke of Luck! An Autobiography*, Paddington Press/Two Continents, New York, 1975

Sturgis, Alexander, ed., *Understanding Paintings: Themes in Art Explored and Explained*, Mitchell Beazley, London, 2000

Summers, Claude J., ed., *The Gay and Lesbian Literary Heritage*, Henry Holt & Co., New York, 1995

Szasz, Thomas, *Schizophrenia: The Sacred Symbol of Psychiatry*, Basic Books, Inc., Publishers, New York, 1976

Tate, Allen, *Memoirs and Opinions 1926–1974*, Swallow Press, Chicago, 1975

Taylor, Dwight, *Joy Ride*, G. P. Putnam's Sons, New York, 1959

Thurber, James, *Credos and Curios*, Harper & Row, New York, 1962

Tomkins, Calvin, *Living Well Is The Best Revenge: Two Americans in Paris 1921–1933*, E. P. Dutton, New York, 1962; Viking, New York, 1971; André Deutsch, London, 1972

Trager, James, *The Women's Chronology*, Aurum Press, London, 1994

Turner, Elizabeth Hutton, ed., *Americans in Paris (1921–1931): Man Ray, Gerald Murphy, Stuart Davis, Alexander Calder*, Counterpoint, Washington DC, 1996

Twain, Mark, *Life on the Mississippi*, Harper and Bros, New York, 1917

Tynan, Kenneth, *Show People*, Berkley Books, New York, 1981

Uglow, Jennifer, *Macmillan Dictionary of Women's Biography*, Macmillan, London, 1982

Vaill, Amanda, *Everybody Was So Young: Gerald and Sara Murphy. A Lost Generation Love Story*, Houghton Mifflin, Boston, 1998; Little, Brown & Co., London, 1998

Van Vechten, Carl, *Parties* (originally published 1930), Avon Books, New York, 1977

Vaughan, Courtney Sprague and Reneau, Patricia Sprague, *Remembered and Honored*, Sentinel Printers, Santa Cruz, 1992

Wagner, Linda M., *Dos Passos: Artist as American*, University of Texas Press, Austin, 1979

Waldron, Ann, *Close Connections: Caroline Gordon and the Southern Resistance*, University of Tennessee Press, Knoxville, 1987

Wilson, Edmund, *The Thirties: From Notebooks and Diaries of the Period*, ed. Leon Edel, Farrar, Straus & Giroux, New York, 1980

——*Letters on Literature and Politics 1912–1972*, ed. Elena Wilson, Farrar, Straus & Giroux, New York, 1977

——*The Twenties: From Notebooks and Diaries of the Period*, ed. Leon Edel, Farrar, Straus & Giroux, New York, 1975

——*A Prelude*, Farrar, Straus & Giroux, New York, 1967

——*The Shores of Light*, Farrar, Straus & Young, New York, 1952

Winthrop Chanler, Mrs, *Autumn in the Valley*, Little, Brown & Co., Boston, 1936

Wiser, William, *The Great Good Place: American Expatriate Women in Paris*, W. W. Norton & Co., New York, London, 1991

Wolfe, Thomas, *Look Homeward, Angel*, Penguin Books, London, 1984

Wolpert, Lewis, *Malignant Sadness: The Anatomy of Depression*, Faber & Faber, London, 1999

Articles, journals, magazines, newspapers

Blackshear, Helen F., 'Mama Sayre, Scott Fitzgerald's Mother-in-Law', *Georgia Review*, winter 1965

Connor, Steve, 'Schizophrenia gene close to discovery say scientists', *The Independent*, 1 Sep. 1998

Dobson, Roger, 'Are schizophrenics the lepers of our time?', *The Independent*, 21 July 1998

Haardt, Sara, 'Alabama', *American Mercury*, 6 Sep. 1925

Harlow, John, 'Hemingway's black sex slave fantasy', *Sunday Times*, 16 Aug. 1998

Heilbrun, Carolyn G., 'Discovering the Lost Lives of Woman', *New York Times*, 24 June 1984

Henley, Ann, 'Sara Haardt and "The Sweet, Flowering South"', *Alabama Heritage* 31, winter 1994

Mitchell, Ted, 'The Doom of the Mountains', *Our State: North Carolina* 66: 10, Mar. 1999

Pattillo, Eddie, 'Last of the Belles – a Remembrance', *Montgomery*, July 1994

Princeton University Library Chronicle, LX:2, winter 1999; LX: 1, autumn 1998

Seldes, Gilbert, 'Spring Flight', *The Dial*, Aug. 1925

Solomon, Wendy E., 'Skin Troubles May Be Tied To Anxiety', *New York Times*, 21 Nov. 1989

Taylor, Robert, 'A Strater Retrospective: No Faces of Fame', *Boston Globe Magazine*, 6 Aug. 1981

Tomkins, Calvin, 'Living Well is the Best Revenge', *New Yorker*, 28 July 1962

Vincent, Sally, 'Georgia O'Keeffe: All Woman', *Guardian Weekend*, 28 Apr. 2001

INDEX